GLOBALIZATION AND THE FUTURE OF LABOUR LAW

How are national and international labour laws responding to the challenge of globalization as it reshapes the workplaces of the world?

This collection of essays by leading legal scholars and lawyers from Europe and the Americas addresses the implications of globalization for the legal regulation of the new workplace. It examines the role of international labour standards and the contribution of the International Labour Organization, and assesses the success of the European experiment with continental employment standards. It explores the prospects for hemispheric cooperation on labour standards in the Americas, and deals with the impact of international labour standards on the rights of women and migrant workers.

As the nature and organization of work around the world is being decisively transformed, new regional and international institutions are emerging that may provide the platform for new labour standards, and for protecting existing ones.

JOHN D. R. CRAIG is a Partner at Heenan Blaikie LLP, Toronto, and is Adjunct Professor at the University of Western Ontario Faculty of Law, London, Ontario.

S. MICHAEL LYNK is Associate Professor of Law at the University of Western Ontario.

GLOBALIZATION AND THE FUTURE OF LABOUR LAW

Edited by

JOHN D. R. CRAIG AND S. MICHAEL LYNK

CAMBRIDGE
UNIVERSITY PRESS

CAMBRIDGE UNIVERSITY PRESS
Cambridge, New York, Melbourne, Madrid, Cape Town, Singapore, São Paulo

Cambridge University Press
The Edinburgh Building, Cambridge CB2 2RU, UK

Published in the United States of America by Cambridge University Press, New York

www.cambridge.org
Information on this title: www.cambridge.org/9780521854900

© Cambridge University Press 2006

First published 2006

Printed in the United Kingdom at the University Press, Cambridge

A catalogue record for this publication is available from the British Library

ISBN-13   978-0-521-85490-0 hardback
ISBN-10   0-521-85490-3 hardback

CONTENTS

Notes on contributors   *page* viii
Acknowledgements   xiii
Table of cases   xiv
List of abbreviations   xvii

Introduction   1
JOHN CRAIG AND MICHAEL LYNK

PART I   **Perspectives on globalization**

1   The international labour dimension: an introduction   15
BRIAN W. BURKETT

2   Who's afraid of globalization? Reflections on the future of
labour law   51
HARRY ARTHURS

PART II   **International labour standards**

3   The impact of globalization on labour standards   77
KEVIN BANKS

4   Globalization, decentralization and the role of subsidiarity in
the labour setting   108
VÉRONIQUE MARLEAU

5   A game-theory account and defence of transnational labour
standards – a preliminary look at the problem   143
ALAN HYDE

v

PART III   **The European Union**

6   Industrial relations and EU enlargement   169
MANFRED WEISS

7   Trends and challenges of labour law in Central Europe   191
ARTURO BRONSTEIN

8   Labour market integration: lessons from the
European Union   225
CATHERINE BARNARD

PART IV   **The Americas**

9   Labour rights in the FTAA   245
LANCE COMPA

10 Globalization and the just society – core labour rights, the
FTAA, and development   274
BRIAN LANGILLE

11 The future of labour integration: the South American
perspective   304
JOSÉ PASTORE

PART V   **The ILO**

12 International labour standards in the globalized economy :
obstacles and opportunities for achieving progress   331
WERNER SENGENBERGER

13 The growing importance of the International Labour
Organization: the view from the United States   356
EDWARD POTTER

PART VI   **Labour rights**

14 Securing gender justice: the challenges facing international
labour law   377
MARY CORNISH, FAY FARADAY AND VEENA VERMA

15   International labour law and the protection of migrant workers:
      revitalizing the agenda in the era of globalization   409
      RYSZARD CHOLEWINSKI

      Bibliography   445
      Index   479

NOTES ON CONTRIBUTORS

John Craig is a lawyer with the Toronto office of the Canadian law firm of Heenan Blaikie LLP. He is also an Adjunct Professor of labour and employment law at the University of Western Ontario, in London, Ontario, where he has been teaching since 1999. He is the author of *Privacy and Employment Law* (1999) based on his doctoral thesis from the University of Oxford. He has also published articles related to labour and employment law in the *McGill Law Journal*, the *Comparative Labour Law and Policy Journal*, the *Industrial Law Journal*, the *Review of Constitutional Studies*, the *European Human Rights Law Review* and the *Canadian Labour and Employment Law Journal*.

Michael Lynk is Associate Professor at the Faculty of Law, the University of Western Ontario, London, Ontario. His teaching and research areas include labour law, domestic and international human rights, and constitutional law. His recent work has centred on fundamental employment rights under the Canadian constitution, disability rights at work, and final status issues in the Middle East peace process. Professor Lynk has also worked with the United Nations in the Middle East on refugee and human rights issues. He is the co-author of *Trade Union Law in Canada*.

Harry W. Arthurs is a Professor and former Dean at Osgoode Hall Law School, and Professor Emeritus of York University. He has published extensively on labour law theory and doctrine, and his recent work has focused on the impact of the new economy – globalization, technological change and neo-liberal policies – on labour law and labour market institutions. His other fields of scholarship include constitutionalism and governance, administrative law and public administration, legal pluralism and the sociology of law, and the legal profession, legal history and legal education.

Kevin Banks is currently the Director of Inter-American Labour Cooperation at Human Resources Development Canada, where he is responsible for the office that negotiates and implements Canada's trade-related labour agreements in the Americas, and for managing Canada's participation in the Inter-American Conference of Ministers of Labour. From 1998 to 2001, he was a Senior Labour Law advisor with the Secretariat of the Commission for Labor Cooperation, in Washington, DC. Mr. Banks has written a number of publications on labour law and related matters, and he recently co-authored a book entitled *North American Labor Relations Law – A Comparative Guide to the Labor Relations Laws of Canada, Mexico and the United States* (2003).

Catherine Barnard is a University Lecturer in Law at the University of Cambridge and a fellow of Trinity College, Cambridge. Professor Barnard specializes in European Community law, labour law and anti-discrimination law. She is currently acting as a consultant for the European Commission on the implementation of the Working Time Directive. Professor Barnard is the author of *EC Employment Law* (2000), and the co-author of *The Exercise of Individual Employment Rights in the Member States of the Community* (1995).

Arturo Bronstein is the Senior Labour Law Policy Advisor within the *In Focus* Programme on Social Dialogue, Labour Law and Labour Administration, at the International Labour Organization, Geneva (ILO). During his 30-year career at the ILO, he has served as Head of the Labour Legislation Section, Director of the ILO multi-disciplinary technical team for Central America, Cuba, Haiti, Mexico, Panama and the Dominican Republic, based in San José, Costa Rica, and as Deputy Director of the Government, Labour Law and Labour Administration Department. Mr Bronstein has written many publications in the field of labour law. In addition to his responsibilities with the ILO, he is also the current Secretary General of the International Society for Labour Law and Social Security.

Brian Burkett is a partner with the Toronto office of the national Canadian law firm of Heenan Blaikie LLP, practising exclusively in the area of management labour relations and employment law. He is a member of the Public Policy Forum and sits on its Advisory Committee on Globalization and Governance. Mr Burkett is also a member of the Canadian Bar Association and the American Bar Association, and serves on the Railway and Airline Subcommittee of the latter organization. In addition, Mr Burkett is a Director of the Canadian Employers Council which represents the interests of the Canadian employer community at the ILO in Geneva, Switzerland.

Ryszard Cholewinski is a Reader in Law at the University of Leicester. Besides teaching constitutional law, human rights and civil liberties, he is also the Director of the Centre for European Law and Integration. He is the author of *Migrant Workers in International Law* (1997), and has published widely on the human and employment rights of migrant workers, and the international protection of refugees.

Lance Compa is a Senior Lecturer at Cornell University's School of Industrial and Labour Relations in Ithaca, New York, where he teaches US labour law and international labour rights. Before joining the Cornell faculty in 1997, Mr Compa was the first Director of Labour Law and Economic Research at the Secretariat of the North American Commission for Labour Cooperation. Prior to his 1995 appointment to the Secretariat, he taught labour law, employment law, and international labour rights as a Visiting Lecturer at Yale Law School and the Yale School of Management. He is the author of the 2000 Human Rights Watch report *Unfair Advantage: Workers' Freedom of Association in the United States under International Human Rights Standards*, and co-editor of the book *Human Rights, Labor Rights, and International Trade* (1996).

Mary Cornish is a senior partner with the Toronto law firm of Cavalluzzo Hayes Shilton McIntyre & Cornish. Her legal practice and advocacy work have included pay and employment equity, human rights, labour law, judicial reform and social protection issues. As an international consultant, she has provided advice to the World Bank, the European Economic Community, and the governments of New Zealand and Sweden on pay and employment equity. In Canada, Ms Cornish has advised the Ontario Government and the Canadian Human Rights Commission on human rights enforcement and alternative dispute resolution.

Fay Faraday is a partner with the Toronto law firm of Cavalluzzo Hayes Shilton McIntyre & Cornish. Her practice focuses on Canadian constitutional law, administrative law, human rights, pay and employment equity law and education law, and has included appearances before the Supreme Court of Canada and the Ontario Court of Appeal. Ms Faraday is widely published on labour law and equality issues.

Alan Hyde is a Professor and Sidney Reitman Scholar at the School of Law, Rutgers University, in Newark, New Jersey. He is the author of *Working in Silicon Valley: Economic and Legal Analysis of a High-Velocity Labor Market* (2003), *Bodies of Law* (1997) and the co-editor of *Cases and Materials on Labor Law* (2nd ed., 1982). Professor Hyde has been a visiting professor at Yale, Columbia, New York University, Cardozo, and the University of Michigan law schools. His current research projects include transnational labour standards as solutions to strategic dilemmas; work relations in labour markets with extremely short tenures and rapid turnover, such as Silicon Valley, California; and new global labour markets characterized by extensive transnational outsourcing of production and labour migration.

Brian Langille is Professor of Law at the University of Toronto Faculty of Law. Professor Langille has written and lectured widely on his principal research areas, which include labour law, contract law and legal theory. His recent work has focused on issues of international labour standards and international economic integration. He has served on Canadian delegations to both the Governing Body and the International Labour Conference of the International Labour Organization (ILO), as a consultant to the ILO, as a rapporteur to the Organization for Economic Cooperation and Development (OECD), as an editor of the *International Labour Law Reports*, and as an executive member of the International Society for Labour Law and Social Security.

Véronique Marleau is a senior officer with the Freedom of Association program at the ILO's International Training Centre, at Turin, Italy. She has previously served as a member of the Canada Labour Relations Board, and practised labour law in Montreal. She has written extensively on international labour law issues.

José Pastore is Professor of Industrial Relations, University of São Paulo, Brazil. He has more than 40 years' experience in teaching and research on industrial relations, labour markets, employment, human resources, trade unionism, institution building in the area of labour, and social change in Brazil and Latin America. He has published 30 books in these fields, including *Trade Union and Managerial Association Reform in Brazil, Social Mobility in Brazil* (with Nelson do Valle Silva), and *Inequality and Social Mobility in Brazil*. Recently, Professor Pastore served as a member of the National Labour Forum, which is responsible for presenting a proposal to the president of Brazil on labour law reform, acted as the coordinator of the technical advisory body of the Minister of Labour in Brazil, and was a member of the governing body of the ILO.

Edward Potter is the President of the Employment Policy Foundation (EPF), based in Washington, DC, a non-profit economic policy research foundation that promotes employment policy reform. He is the co-author of *Keeping America Competitive: Employment Policy for the Twenty-First*

Century (1995), which addresses the critical relationship between employment policy, competitiveness, and the standard of living of Americans. Mr Potter currently serves as the US Employer Delegate to the annual ILO Conference, where he has overall responsibility for US business' negotiating position on multilateral treaties that are intended to establish minimum international labour standards. In addition to his work at the EPF, Mr Potter is a senior partner in the law firm of McGuiness Norris & Williams, LLP in Washington, DC.

Werner Sengenberger is the former Director of the Employment Strategy Department, ILO, Geneva. Previously, he was the Director of the ILO's Employment and Vocational Training Department, and Chief of Programme of New Industrial Organizations at the ILO's International Institute for Labour Studies in Geneva. Dr Sengenberger has also served as Director of the ILO Advisory Team for Central and Eastern Europe in Budapest. After retiring from the ILO in 2001, he has acted as a consultant for various UN agencies and other international organizations.

Veena Verma is an associate lawyer with the Toronto law firm of Cavalluzzo Hayes Shilton McIntyre & Cornish, practising in the areas of labour law and human rights. She has worked in India for *MANUSHI*, a well-known journal about Indian women and minorities, and in Guyana on a Canadian Lawyers Association for International Human Rights (CLAIHR) initiative focusing on the property rights of women. Ms Verma has recently published a study, entitled *The Mexican and Caribbean Seasonal Agricultural Workers Program*, for the North South Institute, Ottawa (2003).

Manfred Weiss is Professor of Labour Law and Civil Law, at the J. W. Goethe University, in Frankfurt, Germany, where he has taught since 1970. He is a past president of the International Industrial Relations Association, and has written over 100 publications on various aspects of German, European and international labour law. Professor Weiss has acted as a consultant to the ILO for over twenty years, and has served with ILO missions to a number of countries in Africa, Asia, the Caribbean and Eastern Europe. Professor Weiss serves as the German correspondent for the *International Labour Law Reports*, the International Encyclopedia of Labour Law and Industrial Relations, and the United States Academy of Arbitrators.

ACKNOWLEDGEMENTS

The editors would like to acknowledge the contributions of the following individuals, without whose help this book would not have been possible: Matt Diskin, Puja Varma, Sandra Konstantinou, Claudia Vicencio, Mathias Link, Sonia Regenbogen-Luciw, Jodi Gallagher, Rhonda Shirreff, Max Khan, Simon Finlayson, Trevor Guy, Andrew Bruntin and Joyce Mendez.

TABLE OF CASES

AG (Canada) v. AG (Ontario) (Labour Conventions Reference) [1937] AC 326

Andrea Francovich, Danila Bonifaci and Others v. Italy [1991] ECR I-5357

Association of Major League Umpires v. American League and National League of Professional Baseball Clubs & Toronto Blue Jays Baseball Club (1995), OLRD No. 0298-95-U

Baumbast and R v. Secretary of State for the Home Department (C-413/99) [2002] ECR I-7091

Bernini v. Minister van Onderwijs en Wetenschappen [1992] ECR I-1071

Bestuur van de Sociale Verzekeringsbank v. Cabanis-Issarte [1996] ECR I-2097

Bickel and Franz (C-274/96) [1998] ECR I-7637

Brian Francis Collins v. Secretary of State for Work and Pensions (C-138/02) [2003] ECR I-000

Commission v. Belgium [1996] ECR I-4307

Commission v. France (C-35/97) [1998] ECR I-5325

Commission v. Germany (C-249/86) [1989] ECR 1263

Commission v. Greece [1998] ECR I-6601

Commission v. Luxembourg (C-111/91)

Commission v. United Kingdom [1994] IRLR 392, 412

Crevier v. AG (Quebec)(1982) 127 D.L.R. (3d) 1

Criminal proceedings against Even (C-207/78) [1979] ECR 2019

Criminal proceedings against Mutsch (C-137/84) [1985] ECR 2681

Defrenne v. Sabena (Case 43/75) [1976] ECR 455

Doe I v. Unocal Corporation, 2003 U.S. App. LEXIS 2716 (9th Cir. 2003) [*Unocal*]

Dole Food Co. v. Patrickson, 538 U.S. 468 (2003)

Dunmore v. Ontario (Attorney General) [2001] 3 S.C.R. 1016

Echternach and Moritz v. Minister van Onderwijs en Wetenschappen [1989] ECR 723

Estate of Rodriguez v. Drummond Co. Inc., 256 F. Supp.2d 1250 (N.D. Alabama, April 14, 2003)

Filartiga v. Pena-Irala, 630 F.2d 876, 879 (2d Cir. 1980)

Fiorini (née Christini) v. SNCF [1975] ECR 1085

Franca Ninni-Orasche v. Bundesminister für Wissenschaft, Verkehr und Kunst (C-413/01) [2003] ECR I-000

Garcia Avello (C-148/02) [2003] ECR I-000

Grzelczyk (C-184/99) [2001] ECR I-6193

Helga Nimz v. Freie und Hansestadt Hamburg (C-184/99) [1991] ECR I-297

Höfner and Elser v. Macrotron GmbH. [1991] ECR I-01979

Kalanke v. Freie Hansestadt Bremen (C-450/93) [1995] ECR I-3051, [1996] 1 CMLR 175

Kang v. U.Lim America, Inc. 296 F.3d 810 (9th Cir. 2002)

Lavigne v. Ontario Public Service Employees Union [1991] 2 S.C.R. 211

Mahlburg v. Land Mecklenburg (Case 207/98) [2000] ECR I-549

Martinez v. Dow Chemical Co., 219 F.Supp.2d 719

Martínez Sala v. Freistaat Bayern (C-8596) [1998] ECR I-2691

Meeusen [1999] ECR I-3289

Meints v. Minister van Landbouw (C-57/96) [1997] ECR 6689

Minister of Labour v. CUPE and SEIU [2003] 1 S.C.R. 539

National Basketball Referees Association v. National Basketball Association (1995) OLRD no. 2919-95-U

Netherlands v. Reed [1986] ECR 1283

New Brunswick (Minister of Finance) v. Mackin and Rice [2002] 1 S.C.R. 405

O'Flynn v. Adjudication Officer [1996] ECR I-2617

ONEM v. Deak [1985] ECR 1873

Parry Sound Social Services Administration Board v. Ontario Public Services Union [2003] 1 S.C.R. 157

Piermont v. France (1995) 20 EHRR 301

Public Service Alliance of Canada v. Canada [1987] 1 S.C.R. 424

R. v. Advance Cutting & Coring Ltd (2001), 205 D.L.R. (4th) 385

Reference re Public Service Employee Relations Act (Alberta) [1987] 1 S.C.R. 313

Reference re Remuneration of Judges of the Provincial Court of Prince Edward Island [1997] 3 S.C.R. 3

Reina v. Landerkreditbank Baden-Wurttemberg (C-65/81) [1982] ECR 33

Retail, Wholesale and Department Store Union, Locals 544, 496, 635 and 955 v. Government of Saskatchewan [1987] 1 S.C.R. 460

Retail, Wholesale and Department Store Union, Local 558 v. Pepsi-Cola Canada Beverages (West) Ltd (2002) 208 D.L.R. (4th) 385

Rodriguez-Fernandez v. Wilkenson, 654 F.2d 1382 (10th Cir. 1981)

Rudy Grzelczyk v. Centre public d'aide sociale d'Ottignies-Louvain-la-Neuve (C-184/99) [2001] ECR I-6193

Sodemare SA, Anni Azzurri Holding SpA and Anni Azzurri Rezzato Srl v. Regione Lombardia (C-70/95) [1997] ECR I-3395

Stöber and Pereira [1997] ECR I-511

Tel-Oren v. Libyan Arab Republic, 726 F.2d 774 (D.C. Cir. 1984)

Trojani v. Centre public d'aide sociale de Bruxelles (C-456/02), judgment of 7 September 2004

Vriend v. Alberta (1998) 156 D.L.R. (4th) 385

Weber v. Ontario Hydro [1995] 2 S.C.R. 929

Wijsenbeek (C-378/97) [1999] ECR I-6207

Youngstown Sheet & Tube Co. v. Sawyer, 343 U.S. 579 (1952)

LIST OF ABBREVIATIONS

ASEAN	Association of Southeast Asian Nations
ASW	Association of Southeast Asian Nations Sub-Committee on Women
ATCA	Alien Tort Claims Act
CAFTA	Central American Free Trade Agreement
Cairo Declaration	Declaration of Human Rights in Islam
CARICOM	The Caribbean Community and Common Market
CEDAW	Convention on the Elimination of all Forms of Discrimination Against Women
CEE States	Central and Eastern European States
CEEP	European Centre of Enterprises with Public Participation and of Enterprises of General Economic Interest
CFA	Committee on Freedom of Association
Charter	European Charter of Fundamental Rights
CLT	Brazilian Labour Code
CMC	Common Market Council
CMG	Common Market Group
CSO	Civil Society Organization
CSR	Corporate Social Responsibility
EC Law	European Community Law
EC Treaty	European Community Treaty
ECHR	European Convention on Human Rights
ECJ	European Court of Justice
ECLAC	United Nations' Economic Commission for Latin America and the Caribbean
ECSC	European Coal and Steel Community
EEC	European Economic Community
EMF	European Metalworkers Federation

EPZ	Export Processing Zone
ESCF	Economic and Social Consultative Forum
ETUC	European Trade Union Confederation
ETUI	The European Trade Union Institute
EU	European Union
EUCOB	European Collective Bargaining Information Network
EWC	European Works Council
FDI	Foreign Direct Investment
FGTS	*Fundo de Garantia por Tempo de Serviço*
FNT	*Forum Nacional do Trabalho*
FTA	Free Trade Agreement between Canada and the United States of America
FTAA	Free Trade Agreement of the Americas
Fundamental Declaration	ILO Declaration on Fundamental Principles and Rights at Work
GATS	General Agreement on Trade in Services
GDP	Gross Domestic Product
GIR	Globalization and Information Revolution
GNP	Gross National Product
GSP	Generalized System of Preferences
HR	Human Resources
IACML	Inter-American Conference of Ministers of Labour
ICB	Institutional Capacity Building
ICCPR	International Covenant on Civil and Political Rights
ICESCR	International Covenant on Economic Social and Cultural Rights
IDB	Inter-American Development Bank
ILO	International Labour Organization
ILS	International Labour Standards
IMF	International Monetary Fund
International Association	The International Association for the Legal Protection of Workers
IOM	International Organization for Migration
IPECL	International Program for the Elimination of Child Labour
IR	Industrial Relations
JS	Just Societies

Maastricht Treaty	Treaty on European Union
Mercosur	Common Market of the Southern Cone
MNE	Multinational Enterprise
MP	Member of Parliament
MWC	UN Convention on the Protection of the Rights of All Migrant Workers and Members of Their Families
NAALC	North American Agreement on Labour Cooperation
NAFTA	North American Free Trade Association
NAO	National Administrative Office
NGO	Non-governmental Organization
NIS	National Innovation System
OAS	Organization of American States
OECD	Organization for Economic Co-operation and Development
OMU	Offshore Mariners United
PICUM	Platform for International Cooperation on Undocumented Migrants
POEA	Administrator of the Philippine Overseas Employment Administration
SEF	Socio-Economic Forum
SEWA	Self-Employed Women's Association
SLC	Social-Labour Commission
SME	Small and Medium-sized Enterprise
SNCF	National Railway Company of France
Social Charter	European Union Community Charter of Basic Social Rights
Strategy	European Union Community Framework Strategy on Gender Equality (2001–2005)
TNC	Transnational Corporation
TPA	Trade Promotion Authority
Trico	Trico Marine Services Inc.
Tripartite Declaration	Tripartite Declaration of Principles concerning Multinational Enterprises and Social Policy
UDHR	Universal Declaration of Human Rights
UN	United Nations
UNCTAD	United Nations Conference on Trade and Development

UNESCO	United Nations Educational, Scientific and Cultural Organization
UNICE	*Union des Industries de la Communauté Européenne*
UNICEF	United Nations International Children's Emergency Fund
WTO	World Trade Organization

INTRODUCTION

JOHN CRAIG AND MICHAEL LYNK

The power to become habituated to his surroundings is a marked characteristic of mankind. Very few of us realise with conviction the intensely unusual, unstable, complicated, unreliable, temporary nature of the economic organisation by which Western Europe has lived for the last half century. We assume some of the most peculiar and temporary of our late advantages as natural, permanent, and to be depended on, and we lay our plans accordingly. On this sandy and false foundation we scheme our social improvement and dress our political platforms, pursue our animosities and particular ambitions . . .

John Maynard Keynes, *The Economic Consequences of the Peace* (1919)[1]

Having lost the comfort of our geographic boundaries, we must in effect rediscover what creates the bond between humans that constitute a community.

Jean-Marie Guehenno, *The End of the Nation-State*[2]

Labour law and globalization

The defining characteristic of globalization in our modern age has been to challenge the stability and isolation of what is local, without always conferring the benefit of what is universal. Economic growth has lifted millions out of poverty over the past fifteen years, yet the prosperity has been unevenly distributed, and economic inequalities and social exclusion within and among nations have actually deepened. Open societies have emerged, but the erection of democratic national and global institutions to manage the volatility of social and economic change has proven largely elusive. New means of communications are enabling the arrival of a truly global conscience, but they have also spread a homogeneous culture that is eroding local identities and distinctiveness. More people are working but, more than ever before, they labour in conditions of employment

1

informality and insecurity. The workplaces of our new world are being transformed by the dynamic push of international trade patterns, capital investment flows, and migratory labour movements, but the regulation of these workplaces, when they are regulated at all, remains the province of national labour and employment laws that are increasingly unable to either protect or adapt.

Compared to the whirl of change in the international economy, domestic labour laws have largely stood still over the past fifteen years. In part, this has been the result of new fiscal and economic policies pursued by governments and international institutions that have opened up labour markets and, in the process, weakened the ability of trade unions and liberal forces in society to seek enhanced employment conditions and improved legislation. Another contributing factor has been the declining role of national governments, where the self-induced policies of lower taxation rates, a reduced state presence in the economy, and more restrictive social programmes have curtailed their desire and their capacity to regulate labour market outcomes. A third factor has seemingly been an exhaustion of ideas, as if the statutory models of labour law regulation that have prevailed over the past half century and more have been depleted of their possibilities to be reformed and regenerated. Moreover, this legislative stagnation shows no sign of any early abatement, as the politics of national labour law reform have become increasingly contingent upon the deference of governments to the real and imagined imperatives of the international market-place.

Let us be clear. National labour laws will remain, far into the future, the primary legal structure for promoting fair employment practices, for enabling workers to achieve collective representation, for regulating the reconcilable differences between employers and employees, and for diminishing the patterns of discrimination and exclusion at work. But, increasingly, these laws are unable to accomplish their public purpose. The declining numerical strength of trade unions, the shrinking public resources devoted to the enforcement of legislative standards, and the rise of contingent and unregulated work relationships all point to a widening gap between labour law norms and workplace realities. Meanwhile, the rising percentage of trade as a component of national economies, the spreading out by companies of their production stages across countries and continents, and the instant transfer of work around the globe by modern technology have meant that globalization is reshaping our workplaces much more decisively than our available legal tools can meaningfully regulate them. Thus, the question becomes: if some of the causes for the malaise in labour law performance lie in the dynamic shifts in the global economy, can some of the solutions also be found in the international sphere?

The driving engine of globalization has been economic, and the struggle at the international level to promote non-mercantile values such as environmental protection, human rights, and social and labour standards, while not forgotten, has often been a distant concern. The law, in particular, has reflected this lopsided emphasis. A fierce commitment has been given within the international sphere to the legal status and enforcement of trade agreements, private capital investments and intellectual property guarantees, complete with elaborate dispute resolution mechanisms that are rules-based, respected and obeyed. Indeed, this nascent system of international economic rights has been regularly identified as a template for a grander law-based approach to manage other sorts of global issues. However, the blueprints for a brave new world of international social and workplace rights have not advanced much beyond drafting tables and noble dreams. To date, the success of international labour law in protecting and promoting employment rights has been confined largely to the issuance of aspirational declarations, advisory standards and tribunal recommendations.

Yet, something profound is stirring. The intense unease that has greeted the promises and the institutions of globalization has spawned a new intellectual climate of criticism and analysis. Among industrial relations and legal academics concerned with employment and labour rights, a recognition is growing that the grand project of regulating the workplace to promote industrial justice is passing through a period of propulsive change, comparable perhaps only to the transition from the common law and traditional contractual principles to statutory labour laws during the years immediately before and after the Second World War. As responses to the challenges of globalization and the limitations of national law, two distinct and complementary approaches are emerging. Domestically, the argument is being made more and more insistently that labour rights, until now expressed primarily through ordinary employment statutes, must acquire a constitutional status as fundamental legal rights if they are to avoid a slide into disrepair. Internationally, the promising achievements of the European experience with supranational agreements as a means to promote labour laws, and the altogether more modest attempts in the Americas to include voluntary labour standards as an adjunct to regional trade agreements, have stirred the intellectual and social imagination about the possibility of new international and continental structures to secure workplace rights.

International labour law has existed as a discrete body of norms and advisory rules since the early years of the International Labour Organization following the First World War. For many years thereafter, there existed in the minds of most labour law scholars a traditional and simple division between the substantive rules of national labour laws and the advisory standards and conventions proclaimed by the ILO. One warranted a respected review, because it was solid, and the other received only a fleeting mention, because it was lighter than air. But over the past twenty years or so, this division no longer accurately represents the growing complexity of modern labour law on the international stage. Building on the promise of the European experiment, and the tentative steps taken elsewhere, it is becoming clear that the creation of new international labour law structures will not occur as a top-down project. Almost certainly, these new structures will evolve out of the growing number of regional and hemispheric economic agreements, which have added labour standards pacts as a political response to the demands for social protection against the shocks of rapid change. While, initially, many of these labour pacts have been humble efforts, they contain within them the potential of becoming the platforms for more substantive institutions and more effective rules that can complement and supplement the body of national labour laws. Yet, for any of this to occur, much depends upon the political will to recognize how globalization's imbalance between economy and society is exasperating social fault lines across the world.

Euclid, when asked by Ptolemy if there was a shorter route to mastering his teachings than by reading the *Elements*, is said to have replied: "There is no 'royal road' to geometry." So it is with the problems of globalization and the modern regulation of work. While the trials now confronting labour law are similar in importance to earlier periods of great transformations in the organization of employment, the challenges of our present era are almost certainly unique in dimension and complexity. The issues of national sovereignty, regional cooperation, the myriad of different systems of labour law regulation, the variety and number of workers falling outside formal protection, and the sheer pace of economic change present problems of an entirely new magnitude. But the very scale of the challenges of globalization to the world of work makes a multilateral response both indispensable and inescapable. As the World Commission on the Social Dimension of Globalization in its landmark report in 2004 pointed out, these problems are solvable and they are manageable, but not without a resolute universal recognition that human dignity, international solidarity and industrial justice are the cornerstone ethical values that can alone provide legitimacy to the globalization project as it affects the workplace.[3]

This volume of essays on globalization and the future of labour law seek to understand some of the problems and possibilities in our new world of work. The authors of these essays share the common starting point that the fundamental premises of contemporary labour law – workplace justice, industrial citizenship and production flexibility – remain intact, but that the ability to realize these goals through conventional regulatory tools are being substantially challenged by the new economic and political realities of the international marketplace. The authors' perspectives traverse through a range of issues, both geographic and topical, and are based on their experiences both in their home countries and regions and on the international stage. Drafts of many of the papers were first presented at a conference held at the University of Western Ontario in London, Ontario on 17 and 18 October 2003. This conference, co-sponsored by the Faculty of Law at the University of Western Ontario, the Canadian national law firm Heenan Blaikie LLP, and the Toronto law firm of Koskie Minsky, was among the first to be held in North America exclusively devoted to the issue of globalization and international labour law.

Part I   Perspectives on globalization

Brian Burkett's introductory paper (Chapter 1) introduces the concept of the "international labour dimension", and sets the stage for each of the papers that follow. In Burkett's view, regional and international labour integration involves the interplay not only of legal norms and standards with regulatory effect, but also of processes and institutions to develop and administer norms and standards at the international level. Burkett suggests that initiatives within the international labour dimension have a long and complex history that predates the founding of the ILO in 1919, and can even be traced back to the early nineteenth century. With the ILO came the birth of modern international labour law, which was premised on three pillars: social, political, and economic. The *social* relates to the shared desire to improve the human condition; the *political* refers to meeting ideological challenges (in 1919, the ideological challenges of communism and socialism); and the *economic* addresses social dumping and the 'race to the bottom'. Burkett is able to identify these three pillars within regional initiatives such as the European Union, the North American Free Trade Agreement (NAFTA), Mercosur, and the Summit of the Americas Process.

In Chapter 2, Harry Arthurs asks the question, "Who's afraid of globalization?" He posed this question when delivering the inaugural Koskie Minsky University Lecture on Labour Law that opened the conference on 17 October 2003. In answering the question, Arthurs focuses first on assessing the actual impact of globalization on substantive domestic labour laws. His conclusion: labour law continues to be viewed as primarily local in nature. This leads him to adopt a "common sense hypothesis" that globalization is formative, as opposed to normative. In other words, globalization changes labour law not by directly amending the substantive rules but instead by transforming the institutions and processes through which those rules are made and administered. Arthurs offers a message of optimism in the face of globalization. He observes that social progress is most enduring when it is built from the bottom-up. While globalization may make grassroots reform a daunting prospect, it is nevertheless possible, particularly if the advantages of globalization – e.g. instantaneous communications and the ability to organize over great distances – can be harnessed.

Part II   International labour standards

Part II focuses on the appropriate role of international labour standards in meeting the challenges of globalization. Each author offers a unique perspective. In Chapter 3, Kevin Banks addresses the phenomenon of social dumping and the link that has been drawn between international trade and labour standards. Banks writes that emerging scholarship has brought into question the theory that trade liberalization without labour standards will inevitably lead to a "race to the bottom". In fact, the evidence suggests that nations that improve their labour standards will generate positive long-term economic benefits. Social dumping is, at best, a short-term economic strategy. The implication is that international labour standards can be justified because of their positive long-term economic impact and not simply because they constitute international barriers to social dumping. However, as Banks observes, the enforcement of international labour standards remains a thorny issue.

Véronique Marleau suggests a different approach to globalization in Chapter 4. In her view, the optimal means of managing labour law in an era of globalization is through the concept of subsidiarity: decisions affecting individuals should, as far as possible, be made by the level of government closest to them. As a principle of social organization, subsidiarity localizes decision-making to the greatest extent possible, thereby creating a link between social and economic phenomena occurring at the global level and the circumstances and priorities of affected individuals and communities. Marleau is able to point to concrete examples of subsidiarity within the European Union and the ILO to bolster her point.

In Chapter 5, Alan Hyde offers a colourful and instructive defence of transnational labour standards, relying for support on Game Theory. In Hyde's "stag hunt", participants are only able to achieve the optimal result (i.e. successfully hunting a stag) if they cooperate and act collectively. If one participant chooses the course of individual action (i.e. prefers to hunt a hare individually instead of a stag collectively) then all other participants will either be left empty-handed (since hunting a stag is no longer possible) or will be forced to engage in the individual hunt for hares. Through the stag hunt model, Hyde is able to draw certain conclusions about transnational labour standards. Foremost among these is that multilateral cooperation in raising labour standards is crucial. However, the fewer the participants, the more likely they will be to develop the level of trust and cooperation that is necessary to ensure compliance with transnational labour standards. As such, Hyde suggests that greater success may be achieved through transnational labour standards negotiated in bilateral or regional trading agreements.

Part III   The European Union

The European Union has the most advanced system of regional labour integration, yet it is experiencing new challenges arising from the addition in 2004 of ten new states: Cyprus, the Czech Republic, Estonia, Hungary, Latvia, Lithuania, Malta, Poland, Slovakia and Slovenia. The future of European labour law is thus the focus of Part III of this book.

In Chapter 6, Manfred Weiss provides an overview of the industrial relations systems in the new member states from Central and Eastern Europe. He observes that these systems have developed over the past decade in reaction to the legacy of communism, and tend to reflect excessive neo-liberalism. As such, collective organizations representing workers and employers are relatively rare in the private sector, tripartite social dialogue is largely absent, and collective bargaining is the exception rather than the rule (and generally only occurs on a plant or company basis). Weiss further observes that while the Central and Eastern European states generally have favourable labour laws, implementation and enforcement are inadequate. Private sector companies are presently able to contract out of labour laws, in any event. Given the fundamental importance of collective organizations and social dialogue in EU-level labour law, Weiss identifies significant structural flaws that could threaten to undermine and delay future initiatives.

Arturo Bronstein's paper in Chapter 7 complements Weiss's paper. Bronstein outlines the evolution of labour laws in the Central and Eastern European states since the fall of communism. He describes their legal systems at the end of the communist era, emphasizing their diverse circumstances and laws. He then plots the approaches taken by these states to modernize their labour laws in the 1990s with a view to EU membership. Like Weiss, Bronstein points to excessive neo-liberalism and deregulation as predominant forces. Interestingly, however, he notes that most of the Central and Eastern European states have ultimately chosen to pursue a labour law model based on the German precedent; they have also sought technical assistance from German and French experts, and the ILO. Moreover, the ILO's standards and principles on freedom of association and collective bargaining have generally been adopted as the institutional framework for newly developing industrial relations systems. Given these developments, Bronstein predicts that the values of the European Social Model will eventually be embedded within the labour law systems of the Central and Eastern European states.

The final paper in Part III, by Catherine Barnard (Chapter 8), explores the development of worker mobility rights within the European Union, and considers whether the European experience holds any lessons for international labour law. Barnard is particularly interested in the implications of the principle of "solidarity", which has emerged within recent European jurisprudence. Solidarity is used to describe the relational bonds of citizens and communities, who share common interests, mutual dependence, and unity of purpose. While solidarity is generally found within states, it is not necessarily present at the transnational level. Indeed, the question arises whether the emergence of transnational solidarity is a precondition to true social and labour integration of the kind pursued by the EU. Barnard's discussion on this point could well be read in conjunction with Hyde's "stag hunt" analogy (Chapter 5). Are states more likely to cooperate in the pursuit of common social goals where solidarity prevails among their citizens? Is solidarity an essential precondition to multilateral action in social fields like labour law?

Part IV   The Americas

Whereas the European Union has decades of experience in harmonizing economic and social policies, the nations of the Americas are only now embarking upon a process to create a common hemispheric market through the proposed FTAA. It remains an open question how labour and other social issues will be treated under the FTAA. Hence, the papers in Part IV consider the challenges and potential outcomes of the FTAA negotiations.

In Chapter 9, Lance Compa adopts a pragmatic approach to worker rights under the FTAA, emphasizing the need to develop a viable, as opposed to a definitive or triumphant, solution for addressing worker concerns in a hemispheric economic zone. To this end, Compa considers in detail the hemispheric systems that already exist – the NAALC regime within NAFTA, Mercosur's Social-Labour Declaration, and Caricom's Charter of Civil Society. He concludes that governments of the Americas do not need to invent a new approach to address workers' rights within the FTAA. Instead, a system can be developed that incorporates features from each of the existing systems.

Brian Langille (Chapter 10) provides a principled justification for the adoption of labour rights within the FTAA. In his view, what is needed is a dramatic shift in attitude towards the social dimensions of trade liberalization. Langille argues that the negotiation of transnational social protections and standards is defensible not simply to prevent the "race to the bottom". More importantly, such measures are essential for socio-economic development and human progress. In developing a labour rights component to the FTAA, Langille states that countries participating in the FTAA talks need to reevaluate their reasons for engaging a labour rights agenda. If countries' mutual objectives include long-term economic development, social progress and political stability, then these objectives can and should inform the outcome of the FTAA negotiations.

José Pastore's paper (Chapter 11) provides a detailed examination of Latin American industrial relations systems, to demonstrate the challenges facing FTAA negotiators in creating viable hemispheric labour standards. Pastore focuses on the nations of Mercosur – Brazil, Argentina, Paraguay and Uruguay – and observes that they each have comprehensive protective labour laws, yet compliance with these laws is problematic. Moreover, informal employment relationships predominate, leaving millions of workers beyond the reach of protective laws. Pastore also points to significant vested interests in Latin American societies that have frustrated previous reform initiatives, both domestically and within Mercosur. With respect to the FTAA, Pastore takes the view that the priority should be to develop hemispheric mechanisms to enhance local compliance with domestic labour laws, as opposed to implementing and enforcing hemispheric labour standards. Hence, a model based on the NAALC system would be preferable.

Part V   The ILO

The ILO's significance in the debate over labour law and globalization cannot be overstated. Particularly since 1998, when it identified the "core" labour rights and promulgated its Declaration on Fundamental Principles and Rights at Work, the ILO has taken centre stage in all discussions related to global economic and social integration. The two papers in Part V consider the ILO's history and its future role in the globalization debate.

Werner Sengenberger's paper (Chapter 12) discusses the pluralist vision of the economy and society that has underscored the ILO's approach. Since 1919, the ILO has advocated processes for reconciling competing interests that emphasize association, consultation, negotiation and social dialogue. As Sengenberger notes, the ILO's pluralist approach to establishing international labour standards has often been challenged by economic orthodoxy, which itself advocates an unfettered free market as the optimal means of achieving greater employment opportunities and stronger worker protection. The pluralist approach has also occasionally been challenged on political and cultural grounds; however, Sengenberger argues that political and cultural objections to international labour standards are often mere pretexts designed to preserve the positions of powerful vested interests. Ultimately, Sengenberger suggests that the greatest challenge to the ILO in the coming years will arise out of the global economic and political environment. Will parochial attitudes and opportunistic local behaviour predominate, or will international cooperation prevail?

In Chapter 13, Edward Potter provides an overview of the United States' approach to the ILO. As the world's only superpower, the United States is a crucial player in the international sphere. Potter explains that the United States has had an uneasy relationship with the ILO since joining in 1934. Prior to 1989, the United States participated in the ILO primarily to fight communism and to limit the scope of international labour standards. Since 1990, however, there has been a remarkable transformation of the United States' attitude toward the ILO. Potter argues that the United States now views the ILO as an important actor in addressing worker rights in the global economy. This is particularly the case since the United States' policy is to link worker rights with trade. Potter argues that the United

States' emphasis on worker rights within international trading agreements has significantly enhanced the legitimacy of the ILO as an international standard-setting body.

Part VI   Labour rights

One of the areas where the attributes of globalization will be most carefully judged will be its impact upon historically vulnerable workers. Women and migrant workers have often lacked adequate protections under national labour laws, and they have become a special target of concern in the debates on the international role of law in regulating the global workplace.

Mary Cornish, Fay Faraday and Veena Verma consider the issue of gender inequality in Chapter 14. They emphasize the unique issues facing women in the new global economy: women's jobs are often precarious, substandard and low wage; the majority of positions in the growing informal economy are held by women; women continue to bear the burden of family and community responsibilities; and women can be easily exploited by low wage employers because of their need for flexible employment. Cornish, Faraday and Verma emphasize that gender inequality is pervasive and structural in nature. Achieving gender equality will require concerted efforts on the part of international bodies, states, employers and unions.

In the final Chapter, Ryszard Cholewinski examines the application of international labour standards developed first by the ILO and then under the auspices of the United Nations towards the plight of migrant workers. After considering some of the specific concerns of the modern migrant labour force, including those of women and temporary workers, Cholewinski argues that the working conditions of migrant employees in the receiving countries are becoming acute because they are ". . . often seen as a tool in maintaining competitiveness at the expense of formal employment and human rights protections". While the ILO has developed a comprehensive set of labour standards for the protection of migrant workers, much needs to be done to ensure these standards are realized at the national level. Paradoxically, he concludes, the process of globalization that has exasperated the traditionally difficult working conditions of migrant workers has also brought together the diverse and geographically distant movements in support of migrant workers' rights that are becoming increasingly effective in their struggle for a fair and just deal.

Conclusion

Labour law is but one of several important public tools and private forces that will shape the future of the global workplace. Economic agreements, trade and investment patterns, technological developments, political institutions, social and civil conventions and non-governmental organizations have all contributed to the dynamic changes in the organization of work, and to the emerging debate about how the employment relationship should now be regulated and protected in the face of new global realities. Our early warning systems – in the form of international institutional reports, scholarly writings, critical journalism and, indeed, the experiences of everyday life – are telling us that globalization in its present form is probably unsustainable, and the new workplace is becoming one of the social canaries that are signalling the coming distress. But this is not a message of despair. While globalization may be inevitable and everywhere, its final course is not predetermined. The role of labour law, both in its present form and in its imagined vision, is part of the larger debate over the ethical and social dimensions of globalization. Where all this will take us is not yet clear, but the newly forged human bonds of community and shared values are illuminating the way forward.

Notes

1. (Penguin Press, London, 1995).
2. (University of Minnesota Press, Minneapolis, 1995).
3. *A Fair Globalization: Creating Opportunities for All* (ILO: Geneva, 2004).

PART I

Perspectives on globalization

The international labour dimension: an introduction

BRIAN BURKETT

Introduction

The treatment of labour issues as a matter of international concern has been the subject of much discussion during the past decade, but it also has a long and complex history dating back to the early part of the nineteenth century. An understanding of this history is essential to any serious consideration of how the international labour dimension might develop in the coming years. Hence, the first objective of this paper is to survey the historical development of the international labour dimension, and to highlight its underlying social, political and economic dynamics. To this end, the focus of this discussion will be on the International Labour Organization (ILO), and three regional systems: the European Union (EU), NAFTA, and Mercosur. The Summit of the Americas Process and the negotiations surrounding the proposed Free Trade Agreement of the Americas (FTAA) will also be considered.

The choice of the term "international labour dimension" suggests a second objective. Although lawyers – both practitioners and scholars – tend to refer to international labour "law", it is quite clear that legal norms are only one element of the diverse efforts to address working conditions and labour standards at a level above the nation-state. The latter part of this paper will consider the broader concept of the international labour dimension, focusing on the diversity of approaches to promulgating norms and standards, and to addressing issues of administration and enforcement. The analysis will show that the international labour dimension should be understood as a complex interplay of norms and standards, institutions, and processes, all with the broad purpose of facilitating regional and international labour integration and cooperation.

Developments in the international labour dimension – a survey

The beginnings

The ILO was founded in 1919. However, this event was hardly the "genesis" of the international labour dimension. Although it is difficult to pinpoint an exact date, it is safe to say that discussions at the international level about working conditions and labour reform predated the ILO by over a century. The year 1818 is particularly notable, being the year of the Conference of the European Powers at Aix-la-Chapelle, France. There, British industrialist Robert Owen forcefully argued that a cooperative international effort to reform the conditions of labour would be in the interests of all classes of society. Having considered the vagaries of the industrial revolution, Owen advanced the theory that shorter hours of work and improved living conditions for workers would help to remove the causes that perpetuated human misery.[1] Owen even proposed an international institution to facilitate reform efforts.

There were a surprising number of international conferences on the subject of labour during the second half of the nineteenth century. These were generally privately organized affairs, with conference participants made up of academics, doctors, lawyers, social workers, and legislators.[2] The first of these was an international conference organized by Edouard Ducpetiaux, a Belgian prison inspector-general, in 1856 in Brussels. At a follow-up conference in 1857 in Frankfurt, a motion was adopted that called for the creation of international conventions regarding working conditions.[3]

Increasing discussion and concern at the international level about working conditions was paralleled by the rise of an international labour movement, through which workers formed transnational associations and demanded the emancipation of labour in all nations.[4] In 1866, at the first conference of the International Workers' Association in Geneva, several proposals were submitted on the reduction of the length of working days and the protection of women and children. Such demands were soon incorporated into the political agenda of socialists, who both responded to, and further fuelled, the demands of international labour. The formation of socialist parties emphasizing worker empowerment accelerated in the last quarter of the nineteenth century, with such parties eventually establishing a presence in countries across Europe.[5]

Despite the efforts of the international labour movement, and pressure applied by domestic socialist parties, it was not until the late 1800s

that state governments were persuaded to pursue international cooperation. At the invitation of the Swiss government, several European states
attended a preparatory conference in Bern on 5 May 1890. The subject
was the negotiation of an international agreement on the improvement
of working conditions. Germany proposed establishing a group of independent persons who would supervise the implementation of multilateral
protective measures. The conference endorsed this proposal, which stimulated the adoption of national labour legislation in several countries,
including Germany, Austria, Denmark and Portugal.[6]

The International Association for the Legal Protection of Workers (the
"International Association"), founded in 1897, held its first constitutive
assembly four years later in Basel. Seven countries participated. In order
to achieve some consensus among the participants, a commission was
formed to prepare general prohibitions on the less controversial subjects
of night work for women and the use of white phosphorous in the match
industry. Two conventions on these subjects were prepared and adopted
at a diplomatic conference in Bern in 1906.[7] These became the first true
international labour conventions when they were ratified and came into
force in 1912.[8]

Inspired by the work of the International Association, France and Italy
negotiated a groundbreaking bilateral labour treaty in 1904, which dealt
with accident indemnity, unemployment insurance, age restrictions, and
welfare conditions for nationals of one country who were working in
the other country.[9] By 1915, over twenty bilateral labour treaties had
been signed in addition to the two 1906 conventions, involving twelve
European countries and the United States. These treaties covered subjects
ranging from social insurance to the migration of workers.[10]

After the Bern conference, the International Association continued its
work on labour questions. In 1913, the Swiss government proposed a
new technical conference to prepare more conventions, which was to be
followed by another diplomatic conference in September 1914. However,
the First World War halted the development of the international labour
dimension for the next five years.[11]

The International Labour Organization

The ILO was created in 1919 by Part XIII of the Versailles Peace Treaty,
which ended the First World War.[12] As discussed above, a number of commentators had advocated the need for such an institution in the nineteenth
century. Specifically, the ideas advanced by Robert Owen, which were

originally reflected in the International Association, were subsequently incorporated into the Constitution of the ILO.

The factors that ultimately led to the creation of the ILO fall into three broad categories: social, political and economic.[13]

Social

It is probably fair to say that the primary factor in the creation of the ILO was a shared desire to improve the human condition. This had been a recurring theme in early discussions about the international labour dimension in the nineteenth century. By the end of the First World War, a consensus had been reached that state intervention was required to protect industrial and agrarian workers from harsh working terms and conditions that failed to take into account their health, their family lives and their advancement. A desire to ameliorate existing labour conditions, and to ensure that employers would abide by certain minimum standards related to matters such as wages, working time and the abolition of child labour, is clearly acknowledged in the Preamble to the ILO Constitution, which states that "conditions of labour exist involving . . . injustice, hardship and privation to large numbers of people".[14]

Political

The creation of the ILO was also a response to the very serious ideological challenges to the status quo made by international socialism and communism. Not surprisingly, scholars have pointed to the 1917 Russian Revolution as a pivotal event in the formation of the ILO, since it impressed upon governments that, absent concrete measures to improve working conditions, growing worker unrest could lead to revolution. The Preamble to the ILO Constitution effectively concedes the ideologically responsive nature of the ILO when it notes that workplace injustice produces "unrest so great that the peace and harmony of the world are imperilled."[15]

It is also interesting to note that growing worker unrest in the years prior to 1919 was paralleled by the increasing political influence of the international labour movement. In several European countries, war conditions brought worker organizations into much closer relations with governments. The reorientation of industry for the production of munitions and for supplying the essential needs of the community gave rise to many problems about which governments found it essential to consult worker organizations. As a result, governments became better informed about, and more sympathetic to, worker concerns, while the influence of worker organizations in domestic policy-making expanded significantly.[16]

Economic

Although the two factors outlined above – social and political – were crucial to the formation of the ILO, neither necessarily had to be addressed through international cooperation. Domestic initiatives could have been taken to safeguard workers and improve working conditions. What elevated the labour dimension to the international level was the third factor behind the formation of the ILO, namely concerns about competitive advantage in international trade. Improving labour conditions was viewed as potentially having an inflationary impact on the cost of production. Individual countries were reluctant to act unilaterally on worker protection initiatives if this could lead to a competitive disadvantage vis-à-vis other countries that did not implement similar reforms. Moreover, there were concerns that countries might roll back protective regulations to gain a competitive advantage. Today, this phenomenon goes by various names – "worker protection erosion", "social dumping", "the race to the bottom" – to mention three. Because of concerns about this phenomenon, a consensus was reached that distortions in competition on the world economic market could be avoided through international labour standards.[17] Hence, the Preamble to the ILO Constitution states that "the failure of any nation to adopt humane conditions of labour is an obstacle in the way of other nations which desire to improve the conditions in their own countries."

The ILO today

The number of ILO member states has grown from the original 42 in 1919, to 177 in 2004. Between 1919 and 2003, the ILO promulgated some 185 conventions and 194 recommendations.[18] These conventions and recommendations relate to a wide variety of matters of labour law and social policy: fundamental rights (freedom of association, collective bargaining, equality in employment), conditions of work, child labour, protection of women workers, hours of work, labour inspection, vocational guidance and training, social security protection, and occupational health and safety.[19]

For the purpose of the present discussion, the ILO's most significant recent accomplishment occurred in 1998, when it promulgated the *ILO Declaration on Fundamental Principles and Rights at Work* (the "Fundamental Declaration").[20] This document provides a consensus definition of the four core labour standards that have become the centrepiece of the global labour standards movement. The Fundamental Declaration holds that the four core standards are: (a) freedom of association and the effective recognition of the right to collective bargaining; (b) the elimination of all forms of forced or compulsory labour; (c) the effective abolition of child labour; and (d) the elimination of discrimination in respect of employment and occupation.

The ILO's position as the preeminent international standard-setting body on labour issues has enabled it to assert substantial influence on the development of regional systems. As will be discussed below, protecting fundamental labour principles has been a focus of discussions within the EU, NAFTA, Mercosur, and the Summit of the Americas Process. Moreover, the debate surrounding a "Social Clause" within the World Trade Organization has largely centred on the proposal to link trade liberalization to respect for the standards set out in the Fundamental Declaration. The ILO thus remains "front and centre" in all discussions about the international labour dimension.[21]

Regional systems

Since the formation of the ILO in 1919, several regional systems have emerged within the international labour dimension. In each case, social, political and economic factors have been driving factors. Below, three existing regional systems are considered, namely, the EU, NAFTA, and Mercosur. Discussion is also included of the Summit of the Americas Process and the negotiations surrounding the proposed FTAA.

The European Union

In discussing the international labour dimension, it is tempting for analytical purposes to group the EU together with other free trade zones, such as NAFTA or Mercosur. However, even a cursory analysis reveals a history, impact and role for the EU beyond that of a trading bloc. The EU is a supranational entity with legislative, judicial and executive powers of its own. The twenty-five member states make up an economic and political confederation, which includes a common currency (among twelve of the member states), common foreign security policy and cooperation on justice and home affairs.

Although the labour dimension of the EU is more advanced than in any other regional system, it is important to observe that the European Community (the EU's predecessor)[22] was created for political and economic, rather than social, reasons. As a consequence, a regional social and labour dimension has only slowly emerged. In fact, the initial motivation behind creating a common economic market in Europe was primarily political: namely, the prevention of another European war.

Following the enormous devastation, both in human and economic terms, of the Second World War, European integrationists argued that the only way to prevent future conflicts was to heighten the interdependence and stability of European nations.[23] This was to be achieved through the creation of a supranational authority with powers independent of, and in some cases superior to, national legislatures.[24] The first step was the creation of the 1952 European Coal and Steel Community (ECSC), through which France, West Germany, Belgium, Luxembourg, the Netherlands and Italy agreed to eliminate tariff and subsidy barriers on their coal and steel industries.[25] The same six countries agreed half a decade later to expand on the ECSC to create a common market and harmonize their economic policies. The European Economic Community (EEC) thus came into existence in January 1958 with the ratification of the Treaty of the European Economic Community.[26] The main economic goals of the EEC were the prevention of distortions in competition, and the abolition of barriers to the free movement of goods, persons (including workers), services, and capital.[27] By mid-1968, internal tariffs had fallen quickly enough to allow the six member states to agree to a common external tariff and to declare that an industrial customs union existed.

It was during the period from 1972 to 1980 that the EEC took its first steps toward creating a distinct social dimension through the adoption of "preliminary guidelines for a community's social policy programme", drafted by the European Commission in 1971.

This led to the Declaration of the heads of state and prime ministers at the 1972 Paris Summit, where the leaders of member states stated that they:

> attached as much importance to vigorous action in the social field as to the achievement of economic union . . . it is essential to ensure the increased involvement of labour and management in the economic and social decisions of the Community.[28]

This Declaration paved the way for the launch of the European Social Fund and the Social Action Programme, adopted by the Council in a resolution in January 1974. The programme concentrated on achieving full and better employment, the improvement of living and working conditions, the movement towards greater industrial democracy for workers, and the increased involvement of management and labour in the economic and social decisions of the Community.[29]

A number of legislative measures also materialized during the 1970s, including Council directives on protecting the acquired rights of workers on redundancy, insolvency and the transfer of an undertaking. A Council directive on equal pay was also adopted, followed by directives on equal treatment in employment and occupational social security.[30]

A breakthrough in the EU's labour dimension came with the 1976 decision of the European Court of Justice (ECJ) in *Defrenne* v. *Sabena (No. 2)*[31], where the Court took the view that Article 141 (equal pay)[32] served both economic and social purposes. In view of the different stages of development of social legislation in the various member states, the aim of Article 141 and other European-level social measures was to avoid "social dumping". The ECJ also stressed that Article 141 forms part of the social objectives of the European Community, which is not merely an economic union, but is intended to ensure social progress and to pursue constant improvement of living and working conditions.[33]

European-level activities within the social dimension slowed noticeably during the 1980s. Stung by slow economic growth and massive unemployment, EEC members generally followed the direction of British Prime Minister Margaret Thatcher, who insisted on deregulation and flexibility, and opposed proposals for numerous Council directives related to labour and social issues.[34]

Even the Single European Act of 1986, the most important advance in European integration since the Treaty of Rome, was almost singularly concerned with economic policy and harmonization. Pursuant to the Act, the members of the EEC (then numbering twelve) agreed to remove all remaining physical, fiscal and technical barriers to trade.[35]

By the mid-1980s, however, Jacques Delors, the then President of the European Commission, linked social policy to the objective of realizing a common Internal Market by 1992. Delors argued that the harmonization of social laws was necessary to prevent social dumping and a "race to the bottom". He envisaged the creation of a "European Social Area" to ensure the protection of social standards in the face of open competition.[36] Delors's vision was at least partly realized in 1989 with the adoption by eleven of the twelve member states[37] of the Community Charter of Basic Social Rights (the "Social Charter"). The Social Charter brought together all of the social policy goals that had been mentioned throughout the life of the Community. Drawing upon the core labour conventions of the ILO, the Social Charter guaranteed social improvements in areas such as freedom of movement of workers, living and working conditions, health and safety in the workplace, social protection, education and training, and equal treatment (including protection against discrimination on grounds of sex, race, colour, opinion, religion, and protection for migrant workers and nationals of third countries).[38]

The adoption of the Social Charter was then followed by further developments respecting economic and social integration. At the Maastricht Summit in December 1991, the member states agreed on a revision of the Treaty of Rome, and signed a new treaty on European Union (the "Maastricht Treaty"). This treaty was eventually ratified by the member states and came into force on 1 November 1993. The treaty created a new legal entity called the "European Union", which was comprised of three pillars: the European Community, and two (mainly) inter-governmental pillars addressing matters relating to justice and home affairs and a common foreign and security policy. The Treaty of Rome was reorganized and renamed the "EC Treaty".[39] In effect, a new union between the twelve member states was created, the jurisdiction of the EU was extended into areas such as consumer protection, public health policy and education, and new rights were given to European citizens, who could now live where they liked in the EU and vote in local and European elections.[40] Moreover, the Maastricht Treaty established social and labour market policy as independent policy areas, and fully recognized the right of the social partners (i.e. employer and worker organizations) to be consulted in European-level decision making.[41]

By the time of the Amsterdam Treaty, signed in 1997, the role of the EU in promoting harmonization within the social dimension was no longer in dispute. In fact, the Amsterdam Treaty explicitly recognized the importance of social issues within the Community:

> The Community shall have as its task, by establishing a common market and an economic and monetary union and by implementing the common policies or activities referred to in Articles 3 and 4, to promote throughout the Community an harmonious and balanced development of economic activities, a high level of employment and of social protection, equality between men and women, sustainable and non-inflationary growth, a high degree of competitiveness and convergence of economic performance, a high level of protection and improvement of the environment, the raising of the standard of living and quality of life, and economic and social cohesion and solidarity among Member States.[42]

Pursuant to the Amsterdam Treaty, a new chapter on employment (Articles 125–130) was inserted into the EC Treaty. Under this chapter, the EU is required to promulgate annual employment guidelines to promote four major goals: employability, entrepreneurship, adaptability, and equal opportunities.[43] The member states themselves must adopt more detailed national action plans in order to implement the guidelines.[44]

Hence, as of 2004, it is clear that the EU and its institutions have a recognized jurisdiction to promote a regional social and labour dimension. Consider the Council of the European Union, the principle legislative institution of the EU, which has formal responsibilities in areas such as:

- free movement of workers (Article 40 EC Treaty);
- the establishment of the internal market (Article 95 EC Treaty);
- workers' health and safety;
- working conditions;
- information and consultation of workers;
- equality between men and women (Articles 137 and 141 EC Treaty);
- employment and incentive measures (Articles 128 and 129 EC Treaty);
- the European Social Fund (Article 148 EC Treaty);
- vocational training (Article 150 EC Treaty); and
- economic and social cohesion (Article 162 EC Treaty).[45]

It is notable that Article 137 grants to the Council, together with the European Parliament, the power to adopt most measures in the labour dimension by a qualified majority.[46] Other matters require either an absolute majority or unanimity.[47]

In recent times, the EU has placed heavy reliance on non-binding declarations, as opposed to binding regulations and directives, as the preferred means of setting the course of policy. This may be occurring at the expense of implementing more individual and collective social rights that are enforceable against the member states. A critical test of the European Union's ability to protect social rights will be the implementation of the European Charter of Fundamental Rights (the "Charter"). The Charter was signed by the Presidents of the European Parliament, the Council and the Commission in Nice on 7 December 2000 and was incorporated into the much anticipated European Constitution[48] as Part II. The European Constitution, which was signed by all heads of member states on 29 October 2004 in Rome, will only become binding once it is ratified by each member state according to their domestic rules. National referenda are expected to be held by a number of member states during the period from 2004 to 2006.[49]

The Charter, which is based partly on the 1950 European Convention on Human Rights, provides for six categories of rights: dignity, freedoms, equality, solidarity, citizens' rights, and justice. Within these categories, the Charter provides for a number of workers' rights, including:

- freedom of assembly and of association (Article II-72);
- freedom to choose an occupation and right to engage in work (Article II-75);
- freedom to conduct a business (Article II-76);
- non-discrimination (Article II-81);
- equality between men and women (Article II-83);
- workers' right to information and consultation within the undertaking (Article II-87);
- right of collective bargaining and strike action (Article II-88);
- fair and just working conditions (Article II-91); and
- prohibition of child labour and the protection of young people at work (Article II-92).

A limitation of the Charter is that it does not apply directly to the domestic affairs of member states. Rather, it binds the institutions, bodies, offices and agencies of the European Union generally and the member states only when they are implementing European Union law.[50] Nonetheless, implementation of the Charter as part of the EU Constitution would have signalled a significant advance in the recognition and advancement of social rights at the EU level.

The EU has therefore evolved to the point where it has the dual objectives of economic and social advancement. A pan-European labour dimension has emerged in response to the same economic and social factors that were discussed above in relation to the ILO. Critical areas within the labour dimension are poised to gain greater protection at the EU level with the possible ratification of the European Constitution, which includes the Charter of Fundamental Rights. There are, however, important elements within the labour dimension that remain beyond the jurisdiction of the EU to enforce against member states in the operation of their domestic affairs, including freedom of association (i.e. union formation), collective bargaining, and the right to strike. Given political sensitivities, it is doubtful whether the member states will ever be willing to cede jurisdiction over these issues to European-level institutions. Nevertheless, the EU has gone further in developing norms and standards within the labour dimension than any other regional system. It is also the most mature regional system in terms of institutions and processes.

Going forward, the greatest challenge facing the EU will be the integration of its ten newest member states, which joined the EU on 1 May 2004.[51]

The new members not only increase the size and population of the EU, but the disparity of wealth between the new and existing member states will result in a dramatic reduction of per person GDP. In addition, harmonizing the less developed labour and social policies of the new member states with those of the existing members may prove exceedingly difficult in the short to medium term. The EU could well find itself in a position similar to participants in the Summit of the Americas Process (discussed below), namely, searching for an integration strategy to address disparate levels of development and significant structural differences among member states.

NAFTA

The Free Trade Agreement between Canada and the United States of America[52] (FTA) came into effect in January 1989, creating a free trade zone between Canada and the United States. The FTA itself contained no discernible social or labour dimension. In fact, a link between trade liberalization and labour or environmental standards was denied by supporters of the FTA. Only two years later, negotiations began for a trilateral free trade agreement that would include Mexico, and would build on and supercede the FTA. After intense national debates respecting the social, political, and economic consequences of such an agreement, Canada, the United States and Mexico concluded the North American Free Trade Agreement (NAFTA) in January 1994.[53] NAFTA essentially creates a free trade zone in goods, and significantly liberalizes the treatment of investment, intellectual property, and services across the continent.

The relationships and histories of the three NAFTA member states have shaped the form and substantive provisions of NAFTA. While there are many reasons for Canada, the United States and Mexico to develop closer economic relations, the social, political and cultural dynamics that drove the creation and evolution of the EEC after the Second World War simply did not exist in North America in the early 1990s. Moreover, as a result of the historical experiences of Canada, the United States and Mexico, each country has manifested a strong desire to preserve its sovereignty in the face of economic integration. The sheer size and power of the United States has made both Canada and Mexico reluctant to integrate socially and politically within North America. This is a dynamic that has traditionally not existed within the European Union, where the member states have been more balanced in terms of political and economic power.[54]

The high priority placed on sovereignty by the three NAFTA countries is most evident in the ancillary nature of the continental social and labour dimensions that ultimately emerged. Rather than attempting to harmonize labour standards as in the EU, the United States, Canada and Mexico agreed to a mechanism that allows each country the opportunity to challenge the enforcement by the other countries of their national labour laws. This mechanism is contained in the North American Agreement on Labour Cooperation (the NAALC),[55] a supplementary side agreement to the NAFTA.

The impetus for the NAALC came predominantly from political circumstances in the United States. During the NAFTA negotiations, the American environmental and labour movements argued that free trade would produce social dumping and a destructive "race to the bottom". Bill Clinton, who was at the time the Democratic Party nominee for President and who had initially supported George H. W. Bush's trade-oriented agenda, made his support of NAFTA contingent, in part, on linking trade liberalization to improved environmental and labour standards. Upon taking power, Clinton responded to the environmental concerns by concluding the North American Agreement on Environmental Cooperation.[56] Further, to assuage fears of American workers and unions about the consequences of the "race to the bottom" (and particularly the loss of jobs to Mexico), Clinton negotiated the NAALC.

The negotiations surrounding the substantive provisions of the NAALC revealed the difficulties of implementing a labour dimension as an aspect of trade liberalization among countries of disparate levels of development. In the United States, the labour movement was most concerned that the creation of a free trade zone between two developed countries (Canada and the United States) and a developing country (Mexico) would lead to significant competitive pressures to lower labour standards in the developed countries. On the other hand, the Clinton administration argued that existing Mexican labour laws were sufficiently protective, and maintained that the problem was the lack of enforcement of these laws.[57] In response, Mexico argued that its labour laws were as progressive as those of Canada and the United States, and that enforcement problems were a result of a lack of governmental resources.[58] For its part, Canada maintained that enforcement procedures should be improved in Mexico, but argued that each member state should remain free to set its own labour standards.[59]

The agreement that was finally negotiated did not commit to harmonizing labour standards of the three countries. Moreover, the inclusion of a NAFTA-level enforcement process for labour issues was rejected. In fact, the NAALC recognizes that laws and standards will differ, and that each nation may chart its own course. As a result, the agreement simply requires the NAFTA countries to enforce their own labour laws, with no formal requirement that those laws be consistent with internationally agreed core labour standards such as those in the Fundamental Declaration.

However, under the NAALC, the NAFTA countries have undertaken to ensure that labour laws and regulations provide for "high labour standards". Pursuant to Article 1, each nation has committed itself to promoting *in its own way* the ideals contained in three tiers in Annex I, which include core labour principles such as: the protection of the right to organize, bargain and strike; the prohibition of forced labour, the protection of migrant labour, the elimination of employment discrimination and the pursuit of equality including equal pay for equal work; the protection of occupational health and safety, the prohibition of child labour and the protection of minimum wages. It is notable that only three areas – occupational health and safety, child labour and minimum wages – are subject to the full dispute resolution and enforcement provisions of the NAALC.

The NAALC obligates member states to enforce their own labour laws in the subject areas set out in Annex I, and provides that if a member state believes that another is not doing so, it may launch a complaint to the Commission for Labour Cooperation. Such a complaint is first referred to a Council composed of the labour secretaries/ministers of each member state. The Council, which establishes its own rules and procedures, first attempts to resolve the complaint through consultation and cooperation. A pattern of non-compliance in certain subject areas could result in the appointment of an outside group of experts to make non-binding recommendations.

Failing resolution at this level, a complaint that deals with laws regarding occupational health and safety, child labour or minimum wages could eventually proceed through various layers of investigation and consultations at the ministerial level to an arbitration before a panel, and the imposition of sanctions. In order for the Council to convene an arbitral panel, the matter at issue must be both trade-related and be covered by mutually recognized labour laws.[60]

The National Administrative Offices (NAOs) of member states may ignore a complaint altogether, investigate the complaint but not report the outcome, or refuse to recommend that the complaint be made the subject of ministerial consultation. Likewise, labour ministers involved in the government-to-government consultations are not bound by rules or guidelines regarding the consideration of individual cases. As a result, the cases that have proceeded under the NAALC in Canada, the United States and Mexico have had varying results. The desire of the NAFTA countries to avoid the harmonization of labour laws and a multinational judicial process has resulted in an instrument that lacks an effective enforcement mechanism.

On balance, it is clear that economic issues have been the central feature of the NAFTA, and that the labour dimension of NAFTA is really ancillary. The NAALC has not made any notable progress in promoting continental social and labour integration, nor has it created an effective enforcement mechanism to ensure that each NAFTA country complies with its own domestic labour standards. However, the NAALC does create a link between trade and labour, and in this sense it breaks new ground by creating labour relations obligations in the context of an agreement to liberalize trade. This is particularly evident in the work of the NAALC Secretariat, which is based in Washington, DC. This unique multinational institution, which includes labour economists, lawyers and other professionals, is devoted to advancing labour standards as an integral part of expanding trade relations. The Secretariat has two principal functions. First, the Secretariat serves as the general administrative arm of the Commission. It provides support to the Council, as well as to evaluation committees of experts and arbitral panels established by the Council. Second, it undertakes research and analysis, and prepares public reports on: labour law and administrative procedures; trends and administrative strategies related to the implementation and enforcement of labour law; labour market conditions such as employment rates, average wages and labour productivity; and human resource development issues such as training and adjustment programmes. The Secretariat supports the cooperative activities of the Commission, including seminars, conferences, joint research projects and technical assistance in relation to the eleven labour principles of the NAALC, as well as labour statistics, productivity, and other related matters. Recent cooperative activities include trilateral seminars of the Labour Boards in North America, technical workshops on occupational health and safety management systems, migrant and immigrant worker forums as well as tri-national conferences on violence in the workplace. The cooperative activities have created a process through which member states may share best practices, exchange knowledge and develop educational programs – potentially a precursor to further regional cooperation in the social and labour dimensions.

Mercosur

The Southern Cone Common Market (in Spanish, Mercado Común del Sur – commonly referred to as "Mercosur") provides another important example of a trading bloc that has pursued the development of a regional labour dimension. Mercosur was formed in 1991 by Argentina, Brazil, Paraguay and Uruguay through the Treaty of Asunción.[61] This treaty provided for the liberalization of trade in goods between the member states, implemented a common external tariff, and proclaimed Mercosur's ambition to become a common market in which goods, services, capital, and labour would circulate freely.[62] With 240 million consumers (compared with 380 million in NAFTA), Mercosur's regional system is one of the world's most important.

Since its creation in 1991, Mercosur's mandate has included a social dimension that links social and labour issues with trade interests. The Treaty of Asunción clearly stipulated the objective of accelerating the processes of economic development through social justice, and securing a better standard of living for the inhabitants of the member countries.[63] This makes Mercosur notable among the world's leading regional trading blocs, since social development was a priority from the outset, as opposed to an ancillary point. This is perhaps not surprising, though, since the member states of Mercosur each shared pressing social and political problems prior to 1991. The development of a common market among these countries was viewed not simply as an economic development project, but also as a means to achieve improvements in social standards and to promote political stability through multilateral interdependence. Running parallel to the humanitarian and political imperatives of Mercosur was a familiar concern about social dumping – given the geographic proximity of member states, capital could all too easily move from jurisdiction to jurisdiction in order to exploit lower (and cheaper) labour standards. Avoiding a "race to the bottom" therefore required proactive and coordinated measures at the Mercosur level on social standards.

A review of Mercosur's achievements with respect to the labour dimension demonstrates a progression from an initial emphasis on process issues, to the creation of Mercosur-level institutions with a labour dimension mandate, to the promulgation of social and labour standards. An appropriate starting point is "Working Subgroup No. 11", a tripartite body fine-tuned in 1991 for the express purpose of giving effect to the labour dimension of Mercosur. At its inception, matters related to the labour market, labour relations, employment and social security were referred to this Subgroup. Through the work of its Technical Commissions, the Subgroup was able to develop diagnostic exercises and comparative studies, detecting asymmetries among the members' systems with a view towards harmonization and convergence in areas such as individual and collective rights, employment, vocational training, labour occupational health and social security. The Subgroup also took on the task of reviewing international labour conventions and identifying those it considered essential for developing multilateral agreements to standardize national labour legislation. The result of this project was the identification of 35 ILO conventions, including those covering the core labour principles that were eventually incorporated into the Fundamental Declaration. The work of the Subgroup, largely completed by 1995, was crucial for gaining insights into the national realities of the member states, and was arguably the necessary first step before any substantive initiatives in the labour dimension could be taken at the Mercosur level.[64]

The "Ouro Preto Protocol" of 1994 was the next notable development, as it triggered the creation of an institutional structure within Mercosur for dealing with the labour dimension. Two bodies emerged. First, "Working Subgroup No. 10" was established in May 1996 with responsibility for labour issues, employment and social security. This Subgroup followed the objectives and tripartite structure of its predecessor, Subgroup No. 11, but its mandate was expanded considerably. Second, an "Economic and Social Advisory Forum" was created for the express purpose of facilitating cooperation between employer and worker representatives. The Forum was also open to other social groups including consumer associations, cooperatives and academics.[65]

During the period 1996–8, Subgroup No. 10 pursued its mandate of considering mechanisms to ensure the effective improvement of social and labour conditions within the region. It focused its deliberations on three main areas: (1) specific labour and social rights to be recognized within Mercosur, (2) the legal nature of these rights, and (3) the development of mechanisms for supervision and follow-up on compliance with these rights. One of the Subgroup's most important accomplishments was the drafting of a Multilateral Treaty on Social Security, which unified existing bilateral treaties and promoted principles such as equal treatment of nationals of the four countries, protection of rights, apportioning of benefits, and ensuring administrative cooperation between social security administrations. Subgroup No. 10 also played a key role in the establishment of a Regional Labour Market Observatory to collect, process and disseminate accurate labour market information within the region.

Subgroup No. 10's work formed the basis for Mercosur's "Social and Labour Declaration" dealing with labour relations, employment and social security. The declaration was a solemn statement delivered by the heads of state of the four member countries in December 1998. It enumerated the fundamental labour rights of workers and employers, and committed member states to pursue the effective implementation of these rights. The declaration also created a third significant body, the Social and Labour Commission. Based on a tripartite structure, the Commission was given the mandate to examine government reports and propose recommendations, programmes and plans of action to ensure the effective observance of the social and labour standards set out in the declaration.[66]

Future lines of action have been identified by Subgroup No.10 and the Social and Labour Commission. These include:

- regional harmonization of labour legislation through a convergence of national and international rules;
- standardization of basic principles to direct national policy and action in areas such as vocational training, occupational health and labour competencies, and regulation of the free circulation of workers;
- regulating border crossings for labour purposes;
- coordination of labour inspection;
- improving control and follow-up mechanisms; and
- broadening consecrated rights.

Overall, then, Mercosur has made notable progress in developing a regional labour dimension. Mercosur's accomplishments include the creation of political and technical bodies responsible for overseeing labour issues, the consolidation of minimum fundamental rights of workers and employers, coordination and harmonization to protect and promote these rights, and improvements in balancing the interests of all actors involved in the social and labour fields through tripartism.[67] Mercosur's success reflects the fact that member states have approached the project of developing a common market not simply as a matter of economic development, but also as a means to achieve social progress and political stability.

The FTAA project, discussed below, is bound to have a significant impact on the development of Mercosur. The Mercosur nations have had a difficult time agreeing on their position towards the FTAA.[68] Brazil has been particularly reluctant to commit to the FTAA, and remains cautious of rushing into an agreement.[69] Despite tensions, Mercosur continues to be a major actor in the negotiations over the FTAA, and internal cohesion at the negotiating table has significantly improved.[70] Assuming the successful negotiation of the FTAA, an obvious issue arises as to the sustainability of Mercosur generally, and of labour dimension initiatives within Mercosur specifically. Could Mercosur be absorbed into the FTAA? Or will it continue to have a separate existence even as its member countries adhere to the FTAA? In either eventuality, the Mercosur member countries will probably insist that the FTAA incorporate safeguards within the labour dimension. Otherwise, Mercosur's accomplishments could be undercut through the creation of a pan-American common market in which a "race to the bottom" is allowed to occur.

The Summit of the Americas

In many ways, the Summit of the Americas Process is the ultimate expression of the political, social and economic dynamics that have traditionally driven the international labour dimension. This is because the present Summit of the Americas Process has, from its inception, treated economic integration under the FTAA as one element of a broader socio-political integration project for the Americas. The breadth of the Summit Process is reflected in the agenda of the First Summit of the Americas, which took place in Miami in 1994. This summit, intended as a platform to discuss a variety of common concerns across the Americas, focused on the following issues:

- the strengthening of democratic institutions;
- the fight against drug trafficking;
- the growth of trade and commerce, better labour conditions, and enhanced environmental protection; and
- addressing social issues, including poverty, health, education and job growth.

The Declaration of Principles and the Plan of Action coming out of the Miami Summit committed participating nations to pursuing a joint agenda for the strengthening of democracies in the Americas.[71] The Miami Declaration established the goals of expanding prosperity through greater economic integration and free trade, eradicating poverty and discrimination, and encouraging sustainable development and environmental protection. The Miami Plan of Action contained a series of specific initiatives, with one or more countries being designated to take on a leadership role with respect to each initiative.[72] One of these initiatives was, of course, an agreement to work towards establishing a hemispheric common market through the FTAA by 2005. To realize this goal, a Tripartite Committee was formed, the members of which included the Inter-American Development Bank (IDB), the Organization of American States (OAS), and the United Nations' Economic Commission for Latin America and the Caribbean ("ECLAC").

The Second Summit of the Americas was held in Santiago, Chile on 18–19 April 1998. Again, the agenda of the summit focused on socio-political issues such as strengthening democratic institutions and protecting human rights. The latter was an especially important issue, given the continued presence in some countries of torture, police brutality, arbitrary detention, the harassment of journalists and extrajudicial executions. The Santiago Summit reaffirmed the Miami Summit's commitments to democracy and economic integration, and established that summits should be organized on a regular basis as an integral component of hemispheric relations.

The Santiago Declaration, like the earlier Miami Declaration, was an umbrella document setting forth general principles to guide governments in their implementation of a detailed Plan of Action.[73] The Santiago Declaration was notable for its emphasis on the need to improve education and living conditions for the peoples of the Americas, and the importance of moving forward with hemispheric economic integration. In the Santiago Declaration, the heads of state and government directed their "Ministers responsible for trade" to begin negotiations for the FTAA. They further restated their determination to conclude the negotiation of the FTAA no later than 2005.

The Santiago Plan of Action set forth 26 separate initiatives, including an initiative on "Modernization of the state in labour matters". The Plan of Action also contained a special section entitled "Summit of the Americas Follow-up", which set forth procedures and steps going forward.

While the First and Second Summits each led to initiatives in the labour dimension, it was the Third Summit of the Americas in Quebec City, Canada (20–22 April 2001) that proved to be a watershed event in developing a hemispheric labour dimension. At the Quebec City Summit, leaders addressed common hemispheric issues and challenges that were identified as a result of the processes established at the previous summits. Social issues, such as access to education, poverty, human rights and democracy, were a significant focus of discussions. Meanwhile, outside the summit, anti-globalization protesters gathered to oppose (in some cases violently) the allegedly corporatist agenda of the summit and its alleged failure to address adequately social issues including labour and environmental standards.

The Quebec City Declaration set out the continued commitment of nations to the principles of democracy, human rights and protection of security.[74] Further goals included reducing drug trafficking, combating the spread of HIV, and strengthening free and open economies. In terms of the labour dimension, the heads of state agreed to work toward compliance with internationally recognized core labour standards as embodied in the Fundamental Declaration.

The Quebec City Plan of Action (Part 11 – 'Labour and Employment')[75] recognized that true prosperity can only be achieved by protecting and respecting basic rights of workers as well as promoting equal employment opportunities and improving working conditions for people across the hemisphere.[76] Governments also agreed to:

- develop new mechanisms to increase the effectiveness of projects and other technical assistance designed to build the capacity of smaller economies and their institutions to implement labour laws and standards effectively, and to foster equality of opportunity (particularly with respect to gender) in strategies to promote employment, training, life-long learning, and human resource development programmes; and,
- promote and protect the rights of all workers, in particular those of working women, and take action to remove structural and legal barriers as well as stereotypical attitudes to gender equality at work, addressing, inter alia, gender bias in recruitment, working conditions, occupational discrimination and harassment, discrimination in social protection benefits, women's occupational health and safety, and unequal career opportunities and pay.

Notably, the Quebec City Plan of Action referred labour matters to the Inter-American Conference of Ministers of Labour (IACML), a body of the Organization of American States (OAS).[77] that is composed of the Ministers of Labour of all the countries participating in the Summit of the Americas Process. The IACML was directed in the Quebec City Plan of Action to develop a process to consider and address the labour and social dimensions of hemispheric economic integration. The fact that labour issues arising within the Summit of the Americas are being dealt with at the highest ministerial level is indicative of the overall significance of the hemispheric labour dimension and the level of acceptance afforded the Fundamental Declaration.

At its twelfth meeting in Ottawa in October 2001, the IACML established a two-year agenda of meetings, conferences and studies designed to fulfil the mandate set down in the Quebec City Plan of Action. Through its own Ottawa Declaration and Plan of Action, the IACML adopted a tripartite process with two working groups:

- Working Group 1: Labour Dimensions of the Summit of the Americas Process – the mandate of this working group was to study and report back to the IACML on the implications for labour and employment of hemispheric integration, and the development of common hemispheric labour standards; and
- Working Group 2: Needs and Capacities of Labour Administration – the mandate of this working group was to study and report back to the IACML on how best practices models could be developed to assist nations in implementing and administering labour laws and standards, training programmes, human resource development, and employment growth strategies.[78]

Working Group 2 was also given the mandate to consider the promotion of the ILO's Fundamental Declaration within the Americas.

The approach taken by the IACML is centred on generating high-level discussions among countries on labour dimension issues, in order to build consensus on future steps. This is an inherently slow process, given the number of countries (34) involved,[79] and the remarkable diversity of these countries on matters ranging from population, language and culture, to economic development, legal traditions, and social policies. However, it is not an unfamiliar process, since (as discussed above) Mercosur's process of regional integration has proceeded under a similar format.

At its thirteenth meeting in September 2003 at Salvador, Brazil, the IACML launched the next two-year phase of its deliberations respecting the social and labour dimensions of the Summit of the Americas Process. The Salvador Plan of Action called for the two working groups described above to continue their work, with a view to developing concrete proposals for addressing the issues of labour integration and labour administration in the Americas.[80] In addition, the Ministers of Labour agreed to conduct a feasibility study on the creation of a mechanism dedicated to facilitating horizontal cooperation initiatives for improving and professionalizing labour administration in the Americas.[81] A final draft of the feasibility study is scheduled to be submitted to the IACML Ministers for approval in late 2004.

In November 2002, the IACML received an unprecedented invitation from the trade ministers of the Americas, who requested[82] that a report on the labour dimension of the Summit of the Americas Process be presented at their next ministerial meeting. Consequently, at the 8th FTAA ministerial meeting held in Miami in November 2003, the IACML's Working Group 1 presented its report entitled "Labour Dimensions of the Summit of the Americas Process: Globalization, Employment and Labour",[83] which emphasized that modern labour policies are key to the success of a global economy. The Labour Dimensions report recommended that the ministers of labour prepare a plan of action to:

- continue studying labour provisions in emerging free trade agreements;
- present options to allow for better implementation of labour commitments, legislation and policies;
- find ways and methods to further study the effects of economic integration on labour markets and labour policy, and find means to enable the smaller economies of the Americas to undertake this type of analysis;
- commission a feasibility study on ways to strengthen labour ministries' capacity to carry out their functions;
- invite officials from trade and other ministries to IACML meetings to address appropriate cross-cutting issues; and
- continue to encourage business and labour representatives and international organizations to actively participate in the IACML.[84]

In the Miami Ministerial Declaration,[85] the trade ministers acknowledged the IACML report, expressed their agreement with the IACML's Salvador Declaration, encouraged further study of the labour dimensions of economic integration and requested that the IACML keep them informed of future findings.

To say that the IACML process is ambitious is, probably, an understatement. Nevertheless, some concrete advances have been made that address the challenges inherent in the pursuit of labour integration among countries of such incredible diversity. Notable among these advances is an emphasis on labour dimension process, as opposed to promulgating norms and standards. Reflecting the need to assist smaller, developing economies to modernize and democratize their labour laws and institutions as a necessary first step to deeper hemispheric labour integration, the IACML has emphasized the development of "horizontal cooperation" mechanisms and processes. Horizontal cooperation is an approach that facilitates information sharing, technical exchanges, and the development of best practices models through a mix of bilateral and multilateral initiatives among nations. It is the opposite of a "vertical" or "top down" model, where norms and standards are promulgated at the supranational level (usually through supranational institutions), and are then implemented within domestic systems. What has become clear through the work of the IACML is that a horizontal cooperation approach to labour dimension issues is not only easier to sell politically (since it is less interventionist), but is also more practical in the short to medium term for addressing the wide disparities among countries. Given the absence of a hemispheric culture of cooperation and solidarity on labour and social issues, and given the disparities among countries with respect to those issues, it is probable that a vertical model akin to the European Union would be unworkable. Horizontal cooperation could, over time, promote the conditions necessary for deeper labour integration under a vertical system of labour norms and standards.

The collective commitment by heads of state of the Americas to develop a hemispheric labour dimension was reinvigorated in January 2004, when a Special Summit of the Americas was held in Monterrey, Mexico. One factor which motivated the early scheduling of the Monterrey Summit (originally planned for 2005) was that one third of the relevant heads of state had taken office since the Third Summit of the Americas, and were therefore not part of the collective Quebec City commitments.

The themes of the Monterrey Summit echoed prior meetings: combating poverty, promoting social development, achieving economic growth with equity, and strengthening democratic governance. The heads of state ratified the Declaration of Nuevo Léon,[86] which included a collective reaffirmation of ILO principles and recognition of the IACML's mandate:

> We are committed to the principles of decent work proclaimed by the International Labour Organization, and we will promote the implementation of the declaration on the fundamental principles and rights at work in the conviction that respect for workers' rights and dignity is an essential element to achieving poverty reduction and sustainable social and economic development for our peoples. Additionally, we agree to take measures to fight the worst forms of child labour. We recognize and support the important work of the Inter-American Conference of Ministers of Labour toward achieving these vital objectives.[87]

Of course, the work of the IACML within the Summit of the Americas Process is still preliminary. It is therefore difficult to predict the nature and form of the labour dimension that could emerge when (or perhaps even if) the FTAA negotiations are completed.[88] However, what is most interesting for present purposes is the strong commitment made by participants to deal with labour issues as an inherent aspect of the hemispheric integration process. This commitment is rooted in several factors. First, the Summit of the Americas Process has been conceived since its inception as a broad-based economic, social and political project to address poverty, political instability and social inequities in participating countries. By defining the Process so broadly, participants are hard-pressed to deny a link between trade and social/labour issues. Second, the two key trading blocs in the Americas[89] – NAFTA and Mercosur – have accepted a link between trade and labour standards, and the need to prevent social dumping among nations in a common market. This approach has been brought forward into the Summit of the Americas, which to a considerable extent builds on the accomplishments of NAFTA, Mercosur and other regional trading systems like CARICOM. Third, and perhaps most significantly, the Summit Process has been under intense scrutiny from the anti-globalization movement. The ideological challenge of anti-globalization, which views international economic integration as little more than a corporate conspiracy to reap profits at the expense of third world workers and first world jobs, has fuelled public demand for substantive measures to address social dimensions issues. Politicians from across the hemisphere may well have concluded that the FTAA would enjoy insufficient popular support absent measures to protect workers and the environment, raise social standards, etc.

What is the international labour dimension?

The social, political, and economic factors behind the earliest discussions of labour issues continue to have influence today. Hence, at the risk of oversimplification, labour issues are appropriately considered at the regional or international level in order to address social disparities, political/ideological challenges and trade distortions. This was true when the ILO emerged in 1919; it remains the case in 2005 as evidenced by the Summit of the Americas Process. Experience suggests, however, that the political objectives of integration largely determine the nature and scope of the labour dimension within a particular multinational system. Since the underlying political purpose of European integration was to create strong institutional links among nations in order to heighten stability and prevent conflict, it is not surprising that the labour dimension within the EU has developed in a comprehensive form that vests considerable authority in relatively strong European-level institutions. In contrast, NAFTA was envisaged as an economic, as opposed to political, project. Its labour dimension was exceptional, emanating from political pressure in the United States to address potential social dumping in Mexico. This largely explains the narrow application of the NAALC.

Interestingly, the Summit of the Americas Process has much broader social and political ambitions than the negotiations for NAFTA. Because the goals of the Summit of the Americas Process include strengthening democracy and addressing social issues such as poverty, unemployment and underemployment, the labour dimension has been defined broadly to include matters ranging from professionalizing labour administration, to improving skills training, to developing mechanisms for collecting and disseminating labour market information.

Developments since 1919 – particularly within regional models – demonstrate the complexity of the international labour dimension. Although there may be a tendency to think first in terms of norms and standards, and how these are given expression at the international level, the international labour dimension is broader and more systemic in nature. In fact, it has three distinct components: (1) norms and standards; (2) processes; and (3) institutions.

International norms and standards

The promulgation of standards respecting labour rights and working conditions is an important function within the international labour dimension. The ILO is, of course, the predominant international standard-setting body in the labour field. As discussed above, the regional systems also have an important role to play in developing standards. Hence, the EU has a formal (albeit limited) standard-setting function in areas related to work, and the NAALC purports to commit member states to adhere to certain core labour standards. One of the focuses of the Summit of the Americas Process has been to identify the principles and standards that should be applied to countries participating in the FTAA. This mirrors a similar search by Mercosur nations for common ground on matters of worker protection.

Reference is often made to the ILO's Fundamental Declaration as the basis for international and regional labour standards. Of course, the principles in the Fundamental Declaration are few in number, and are by definition "core" matters that should be protected in the labour systems of all civilized nations. Agreeing to adhere to the Fundamental Declaration should, for the vast majority of countries, be a simple matter.

The standard-setting function within the international labour dimension becomes considerably more complicated and controversial once one moves beyond the fundamental issues. Certainly, the ILO has made substantial progress on a diverse range of worker protection issues, through its numerous conventions and recommendations. However, compliance has long been a concern. Experience suggests that as the focus of international labour discussions moves from the protection of fundamental principles to more detailed regulation of the local workplace, state resistance is bound to increase. Smaller, developing countries view such regulation as intrusive and harmful to attracting foreign investment and achieving economic development; larger, wealthier countries view such regulation as unnecessary, rigidifying and/or inconsistent with collective laissez-faire traditions. One would expect that common ground on labour standards would be most difficult to achieve as between countries of disparate economic development. It will therefore be very interesting to observe the development of the labour dimension within the EU, in the face of recent expansion. The EU's progress in labour standard-setting has been slow even though its members share high levels of development and (in most cases) similar legal and industrial traditions. The recent introduction of former Soviet-bloc and relatively less developed countries into the mix presents great challenges.

The challenges faced by the EU in the area of standard-setting pale in comparison to those facing the countries participating in the Summit of the Americas Process. No regional integration process has ever involved countries of such disparate economic and social development. The search for common ground on matters of labour rights and worker protection is bound to be contentious and, in some cases, futile. It is in recognition of this that the IACML has limited its discussions to the implementation at the regional level of the core labour principles of the Fundamental Declaration. At the same time, the IACML has focused its efforts on institutions and processes – the two other elements of the international labour dimension discussed below.

A significant recent phenomenon in the area of international labour standards is the increasing focus of both national and multinational corporations on corporate social responsibility (CSR) and the adoption of voluntary codes of conduct.[90] Such codes are being promulgated by companies in response to mounting criticism from consumers, non-governmental organizations (NGOs) and governments concerning inadequate labour conditions in supplier and subcontractor workplaces in developing countries. Some have criticized voluntary codes of conduct as public relations exercises and marketing tools, while others have raised concerns about the "privatization" of the international labour dimension. What is most important, however, is that the companies who are adopting and complying with these codes of conduct are doing so for "bottom line" reasons, and not simply for altruistic purposes. Public concern about labour rights, employment standards and working conditions has grown to such an extent that companies who fail to respond with protective measures could face consumer boycotts. Conversely, companies who are genuinely committed to implementing and monitoring compliance with their codes of conduct can expect to benefit via a more favourable corporate image, and even increased sales and shareholder investment. This is surely an indication that the public is now more deeply engaged in the debate about the international labour dimension than ever before.

International processes

Many of the most significant recent developments in the international labour dimension have been process-based, primarily because of the challenges presented where integration is being pursued among countries of disparate economic, social and political development. The issues in such an integration scenario are much more complex. For example, the IACML within the Summit of the Americas Process quickly concluded that the promulgation of hemispheric norms and standards on labour issues could not occur unless and until the structural problems of domestic labour systems were first addressed. Through the IACML's research and consultations, it has become clear that there are significant inadequacies in domestic labour laws, labour administration mechanisms and labour market information systems. The obvious conclusion was that regional efforts to develop a labour dimension had to focus first on the provision of technical assistance to promote the improvement of domestic systems.

The IACML's work, and the prior work of the Mercosur countries, demonstrates that the international labour dimension is not (and should not be) primarily focused on the promulgation of norms and standards. While multilateral agreements to respect the principles of the Fundamental Declaration, or other important labour standards, are clearly important, such agreements should ideally be one goal of a labour dimension process in which a range of issues can be addressed.

What should such an international process look like? Of course, it should be tailored to fit the needs and circumstances of participating nations, and must necessarily respond to political exigencies. Nevertheless, certain features should generally be incorporated. First, the process should always be tripartite, with the full involvement of worker and employer representatives. Workers and employers should not merely be observers, watching on the sidelines as government officials debate the issues. Instead, these groups should be actively involved at all stages, from researching and identifying issues, to negotiating and drafting agreements, to administering those agreements and engaging in necessary follow-up. In order to support tripartism, governments should be prepared to fund worker and employer organizations to ensure their active participation. There will, of course, be other actors who should be appropriately consulted within labour dimension processes. Because of the ILO's unique experience and expertise, it will always be in a position to provide meaningful contributions. There are a wide variety of other groups that have a role to play. Nevertheless, their participation should not detract from the predominant roles of the social partners – workers, employers and governments – in the international labour dimension.

Second, the process should be comprehensive, in the sense that it should be capable of addressing the full range of issues that arise within an international labour *system*. As the Summit of the Americas Process has made clear, the international labour dimension can be defined broadly to include not only the promulgation of norms and standards, but also the search for solutions to joint domestic problems such as inadequate labour administration and enforcement, poorly developed skills training, etc. The breadth of the international labour dimension clearly lends itself to a comprehensive approach that can address a diversity of domestic, regional and international issues.

Third, cooperation should be a defining feature of any international labour process. Where diverse nations are engaged in an integration process, there are bound to be numerous opportunities to share experiences with, and solutions to, common problems. Moreover, countries can pool their resources in order to encourage innovation in addressing shared concerns. It is reasonable to conclude that nations within a regional system are more likely to embrace a labour dimension that is premised on cooperative efforts and voluntarism, than one which calls for sovereign power to be ceded to transnational authorities empowered to impose solutions on member states.

International institutions

Finally, the international labour dimension must be defined to take into account the need for effective institutions to facilitate integration and cooperation processes, promulgate and enforce standards, and generally administer labour matters. The discussion above illustrates tremendous diversity in the nature, roles and powers of the international labour institutions that exist today. Of course, the ILO is the ultimate institution in the field, but there are many others: the various bodies of the EU, the NAALC Secretariat, Mercosur's Social and Labour Commission and the IACML.

The vesting of powers and jurisdictions in a supranational authority is often a matter of heated debate, since this may involve the perceived or actual loss of sovereignty by domestic governments. Certainly, some supranational institutions (such as those within the EU) do appear to wield considerable formal authority over national governments and domestic workplaces. However, the success of an international labour institution does not necessarily depend on formal, "top-down" power to impose or enforce standards. Much depends on the purposes of, and expectations for, an institution. The NAALC Secretariat, which was never designed to pursue labour integration among the NAFTA countries, has nevertheless been surprisingly successful in promoting awareness of, and cooperation on, labour matters within North America through its research and education functions. An even better example is the ILO, which wields remarkable influence in all corners of the world despite its very limited ability to enforce its conventions.

The institutions that emerge within an international labour system will naturally reflect the political realities and legal traditions of the countries involved. These institutions may also need to evolve over time as issues and concerns within the labour dimension develop. It is therefore difficult to generalize about the composition and mandate of such institutions. One generalization, however, can be suggested. In every case, the governance structures of international labour institutions should be designed to reflect the tripartite model, so that employers and workers have assured access and influence at the institutional level.

Notes

1. John W. Follows, *Antecedents of the International Labour Organization* (Clarendon Press, Oxford, 1951), 1–9.
2. Anthony Alcock, *History of the International Labor Organization* (Octagon Books, New York, 1971), at 12.
3. Lammy Betten, *International Labour Law: Selected Issues* (Kluwer, Deventer, 1993), 1–2.
4. In 1864, at the Assembly of the International Workers' Association in London, a provisional constitution drafted by Karl Marx was adopted that contained a

paragraph stating that the emancipation of workers was not simply a local or national problem, but one which concerned all civilized nations.

5. Alcock, *History,* 8.
6. Betten, *International Labour Law,* 3.
7. James T. Shotwell (ed.), *The Origins of the International Labor Organization,* vol. 1 (Columbia University Press, New York, 1934), 485–8.
8. Betten, *International Labour Law* p. 4.
9. Alcock, *History,* 11.
10. Alcock, *History,* 13.
11. Betten, *International Labour Law,* 7.
12. For an excellent discussion of the events surrounding the Peace Treaty, see Margaret Macmillan, *Paris 1919: Six Months that Changed the World* (Random House Publishing, New York, 2002).
13. "About the ILO", online: http://www.ilo.org/public/english/ about/history.htm (About the ILO).
14. Betten, *International Labour Law,* 1; see "ILO Constitution", online: http://www. ilo.org/public/ english/about/iloconst.htm#pre (ILO Constitution).
15. ILO Constitution.
16. George A. Johnston, *The International Labour Organisation: Its Work for Social and Economic Progress* (Europa Publications Limited, London, 1870), 1.
17. Betten, *International Labour Law,* 7–8.
18. "ILO Declarations, International Labor Conventions and Recommendations", online: http://www.ilo.org /public/english/comp/civil/standards/ilodcr.htm. More generally, see the ILO's ILOLEX database of Conventions and Recommendations, online: http://www.ilo.org/ilolex/english/index.htm.
19. About the ILO.
20. ILO Declaration on Fundamental Principles and Rights at Work, adopted by the 86th session of the International Labour Conference, Geneva, 18 June 1998, online: http://www.ilo.org/dyn/declaris/declarationweb.index.
21. The importance of the ILO on the world stage in relation not only to the international labour dimension, but also with regard to global social issues in general, is evidenced by the February 2004 publication of *A Fair Globalization: Creating Opportunities for All,* the groundbreaking report of the ILO's World Commission on the Social Dimension of Globalization. Over two years in the making, the report sets out a number of key conclusions and recommendations on how the negative aspects of globalization can be overcome through a re-evaluation of the existing policies and institutions of global governance. See ILO Homepage, online: http://www.ilo.org/public/english/wcsdg/docs/report.pdf.
22. Initially, the European Economic Community, later the European Community.
23. Walter Cairns, *Introduction to European Union Law,* 2nd edn (Cavendish Publishing, London, 2002), 14. The concept of European integration had been advocated in one form or another since the mid-nineteenh century with the writings of Einaudi and

Victor Hugo. The idea of a European government was also raised, unsuccessfully, at the end of World War I during the Versailles Peace Treaty discussions, by the Pan Europa movement of the 1920s, by Winston Churchill during and shortly after WWII, and by the Council of Europe. See Cairns, *Introduction*, 13. Also see John McCormick, *The European Union: Politics and Policies*, 2nd edn (Westview Press, Boulder, 1999) 44; Derek Urwin, *The Community of Europe*, 2nd edn (Longman, Essex, 1994), 34; John Gillingham, *Coal, Steel, and the Rebirth of Europe, 1945–1955* (Cambridge University Press, Cambridge, 1991), 118–19.

24. McCormick, *The European Union*, 47.

25. McCormick, *The European Union*, 58–9. The architect of the ECSC, French Foreign Minister Robert Schuman envisioned the ECSC as "a first step in the federation of Europe", which would make war between France and Germany "not merely unthinkable, but materially impossible". See David Weigall and Peter Stirk (eds.), *The Origins and Development of the European Community* (Leicester University Press, Leicester, 1992), 58–9.

26. "European Union", *The Columbia Encyclopedia*, 6th edn (Columbia University Press, New York, 2003), online: www.bartleby.com/65/. Also referred to as the Treaty of Rome.

27. R. Nielsen, *European Labour Law* (DJOF Publishing, Copenhagen, 2000), 28.

28. Nielsen, *European Labour Law*, 43.

29. Roger Blanpain, *European Labour Law*, 8th rev. edn (Kluwer Law International, The Hague, 2002), at para. 252. Note that free movement of workers was one of the first labour measures included in the EEC Treaty, effectively having been transposed from the ECSC: see para. 47.

30. Nielsen, *European Labour Law*, 44. An Action Programme was adopted in the field of health and safety at work and, within this framework, a number of directives were adopted dealing with the classification, packaging and labelling of dangerous substances, electrical equipment, vinyl chloride monomer, and safety signs at the workplace.

31. Case 43/75, [1976] ECR 455.

32. The equal pay provision, based on French legislation, was present in the Treaty of Rome.

33. Nielsen, *European Labour Law*, 29.

34. Blanpain, *European Labour Law*, para. 225.

35. McCormick, *The European Union*, 65–7. The Single European Act would also cover areas such as environment, research and development, and regional and foreign policy. The new single market did not technically come into force until January 1993 due to the time-consuming task of adopting and transposing the provisions of the Act into the national laws of the member states.

36. Nielsen, *European Labour Law*, 45.

37. McCormick, *The European Union*, 254–5. There were plans to incorporate the Social Charter (a non-binding declaration) into Maastricht in 1991, but the British government refused to agree. This led to a compromise – a social protocol (the social

chapter) was attached to Maastrict and Britain was excluded from voting in the Council on social issues, while the other eleven member states formed their own ad hoc Social Community. In 1997, the newly elected government under Tony Blair committed Britain to the goals of the social protocol, and it was incorporated into the Treaties by the Treaty of Amsterdam.

38. McCormick, *The European Union*, 253–4.
39. Nielsen, *European Labour Law*, 45.
40. McCormick, *The European Union*, 72. On 1 January 2002, the member states (excluding Britain, Sweden and Denmark) also adopted a common currency, the Euro.
41. Perhaps the most important employer organization at the European level is the Union of Industrial and Employers Confederations of Europe (UNICE), which organizes central federations of industry and national confederations of employers' organizations from 31 countries. The most important European trade union is the European Trade Union Confederation (ETUC). Created in 1972, ETUC presently represents some 60 million members, who belong to 66 national trade unions in 33 countries. See Blanpain, *European Labour Law*, paras. 118–36.
42. Article 2. This competence relates, according to Article 3, among others to:

- measures concerning the entry and movement of persons in the internal market;
- the approximation of the laws of Member States to the extent required for the functioning of the common market
- the promotion of coordination between employment policies of the Member States with a view to enhancing their effectiveness by developing a coordinated strategy for employment
- a policy in the social sphere comprising a European Social Fund; the strengthening of economic and social cohesion;
- a contribution to a high level of health protection;
- a contribution to education and training of quality and to the flowering of the cultures of the Member States.

See Blanpain, *European Labour Law*, para. 40.
43. The 2003 Adopted Employment Guidelines and the 2004 Proposal for Employment Guidelines are available online: http://europa.eu.int/comm/employment_social/ employment_strategy/ guidelines_en.ht.
44. Nielsen, *European Labour Law*, 45.
45. Blanpain, *European Labour Law*, para. 59.
46. From 1 November 2004, a qualified majority will be reached if two conditions are met: (a) if a majority of member states approve in some case a two-thirds majority; (b) a minimum of 232 votes is cast in favour of the proposal, i.e. 72.3 per cent of the total (roughly the same share as under the previous system).

In addition, a member state may ask for confirmation that the votes in favour represent at least 62 per cent of the total population of the Union. If this is found

not to be the case, the decision will not be adopted. The distribution of votes for
each member state is (from 04/11/01):

Germany, France, Italy, United Kingdom	29
Spain, Poland	27
Netherlands	13
Belgium, Czech Republic, Greece, Hungary, Portugal	12
Austria, Sweden	10
Denmark, Ireland, Lithuania, Slovakia, Finland	7
Cyprus, Estonia, Latvia, Luxembourg, Slovenia	4
Malta	3

47. Nielsen, *European Labour Law*, 46–7. Article 250(1) of the EC Treaty provides that, "unless otherwise provided in this Treaty, the Council shall act by a majority of its members".

48. Treaty establishing a Constitution for Europe, CIG 86/04. The European Constitution is divided into four parts. Part I defines the values, objectives, powers, finances, citizenship decision-making procedures and institutions of the EU. Part II contains the Charter of Fundamental Rights. Part III describes the policies, the internal and external action, and the functioning of the EU. Part IV contains general provisions, including the procedures for adopting and revising the Constitution.

49. See "Blair confirms EU constitution poll", 20 April, 2004, BBC News – World Edition, online: http://news.bbc.co.uk/2/hi/uk_news/politics/3640949.stm.

50. Article II-111 and Article II-112 of the Charter of Fundamental Rights, which forms Part II of the European Constitution.

51. See Horst Hanusch and Marcus Balzat, "A New Era in the Dynamics of European Integration?" May 2004, online: http://www.wiwi.uni-augsburg.de/vwl/institut/paper/261.pdf.

52. *Canada–United States Free Trade Agreement*, 22 December 1987, Can. T.S. 1989 No. 3, 27 I.L.M. 281 (entered into force 1 January 1989).

53. *North American Free Trade Agreement Between the Government of Canada, the Government of Mexico and the Government of the United States*, 17 December 1992, Can. T.S. 1994 No.2, 32 I.L.M. 289 (entered into force 1 January 1994).

54. Some EU Member States have recently expressed concerns about the balance of power between larger and smaller members. Ireland, for example, rejected the Nice Treaty by referendum in June 2001 for a number of reasons, including the fact that the Treaty will change the Council voting structure in the EU, and some believe that the power of smaller states, such as Ireland, will be dwarfed by larger countries such as Britain and Germany. The treaty was endorsed in a second referendum in October 2002.

55. *North American Agreement on Labour Cooperation Between the Government of Canada, the Government of Mexico and the Government of the United States*, 13 September 1993, Can T.S. 1994 No. 4, 32 I.L.M. 1499 (entered into force 1 January 1994).

56. *North American Agreement on Environmental Cooperation Between the Government of Canada, the Government of Mexico and the Government of the United States*, 13 September 1993, 32 I.L.M. 1480 (entered into force 1 January 1994).

57. Pharis J. Harvey, "The North American Agreement on Labour Cooperation: A Non-Governmental View", presented to a conference on Social Clauses and Environmental Standards in International Trade Agreements: Links, Implementation and Prospects, held 31 May 1996 (Brussels), online: http://www.laborrights.org/publications/naalc.html.

58. Robert Paterson et al., *International Trade and Investment Law in Canada*, Second Edition (Carswell, Toronto, 2003), loose-leaf, § 3.11(b)(i).

59. Paterson et al., *International Trade*.

60. Paterson et al., *International Trade*, § 3.11(b)(iii).

61. "Trade and Investment Report – Mercosur", Department of Foreign Affairs and International Trade, online: http://www.dfait-maeci.gc.ca/latinamerica/mercosur-en.asp.

62. Michael Reid, *Mercosur: A Critical Overview* (Chatham House, London, Mercosur Study Group, 2002), at 2.

63. Reid, *Mercosur*.

64. Reid, *Mercosur*.

65. Reid, *Mercosur*.

66. J. Bosch, "Mercosur: Recent Experience and Future Prospects for Social and Labour Institutions" (Panel No.2 of the XIIth Inter-American Conference of Ministers of Labour, First Meeting of Working Group 1, 9–11 April 2002); transcript available online: http://www.xii.iacml.org.

67. Bosch, "Mercosur".

68. Reid, *Mercosur*, 6.

69. Reid, *Mercosur*, 6.

70. José M. Salazar-Xirinachs, "The Summit Process and Plan of Action: Goals and Strategies for Hemispheric Integration", in *Labour Issues in the Context of Economic Integration and Free Trade* (ILO Caribbean Office, 1999), at 147–58.

71. First Summit of the Americas, Declaration of Principles (1994).

72. First Summit of the Americas, Plan of Action (1994).

73. Second Summit of the Americas, Declaration of Principles (1998).

74. Third Summit of the Americas, Declaration of Principles (2001).

75. Third Summit of the Americas, Plan of Action (2001).

76. Third Summit of the Americas, Plan of Action (2001) .

77. For general background on the OAS, see online: www.oas.org.

78. XIIth IACML, Ottawa Declaration and Plan of Action (19 October 2001).

79. There are actually 35 members countries, but the government of Cuba has been excluded from participating in the OAS since 1962.
80. XIIIth IACML Salvador Declaration and Plan of Action (26 September 2003).
81. XIIIth IACML, 'Feasibility Study for an Inter-American Co-operation Mechanism for Professional Labour Administration' (26 September 2003).
82. Ministerial Declaration of Quito, Free Trade Area of the Americas Seventh Ministerial Meeting, Quito, Equador, 1 November 2002, online: http://www.ftaa-alca.org/ministerials/quito/Quito_e.asp at para. 10.
83. Available online: http://www.oas.org/documents/ConferenciaTrabajoBrazil/Reporte TrabajoGrupo1_eng.pdf.
84. HRSDC, "Labour Ministers from Canada, Brazil and Mexico present IACML report to the Trade Ministers of the Americas", News Release (20 November 2003), online: www.hrsdc.gc.ca/en/cs/comm/news/2003/031120b.shtml.
85. Miami Ministerial Declaration, Free Trade Area of the Americas Eighth Ministerial Meeting, Miami, Florida, 20 November 2003, online: http://www.ftaa-alca.org/Ministerials/Miami/Miami_e.asp.
86. Monterrey, Declaration of Nuevo Léon (January 13, 2004), online: www.ftaa-alca.org/Summits/Monterrey/NLeon_e.asp (Monterrey Declaration).
87. Monterrey Declaration, 6.
88. Despite a number of setbacks, including a disappointing outcome to the 8th Ministerial Meeting of the FTAA in Miami in November 2003, the 34 future FTAA member states remained committed to concluding negotiations for the FTAA by the January 1, 2005 deadline. The FTAA is now delayed indefinitely.
89. Poised to become a key trading block in this region is the market established under the United States–Dominican Republic–Central America Free Trade Agreement (DR-CAFTA), which was signed in August 2004 and remains to be ratified by the participating countries.
90. For a more fulsome discussion of corporate social responsibility, see Rhys Jenkins, "Corporate Codes of Conduct, Self Regulation in a Global Economy", Technology, Business and Society Programme Paper Number 2, April 2001, United Nations Research Institute for Social Development, online: http://www.unrisd.org; "Corporate Social Responsibility: an IOE Approach", International Organization of Employers Position Paper, online: http://www.uscib.org/docs/03_21_03_CR.pdf; and Jill Murray, "Corporate Codes of Conduct and Labour Standards", International Labour Organization Bureau for Workers' Activities, online: http://www.itcilo.it/english/actrav/telearn/global/ilo/GUIDE/ JILL.HTM.

2

Who's afraid of globalization? Reflections on the future of labour law

HARRY ARTHURS

Introduction

My challenge in this paper can be summed up by the following question: "Who's afraid of globalization?" My short answer is "just about everyone, if they have any sense": CEOs of companies, small business people, local executives of branch plants, fundraisers for charities, practising professionals in law, epidemiology, advertising and finance – and, of course, workers and unions. In fact, since I am being autobiographical, add to my list of fearful Canadians at least one labour law professor. However, like many other people, my own feelings about globalization are mixed. It has turned much of my world upside down, but at the same time, it has provided me with ten years of interesting work.

My common sense assumptions about globalization and labour law – and why they had to be revised

My work on globalization and labour law began with what seemed like common sense assumptions: that globalization was reshaping the economies of almost all countries, albeit in different ways; that to govern this new economic order, a new transnational legal system would surely emerge; that this new transnational legal system would somehow reproduce at the international level the institutions and processes of our domestic systems of labour law; that *en route* to this transnational system, employers would likely enjoy significant but time-limited advantages; but that ultimately, transnational labour law – global labour law – would reach the standard we have set for our domestic systems: it would ensure a decent level of social justice for workers and social peace for employers.

I have described these beginning assumptions as "common sense". Let me explain why. Much of the literature on the globalization of law is clustered around two themes. The first is that a transnational frame-work of law has already developed to regulate business transactions. Often called the new *lex mercatoria*, its sources include contracts, commercial custom, arbitration awards, and international treaties and conventions, which have gradually coalesced into a body of legal principles, rules, pro-cesses and institutions. And, the literature suggests, this new transnational legal system has somehow leached back into national legal systems, much as the original law merchant did in Mansfield's time.[1] All of these transna-tional sources of business law have their counterparts in the labour field, I thought, so we can reasonably expect to see something similar hap-pening in labour law as well. The second theme converged with the first: the architects of the new *lex mercatoria* were, understandably enough, not national legislatures or courts, but rather the major actors in the global economy – transnational institutions, corporations, consultants, law firms, arbitrators and scholars – all of whom again have counterparts in the labour field.[2] One could therefore expect that somehow enlightened employers, unions, social movements and international agencies would be developing something analogous to the *lex mercatoria*, what one might call the *lex laboris*. Armed with these common sense assumptions, then, I launched several research projects to try to determine the normative effects of globalization on labour law.

The first was a study of how often Canadian labour law decision-makers actually dealt with globalization in the ordinary course of business. To my surprise, an electronic search of the decisions of all Canadian courts and tribunals involving employment or labour law, reaching back to the 1930s, showed that references to globalization, free trade, NAFTA, the WTO, the ILO and so on appeared in less than 60 cases.[3]

About half of those cases dealt with the possible application of inter-national labour norms. By and large, these norms were used, if at all, only to bolster interpretations of domestic law. About a quarter of the cases involved judges and labour boards considering record evidence or taking "judicial notice" of background events which involved globalization or free trade. This apparently had little impact on their findings of fact or interpretations of law. The remaining cases dealt mostly with situations potentially involving conflicts of laws issues, such as whether Canadian or foreign law applied to the labour agreement or conflict being litigated. However, conflicts issues were often ignored in these cases, as doubtless they were in many other cases which did not turn up in my survey. All in all, these are not the findings one might expect, given the supposedly transfor-mative effects of globalization on national labour law systems. Nor are they

the findings one might expect given the long and well-documented history of foreign influence on Canada's economy, corporate culture, union
structures and labour law. Parenthetically, my survey also turned up fewer
references to the United States than one might expect, though obviously
we cite American court, board and arbitration decisions, and scholarly
writing, fairly often.

My second research project involved a survey of management-side
labour lawyers in seven countries – the three NAFTA countries and four
EU countries.[4] These lawyers all acted for transnational companies, so
presumably they were well placed to respond to my question: "has globalization produced a *lex laboris*, a transnational system of labour law?" Their
virtually unanimous response was: "Of course not. Labour law is local
law." None of them viewed international labour standards as a significant
factor in their practice; only a very few had been even peripherally involved
with the NAALC or the ILO or corporate codes of conduct or even with
European labour law. Indeed, all of these lawyers reported that their foreign clients were generally willing to live with the local labour law system
as they found it, though some shared with me anecdotes about American clients who were indignant when they discovered that they could not
conduct their employment relations abroad exactly as they did at home.
Of course, the most thoughtful amongst these lawyers acknowledged that
the restructuring of the global economy would ultimately have repercussions on national labour law. However, even the EU lawyers mostly felt
that those repercussions had not yet become obvious. Again, surprisingly
little evidence that globalization has had normative effects – that it has
changed the actual substantive rules of labour law.

In a third project, I tried to map out how the "hollowing out of corporate Canada" affected the content of Canadian labour law.[5] To explain:
Canadian-based companies are being taken over by foreign firms, while
Canadian subsidiaries of foreign – especially US – parent firms are being
stripped of their autonomy and their executive functions, and subjected
to more detailed control from their American head offices. How does this
affect the informal norms of labour law, the law of the workplace? My
concern was similar to that of people who used to complain of American
domination of the Canadian labour movement: perhaps attitudes, ideolo-
gies, organizational structures and especially human resources/industrial
relations practices are being developed in the US and then shipped off to
Canada with no regard for their possible lack of fit with our industrial
relations culture and labour law. Once again, it proved difficult to document direct normative consequences. Relatively few transnational parent

companies seem to intervene directly on a daily basis in HR/IR practices of their Canadian subsidiaries. For sure, some American companies have successfully exported to Canada their philosophy of remaining union-free, and for sure their HR/IR personnel must have been educated in that philosophy. In that sense, workplace practices will have migrated across the border. But to a greater extent than I had anticipated, workplace norms seem to develop at the local level, rather than at head office.

All three of my studies are open to reasonable objections on method-ological and other grounds. However, I had to face facts: I found little direct evidence of the normative effects of globalization on Canadian labour law. Perhaps a transnational labour law system, a *lex laboris*, is emerging somehow, somewhere; but it does not seem so far to have influ-enced the substantive rules of Canada's domestic labour law system. On the contrary, according to those who should know best – the very lawyers who are supposedly building that *lex laboris* – transnational labour law does not exist in any functional sense. And finally, while changes in cor-porate structures and decision-making processes must surely affect the informal law of the workplace, we cannot say exactly how. At this point, I recalled the old adage: "if everyone around you is losing their heads, and you are perfectly calm, it's likely that you haven't grasped the situation".

The role of corporations in shaping labour law in the global economy

Well, how to grasp the situation? I began by taking a step backwards. As we all know, the basic assumptions which have underpinned our labour law system from the 1940s onwards have been radically revised. Employ-ment has become more technology-intensive and knowledge-based, but also more flexible and insecure. The workforce has become more demo-graphically diverse and more concentrated in the service sector. Other identities have become more important than class solidarity. Policy has shifted from promoting full employment and protecting workers to man-aging consumer demand and encouraging competitiveness. Most of these developments originated in the United States, and to a lesser extent in Japan and Europe, and were then adopted by other countries – includ-ing ours – in response to the influence, pressure or example of the three economic superpowers.

The result has been what is sometimes called a new international divi-sion of labour – a hub-and-spoke relationship between the economic superpowers and the rest of the world.[6] This new relationship is inscribed in trade regimes, such as the WTO and NAFTA; it is reinforced by institutions such as the World Bank and the OECD; it is made respectable by mainstream economic scholarship; it is welcomed and given effect by the governments of most countries which would rather be spokes than ignored altogether. And finally, this new international division of labour is accomplished largely by the operation of global capital, product and service markets dominated by global corporations which are almost exclusively located – no surprise – in the United States, the EU and Japan.

This, then, is the moment to say something about global corporations and especially their influence over labour law. First, they are enormous: the revenues of any of the top 100 or so global firms exceed the GDP of many nations.[7] They have deep pockets: they can buy new identities, litigate forever, stare down most strikes and wait out most consumer boycotts. Workers, knowing this, have become very nervous. This gives global firms a tremendous edge in all aspects of their employment relations. Second, these firms are influential: most states make great efforts to attract them as investors, purchasers of local goods and services and, especially, prospective employers and taxpayers. One way to attract global firms is to ensure that domestic labour laws are acceptable to them. Third, global firms generally have a national character: their boards, senior executives, key functionaries, bankers and suppliers are often concentrated around a head office in their home country. They therefore wield huge influence over the formation and execution of their home country's foreign, trade, fiscal, social and labour policies. In effect, they are able to borrow state power to protect their interests at home and abroad.

Fourth, these corporations are highly centralized: precisely because they do business all over the world, head office has to control most important decisions; hence the "hollowing out" effect I described earlier. However, personnel practices, collective bargaining strategies or compliance with labour standards at the local level are not usually considered "important decisions" or managed by head office on a daily basis. There appear to be four exceptions to this general principle: if local developments seriously increase production costs; if they threaten to damage the firm's reputation and market share; if they might set precedents for the firm's labour relations elsewhere; or if – in the unique case of Canada – local decisions can conveniently be dealt with by the home country management. These exceptions to one side, however, instead of intervening directly, head office tends to shape local labour practices through its global business strategies: to expand or contract home country operations; to establish or close foreign subsidiaries; to own or out-source foreign operations; to set cost

targets or profit margins for suppliers and subsidiaries which either permit local managers to treat workers decently or force them to do the
opposite; and to adopt a worldwide policy of obeying, ignoring or rewrit-
ing local labour law.[8]

Finally, you may be relieved to know, these corporations do have an
Achilles heel. Their political visibility, size, ubiquity and complexity makes
them potentially vulnerable to hostile action by politicians, investors, consumers and other actors with power to disrupt their global production
and distribution chains. How vulnerable we do not know; nor do they.
Consequently, they treat their workers as well as they need to in order to
avoid adverse market reactions, embarrassing legal proceedings or political awkwardness at home or abroad. As well as they need to: but no
better.

The implications of globalization for the future of Canadian labour law

Armed with this more refined understanding of the character and structure of large, transnational corporations, I adopted a new common sense
hypothesis about the implications of globalization for Canadian labour
law: globalization is formative, not normative. It changes labour law not
by directly amending the substantive rules but by transforming the institutions, structures and processes through which those rules are made and
administered.

To explain how and why that is happening in Canada, I have to clarify
just what globalization means for us. To cut to the chase, for Canada globalization essentially means integration into the American economy. The
United States is our biggest supplier of capital; American firms dominate
important sectors of our economy; the United States is virtually our only
significant export market – four times larger than all other markets combined – but a very high proportion of our exports move across the border
intra-firm, from Canadian subsidiaries to American parents.[9] Finally, the
United States is also the place from which we import a significant proportion of our public policies, management practices and business culture –
all of which, for better and worse, have been crucial in shaping Canadian
labour law.

I do not want to overstate my case. Canada so far remains a different
country from the United States, not just in terms of formal sovereignty, but
in many other respects which are pertinent to the discussion in this chapter. So far, we see things from the periphery of empire, not its epicentre;
our public spending priorities are different, notably in terms of health

care and social equity; our social attitudes remain somewhat more liberal; our labour law system is not quite as moribund; our unions are not as decrepit and discouraged. So far. But the question is whether Canada is bound to follow America down the path of state disengagement from labour policy, almost total de-unionization, growing personal insecurity, a highly racialized underclass and startling economic inequalities. Given our ever-closer integration with the United States, obviously that is a real possibility. "And a good thing too" – some people say – "Canada should imitate the United States in order to make our economy more internationally competitive. Like the United States, Canada should get the state out of the labour market, and free business from the burden of expensive social programmes, strong unions and unrealistic labour standards. These are the policies which will reverse years of under-investment, low productivity and declining living standards."

This strategy of making labour law more business-friendly is but one aspect of a broader neo-liberal ideology which has gained widespread acceptance in Canada as a result of what I refer to as "globalization of the mind" – the emergence of a broad international consensus amongst right-thinking governments, business executives, policy wonks, currency traders, academics and editorial writers.[10] True, many neo-liberal laws and policies do not bear a "labour" or "employment" label. Nonetheless, free trade is labour policy; so too is balanced budget and tax-cutting legislation; so too is the rigorous anti-inflation strategy of the Bank of Canada; and so too, for that matter, are cutbacks in welfare and social housing, and the privatization of medical care and pensions. All of these neo-liberal strategies – which are designed to restructure and reinvigorate the economy in the context of globalization – have very predictable labour market consequences. They sometimes increase but often decrease workers' opportunities, confidence and solidarity; they generally undermine – but occasionally reinforce – the bargaining power of unions; they allow some firms and their employees to prosper, but expose others to foreign competition, ownership or dependency; they tend to take the state out of the power equation, though preserving its disciplinary and tutelary role. That is what I mean by the formative effects of globalization on labour law.

The future of Canadian labour law

And now, finally, to reflect on the future of Canadian labour law. I am going to mention five general developments which are associated, at least to some extent, with globalization.

First, globalization has helped to politicize labour law. Once upon a time, Canadian governments enacted labour legislation in a rather leisurely fashion, on the advice of experts and after consultation with the parties, and then administered that legislation in a relatively even-handed fashion.[11] Business wasn't wholly satisfied; labour wasn't wholly outraged; experts weren't wholly impressed; but we gradually created a decent system which the parties and the public generally accepted. But globalization operates at high velocity and has little concern with political continuity or social cohesion.[12] Arguably, that is why Ontario's social democratic government, in an attempt to reverse the union job losses it attributed to the advent of free trade, enacted extensive labour law reforms in 1993.[13] It is also why the neo-liberal government of Premier Harris moved so aggressively in the opposite direction, after its election in 1995, to signal that Ontario was "open for business" by repealing all of the previous government's reforms and then introducing new, restrictive legislation of its own.[14] It is not that all legislation enacted by either government – or others I could name – was so totally outrageous in itself; it was rather the aggressively partisan spirit in which it was introduced. That partisanship, that politicization, was even more evident when it came to administering the law, especially under the Harris government which outsourced policy-making to private law firms, got rid of incumbent members of the labour board,[15] laid off labour department staff and reduced workplace inspections,[16] dismantled consultative forums such as the women's directorate and the anti-racism secretariat,[17] and attempted to fix the outcomes of interest arbitration by removing knowledgeable arbitrators from the process.[18]

I do not mean to single out Ontario. The politicization of labour law has become widespread. However, Ontario's experience underlines the point that governments confronted with crises, such as that provoked by globalization, must make a conscious, political choice as to whether labour law will be used to shelter workers from the new reality or to force them to adapt to it, whether new labour laws will emerge slowly by consensus, or whether radical innovations will be pushed through rapidly. Which approach a government chooses will establish not only new rules but a new dynamic in the lawmaking process. Based on recent experience, then, Canadian labour law is almost surely going to be much more highly politicized and more volatile, and therefore less expert-driven and less consensus-based, than it used to be.

A second trend is the increasing privatization of labour law. To some extent, Canadian labour law has always been privatized: the parties make their own individual or collective contracts of employment, subject to a few statutory "dos" and "don'ts"; they fill in contractual blanks with a host of workplace-specific rules and practices; they resolve workplace disputes through private procedures and, in unionized contexts, through private arbitration. But now the scope of private regulation is widening, as the state shifts responsibility for enforcing human rights and labour standards legislation to private arbitrators,[19] as some fixed labour standards – such as maximum hours – are made more negotiable,[20] and as governments move to maintain or restore unilateral employer control of the workplace.[21] The American Supreme Court has confirmed and legitimated this trend to privatization by ruling that employees may bargain away their statutory rights and remedies.[22] Our Supreme Court has not gone quite that far, but in *Weber*[23] and in *Parry Sound*[24] it did confirm the exclusive right of arbitrators to decide Charter, human rights, tort and employment standards claims in unionized workplaces.

At the national level, privatization is being actively promoted through government endorsement of corporate social responsibility and corporate self-regulation.[25] In the international sphere, it is being legitimated by the UN's sponsorship of the Global Compact and by the proliferation of corporate codes of conduct.[26] In academe – in academe! – privatization has proceeded apace as even progressive scholars have begun to give up on state labour legislation, and accept as the "new normal" reflexive labour law and RLS – the so-called ratcheting of labour standards.[27]

All of which would be fine if we could simply say: "let's see how it all works out; let's see if in fact corporations, the market and public opinion can safeguard labour standards and labour rights as well as the state did". However, if privatization doesn't work out, there may be no going back. Negotiations are currently under way to implement the General Agreement on Trade in Services – the GATS. Depending on the outcome of these negotiations, the GATS treaty may effectively prohibit governments from reassuming control of privatized state functions – including regulation – unless they compensate private providers of regulatory services.[28] Privatization, like diamonds, may be forever.

So much for politicization and privatization. Now I want to say something about how globalization has brought labour law face to face with the new paradigm of flexible employment. American labour law has for some time rested on the rickety foundation of employment-at-will.[29] However, until recently the reality of employment in America was otherwise: people worked years and decades in the same auto plant or insurance office. But now, because of new technologies, new methods of organizing work and new conceptions of job tenure, employment is again, in fact as well as law, pretty much "at-will".[30] Recent studies have revealed that the average job tenure for American workers is now less than three years, that over half (or their family members) have been laid off at some point during their careers, and that during the latest recession (2000–2003), while almost 20 per cent of American workers were unemployed at some point, less than half of them received any form of income replacement.[31] Flexible employment, then, is insecure employment and the implications for labour law are potentially enormous, not just in the United States but in all countries whose economies are linked to the American economy – including ours. Essentially, we will have to reexamine many doctrines and processes in Canadian labour law which were based on assumptions about people having fairly long-lasting, fairly secure work. What will happen to, say, the "reasonable notice" requirements of common law employment contracts? To the definition of bargaining units based on "community of interest"? To union solidarity and democracy premised on workers having lengthy periods of shared experience on the shop floor? To pensions and employment insurance based on protracted periods of contribution? In fact, what will happen to the very concept of employment – a term which fails utterly to capture the motley congregation of contractors, temps, franchisees, homeworkers and consultants who do work which "employees" used to do?[32]

The transnationalization of employment represents a fourth way in which globalization has exercised a formative influence on labour law. Employment relations were once largely conducted within the boundaries of a single jurisdiction. Of course there were exceptions: travelling salesmen, truck drivers and sailors crossed borders; so too did the odd labour dispute; and enterprise- or industry-wide bargaining structures occasionally included workers from several provinces or, more rarely, from both Canada and the United States. But these exceptions were rare enough that we could – and did – ignore them. Now globalization has changed all that.

First, more employees actually cross borders. Take professional athletes, who play in leagues with teams in two or more countries. It is generally assumed that collective bargaining in the North American baseball, basketball and hockey leagues will be conducted under American law, even for Canadian teams, although Ontario's Labour Relations Board, without so much as a second thought, applied Ontario law in two cases in the mid-1990s.[33] Whose law should govern? Second, work processes cross borders, even when workers themselves do not: take the call centres in Baltimore or Bangalore, which now service the Canadian customers of Canadian enterprises. Does Canadian anti-discrimination law apply to these call centres? Should it? Can it? Third, even when work and workers do not move, goods do: DVD players are produced in, say, China for Canadian retailers. We have no difficulty in insisting that Chinese manufacturers comply with Canadian consumer and patent laws; but should we – can we – insist that they must also comply with Canadian labour standards? And finally, the effects of labour disputes cross borders: a work stoppage in a Canadian feeder plant may interrupt automobile production in Michigan, a lockout by an employer in Seoul may provoke sympathetic union action in Saskatoon. Will strikes or picketing or boycotts with a foreign cause or consequence be subject to the same legal rules as purely domestic conflicts? In short, since the legal relations of employment are now more often transnational, Canadian lawyers will likely have to pay more attention to issues of conflicts of labour law as between national labour law regimes and, I predict, also amongst provincial labour law regimes.[34]

This in turn may force us to revisit the longstanding assumption that provincial jurisdiction over labour law is the default position under the Canadian constitution.[35] The unreality and unworkability of that assumption in the context of globalization has already become clear. The NAFTA labour side agreement – the North American Agreement on Labour Cooperation (NAALC) – provided that Canada's commitments would become operational only after approval by a specified number of provinces, and even then, only with regard to industries concentrated in those provinces.[36] As it happens, Ontario has not approved. As a result, the auto industry – Canada's single largest contribution to the global economy – is not subject to the NAALC. Surely we have to think again about our self-imposed incapacity to participate in a transnational regime of labour law? It was one thing for the Privy Council in 1937 – in an era of protectionism and isolationism – to excuse Canada from its obligations under ILO labour conventions.[37] It is quite another today – in an era of globalization – for Canada to continue to operate on the premise that its national government can sign treaties promising to observe international labour standards, but cannot constitutionally make good on its promise.

This brings me to a fifth tendency – the tendency to locate labour law within a universal discourse of human rights and fundamental freedoms.[38] What has this discourse to do with globalization? In part, it represents an attempt to make the message of neo-liberal globalization more benign; in part it represents the resurgence of the older, more idealistic one-world view of globalization which was associated with the birth of the ILO and the United Nations; and in part it represents an extrapolation into the international domain of the hopes and aspirations embodied in national bills and charters of rights.

At this point these may be some readers who are thinking that I am going back on my earlier claim that the effects of globalization are formative, not normative. Well, have no fear. I will be not only consistent, but consistent to a fault. I never denied that the ILO and other global and regional human rights regimes articulate normative standards which protect the fundamental rights of workers. But their normative influence is seriously diminished by the absence in most of these rights-based regimes of effective investigative, adjudicative and sanctioning systems. Ironically, such systems do exist within trade regimes, whose normative – and formative – effects are therefore much greater than those of most labour and human rights regimes. However, attempts to pin human and labour rights onto the elusive coat-tails of trade regimes have not so far come to much.[39] It is true that the EU has some jurisdiction over employment and social rights[40] that NAFTA deals with labour mobility,[41] and that a few scholars argue that fundamental human and labour rights are implicitly embedded in the WTO charter.[42] But essentially, the NAALC and the bilateral free trade agreements modelled on it are the only trade agreements which deal directly with labour matters.[43] That is a modest exception, however, since the NAALC merely obliges member states to adhere to their own labour laws, not to meet ILO or other international standards.[44]

For these reasons, it strikes me as rather odd that some distinguished scholars and practitioners view international human rights discourse as the last, best hope of labour law.[45] Of course I understand that they want to lodge the core principles of labour law in binding international treaties, where they will be safe from hostile or indifferent governments. Of course I follow their argument that core labour standards already comprise a body of "soft law" which will gradually permeate and reshape the "hard law" of trade treaties and national legislation. Of course I admire this new and idealistic project of globalization which will promote not only markets but also democratic societies which respect fundamental human rights and core labour rights. And finally, of course I know that this attractive project is endorsed not only by all the usual suspects – ILO supporters, human rights activists, trade unions and social movements – but also by enlightened pragmatists at the UN, the EU, the OECD and even the World Bank. For all these reasons, I wish I could be more enthusiastic. But as a scholar, I have to register a number of *caveats*: that traditions and structures of labour organization differ too much from one country to the next; that workers in different countries are essentially competing with each other for jobs; that international labour standards are therefore unlikely to be agreed, or if they are, to be agreed at any meaningful level of specificity; and that international standards are too remote – institutionally, symbolically and practically – to gain legitimacy and force from grassroots participation. These are pretty powerful *caveats.*

However, I mostly want to make a different point. The argument for internationalizing labour rights is very like that for embedding those same rights in national constitutions: to make them unassailable.[46] In fact, the two strategies are linked in the sense that ILO Conventions and other international norms have sometimes been used as a template for guarantees in national constitutions of "freedom of association, expression and assembly", of "the right to strike" or of entrenched social rights.[47] Likewise, they have been used by good advocates to pour meaning into such open-ended constitutional provisions, which in Canada has produced some memorable Supreme Court judgments.

However, close study of those judgments reveals the limits of the exercise. Our Supreme Court got off to a disappointing start in the mid-1980s, when it was asked in a trilogy of cases to constitutionalize labour rights.[48] That trilogy ended with the score of management three, labour nil. The Court muddled along for another decade or so, occasionally inflicting collateral damage on the system, as in *Weber*,[49] occasionally reinforcing long-standing arrangements, as in *Lavigne*,[50] and occasionally wandering off in surprising but attractive directions, as in *Vriend*.[51] However, the Court recently decided its second labour rights trilogy – *Dunmore, Pepsi Cola* and *Advance Cutting and Coring* – which seemed to extend Charter protection to agricultural workers, secondary picketing and legislatively imposed union membership.[52] The score this time round appeared to be labour three, management nil. But appearances deceive. On closer examination, the Court merely instructed legislatures to carefully balance labour rights against economic exigency, public safety and private rights of property, person and reputation. If they do that, said the Court, legislation restricting labour rights will be upheld.

That said, the equality provisions of the Charter have been repeatedly invoked over the past twenty years to force governments and employers to address issues of systemic discrimination.[53] How then can I be so dismissive of the influence of the Charter and, by extension, of international law on labour law? For three reasons: because ordinary legislation, not the Charter, has been invoked most often and most successfully against systemic discrimination; because foreign jurisdictions with no counterpart to the Charter have made as much progress or more in ensuring dignity and opportunity in the workplace for disadvantaged groups; and because, to be frank, it is by no means clear that the Supreme Court's judgments have in fact much changed employer or government behaviour: according to various indicators, some groups supposedly protected by the Charter continue to suffer significant disadvantages at work.[54] Ironically, the only exception, the only group whose employment rights have been truly entrenched, is the judiciary.[55]

All in all, I have to say, rights discourse has had three major impacts on Canadian labour law, none of them positive. The first was the decision in *Crevier*, which by constitutionally guaranteeing access to judicial review brought to an end forty years of legislative effort to preserve the uniqueness and autonomy of specialized labour tribunals.[56] The second has been the juridification of labour board and arbitration proceedings, which has led to legal costs, delays, distortions and frustrations.[57] The third has been the diversion of scarce labour resources and energies into litigation strategies, and away from industrial, political and social mobilization.

My reservations about reliance on international or universal labour rights, then, are very like my reservations about reliance on constitutional rights: at best they are feeble; at worst, they may be hurtful. All things considered, those who want to protect workers against the ravages of globalization, neo-liberalism and other pathologies of advanced capitalism would far be better off to attempt to reform labour law by political means. If workers cannot find ways to mobilize their potentially great political strength, if they cannot work out an understanding with the state and with their social partners concerning fair arrangements for the sharing of wealth and power, if people who care about industrial democracy cannot persuade their fellow citizens of the rightness of their cause, why do we imagine that the Supreme Court or the ILO or the international human rights system will do the heavy lifting for them? Why, indeed, would we continue to believe – against all evidence and experience – that these bodies are capable of the heavy lifting? And why, for that matter, would we want them to: what do they know about the specific macro-economic policies, labour markets, workplace dynamics, technologies, histories and cultures – about the deep structures of class and power – which give unique shape and effect to each country's labour law? And finally, why would we want to permanently entrench any particular regime of labour law in a domestic or international Charter at precisely the moment when we are experiencing transformative social, economic, political and cultural changes whose direction and duration no-one can yet predict?

None of this, I know, is going to dissuade clever and well-intentioned lawyers who must do their best for their clients, judges who must "do justice though the heavens fall", and law professors who must explore the full creative potential of law, wherever it leads them. I wish them all well in their efforts; truly I do. But there is little reason to believe that recourse to the Charter or to emerging international labour norms is likely to alter the powerful formative effects of globalization; to make markets less predatory; to force states to resume their engagement with issues of social justice; to help labour regain its solidarity and strength; to produce even in formal terms legal outcomes which are less equivocal and more efficacious.

Conclusion

This, I want to stress in conclusion, is not a pessimistic response to the challenges globalization poses for labour law. On the contrary: I am an optimist for three distinct reasons. First, labour law has always been built not from the top down, but from the bottom up. This involves much experimentation, repeated failures and many new beginnings before we achieve something like a sensible system. In this era of globalization, "building from the bottom up" may seem a particularly daunting prospect; but it has been done before under equally discouraging conditions – during the industrial revolution of the nineteenth century, the Great Depression of the 1930s and the period of post-war reconstruction after 1945. It can be done again if there is a will to do so.

Second, workers can rely with greatest assurance on the rights they have won for themselves, whether through industrial or political action. Such action is difficult in a globalized world, but not impossible. As I suggested earlier, the unique strengths of global corporations are potentially their unique weaknesses as well. Every border these corporations must cross, every national labour law system they must negotiate, every new cultural context they must adapt to or bend to their will presents workers with opportunities for resistance, civil society with opportunities for political and economic brokerage and states with opportunities to re-engineer their formal structures of law and industrial relations. The question is whether, and if so with what effect, these opportunities will be exploited.

And third, globalization in its present form is making everyone afraid, not just professors of labour law. Even the most devoted theoreticians, practitioners and beneficiaries of globalization are coming to accept the need to put a human face on it, if only to protect it from its own excesses. They are clever people. They know that only if labour's rights and interests are respected to some decent degree will communities, states, corporations and global markets enjoy the social and political stability that is so necessary for their long-term economic success.

That is why I am an optimist. But, I have to confess, I am a particular species of optimist. I am an optimist who accepts the mixed messages of history, an optimist who acknowledges that all human enterprises are likely to be imperfect and transitory – neo-liberal globalization included. I am therefore an optimist who believes that law is shaped more by the interplay of social forces than by great declarations of principle, whether domestic or international. This species of optimism, I quite cheerfully admit, makes me agnostic about the ability of constitutions or Charters – or UN Conventions – to correct deep-rooted injustice, to redress structural imbalances of power or to transform people's world views and the cultural and social relations in which they are embedded. At most, I believe, law becomes effective only when it transcribes and implements and, let me say, legitimates and reinforces decrees written in the domain of political economy. In that domain, for reasons I have just explained, change is almost inevitable, and its direction can be – almost inevitably is – shaped by human agents.

By us.

Notes

1. Various perspectives on transnational business law are captured in Richard Appelbaum, William L.F. Felstiner and Volkmar Gessner (eds.), *Rules and Networks: The Legal Culture of Global Business Transactions* (Hart Publishing, Oxford, 2001).
2. Yves Dezalay and David Sugarman, (eds.), *Profession Competition and Professional Power: Lawyers, Accountants and the Social Construction of Markets* (Routledge, London/New York, 1995); Yves Dezalay and Bryant Garth, *Dealing In Virtue: International Commercial Arbitration and the Construction of a Transnational Legal Order* (University of Chicago Press, Chicago, 1996); Bryant Garth, "Transnational Legal Practice and Professional Ideology" (1985) 7 *Michigan Year Book of International Legal Studies* 3; Gunther Teubner (ed.), *Global Law Without a State* (Tyne & Wear, Gateshead, 1997); J. Flood, "Mega-lawyering in the Global Order – The Cultural, Social and Economic Transformation of Global Legal Practice" (1996) 3 *International Journal of the Legal Profession* 169; David Trubek et al., "Global Restructuring and the Law: Studies of the Internationalization of Legal Fields and the Creation of Transnational Arenas" (1994) 44: 2 *Case Western Reserve Journal of International Law* 407.

3. Search procedures and parameters will be provided on request.
4. Harry W. Arthurs, "The Role of Global Law Firms in Constructing or Obstructing a Transitional Regime of Labour Law", in Richard Appelbaum, *Rules and Networks* 273–300. For a contrary view, see S. Bisson-Rapp, "Exceeding our Boundaries: Transactional Employment Law Practice and the Export of American Lawyering Styles to the Global Market" (forthcoming; unpublished MS in possession of the author).
5. Harry W. Arthurs, "The Hollowing out of Corporate Canada?", in Jane Jenson and Boaventura de Sousa Santos (eds.), *Globalizing Institutions: Case Studies in Social Regulation and Innovation* (Ashgate Press, London, 2000), 29; Harry W. Arthurs, "Reinventing Labour Law for The Global Economy" 2001 22 *Berkeley Journal of Employment and Labor Law* 271–92.
6. Alejandro Portes and John Walton, *Labor, Class and the International System* (Academic Press, New York/London, 1981), 189–91.
7. See e.g. estimates provided by Jill Rubery and Damian Grimshaw, *The Organization of Employment: International Perspectives* (Palgrave, Basingstoke, 2003), at 198, and Leslie Sklair, *Globalization: Capitalism and its Alternatives* (Oxford University Press, Oxford, 2002), 37; but Alan Rugman, *The End of Globalization* (Random House, London, 2001), 58 argues that these estimates are much too large.
8. The relative importance of local and head office influences has engendered considerable debate. See e.g. Ruth Milkman, *Japan's California Factories: Labor Relations and Economic Globalization* (Institute of Industrial Relations, Los Angeles, 1991), 39–49; Stephen Frenkel, "Patterns of Workplace Relations in the Global Corporation: Toward Convergence?", in Jacques Belanger et al. (eds.), *Workplace Industrial Relations and the Global Challenge* (Ithaca: ILR Press, 1994), 247 at 267–9; Daniel Drache, "Lean Production in Japanese Auto Plants in Canada" (1994) 2(3) *Canadian Business Economics* 45 at 45–8; Anthony Ferner, "Country of Origin Effects and HRM in Multinational Companies" (1997) 7 *Human Resource Management Journal* 19 at 19–20; Laura Nielson, "Paying Workers or Paying Lawyers: Employee Termination Practices in the United States and Canada" (1999) 21 *Law and Social Policy* 247 at 260; Jacques Belanger, A. Giles and J. Grenier, "Patterns of Influence in the Host Country: A Study of ABB in Canada" (2003) 14 *International Journal of Human Resource Management* 469.
9. A fact sheet distributed by the Heenan Blaikie firm notes that 72 per cent of all foreign direct investment in Canada comes from the United States, and that US trade accounts for 40 per cent of Canada's GDP and 86 per cent of Canada's exports. Other studies show that about 90 per cent of Canada's exports to the United States are by way of intra-firm transfers between Canadian subsidiaries and their parent companies. For a comprehensive recent examination of the Canada-USA relationship, see Stephen Clarkson , *Uncle Sam and Us: Globalization, Neoconservatism and the Canadian State* (University of Toronto Press, Toronto, 2002).
10. Harry W. Arthurs, "Globalization of the Mind: Canadian Elites and the Restructuring of Legal Fields" (1998) 12:2 *Canadian Journal of Law and Society* 219.

11. Harry W. Arthurs, "Understanding: Industrial Relations Research and Policy in Canada from 1969 to 1984 . . . and Beyond" (1984) 39 *Relations Industrielles* 753.

12. William Scheuerman, "Globalization and the Fate of Law" in David Dyzenhaus (ed.), *Recrafting the Rule of Law* (Hart Publishing, Oxford, 1999), 243–66.

13. H. C. Jain and Subba Muthuchidambam, *Ontario Labour Law Reform: A History and Evaluation of Bill 40* (IRC Press, Kingston, 1995), 17; Patrick Monahan, *Storming the Pink Palace: The NDP in Power: A Cautionary Tale* (Lester Publishing, Toronto, 1995), 126; Bob Rae, *From Protest to Power: Personal Reflections on a Life in Politics* (Viking, Toronto, 1996), 207.

14. See e.g. Savings and Restructuring Act, 1996, S.O. 1996 c. 1, Schedule Q (Amendments to various statutes with regard to Interest Arbitration); *An Act to Provide for Expeditious Resolution of Disputes During Collective Bargaining in Certain Sectors and to Facilitate Collective Bargaining Following Restructuring in the Public Sector and to Make Certain Amendments to the Employment Standards Act and the Pay Equity Act*, 1997, S.O. 1997, c. 21 (Schedules A, B, C); H. C. Jain and Subba Muthuchidambam, "Ontario Labour Law Reforms: A Comparative Study of Bill 40 and Bill 7" (1996) 4 *Canadian Labour & Employment Law Journal* 311; William Hayter, "Bill 7: Advance or Retreat?" (1996) 4 *Canadian Labour & Employment Law Journal* 331; Sara Slinn, "The Effect of Compulsory Certification Votes on Certification Applications in Ontario: An Empirical Analysis" (2003) 10 *Canadian Labour & Employment Law Journal* 367; Joseph B. Rose, "The Assault on School Teacher Bargaining in Ontario" (2002) *Relations Industrielles* 100; David Wilken, "Manufacturing Crisis in Workers' Compensation" (1998) 13 *Journal of Law and Social Policy* 124; Gavin Leeb, "A Global Experience Up Close and Personal: Ontario Government Workers Resist Privatization" (2002) 9 *Canadian Labour & Employment Law Journal* 7; Yonatan Reshef and Sandra Rastin, *Unions in the Time of Revolution: Government Restructuring in Alberta and Ontario* (University of Toronto Press, Toronto, 2003).

15. See Ron Ellis, "An Administrative System in Jeopardy: Ontario's Appointments Process" (1998) 6 *Canadian Labour & Employment Law Journal* 53; Kevin Burkett, "The Politicization of the Ontario Labour Relations Framework in the 1990s" (1998) 6 *Canadian Labour & Employment Law Journal* 161; Judith McCormack, "Comment on 'The Politicization of the Ontario Labour Relations Framework in the 1990s'" (1999) 7 *Canadian Labour & Employment Law Journal* 325.

16. According to the *Line in the Sand* Canadian Auto Workers Newsletter – online: http://www.caw.ca/news/allCAWnewsletters/lineinthesand/ – in its first months the Harris Government cut the Ministry of Labour budget by 46 per cent, and made redundant 52 of 257 health and safety inspectors (vol. I, no. 3, 20 Oct. 1995) as well as 4 of 7 ministry doctors, 17 of 34 engineers, 10 of 20 hygienists, all 13 air quality technicians, all 6 nurses, all 5 ergonomists and 2 of 3 divers (vol I, no. 4, Oct. 25, 1995); it also disbanded the Workers' Health and Safety Agency (vol. I, no. 10, July 1996). Similar redundancies occurred in other branches of the Labour Ministry.

17. See Ontario, Legislative Assembly, Official Report of Debates (Hansard), 36th Parliament 1st session (29 May 1996) at 3145–7 (Hon. David Johnson).

18. See *Minister of Labour* v. *CUPE and SEIU* [2003] 1 S.C.R. 539, and see David Mullan, "Judging the Judgment of Judges: *CUPE v Ontario (Minister of Labour)*" (2003) 10 *Canadian Labour & Employment Law Journal* 431.

19. See e.g. Employment Standards Act, 2000., S.O. 2000 c. 41 s. 99; Ontario Labour Relations Act, 1995, S.O. 1995, c. 1, s. 48 (12)(j); Ontario Human Rights Code, R.S.O., c. H. 19, s. 34 (1)(a).

20. See e.g. Employment Standards Act, 2000, S.O. 2000, c. 41, s. 17 (2).

21. See e.g. Agricultural Employees Protection Act, 2002, S.O. 2002.

22. Katherine Stone, "Mandatory Arbitration of Individual Employment Rights: The Yellow Dog Contract of the 1990s" (1996) 73 *Denver University Law Review* 1017; Calvin Sharpe, "Integrity Review of Statutory Arbitration Awards" (2003) 54 *Hastings Law Journal* 311.

23. In *Weber* v. *Ontario Hydro*, [1995] 2 S.C.R. 929 the Supreme Court of Canada held that an employee was obliged to take to grievance arbitration – rather than to a civil court – claims founded in tort and on an alleged violation of the Canadian Charter of Rights and Freedoms. The Court did not address several issues: neither grievance arbitrators nor advocates are necessarily legally trained; if legally trained, they may be experts in labour law but not in torts or Charter law; the union – rather than the individual employee – can initiate and settle grievances and controls access to grievance arbitration proceedings; and the arbitrator's mandate is confined strictly to disputes arising out of the application, interpretation or alleged violation of the agreement.

24. In *Parry Sound Social Services Administration Board* v. *Ontario Public Services Union* [2003] 1 S.C.R. 157 at para. 53, the Court held that "the fact that the Human Rights Commission currently has greater expertise than [a grievance arbitrator] in respect of human rights violations is an insufficient basis on which to conclude that a grievance arbitrator ought not to have the power to enforce . . . the Human Rights Code". As in *Weber*, the result is that employees are obliged to settle for adjudication of their human rights claims in an inappropriate forum.

25. Harry W. Arthurs, "Private Ordering and Workers' Rights in the Global Economy: Corporate Codes of Conduct as a Regime of Labour Market Regulation", in Joanne Conaghan, Karl Klare and Michael Fischl (eds.), *Labour Law in an Era of Globalization: Transformative Practices and Possibilities* (Oxford University Press, Oxford, 2001), 471–88.

26. Harry W. Arthurs, "Corporate Codes of Conduct: Profit, Power and Law in the Global Economy", in Wesley Cragg (ed.), Ethics *Codes: Corporations and the Challenge of Globalization* (Edward Elgar Press, Northampton, 2005), 51–71.

27. Harry W. Arthurs, "Corporate Self-regulation: Political Economy, State Regulation and Reflexive Labour Law", in Ton Wilthagen and Rolf Rogowski (eds.), *Reflexive*

Labour Law: Studies in International and European Employment Law and Labour Market Policy (Kluwer Law International, forthcoming).

28. See General Agreement on Trade in Services Article I (3) (a)–(c). According to a schedule adopted in 2002 by the WTO at Doha, negotiations over implementation are due to be completed in 2005. However, this seems unlikely.

29. See e.g. Sanford Jacoby, "The Duration of Indefinite Employment Contracts in the United States and England: An Historical Analysis" (1982) 5 *Comparative Labor Law Journal* 84; Clyde Summers, "Employment at Will in the United States: The Divine Right of Employers" (2000) 3 *University of Pennsylvania, Journal of Labor and Employment Law* 65.

30. Katherine Stone, *From Widgets to Digits: Employment Regulation for the Changing Workplace* (Cambridge University Press, 2004).

31. Carl E. Van Horn and K. A. Dixon "The Disposable Worker: Living in a Job-Loss Economy" (2003) 6:2 Work Trends, John J. Heldrich Center for Workforce Development, Rutgers University and Center for Survey Research and Analysis, University of Connecticut, Rutgers University.

32. See e.g. Guy Davidov, "The Three Axes of Employment Relationships: A Characterization of Workers in Need of Protection' (2002) 52 *University of Toronto Faculty of Law Review* 357; Judy Fudge, Eric Tucker and Leah Vosko, "Employee or Independent Contractor? Charting the Legal Significance of the Distinction in Canada" (2003) 10 *Canadian Labour and Employment Law Journal* 193.

33. See *Association of Major League Umpires* v. *American League and National League of Professional Baseball Clubs & Toronto Blue Jays Baseball Club*, (1995) O.L.R.B. Rep. April 540; *National Basketball Referees Association* v. *National Basketball Association* (1995) O.L.R.B. Rep. November 1389.

34. See e.g Jean Gabriel Castel and Janet Walker, *Canadian Conflicts of Laws* (Butterworths, Markham, 2002), chapter 31.

35. The Constitutional Law Group, *Canadian Constitutional Law* (Emond Montgomery Publications, Toronto, 2003), 187–97; Peter Hogg, *Constitutional Law of Canada, Student Edition* (Carswell, Scarborough, 2003), s. 28; Thomas Kuttner, "Federalism and Labour Relations in Canada" (1997) 5 *Canadian Labour and Employment Law Journal* 195.

36. NAALC, USA Canada-Mexico, 14 September 1993, 32 I.L.M. (entered into force 1 Jan. 1994) Annex 46.

37. The Privy Council in the United Kingdom, until 1949 Canada's court of last resort, held in *AG (Canada)* v. *AG (Ontario) (Labour Conventions Reference)* [1937] AC 326 that the constitutional authority of the federal government to make treaties – in this case, ILO conventions – did not entitle it to enact legislation necessary to implement those treaties. See Robert Howse, "The Labour Conventions Doctrine in an Era of Global Interdependence: Rethinking the Constitutional Dimension of Canada's External Economic Relations" (1990) 16 *Canadian Business Law Journal* 160.

38. Roy Adams, "On the Convergence of Labour Rights and Human Rights" (2001) 1 *Relations Industrielles/Industrial Relations* 56; John Godard, "Labour Unions, Workplace Rights and Canadian Public Policy" (2003) 4 *Canadian Public Policy* 29; Adelle Blackett and Colleen Sheppard, "Collective Bargaining and Equality: Making Connections" (2003) 4 *International Labour Review* 419–57; Robert Howse and Makua Mutua, *Protecting Human Rights in the Global Economy: Challenges for the World Trade Organization* (Rights and Democracy, Montreal, 1999), online: International Centre for Human Rights and Democratic Development, http://www.ichrdd.ca/111/english/commdoc/publications/globalization/wtoRightsGlob.html.

39. Steve Charnowitz, "The Influence of International Labor Standards on the World Trading Regime: A Historical Overview" (1987) 126 *International Labour Review* 565; Brian Langille, "Canadian Labour Law Reform and Free Trade" (1991) 23 *Ottawa Law Review* 3; Adelle Blackett, "Whither Social Clause? Human Rights, Trade Theory and Treaty Interpretation" (1999) 3 *Columbia Human Rights Law Review* 1; Tim Armstrong, "Labour Issues in International Trade Agreements: Two Solitudes? Where Does Canada Stand vis-à-vis the Integration of Labour Standards and International Trade Agreements? Are We Making Progress?" (2000) 4 *Behind the Headlines* 57; Adelle Blackett, "Mapping the Equilibrium Line: Fundamental Principles and Rights at Work and the Interpretative Universe of the World Trade Organization" (2002) 65 *Saskatchewan Law Review* 369; C. Yates, "The ILO Declaration on Fundamental Principles and Rights at Work: The Limitations to Global Labour Standards", in Maureen Irish (ed.), *The Auto Pact and Beyond* (Kluwer Law International, London, 2004), 243–256; Robert Wai, "Countering, Branding, Dealing: Using Economic and Social Rights in and around the International Trade Regime" (2003) 14 *European Journal of International Law* 35.

40. Treaty Establishing the European Community as Amended by Subsequent Treaties, Rome, 25 March 1957. online: http://europa.eu.int/abc/obj/treaties/en/entoc05.htm. Title III, (Free Movement of Persons Services and Capital, Chapter 1, Workers, Articles 48–51. online: http://europa.eu.int/abc/obj/treaties/en/entr6d03.htm#112; and see generally Paul Davies, Silvana Sciarra, Antoine Lyon-Caen, Spiros Simitis (eds.), *European Community Labour Law: Principles and Perspectives* (Clarendon Press, Oxford, 1996).

41. North American Free Trade Agreement (NAFTA, 1 January 1994), online: http://www.nafta-sec-alena.org/DefaultSite/ index_e.aspx?CategoryID = 42 at Chapter 16 – Temporary Entry for Business Persons.

42. Robert Howse, "The World Trade Organization and the Protection of Workers' Rights" (1999) 3 *Journal of Small and Emerging Business Law* 131 at 142; Blackett, "Whither Social Clause".

43. John McKennirey, "Labor in the International Economy" (1996) 22 *Canada-U.S. Law Journal* 183 at 189–90. Canada has recently been using the NAALC as a template for bilateral free trade agreements with a number of Latin American countries.

44. North American Agreement on Labor Cooperation (NAALC, 13 September 1993) Article 2, online: http://www.naalc.org/english/agreement.shtml.

45. David Beatty, *Putting the Charter to Work: Designing a Constitutional Labour Code* (McGill-Queens University Press, Kingston and Montreal, 1987); Virginia Leary, "The Paradox of Workers' Rights as Human Rights", in Lance Compa and Stephen Diamond (eds.), *Human Rights, Labor Rights and International Trade* (University of Pennsylvania Press, 1996); Roy Adams, "The Convergence of Labour Rights and Human Rights" (2001) 56 *Relations Industrielles/Industrial Relations* 199; Roy Adams, "Implications of the International Human Rights Consensus for Canadian Labour and Management" (2002) 9 *Canadian Labour and Employment Law Journal* 125. For a relatively modest statement of the position, see Dennis Davis, Patrick Macklem and Guy Mundlak, "Social Rights, Social Citizenship and Transformative Constitutionalism: A Comparative Assessment", in Joanne Conaghan, Richard Fischl and Karl Klare *Labour Law in an Era of Globalization: Transformative Practices and Possibilities* (Oxford University Press, 2002), 511–34.

46. David Beatty, *Putting the Charter to Work*; Thomas Kuttner, "Constitution as Covenant: Labour Law, Labour Boards and the Courts from the Old to the New Dispensation" (1988) 13 *Queens Law Journal* 32.

47. For a recent comparative study, see David Beatty, *The Ultimate Rule of Law* (Oxford University Press, 2004), chapter 3 ("Equality") and chapter 5 ("Fraternity").

48. The Supreme Court's first so-called "labour trilogy" comprised: *Reference re Public Service Employee Relations Act* (Alberta) [1987] 1 S.C.R. 313; *Retail, Wholesale and Department Store Union, Locals 544, 496, 635 and 955* v. *Government of Saskatchewan* [1987] 1 S.C.R. 460: *Public Service Alliance of Canada* v. *Canada* [1987] 1 S.C.R. 424. In each of these cases the Supreme Court declined to use the Charter of Rights and Freedoms to protect the right of workers to bargain collectively or to strike. The literature criticizing the trilogy is extensive. See e.g. David Beatty and Steven Kennett, "Striking Back: Fighting Words, Social Protest and Political Participation in Free and Democratic Societies" (1988) 67 *Canadian Bar Review* 573; John Kilcoyne, "Developments in Employment Law: The 1986–87 Term" (1988) 10 *Supreme Court Law Review* 183; Paul Weiler, "The *Charter* at Work: Reflections on the Constitutionalizing of Labour and Employment Law" (1990) 40 *University of Toronto Law Journal* 117; Brian Etherington, "An Assessment of Judicial Review of Labour Laws under the *Charter*: Of Realists, Romantics, and Pragmatists" (1992) 24 *Ottawa Law Review* 685.

49. *Weber* v. *Ontario Hydro* [1995] 2 S.C.R. 929.

50. In *Lavigne* v. *Ontario Public Service Employees Union* [1991] 2 S.C.R. 211, the Court declined to find that compulsory payment of union dues violated the plaintiff's freedom of association, even though the union used its dues revenue to support various social and political causes of which the plaintiff disapproved.

51. In *Vriend* v. *Alberta* (1998) 156 D.L.R. (4th) 385 the Court held that Alberta's failure to extend the protection of its human rights code to homosexuals violated

their equality rights under the Canadian Charter of Rights and Freedoms. Though the Charter does not designate homosexuals as entitled to equality rights, in an earlier ruling the Court had held that they were entitled to protection as a group "analogous" to those named.

52. The second labour trilogy comprised: *R. v. Advance Cutting & Coring Ltd* (2001), 205 D.L.R. (4th) 385 (Quebec legislation requiring union membership for all construction workers upheld); *Dunmore v. Ontario (Attorney General)* [2001] 3 S.C.R. 1011 (total exclusion of agricultural workers from collective bargaining struck down); *Retail, Wholesale and Department Store Union, Local 558 v. Pepsi-Cola Canada Beverages (West) Ltd* (2002) 208 D.L.R. (4th) 385 (common law prohibition of secondary picketing as illegal per se struck down); see e.g., Dianne Pothier, "Twenty Years of Labour Law and the Charter" (2002) 40 *Osgoode Hall Law Journal* 369; Michael McNeil, "Unions and the *Charter*: The Supreme Court of Canada and Democratic Values" (2003) 10 *Canadian Labour and Employment Law Journal* 3; Jamie Cameron, "The Second Labour Trilogy: a comment on *R. v. Advance Cutting, Dunmore v. Ontario,* and *R.W.D.S.U. v. Pepsi-Cola*" (2002) 16 *Supreme Court Law Review* 66.

53. See generally George Adams, *Canadian Labour Law* (Aurora: Canada Law Book, 2nd edn revised 2004), para. 3.720.

54. See Harry Arthurs and Brent Arnold, "Does the Charter Matter?" (forthcoming 2004).

55. The Supreme Court of Canada has upheld the right of judges to have their salaries determined by an independent judicial salary commission, *Reference re Remuneration of Judges of the Provincial Court of Prince Edward Island* [1997] 3 S.C.R. 3, and is about to consider several cases challenging the right of governments to override the recommendations of such a commission: *Provincial Judges Association of New Brunswick v. New Brunswick (Minister of Justice)* leave to appeal granted 4 December 2003 (and two similar cases involving judges in Alberta and Ontario). The Court also struck down an attempt to repeal a recently enacted statute which allowed so-called "supernumerary" judges to work half-time for full pay: *New Brunswick (Minister of Finance) v. Mackin and Rice* [2002] 1 S.C.R. 405.

56. *Crevier v. A.G. Quebec* (1982) 127 D.L.R. (3d) 1. Subsequent developments are traced out in Harry Arthurs, "Protection Against Judicial Review" (1983) 43 *Revue du Barreau* 277–90, reprinted in Canadian Institute of Administrative Justice, *Judicial Review of Administrative Rulings* (Montreal, Editions Yvon Blais, 1983); Brian Langille, "Judicial Review, Judicial Revisionism and Judicial Responsibility" (1986) 17 *Revue générale de droit* 169; Paul Cavalluzzo, "The Rise and Fall of Judicial Deference", in Neil Finkelstein and Brian Rogers (eds.), *Recent Developments in Administrative Law* (Carswell, Toronto, 1987), 213–42; Brian Etherington, "Arbitration, Labour Boards and the Courts in the 1980s: Romance Meets Realism" (1989) 68 *Canadian Bar Review* 405.

57. Paul Weiler, "The Charter at Work: Reflections on the Constitutionalizing of Labour and Employment Law" (1990) 40 *University of Toronto Law Journal* 117 at 186–90; Harry Arthurs, "The New Economy and the New Legality: Industrial Citizenship and the Future of Labour Arbitration" (1999) 7 *Canadian Labour and Employment Law Journal* 45 at 50–63.

PART II

International labour standards

3

The impact of globalization on labour standards
A second look at the evidence

KEVIN BANKS

Introduction

The impact of international economic integration on labour standards[1] has occupied an important place in Canadian public debate over trade policy for at least fifteen years. This debate was first ignited by the negotiation of the Canada–United States Free Trade Agreement (FTA) in the late 1980s. Canadian critics of the FTA argued that deeper economic integration with the United States would inevitably lead to a deterioration in working conditions in Canada, as Canadian enterprises faced more competition from less regulated southern states with lower wage rates and levels of unionization.[2] Eventually, the critics argued, economic pressures would inevitably put political pressure on Canadian labour legislation. The conclusion in rapid succession of the North American Free Trade Agreement (NAFTA) and the Uruguay Round of the GATT negotiations, and the emergence of globalization as a focus of public attention, vaulted such concerns to greater international prominence. Increased economic integration with low wage developing countries led to the prospect of a "race to the bottom" in labour standards, an issue which became a topic of debate and research throughout much of the industrialized world, and provided one of the key arguments for linking labour standards and international trade by including a set of binding labour standards alongside or within free trade agreements.

That linkage is now firmly established in North America[3] and concern about the potential impacts of globalization on labour standards remains significant among the package of policy arguments for the trade-labour linkage.[4] Yet, trade and international relations scholars increasingly question whether such concerns have any real basis. It would certainly be difficult to argue that the content of reforms to Canadian labour legislation over the last fifteen years has been determined by international competitive pressures.[5] Such reforms have in fact moved in dramatically different directions, at times favouring workers and at times favouring employers, depending upon the political orientation of the party in power. The Canadian experience suggests that governments still have a great deal of room to manoeuvre in writing labour laws. As research into the question accumulates, a consensus appears to be emerging that there is no empirical evidence to support a negative relationship between globalization and labour standards. Some have pressed the point further, arguing that the "race to the bottom" argument is little more than rhetoric and a cover for protectionism.[6]

This emerging consensus view provides a valuable corrective for overblown rhetoric about the dangers of globalization. However, this paper will argue that it is too sanguine and not really supported by the evidence upon which it relies. Critics are right to discount the prospect of a wholesale "race to the bottom" in labour laws or wages and working conditions in the wealthy industrialized countries. However, a closer look at conditions in the developing world suggests that globalization may well be exerting important competitive pressures on labour standards there. Many sectors within developed economies are unlikely to remain immune to such pressures and some have already felt them. Rather than a race to the bottom, the risk posed by globalization is that of deepening segmentation between high standards and low standards regions, sectors and occupations within the international industrial economy. This segmentation is not inevitable, but has potential to undermine the quality of life of affected workers and prospects for economic development in both the developing and industrialized world.

This paper has four parts. The first part provides necessary background. It summarizes the main theories on the relationship between globalization, labour markets and labour standards, considers which predicted effects of globalization are relevant to whether labour standards obligations should be linked to trade law or other initiatives to deepen international economic integration. It then outlines what types of evidence are best suited to determining whether those effects are in fact occurring. The second part summarizes the evidence upon which the emerging consensus is based. The third offers a reconsideration of that evidence, in light of industrial and political conditions that often prevail in developing countries, inherent defects in "race to the bottom" arguments, and sources of evidence that are often disregarded or remain underdeveloped. The conclusion briefly draws out implications for policy.

The effects of economic integration on labour laws and labour markets:
predictions and policy implications

A great deal has been written in recent years about the effects of economic integration on labour laws and labour markets. Most of this writing has focused on theories or empirical evidence of different causal relationships. Relatively little attention has been given to carefully exploring the policy implications of those relationships. This is unfortunate, because different causal relationships between globalization and labour standards have very different policy implications. Specifically, two potential causal connections need to be clearly distinguished: competition on the basis of low wage comparative advantage, and competition on the basis of unit labour costs attributable to labour standards. Failing to do so has lead to confusion about what is at stake in policy debates. This section will therefore preface the argument of the paper by identifying the driving forces hypothesized by theories of how economic integration affects labour laws and labour markets; by explaining the difference in causal and policy terms between competition on the basis of comparative advantage and competition on the basis of unit labour cost differences, and by clarifying which types of empirical data best allow us to isolate the latter from the former.

International integration of product and capital markets has been spurred by advances in transportation and communications technology and the development of sophisticated private markets for finance, insurance, dispute settlement, and so on – developments that have made it increasingly feasible to relocate production in search of competitive advantage.[7] Integration has been deepened and reinforced by international legal structures: by providing greater security of market access, the international trading system seeks to enable producers to enter product markets from any location where they can operate competitively. Each of these strands of integration allows production cost advantages in different countries to have more of an effect on international product market share, and encourages international investment in production facilities. Economic integration thus stands to increase international competition for product and service market share, as well as international competition to attract investment.

Economics and political economy provide a number of coherent theories that predict how such competition will affect labour laws and labour markets.[8] What these theories have in common is that their predictions are driven by the leverage that increased mobility of production and investment give to employers in the workplace. This leverage enables and perhaps requires them to treat labour costs as competitive disadvantages that must be reduced in the short term, even if the employer and wider society might realize longer term productivity or stability advantages from increased income shares for workers, or from respect for the norms embedded in labour laws. Predicted effects include shifts in bargaining power and in the incidence of regulatory costs from workers to employers, downward pressures on the level of protection offered to workers by labour laws and policies, and increases or decreases in inequality between skill groups in the workforce.

International competition for market share and investment thus bring into play differences between the labour laws, policies and programmes of competing jurisdictions. The key economic variables fuelling these competitive pressures are (1) comparative advantage in labour supply, and (2) international differences in unit labour costs.[9] The policy implications of each of these variables are quite different, and therefore it is important to be able to distinguish them and to find sources of evidence that separate their effects.

An open international trading system induces national economies to specialize in industries in which they have comparative advantages.[10] The international community has generally recognized that the benefits of allowing specialization according to comparative advantage are a key underpinning of the international trading system, and that one important and legitimate source of comparative advantage is the relative abundance of skilled or unskilled labour.[11] In a country with a relatively abundant supply of unskilled labour, pressures to make use of comparative advantage can be expected to induce a shift towards industries that rely more heavily on low skill production methods. This will in turn shift the demand for different kinds of workers in competing economies, resulting in increases or decreases in their employment incomes. Conversely, economists have long predicted that growing international trade should lead to increased inequality between skilled and unskilled workers in industrialized countries, as their economies shift away from unskilled labour, and the opposite trend in developing countries. Thus increased trade should lead to an equalizing trend in wages across borders.[12]

From a contemporary policy perspective, these shifts are a generally accepted consequence of participating in the international trading system. The system is based on the principles that comparative advantage should be allowed to operate, and that competition from abroad should not per se be treated differently from competition from domestic producers. Thus, low wages resulting from an abundant supply of labour have been recognized as a legitimate comparative advantage that must be allowed to drive market outcomes. In turn, the resulting consequences of shifts in demand for workers, such as unemployment or increased inequality within the labour market are implicitly accepted once the free trade bargain is struck. They are addressed simply as matters of adjustment. Because of the importance of the principles of comparative advantage to trade policy, any other approach would call into question the fundamental underpinnings of today's international trading system.

On the other hand, while competition on the basis of international differences in unit labour costs attributable to labour standards themselves is also a potential by-product of economic integration, it is one about which trade policy has relatively little to say. Entering into an open international trading system does not imply an acceptance that national labour policies or policy autonomy will be eroded. Further, there is now a firm international consensus that certain fundamental labour principles and rights should be promoted and respected in the international economy by all countries, whatever their level of development.

The key issue is thus whether labour standards themselves can spur competitive pressures leading to their own erosion, by negatively affecting the ability to attract investment and to succeed in international product markets. This is not a question about comparative advantage, since low labour standards per se are not recognized as a legitimate source of such advantage.

The best reason to believe that labour standards may be subject to international competitive pressures is that there are significant unit labour cost differences attributable to labour standards levels themselves. Unit labour cost differences can be expected to generate competition between jurisdictions, since lower unit labour costs are by definition a competitive advantage – one that can have a significant impact at the margin. They can matter regardless of the political and economic environment in which they are embedded, if one assumes that raising or lowering labour standards leaves all other things equal, or when, even if short term cost advantages are outweighed by potential longer term gains, economic actors cannot be sure of obtaining the benefits of those gains and thus tend to discount them heavily. Such a situation can arise, for example, when obtaining such longer term benefits requires coordination among potential competitors that is difficult to achieve.[13]

There are well documented differences in unit labour costs between countries which have persisted over relatively long periods of time.[14] They result from a variety of factors particular to national economic, political and social environments.[15] They can reflect international differences in levels of supply and demand for particular types of workers. Labour laws, policies and programmes can also exert an important influence on unit labour costs. Recent studies comparing manufacturing labour costs across countries have found that countries ranking lower on various indices of labour standards implementation tended to have substantially lower labour costs, even after controlling for other factors including worker productivity.[16] While some labour standards have also been shown to have efficiency enhancing effects, many nonetheless entail a net redistribution of income and risk from workers to employers.[17] Thus, even if labour standards have long-term efficiency and productivity enhancing effects, there is potential for competitive pressures at the margin to reduce their redistributive effects.

For policy purposes it is therefore important to separate the effects of accepted sources of comparative advantage from those of competition on the basis of low labour standards. Evidence of labour market effects associated with economic integration thus needs to be handled with caution. It may be a symptom of competitive pressures on labour standards, but often it may simply reflect the operation of legitimate forms of comparative advantage. Without isolating the effects of the two sources of pressure it would be difficult to say anything with clear policy implications.

Similarly, evidence of effects on labour standards associated with international economic integration needs to be handled with caution. From a narrow bottom line perspective, cost savings achieved through market adjustments are economically equivalent to those being achieved through low or lowered labour standards. Pressure on labour standards may thus be an unintended consequence of the operation of legitimate comparative advantage (which raises important policy questions that lie beyond the scope of this paper).

The best evidence of the impact of globalization on labour standards is thus found in studies that directly examine the relationship between labour standards and the economic variables that can generate competitive pressures – trade and investment flows. This evidence can be usefully complemented by evidence of associations between effects on labour standards and deepening international economic integration, such as shifts in the incidence of regulatory costs of paid holidays or days of rest on to workers, shifts in bargaining power which undermine the capacity of workers to organize or bargain collectively, or competitive pressures on labour legislation itself.

The case for the emerging consensus

Since the early 1990s, both trade and labour economists have generated a substantial empirical literature on the effects of labour standards on international trade and investment flows. Much of this work has been compiled in seminal studies undertaken by the Organization for Economic Cooperation and Development in 1996 and 2000,[18] and more recently under the auspices of the International Labour Organization's World Commission on the Social Dimensions of Globalization.[19] At the same time, legal scholars and political economists have begun to look directly at whether international economic integration has led to regulatory competition or to policy convergence between states in a variety of fields. A number of these studies have examined patterns in the evolution of labour laws and social programmes under deepening integration.

Most reviews of this body of work have concluded that there is no evidence of a regulatory "race to the bottom" in labour affairs or similar policy fields, and that there is little evidence that labour standards are driving outcomes of competition for investment or success in international trade. Some key findings are summarized below.

Studies of policy convergence and regulatory competition

Scholars and activists have documented some quite compelling case examples in which legislators have sought to attract investment by weakening legal protections for workers, or by touting the absence of such protections.[20] However, the relatively few systematic studies attempting to show how regulatory competition affects labour and employment laws and policies have suggested that these cases are outliers rather than part of a strong trend.[21]

Within the European Union there have been prominent cases in which multinational corporations have relocated in search of lower labour costs or have obtained concessions from unions after publicly considering such relocation.[22] Despite the public concern that these cases have generated, there is little evidence that labour legislation in Europe has been amended in response to international competitive pressures within the EU, and labour affairs officials at the EU concede (privately at least) that there is no immediate threat of large-scale capital movements within the Union in search of lower labour costs.[23]

In the United States, national legislation actively seeks to harmonize the labour and employment standards that apply to the majority of the work force, providing little opportunity for regulatory competition between states.[24] One notable exception lies in the right of states to enact so-called "right to work" laws.[25] Such laws are widely understood to impede unionization and to reflect the preference of a substantial part of the local employer community to operate in a "union-free" environment.[26] Thus, some have argued that the pattern of adoption of "right to work" legislation provides one possible test of the thesis that economic integration can lead to downward pressures on labour laws.[27] However, the geographic pattern of right to work laws coincides with historical patterns of receptiveness or hostility to unionism within state politics, reflecting the local political strength of the labour movement and its political allies, rather than any pattern of inter-state regulatory competition. Right to work laws were passed by a number of states in the South, the West and the central plains in the 1940s and 1950s. Since the end of the 1950s only four states have passed such legislation notwithstanding the long-term movement of capital from the more heavily unionized North to the South after the 1930s.[28]

Case studies of social programme reforms in Southern and Eastern Europe, East Asia and Latin America have found no evidence that those reforms were driven by competitive pressures from economic globalization.[29] In each case it appears that the policy direction of governments was determined by political factors other than a desire to enhance or maintain international product market competitiveness. In many cases the relevant political factors included international influences, but these operated at the level of persuasive argumentation rather than economic compulsion. European countries outside of the European Union, for example, have been drawn to emulate the social policies of countries playing a leading role within the EU.[30] Other countries have been strongly influenced by World Bank or IMF policy advice.[31]

Finally, social spending and levels of taxation have tended to increase in tandem with international economic integration. This is consistent with predictions that globalization would create demands for additional social protection in the face of the economic instability and competitive pressures that it brings.[32]

Patterns in foreign direct investment and international trade

Overall foreign direct investment (FDI) and trade patterns show little sign of being influenced by labour laws, labour policies or labour markets. Consider first the case of foreign direct investment. In 1997, 77 per cent of FDI flowed into OECD countries,[33] although unit labour cost differences between these countries are much smaller than those between North and South. That percentage was roughly the same as it was in 1990, notwithstanding a substantial expansion of total FDI between 1990 and 1997.[34] As of 1991, 81 per cent of the world stock of FDI was located in the high wage and relatively high tax countries of the OECD. This represented an increase of 12 per cent since 1967.[35]

These patterns suggest that the bulk of aggregate FDI is drawn by factors other than low labour costs – in other words, by factors most often associated with advanced capitalist development. If anything, protection of worker rights seems to be associated with environments conducive to FDI. A recent comprehensive literature review and study of the effects of worker rights and unionization rates on FDI concludes that FDI tends to be greater in countries with stronger worker rights, and that evidence on the effect of unionization rates was inconclusive.[36] This result holds for both developing and developed countries.

Surveys of investors tend to show that FDI decisions depend more on factors other than low labour costs. These include the size and growth potential of the receiving country's domestic market; political and social stability; the quality of the labour force; the quality of infrastructure; the transparency of the legal system; and the manufacturing and services environment.[37] When foreign direct investors consider whether to locate production in developing countries, they will in fact often look for a stable, well-trained labour force rather than the lowest possible labour costs. They will often bring with them management techniques that are more respectful of workers than those that prevail in developing economies, and often pay higher wages than local producers.[38]

Similar patterns hold for international trade. The vast majority of trade takes places between the wealthy industrialized nations of the North, and there has been little change in this aggregate pattern since 1970.[39] Trade flows continue to depend directly upon a range of institutional, cultural and geographic factors, and those flows are concentrated in intra-regional patterns in Europe, Asia and the Americas.[40] For the most part, each OECD country continues to have only two or three significant trading partners. The main exceptions are the smaller countries; but even in those cases, trade partners have been established over a long period, reflecting ties of geography, empire, culture and corporate organization.[41] While figures on intra-firm trade are probably inflated by corporate transfer pricing,[42] such trade probably accounts for a significant fraction of total imports and exports in major industrialized economies – perhaps a third or more.[43] Garrett finds that in fact the increase in trade activity between the early 1960s and 1992 seems to be attributable to intra-industry trade between OECD countries.[44]

Since there is less difference in unit labour costs between OECD countries than between countries within and outside the OECD, other competitive advantages clearly override labour cost differences in determining the bulk of trade flows. Not surprisingly, OECD researchers found: (1) that there is little relationship between changes in total country shares in manufacturing export markets and the application of International Labour Organization (ILO) core labour standards; (2) that other forces such as resource and technological endowments provide a more cogent explanation of those changes; and that (3) resource-based and technology-based patterns of comparative advantage in manufacturing were not altered by different levels of enforcement of core labour standards.[45]

In short, despite significant unit labour cost differences between industrialized and developing countries, and despite increasing economic openness between the developing and developed world in key sectors such as manufacturing, there is no evidence that such openness has had a widespread impact on labour laws or labour markets in industrialized countries. Competition for investment and product market share appears instead to continue to favour the advanced industrialized economies as much as it ever did.

In fact, there is increasing evidence that high labour standards make a positive contribution to economic competitiveness. In its 1996 study, the OECD concluded that there appears to be a mutually supportive relationship between successful trade liberalization and respect for the core labour standards subsequently recognized in the ILO Declaration on Fundamental Principles and Rights at Work.[46] The OECD later recognized that stronger core labour standards can increase growth and efficiency by raising skill levels in the work force and by encouraging innovation and higher productivity.[47] Kucera's 2001 review suggested that core labour standards may in fact be integral to the other elements of the social, political and regulatory environment necessary to attracting significant FDI, because they promote social and political stability and growth in the domestic market.[48]

Given these findings, it is perhaps not surprising to see an emerging consensus among writers that there is no economic basis for fears that international economic integration poses a threat to core labour standards.[49] This consensus could in principle be extended to most labour standards and labour laws. The OECD concluded that low standards countries are unlikely to gain market share at the expense of high standards countries and that developing countries need not worry that adopting high labour standards will impede their economic performance.[50] Even commentators sympathetic to linking labour standards to international trade law now argue that competition on the basis of low labour standards can only be explained as a political rather than an economic phenomenon, reflecting little more than misguided attempts to secure short term political payoffs – attempts which may be imitated by others.[51]

Consensus conclusions reconsidered

As critics have pointed out, the failure to consider other sources of competitive advantage often associated with high labour standards reflects a more general problem with such regulatory competition or "race to the bottom" theories, a problem that has been observed in attempts to test them across a number of policy fields.[52] Such theories tend to assume that cost differences due to differences in national labour markets and labour laws are sufficient to overcome other factors that affect the location of production and competitiveness in product markets. They also tend to assume that the state responds exclusively to the preferences of capital and not to other constituencies such as voters, bureaucracies or interest groups. And they tend to assume that regulatory standards will not have offsetting economic advantages for business either directly or as an inextricable element of a larger social, political or regulatory environment. These assumptions reflect a more general tendency to abstract relationships between international economic integration, labour markets, and labour policies from the industry conditions and political systems in which they are embedded.

However, critics of the "race to the bottom" argument have failed to push this line of argument to its logical conclusion. If context matters, then differences in context matter as well. The evidence upon which the emerging consensus is based is dominated by dynamics within the developed world – by industries where competitiveness clearly turns on factors other than unit labour costs, and by political contexts where democracy and modern labour laws are firmly established and generally well-implemented. To generalize on the basis of this evidence is to assume that the competitive advantages of established industrial democracies can also be secured relatively easily in the developing world, and that something will similarly offset competitive pressures on labour standards. It also requires the assumption that there will be no major political obstacles to moving towards higher labour standards during a period of transition. It is necessary to consider whether those assumptions are well-founded.

There are at least two plausible scenarios in which labour cost considerations may drive inter-jurisdictional competition for investment and market share, notwithstanding the greater weight that investors give to infrastructure, political stability and the like. The first involves what may be termed horizontal competitive pressure. In this scenario, the two or more jurisdictions are similarly situated with respect to the main advantages that have been found to determine investment location decisions: they have similar levels of physical and legal infrastructure, political and social stability, and proximity to major markets. Between such jurisdictions, the marginal competitive advantage presented by lower unit labour costs and a less constraining regulatory environment becomes much more significant. For example, within the United States, advantages of infrastructure and market access are relatively evenly distributed between states, and those with high rates of unionization and high wages rates have had significantly lower rates of manufacturing growth over a long period of time.[53] This suggests that over time these variables have significantly influenced the rate of new plant openings, the rate of expansion or contractions of existing plants, or the rate of closure of obsolete plants.

A second and perhaps more important case involves what may be called vertical competitive pressures. These pressures result where less developed economies rely heavily on low labour costs to compensate for shortcomings in other factors that attract investment and gain market share. Such jurisdictions will face significant short-term pressures to hold labour standards down. This may prove to be only a transitional strategy in some states. In others, it may last a long time – for example where infrastructure and political stability are slow to develop, where major markets are distant, and where strong employment growth is needed to supply jobs to a burgeoning population. In such scenarios, the long-term advantages of high labour standards may seem too distant to elicit enlightened self-interested behaviour.

A preliminary consideration of differences between the political and industrial context of the developed world and that of many developing countries suggests that both horizontal and vertical competitive pressure are far more likely to operate in the latter than in the former. To the extent that those pressures do affect the industrialized states, this is likely to be in industries and occupations that are particularly vulnerable to vertical competition from the developing world.

Within the advanced industrialized economies, horizontal competitive pressures are likely to be offset by institutional and political constraints that allow the longer term advantages of high labour standards to prevail. The institutional and regulatory environment will have influenced employer strategic choice in responding to competitive pressures over many years, providing incentives for investment in human and physical capital to improve productivity. In many industries, labour costs will be a relatively small share of total costs of production, as producers will long ago have substituted human and physical capital for labour. Skills developed on the job will be important to productivity. This entails a greater need to retain workers, and thus creates pressures for better compensation and working conditions. Production facilities themselves may be highly dependent upon advantages specific to their location, such as a reliable network of suppliers. In some countries, strong unions and centralized collective bargaining will insulate groups of workers from competitive pressures on remuneration, imposing solidaristic wage policies such as industry-wide wage bargains or contractual prohibitions on contracting of work outside the reach of collective bargaining agreements.[54] Employer responses will reflect this institutional environment, and as a consequence will not necessarily place primary emphasis on labour cost reduction.[55] Furthermore, workers and the public in general will often vigorously resist efforts by employers and governments to lower the established floor of labour standards.

By contrast, in the developing world, a number of mutually reinforcing tendencies make competition on the basis of low labour costs and pressures on labour standards more much more likely.

First, a far greater share of employers are likely to rely on low labour costs for competitiveness, and they will face obstacles in pursuing other strategies. In accordance with their comparative advantage, many developing countries have a high concentration of low skill, labour-intensive producers for whom labour costs are a large part of total costs of production. Relative ease of entry into such industries often means that product markets are highly competitive, and relatively small production cost differences are likely to matter at the margin. A large supply of unskilled labour reduces the need to improve compensation and working conditions in order to retain workers. A relatively small supply of skilled workers and capital makes trying to substitute human and physical capital for unskilled labour less attractive and more difficult.

Second, many developing economies have a relatively high proportion of production that can be easily relocated. Much of this is structured for mobility in order to maintain low labour costs and to insulate against political instability, currency fluctuations and other risks often associated with developing economies. A higher share of FDI in developing countries is put into export oriented industries and thus not dependent on local markets. It is also concentrated in labour-intensive manufacturing, and is relatively footloose.[56] Perhaps more importantly, a significant part of manufacturing for export takes place within supply chains in which the decision that allocates work and employment is not whether to invest in production facilities but rather whether to award a contract for the production of intermediate inputs or even finished products. This greatly increases the mobility of production.

It is difficult to provide an overall description of global patterns of multinational enterprise sub-contracting practices because of the lack of data and complexity of the arrangements.[57] However, there is evidence in trade statistics that out-sourcing of intermediate inputs has increased significantly in recent years in the manufacturing sectors of a number of OECD countries, and that it now accounts for a significant percentage of total intermediate input production.[58] The fact that two-thirds of enterprises in export processing zones are locally owned or are joint ventures between local and foreign capital[59] suggests that much of their production is channelled through supply contracts.

Third, the legal and institutional environment in many developing countries may offer little buffer against market pressures. Trade unions are often weaker than in the industrialized world, and labour laws, though at times quite protective of workers on paper are often ineffectively enforced.[60] Thus the institutional environment is much less likely to induce employers to adopt competitive strategies that coexist easily with or generate high labour standards.

Finally, in many developing countries the economy and the balance of payments increasingly depend upon low-skill labour intensive exports into competitive markets. This raises the political stakes of maintaining a regulatory environment that does not threaten low labour cost advantages. Vulnerability to financial crises can accentuate this dependence, by creating a need for hard currency export earnings to repay foreign currency denominated obligations and thus further strengthening the political hand of export industries. This political climate will in turn make the country in question a more attractive location for other similar producers. Moreover the operation of such pressures in one country will encourage their operation in other similarly situated countries, since none of them will be able to afford to raise labour standards without fear of losing market share to another.

In this context, immediate political and economic incentives to avoid raising labour standards are likely to persist even if infrastructure building and skills development bring some of the competitive advantages of the advanced industrialized economies. Thus, there is little reason to believe that higher standards will come about automatically in the process of development. In fact, as more developing countries seek to industrialize under similar conditions, there is a real risk that competitive pressures on labour standards will intensify. We may already be seeing this. As the OECD notes, the advantages of export processing zones as a means of generating employment for low-cost, low-skill labour are increasingly undermined by intensifying international competitive pressures, which render employment precarious and subject to a logic of labour cost minimization.[61]

There is no reason to believe that the industrialized countries can immunize themselves against such competitive dynamics. It is well known that labour-intensive industries in the industrialized world face stiff competition on the basis of low labour costs, and there is evidence that this is translating into lower labour standards through the advent of bargaining dynamics that reduce the value of legal rights.[62] Moreover, a wide range of labour-intensive operations across many skill sets can be isolated and outsourced through supply chains that seek to minimize labour costs.[63] As Harrison has documented, in many industries employers increasingly segment their work force into core and contingent groups, and this competitive strategy has accelerated with globalization.[64]

In short, rather than a uniform "race to the bottom", competitive pressures resulting from international economic integration may well produce a segmentation within the international industrial economy. On the one hand, major parts of the developing world and certain sectors within industrialized economies will continue to experience pressures that will make a strategy of competing on the basis of absolute labour cost minimization not only economically rational but self-perpetuating. On the other hand, much of the industrialized world will seek to insulate itself against such pressures by relying increasingly upon non-labour cost advantages, or by segmenting work vulnerable to competitive pressures through low-cost outsourcing options or other forms of restructuring.

The shortcomings of the evidence on trade and investment patterns underpinning the emerging consensus are now clear. First, the very general trade and FDI trends upon which that consensus is based are dominated by dynamics within the industrialized world. The picture may be very different in the developing countries and in specific industries in the developed countries. Second, the data on investment decisions fail to include supply chains, which are a form of economic organization conducive to low labour cost competitive strategies. Third, the evidence fails to separate the effects of high labour standards on investment and trade from the much larger effects of advantages in infrastructure and stability that prove decisive in the competitive advantage of the industrialized world. Fourth, the OECD studies fail to distinguish between local market oriented investment within OECD countries, which still represents the majority of FDI flows, and the movement of investment between the industrialized and developing world. Finally, studies of effects of economic integration on labour laws and labour markets focus mainly on the industrialized world, leaving a very incomplete picture.

There is a small and incomplete body of evidence that begins to redress these deficiencies, and which suggests that the emerging consensus view is too sanguine. Studies focusing on the developing world have found a negative association between ILO core conventions and export performance, and a negative association between higher unit labour costs and FDI. Studies have also noted that within multinational firms labour demand in each affiliate is related to the cost and demand conditions of other affiliates owned by the same firm, with the result that production location decisions are correlated with declines in wages.[65] Rodrik found that one measure of comparative advantage in labour intensive goods – the ratio of textile and clothing exports to other exports, excluding fuels – was associated with a number of indicators of low labour standards.[66] Since he also found that US foreign direct investment was positively correlated with indicators of democracy and human rights enforcement, he hypothesized that poor labour standards may attract outsourcing in labour intensive industries, but may not attract foreign direct investment from the United States. Many major producers of goods such as clothing, footwear, consumer electronics and automobile parts have concentrated the decision-making power and profitable functions of their enterprise (such as the development of technology and brand loyalty) in corporate central offices located within the developed world, while production requiring manual labour is outsourced to lowest cost suppliers in the developing world.[67]

Finally, it should be kept in mind that studies noting the absence of a "race to the bottom" in labour laws do not tell us much. In some cases it is because such findings are easily explained. Within the European Union, for example, differences in worker productivity most often offset differences in wages[68] and thus neutralize incentives to relocate in search of cheap labour. Perhaps more importantly, most governments are less likely to downgrade labour laws than to choose other political responses to competitive pressures. As Gunderson notes, since labour and employment laws often have as a stated purpose the protection of the economically disadvantaged, reducing such regulations risks making a government look mean-spirited.[69] Moreover, labour and employment laws are often of general application, so levels of protection cannot be reduced without affecting a substantial part of the voting public. Governments that do respond to competitive pressures are likely to prefer measures that have relatively low visibility. Such responses may take the form of neglect, for example by reducing administrative and enforcement resources or the failure to introduce new legislation. They may also take the form of targeted reductions of standards that affect limited classes of workers rather than the population at large.

In this light, it is interesting to note three points. The first two arise from comparisons between US states. As noted above, these are jurisdictions which are highly integrated economically and which have relatively small differences in the quality of their governance and infrastructure by international standards. Thus differences in labour standards would be expected to matter. First, Elmslie and Milberg report that until the US Congress passed the Fair Labor Standards Act of 1938 there was in fact considerable competition between US state legislatures in setting lax child labour laws.[70] Second, states such as Massachusetts, Michigan, New York and Pennsylvania offer a wide array of supports and commit extensive resources in an effort to promote the expansion of existing firms and the creation of new one, while others, such as Arizona and Texas, have been much more restrained and focused on attracting firms from other states, in large part by offering a low-tax, anti-union business climate.[71] Thus, competitive pressures on labour standards appear to have been diverted into less visible fiscal policy means of providing offsetting advantages where it is more politically convenient to do so. The third point is that shifts in fiscal policy broadly consistent with this pattern can be seen in other countries. A number of studies suggest that globalization has been associated in many countries with a shift in the burdens of taxation from capital to labour, through increased reliance on consumption taxes, payroll taxes and income taxes falling on wages.[72] In addition, a growing number of countries are deciding to pursue a strategy of offering tax holidays in order to attract foreign investment.[73] This could, in turn, accelerate competitive pressures on domestic tax regimes, a problem which the OECD has sought to address in a recent report.[74]

In short, a closer look at the pressures and incentives flowing from economic integration shows that there is a real risk that competitive strategies based on low labour standards will have an enduring attraction in the developing world, even though such strategies impede rather than assist long-term competitiveness and economic development. Many developing countries and their producers face a combination of horizontal and vertical competitive pressures to seek short-term competitive advantages through low standards. This can be expected to have an impact in the industrialized world, especially in the labour-intensive and internationally integrated sectors where producers can expect to face increasing pressures on labour costs and standards. The risk that these pressures present is that the international economy will increasingly be segmented into high and low standards economic sectors and regions. Once established, low standards methods of production will have a propensity to reproduce themselves through self-reinforcing complexes of institutions, incentives and competitive strategies.

The more sanguine views of the emerging consensus are based on an inherently incomplete and insufficiently disaggregated picture of trade and investment trends operating mainly within the industrialized world. Analysts have also looked in the wrong places for trends in labour standards themselves, searching for a "race to the bottom" in highly visible and broadly based public laws and institutions, rather than focusing on the restructuring of private sector production or trends in the administration of labour laws. Research would do well to probe below the level of national legislation, one of the least likely elements of labour standards to yield to competitive pressures, examining instead the extent to which laws are enforced, the formative effects that competitive pressures exert on employer practices in the workplace and on bargained terms and conditions of employment, and the incidence of regulatory costs as between workers and employers.

Conclusion

The emerging consensus view on globalization and labour standards correctly points out that the most successful economies in today's integrating world are those with high labour standards, that such standards appear to make a positive contribution to economic success, and that there is little risk of a wholesale "race to the bottom" in labour standards in the industrialized world. Yet this does not entail, as the consensus suggests, that globalization is unlikely to have any significant negative impacts on labour standards.

The proponents of the emerging consensus have failed to look closely enough at industrial and political conditions that shape short-term interests, and thus outcomes, within international competition for market share and investment. Despite the long-term advantages of high labour standards, international economic integration creates the potential for self-perpetuating cycles of low standards competition, in both low and high skilled forms of production, especially but not only in the developing world. These cycles, unless checked, will tend to create a deepening gap in the international industrial economy between those fortunate enough to be located within prosperous core centres of production, largely in the industrialized world, and those in more precarious operations that can be outsourced or easily relocated, or that for other reasons have come to depend upon absolute labour cost minimization as a competitive strategy.

In many developing countries strengthening the application of labour standards stands to improve the lives of working men and women entering the growing international industrial economy, to reduce the social and political strife over working conditions that plagued so many of the early industrializing states, and to gain opportunities for economic growth and political stability. The somewhat uncomfortable conclusion that flows from this paper is that achieving these goals may require stronger forms of international coordination to maintain and even raise labour standards. History provides little reason to believe that these problems will simply sort themselves out.[75]

Today, however, many if not most developing country governments resist the prospect of stronger international governance with respect to labour standards. Their reasons are varied. Many would not agree with this paper's arguments. Many fear yet another incursion into national sovereignty after many years of structural adjustment pressures or experience with trade agreements that they view as unbalanced. Some see a threat of disguised protectionism on the part of the industrialized world.

Yet, this was not always the case. At the founding of the multilateral trading system, it was developing countries who argued most strongly for a fair labour standards clause in the Charter of the International Trade Organization.[76] Their arguments were precisely that increased international economic integration created a risk of competitive pressures undermining their efforts to develop and maintain high labour standards. Clearly, developing country governments at that time saw their interests differently at that time. They may do so again in the future. However, in order for this to happen, public debate over globalization will need to develop and examine models of international coordination that can promise effectiveness while addressing today's concerns about national autonomy over labour policy and protectionist misuse.

Today, as in the past, the prospect of destructive international competition impacting on labour standards most often evokes calls for stronger international commitments backed by more binding enforcement procedures. The incentives provided by such procedures are meant to offset those generated by international competitive pressures, disciplining states to maintain or adopt a policy stance that favours and enforces high labour standards. This "command and control" mode of international regulation proposes a direct trade-off of national policy autonomy for freedom from competitive pressures through effective international coordination.

Yet the analysis of this paper points to a number of reasons to believe that such an enforcement-based approach is unlikely to be sufficient to its task. The effectiveness of labour standards implementation at the national level is likely to be bound up in a complex interdependence with the competitive strategies of employers in key industries. Shifting from economic structures that are accustomed to or rely upon low labour standards entails significant social and economic change. In most countries where they succeed, labour law and policy have been built up gradually through local and national struggles and dialogue. Thus the basic challenge is probably not that of restraining government action (to reduce labour standards) through threats of sanctions, but rather that of seeking to induce government and civil society buy-in to a process of complex structural reform over a long period of time. One may question on the basis of experience whether any regime based only on adjudication and sanctions is sufficient to bring this about.[77]

Perhaps enforcement regimes should be treated not as backing up an international contract, but rather as underpinning an effort to build an international community in which the idea of development includes the improvement of labour standards and all of the structural reform that this entails. In such a system international institutions could build on rather than constrain democratic politics at the national level – deliberately aiming to heighten the pace at which political reforms required to implement high labour standards are discussed, considered and achieved.

Notes

1. Understood as the application in practice of labour norms that are important from a policy perspective (generally those embodied in key national laws or international conventions).

2. For a review and commentary on the debates of that time, see Brian Langille, "Canadian Labour Law Reform and Free Trade" (1991) 23 *Ottawa Law Review* 583.

3. Since the NAFTA, Canadian policy makers have insisted upon labour cooperation agreements in tandem with each of Canada's new free trade agreements in the Americas, on each occasion consolidating a practice that now effectively amounts to a policy. Meanwhile in the United States the drive by unions, human rights groups and Democratic Party legislators to link labour standards to future trade agreements lay at the centre of an eight year deadlock in Congress over the terms of the US Administration's mandate to negotiate new trade agreements. The eventual hard fought compromise, set out in the Trade Act of 2002, requires that the Administration seek to include in each new trade agreement labour standards protections enforceable though procedures equivalent to those that enforce the rest of the agreement. The USA has since negotiated and ratified trade agreements containing labour chapters with Singapore and Chile, is seeking such provisions in negotiations for a Central America Free Trade Agreement, and has begun to press for a labour chapter in the FTAA. Today, as Canadians look ahead to a possible Free Trade Area of the Americas, polling data suggest that they support linking some form of protection for worker rights to international trade more strongly than they support free trade itself. (See e.g. the Canadian Broadcasting Corporation News poll conducted between 3 and 9 April 2001, finding that 57 per cent of Canadians thought that expanding the free trade area between Canada and other countries would be a good thing for Canadians, that 11 per cent strongly opposed creating a Free Trade Area of the Americas (FTAA) and 45 per cent somewhat supported it, while 85 per cent said that a commitment to minimum labour standards should be included in the FTAA. The margin of error was less than 3 per cent. "CBC News Poll", CBC News, (2001) online: http://cbc.ca/news/indepth/summit_poll.html. In view of the US position, and in view of public opinion at home, the Canadian government would have great difficulty backing away from its current practice of linking labour rights and trade, even if it wanted to.

4. In addition to concerns about competitive pressures, there are three principal arguments for linking labour standards to trade. The first is based on ethical norms of fairness – that the international economy opened up by trade regimes should respect at least a basic set of norms with respect to decent working conditions, and the ability to earn a fair share enterprise income. This argument is most powerfully based on internationally recognized fundamental human rights at work, but may also be based on strongly held beliefs within a national polity about such matters as basic occupational safety and health or minimum wages. The second is that linking labour standards to trade serves the larger purpose of promoting sustainable development by promoting equity, the effective use of human resources, and social and political stability. While neither of these two arguments depends upon the competitive pressures argument, each is reinforced by it: to the extent that their aims are put at risk by economic competitive pressures it becomes easier to justify creating

enforceable commitments to labour standards rather than relying upon strategies
that are simply promotional. The third argument is the pragmatic one that doing
something about labour standards is simply politically necessary to maintain public
support for open trade.

5. See Michel Gauvin and Charles-Philippe Rochon, *Labour Legislation in Canada: Major Developments and Trends 1989–2003* (HRSDC, 2003).

6. Jagdish Bhagwati, "Free Trade and Labour", *Financial Times*, 29 August 2001.

7. For a good description of these interconnected processes, see United Nations Conference on Trade and Development, *World Investment Report* (UNCTAD, 1994), Ch. 3.

8. See e.g., Paul Samuelson, "International Trade and Equalization of Factor Process" (1948) 7 *Economic Journal* 163, showing increasing or decreasing inequality between skill groups in the labour force; Dani Rodrik, *Has Globalization Gone Too Far?* (Institute for International Economics, Washington DC, 1997), Ch. 2, demonstrating shifts in the incidence of regulatory costs and bargaining power; Brian Langille, "Competing Conceptions of Regulatory Competition in Debates on Trade Liberalization and Labour Standards", in William Bratton et al. (eds.), *International Regulatory Competition and Coordination* (Clarendon Press, Oxford, 1996) at 479–90; Geoffrey Garrett, *Partisan Politics in the Global Economy* (Cambridge University Press, 1998), setting out and examining arguments for downwards pressures on social policies; Adrian Wood, *North-South Trade, Employment and Inequality: Changing Fortunes in a Skill-Driven World* (Clarendon Press, London, 1995), showing increased unemployment and shifts in income shares and downwards pressures on labour laws and policies – dynamics captured in the model of the prisoner's dilemma.

9. Unit labour cost is the ratio between absolute labour cost and labour productivity. It is thus a direct measure of the labour cost of producing a given quantity of product, and an indirect measure of the share of the income stream generated by that product that accrues to workers.

10. A comparative advantage is an advantage that is more significant than advantages that may obtain in other industries within that economy

11. See World Trade Organization, Singapore Ministerial Declaration, Singapore, 13 December 1996, (1997) 36 I.L.M. 220.

12. See e.g., the classic article by Paul Samuelson, "International Trade and Equalization of Factor Prices" (1948) 58 *Economic Journal* 163.

13. See Alan Hyde, "A game-theory account and defence of transnational labour standards – a preliminary look at the problem" chapter 5 of this volume.

14. Dani Rodrik, "Democracies Pay Higher Wages" (1999) 64 *The Quarterly Journal of Economics* 707; UNCTAD, *Trade and Development Report 1997* (United Nations Conference on Trade and Development, 1997), 90, table 31; Jim Stanford, Christine Elwell and Scott Sinclair, *Social Dumping Under North American Free Trade* (Canadian Centre for Policy Alternatives, Ottawa, 1993), 17.

15. According to standard economic theory wages in any particular industry will be influenced by the productivity of workers throughout the economy as a whole, owing to the mobility of workers between places and industries. Thus in an economy in which overall productivity is very low, one would expect that wages in industries with high productivity would nonetheless be low relative to the wages of workers with similar productivity situated in a country in which overall productivity was higher. Unit labour cost differences can also be the product of a structural imbalance of labour supply and demand: the disparity between large and rapidly growing working populations and inadequate social, physical and productive infrastructure which condemns them to subsistence labour and meagre opportunity. See generally Gerald Meier, *Leading Issues in Economic Development* (Oxford University Press, 1964), ch. 3. In addition, fluctuations in international currency exchange rates, which often have little to do with industry cost structures, can nonetheless create differences in unit labour costs measured in the currency of an importing country. See Kenichi Ohno, "The Case for a New System" in *Bretton Woods: Looking to the Future*, Commission Report Staff Review Background Papers (Bretton Woods Commission, Washington, 1994) C-5–C 12.

16. Rodrik, *Has Globalization Gone Too Far?* The indices included (1) total number of ILO Conventions ratified by the country; (2) the number of ratifications of ILO Conventions relating to the ILO's Declaration on the Fundamental Principles and Rights at Work – Conventions 29, 87, 98, 105, 111, 138; (3) the Freedom House indicators of civil and political rights, which are based on actual practice rather than formal ratifications; (4) an indicator of the extent to which child labour is condoned in a country, based on US embassy and ILO reports; (5) statutory hours of work in a normal work week; (6) days of annual leave with pay in manufacturing; (7) percentage of the labour force that is unionized. Morici and Schultz performed a similar regression, correcting for perceived methodological problems and using additional and more recent data. They obtained even stronger findings than Rodrik, estimating that annual manufacturing costs per worker, after taking into account national differences in productivity, are reduced by an average of more than $6000 per year in economies where both freedom of association and prohibitions against child labour are not effectively implemented. See Peter Morici and Evan Schultz, *Labour Standards in the Global Trading System* (Economic Strategy Institute, Washington DC, 2001). Rodrik followed up on his 1997 study with a study of the effects of democratic institutions on labour market outcomes: see Rodrik, "Democracies Pay Higher Wages". He found a very significant association between national levels of democracy and manufacturing wage levels. This is consistent with the view that authoritarian regimes tend to transfer income from labour to employers. The relationship between democracy and wages may be a consequence of political competition and political participation at large, which can serve to raise wages through competition between political parties to provide income enhancing labour legislation such as job security provisions, minimum wages and social security. Democratic

institutions may also be associated with an environment in which trade unions can bargain effectively.

17. Laws facilitating or promoting the practice of collective bargaining are probably the clearest example. Studies of union and non-union wage differentials consistently show that unionization results in a wage premium to workers both in industrialized and industrializing countries. World Bank, *Collective Bargaining and Country Economic Performance: A Review of the Empirical Literature* (2000) (unpublished draft paper on file with author). Restrictions on hours of work can also have important cost implications for employers, and were in fact the focal point of competitive pressure arguments during the industrial revolution. Juliet B. Schor, *The Overworked American: The Unexpected Decline of Leisure* (Basic Books, New York, 1991). Thus, as Gunderson concludes, it is likely wishful thinking to believe that labour and employment laws will as a whole pay for themselves from the point of view of the individual employer looking at immediate competitive pressures. Morley Gunderson, "Harmonization of Labour Policies Under Trade Liberalization" (1998) 53 *Relations Industrielles* 1 at note 26 and accompanying text.

18. "International Trade and Core Labour Standards", Policy Brief, Organisation for Cooperation and Economic Development, (2000) online: http://www.oecd.org/dataoecd/2/36/1917944.pdf; OECD, *Trade, Employment and Labour Standards: A Study of Core Worker Rights in International Trade* (OECD, Paris, 1996).

19. David Kucera, "The Effects of Core Workers Rights on Labour Costs and Foreign Direct Investment: Evaluating the Conventional Wisdom", *Decent Work Research Programme*, Discussion Paper No. 130/2001 (International Institute for Labour Studies, Geneva, 2001), online: http://www.ilo.org/public/english/bureau/inst/download/dp13001.pdf.

20. Harry Browne and Beth Sims, *Runaway America: US Jobs and Factories on the Move* (Interhemispheric, London, 1993); Mark Aspinwall, "Globalization, Exit and Free Social Riders: A Dysfunctional Integration Theory" (1998) 33 *European Journal of Political Research* 323.

21. Gunderson concludes that little systematic evidence exists on the extent to which jurisdictions are willing to reduce regulation to attract business. See Gunderson, "Harmonization of Labour Policies".

22. David Goodhart, "Social Dumping within the EU" in David Hine and Hussein Kassim (eds.), *Beyond The Market: the EU and National Social Policy* (Routledge, London, 1998), 79–90.

23. Goodhart, "Social Dumping within the EU" at 87. See surveys in Hugh Mosley, "The 'social dumping' threat of European integration: a critique", in Brigitte Unger and Frans van Warden (eds.), *Convergence or Diversity? Internationalization and Economic Policy Response* (Ashgate Publishing Ltd, Aldershot, 1995), 182–99.

24. Kevin Banks and Tequila Brooks, *Legal Rights of Migrant Agricultural Workers in North America* (Commission for Labor Cooperation, Dallas, 2000).

25. The National Labour Relations Act was amended in 1948 to allow states to forbid unions and employers from agreeing to require that employees pay to the union the equivalent of union dues as a condition of employment. Unions are nonetheless required by federal law to represent each employee in a bargaining unit of workers for which they hold collective bargaining rights, regardless of whether the employee is a union member or pays anything to the union to support such representation. Twenty-one states have enacted such laws.

26. Unions have long argued that right to work laws make it possible for many workers to "free-ride" on the dues of other workers, undermining solidarity among union members and eroding the financial base for union operations. Unions represent more than 20 per cent of the work force in states where there are no right to work laws, but only 10 per cent in states with them. See Kevin Banks, Lance Compa, Leonico Lara and Sandra Polaski, *North American Labor Relations Law – A Comparative Guide to the Labor Relations Law of Canada, Mexico and the United States* (Commission for Labor Cooperation, Washington DC, 2000), 199. While this difference in union density cannot be attributed solely to right to work laws, it is well-understood in the labour relations community that right to work laws send a message to employers that the state government does not actively encourage unionization.

27. Lane Kenworthy, "Economic Integration and Convergence: A Look at the US States" (1999) 80 *Social Science Quarterly* 4.

28. See Mike Davis, *Prisoners of the American Dream: Politics and Economy in the History of the US Working Class* (Verso Press, London, 1986), 137.

29. See the various case-studies contained in (2000) 10 *Journal of European Social Policy* 2.

30. For example, Spain and Greece each substantially increased social expenditures as a fraction of GDP between the early 1980s and the mid-1990s following their accession to the European Union. The increases paid for new programmes and increased and/or extended benefits. In Greece rising wages and payroll taxes were offset by increased productivity during the 1980s and 1990s, and as a result unit labour costs declined. In Spain on the other hand productivity increases were not high enough to offset the cost of increased wages, and thus unit labour costs rose. Guillen and Matsaganis attribute social welfare policy changes primarily to domestic political pressures for a "social convergence" with the rest of Europe, assisted by political activism in response to a need to legitimate and stabilize new democratic orders. Subsequent retrenchment of social spending in the 1990s was due to domestic political pressures resulting from deficit spending and the clientelistic provision of benefits which segmented the population into privileged insiders and neglected outsiders. At no point did national policy link competitiveness and social policy. Ana M. Guillen and Manos Matsaganis, "Testing the 'Social Dumping Hypothesis' in Southern Europe: Welfare Policies in Greece and Spain during the last 20 Years'" (2000) 10 *Journal of European Social Policy* 2. Similarly, in post-Communist Central

and Eastern Europe the key social welfare policy question in a number of countries appears to have been whether social policy would gradually evolve towards a Western European corporatist model, or towards a US-style targeted and more limited model. Deacon finds that the outcomes of these debates depended upon political battles involving both national and supra-national actors. "The supranational struggle between the ILO, endorsing the corporatist model, and the IMF and World Bank advocating targeted schemes and privatization, found its expression on the national level in struggles between ministries of labour mostly siding with the ILO and the European welfare model, and ministries of finance believing in the selective US model." See Bob Deacon, "The Prospects for Equitable Access to Social Provision in A Globalizing World", in Andrea Krizsan and Violetta Zentai (eds.), *Reshaping Globalization* (Central European University Press, Hungary, 2002), 109.

31. Kay, examining recent reforms to national pension systems in Latin America, found that government initiatives throughout Latin America to replace or complement state sponsored pay-as-you-go defined benefit plans with defined contribution savings programmes were driven mainly by a combination of political pressures of domestic and international origins not directly related to international trade integration: ageing populations combined with massive tax evasion in response to high payroll taxes; popular dissatisfaction with increasingly clientelistic privileges for specific groups; financial pressures on pension systems resulting from the deteriorating fiscal position of governments; the endorsement, technical support and financing of reforms by the World Bank, the IMF and the Inter-American Development Bank. Stephen J. Kay, "Recent Changes in Latin American Welfare States: Is there Social Dumping?" (2000) 10 *Journal of European Social Policy* 2.

32. Garrett finds that total revenues to OECD governments increased between 1966 and 1990 as a percentage of GDP. On average, the increase in revenues was largely accounted for by increased personal income tax revenue and increased employer social security contribution revenue, with consumption tax and corporate tax revenue remaining relatively stable. Geoffrey Garrett, *Partisan Politics in the Global Economy* (Cambridge University Press, 1998), 86.

33. Garrett, *Partisan Politics*, 34.

34. Garrett, *Partisan Politics*.

35. Linda Weiss, *The Myth of the Powerless State* (Cornell University Press, Ithaca, 1998), 185.

36. Kucera, *The Effects of Core Worker Rights on Labour Costs*.

37. Fabrice Hatem, *International Investment: Towards the Year 2002* (Renouf Pub. Co. Ltd, Paris, 1998). Horizontal FDI designed to serve domestic markets (and thus less directly implicated in global markets) appears to be more important as a fraction of total FDI than vertical FDI designed to serve international markets.

38. Debora Spar, "Foreign Investment and Human Rights: International Lessons" (1999) 42:1 *Challenge*, 55–80.

39. Weiss, *The Myth of the Powerless State*, 176. Over the 1970–89 period the North's share of trade grew from 81 to 84 per cent. Despite strong increases in the volume of international trade in recent decades, there is little if any evidence as yet of gains in the share of international trade of low wage countries. Between the early 1960s and 1992 imports and exports increased as a fraction of total OECD gross domestic product from just under 50 per cent to almost 70 per cent. See Geoffrey Garrett, "Global Markets and National Politics: Collision Course of Virtuous Circle?" (1998) 52:4 *International Organization* 787, at 805. OECD imports from low-wage countries varied little as a fraction – around 20 per cent – of total OECD gross domestic product.

40. Weiss, *The Myth of the Powerless State*, 176–7.

41. Weiss, *The Myth of the Powerless State*, 172.

42. Weiss, *The Myth of the Powerless State*, 171.

43. See United Nations, World Investment Report (1994) at 143. Figures for the United States and Japan.

44. Garrett, *Global Markets and National Politics,* 806.

45. *OECD* (1996).

46. *OECD* (1996) at 111–12.

47. *OECD* (2000) at 19.

48. Kucera, *The Effects of Core Worker Rights.*

49. Drezner states simply that "there is no empirical evidence to support a negative relationship between globalization and labour standards". Daniel Drezner, "Who Rules? State Power and the Structure of Global Regulation", Paper presented at the 97th annual meeting of the American Political Science Association, San Francisco, California (September 2001). Langille concludes as follows: "The net effect of these observations . . . is that the argument for international labour standards shifts from a 'rational' economically based 'race to the bottom' to a race which should not occur at all because it is based upon an economic mistake". See Brian Langille, "The Coherence Agenda – A New Approach to International Labour Obligations", Unpublished Paper, Department of Foreign Affairs and International Trade (2002), 26.

50. *OECD* (1996) at 125.

51. See e.g., Langille, "The Coherence Agenda".

52. See Drezner, *State Power.*

53. Robert W. Crandall, *Manufacturing on the Move* (Brookings Institution, Washington DC, 1993). He provides a regression analysis covering the period 1967–89.

54. Richard Locke and Kathleen Thelen, "Apples and Oranges Revisited: Contextualized Comparative Labour Politics" (1995) 23 *Politics & Society* 3.

55. Models of competitive strategy are often quite specific to particular industries and can produce very different responses to similar competitive pressure. Michael Piore, "Trade and the Social Structure of Economic Activity", in Susan Collins (ed.),

Imports, Exports and the Aerocan Worker (Brookings Institutions Press, Washington DC, 1998), 257–86.

56. Piore, "Trade and Social Structure", 280.
57. *OECD* (1996) at 120–21.
58. Robert Feenstra, "Integration of Trade and Disintegration of Production in the Global Economy"(1998) 12:4 *Journal of Economics Perspectives* 31–50.
59. Keith Maskus, "Should Core Labour Standards be Imposed Through International Trade Policy", in *World Bank Policy Research Working Paper No. 1817* (The World Bank Group, 1997).
60. See e.g., *Annual Survey of Violations of Trade Union Rights, 1999* (International Confederation of Free Trade Unions, Brussels, 1999); Jeffrey Harrod, "Social Relations of Production, Systems of Labour Control and Third World Trade Unions", in Roger Southall (ed.), *Trade Unions and The New Industrialization of the Third World* (Zed Books Ltd, London, 1988), 41–58.
61. *OECD* (1996) at 120–21.
62. Competitive pressures appear however to have had significant effects on worker bargaining power in import competing industries in the USA, where Rodrik notes that:

> One can debate the quantitative significance of the decline in bargaining power engendered by the differential global mobility of employers versus employees. But there can be little doubt that this has changed the nature of employment contracts in many tradable goods industries, and through example and spill over, in many non-tradable ones as well . . . Mitchell has documented a striking transformation in union contracts starting in the early 1980s, a transformation that is not well accounted for by either the disinflation of those years or the above average unemployment rate. The transformation was reflected in wage freezes and cuts, which first showed up in a narrow range of industries in 1981 and then spread to others. Management has appeared increasingly to take a harder stance. Mitchell calls this a "norm shift" in wage determination. While not all the sectors in which this happened were those that came under increased exposure to trade in the early 1980s (e.g. construction and retail food stores), many were (e.g., metal manufacturing, machinery, lumber and paper, aerospace). The pattern set in the early 1980s survived even through the trade deficit that was eventually reduced . . . The first order effect of trade [in industries such as autos or steel] appears to have been a redistribution of the enterprise surplus towards employers rather than an enlargement of that surplus.

See Rodrik, *Has Globalization Gone Too Far?* 24–5 citing Daniel Mitchell and Katherine Abraham, "Shifting Norms in Wage Determination" (1985) (Brookings Papers on Economic Activity, 575–608. Moreover, there is mounting evidence that employers in the United States use "predictions" that they might move to abroad (most often to Mexico) in order to discourage workers from unionizing. Kate Bronfenbrenner, "Uneasy Terrain: The Impact of Capital Mobility on Workers, Wages and Union Organizing" (US Trade Deficit Review Commission, 2000).

63. As the OECD notes, this is true not only of low-skilled work but also with respect to highly skilled tasks that are nonetheless easily relocated:

> In the wake of internationalization of costs, many businesses are moving their software and programming services to countries such as India and the Philippines. Air carriers, such as Cathay Pacific or Lufthansa, employ a small number of experts in India to process flight tickets, the aircraft maintenance is carried out in Ireland and China, and a fixed percentage of flight personnel is hired abroad at local conditions. These changes in the internal organization of MNEs underline the importance of cost considerations.
>
> See *OECD* (1996) at 120–1.

64. Bennett Harrison, *Lean and Mean: The Changing Landscape of Corporate Power in the Age of Flexibility* (Basic Books, New York, 1994). Harrison argues that these structural changes account for account in significant measure of the growing wage inequality within skill and education groups in the United States.

65. Patrick Belser, "Does Latin American and Caribbean Unemployment Depend on Asian Labor Standards?", Working Paper No. 380, Inter-American Development Bank (1998). Kucera notes that FDI in developing countries is negatively affected by higher unit labour costs, which may reflect the higher share of vertical FDI in developing countries with such FDI being more export oriented, concentrated in labour-intensive manufacturing, and footloose. Kucera, note 19 above at 28.

66. He cautions that many of these associations were not statistically significant, but concludes that given the weakness of the data on labour standards enforcement and the difficulty of quantifying differences across countries on such a complex set of issues, his results are suggestive. See Rodrik, *Has Globalization Gone Too Far?*

67. Harrison, *Lean and Mean*; Gary Gereffi, "The Organization of Buyer Driven Global Commodity Chains: How US Retailers Shape Overseas Production Networks" in Gary Gereffi et al. (eds.), *Commodity Chains and Global Capitalism* (Praeger, Westport, Conn. 1994), 95–122.

68. See Goodhart, "Social Dumping" at 82.

69. Gunderson, "Harmonization of Labour Policies" at 41.

70. Bruce Elmslie and William Milberg, "Free Trade and Social Dumping: Lessons From the Regulation of US Interstate Commerce" (1996) 39 *CHALLENGE* 46–52.

71. Kenworthy, "Economic Integration and Convergence" at 863.

72. At least three studies have found that tax rates on labour in industrialized countries have increased in recent decades while tax rates on capital have tended to remain stationary or to decrease. These studies have drawn on national income accounts to separate taxes on consumption (general taxes on goods and services plus excise taxes), taxes on labour (income tax on wages plus social security taxes including both

employer and employee portions, and (other) payroll taxes), and taxes on capital (personal income tax on non-wage income, corporate income taxes, and taxes on financial transactions). The first found that taxes on labour in the G-7 countries from 1965 to 1988 followed an increasing trend in all countries, while taxes on consumption and capital remained stationary: Enrique Mendoza, Assaf Razin and Linda Tesar, "Effective Tax Rates in Macroeconomics: Cross-Country Estimates of Tax Rates on Factor Incomes and Consumption" (1994) 34 *Journal of Monetary Economy* 297. The second found similar trends in eighteen OECD countries between 1965 and 1991, and that in regression analyses taxes on labour responded positively and significantly to a lagged economic openness variable, while the opposite was true for taxes on capital: Enrique Mendoza, Gian Maria Milesi-Ferreti and Patrick Asea, "On the Ineffectiveness of Tax Policy in Altering Long-run Growth: Harberger's Superneutrality Conjecture' *Center for Economic Policy Research Discussion Paper No. 1378* (CEPR, 1996). Finally, Rodrik calculated the unweighted average effective tax rated on capital and labour for France, Germany, the United Kingdom and the USA for the period from 1971 to 1991, finding that tax rates on both rose steadily until about 1980, at which point tax rates on labour continued to increase at roughly the same rate while tax rates on capital began to fall. Rodrik, *Has Globalization Gone Too Far?* 63–4.

These findings should be approached with some caution because they are based on a method which attributes the entire burden of social security and other payroll taxes to employees. This may be a safe assumption in many cases, but there are circumstances, particularly where collective bargaining institutions are strong, in which the incidence of payroll taxes falls more heavily on employers. Payroll taxes may fall on employees if they result in reduced wage growth or wage reductions. There is some evidence suggesting that in many cases the majority share of such taxes has been borne by workers in this way. See Bev Dahlby, "Payroll Taxes" in Allan Maslove (ed.), *Business Taxation in Ontario* (University of Toronto Press, 1993). However, Alesina and Perotti find that in OECD countries increases in payroll taxes to pension and unemployment insurance benefits resulted in increased unit labour costs in countries that had an intermediate level of centralization in collective bargaining institutions: Alberto Alesina and Roberto Perotti, "The Welfare State and Competitiveness", unpublished paper, cited in Rodrik, *Has Globalization Gone too Far?*; 45. Moreover, some of the patterns in taxation described above might be accounted for by a general rightward shift in politics within OECD nations, a shift which may have been relatively independent of international competitive pressures. Nonetheless, they do provide suggestive evidence that in recent decades international economic integration has been associated with a shift in the tax burden from capital to labour. The more limited available evidence for developing countries shows increases in the importance of general consumption taxes. Reuven S. Avi-Yonah, "Globalization, Tax Competition and the Fiscal Crisis of the Welfare State" (2000) 113 *Harvard Law Review* 1573 at 1620–1.

73. Avi-Yonah concluded on the basis of his own research and a review of the literature that:

> Tax competition has led to the proliferation of production tax havens. Currently at least 103 countries offer special tax concessions to foreign corporations that set up production or administrative facilities within their borders. They include such developed countries as Belgium, Ireland, and Israel and such developing countries as Malaysia and India. The extent of the tax holiday varies, but in general the tax haven reduces its statutory tax rate to 10% or less for foreign corporations investing in specified types of facilities or areas within the jurisdiction. However, the jurisdiction imposes a higher rate of between 30% or 40% on local corporations, a personal income tax at even higher rates on individuals, and a value added tax . . . Studies by economists have shown that such tax incentives are quite widespread and that investments in these countries are significant.
>
> Avi-Yonah, "Globalization, Tax Competion" at 1588.

74. See OECD, *Harmful Tax Competition: An Emerging Global Issue* (OECD, 1998).
75. While some have argued that the first wave of globalization in the late nineteenth and early twentieth century did not inhibit the development of modern labour laws in the industrialized world, it should be noted that most labour law systems were consolidated and fully developed only after World War I, by which time the tides of international economic integration were receding. In fact, the argument that no jurisdiction could improve its labour laws without risking its industrial competitiveness appears to have exerted a profound restraining influence on labour policy in Europe during much of the nineteenth century, and was the most important reason for the founding of the International Labour Organization. See Kevin Banks, "Trade, Labour, and International Governance", Doctoral Dissertation, Harvard Law School, (2003), App. A.
76. The negotiating history of the ITO Charter's fair labour standards clause is reviewed and analyzed in Banks, "Trade, Labor, and International Governance" at App. B.
77. Banks, "Trade, Labor, and International Governance" at Ch. V.

4

Globalization, decentralization and the role of subsidiarity in the labour setting
in memory of Marco Biagi

VÉRONIQUE MARLEAU

Introduction[1]

> *La gloria di colui che tutto move*
> *per l'universo penetra, e*
> *risplende*
> *in una parte più e meno altrove.*
>
> Dante Alighieri, *Paradiso*[2]

The principle of subsidiarity prescribes that decisions should be made at the level where they can be most effective and, as far as is reasonable, by the level closest to the individuals affected. In the context of discussions over the appropriate direction of labour law reform in Italy, Marco Biagi[3] argued that subsidiarity should be the leading principle of collective bargaining to respond to concerns about employer competitiveness in an increasingly global trading environment.[4] In keeping with subsidiarity, Marco Biagi also believed that the scope of bargaining at the local level should not be dictated to the parties on the basis of some predetermined bargaining structure, but that it should "fall to the contractual agents themselves to define the field of application."[5]

The purpose of this paper is to take a fresh look at the role of subsidiarity in the labour context by focusing on the links between globalization and labour regulation in light of the current trend towards decentralization of collective bargaining. To that end, the key notions of globalization and decentralization will be examined and related to the structural and functional dimensions of subsidiarity in the context of labour regulation. The discussion will emphasize the potential of subsidiarity as a means to promote an inclusive democracy, and stress its pivotal role as an operative principle of social justice. The paper will also defend the view that the principle of subsidiarity is the best tool yet devised to offset some of globalization's unwanted consequences and thereby more effectively protect workers' interests.

From integration to fragmentation

The proposal to make subsidiarity the leading principle of collective bargaining brings to the surface a very old problem in a contemporary context: how to find the appropriate balance between the broad and the narrow, the central and the local in order to ensure that labour relations systems can adapt to what lies ahead. This question raises another important issue: How much design is possible? Can we articulate the One-in-many?

Such questions cannot be answered in isolation. An understanding of the forces at play and their relationship to existing frameworks is necessary to come to grips with the challenges facing existing labour relations systems. Yet what makes this task necessary is also what makes it so difficult: globalization is shaping a new social order that often seems to be working at cross-purposes. It is perplexing to realize that a process of integration (in the sense of increased globalism) can trigger a process of decentralization (in the sense of increased localism). Marco Biagi underscored this apparent contradiction when he observed: "Paradoxically, as has been mentioned on various occasions, globalization and internationalization of markets have led to diversification and to a drive towards the local dimension, thus increasing the pressure on employers and unions to enter into wage agreements in line with the conditions of the local labour market."[6]

The meaning of "Globalization"

As Vidya Kumar stressed in his critical assessment of globalization methodology, "the fundamental question of what globalization is seems to have been eclipsed by its arrival."[7] For "the debate about what to do about globalization is still very much a debate about what globalization is."[8] Although the aim here is only to clarify the meaning of globalization, and not to reflect upon the relationship between globalization's definition and what globalization theorists propose as appropriate responses to its effects, it remains important to emphasize the epistemological implications of such a relationship.

Like the meaning of law, the meaning of globalization is in one sense self-evident and in another, as vague and obscure as its reaches are wide and constantly shifting.[9] To some extent this is because the reality of globalization is theory-laden: the facts about globalization are constructed facts (their identification depends entirely upon the theory that asserts their relevance as "globalization facts"), and the definition of globalization is part and parcel of the reality it asserts.[10] This implies that globalization is both an objective and subjective phenomenon,[11] and that it is as normative (prescriptive) as it is factual (descriptive).[12]

In the face of such potential for distortion, a stipulated definition of globalization (a "working ontology") becomes necessary to bring to the surface the assumptions implied in the factual analysis. To that end, a first step to clarify what we are talking about when we refer to "globalization" is to distinguish between the narrow and broad view of the concept. A second step is to articulate a "vision" of globalization from which likely implications can be drawn.

The narrow and broad views of globalization

Under the narrow view, globalization is conceived as a particularly advanced state of cross-border economic interdependence, i.e. the *economic integration* resulting from the cross-penetration of markets and the growing significance of intra-firm trade (the globalizing economy). The key characteristics of globalization so conceived are the liberalization of international trade, the expansion of foreign investment and the emergence of massive cross-border financial flows, all resulting in increased market competition.[13] This view places the multinational corporation at centre stage, positioning it as the engine of this economic interdependence.[14] This is in keeping with the original meaning of the term "globalization", which was first used to describe trends in multinational corporate strategies in the early 1980s.[15]

By contrast, the broad view of globalization encompasses all theories of social change that rely upon the core concept of globalization to explain current fundamental, causal trends of social reality, drawing on a variety of different and sometimes contradictory perspectives. As W.E. Scheuerman notes, although major disagreements remain about the precise nature of the causal forces behind globalization, a consensus about the basic features characteristic of the concept appears to be emerging.

First, social theorists associate globalization with deterritorialization, "according to which a growing variety of social activities takes place irrespective of the geographical location of participants."[16] Second, globalization is linked to the growth of social interconnectedness across existing geographical and political boundaries. Here globalization refers "to

processes of change which underpin a transformation in the organization of human affairs by linking together and expanding human activity
across regions and continents."[17] Third, observers agree that globalization is characterized by reference to the speed or velocity of social activity
and, more generally, a sense of acceleration of change. This is a way of
saying that globalization is not only spatial in nature, it is also temporal.[18]

Globalization is also widely recognized as a long-term and multi-
pronged process. It is a long-term process because the linking together
and expansion of activities across borders only makes more readily apparent what many thought existed all along. At the same time, globalization
is multi-pronged because "deterritorialization, social interconnectedness,
and acceleration manifest themselves in many different (economic, political, and cultural) arenas of social activity."[19]

Whether one favours the narrow or broad view of globalization, everyone concedes that globalization is a matter of degree because any given
activity may influence events more or less faraway and each manifestation
of globalization generates distinct conflicts and dislocations.[20] Indeed,
while each facet of globalization is linked to the core components of globalization, at the same time "each consists of a complex and relatively
autonomous series of empirical developments, requiring careful examination in order to disclose the causal mechanisms specific to it."[21]

Globalization as compound interdependence

Globalization is a dynamic concept, and like any dynamic concept it
embodies the idea of change. The change involved here refers to a process
of progressive interdependence driven by factors that bring societies and
citizens closer together, and by policies, institutions and private initiatives
that support the integration of economies and countries.[22]

If one accepts that social order is an emergent, complex relationship
between human intentionality and unintended social consequences, it
becomes clear that globalization is the ever evolving outcome of the profound tension between the goals of designed institutions and the resulting
spontaneity of an evolving order: "A synthesis results, which has greater
social significance that any of its isolated individual components."[23] That
synthesis is one of *compound interdependence*. It describes a new reality, a
new blueprint with profound social and political implications. That new
blueprint is "a degree of interdependence which goes far beyond simple
expansion of international trade, the main indication of the internationalization of the economy in the past."[24]

While globalization supports integration, it also seems to embody two distinct, yet interdependent phenomena: one of increased integration and another of increased fragmentation. This remains true whether one takes the narrow or broad view of globalization; in all cases the logic of globalization seems to imply the simultaneous appearance of both phenomena. In this sense, globalization is a dialectical phenomenon, as it expresses the synergy of two complementary and interdependent "spins" operating in reverse directions, the local and the global.

Hence, globalization is a paradox of compound interdependence. Its impact is not always in the direction of centralization or the creation of larger units or even of homogenization, no matter how much it changes the significance of existing boundaries.[25] This apparent contradiction, underscored by Marco Biagi in the labour relations context, has also been noted elsewhere. In the socio-political sphere, Twinning observed that although the processes of globalization tends to make the world more interdependent:

> This does not mean that we are moving inexorably towards a single world government nor does it mean the end of nation-states as the most important actors. The post-modern mood stresses cultural relativism. At the same time as the European Union grows in size, we are also witnessing the revival or growth of smaller nationalisms and local identities. It [is] by no means only the Balkans that are becoming balkanized. The global does not exclude the local, but rather they interact in very complex, sometimes contradictory ways.[26]

Similar observations have been made in relation to the emergence of multinational corporations (MNCs). In this respect, Duncan Campbell has noted that the redefinition of subsidiary from a geographically oriented principle to a component within a global network seems to affect its autonomy, but how it does so is unclear:

> In one sense, responsibility for worldwide production of a key product or component may be becoming increasingly decentralized to subsidiary level. In another, the subsidiary's increasing role within a centrally coordinated production web may result in a decline in the relative autonomy formerly held by the subsidiary for marketing, finance or local strategic decision-making.[27]

Hence Campbell's conclusion that "what seems to be implied by the logic of globalization is that there may be simultaneously greater centralization (such as the coordination of overall product strategy), and greater decentralization (such as is occurring with research and development in the pharmaceutical industry)."[28]

As a force of far-reaching change, globalization seems to intensify all existing polarities, both at global and local levels. Globalization affects everyone but its impact is uneven. And in this, the traditionally disadvantaged groups and nations are once again the great losers.[29] One explanation might be that the economically driven forces at play merely compound preexisting conditions: with globalization the Wheel of Fortune does not change direction – it only spins faster.

On this account, one could think that "globalization" is a misnomer and that a better term might be "glocalization" to reflect the inherently dialectical nature of the phenomenon. The suggestion was made by Bob Hepple, who has argued that the term "glocalization" would more accurately emphasize the tensions between global integration and movements of capital, goods and services, etc., and growing local dislocations and awareness of local cultural and social diversity.[30] As he puts it, globalization suggests global unity, while in fact the so-called "free" circulation of capital goods and services is concentrated within specific regions (particularly the free trade areas).[31] At the same time, globalization suggests global integration, while in reality it results in growing inequality, unemployment and exclusion.[32]

Another dialectical characteristic of globalization adds to its complexity. This is highlighted by the transformation within firms that show that the "micro" can achieve a global reach (such as where responsibility for worldwide production of a key product or component becomes decentralized to subsidiary level).

Along related lines, Boaventura de Souza Santos has argued that in assessing globalization's implications, we need to distinguish between situations where some local phenomenon becomes successfully globalized ("globalized localism") and situations where local conditions, structures and practices change in response to transnational influences ("localized globalism"). Examples of this include the spread of the English language and Coca-Cola as instances of "globalized localism," and the adaptation of local commercial laws to deal with transnational transactions or deforestation to pay for foreign debt as cases of "localized globalism."[33] Souza Santos has relied on this distinction to map two extremes of North-South relations, arguing that "the core countries specialize in globalized localisms, while upon the peripheral countries is imposed the choice of localized globalism."[34]

While this logical framework helps emphasize deeply-seated imbalances between developed and developing countries, by itself it cannot explain these trends, as other more complex interactions occurring on many levels must also be factored into the equation.[35] The value of Souza Santos' distinction lies more in its ability to capture the fundamental nature of globalization phenomena, namely a profound relationship of complementarities between whole (global) and part (local).

Indeed, the distinction offers a conceptual matrix based upon a "universals-particulars" frame of reference, which helps reveal that each local instance has a global counterpart and vice versa. Each global trend has its local manifestation. In classical epistemology, the universal always refers to the concept, while the particular refers to an individualized instance of the concept (the recurring question being whether we access the concept through the particular or whether the particular is created by the concept). The new dimension here is that each phenomenon refers individually to both the universal and the particular (i.e. there is a universal concept of globalized localism and particular instances of its manifestation as well).

By way of illustration, let us take the example of informal sector growth in non-rural areas, which is now well-documented.[36] On the one hand, informal sector growth can be regarded as an instance of globalized localism if we focus on the *development* of the phenomenon. Informal sector growth in non-rural areas can be said to have started locally with the spread of a new "core-periphery" model of work organization. Indeed, this new model originated from flexible methods of organizing production pioneered by the Japanese.[37] In this sense, informal sector growth was an isolated localized instance before becoming a process that turned into a global trend (i.e. the displacement of workers outside the parameters of the formal system).

At the same time, informal sector growth in non-rural areas can be characterized as a case of localized globalism when we focus on *outcomes*. Informal sector growth is observed in all countries of the world and this growth can be linked in varying degrees to transnational influences. However, the nature and extent of the phenomenon clearly varies according to local conditions, structures and practices. In recent years the majority of new jobs and income opportunities created in the world have emerged in the informal economy, but the trend is much more acute and its effects are far more dramatic in developing countries and transition economies, where informal employment now absorbs half to three-quarters of non-agricultural employment.[38]

The examples could be multiplied, but the point here is mainly to stress that a logical framework premised upon a "universal-particulars" complementarity captures an essential characteristic of globalization phenomena, namely a fundamental relationship between part (local) and whole (global) that is inextricably linked to the conditions of "observation", i.e. the perspective taken to construe phenomena (process or outcome).

This suggests fascinating parallels with quantum reality, which (like the social reality of globalization) is not open to direct observation. The nature of quantum phenomena has been found to be fundamentally dual (wave-particle dualism or coexistence) because quanta exhibit two properties depending on observational conditions.[39] Moreover, the discovery of nonlocality by micro-physicists (i.e. instantaneous interconnections or correlations among parts of a system, which in turn cannot be localized in a given region of space and time, or true instantaneous action-at-a-distance)[40] has revealed the existence of a profound new relationship of complementarities and interdependence between parts (quanta) and whole (universe). This part-whole coexistence, which is known as non-separability, results from nonlocality, and is now claimed to be one of the most certain general concepts of physics.[41]

That globalization is shaped by "observer-created reality" seems to be similarly governed by a profound relationship of complementarities and interdependence between parts (local) and whole (global), linked to the conditions of "observation". At the same time, globalization as a whole appears to be characterized by instances of instantaneous connections or correlations among parts of systems that in turn cannot be localized in a given region of space and time. At the least, globalization phenomena offer paradigmatic examples of Niels Bohr's complementarity principle[42] manifesting not through the wave-particle nature of light, but rather through the process-outcome nature of social phenomenon.

If the social reality of globalization is fundamentally dual and characterized by the profound complementarity of the relationship between part and whole, and if nonlocality is a property of the entire universe, it may well be that an undivided wholeness exists in all aspects of reality – physical *and* social – and that there is accordingly no basis for the stark division between mind and world sanctioned by classical physics from which the assumptions of free market economics are derived.

That the character of social reality may be ruled by the same fundamental principles that govern physical reality should not surprise us. In real life there is no closed and hermetically sealed social system divorced from the physical parts of the universe. Both globalization phenomena on the social plane and quantum phenomena on the material plane appeal to the idea that wholeness requires a complementary relationship between unity and difference, and that in some sense within all parts. With complementarity there is interdependence, and all developments and trends observed so far lead to the same conclusion that each local instance has a global counterpart and vice versa, i.e. the global trend and its local manifestation. There is interdependence of the local and global dimensions.

Interestingly, this all brings us back to Heraclitus and his doctrine of the inseparability of opposites and unity in difference, and his claim that things *are* interdependent. Heraclitus was telling us all along that reality is a dialectical process of constant interaction of opposites in an undivided and yet constantly changing universe.[43]

In the final analysis, no matter how we label the forces at play ("globalization", "glocalization" or something else), it is clear that they produce a dialectic of greater integration and greater fragmentation, whose resulting synthesis can be characterized as one of compound interdependence. While this refers to a new social blueprint characterized by economic hegemony, it also describes a new reality marked by the acceleration and intensification of existing polarities.

The implications of decentralization

Like globalization, decentralization embodies the idea of change. In this case, however, the change refers to a movement of means of action and decision-making power to regional or local levels. As such, decentralization does not impose a specific mode of ordering, rather, it describes a form of organization in which the local dimension plays a significant role.

Decentralization and power articulation

The concept of decentralization is at least as old as the Bible, where we find an early articulation of the principle in discussions about the judiciary. In the Book of Exodus, Moses struggles with the problem of a heavy caseload. Because he alone sits as a judge for the people, he finds himself performing judicial functions from morning till evening, with no time for anything else. Jethro, Moses's father-in-law, has a practical suggestion to this problem. He tells Moses:

> What you are doing is not good. You and these people who come to you will only wear yourselves out. The work is too heavy for you; you cannot handle it alone. Listen now to me and I will give you some advice, and may God be with you. You must be the people's representative before God and

bring their disputes to him. Teach them the decrees and laws, and show them the way to live and the duties they are to perform. But select capable men from all the people – men who fear God, trustworthy men who hate dishonest gain – and appoint them as officials over thousands, hundreds, fifties and tens. Have them serve as judges for the people at all times, but have them bring every difficult case to you; the simple cases they can decide themselves. That will make your load lighter, because they will share it with you. If you do this and God so commands, you will be able to stand the strain, and all these people will go home satisfied.

(Exodus 18: 17–23; see also Deuteronomy 1: 9–18).

This example shows that a measure of decentralization becomes inevitable as institutions begin to grow. From that perspective, decentralization is rooted in common sense, since effective resource management requires a sharing of decision-making tasks. Certainly, decentralization makes perfect sense in the judicial context, where it would be futile to proceed differently.

Models of decentralization run across a spectrum of possibilities concerning the form of distribution of powers and the operating principles shaping the exercise of power by the centre and the regions. Alongside models of decentralization allocating powers on the basis of exclusivity, decentralization can also be "articulated" on the basis of complementarity (shared competence), according to different principles of organization. One of these principles is subsidiarity, which assigns primary responsibility for the exercise of authority to the local level, while leaving to the central level the power to intervene to supplement this authority to ensure the effectiveness of the scheme.

In the example taken from the Exodus, Moses has a job to do but he cannot do it alone. And so the suggestion is the adoption of a scheme in which decision-making power is to be distributed between the central figure (Moses) and the local officials (capable souls who hate dishonest gain) according to a guiding criterion of complexity.

At first sight, the scheme might seem like a form of decentralization on the basis of delegated authority (based upon hierarchical decision-making power). On another reading, it might look like decentralization on the basis of exclusivity because no provision is made for the review of local officials' decisions on matters of jurisdiction (it would seem that their power in this respect is complete). However, a third reading and one more in keeping with the spirit of the text, suggests rather a scheme based on an articulated sharing of powers, for it is clear that a measure of complementarity was intended through subsidiarity as an articulating device. Certainly Jethro was not suggesting that his son-in-law "decentralizes" judicial functions without retaining any oversight power or ultimate discretion. To be sure, Moses could have derived a power to review a simple-case-turned-complicated from his residual power to dismiss judges altogether. He could also have found an implied power to review local officials' decisions on grounds of natural justice. Whatever the rationale, the main point here is to illustrate that the existence of such an overseeing authority is an essential component of the principle of subsidiarity operating as a check against abuse (in this case, abuse or excess of jurisdiction).

Decentralization and bargaining articulation

In the labour relations sphere, the phenomenon labelled "decentralization" generally refers to an increase in collective bargaining at the local level, i.e. the "widely observed trend towards the decentralization of bargaining to the company level".[44] Indeed, as is noted in the latest ILO Global Report, *Organizing for Social Justice*:

> Since the end of the 1970s, there has been a growing tendency towards decentralization of collective bargaining in most parts of the world. Enterprise-level collective bargaining is developing; and where this level is predominant, it is diversifying further . . . In most countries, negotiation at this level has been aimed at enhancing enterprises' capacity to adapt to product and labour market requirements."[45]

Western Europe is the region where this trend has been noted with the greatest alarm.[46] In most cases, however, collective bargaining did not cease at multi-employer levels in countries of the "old EU". For the most part, collective bargaining systems remain centralized, with sectoral level bargaining and national level agreements being predominant.[47] As Roy Adams points out, what is called decentralization in this context is more properly bargaining articulation (or "re-articulation").[48] Following F. Traxler, Philippe Barré echoes this view by using the term "organized decentralization" to describe the phenomenon, stressing that it is in fact characterized by simultaneous "re-centralization" and "decentralization" of collective bargaining.[49]

Indeed, such bargaining articulation operates as well in the reverse direction. Since the beginning of the 1990s, centralized national agreements (which had often disappeared for many decades), have reappeared in many countries of Western Europe.[50] As Marco Biagi had observed, "it is clear that alongside the drive to decentralization of the structures of collective bargaining, we are also witnessing the growing strategic importance of the European level."[51]

On the whole, however, articulation upward (beyond the national level) remains a rare phenomenon.[52] For that reason, the trend towards increased bargaining at the local level does give legitimate reason to fear that, in a context where employers' bargaining power is increased regardless of the bargaining structure in place, decentralized bargaining will translate into "bargaining downward," i.e. lead to less bargaining and to a general deterioration of working conditions.

In this respect, bargaining articulation within multi-level bargaining regimes must be contrasted from instances where bargaining actually has become more decentralized in the sense that less bargaining takes place at higher (multi-employer) levels. While the first scenario mostly involves changes regarding the object and content of bargaining at the various levels, the second scenario produces a (sometimes major) decline in bargaining coverage and generates a widening of income differentials (as happened in Great Britain and New Zealand).[53]

Similarly, the European trend towards the decentralization of bargaining to the company level must be contrasted from decentralized collective bargaining regimes, i.e. regimes such as those of Canada and the United States that were designed as decentralized (single-level bargaining, single-employer and single bargaining unit). These regimes were intended to operate fundamentally at the local level.[54] In single enterprise-level regimes there is no trend toward greater centralization. On the contrary, it is met with an intensification of existing tendencies, that is, by a trend towards greater decentralization. And since collective bargaining cannot move to a more local level, greater decentralization in this context inescapably translates into a disintegration of collective bargaining altogether. Therefore, what we have here is a much more alarming trend towards the elimination or disintegration of collective bargaining, due to a decline in bargaining coverage at the local level.

The fully decentralized Canadian labour relations setting is particularly problematic in this respect. The Canadian model supports a fully decentralized version of labour law and labour relations as a result of the superposition of separate labour jurisdictions (constitutional framework), separate regulatory regimes (regulatory framework), and decentralized collective bargaining (labour relations framework). At all three levels, the decentralized framework follows a model of power allocation (and exercise) on the basis of exclusivity (no complementarity or sharing of powers between a central authority and a local level). In this scenario of complete decentralization all existing structures and trends operate in the same direction. The dynamic interaction of these structural layers thus produces a synthesis of compound decentralization, characterized by mutually reinforcing patterns.

The significance of this in the context of globalization should not be underestimated. If globalization means that pressures and readjustments downward are unavoidable, there is a need for structural adjustment or articulation that would allow existing systems to continue to serve the purpose for which they were designed. In a fully decentralized regime, no such articulation is possible because there is no central power or level vested with a power to intervene (nor even coordinated strategies between jurisdictions) to contain existing debasing pressures.

A fully decentralized framework favours the development of a regulatory race to the bottom because there is no countervailing force capable of offsetting the tendency of jurisdictions to compete for investments and jobs by bringing existing protections to the lowest common denominator. Canadian developments in labour regulation and practice over the last ten years in the various political jurisdictions confirm this prognostic, by showing that the risks of dismantling and regulating downward are real in the absence of a central regulating authority and broad-based bargaining structures.[55] This emphasizes the pivotal role of such structures and the importance of building adequate safeguards into existing frameworks.

To ensure a labour relations system's ability to maintain its equilibrium in the face of profound external and internal pressures, full centralization is not a viable option (nor a satisfactory one in the labour setting), while complete decentralization can in turn have devastating effects. A better approach therefore seems to be to resort to an articulating device premised on proportionality to ensure a measure of complementarity (checks and balances) within the system in order to counter the risks of downward regulation. As will be discussed next, subsidiarity can serve this purpose as the principle of articulation most capable of ensuring the necessary compromise between the need for flexibility and autonomy of action on the one hand, and the need for support and protection against abuse on the other.

Subsidiarity for wholeness

Although subsidiarity is better known as a guiding principle of political organization in instances of shared competences of federal states, it is first and foremost a principle of social organization. We find an early articulation of the principle in the papal encyclical Quadragesimo Anno of 1931:

> It is a fundamental principle of social philosophy, fixed and unchangeable, that one should not withdraw from individuals and commit to the community what they can accomplish by their own enterprise and industry. So, too, it is injustice and at the same time a grave evil and a disturbance of right order, to transfer to the larger and higher collectivity functions which can be performed and provided for by lesser and subordinate bodies. In as much as every social activity should, by it very nature, prove a help to members of the body social, it should never destroy or absorb them.[56]

The principle of subsidiarity was originally developed as part of a social system based upon self-reliance, participation and solidarity as structural principles. This social system was proposed as a qualified response to Marxism, situating itself between the liberal doctrine of individualism and that of collectivism.[57] This neo-Christian doctrine (solidarism) was meant to preserve the Christian value of charity by personalism, not by rigorous claims of justice but by equity.[58]

The subsidiarity doctrine is premised upon the complementarity and interdependence of two distinct, yet fundamentally related dimensions, the relationship between individuals and the whole on the one hand, and the relationship between economic and social interests on the other. In this context, the principle of subsidiarity conceived as an articulating device is also based upon complementarity, but one between decision-making levels. Subsidiarity can extend the state's action when circumstances so warrant and conversely limit such action (or justify that it ceases) when circumstances no longer justify the intervention.[59] This implies as a necessary corollary the principle of proportionality.[60]

The structural dimension of subsidiarity

From a structural standpoint, an articulating device is needed to allow a system to readjust to powerful debasing pressures. At the same time, checking devices are needed to offset the risks of regulation downward. Subsidiarity can offer both devices at the political level within a federal union as well as within labour relations schemes as the chosen principle of collective bargaining articulation.

Subsidiarity and the race to the bottom

As a principle of political organization, subsidiarity (which presupposes federalism) guides the exercise (articulation) of shared competences between the central and local levels (political units). As with decentralization, which reflects certain models of federalism, federal unions run across a spectrum of possibilities, each having their own model of distribution of powers and operating principles shaping the actual balance of power between the central and regional. In this context, subsidiarity represents one of the approaches available for the articulation of legislative power, when this is done on the basis of complementarity.[61]

In the European Union, which operates as a de facto federal union, subsidiarity has been retained as the principle guiding the exercise of shared and complementary powers.[62] The principle provides that, in areas outside its exclusive jurisdiction, the EU must take action in accordance with the principle of subsidiarity, that is to say, "take action . . . only and in so far as the objectives of the proposed action cannot be sufficiently achieved by the Member States and can therefore, by reason of the scale or effects of the proposed action, be better achieved by the Community. Any action of the Community shall not go beyond what is necessary to achieve the objectives of this Treaty."[63]

The EU subsidiarity scheme ensures that consideration be given to setting minimum standards at EU level and to allowing member states to set higher national standards.[64] In this context, Community law is to be general and not detailed, its role being to help level the "playing field" in a manner that serves the economic and social objectives of the Union. Such a framework is of paramount importance in the area of social policy, where there are pressures to deregulate to the lowest common denominator (or worse, to a lower denominator). In this context, the central authority serves a stabilizing function by ensuring a minimum of protection to workers across the Union.[65]

In addition to this stabilizing function, the subsidiarity principle can also operate "reactively" to compel a recalcitrant member state to take positive action to comply with the principle of subsidiarity. An example on point is the United Kingdom, where workers have benefited from ECJ rulings forcing the United Kingdom, on grounds of failure to comply with the principle of subsidiarity, to bring forward legislation to provide for the designation of workers' representatives for the purposes of consultation under the directives on collective redundancies and transfer of undertakings.[66]

In both instances, subsidiarity operates as a checking device against abuse. Checking devices refer to those mechanisms that are built into a system to preclude an excessive concentration of power. Strictly speaking, they are the constitutional controls whereby separate branches of government have limiting powers over each other so that no branch will become supreme. However, broadly understood as an operative component of the democratic principle, checks and balances also operate vertically through the distribution of powers between a central authority and several regional authorities.[67] In this vertical form, the powers are distributed in such a way that every individual in the political union is subject to the laws and regimes of at least two authorities, a central authority and a regional authority.

A structure that incorporates vertical and/or horizontal checks and balances adds layers of complexity, thus opening the door to jurisdictional disputes. At the same time, regulating is made more difficult because the dispersal of power makes it harder to adopt and implement terms and policies. In a context of global integration, however, it should be readily apparent that the supervisory and stabilizing role of a central authority is needed to effectively contain pressures for downward regulation.

To ensure this balance in the social sphere, and particularly in the area of labour and employment regulation, an effective power allocation scheme should be one articulated on the basis of complementarity and governed by a subsidiarity scheme to ensure that decisions (particularly legislation) affecting workers' interests be subjected to the checking device provided by the existence of at least two authorities.

Subsidiarity and collective bargaining schemes

Throughout the industrialized world, there is a widespread consensus that a defining attribute of a sound labour relations system is that it be devised along democratic lines. Certainly, representation schemes have become linked with the idea of democracy as well as with ideas of liberty and justice.[68] As has been noted: "One of the most cherished hopes of those who originally championed the concept of collective bargaining was that it would introduce into the workplace some of the basic features of the political democracy that was becoming the hallmark of most of the western world. Traditionally referred to as industrial democracy, it can be described as the substitution of the rule of law for the rule of men in the work place."[69]

On this logic, we should expect to find effective checks and balances in all labour relations systems. This is not an unreasonable proposition since, as systems of collective representation, these systems were designed (or they developed) through considerable modelling and borrowing from political tradition.[70] From that vantage point, it is legitimate to ask whether current labour relations systems contain sufficient checks and balances and, in this context, whether subsidiarity should be the

preferred articulating device. An enquiry along these lines can help identify our systems' strengths and shortcomings from the twin standpoint of
their ability to contain some of globalization's debasing pressures and their
capacity to ensure effective worker participation and fair representation
to all concerned.

Vertical checks and balance in the bargaining context suggest the existence of a supplemental level, creating a structure with a centralized multi-
partner approach accompanied by somewhat more flexible single-partner
enterprise-based bargaining.[71] To work, checks and balances require a
measure of coordination between levels. As we have seen, such coordination is a necessary component of an approach articulated in accordance
with subsidiarity, where the general framework agreement is meant to
exert a stabilizing function over the specific local (enterprise) agreement.
Horizontal checks and balances in the collective bargaining setting can
in turn be seen as referring to the existence of other – supplementary
or complementary – forms of employee representation, which serve to
ensure universality of participation and a freedom of choice based on
needs.

For the most part, vertical checks and balances are absent in the single
level collective bargaining frameworks of countries such as Canada and
the United States. North American industrial relations regimes also lack
other forms of employee representation besides collective bargaining. The
reason for this is twofold: exclusive trade union representation is a fundamental tenet of the representation scheme,[72] and collective bargaining
has been chosen as the sole method of determining terms and conditions
of employment for unionized workers.

What these single-level enterprise-based systems lack in checks and balances, they gain in simplicity and effectiveness (features which do matter
to covered workers). Under such schemes, workers can know rather easily
where they stand: only one trade union represents them (in the unit), only
one collective agreement can apply at any given time (to the unit), and
this agreement sets all the terms and conditions of employment of the
group (for the unit). However, these virtues are of little significance if the
regime itself loses its relevance in a context of global competition. As we
have seen, fully decentralized bargaining frameworks are ill-equipped for
making the necessary adjustments to continue to provide a majority of
workers with the benefits of (and real access to) collective representation.

In the case of multi-levelled collective bargaining frameworks (such
as those found in continental Europe), the strengths and shortcomings
are of a completely different nature. In such systems, checks and balances

exist both horizontally (different forms of worker representation) and vertically (central and local levels, with or without additional bargaining levels at branch, region, etc.), but it is difficult to find clearly articulated guiding principles. It is not that such principles do not exist, but rather that the rules governing articulation are very complex and often conflicting. Here, the benefits of the systems are somehow diluted by their inherent complexities and rigidities (the build-up effect resulting from the constant addition of new rules to resolve new situations and conflicts).

In this context, the twin-level approach of the broad and the narrow (which can of course introduce additional levels or layers of bargaining in between) may or may not operate on the basis of subsidiarity. In this context, a subsidiarity-based approach would be one leaving the choice of bargaining format to the bargaining parties' mutual agreement (i.e. the determination of the bargaining level at which to address specific issues or the scope of bargaining at each level). This requires a scheme premised upon complementarity between levels and operating on an articulated basis.

As with federalism, one difficulty is that no multi-level bargaining system is pure. Existing schemes reflect more decentralized or centralized patterns (as the case may be) with various degrees of coordination, combining different principles of articulation and methods of arbitration to choose between competing provisions. An added complexity is that these different operating principles must often accommodate the principle of the most favourable term or "derogation *in melius*" (i.e. benefits cannot be reduced but can only be enlarged upon, and the most favourable standard must be applied regardless of the level at which it was set); this, in a context where such determinations are becoming more and more difficult to make.[73] Moreover, exceptions are now allowed in certain instances that disrupt the system's unity ("derogation *in peius*").[74]

If articulated systems seem better suited than single-level systems to face globalization's debasing pressures, it begs the question as to what should be the preferred model. Some contend that centralized systems provide for more stability and ensure a better distribution of burdens and benefits, thus minimizing the risks of distortions of competition. Others claim that decentralized systems are better equipped to deal with current needs for adjustments in the face of a changing workforce and growing pressures to meet the demands of competition.[75]

As was observed in the latest ILO Global Report, *Organizing for Social Justice*: "Recent studies throw doubt upon the validity of all these arguments, finding no systematic impact of the extent of bargaining centralization on aggregate wage increases, inflation and unemployment. Reality is richer and more complex than hypothetical models . . . It would seem that there is no 'optimum' bargaining structure."[76]

If there is no optimum structure, this should suggest that none should be dictated to the bargaining parties and that they should be able to establish the format for bargaining best suited to their needs at a particular time. Such an approach would be in keeping with international labour standards and principles on the subject, which establish that the fundamental principles of voluntary negotiation and bargaining require that bargaining partners must be the master of their own bargaining relationship.[77]

While this precludes the imposition of a specific bargaining format limiting the parties' freedom to select the level at which they wish to bargain, it also implies that parties must be free to bargain at more than one level and that they must be at liberty to determine the level at which each specific issue will be addressed. In this context, it should not matter to us whether the bargaining format ultimately turns out to be centralized or decentralized. What should matter is that the bargaining scheme adopted be one capable of allowing the parties to bargain at more than one level in a coordinated manner. A collective bargaining scheme which contains no mechanism for collective bargaining articulation and no structure for regulating higher-level bargaining (such as a mechanism for determining representativeness in a multi-party structure) is not a scheme which can be said to provide parties with real choices.

This view is supported by Article 4 of ILO Convention No. 98 on the Right to Organize and Collective Bargaining, which prescribes that voluntary collective bargaining must be promoted at all levels where it can be undertaken. This implies that a measure of state intervention is necessary to allow the parties to take advantage of the full range of options available to optimize voluntary collective bargaining initiatives.[78] ILO Recommendation No. 163 confirms this by stating that "measures adapted to national conditions should be taken, if necessary, so that collective bargaining is possible at any level whatsoever, including that of the establishment, the undertaking, the branch of activity, the industry, or the regional or national levels."[79]

In an increasingly global trading environment where employers' bargaining power is increased, trade unions' ability to influence the choice of appropriate bargaining level may be undermined if the overall bargaining framework is devoid of adequate structural protections. As was noted by the ILO Committee of Experts, necessary measures must be taken by public authorities to ensure that structural change is not used to undermine trade unions.[80] In this respect, subsidiarity as a principle of bargaining articulation can operate as a structural safeguard to minimize this risk by ensuring the necessary compromise between the need for flexibility of choice (of bargaining level and scope of bargaining) and the need for protection against abuse (i.e. inability of choice).

A subsidiarity-based approach requires coordination between bargaining levels to ensure a minimum of protection and representation to all workers concerned (through proportionality). In itself collective bargaining never guarantees specific results but only a fair process that can lead to desired outcomes. As the principle for collective bargaining articulation, subsidiarity operates much in the same manner. While it does not guarantee specific bargaining content and outcomes at a higher (broader) level, it does guarantee that there will be a measure of broader-based bargaining, which implies something more than pure social dialogue in the form of consultation.[81]

A subsidiarity-based collective bargaining scheme is also likely to prove mutually beneficial to the parties by offering a fair compromise between workers' need for "protective bargaining" and "representational security" on the one hand, and employers' need for "pragmatic bargaining" (i.e. bargaining to find innovative solutions aimed at enhancing an enterprise's capacity to adapt to product and labour market requirements in exchange for new protective mechanisms for workers) and "operative flexibility" on the other hand.

The functional dimension of subsidiarity

The previous discussion shows that in addition to acting as an articulating principle and a checking device against abuse, subsidiarity can also be conceived functionally as a device that fosters and protects worker participation, representation and empowerment in the labour setting.

Expanded representation and effective participation

As a principle ruling the relationship between individuals and the whole, subsidiarity favours individual action. The subsidiarity doctrine recognizes that the individual is society's most fundamental "social unit" and consequently, that individual autonomy and freedom of choice and industry must be encouraged. To that end, public authorities must support individual freedom of action, association and organization. This approach is not meant to compromise the unity of society or the state. On the contrary, it is meant to reinforce the legitimacy of such unity by ensuring that it be the true reflection of the will of the people.

In this way, subsidiarity fosters an inclusive democracy by allowing a democratizing downward expansion of representation. Such expanded representation is made possible through political articulation and the exercise of people's freedom of association and right to organize. An expanded version of the concept of representation gradually emerges as society differentiates itself and organizes for action.[82] "When articulation expands throughout society, the representative will also expand until the limit is reached where the membership of the society has become politically articulate down to the last individual, and correspondingly, the society becomes the representative of itself."[83]

This is in keeping with the International Labour Organization's long-established principles on freedom of association for trade union purposes, which assert the importance of governmental *support for* rather than *interference in* the right to organize and to bargain collectively.[84] The ILO approach is also premised upon subsidiarity in requiring that the implementation and enforcement of international labour standards be done at the level where it can be most effectively achieved (i.e. state level). In keeping with subsidiarity, the ILO approach is to foster such compliance through active support, by way of ongoing monitoring, technical assistance and persuasive policing. The ILO has been particularly active in this respect in the area of freedom of association and collective bargaining because of the importance attached to these principles in the labour setting.[85]

Equal concern for social and economic interests

Although the subsidiarity doctrine favours the individual as the most fundamental social unit, it differs fundamentally from liberalism and its ethic of individualism in two fundamental respects. Firstly, unlike liberalism, which does not consider state support necessary (deeming everyone to have free will and free choice), subsidiarity recognizes as essential the need to strengthen the ability of individuals to take action (support for rather than interference in).[86]

Secondly, while liberalism does not take into account the starting position of the parties but only the transaction itself (being premised upon formal equality or equality of process), the doctrine of subsidiarity regulates differently the relationship between economic and social considerations, holding that the state must attend equally to the social and economic interests of citizens. This was made clear in the original statement of the subsidiarity doctrine articulated by the Catholic Church in response to the rise of fascism in Italy in the 1930s:

> It is therefore necessary that the administration give wholehearted and careful attention to the social as well as to the economic progress of citizens, and to the development of the productive system.[87]

These two dimensions of the subsidiarity doctrine produce an overall approach to social organization and regulation premised upon *substantive* equality between social and economic interests. Such an approach admits the need for corrective measures to take into account the starting position of the parties (i.e. more favoured – least advantaged) to ensure more equitable outcomes. To state the matter differently, unlike liberalism, the subsidiarity doctrine recognizes that a "visible hand" is needed as an effective counterpart to the "invisible hand" of economic progress, which cannot produce on its own the good of society.[88] The Zen master might suggest that this should be self-evident, referring us to this famous *koan*: "You can make the sound of two hands clapping. Now what is the sound of one hand?"[89] Indeed, what is the sound of a single hand, especially an invisible one?

Labour law gives concrete form to the reality of the visible hand by introducing a measure of fairness in the labour market. As Harry Arthurs has observed, all systems of labour law built up some fifty years ago have had a considerable boost from the state, and without state intervention collective bargaining systems could never have worked as well as they did: "The state acts to promote collective bargaining and ensure workers' entitlements to various job-related benefits, to end oppressive, unsafe and discriminatory practices in the workplace and, within limits, to buffer workers from temporary employment and illness and poverty after retirement."[90]

The logic of subsidiarity is at work in labour law by calling for a measure of public intervention to establish adequate safeguards to ensure the free and effective exercise of workers' rights to collective action, to prevent workers' exploitation by setting a floor of rights (minimum labour standards), and by imposing a positive obligation on states to extend protective legislation to unprotected groups.[91] Collective bargaining itself embodies the spirit of subsidiarity as the device effectively enabling self-regulation on a more equal footing through worker empowerment.

Of course with globalization, this approach is now under considerable strain. The logic of economic integration does not follow the logic of subsidiarity, which recognizes the importance of balancing economic and social interests. What aggravates the problem is the fact that the central legitimating principle of free market economics (the invisible hand), calls for an approach co-mingling social considerations with economic priorities (no need for a visible hand when we have an invisible one). The theory does not work otherwise because the invisible hand, conceived as a law-like force freeing the units to pursue their best interests, cannot operate outside a closed or hermetically sealed system governed by a frame of reference absolutely at rest (i.e. the Newtonian construct of three-dimensional absolute space existing separately from absolute time).[92]

The obvious problem with this construct (as the adverse social side-effects of globalization attest) is that there is no closed and hermetically sealed system in which the invisible hand of economic forces can result in a healthy growth economy producing universal social goodness. In the real economy, there are impediments that cannot be removed because economic and social dimensions are not hermetically sealed off from each other and interact as two complementary and interdependent aspects of the same seamlessly interactive system. In the real economy, the interaction between parts is intimately related to the whole, and expanding economic systems are embedded in a web of relationships with the entire universe.[93]

The discrepancy between the real economy (where there is nothing free about free trade) and the virtual economy (where free trade is not only assumed but also said to promise universal social goodness) generates all kinds of dysfunctions and adverse side effects, which are aggravated by the beliefs conveyed by current economic wisdom. The dysfunctions of the model are manifested in the huge gap that exists between the outcomes promised and the actual results achieved so far. In this respect, it is striking that since 1990, the period in which globalization has been most pronounced, global GDP growth has been slower than in previous decades,[94] while at the same time, "the income gap between the richest and poorest countries has increased significantly."[95]

If the origin of these dysfunctions can to a large extent be traced to market integration theories demanding that social considerations be subsumed with economic priorities (interference from a visible hand is not only unnecessary, but also upsets the model's proper functioning), the forces of globalization, as we have seen, compound the problem by intensifying existing polarities. Globalization becomes economic hegemony with an invisible social dimension, while globalization dialectics turn this imbalance into a "universal-particulars" kind of phenomenon resulting in this asymmetry being felt everywhere, at all regulatory levels in various degrees and measures.

The adverse side effects of globalization make state intervention and institutional support in the social sphere more necessary than ever, particularly because the basic assumptions underlying labour regulation are also in need of revision to ensure labour law's relevance in a labour market which is no longer characterized by a single, clearly defined model of employment. At the same time, the resulting debasing pressures make state intervention much less effective and much more difficult to secure. On this the facts are clear: the greater portion of the world's working population is now absorbed by the informal sector, i.e. left without any form of social protection,[96] while new forms of exploitation through labour are increasing (for example, while there were 79 export processing zones (EPZs) in 25 countries in 1975, by 2002 this had grown to 3,000 in 116 countries).[97] This again emphasizes the importance of having a subsidiarity scheme in place (especially at the constitutional and labour relations levels), to contain powerful debasing pressures.

Conclusion

The new labour law – the labour law of globalization – is, to borrow Harry Arthurs' a phrase, a *labour law without the State*.[98] It is a labour law of informal regulation producing standards shaped by global competition.

As a strategic response to contain this phenomenon, this paper has stressed the importance of conditioning frameworks and, in this context, of subsidiarity as a device for ensuring an inclusive democracy and facilitating the achievement of social justice. The great richness of the doctrine lies in its potential to foster both inclusive democracy and social justice in a complementary and mutually reinforcing way. The subsidiarity doctrine not only recognizes the interface that exists between the twin objectives of justice and democracy; it also offers feasible means to ensure their achievement.

As was seen, on the one hand subsidiarity operates as the instrumental device of an inclusive democracy by fostering greater participation and expanded representation (representational security), while simultaneously operating as a check and balance principle against abuse of political power and the excesses of too much centralization and decentralization. On the other hand, subsidiarity acts as the operating principle of social justice through its ability to generate a fairer distribution of outcomes by placing economic and social interests on an equal footing, while simultaneously recognizing that this balance cannot be ensured without a measure of corrective action and the promotion of individual empowerment.

In this respect, it is noteworthy that a subsidiarity-premised approach has been the ILO approach all along. This is reflected not only in the ILO policy of technical assistance, but also in ILO standards and ILO supervisory functions, particularly in the field of freedom of association and collective bargaining, where subsidiarity also forms the basis of the long-established principle of non-interference and the rationale for the effective recognition of the right to collective bargaining.

In light of the foregoing, what are we to say of Marco Biagi's suggestion to make subsidiarity the leading principle of collective bargaining articulation to answer concerns over employer competitiveness? From this discussion, it should be fairly clear that a subsidiarity-based collective bargaining scheme would be beneficial for all involved by guaranteeing workers' "representative security", while at the same time ensuring that decisions (such as those affecting employer competitiveness) be made at the level where the interests at stake can be best addressed. Subsidiarity so construed can promote a fairer globalization in a cost-efficient manner, by offering a mutually beneficial compromise between the need for broader-based protection and the need for tailor-made flexibility in a context where the risks of dismantling are real.

Notes

1. This paper was first presented under the title "Globalization and the Problem of Compound Decentralization" at the International Seminar on "The Decentralization of Labour Policies and Collective Bargaining", which took place in Modena on 19–20 March 2003, to commemorate the first year marking the tragic death of Marco Biagi on 19 March 2002. It was updated and shortened to reflect recent developments and to fit the format of this book. The views expressed in this paper are those of the author and do not commit the ILO.

2. "The glory of the One who moves all things permeates the universe but glows in one part more and in another less" (translation of the opening line of the *Paradiso* in *The Divine Comedy*).

3. On the evening of 19 March 2002, Marco Biagi was murdered on the doorsteps of his house in Bologna. Responsibility for the murder was claimed on the following day by the Red Brigades terrorist group. A professor of labour law at the University of Modena, Marco Biagi was highly respected for his independence of mind, broad

expertise and commitment to social dialogue. Like Massimo D'Antona, another respected professor of labour law killed at the hands of the Red Brigades, Marco Biagi had been involved in reforms of labour legislation in Italy, as a government consultant working for ministers of labour in three successive governments. His murder shocked everyone and brought protest and condemnation from all corners of the world. In Italy, the three main trade union confederations (Cgil, Cisl and Uil) called a nationwide two-hour general strike in protest, with demonstrations in several cities across the country. This was followed by a joint national mobilization for democracy and against terrorism. I had the privilege of knowing Marco Biagi and of working with him on the editorial board of *The International Journal of Comparative Labour Law and Industrial Relations*. A trusted colleague of wise counsel, a dynamic editor-in-chief, a good friend gifted with a sense of humour, Marco Biagi was all these things and more. This paper, on a topic close to his heart, is dedicated to his memory.

4. Marco Biagi, "Changing Industrial Relations – A Few Comments on the Report of the High-Level Group on Industrial Relations and Managing Change in the European Union", in Michele Tiraboschi (ed.), *Marco Biagi, Selected Writings* (Kluwer Law International, The Hague, 2003), 29–44 at 34.

5. Biagi, "Changing Industrial Relations", 35. In considering the feasibility of such proposals, Marco Biagi was keenly aware that much would depend on how the institutional framework would stand once the Constitutional Court had interpreted the new provisions of Title V of the Italian Constitution, which distribute powers between state and regions (article 117 *Cost*): see p. 36. The new provisions were adopted pursuant to the Constitutional law of 18 October 2001, no. 3. For an English translation of the Italian Constitution, see International Constitutional Law Project Information, online: http://www.oefre.unibe.ch/law/icl/home.html.

6. Biagi, "Changing Industrial Relations", 33–4.

7. Vidya S.A. Kumar, "A Critical Methodology of Globalization: Politics of the 21st Century?" (2003) 10 *Indiana Journal of Global Legal Studies* 87.

8. Kumar, "A Critical Methodology of Globalization."

9. See C. Poppi, "Wider Horizons with Larger Details: Subjectivity, Ethnicity and Globalization" in Alan Scott (ed.), *The Limits of Globalization: Cases and Arguments* (Routledge, London, 1997), 300, n. 1.

10. In this sense it can be said that "in attempting to define globalization, theorists create globalization": Kumar, "A Critical Methodology of Globalization", at 88.

11. James H. Mittelman, "How Does Globalization Really Work?" in James H. Mittelman (ed.) *Globalization: Critical Reflections* (Lynne Rienner Publishers Inc., Colorado, 1996), 229–30.

12. Mittelman, 'How Does Globalization Really Work?' at 90, referring to John Baylis and Steven Smith (eds.), *The Globalization of World Politics: An Introduction to International Relations* (Oxford University Press, Oxford, 1997), 6–10: "the nature of globalization is contingent upon one's theoretical perspective".

13. See World Commission on the Social Dimension of Globalization, *A Fair Globalization: Creating Opportunities for All*. Report of the Commission (International Labour Office, Geneva, 2004) (*A Fair Globalization*), 24, para. 132, stressing that new technology and policy decisions to reduce national barriers to international economic transactions have created the enabling conditions. See also generally, 24–36, paras. 131–77 (key characteristics of globalization).

14. Multinationals are not only conceived as the engine of this economic interdependence, but also as the true "managers" of globalization: Duncan Campbell, *Globalisation and Strategic Choices in Tripartite Perspective: An Agenda for Research and Policy Issues*, New Industrial Organisation Programme, International Institute for Labour Studies, DP/46/1991 (International Labour Office, Geneva, 1991), 31, citing Riccardo Petrella, 'Une même logique inégalitaire sur toute la planète', *Le Monde Diplomatique*, January 1991, 6 (the "globalization of the economy is for the moment 'governed' above all by a private actor, the global enterprise-network").

15. Campbell, *Globalisation and strategic choices*, 1.

16. William E. Scheuerman, "Globalization" in Edward N. Zalta (ed.), *The Stanford Encyclopedia of Philosophy, Fall 2002 Edition* (Stanford Metaphysics Research Lab, Center for the Study of Language and Information, 2002), online: http://plato.stanford.edu/archives/fall2002/entries/globalization: globalization refers to those processes whereby geographically distant events and decisions impact to a growing degree on "local" life and regional endeavours.

17. David Held, Anthony McGrew, David Goldblatt and Jonathan Perraton, *Global Transformations: Politics, Economics and Culture* (Stanford University Press, Stanford, 1999), 15.

18. Scheuerman, "Globalization", 4.

19. Scheuerman, "Globalization", 5; see also Held and others, *Global Transformations*.

20. See Scheuerman, "Globalization", 3–4; and Martin Heidegger, 'The Thing' in *Poetry, Language, Thought*, tr. Albert Hofstadter (Harper & Row, New York, 1971) 165–6 (on the "abolition of distance" as a constitutive condition of our contemporary condition). Even within the narrow view, globalization theorists recognize that forces of deterritorialization and interconnection are at play, for it is hardly disputed that events beyond the firm have also contributed to economic integration: "in particular, the deregulation of financial markets and the considerable political will that has galvanized adjacent nations to integrate their markets for goods, services, capital": Scheuerman, "Globalization", 5.

21. Scheuerman, "Globalization", 5.

22. See generally *A Fair Globalization*; and on the webpage of the World Commission on the Social Dimension of Globalization (established by the ILO), "The Social Dimension of Globalization", International Labour Organization website, online: http://www.ilo.org.

23. Chris M. Sciabarra, *Marx, Hayek, and Utopia* (State University of New York Press, Albany, 1995), 33.

24. International Confederation of Free Trade Unions (ICFTU), *A Trade Union Guide to Globalisation* (Brussels, December 2001), at 9: globalization as "the result of several developments and processes which are generally linked together". See also William Twining, *Globalisation and Legal Theory* (Butterworths, London, 2000), 4: globalization referring to those processes which tend to make the world more interdependent; and Giddens, *The Consequences of Modernity* (Stanford University Press, California), 64: globalization as "the intensification of world-wide social relations which link distant localities in such a way that local happenings are shaped by events occurring many miles away and vice versa".

25. Twining, *Globalisation and Legal Theory*, 5, referring to Roland Robertson, "Mapping the Global Condition: Globalization as the Central Concept", in Mike Featherstone (ed.), *Global Culture: Nationalism, Globalization and Modernity* (Sage Publications, London, 1990), vol.7 (2–3), 15–30.

26. Twining, *Globalisation and legal theory*, 5.

27. Campbell, *Globalisation and Strategic Choices*, 21.

28. Campbell, *Globalisation and Strategic Choices*, 21, referring to C. de Granut, 'La mondialisation de l'économie: Éléments de synthèse', Forecasting and Assessment in Science and Technology, Working Paper 'Commission of the European Communities' Brussels, 1990).

29. See generally *A Fair Globalization*, and notably p. x, and pp. 35–49, paras. 170–224 (Globalization and its impact).

30. Bob Hepple, "New Approaches to International Labour Regulation" (1997) 26 *Industrial Law Journal* 353, at 358, referring to Sol Picciotto, "The Regulatory Criss-Cross: Interaction between Jurisdiction and the Construction of Global Regulatory Networks", in W. Bratton et al. (eds.), *International Regulatory Competition and Coordination: Perspectives on Economic Regulation in Europe and the United States.*

31. Hepple, "New Approaches", 358.

32. Hepple, "New Approaches", 366.

33. See Boaventura De Sousa Santos, *Toward a New Common Sense: Law, Science and Politics in Paradigmatic Transition* (Routledge, New York, 1995), 263.

34. Sousa Santos, *Toward a New Common Sense*, 263.

35. The point is stressed by Twining in *Globalisation and Legal Theory*, 5.

36. See generally ILO, *World Labour Report 1997–98: Industrial Relations, Democracy and Social Stability* (International Labour Office, Geneva, 1997). The informal sector can be loosely defined as referring to the part of the labour market encompassing all forms of work characterized by precarious conditions and an absence of formal protection: see ILO, Report of the Director-General: *Organizing for Social Justice*, Global Report under the Follow-up to the ILO Declaration on Fundamental Principles and Rights at Work, International Labour Conference 92nd Session 2004, Report I (B), (International Labour Office, Geneva, 2004), 44, para. 170; and generally 44–46 (the challenges of the informal economy). The meaning of term "informal economy is discussed at 45, para. 174–5. See also ILO, *Decent work and the informal*

economy, Report VI, International Labour Conference, 90th Session (International Labour Office, Geneva, 2002).

37. See Philippe Barré, "Production des normes de temps de travail et décentralisation organisée de la négociation collective en Europe", in Claude Durand and Alain Pichon (eds.), *La puissance des normes* (L'Harmattan, "Logiques sociales", Paris, 2003) 237–54 at 246, referring to B. Coriat, "Penser à l'envers. Travail et organisation dans l'entreprise japonaise" (Bourgeois, "Choix-essais", Paris, 1991). This new model has given the impetus for the development of "flexible work" strategies (precarious work), leading the way towards increased externalization/delocalization of work. The resulting development has been internal labour market segmentation.

38. See ILO, *Employment statistics in the informal sector*, 15th International Conference of Labour Statisticians, Geneva, 19–28 January 1993, Report III, 6; ILO, *World Labour Report 1997–98*, 189 ff.; and ILO, *Organizing for Social Justice*, 44, para. 170.

39. For an accessible description of quantum theory and wave-particle dualism or coexistence, see Robert Nadeau and Menas Kafatos, *The Non-Local Universe: The New Physics and Matters of the Mind* (Oxford University Press, Oxford 2001), 41–6; see also Nick Herbert, *Quantum Reality: Beyond the New Physics* (Doubleday, New York, 1985), 66–67.

40. See Nadeau and Kafatos, *Non-local Universe*, 3–5. The experiment of microphysicists Alain Aspect and Nicolus Gisin have provided dramatic evidence that nonlocality is a fact of nature: see pp. 77–80.

41. See Nadeau and Kafatos, *Non-local Universe*, 78, referring to French scientist Bernard d'Espagnat, *Physical Review Letters* 49 (1981): 1804. At p. 46 the authors stress that the two-domain distinction between micro and macro phenomena in the orthodox quantum measurement theory has led to enormous confusion about the character of quantum reality.

42. See Nadeau and Kafatos, *Non-local Universe*, 88–9 (explaining that the dual character stems from the recognition that since one of the paired constructs cannot define the situation in the absence of the other, both are required for a complete view of the actual situation).

43. See Frederick Copleston, S.J., *A History of Philosophy*, Book One (Doubleday, New York, 1985), Vol. 1, 38–46.

44. European Industrial Relations Observatory Online (EIROnline), *Industrial Relations in the EU, Japan and USA, 2001* (2002), 2; Eironline, *Industrial Relations in the EU Member States and Candidate Countries* (2002), 8, online: http://www.eiro.eurofound.ie/.

45. ILO, *Organizing for Social Justice*, 60, para. 222, referring to ILO, *World Labour Report 1997–98*. For example, in the case of enterprises whose production is oriented mainly to export markets, enterprise-level negotiation may help them adjust to business constraints: see *Organizing for Social Justice*, 64, box 3.2. See also Harry C. Katz, "The Decentralization of Collective Bargaining: A Literature Review and Comparative Analysis" (1993) 47/1 *Industrial and Labor Relations Review* 3 (identifying

three mains factors having contributed to this trend: (1) reduction of trade unions' bargaining power; (2) growing diffusion of new forms of flexibility-premised work organization, requiring greater worker participation; and (3) decentralization of productive structures along with diversification of workers' interests and preferences).

46. For a recent review of these trends, see EIROnline, *Industrial Relations.*

47. "Despite a widely observed trend towards the decentralization of bargaining, most EU countries have centralized systems": ILO, *Organizing for Social Justice,* 60, para. 212; see also table 3.6. Bargaining at sectoral level is less prevalent in the transition countries of the new eastern European EU member states (in spite of the legacy of centralized pay and grade classification systems of the earlier era of central planning): see p. 65, para. 231.

48. As suggested by Roy J. Adams, *Assessing the Extent of Freedom of Association and the Effective Right to Bargain Collectively in Light of Global Developments* (ILO, Research & Publications, Geneva), online: http://www.ilo.org, 3.

49. See Barré, "Décentralisation organisée", 239 and 247, referring to F. Traxler, "Farewell to Labour Market Associations? Organized versus Disorganized Decentralization as a Map for Industrial Relations", in F. Traxler (ed.), *Organized Industrial Relations in Europe: What Future?* (Aldershot, Ashgate, 1995).

50. See Barré, "Décentralisation organisée", 148.

51. Biagi, 'Changing Industrial Relations', 39.

52. See ILO, *Organizing for Social Justice,* 69, para. 231. The report offers a relatively comprehensive review of existing trends in this respect: see 69–80, paras. 242–52 (International frameworks agreements) and paras. 253–65 (Other forms of supranational negotiation and social dialogue). Revised figures now show that at least 31 IFAs have been signed: see ICFTU online at http://www.icftu.org.

53. Adams, *Assessing the Extent of Freedom of Association,* 3.

54. Certain limited exceptions exist, such as the construction industry (Canada and the United States) and certain branches of the public sector and longshore industry (Canada). There is also a practice of pattern bargaining in the automobile industry in both countries, while multi-employer supranational bargaining (multi-jurisdictions) is found in professional sport: see *Brown v. Pro Football, Inc.* (95–388), 518 U.S. 231 (1996), where the US Supreme Court held that US Federal labour laws shielded from antitrust attack an agreement among several employers bargaining together to implement after impasse the terms of their last best good faith wage offer.

55. The review of such developments cannot be included here for reasons of space. However, an overview of existing approaches (focusing primarily on the public sector) can be found in ICFTU, *Report for the WTO General Council Review of the Trade Policies of Canada* (Geneva, 12 and 14 March 2003), under Trade & Labour Standards: Country Reports: WTO & Labour Standards on Trade & Labour Standards, online: http://www.icftu.org.

56. Pope Pius XI quoted by R.E. Mulcahy, "Subsidiarity" in *New Catholic Encyclopedia*, vol. 13 (McGraw Hill, New York, 1967), at 762.

57. See Geza Ankerl, *Towards a Social Contract on a World-wide Scale: Solidarity Contracts*, Research Series, no. 47, International Institute for Labour Studies (International Labour Office, Geneva, 1980), 3.

58. Ankerl, *Solidarity Contracts*, 3. This reflects the Aristotelian distinction between equity and justice, according to which the first (based upon distributive justice) is higher than the second (based upon formal equality): see Aristotle, *Ethics*, 5, 10.

59. For an application in the political setting, see e.g. section 3 of the *Protocol on the application of the principles of subsidiarity and proportionailty* ("Protocol") originating from the Treaty of Amsterdam (in the form of guidelines), annexed to the *Treaty instituting the European Community* (consolidated version) Art. 5 (formerly 3B) ("EC Treaty").

60. Within the EU, the principle of proportionality implies that Community action should be minimized and should be proportionate to the objective to be achieved, i.e. any action by the Community must not go beyond what is necessary to achieve the objectives of the Treaty, and its form must comply with the principle of simplicity and generality. Inasmuch as possible, preference must be given to action by way of directives or framework-directives (Protocol, s. 6) respecting well-established national practices and the internal organization of member states and leaving the greatest possible scope for national decision. If necessary, a range of different solutions must be offered (Protocol, s. 7).

61. These approaches can be grouped in two broad categories, namely: (1) Complementarity (shared competence): (a) subsidiarity (local dominance, i.e. primary responsibility from the bottom up); (b) supremacy (federal dominance, i.e. primary responsibility from the top down); (2) Exclusivity (exclusive competence): (a) plenary (complete, i.e. exclusive to the central or local level); (b) fragmented (divided between levels, i.e. plenary on a jurisdictional basis or exclusive to the Legislature to which the powers are assigned). A third approach is the horizontal coordination of policies between political jurisdictions, which can also be rendered compulsory in certain areas. This can be done (as at the EU) by inserting in the founding agreement a provision defining the open method of coordination and its procedure, and specifying instances of application.

62. See Art. 5 (formerly 3B) EC Treaty. When a constitution does not specify the applicable principle in cases of shared powers, courts of last resort have inferred, on their reading of the constitution, the principle of articulation that they find appropriate to determine a constitutional challenge involving the allocation of legislative power.

63. EC Treaty, Art. 5 (formerly 3B). The Protocol spells out how the subsidiarity principle must be applied: First, the principle of subsidiarity does not apply to matters falling within the EU's exclusive competence. Second, the question of whether the objectives of the proposed action cannot be sufficiently achieved by the member

states and can be better achieved by the Union must be examined in the light of the guidelines articulated in the Protocol, which include the need to strengthen economic and social cohesion (Protocol, s. 5).

64. Current proposals for the reform of subsidiarity at the EU are process-related to address legitimacy deficits (early warning system and expansion of the scope for referral to the ECJ on grounds of failure to comply with the principle of subsidiarity). Subsidiarity as a concept remains unchanged: see CONV 579/03, Brussels 27 February 2003. For a critical analysis of these issues, see Anna V. Bausili, "Rethinking the Methods of Dividing and Exercising Powers in the EU: Reforming Subsidiarity and National Parliaments", Jean Monnet Working Paper 9/02, NYU School of Law, online: http://www.jeanmonnetprogram.org/ at 2.

65. The principle of subsidiarity is complemented by the provision indicating that when action at the central level cannot be justified by virtue of the application of subsidiarity, member states are still bound under the Treaty to avoid taking action that might compromise the fulfilment of the Treaty's objectives (Protocol, s. 8).

66. See e.g. joined cases. C-382 and 383/92, *Commission* v. *United Kingdom* [1994] IRLR 392, 412; commented by Bob Hepple in "The Future of Labour Law" (1995) 24 *Industrial Law Journal* 303 at 303–304 (directive on collective redundancies and transfers of undertakings).

67. The principle of checks and balances is typically conceived as a system of formal division of governmental powers between executive, legislative and judiciary branches of government. However, from the vantage point of democratic safeguards, the division of governmental power inherent in a federal system operates to preclude an excessive concentration of power, and thus as a check against tyranny: see Albert V. Dicey, *The Law of the Constitution*, 10th edn (Wade, Macmillan & Co. Ltd, London, 1960), 171; Donald V. Smiley, *The Federal Condition in Canada* (McGraw-Hill Ryerson, Toronto, 1987), 19–22. There are other models of checks and balances. In India, for instance, it has been suggested that the doctrine of dharma along with the corollary principle of karma have served that purpose in the past (a sort of mystic version of the doctrine of checks and balances): see H. Patrick Glenn, *Legal Traditions of the World* (Oxford University Press, Oxford, 2000), 263–4.

68. See Hannah F. Pitkin, *The Concept of Representation* (University of California Press, Berkeley, 1972), 2.

69. *Canadian Industrial Relations: The Report of the Task Force of Labour Relations*, Canada, Privy Council Office, December 1968 (H. D. Woods, Chairman), 96, para. 296; see also Sidney and Beatrice Webb, *Industrial Democracy* (Longmans Green, London, 1897).

70. Even trade unions borrowed from political traditions. For example, the American Federation of Labor, which was founded in 1886, modelled its structure on federalism, and this became the pattern in North America: see Archibald Cox, Derek C.

Bok, Robert A. Gorman and Matthew W. Finkin, *Labor Law, Cases and Materials*, 12th edn (Foundation Press, University Casebook Series, Westbury, 1996), 11.

71. Legislatively imposed labour standards and procedures operate also as "checks and balance" in the context of collective bargaining. However, they are not *bargained* terms; as such, they do not replace bargaining at a level sufficiently broad in scope to allow the setting forth of policies shared by the partners with reference to a set context of production or services, and which may be further detailed in local level agreements, according to the size of the enterprise and the scope of the bargaining unit.

72. Historically, the concurrent existence of more than one trade union in the same field generated divided authority and loyalty, and was consequently perceived as sapping the trade unions' strength. Thus the notion emerged that in each recognized field of activity, there should only be one union, which would have exclusive jurisdiction.

73. Over the years an increasingly complicated range of issues has found its way on to the bargaining table, adding to the difficulty of choosing between divergent trade-offs (particularly on the basis of the "*in melius*" doctrine). The introduction of employment issues (commitments to hire and limit lay-offs, restrictions on contracting out, etc.) has profoundly altered the concept of "equivalent standard". These new grounds for bargaining seem to demand a new logic because they give rise to bargained terms and conditions over employment issues that can conflict with traditional labour standards (particularly when the positive/adverse effect of two sets of agreed-upon terms depends upon the worker's status).

74. On this, see Biagi, "Changing Industrial Relations", at 35–6 (discussing the practice of "protected derogation", the grounds for "exiting" from first-level bargaining and other approaches developed in other EU countries to do away with this requirement in certain circumstances). In France, where this sort of arbitration is particularly complex, certain derogations *in pejus* were formally authorized in 1982: see Jean-Claude Javillier, *Droit du travail*, 7th edn no. 94–95, (Paris, LGDJ, 1999), 150–1.

75. ILO, *Organizing for Social Justice*, 62, para. 215; see also para. 214 (reviewing economic arguments for and against different levels of bargaining).

76. ILO, *Organizing for Social Justice*, 62, paras. 216 and 217.

77. Pursuant to the principle of free and voluntary collective bargaining stated at article 4 of ILO Convention no. 98, the choice of bargaining level should essentially depend on the will of the parties and legislation should neither forbid nor serve to frustrate collective bargaining at a higher level (e.g. the industry level): see ILO, *Freedom of Association, Digest of Decisions and Principles of the Freedom of Association Committee of the Governing Body of the ILO*, Fourth [revised] edition (International Labour Office, Geneva, 1996), paras. 844 and 845; 851–853 and 855. See also ILO, *Freedom of Association and Collective Bargaining*, International Labour Conference 81st Session 1994, Report III (Part 4B): General Survey of the *Committee of Experts* on the

Application of Conventions and Recommendations on the Freedom of Association and the Right to Organize Convention (No. 87), 1948, and the Right to Organize and Collective Bargaining Convention (No. 98), 1949 (International Labour Office, Geneva, 1994), paras. 248–9.

78. "This provision contains two essential elements: action by the public authorities to *promote* collective bargaining, and the *voluntary* nature of negotiation, which implies autonomy of the parties": ILO, *Committee of Experts*, para. 235.

79. R163 Collective Bargaining Recommendation, 1981, available online through the ILOLEX database: http://www.ilo.org/ilolex/english/index.htm.

80. See ILO, *Committee of Experts*, para. 236.

81. Although the refusal by employers to bargain at a specific level does not in principle constitute an infringement on trade union freedom (see ILO, *Freedom of Association*, para. 852), this right must not operate to frustrate the obligation to bargain in good faith at the level corresponding to the representation rights obtained (on the principle of bargaining in good faith, see ILO, *Freedom of Association*, para. 814–5).

82. See Eric Voegelin, *The New Science of Politics* (University of Chicago Press, Chicago, 1952) 50, see also Pitkin, *The Concept of Representation*, 45.

83. Voegelin, *The New Science of Politics*, 40, cited by Pitkin, *The Concept of Representation* at 45, who notes that: "Probably, the articulation must grow organically from the society's own history rather than be imposed or borrowed from the outside."

84. See e.g. ILO, *Your Voice at Work*, at p. ix.

85. In addition to its regular system of supervision, the ILO has established special machinery for promoting their enforcement, namely the Committee on Freedom of Association and the Fact-Finding and Conciliation Commission on Freedom of Association.

86. In keeping with the Latin origin of the term: subsidiarity derives from *subsidium*.

87. Mulcahy, "Subsidiarity", quoting *Pacem in terris*.

88. See generally ILO, "The Social Dimension of Globalization".

89. See Fritjof Capra, *The Tao of Physics*, 3rd edn (Shambhala Publications, Boston, 1991), at 49; see also Philip Kapleau, *Three Pillars of Zen* (Beacon Press, Boston, 1967), 135.

90. Harry W. Arthurs, "Labour Law in the New Economy" Remarks to the Conference of Labour Board Chairs of Canada, 9 August 1995 (unpublished).

91. See e.g. *Dunmore* v. *Ontario (Attorney General)* [2001] 3 S.C.R. 1016.

92. See Nadeau and Kafatos, *Non-local Universe*, 200, and generally 198–201 (classical physics and economic theory), stressing that the model of free market economics is inherently flawed because it is based on the same assumptions from classical physics featured in previous neoclassical economic theory, which have been refuted by the findings of contemporary physics.

93. See Nadeau and Kafatos, *Non-local Universe*, 200.

94. *A Fair Globalization*, 35, para. 174, referring to fig. 10 and para. 175.
95. *A Fair Globalization*, 36, para. 176, referring to fig. 11.
96. See e.g. ILO, *Organizing for Social Justice*, p. 44, para. 170.
97. See ILO, *Organizing for Social Justice*, 37–8, para 137; Alan Hyde, Chapter 5 in this book.
98. See Harry W. Arthurs, "Labour Law without the State" (1996) 46 *University of Toronto Law Journal* 1.

5

A game theory account and defence of transnational labour standards – a preliminary look at the problem

ALAN HYDE

Introduction

Information and communications technologies have not only annihilated space and time to create a global labour market, they have also simultaneously helped publicize the appalling labour standards in many developing countries, including, though by no means limited to, their sectors producing goods for export to the developed world. Suddenly, the world of transnational labour standards, long the private preserve of specialists at organizations like the International Labour Organization (ILO), has come under increased scrutiny from demonstrators in the streets outside trade negotiations to American presidential debates, which have lately included intense, if confusing, discussions about labour standards in trade agreements.

The scholarly literature on transnational labour standards is still some way from shaping these intense political controversies. To be blunt, it is remarkable how little is known in an academic sense about transnational labour standards. We know very little about when such standards will be promulgated and less still about their systematic effects. In this near-vacuum, it is hard to argue effectively for the rejection of any of the common political positions, such as either the naive proliferation of labour standards (four hundred conventions of the International Labour Organization, on this way of thinking, being self-evidently twice as good as two hundred) or their total rejection as impediments to trade or development.

The most significant gap in the literature is the lack of systematic knowledge about the real-world impact of existing labour standards. Our ignorance here is close to total. It is difficult to find a single case in which one can be confident that attempts to enforce transnational labour standards have in fact improved working conditions. Most Americans know that the television performer Kathie Lee Gifford cried on television when confronted with working conditions at the factories in Honduras producing clothing sold under her name, but few know much about whether this resulted in any improvements there. Most people know that pressure was placed on manufacturers of soccer balls in Sialkot, Pakistan, to end child labour, and the United Nations International Children's Emergency Fund (UNICEF) and the ILO have now declared the industry to be free of child labour.[1] One may, however, read directly conflicting reports as to whether production shifted to Pakistani stitching centres monitored to make sure no children were sewing[2], or instead to India under even lower working standards;[3] whether the displaced children ended up in school[4] or deprived of home schooling,[5] or working in non-export industries with even lower labour standards, perhaps even as child prostitutes.[6] The impact of other initiatives to raise labour standards, such as conditioning trade preferences in the Generalized System of Preferences programme on particular labour standards in the exporting country,[7] is similarly known entirely through anecdote.[8] The lack of systematic empirical research into the impact of transnational labour standards casts its shadow over the entire field. Economic analyses, including the analysis herein, revert to modelling standards in ideal labour markets, when the one thing we know about labour regulation is that it often has different real-world consequences than would be predicted by economic theory that assumes classical labour markets.[9]

Despite this major empirical uncertainty, legal scholars who examine transnational labour standards typically focus on three major features of the current legal regime that seem anomalous or puzzling from a legal point of view; first, the multiplicity of lawmaking sources; second, particularly in the United States, the choice among international, transnational, or distinctly American standards (whether created specially for foreign workplaces, or the same standards applied at home); third, the ineffectiveness, approaching absence, of current sanctions. I shall refer to these three questions as the "legal scholar's questions". Let me explain these further.

First, a complete picture of transnational labour standards includes a bewildering array of public and private laws. In no particular order, one encounters genuinely international standards, typically promulgated as conventions of the ILO but possibly also including provisions of international covenants such as the Universal Declaration of Human Rights and the International Convention on Economic, Social and Cultural Rights. There are also labour rights provisions in formal treaties, such as the North American Agreement on Labor Cooperation[10] (NAALC, the so-called "side agreement" to the North American Free Trade Agreement), that are transnational but not international, and thus unsatisfactory to many people for that very reason.[11] Some labour standards are found in domestic legislation. In the United States such domestic legislation includes very different models of regulation. The Civil Rights Act applies to the foreign operations of American firms, but only to the American citizens employed there.[12] US trade laws now stipulate that trade agreements must require, and condition some trade benefits on, the exporting country's observance of specified labour standards that are similar, but not identical, to the ILO's truly international standards.[13] The Alien Tort Statute may require US corporations to respect, in their overseas operations, those international human rights that have become part of the "law of nations", and these international human rights might include some ILO standards.[14]

US corporations may also be liable for failing to observe basic health and safety norms of unclear provenance, violated when pesticides banned for domestic use are used in their overseas operations.[15] Finally, labour standards are found in purely private compacts and commitments of the corporations themselves.[16] To the legal scholar, this multiplicity of law-making authority normally appears as a weakness of transnational labour standards. We lack any model that would explain why this multiplicity might be functional, so it naturally appears susceptible to exploitation by corporations seeking the lightest form of regulation.[17]

Second, in the United States, this regulatory redundancy creates painful choices for advocates for workers in developing countries, from the public interest lawyers at the International Labor Rights Fund, to the personal injury lawyers who sued the banana growers hoping to do well by doing good. Bluntly, the efficacy of the law seems inversely related to its international character. The developments summarized at notes 12–15 represent a new aggressive unilateralism by American courts, applying American law to the overseas operations of American firms, with little or no reference to any international standards. Advocates may thus choose law applied by US courts, with US procedure and real monetary remedies (tort law in the banana worker cases; Alien Tort Claims Act; Civil Rights Act in *Kang*). It is hard to explain why they should instead explore transnational regimes with vaguer remedies (NAALC); or international standards with no remedies at all (ILO Conventions, UN Covenants). Advocates may hardly be criticized for selecting strategies with remedies. Academics and others who favour genuinely transnational standards are hard-pressed to explain exactly why internationalism is important, in the teeth of this recent American unilateralism.

Third, the vagueness or absence of remedies for many regimes of labour regulation naturally make them seem precious and artificial, and limit their interest to many legal scholars and advocates. People who think that standards without sanctions might nevertheless be worth fighting for have not advanced any theory explaining why this might be so.

The thesis advanced herein is that these three questions–regulatory multiplicity, the value of internationalism, and sanctions – are related, and are answered by the same model. I shall argue that transnational labour standards (of all types) arise to solve coordination problems in which countries will gain by cooperation but will be disadvantaged if their trading rivals defect. As such, transnational labour standards fall into a class of strategic problems extensively studied, and formalized, by game theorists. Understanding the strategic aspects of regulating labour standards will help explain why there are multiple sources of legal standards; why international standards are necessary but insufficient; why negotiated bilateral standards are also necessary but insufficient; and how standards without immediate sanctions can build the trust that permit countries to maintain standards that are mutually beneficial. On this view, it also follows that some transnational labour standards enhance efficiency and are fully compatible with comparative advantage, as they will be adopted only when in the interest of the affected country.

These are large claims. I advance them in the spirit of provoking and enriching our mutual enquiries. Ultimately, the test of any legal standard is its impact in the observable world. As I have already argued, our empirical knowledge about the impact of labour standards is particularly weak. However, I hope that the model proposed here will sharpen and guide the search for such understanding.

The following section of this chapter models transnational labour standards as solutions to coordination games, specifically, the game called "Stag Hunt". The next section reviews the behavioural literature on the actual play of Stag Hunt games in laboratory settings and shows how well it predicts some version of our existing regulatory regime. In the final section the model is applied to specific regulatory standards, showing how understanding their strategic function explains the level of regulation and the presence or absence of sanctions.

The value of cooperation: transnational labour regulation as a Stag Hunt

Stag Hunts

A Stag Hunt is a game in which players can gain by cooperating, but only if everyone else does. If one is selfish, other players are also better off acting selfishly. The game takes its name from a brief observation in Rousseau's *Discourse on Inequality*. Rousseau describes the beginnings of morality in societies of hunters. The entire passage reads:

> Voilà comment les hommes purent insensiblement acquérir quelque idée grossière des engagements mutuels et de l'avantage de les remplir, mais seulement autant que pouvait l'exiger l'intérêt présent et sensible; car la prévoyance n'était rien pour eux, et loin de s'occuper d'un avenir éloigné, ils ne songeaient pas même au lendemain. S'agissait il de prendre un cerf, chacun sentait bien qu'il devait pour cela garder fidèlement son poste; mais si un lièvre venait à passer à la portée de l'un d'eux, il ne faut pas douter qu'il ne le poursuivit sans scrupule, et qu'ayant atteint sa proie il ne se souciât fort peu de faire manquer la leur à ses compagnons.[18]

The point is that stag makes a much better dinner than hare but can only be hunted in a group in which everyone cooperates, while hare may be hunted individually.[19] If you think that everyone will cooperate, you are better off hunting stag. But if you expect that even one person will go off to hunt hare, then you had better hunt hare yourself.

This phenomenon can be depicted in formal game theory terms, with two players, "Row Player and Column Player", and payoffs indicated, as is customary (Row, Column).[20]

	Column Player	
Row Player	hunts stag (cooperates)	hunts hare (defects)
hunts stag	2,2	0,1
hunts hare	1,0	1,1

That is, if both players hunt stag they will both get a payoff of 2 for the stag. If either defects to hunt a hare, he will get 1 for the hare and his companion will get nothing. If both know or decide that it is hare that shall be hunted, each will catch a hare for a payoff of 1.

A helpful formal feature of this game is that it may be extended to n-number of players. The selfish strategy (hunting hare) yields a fixed payoff no matter what the other players choose (anyone can catch a hare, apparently), while a cooperative strategy yields increasing payoffs depending on the number of players (the more hunters, the bigger the big game that may be landed).

For simplicity, return to the payoff matrix involving two players. This game has two Nash equilibria: either everyone hunts stag, or everyone hunts hare. Hunting stag is "payoff dominant" (or Pareto optimal) but risky since one can easily be left with nothing. Hunting hare is "risk dominant", "secure", or "maximin", since it has the highest guaranteed payoff.[21] Thus there is one Nash equilibrium (each hunts hare) that is not Pareto optimal. There is no strategy that is dominant in the sense of being the best regardless of what others do. The best strategy depends directly on what others do, specifically, whether they will cooperate or not. The n-player Stag Hunt is similar, except that it has a n number of Nash equilibria, each short of the Pareto-optimal solution in which everyone cooperates to hunt stag.

The Stag Hunt is easily confused with the more familiar Prisoner's Dilemma, in which players similarly weigh the returns from decisions to cooperate or defect, depending on what a partner does. In fact, in behavioural experiments, subjects often turn Prisoner's Dilemmas into Stag Hunts, cooperating until the partner defects.[22]

However, in strict modelling, the games are different. In the classic Prisoner's Dilemma, the highest payoff that a player can receive comes not through cooperation but through being the lucky one who rats on a confederate and is thus rewarded by the prosecutors with a lighter or no sentence. If both prisoners remain silent, they will be convicted of some lesser charge. If both rat, they will be convicted of the main charge. If only one rats he will be set free and his confederate will serve a long sentence. These payoffs might be represented with years of prison, minuses in front to show that the longer term is the worse payoff:

	Column Player	
Row Player	Stays silent (cooperates)	rats (defects)
stays silent	−3, −3	−10, 0
rats	0, −10	−6, −6

In such a Prisoner's Dilemma, people can always do better by being selfish, whatever the other does. They prefer mutual cooperation to mutual non-cooperation. That is, mutual cooperation achieves the highest social product (here, $-3 + -3$). But they cannot achieve it, because each rational player will always select non-cooperation.

Non-cooperation (ratting) always gives the higher payoff, whatever the partner chooses.

Free rider problems are Prisoner's Dilemmas in this sense. "Solving" free rider problems (like other Prisoner's Dilemmas) hence requires enlarging people's possible motivations, by for example legal or social sanctions against free riders or repeated contexts in which free riding now might make people not cooperate with you later. "Solving" coordination problems (like Stag Hunts), however, does not require changing people's motivations: "when everyone cooperates, each person wants to do so because everyone else is."[23] In a Stag Hunt or coordination or assurance game, unlike a Prisoner's Dilemma, cooperation is always rational – but only if everyone else does.

Transnational labour regulation as a Stag Hunt

We model the adoption of transnational labour standards as solutions to Stag Hunts, in which everyone is better off if all cooperate (hunt stag), but there is a risk that any individual actor might pursue short-term advantage by defecting (hunting hare and leaving the others with only the gains from hare hunting). Actors are countries that choose whether or not to adopt and enforce labour standards. They are assumed to be rational in the sense of favouring Pareto-optimal actions that improve living standards in their population at least where this can be accomplished without taking away from any.[24]

Consider the following highly stylized statement of the problem. It is clearly in the long-term interest of India, Bangladesh and Pakistan that all their children go to school and do not work in factories. Going to school builds human capital, attracts more and better foreign investment, and generally results in a richer society for all.[25] However, if India and Pakistan actually succeeded in getting all their children out of workshops and into schools, there are certain specific foreign investments that would flow to Bangladesh to take advantage of its child labour, and this would be true even if (as we suppose) Bangladesh knows that it is in its long-term interest that children learn instead of work. This is a classic Stag Hunt. If all countries cooperate in ending child labour, all will be better off. Jobs will be taken by unemployed adults, and children will go to school. But if even one country defects by letting children work, it will capture a certain stream of foreign direct investment that others will not. So, if you think one of your rivals will be selfish, it is rational for you to be selfish, too. There are thus two Nash equilibria: one that is Pareto optimal (no children work), the other that is Pareto suboptimal (children work).

So stated, this is not exactly a new insight, nor one that can only be appreciated through the application of formal game theory.[26] Child labour, noted John Stuart Mill in 1832, is a case "in which it would be highly for the advantage of every body, if every body were to act in a certain manner, but in which it is not the interest of any *individual* to adopt the rule for the guidance of his own conduct, unless he has some security that others will do so too."[27] The value of turning toward game theory is the illumination that it offers, particularly in its behavioural version, to the legal scholars' questions of regulatory multiplicity, choosing between unilateral and multilateral norms, and sanctions.

Just these legal scholars' questions elude the many interesting attempts, by economists of trade, to model trade agreements in similarly strategic terms. There is a long tradition of economic analysis of trade agreements, such as customs unions or agreements to reduce tariffs, as formal cooperative solutions to similar strategic dilemmas.[28] To oversimplify, in these models trade between two countries can reach at least two equilibria, a low equilibrium in which they may not trade at all (perhaps because of high tariffs), and a higher one marked by low tariffs and more trade. A formal trading agreement may assure the country that is lowering its tariff that its partner will do the same. In this analysis, however, agreements of this type are self-enforcing, requiring no formal enforcement mechanism. If one partner defects (by refusing to lower the tariffs that it had promised to lower, for example), the other simply retaliates by refusing to lower its tariffs.

While we will show that labour standards, like trade agreements, similarly enforce high-equilibrium cooperative solutions to games with non-unique equilibria, we will not be able to adopt these economic models of trade agreements. In the world of labour standards, such self-enforcement-through-retaliation is neither feasible nor desirable. To return to our example, if Bangladesh breaks a labour standards agreement by letting children work in factories, it accomplishes nothing if India now lets children start working in its own factories.[29]

Can countries cooperate to lift labour standards if there are short-term advantages in defecting, and little effective sanction against defectors? Game theory suggests at least three possible areas of research: first, make the theory dynamic by repeating the game; second, examine the behaviour of countries that adopt labour standards to see whether they are compatible with the model; and third, examine behavioural experiments on how people actually play these games.[30]

Repeat the game: The Stag Hunt game of labour standards that we have developed so far, like Rousseau's original, is a static game. A hunter chases hare; the stag hunt aborts; one hunter eats hare; everyone else is hungry. Rousseau does not explain why the other hunters will tolerate this situation or what, if anything, they might do to enforce the joint project.

A closer approximation to reality is to play the game over and over again, to see whether those with a taste for stag can develop ways of keeping the hare hunters' mind on stag hunting. The theory of repeated games is complex and beautiful, and revolves around a so-called Folk Theorem that states that any Pareto-optimal outcome can be maintained as a Nash-equilibrium if the game is repeated.[31] The implications for transnational labour standards are obvious. However, for present purposes I will not develop my argument with reference to the theory of repeated games.

Examine countries' behaviour: one could also examine the behaviour of countries that adopt or ratify transnational labour standards, to see whether this behaviour is consistent with the model that treats such actions as cooperative attempts to realize gains from cooperation and prevent defection to secure short-term advantage.[32] Nancy H. Chau and Ravi Kanbur have examined just this relationship, by studying the time patterns of ratification of four recent ILO conventions dealing with core labour rights. They found that the crucial variable was indeed peer effects. Countries ratify agreements that their peer group has ratified. Peer group, in turn, is defined by countries' export orientation, level of development and geographic region. There is also some influence on ratification behaviour of the origin of each country's legal system. However, economic and other political variables do not explain propensity to ratify ILO conventions.[33]

Examine behavioural experiments: Finally it may be possible to examine behavioural experiments in Stag Hunt games. This has not previously been done in discussions of transnational law. We shall see that observable attempts to create and sustain cooperative behaviour tell us a great deal about the structure of transnational labour standards.

Experimental Stag Hunt games

I have been complaining of the paucity of attempts to accommodate theoretically the range of attempts to regulate labour standards. The same complaint has been made about game theory experiments.[34] Certainly our knowledge of cooperative behaviour in games is not adequate to design a system of transnational labour standards from the ground up. However, the behavioural literature on games is quite illuminating on the legal scholars' three problems: understanding regulatory redundancy (that is, comparing norms that bind two parties with those that bind n parties); understanding unilaterally imposed norms; and sanctions.

The first and most basic point is the most transcendentally hopeful: "It is now theoretically well established that when individuals, modelled as freely rational actors with low discount rates, interact in an indefinitely repeated social-dilemma situation, it is possible for them to achieve optimal or near optimal outcomes and avoid the predicted strategies of one-shot and finitely repeated games that yield suboptimal outcomes."[35] We must not lose sight of this insight. Countries need not be stuck forever in a low-level equilibrium. If decent working conditions are in their long-term interest, one can be assured that all will move together to the Pareto-optimal equilibrium, even if (as is surely true) it is difficult to know just how this will be accomplished.

Second, in experimental Stag Hunt games, pairs of players nearly always coordinate on the highest payoff.[36]

Third, coordination on the Pareto-optimal equilibrium has never been observed experimentally in large groups. In groups with 14 to 16 participants, after three rounds of play all sessions converged on the lowest possible choice.[37] Even groups as small as six routinely converge on the least efficient outcome.[38]

This might seem to create a role for formal legal standards. Legal scholars who write about game theory love to assert that the communication of a formal legal standard in such a situation will provide a coordination point around which parties will converge.[39] Unfortunately, there is no experimental support for this in the literature on Stag Hunts. When leaders are introduced into experimental games to urge parties to adopt the Pareto-optimal position, they are largely ineffective in changing payoffs. Pairs still find the optimal solution, and large groups (in this experiment, groups of nine or ten) do not. (However, participants inaccurately attribute effects to the leaders. The pairs inaccurately attribute their success to good leadership, while the large groups inaccurately blame their failure on poor leadership).[40]

A more promising vehicle for enabling large groups to move to Pareto-optimal cooperative solutions is the "peer effect" model mentioned above and explored in Brian Skyrms' new book.[41] Small subgroups of "neighbours" converge on Pareto-optimal solutions, and then, as each bargains with other neighbours, justice is "contagious".[42] I shall explore the implications of this model for transnational labour standards. So far as I know, however, there is no experimental support for the spreading of "justice" in just this way.

Working hypotheses and tentative conclusions

Working hypotheses

Applied to the problem of transnational labour standards, the experimental literature suggests the following working hypotheses:

- The project of transnational labour standards is neither foolish nor hopeless. High standards can be associated with strategies of high labour productivity and do not, in general, deter trade or foreign investment.
- Nations of the world will not, however, necessarily converge on high labour standards naturally. It is possible to become stuck at a low level equilibrium in which it is not in the interest of any one country to improve its standards unless others also do.
- The most important factor in any country's improving its labour standards is the "assurance" (in Amartya Sen's word) that its trading rivals will do the same.
- It is far more likely that such trust and assurance will be achieved in groups of two than in groups of six or more. Consequently, labour standards provisions in negotiated trade agreements (such as the NAALC, or bilateral trade agreements between two countries) perform an important function and do not detract from true international standards (such as ILO conventions). In other works, multiplicity of regulatory institutions may well be functional and does not necessarily denote a weak or ineffective system.
- International standards (such as ILO conventions) will probably not be effective in overcoming a low-level equilibrium and moving large groups of countries to a higher-level equilibrium. However, the process of defining such standards may play a role in building trust. For example, they may provide means of showing trading rivals that one is genuinely committed to lifting labour standards. They may also provide coordination points that will influence bilateral and other negotiations among smaller groups.
- Game theory models of labour standards cannot definitively answer the question of the need for sanctions. Since a high-equilibrium state in which all countries lift labour standards is itself Pareto-optimal, sanctions are not necessary to prevent defection. (By contrast, in a Prisoner's Dilemma, players can always gain by defecting; sanctions, or other tools for reordering incentives, are therefore necessary). On the other hand, the chief obstacle to the growth of labour standards is low trust, or lack of assurance that others won't defect to pursue short-term advantage,

as may happen if defectors themselves do not trust the group. Sanctions against defection thus may be part of a strategy of moving to a higher equilibrium, so long as they do not destroy the trust and assurance that ultimately must underlie transnational labour standards.

This is an extraordinarily difficult problem in modelling to which I will have to return in subsequent work. However, some aspects are clear. Transnational labour standards that are unilaterally imposed by one country, as the United States does in its GSP programme, other trade legislation, banana worker litigation, and Alien Tort Claims Act, run a risk of creating justified anxiety that the United States will not abide by true international standards and thus that other countries would be foolish to do so. Second, it is clear that agreements on labour standards will never be self-enforcing in the manner of tariff agreements or customs unions. To threaten a trading rival that, should it lower its labour standards, you will lower yours, is neither efficacious nor attractive.

Tentative conclusions on legal issues

However tentative, these working hypotheses suggest answers to the three scholars' three questions about transnational labour standards: regulatory redundancy; the role of unilateralism; and the problem of sanctions.

Regulatory redundancy

Regulatory redundancy, at least between truly international standards (like ILO Conventions) and standards in treaties (such as NAFTA or bilateral trade agreements), now appears functional. The standards in the bilateral and small-group treaties can create the assurance that trading partners will also raise labour standards. Such an assurance will move all parties from a suboptimal Nash equilibrium to a Pareto-optimal cooperative solution. The experimental literature suggests that such small groups can achieve such solutions. The international standards will not by themselves create such an assurance, but can provide coordination points for the smaller-scale bargaining.

This emphasis on trust and assurance implies that transnational regulation may be more effective by concentrating on issues that do not evoke national pride or tradition, and therefore are better suited for building trust and assurance. For example, the ILO might be much better off adding a right to basic health and safety to its core labour values, and emphasizing it, if necessary, perhaps even over such issues as child labour or antidiscrimination, important as those are. The latter are issues on which national variation is probably inevitable, because of differing social and religious traditions. It also appears that nearly all countries voluntarily end child labour when annual family income exceeds US $7000 in current values, so ending child labour really requires a commitment to general economic development as opposed to targeted enforcement.[43]

By contrast, a proposed ILO effort on workplace toxins would have no conflict with national or religious traditions. Teams of technical experts might annually identify twenty or thirty of the most dangerous work processes or toxins in use in the world. This process would be technical, non-political, and draw on expertise. Countries would then commit to the eradication of processes and chemicals appearing on the annual list. The ILO would provide technical assistance in this process, for example by suggesting alternatives. The ILO's health and safety standards could then become reference points for national legislation and negotiated treaties. The point is that such a calm, technical process would itself become the means of building trust and respect for ILO standards that would carry over into more controversial efforts such as initiatives against child labour or discrimination.

The model also implies that the real negotiations over labour standards for developing countries should probably be among those countries themselves. If powerful countries impose labour standards on developing countries, these will probably reflect in many, though not all, cases an agenda of protecting standards in the developed country. This objection cannot be raised when the developing countries themselves are encouraged to set the standards that overcome collective action problems and punish defectors. As we have seen, even when standards are international, such as ILO conventions, peer group effects will play a large role in determining which countries ratify them.[44]

Under the model presented here, transnational labour standards are basically pacts among developing countries, or countries at similar levels of development and with a similar export orientation.[45] However, there is a mismatch between this feature of labour standards and the existing institutions that promulgate those standards. The latter are either international institutions dominated by the more powerful countries, or, worse yet, standards propounded unilaterally by those countries, to which we now turn.

Unilateralism

We can now say precisely what is potentially wrong with the unilateral imposition by a country of its own standards as transnational labour standards applicable to its own corporations, as has been true of the US

Congress in trade legislation such as the Trade Act of 2002,[46] the US version of the Generalized System of Preferences,[47] the Caribbean Basin Economic Recovery Act,[48] and the African Growth and Opportunity Act.[49] Such unilateralism has similarly characterized courts in the United States holding banana growers to domestic safety standards[50] or US employers to US antidiscrimination laws.[51] As a mode of transnational labour regulation, such American unilateralism offers many attractive features to those who advocate for workers abroad. These cases take place in US courts, with efficient procedures for trying class actions and compensating advocates. The most ardent free-trader cannot object to them, for they do not destroy any comparative advantage of Mexico or Honduras. In fact, free-traders who oppose labour standards, as restrictions on trade, have instead advocated precisely the imposition by importing nations of their own standards on the overseas operations of their own employers.[52] Objection to such unilateralism should be based on something more substantial than a taste for the global or a distaste for American unilateralism, however common and indeed defensible (indeed, shared by this American author) are such attitudes.

We can now explain exactly what might be the cost of such unilateralism whether, by Americans or others. The game theory perspective suggests that the main obstacle to countries lifting their own standards is the fear that their trading rivals will not, leaving them with the "sucker's payoff" (a hare). Overcoming this fear does not require fundamental reordering of motivation, but rather the building of the trust and assurance needed to overcome short-term advantage (the hare within reach) in favour of longer-term cooperation (bringing down a stag). Unilateralism of the kind seen recently in America potentially destroys this trust and assurance, for it graphically suggests that all countries would be wise to pursue their own labour standards since everyone else, particularly the biggest player, is doing the same. This has certainly been true of the administration of Generalized System of Preferences, not merely in theory but in practice, and, apparently, in legal findings as well.[53]

Dan Danielsen and Karl Klare have recently explored a recent example of US unilateralism that seems to exemplify the costs of unilateralism.[54] US growers of commercial catfish have recently succeeded in obtaining anti-dumping tariffs against Vietnamese catfish fillets. Since the tariffs are prohibitive, Vietnamese catfish is effectively barred from the US market. The successive finding by the US Department of Commerce and US International Trade Commission, that Vietnam was "dumping" catfish, rested entirely on the finding that Vietnam is a "non-market economy".

This permitted the US authorities to ignore the inability of the US catfish producers to show that catfish in fact are sold for less in the United States than in Vietnam. This is a unilateral imposition by the United States of its own version of labour standards. It plainly merely protects a politically powerful domestic industry and will do nothing to raise labour standards in Vietnam. Such unilateral linking of trade benefits to labour or other standards potentially accomplishes little for labour standards and seriously undermines transnational institutions and multinational trust. It is entirely different from a hypothetical proceeding in which the ILO, or some other transnational authority, or, preferably, Vietnam's peers, actually found Vietnam to be out of compliance with core labour standards and permitted countries to invoke trade remedies. Under the model presented in this Chapter, it is possible to imagine how such targeted invocation of trade remedies might induce Vietnam to permit free trade unions, or end some other specified labour practice. By contrast, the US approach is linked to no specific labour practice and effectively punishes Vietnam for its entire economic system. It will result in no change in Vietnam and reinforces the perception that the US does not and will not play by the rules of free trade that it imposes on others.

As with all other claims in this paper, this one, too, is ultimately empirical. One would need to study the relationship between unilateral imposition of standards and later ability to reach cooperative solutions.

The problem of sanctions

While a game theory perspective may illuminate the problem of sanctions in transnational labour regulation, it cannot answer this question without much more precise empirical specification of the costs and benefits. From a game theory perspective, we can certainly see a case for, and a case against, tougher sanctions.

The case for sanctions is that they can increase the assurance that other countries will indeed comply with negotiated standards and thus increase voluntary compliance by all the others. The case against sanctions is that sanctions that are seen as harsh or arbitrary may destroy the very trust and cooperation that is the only long-term hope for labour standards.

The empirical and experimental literature on games does not answer this question. In a Prisoner's Dilemma optimal solutions can be achieved by cooperating until a partner defects and then by sanctioning the defector.[55] However, for reasons we have explored, transnational labour regulation is not a Prisoner's Dilemma but a Stag Hunt, and there has been little experimental enquiry into the role of sanctions in overcoming the low trust that often prevents large groups from reaching Pareto-optimal cooperative solutions. This is a question to which I hope to return in future work.

Notes

1. "UNICEF, ILO, Declare Soccer Ball Industry Child Labour Free", *Pakistani Newswire*, 27 April 2002.
2. International Program on the Elimination of Child Labor (IPECL) , *Child Labor in the Soccer Ball Industry: A Report on the Continued Use of Child Labor in the Soccer Ball Industry in Pakistan* (International Labor Rights Fund, 1999) online: http://www.laborrights.org/projects/foulball/index.html; Kimberly Ann Elliott and Richard B. Freeman, *Can Labor Standards Improve Under Globalization?* (Institute for International Economics, Washington DC, 2003), 114–15.
3. Günseli Berik, "What Happened after Pakistan's Soccer Ball Industry Went Child Free", Conference on Child Labor, Graduate School of Social Work, University of Utah, 7–8 May 2001.
4. IPECL, *Soccer Industry Report*; Elliott and Freeman, *Can Labour Standards Improve?*
5. "It is commonly the case in Sialkot [Pakistan] for women and their children to stitch soccer balls in between other household chores. In order to prevent families from putting their children to work stitching soccer balls, work has been moved from homes to sewing centers. However, . . . mothers who work outside of the home place their daughters at risk for fulltime home-work. However, when mothers work in a household enterprise, such as soccer ball stitching, daughters can more readily combine home-work with schooling. As a consequence, this program [Partners' Agreement to Eliminate Child Labour in the Soccer Ball Industry in Sialkot, Pakistan] has the potential to undermine the efforts that Pakistani families are making to educate their daughters." Drusilla F. Brown, Alan V. Deardorff and Robert M. Stern, "Child Labour: Theory, Evidence, and Policy", in Kaushik Basu, Henrik Horn, Lisa Román and Judith Shapiro (eds.), *International Labour Standards: History, Theory, and Policy Options* (Blackwell, Oxford, 2003), at 232–3.
6. "Working in other industries: Violation of Labour Rules in Sialkot District", *Pakistani Newswire*, 3 March 2002; Bureau of Democracy, Human Rights and Labour, "Country Reports on Human Rights Practices, Pakistan – 2001", Sec. 6d (US Department of State, 2002) available online: http://www.state.gov/g/drl/rls/hrrpt/2002/sa/8237.htm. On child prostitution, I have seen references to a report that I have not been able to find online or in any library and suspect has been suppressed: ILO-IPECL and National Commission for Child Welfare and Development (Pakistan), *Combating Child Trafficking, Sexual Exploitation and Involvement of Children in Intolerable Forms of Child Labour: Pakistan country report* (1998).

However, see also, Economic and Social Commission for Asia and the Pacific, *Sexually Abused and Sexually Exploited Children and Youth in Pakistan: A qualitative account of their health needs and available services in selected provinces* (United Nations, 2001) available online: http://www.unescap.org/esid/hds/sexual/pakistan.pdf. "To make conversation at a dinner party at the World Economic Forum in Davos, I once asked the then finance minister of Pakistan whether child labour was a problem in his country. Perhaps thinking I was a potential investor, he replied, 'No, child labour is not a problem. You can hire all the children you want.'" Alan B. Krueger, "The Political Economy of Child Labour", in K. Basu et al. *International Labour Standards*, at 248.

7. The US legislation is codified at 19 U.S.C. §2461 et seq., the requirement that beneficiaries observe labour rights is at 19 U.S.C. §2462(b)(2)(G) and (H). See generally, Lance Compa and Jeffrey S. Vogt, "Labor Rights in the Generalized System of Preferences: A 20-Year Review" (2003) 22 *Comparative Labor Law & Policy Journal* 199. Similar GSP programs are found in other developed countries.

8. See e.g., Henry J. Frundt, *Trade Conditions and Labor Rights: U.S. Initiatives, Dominican and Central American Responses* (University Press of Florida, Gainesville, 1998), attributing effectiveness to US threats to suspend GSP benefits, particularly to the Dominican Republic.

9. See e.g., David Card and Alan B. Krueger, *Myth and Measurement: The New Economics of the Minimum Wage* (Princeton University Press, Princeton, 1995); Truman F. Bewley, *Why Wages Don't Fall During a Recession* (Harvard University Press, Cambridge, Mass., 1999).

10. Online: http://www.dol.gov/ilab/regs/naalc/naalc.htm.

11. For some free-traders like Jagdish Bhagwati, any smaller trading pact, such as NAFTA, necessarily detracts from the free trade system. See Jagdish Bhagwati, "NAFTA 'a pox on the world trading system'" in *Free Trade Today* (Princeton: Princeton University Press, 2002), 95.

12. Civil Rights Act of 1991, §109, amending Civil Rights Act of 1964 §§ 701(f) and 702(c), 42 U.S.C. §§2000e(f) and 2000e-1(c), and Americans with Disabilities Act of 1990 §102(c), 42 U.S.C. §12112(c). For a remarkable application, see *Kang v. U.Lim America, Inc.* 296 F.3d 810 (9th Cir. 2002), where the court applied the Civil Rights Act to a California corporation without the requisite facilities and size to be covered by the Act, by combining it with a maquiladora electronics factory that it owned in Tijuana, Mexico. This permitted a claim by an executive of Korean origin, now an American citizen, working at the Tijuana plant. The court explained that the statutory reference to US citizens did not mean that the legislation was restricted only to such US citizens. It is not easy to explain how a Mexican citizen, working in Mexico for a plant owned by a US employer, can be a statutory employee under the US Civil Rights Act for purposes of counting employees, but not for purposes of complaining about discrimination.

13. Frundt, *Trade Conditions*; 19 USCS § 2467(4); 19 U.S.C. §2702(b)(7); 19 U.S.C. §2462(b)(2)(G) & (H); 19 U.S.C. §3703(a)(1)(F); 19 U.S.C. §3804.

14. Alien Tort Statute, 28 U.S.C. §1350; *Doe v. Unocal* 2002 U.S.App.LEXIS 19263 (9th Cir. 2002), vacated for rehearing en banc, 2003 U.S.App.LEXIS 2716 (9th Cir., 14 Feb. 2003), argued and submitted 13 June 2003. Now see *Sosa v. Alvarez-Machain* 124 S.Ct. 2739, 2761–2, 159 L.Ed.2d 718, 749 (2004), which suggests that the "law of nations" enforceable under this statute must "rest on a norm of international character accepted by the civilized world and defined with a specificity comparable to the features of the 18th-century paradigms we have recognized", namely, mercantile questions, law merchant, violation of safe conduct, infringement of rights of ambassadors, and antipiracy.

15. *Martinez v. Dow Chemical Co.* 219 F.Supp.2d 719 (E.D. La. 2002), rejecting numerous motions to dismiss. The suits on behalf of classes of overseas banana workers are currently being remanded to state courts, following the destruction in *Dole Food Co. v. Patrickson* 538 U.S. 468 (2003), of the devices that had been used to create federal jurisdiction.

16. See generally Dara O'Rourke, "Outsourcing Regulation: Analyzing Non-Governmental Systems of Labour Standards and Monitoring", online: http://web.mit.edu/dorourke/www/PDF/OutsourcingReg.pdf; Ingeborg Wick, "Workers' tool or PR ploy?: A guide to codes of international labour practice", online: http://www.suedwind-institut.de/Workers-tool-2003.pdf.

17. Harry Arthurs, "Private Ordering and Workers' Rights in the Global Economy: Corporate Codes of Conduct as a Regime of Labour Market Regulation", in Joanne Conaghan, Richard Michael Fischl and Karl Klare (eds.), *Labour Law in an Era of Globalization: Transformative Practices and Possibilities* (Oxford University Press, Oxford, 2002), 471–87.

18. Jean–Jacques Rousseau, *Discours sur l'Origine et les Fondements de l'Inégalité*, Seconde Partie, 3 Oeuvres Complètes (1755) (Jean Starobinski ed., Pléiade edition 1964), 166–7. The English translations that I consulted all have basic grammatical errors or sound stilted because of reliance on cognates, so with some hesitation I will offer my own translation: *That is how men could imperceptibly acquire some rough idea of mutual obligations, and of the advantages of keeping them, but only in so far as present and perceptible interest might require; for foresight meant nothing to them, and far from concerning themselves with the remote future, they did not even think about the next day. In hunting a stag, each well knew that for this purpose he had faithfully to maintain his post; but if a hare happened to pass within reach of one of them, no one can doubt that he would pursue it without scruple, and having attained his prey he cared little about having made his companions lose theirs.* The amenability of this passage for analysis as a formal game was apparently first noticed independently by Amartya Sen in, "Isolation, Assurance, and the Social Rate of Discount" (1967) 81(1) *Quarterly Journal of Economics* 112, and David K. Lewis, *Convention: A Philosophical Study* (Harvard University Press, Cambridge, Mass. 1969). Of course, game

theorists do not treat the Stag Hunt as a primitive stage in moral development but rather as a dilemma that might arise in any situation involving gains from cooperation. Interestingly, recent primate research suggests that Rousseau was indeed correct to locate the origins of morality in hunting bands, though the account might apply to species other than human. Sarah F. Brosnan and Frans B.M. De Waal, "Monkeys Reject Unequal Pay" (2003) 435 *Nature* 297–9. This article indicates that capuchin monkeys, who cooperate in hunting, will reject the cucumber that they otherwise regard as fair payment for a pebble if they witness another monkey receiving a grape for the same pebble.

19. As a native of Los Angeles and current resident of New York City, I take on faith all assumptions about hunting.

20. The mnemonic for this is Roman Catholic.

21. Ken Binmore, Alan Kirman and Piero Tani, "Introduction", in *Frontiers of Game Theory* (MIT Press, Cambridge Mass., 1993), 18. Other general introductions to Stag Hunts are Douglas G. Baird, Robert H. Gertner and Randal C. Picker, *Game Theory and the Law* (Harvard University Press, Cambridge Mass., 1994), 35–9; Colin F. Camerer, *Behavioral Game Theory: Experiments in Strategic Interaction* (Russell Sage Foundation, New York and Princeton University Press, Princeton, 2003), 375–95; Brian Skyrms, *The Stag Hunt and the Evolution of Social Structure* (Cambridge University Press, Cambridge, 2004). Stag Hunts are also sometimes called "coordination games" or "weak link" games (since if one player, the "weak link", defects, the others will drop to his level); Amartya Sen calls them "assurance games": Sen, "Isolation, Assurance", 18. I have found two valuable applications of Stag Hunt models to problems in international law or diplomacy: Carlo Carraro, "Modelling International Policy Games: Lessons from European Monetary Coordination" (1997) 24 *Empirica* 163–77 (examining monetary policy decision in four European countries over a decade and finding them best represented as a stag hunt game); Robert A. Green, "Antilegalistic Approaches to Resolving Disputes Between Governments: A Comparison of the International Tax and Trade Regimes" (1998) 23 *Yale Journal of International Law* 79–139 (analyzing tax treaties, which typically lack enforcement provisions, as solutions to Stag Hunts, and suggesting they work better than a legalistic approach associated with trade law).

22. Camerer, *Behavioral Game Theory*, 377.

23. Michael Suk-Young Chwe, *Rational Ritual: Culture, Coordination, and Common Knowledge* (Princeton University Press, Princeton, 2001), 11–12.

24. This is just a formal requirement of the game. If the leaders have no long-term gains from cooperation, it is not a Stag Hunt. Examples might be kleptocracies that survive by skimming off from current unregulated foreign investment and would lose if any of that investment is lost: Daniel Haile, Abdolkarim Sadrieh and Harrie A. A. Verbon, "Self-Serving Dictators and Economic Growth", Working Paper 1105, Center for Economic Studies and IFO Institute of Economic Research, (2003) online: http://www.CESifo.de; or countries with extremely low time horizons, where the

population would die of famine in the time interval between passing up the available hare and cooperating to bring down a stag. In such situations, there are no net gains from cooperation and the game is a Prisoner's Dilemma or something else. My assumption, however, is that such situations without gains from cooperation are atypical, and that we may helpfully approach the problem of transnational labour standards as a problem in the institutional arrangements that might help countries achieve gains from cooperation. Ultimately, however, it is an empirical question whether one or the other describes reality.

25. I hope in future work to specify more precisely the payoffs from cooperating on high labour standards and from deviating for short-term advantage. For present purposes, the payoffs will be crude and ad hoc. However, the crude ad hoc payoffs assumed here are in fact compatible with the limited empirical literature on the economic effects of labour standards. That is, there is no general "race to the bottom" and flows of trade and investment do *not* create inexorable pressure on each country to lower its labour standards so as to attain comparative advantage. My assumption here is that this race, if it exists at all, is limited by each country's self-interest that places serious constraints on how much it will reduce its labour standards in order to attract foreign direct investment. Nevertheless, there may be advantages to a country in lowering its standards, advantages that I model as short-term.

In fact, there is no evidence of any general "race to the bottom." Every study to examine the question has failed to find a relationship between low labour standards and either foreign direct investment or the competitiveness of exports. See generally Theodore H. Moran, *Beyond Sweatshops: Foreign Direct Investment and Globalization in Developing Countries* (Brookings Institution, Washington DC, 2002), 79–83; Organization for Economic Cooperation and Development (OECD), *Trade, Employment, and Labour Standards: A Study of Core Workers' Rights and International Trade* (OECD, Paris, 1996) (no relationship between low labour standards and any measure of export performance); OECD, *International Trade and Core Labour Standards* (OECD, Paris, 2000); Mita Aggarwal, "International Trade, Labour Standards, and Labour Market Conditions: An Evaluation of the Linkages", Working Paper No. 95–06–C U.S., Office of Economics (International Trade Commission, 1995) (almost half of US foreign direct investment is in Canada, Japan, Germany, the United Kingdom and France, 11; little goes to countries that do not observe core labour standards); Drusilla K. Brown, Alan V. Deardorff and Robert M. Stern, "The Effects of Multinational Production on Wages and Working Conditions in Developing Countries", Working Paper 9669 (National Bureau of Economic Research, 2003) (multinational firms routinely provide higher wages and better working conditions than their local counterparts and are typically not attracted preferentially to countries with weak labour standards); Dani Rodrik, "Labor Standards in International Trade: Do they matter and what do we do about them?", in Robert Z. Lawrence, Dani Rodrik and John Whalley, *Emerging Agenda for Global Trade: High Stakes for Developing Countries* (Overseas Development Council, Washington

DC, 1996), 35–79 (no significant relationship between trade flows and various measures of labour standards, unionization or standards of political democracy); Peter Morici and Evan Schulz, *Labor Standards in the Global Trading System* (Economic Strategy Institute, Washington DC, 2001), 48–57 (reviewing and correcting analysis in the Aggarwal and Rodrik studies and nevertheless concluding that "violations of workers' rights do not positively affect aggregate investment", at 57); Vivek H. Dehejia and Yiagadeesen Samy, "Trade and Labour Standards – Theory, New Empirical Evidence, and Policy Implications", Working Paper No. 830, (CESifo, 2002) (long hours worked is negatively correlated with export performance; unionization, civil liberties, and occupational injuries all lack significant relation to export performance; "there is no robust evidence that countries with low labour standards are attracting more [foreign direct investment] than those with high labour standards", at 27); Matthias Busse and Sebastian Braun, "Export Structure, FDI and Child Labour", Discussion Paper 216 (Hamburgisches Welt-Wirtschafts-Archiv, 2003)(foreign direct investment flows are negatively correlated with child labour, even among developing countries); Mahmood Hussain and Keith E. Maskus, "Child Labour Use and Economic Growth: An Econometric Analysis" (July 2003) 26 *World Economy*, at 993–1017 (countries with higher amounts of child labour have lower amounts of human capital in the future). The largest recipients of foreign direct investment are (in order) Luxembourg, China, France, Germany, the United States, the Netherlands and the United Kingdom. United Nations Commission on Trade and Development (UNCTAD), *World Investment Report 2003: Overview*, Figure 2 at 4, online: www.unctad.org/en/docs//wir2003overview_en.pdf. Particular flows of foreign direct investment that are contingent on host countries lowering labour standards of course exist, but are more consistent with the Stag Hunt model presented here (a hare, not particularly nutritious but passing within reach), than with any supposed "race to the bottom".

26. A number of economists have noted in passing that labour standards might solve strategic interactions in which countries might get stuck in a low level Nash equilibrium, e.g. Kaushik Basu, "Child Labour: Cause, Consequence, and Cure, with Remarks on International Labour Standards" (1999) 37 *Journal of Economic Literature* 1083–119 at 1107, but I have located no formal models.

27. John Stuart Mill, "Employment of Children in Manufactories", in Ann P. Robson and John M. Robson (eds.) *Newspaper Writings August 1831–October 1834*, vol. 23 *Collected Works of John Stuart Mill* (University of Toronto Press, Toronto, 1986) [1832], 398–401 at 399.

28. The most recent is Kyle Bagwell and Robert W. Staiger, *The Economics of the World Trading System* (MIT Press, Cambridge, Mass., 2002). Earlier reviews include John McMillan, *Game Theory in International Economics* (Harwood, Chur, 1986), and Avinash Dixit "Strategic Aspects of Trade Policy", in Truman F. Bewley (ed.), *Advances in Economic Theory Fifth World Congress* (Cambridge University Press, Cambridge, 1987), 329–62.

29. Sensing this problem, the authors of one game theory model of labour standards assume that, if one country defects by lowering labour standards, its partner will retaliate on some other dimension of trade policy, such as by raising a tariff: Kyle Bagwell and Robert W. Staiger, "The Simple Economics of Labor Standards and the GATT", in Alan V. Deardorff and Robert M. Stern (eds.), *Social Dimensions of U.S. Trade Policies* (University of Michigan Press, Ann Arbor, 2000), 195–231. This assumes away what is precisely of interest to the legal scholar. In the real world, as everybody (including of course Bagwell and Staier) knows, parties to the GATT system are *not* permitted to raise tariffs or otherwise retaliate because of partners' low labour standards. That is what the fight has been about for years!

30. Again, I recognize that there are many areas of research that lie outside game theory, most important being the comparative empirical study of competing public and private attempts to improve labour standards.

31. A standard reference is Drew Fudenberg and Jean Tirole, *Game Theory* (MIT Press, Cambridge, Mass. 1991), 150–60. I will not be pursuing the literature on repeated games in this Chapter.

32. See also Carraro, "Modelling International Policy".

33. Nancy H. Chau and Ravi Kanbur, "The Adoption of Labour Standards Conventions: Who, When, and Why?" Discussion Paper 2904 (Centre for Economic Policy Research, 2001) online: http://www.cepr.org/pubs/dps/DP2904.asp. Chau and Kanbur do not specifically model the adoption of labour standards as a Stag Hunt, or any other formal game. However, their findings are a kind of real-world experiment that, like some models, shows the importance of peer groups or location in realizing cooperation. It is both theoretically and empirically much more likely that cooperative solutions will obtain in large groups if players bargain with neighbours and imitate their successes. Jason McKenzie Alexander and Brian Skyrms, "Bargaining With Neighbors: Is Justice Contagious?" (1999) 96 *Journal of Philosophy* 588; Skyrms, *The Stag Hunt*, 23–9. We will return to this point.

34. Elinor Ostrom, "Toward a Behavioral Theory Linking Trust, Reciprocity, and Reputation", in Elinor Ostrom and James Walker (eds.), *Trust and Reciprocity: Interdisciplinary Lessons from Experimental Research* (Russell Sage, New York, 2003), 20.

35. Ostrom, "Toward a Behavioral Theory", 23–4. "Social-dilemma situation" is Ostrom's general term for situations in which rational participants making individual choices will not reach Pareto-optimal outcomes. She cites Drew Fudenberg and Eric Maskin, "The Folk Theorem in Repeated Games with Discounting or with Incomplete Information" (1986) 54(3) *Econometrica* 533.

36. John B. Van Huyck, Raymond C. Battalio and Richard O. Beil, "Tacit Coordination Games, Strategic Uncertainty, and Coordination Failure" (1990) 80(1) *American Economic Review* 234 at 244–6; Marc J. Knez and Colin F. Camerer, "Increasing Cooperation in Prisoner's Dilemmas by Establishing a Precedent of Efficiency in Coordination Games" (2000) 82(2) *Organizational Behavior & Human Decision Processes* 194. The ability of two (but no more) players to reach the Pareto-optimal

strategy is demonstrated theoretically in Hans Carlsson and Eric van Damme, "Equilibrium Selection in Stag Hunt Games", in Ken Binmore, Alan Kirman, and Piero Tani (eds.), *Frontiers of Game Theory* (MIT Press, Cambridge, Mass., 1993), 237–53.

37. Van Huyck et al, "Tacit Coordination Games".

38. Marc J. Knez and Colin F. Camerer, "Creating Expectational Assets in the Laboratory: Coordination in Weakest-Link Games" (1994) 15 *Strategic Management Journal* 101–19.

39. See e.g., Cass R. Sunstein, "On the Expressive Function of Law" (1996) 144 *University of Pennsylvania Law Review* 2021.

40. Roberto Weber, Colin Camerer, Yuval Rottenstreich and Marc Knez, "The Illusion of Leadership: Misattribution of Cause in Coordination Games" (2001) 12(5) *Organizational Science* 582–98.

41. Skyrms, *The Stag Hunt*.

42. Chau and Kanbur, "The Adoption of Labour Standards"; Alexander and Skyrms, "Bargaining With Neighbors"; Skyrms, *The Stag Hunt*.

43. Drusilla K. Brown, "A Transaction Cost Politics Analysis of International Child Labour Standards", in Alan V. Deardorff and Robert M. Stern (eds.), *Social Dimensions of U.S. Trade Policies* (University of Michigan Press, Ann Arbor, 2000), 246–64 ("Historically, the most effective strategies for reducing child labour have been the by-product of economic growth," at 247); Avinash K. Dixit, comment in Deardorff and Stern *Social Dimensions*, 267–70 (United States began to get rid of child labour when real GNP per capita reached $7000 in current dollars). Eric Edmonds and Nina Pavcnikin "Does Globalization Increase Child Labour? Evidence From Vietnam", *Working Paper* 8760 (National Bureau of Economic Research, 2002), confirm the decline in child labour following the removal of price controls on rice, export of rice at world prices, and the resulting increase in income to farmers. Brown and her associates caution, however, that "the well-being of today's children and perhaps even economic growth itself may depend on getting children out of the labour force and into schools *today*": Brown, Deardorff, and Stern, "Child Labour" at 218 (emphasis original).

44. Chau and Kanbur, "The Adoption of Labour Standards".

45. See also Kaushik Basu, "Globalization and Marginalization: A Re-examination of Development Policy", Working Paper no. 026 (Bureau for Research in Economic Analysis of Development (BREAD), 2003); Nancy H. Chau and Ravi Kanbur, "The Race to the Bottom, From the Bottom", Paper 2687 (Centre for Economic Policy Research Discussion, 2001).

46. 19 U.S.C. §3804.

47. 19 U.S.C. §2462(b)(2)(G) & (H)(country not eligible for GSP treatment if : "(G) Such country has not taken or is not taking steps to afford internationally recognized worker rights to workers in the country (including any designated zone in that country)" or "(H) Such country has not implemented its commitments to eliminate the worst forms of child labour").

48. 19 U.S.C. §2702(b)(7) (countries not eligible for favorable tariff treatment unless "taking steps to afford internationally recognized worker rights (as defined in section 507(4) of the Trade Act of 1974 [19 USCS § 2467(4)]) to workers in the country (including any designated zone in that country)".

49. 19 U.S.C. §3703(a)(1)(F) (country eligible if it "has established, or is making continual progress toward establishing, protection of internationally recognized worker rights, including the right of association, the right to organize and bargain collectively, a prohibition on the use of any form of forced or compulsory labour, a minimum age for the employment of children, and acceptable conditions of work with respect to minimum wages, hours of work, and occupational safety and health".

50. *Martinez* v. *Dow Chemical Co.*, 219 F.Supp.2d 719 (E.D. La. 2002) and *Dole Food Co.* v. *Patrickson*, 538 U.S. 468 (2003).

51. *Kang* v. *U.Lim America, Inc.*, 296 F.3d 810 (9th Cir. 2002).

52. Jagdish Bhagwati, "The Demands to Reduce Domestic Diversity among Trading Nations", in Jagdish Bhagwati and Robert Hudec (eds.), *Fair Trade and Harmonization: Prerequisites to Free Trade?* (MIT Press Cambridge, Mass., 1996), 9–40 at 33.

53. Under a recognized exception to the General Agreement on Trade and Tariffs, importing countries may create "Generalized Systems of Preference" under which imports from developing countries may enter free of duties if the exporting country agrees to a list of conditions. The United States, European Union, Canada, and Australia all have such GSP programs. Importing countries have almost total discretion whether to create such a GSP program and, if so, what conditions to place on it. Heavy political interference has always characterized the administration of the US GSP program generally: James M. DeVault, "Political Pressure and the U.S. Generalized System of Preferences" (1996) 22 *Eastern Economic Journal* 35–46; and the labour provisions added in 1984: see generally, Lance Compa and Jeffrey S. Vogt, "Labour Rights in the Generalized System of Preferences: A 20-Year Review" (2002) 22 *Comparative Labour Law & Policy Journal* 199. India has invoked a Dispute Settlement Panel of the World Trade Organisation to consider its allegations of discriminatory application of the European Union's GSP program, specifically its special benefits for fighting drug trafficking and its labour and environmental standards. It has been reported that the Panel has recently upheld this complaint in a ruling that is still interim and confidential: "WTO Panel Rules in India's Favour (World Trade Organisation Panel Dismisses EU's GSP Scheme)", *India Business Insight*, 7 September 2003.

54. Dan Danielsen and Karl Klare, "Trade, Labour and Catfish: A Case Study" presented at INTELL 7, Kyoto, Japan, 26–29 March 2004.

55. Robert Axelrod, *The Evolution of Cooperation* (Basic Books, New York, 1985); Camerer, *Behavioral Game Theory*, 221–3.

PART III

The European Union

6

Industrial relations and EU enlargement

MANFRED WEISS

Introduction

The history of the European Union (EU) is one of enlargement. In 1957, the European Economic Community (EEC, later transformed into the European Community, the EC) began with six relatively homogenous countries: Belgium, France, Germany, Italy, Netherlands and Luxembourg. The EC, and later the EU, subsequently grew to 15 member states, many of whom differed significantly from each other. This increase occurred in several stages, a few countries at a time. In 2004, the composition of the EU underwent a radical transformation, with the addition of ten countries: Cyprus, the Czech Republic, Estonia, Hungary, Latvia, Lithuania, Malta, Poland, Slovakia and Slovenia. This enlargement is without a doubt the biggest challenge the European community has ever faced, not only in terms of quantity, but also in terms of quality. The surface area of the EU has increased by one third and the population has grown by sixty million people. At the same time, the EU's GDP has only increased by 5 per cent, meaning that within the EU, the per capita GDP has declined by approximately 18 per cent.[1] In addition, the number of languages spoken in the EU has almost doubled, and the need to find a fair balance between smaller and larger EU member countries has taken on a new sense of urgency.

In the context of this growth, the Central and Eastern European states (CEE states) are of specific interest. They have had to make the transition from state-controlled to market-based economies, while developing systems of industrial relations that not only function efficiently, but are also adapted to the particular socio-cultural environment of the country concerned. There are significant differences between the various CEE states, and it would be incorrect to lump them together in this respect.[2] Nevertheless, it is possible, to varying degrees, to identify common characteristics between them.[3]

The focus of this paper is the question of how the transformation process in the CEE states is compatible with both the need for industrial
relations in their respective countries and with the need for the harmonization of industrial relations within the EU community as a whole. The
role of EU enlargement in this process will also be examined. Although
Cyprus and Malta are not specifically addressed, these countries are by
no means free from industrial relations integration challenges. However,
their challenges are less difficult, and are similar to those that were resolved
in the course of former, less dramatic enlargement situations.

After briefly setting out the basic elements of industrial relations in
the CEE states, I will attempt to describe the EU's structure of industrial
relations, culminating in a discussion of whether, and how, the two systems
can be made compatible.[4]

Industrial relations in the CEE states

The CEE States were confronted with the dilemma of simultaneously
transforming an authoritarian regime into a democracy, a planned economy into a market economy, and a party-dictated system of industrial
relations into one compatible with political freedom and a market economy. The development of a modern industrial relations system has not
kept pace with the process of developing democratic freedoms and a market economy. In terms of these two aspects of change, the CEE States
have achieved admirable success in a relatively short time. However, the
present structure of industrial relations in the CEE states can, to an extent,
be explained as both a reaction to, and a legacy of, the communist system
of the past.[5]

Trade unions

In the period preceding political change, the CEE states were governed
under a monistic system, wherein trade unions were more or less instruments of the ruling party. An important exception was the *Solidarnosz*
movement in Poland, which was created as an autonomous alternative
to the existing trade union structure. The monistic pattern of the communist period was subsequently replaced by one of excessive pluralism.
It now often appears as though trade unions in the CEE states are more
concerned about competing with each other than understanding their
role as a counterpart to employers' associations. This necessarily weakens the strength of the labour movement as a whole.[6] Furthermore, the

creation of a private sector in the economy has led to an extensive erosion of the system of trade union representation. The backbone of the private sector in these countries is composed of small and medium-sized enterprises (SMEs), where trade unions are practically non-existent and do not play any role.[7] The result of no organized body representing employees' interests in SMEs is the total individualization of the employee/employer relationship. Trade unions only play a role in the larger (still, or formerly, state-owned) enterprises. On the whole, the organization rate of trade unions in CEE states has significantly declined.[8]

Employers' associations

The state of employers' associations in CEE states is even more deplorable. Employers' associations exist only to a very limited and rudimentary extent, and they mainly represent the interests of big enterprise, much of which is still not yet privatized. SME employers generally do not yet see the need to organize. If employers' associations are founded, this is not done for the purpose of acting as a counterpart to trade unions, but with the intention of lobbying for common business interests.[9] Therefore, up to the present time, employers' associations in CEE states may be considered to be rather marginal players.[10]

Tripartite arrangements

A characteristic feature of most CEE states is the existence of tripartite arrangements on a national level. These bodies discuss issues such as restructuring the economy and the promotion of social justice. There is no doubt that tripartite social dialogue has its merits, and that it has played an important role in the process of restructuring industrial relations in the CEE states. However, this social dialogue is asymmetrical. The state still dominates weak trade unions and even weaker employers' associations. Accordingly, these discussion forums largely serve only to legitimize the respective Government's policy.[11] In spite of this structural deficiency, many decisions are made through tripartite social dialogue, thereby retarding, to a certain extent, the evolution of autonomous, bilateral collective bargaining structures. At present, there is no alternative to the tripartite social dialogue that exists, and it is absolutely necessary to garner approval for the transformative work that must be performed. It must also be stressed that these arrangements on the national level do not have a supporting structure at lower levels.

Collective bargaining

In view of the weakness of the employers' associations and the non-existence of collective actors in large parts of the economy, it is no surprise that collective bargaining in CEE states is the exception rather than the rule, and that – at least in principle – it only takes place on a company or plant-wide level. Multi-employer bargaining only takes place in companies which were formerly parts of a large state-owned enterprise.[12] However, practically no bargaining is being conducted at higher levels, either sectorally or nationally.[13] Ultimately, collective agreements and collective bargaining have little impact on most of the private sector.

Employees' involvement in management's decision-making

Due to the experiences gained prior to the fall of the Iron Curtain, there remains great reluctance in CEE states to accept workers' participation in the new market economy.[14] Nevertheless, a considerable amount of legislation institutionalizing workers' participation does exist,[15] in most cases without the support of the social partners. Notably, there is scepticism and opposition in the trade union camp. The difficulty is three-fold: first, employee involvement in management decision-making generally only takes place in very large companies;[16] second, in some cases the institutional arrangements are modelled on the systems of Western Europe and therefore do not really fit into the overall structure of the respective country; and third, there is no appropriate division of labour between trade unions and workers' participation bodies. This lack of a consistent and coherent concept of a broader system of industrial relations creates rivalry and suspicion, and ultimately weakens and de-legitimizes the position of both the workers' elected representatives and the trade unions. It must, however, be reiterated that in the large majority of companies in the private sector, neither trade unions nor other representative bodies exist. Where they are formally present, they are quite often under management control and are mere "extensions of managerial structures".[17]

Law in the books and law in action

The creation of legislation after the political change in all CEE states has been quite impressive, and is still continuing to an enormous extent.[18] This ties in with the legalistic approach still commonly found in the CEE states, whereby a problem is deemed to be resolved if a law or regulation has been passed to deal with it. There remains, however, a considerable gap between the normative level and day-to-day practice.[19] There are many explanations for inadequate implementation, ranging from resentment toward legislative intervention, to the inefficiency and lack of controls existing in the judicial system (or other conflict resolution bodies). In view of their weaknesses, neither trade unions nor other representative bodies are in a position to monitor the implementation of statutory law.

It must also be stressed that in actual practice labour law plays no role whatsoever within the large number of companies in the private sector of the CEE countries. It is far too easy for companies to sign contracts on the basis of general civil law, thereby avoiding the statutory labour and social provisions aimed at providing employees with a degree of protection.[20] This naturally leads to a constant process of de-legitimization of labour and social security legislation, and ultimately results in a mentality which praises the freedom of market forces in the absence of labour and social security laws. This effective absence of collective structures is simply not a precondition for prosperity.

The framework for industrial relations in the EU

Fundamental social rights

After a long and very controversial debate in 2000, the Charter of Fundamental Rights of the EU (the "Charter") was passed as a legally non-binding declaration expressing the consensus of all present member states.

In the meantime, the "Convention" (a group of MPs from member state governments and opposition parties, along with representatives from the EU's institutions), presented the member state governments with a draft of a document that would amend and replace the EU and EC treaties – a new treaty establishing a Constitution for Europe (the "EU Constitution"). The draft was discussed by the Governmental Conference beginning in October 2003, and signed by leaders of the member states on 29 October 2004. Unfortunately, the EU Constitution has been stalled due to the failure of several countries to ratify. The Charter is an important component of the EU Constitution and will become legally binding upon ratification.

Within the Charter there is a specific chapter on fundamental social rights under the title "solidarity", but beyond this chapter, there is a whole set of fundamentally important social rights (e.g. freedom of association, which implies the right of everyone to form and to join trade unions for the protection of his or her interests) (Article 12). The chapter on "solidarity" contains twelve core rights, including the worker's right to working conditions that respect his or her health and dignity (Article 31 para 1), the right of collective bargaining and collective action, which is guaranteed as a subjective right either for workers and employers or for their respective organizations (Article 28), and participation rights to information and consultation in good time with respect to management's decision-making (Article 27). The latter two fundamental rights (collective bargaining and consultation) are of utmost importance in the context of this paper.

In evaluating the content of the chapter on "solidarity", it must be stressed that it includes collective rights. It insists on Community and member state responsibility for providing job security, healthy working conditions, safety and dignity, and for protecting young people at work. Furthermore it insists on measures to make family and professional life compatible, and to provide social security as well as social assistance. Taken collectively, it becomes clear that this is a concept that would be incompatible with mere de-regulation, de-collectivization and de-institutionalization. To put it more broadly, it would be incompatible with a strict neo-liberal approach.[21] The chapter on "solidarity", therefore, outlines the structure of the European social model and the values on which it is based. Evidently, this is also an important message to the CEE states, where the ideology of pure individualism and anti-collectivism is still widespread.

Minimum standards

As opposed to other regional arrangements such as NAFTA or Mercosur, the EU is not merely a free trade zone, but a supranational entity with legislative, judicial and executive powers of its own. The EC has the power to pass legislative acts, either by way of directly applicable regulations or by directives to be transposed into the national law of the member states. In the field of social policy, the regulation as an instrument is too rigid. Therefore, in most cases, the directive is chosen for its flexibility, and member states integrate the legislative goal of the directive into their respective legal and institutional framework. Despite the fact that many topics are addressed by directives that influence domestic law of the member states, directives are increasingly shaped in a way that gives the social partners and workers' representatives a role in their implementation. A very good example of this is the directive on working time.[22]

Up to now, the EC's legislative activity has not been characterized by a systematic approach. This is mainly due to the fact that social policy only gradually became a relevant factor in the context of the Community.

There is presently a far-reaching power to legislate in the field of labour law and social security. However, the EC still has no power to legislate in reference to "pay, the right of association, the right to strike or the right to impose lock-outs". The new Constitutional Treaty has not changed this reality.

Social dialogue

European trade unions and employers' associations have umbrella organizations at the EU level; ETUC on the trade union side, and UNICE (for the private sector) and CEEP (for the public sector) on the employers' association side. These actors are not involved in collective bargaining, but are considered to be a lobby for the interest groups they represent. For a long time, these bodies cooperated informally with the Commission. This "social dialogue" was formalized by the Treaty in 1986, and it has achieved a very elaborate structure by virtue of Article 138 and 139 of the EC Treaty.

At the present time, the aforementioned umbrella organizations are integrated into the legislative machinery. Prior to submitting legislative proposals, the Commission has to consult with them "on the possible direction of Community action". If the Commission wishes to continue to elaborate a proposal, there must be a second consultation of the parties to the social dialogue "on the content of this proposal". On such an occasion, the social partners may take over the Commission's initiative and try to regulate the matter by reaching an agreement. They have nine months to reach an agreement, which – without the involvement of the European Parliament – can be transformed into a legally binding directive by the Council. The directives on parental leave, fixed-term contracts and part-time work are the result of such a procedure. If the social partners cannot reach an agreement within the prescribed nine month period, the Commission itself is given the task of drafting a proposal.

The social partners have an alternative possibility. They are free to conclude agreements – even in matters where the EC has no legislative power – to be implemented "in accordance with the procedures and practices specific to management and labour and the member states". Such agreements are not legally binding. It is up to the social partners at the EU level to convince actors in the member states to integrate the ideas contained in such agreements into their respective national structures. A recent example of such a strategy is the agreement on tele-work of 2002, the possible impact of which is a topic of vivid discussion in the different member states.

In addition to the cross-sectoral social dialogue, there are an increasing number of sectoral social dialogues.[23] They are not integrated into the legislative machinery; rather, their task is the representation of the specific interests of their sector within the EU, as well as the conclusion of legally non-binding agreements.

Collective bargaining

Collective bargaining has been and will continue to be a policy matter lying within the exclusive jurisdiction of member states. The legal pattern of collective bargaining and collective agreements varies widely throughout the EU. In some countries there is a duty to bargain, while in other countries there is no such duty. In some countries, negotiation is highly formalized, while in others it is more or less left to the discretion of the actors. The prerequisites for the actors are significantly different as well. The criteria for representation in pluralistic union movements follow a different legal pattern from the criteria applied in systems with amalgamated unions. The process of conflict resolution is also regulated very differently. There are different institutions for conciliation and arbitration in some countries, while others are not even aware of the existence of such resolution processes. In some countries, going on strike is an individual right, while in others it is a collective one. The legitimate goals and the effects of strikes are regulated differently in various new member states. Finally, the implementation of collective agreements differs from country to country.

In some, there is access to specialized labour courts; in others to ordinary courts; in others, to alternative institutions; in still others, there is no such access at all. Whereas in one country collective agreements are not enforceable, they are strictly legally binding in others. The possibilities of normative regulation are also varied. In one country, collective agreements apply only to union members, in other countries to all employees. Some countries observe a strict peace obligation, while others do not. Rules regarding the relationship between agreements on different levels and between old and new agreements differ from country to country. Subject matter for regulation by collective agreements varies greatly: in some countries, there are significant limitations, while in others there are almost none. The rules on broadening the scope of collective agreements are also very different.

Against this background, it would be totally unrealistic to think of a European Collective Agreement as an instrument to promote uniformity. Nevertheless, the need for more cooperation and coordination in collective bargaining throughout the EC has definitely increased due to the introduction of European monetary union. The new currency has increased transparency as prices, wages and other working conditions can be easily compared. The discrepancies of working conditions between member states are becoming more evident. This may increasingly create pressure to develop strategies directed to the goal of gradual convergence over the longer term.

Monetary union has had a second impact on collective bargaining, which may be of even more significance. Up until the point of monetary union, it had been possible to cope with labour market problems through national monetary policy. There was a sort of interaction between the collective bargaining participants and the National Reserve Banks. This context has now changed, and monetary policy is now centralized and conducted by the European Central Bank. The question of whether a collective bargaining structure can be established that would correspond to European monetary policy (as it did before to national monetary policies) must therefore be asked.[24]

This task would require improving transnational coordination. In this respect, at least some progress has been achieved in the last fifteen years. The first important step was the so called Doorn Declaration of 1988, named after the Dutch town of Doorn where the Declaration was signed, in which the trade unions of Belgium, the Netherlands, Luxembourg and Germany agreed on three core principles to be observed in collective bargaining throughout the European Community: (a) wage settlements in collective agreements should correspond to the sum total of the evaluation of prices and the increase in labour productivity; (b) collective agreements should attempt to strengthen mass purchasing power and focus on job creation measures (shorter working time etc.); and (c) there should be regular information and consultation between the participating trade unions on developments in bargaining policy. In short, the idea was for the first two principles to influence the content of collective bargaining, and for the third to strengthen horizontal communication. The principles on content have been redefined and have shifted from wage issues to non-wage issues, as is evidenced, for example, by the enunciation of a principle of life-long learning. Further, the attempt of more intensive communication has been extended to continuous evaluation.

A number of general initiatives on the sectoral level have also commenced. In 1997, the German metalworkers' trade union launched a cross-border collective bargaining network. The idea was that each individual district of this trade union was supposed to develop a solid network of collective bargaining cooperation with the metalworkers' trade unions of neighbouring countries. Representatives of the different trade unions were supposed to participate as observers in each others' collective bargaining, which would then provide the basis for future joint planning of collective bargaining. So far, the mutual exchange of observers has worked quite well, and has led to a better understanding of different bargaining cultures. A common day-to-day information system on collective bargaining has been established, and common working groups on specific bargaining issues have also come into existence. The example of the German metalworkers' trade union has been followed in Scandinavia by the Nordic metalworkers' trade union and by trade unions from other sectors, including the construction and chemical industries.

The most promising and far-reaching initiative was undertaken by the European Metalworkers Federation (EMF) in the late 1990s. The EMF, which covers member countries as a whole, developed guidelines for national collective bargaining in order to prevent downward competition. Further, it developed Charters on specific bargaining issues, such as wages, working time and bargaining conditions. To illustrate this approach, the Charter in the case of wage bargaining reads, "the point of reference to wage policy in all countries must be to offset the rate of inflation and to ensure that workers' incomes retain a balanced participation in productivity gains". This, of course, is nothing more than a recommendation.

The responsibility for the Charter's implementation remains with the individual negotiating trade union. The EMF initiative has been accompanied by a remarkable process of institution-building. There is now an EMF Collective Bargaining Committee for assessing and further developing the structure of this initiative, and there are working parties for the specific issues. All this has led to continuous evaluation, intensified continuous communication, and a strengthening of personal links between representatives of EMF affiliates. In 1999, the EMF established a European Collective Bargaining Information Network (EUCOB), an excellent database on recent developments in collective bargaining in the metal industries. In the meantime, the EMF has been followed by other European trade union federations in the chemical, construction, food, public service and textile industries.

In view of all these initiatives, the ETUC passed a resolution on a "European system of industrial relations" in 1999 urging in particular a "European solidaristic pay policy" intended to (a) guarantee workers a fair share of income, (b) counter the danger of social dumping, (c) counter growing income inequality, (d) reduce disparities in living conditions, and (e) contribute to an effective implementation of the principle of equal treatment of the sexes. In addition, the resolution stresses the European Federations' responsibility to coordinate collective bargaining.

In 2000, ETUC passed a "European guideline for wage increases", which largely derives its shape from the model of the EMF guideline on wage bargaining. The European Trade Union Institute (ETUI), the research arm of ETUC, is now annually evaluating the wage bargaining policy in light of the guideline.

The evaluation of all these initiatives is merely meant to illustrate that the need for transnational cooperation and coordination has been understood by the trade unions. Even if the structures are still at a rudimentary stage, they represent an important step towards the development of a transnational perspective, and they thereby shape collective bargaining in the national context. There is, however, an evident deficiency; this development has taken place exclusively on the trade union side,[25] and there are no similar attempts on the employers' side. The more the strategy of trade union coordination and cooperation succeeds, the less it will be possible for the employers' associations to simply ignore this new reality.

The process of transnational coordination and cooperation could be significantly stimulated by cross-sectoral and sectoral social dialogue. The cross-sectoral social dialogue should focus on agreements to be implemented according to national law and practice, with a lesser emphasis placed on the preparatory steps of legislation. By doing so, topics that might be of primary interest for regulation may be determined in a more coordinated way. Model agreements could present frameworks to enrich the imagination of the national actors.[26] Even if the actors cannot reach an agreement on a European level, each side could at least communicate its respective view to its constituency. Of course, all such framework agreements and communications would not be legally binding, but they could stimulate discussions on the domestic bargaining scene concerning how best to cope with such proposals. Such a communication strategy can only be effective if there is a vertical dialogue between the European umbrella organizations and the different national constituencies.

It should be noted that the recent developments in promoting the transnational coordination of collective bargaining in the EU context are indeed very promising. However, all available instruments should be used to intensify and accelerate this process. The task is to build up a multi-level system with specific articulation on each level, with feedback from one level to the other, and with mutual learning in the coordination process. Such a system should leave lower level actors with the utmost bargaining autonomy but at the same time put pressure on them to cope with the higher level frameworks. In the meantime, this "open method of coordination" has become the catchword for the flexible strategy of balancing the need for centralization and decentralization in a multi-level system of collective bargaining.[27]

Employment policy

The "open method of coordination" refers not only to coordinated collective bargaining, but to practically all policy areas in which the social partners are supposed to be integrated. A good example is the employment policy for "a coordinated strategy for employment" (Article 125), which was institutionalized in the Amsterdam amendment to the EC Treaty. The genuine competence of the member states in this area remains uncontested. The Community is required to contribute to a high level of employment "by encouraging cooperation between member states and by supporting and, if necessary, complementing their action".

To ensure that this goal is realizable, the Chapter on Employment provides for several institutional arrangements. There is the Employment Committee, which primarily monitors the labour markets and employment policies in the member states and the Community, to help prepare the joint annual report by the Council and the Commission. In fulfilling its mandate, the Employment Committee is required to consult with the social partners. In order to ensure that the activities of the Employment Committee and the joint annual report by the Council and the Commission are not fruitless, the Chapter on Employment establishes additional powers for the Community. After examination of the joint annual report by the European Council and on the basis of the European Council's conclusions, the Council "shall each year draw up guidelines" (Article 128 para. 2). The decision requires only a qualified majority.

This arrangement has led to the adoption of numerous measures, and has significantly increased the interrelated activities between the member states. The summits of Luxembourg, Cologne and Lisbon are important steps on this road,[28] the details of which are of less importance in the context of this discussion. What is important is the fact that the Chapter on Employment establishes a mutual learning process for the Community and the member states, including not only governments, but also the social partners. None of the member states can escape the dialogue and the permanent pressure which it applies. Best practices do not have to be continuously reinvented, but they can easily be communicated and imitated. Media awareness has also increased significantly, and the whole structure is understood as a joint European activity. The goal – in spite of the wording of the Treaty – is a gradual denationalization and Europeanization of employment policy.

Employees' involvement in management's decision-making

Perhaps the most important impact of the EC on the field of industrial relations occurred in the area of employee involvement in management decision-making.[29] From the very beginning, the situation in the different member states was characterized by extreme diversity. Some countries had highly elaborate systems of worker participation, including co-determination. Other countries had very weak systems of information and consultation, and some countries did not abide by a philosophy of cooperation, but rather focused exclusively on conflict and collective bargaining. In the 1970s, in order to guarantee at least a minimum of employee influence in management decision-making, European legislators prescribed patterns of information and consultation in the case of collective redundancies[30] and transfer of undertaking,[31] and later, in the 1980s, on health and safety.[32] However, this was only a beginning and the programme has subsequently become much more ambitious. Attempts to establish patterns of employee involvement on a transnational scale have been successful, and this has significantly increased the minimum level of participation in the national context.

The first step in this direction was the directive on European Works Councils (EWCs) in 1994.[33] Instead of relying on substantial regulation, EWCs provide for a procedural arrangement, establishing a special negotiating body to represent workers' interests. Negotiations are left to this specialized body and the central management of a transnational undertaking or group of undertakings. It is up to the special negotiating body to decide (with a two-thirds majority) not to request an agreement. The subsidiary requirements set out in the annex to the directive apply only if central management refuses to commence negotiations within six months of receiving such a request, or if the two parties are unable to reach an agreement after three years. These subsidiary requirements are the only form of pressure available to the special negotiating body. Until the date of implementation into national law of the member states, the directive allows for voluntary agreements where even the minimal conditions of the directive do not play a role. In the meantime, over a third of the undertakings covered by the directive have actually implemented it.[34] Where subsidiaries of CEE states are involved, representatives of those countries have voluntarily become included in the EWCs. This has turned out to be an excellent strategy to reduce employees' reservations about involvement in management decision-making as still exists in the CEE states.[35]

The same pattern as in the EWC directive is followed by the second step, the directive of October 2001 on employees' involvement in the European Company.[36] This Directive has to be read together with the Statute on the European Company, which contains the rules on company law. The main reason for establishing a European Company is to save on transaction costs, and to increase efficiency and transparency. It should no longer be necessary to create complicated holding company structures in order to overcome the problems arising from national company law. Ideally, this goal will only be achieved if the Statute comprehensively regulates the details of corporate law. Then, the structure of company law for the EC would be identical, a goal that the Statute only partially meets.

A European Company can only be registered if the directive's requirements are met. Accordingly, the provisions on workers' involvement cannot be ignored. The structure of the directive is very much the same as that contained in the directive on the EWCs. It provides for a special negotiating body, lists the topics for negotiation, and leaves everything to those negotiations. In case negotiations fail, there is a fall-back clause, the so called "standard rules". The directive contains two different topics that have to be carefully distinguished. The first refers to information and consultation. Here, the structure is very similar to the one developed in the directive on EWCs, the application of which is excluded in the European Company.

It is the directive's critical second topic that is of most interest. It relates to employee participation, which is defined as "the influence of the body representative of the employees and/or employees' representatives in the affairs of a company by way of (1) the right to elect or appoint some of the members of the company's supervisory or administrative organ, or (2) the right to recommend and/or oppose the appointment of some or all members of the company's supervisory or administrative organ". Normally, how such a scheme should look is left to negotiation, and only in the case of transformation must the agreement "provide at least the same level of all elements of employees' involvement as the ones existing within the company to be converted into a European Company". If, in other cases, negotiations result in a reduction in the participation level, the qualified majority requirement applies to ensure that, by way of agreement, the present highest level cannot be derogated from easily or carelessly. If no agreement is reached, the standard rules apply and ensure that the level of the scheme is maintained in cases where a scheme of workers' participation already existed to a significant extent prior to the conversion into a European company. However, a participation scheme is not needed if none of the participating companies have been "governed by participation rules prior to the registration of the European Company".[37]

The third, and perhaps most important step, is the directive of March 2002 on the minimum framework for information and consultation at national level.[38] It is shaped according to the same philosophy, establishing some minimum conditions, but leaving everything else to the member states. The directive applies to establishments of at least 20 employees and to undertakings of at least 50 employees. In the original version of the proposal, reference was only made to undertakings. This change is due to the fact that, in some member states, the entity which serves as reference point for information and consultation is predominantly the establishment (as for example in Germany).

The purpose of the directive is "to establish a general framework setting out minimum requirements for the right to information and consultation of employees in undertakings or establishments within the Community". The directive defines the structure of information and consultation in a much more comprehensive way than in other directives. The definitions contain important procedural requirements. Timing, content and manner of information must correspond with the directive's purpose, and the directive allows the employees' representatives to examine the information and to prepare for consultation. The consultation itself must meet several requirements: (1) the timing, the method and the content must be effective; (2) information and consultation must take place at the appropriate level of management and representation, depending on the subject under discussion; (3) the employees' representatives are entitled to formulate an opinion on the basis of relevant information to be supplied by the employer; (4) the employees' representatives are entitled to meet with the employer and to obtain a response to any opinion they may formulate along with reasons for that response; and finally (5) in case of decisions within the scope of the employer's management powers, an attempt must be made to seek prior agreement on the decisions covered by information and consultation. Unfortunately, the directive does not cover a situation where an agreement is reached but the employer does not implement it.

Information must cover the recent and probable development of the undertaking or establishment's activities and economic situation in the broadest sense. Information and consultation must take place with respect to the structure and probable development of employment within the undertaking or establishment, or with regard to any anticipatory measures, particularly where there is a threat of unemployment.

Finally, information and consultation must take place on decisions likely to lead to substantial changes in work organization or in contractual relations, including those covered by the Community provisions.

On the whole, the directive remains very flexible, and to a great extent leaves the structural framework and the modalities to the member states. Nevertheless, it turned out that the opposition of some countries could only be overcome by granting transitional provisions. These provisions are supposed to apply if, at the date of the entry into force of the directive in the respective member state (March 2005), there is "no general, permanent and statutory system of information and consultation of employees, nor a general, permanent and statutory system of employee representation at the workplace allowing employees to be represented for that purpose". In these countries, for the first two years after implementation into national law, the directive only applies to companies with at least 150 employees, or to establishments employing at least 100 employees. In the third year, these figures are lowered to 100 and 50 employees respectively. Thereafter, the directive applies as it does everywhere else. In short, those who are unfamiliar with an institutionalized system of employees' information and consultation are not subjected to shock-therapy, and have the opportunity to experience a smoother transition. Since the directive only provides for a minimum framework, it does not affect more favourable arrangements in member states. Additionally, the directive cannot be used to justify the reduction or destruction of existing patterns.

The mere existence of these directives leaves no doubt that the promotion of employees' involvement in company's decision-making has become an essential part of the Community's strategy in its social policy agenda. It has passed the "point of no return". This policy is in line with Article 27 of the Charter of Fundamental Rights of the EU, which guarantees workers' rights to information and consultation. This has important implications for countries with a tradition of exclusively adversarial structures; they no longer have a choice but to reshape their systems to promote partnership and cooperation.

The directives do have their weaknesses. They are unnecessarily complicated, not always consistent, and above all are very vague in their terminology. The directive supplementing the Statute of the European Company, as well as the directive on a national framework for information and consultation, have been watered down during the legislative process, resulting in the acceptance of the lowest common denominator. However, in assessing the importance of these measures for the future of industrial relations in the EU, these deficiencies should not be overstated. The decisive element is the fact that, when taken as a whole, these instruments force all actors involved – trade unions and workers' representatives, employers' associations, employers and employees – to discuss and reflect on the potential of consulting with and sharing information with employees and providing for worker participation on company boards. Finally, it has to be stressed that the Community's approach does not focus on introducing specific institutional patterns, but rather on stimulating and initiating procedures for the promotion of employee involvement in management decision-making.

Integration of industrial relations in an enlarged EU

The insufficiency of the mere transposition of the *acquis communautaire*

The CEE states as well as all other candidate countries were required to transpose all EC legislation (the so called *acquis communitaire*) into their respective legal systems. In view of the tremendous amount of such legislation, this was a difficult task to achieve in a relatively short time. In general, the candidate countries – including the CEE states – had no difficulty meeting this precondition for accession. With the help of external experts (the so called process of "screening"), they largely succeeded in transposing EU law into their respective legal structures.[39] However, the gap between the law as written and the law in action, as examined above, also plays a role in this context. The focus remains on the normative level; as long as the institutions and actors that guarantee satisfactory implementation in actual practice are not available, it would be erroneous to assume that the mere transposition of EU law has an effective impact on the reality of the CEE states[40] and amount to anything more than mere window-dressing.

As indicated above, quite a few of the directives (such as those on working time or on health and safety, two areas where the CEE states are still lagging far behind the present EU average[41]) require the involvement of social partners and/or workers' representatives in order to be implemented effectively. This is not possible, as long as the requisite actors and instruments remain absent.[42]

Social dialogue and collective bargaining

Participation in cross-sectoral, as well as sectoral, social dialogues at European level requires appropriate structures in the national context.

The same is true for the strategy of coordinated collective bargaining described above. Here, the deficits in the CEE states are significant. In particular, social dialogue and collective bargaining at the sectoral level require further development. Without intermediary structures, there will be no input in the European social dialogue from the CEE States nor will these states be able to cope adequately with any input provided by the social dialogue. Neither framework agreements concluded in the context of the European cross-sectoral social dialogue (like the one on tele-work) nor similar agreements and guidelines developed in the context of European sectoral social dialogue will have any relevance for the CEE states as long as there are no intermediary structures in place. Furthermore, as long as trade unions and employers' associations do not have an appropriate organizational structure, they will not be able to play their respective roles in the mutual learning process, as set out above in the example of employment policy. It cannot be denied that social partners and industrial relations in the CEE states are in danger of remaining disconnected from the patterns established on a European level.[43] If they do, then the highly praised open method of coordination may not work at all. This is a challenge, not only for the trade unions, but particularly for the employers' associations. It is also a challenge for the social partners of the present member states and the present EU to support this development, as was promised at the summit in Laeken when Belgium last held the Presidency of the EU.

Employee involvement in management decision-making

As illustrated above, employee involvement in management decision-making has become one of the core activities in the mainstream of the EC social policy. Furthermore, it has reached a point where member states can no longer escape the consultation requirement. With the recent directive on a framework of information and consultation, the question is no longer whether the member states may adopt such an institutional arrangement, but how they choose to shape it. But even in this respect, the amount of leeway afforded to member states is narrowed as all the topics mentioned by the directive are to be covered and the requirements for adequate information and consultation schemes are to be met. There is no doubt that the arrangements established so far in the CEE states do not yet live up to these standards. Of course, it is up to the CEE states whether to select a system exclusively based on trade union representation or a dual system with special elected bodies in addition to existing trade unions. It is also up to the CEE states to establish different structures for enterprises where trade unions are present or where they are absent. The directive is silent in this regard, since it refers to workers' representatives according to national law and practice. The directive, however, is only adequately implemented if workers' representatives are available in the establishments and undertakings covered by the directive. It should be noted that this implementation problem exists not only in the CEE states, but also in quite a few older member states. There will accordingly be a unique opportunity for old and new member states to learn from each other.

Unfortunately, the problem for the CEE states is not only confined to the question of how to shape the pattern of information and consultation. There is also a need to develop a consistent and coherent multi-level system of industrial relations in which employee involvement in management decision-making has its proper place. It is of utmost importance to organize a clear-cut division of labour between the system of information and consultation in management's decision-making and collective bargaining. If there is too much overlap, the industrial relations machinery will not be able to function properly and it will not gain the acceptance of the trade unions. It is important to develop the respective systems in cooperation with the trade unions. However, whether they are in a position to fulfil this role is perhaps doubtful.

Conclusion

The CEE States are still undergoing a transformation in their industrial relations regimes. Systems of employee involvement in management decision-making are the exception rather than the rule, and even where such systems exist, they are weak. There is not yet a consistent multi-level system of industrial relations. Collective bargaining is still a rudimentary phenomenon, mainly taking place at company level. Intermediary levels of collective bargaining and social dialogue are missing, and, to a great extent, the private sector is lacking any collective representation whatsoever.

In such a situation, the accession to the EU presents a particular challenge for both the EU in its attempt to develop an integrated system of industrial relations, and for the CEE States in their aspiration not to be disconnected from the EU pattern. EU enlargement can be a catalyst in this process. As shown above, there is a likelihood that integration will accelerate and shape the dynamics of transformation, and this again will have an impact on the future structure of the EU arrangements. Most important in this context are the fundamental social rights as contained in the Charter of Fundamental Rights of the EU. The value system expressed therein is incompatible with the excessive neo-liberalism that is still largely entrenched in the CEE States.

Notes

1. See M. Ladó, "EU Enlargement: Reshaping European and National Industrial Relations" (2002) 18 *The International Journal of Comparative Labour Law and Industrial Relations* 101.
2. For these very significant differences see the enlightening report by M. Ladó, "Industrial relations in the candidate countries", European Industrial Relations Observatory (2002), online: http://www.eiro.eurofound.eu.int/2002/07/feature/TN0207102F.htm.
3. It should be noted that in many respects Slovenia is an exceptional case whose special features are beyond the scope of this brief paper.
4. For a brief discussion of this challenge, see also M. Weiss and K. Petkov, "The social dimension", in R. Langewiesche and A. Toth, (eds.), *The Unity of Europe: political, economic and social dimensions of EU enlargement* (European Trade Union Institute, Brussels, 2001), 123, and M. Weiss, "Industrial Relations and EU-Enlargement", in R. Blanpain and M. Weiss (eds.), *Changing Industrial Relations and Modernisation of Labour Law* (Kluwer Law International, The Hague, 2003), 438.
5. M. Stanojevic and G. Gradev, "Workers' representation at company level in CEE countries" (2003) 9 TRANSFER 31 at 44.
6. H. Kohl and H.W. Platzer, "Labour Relations in central and eastern Europe and the European social model" (2003) 9 TRANSFER 11 at 15.
7. For details see M. Ladó and D. Vaughan-Whitehead, "Social dialogue in candidate countries: what for ?" (2003) 9 TRANSFER 64 at 69.
8. Ladó and Vaughan-Whitehead, 'Social dialogue', 66.
9. See Ladó, "Industrial Relations", under subtitle "Diversity in industrial relations – heritage of the past".
10. Ladó and Vaughan-Whitehead, "Social dialogue", 70.
11. Ladó,"EU Enlargement", 111.
12. See Ladó, "Industrial Relations", under subtitle "Sectoral collective bargaining – current state of affairs".
13. Ladó and Vaughan-Whitehead, "Social dialogue", 73.
14. See M. Sewerynski, "Employee Involvement and EU Enlargement – Polish Perspective", in M. Biagi (ed.), *Quality of Work and Employee Involvement in Europe* (Kluwer Law International, The Hague, 2002), 270.
15. For an overview, see Kohl and Platzer, "Labour relations", 15, and Ladó, "Industrial Relations", under subtitle "Information and Consultation of workers".
16. Stanojevic and Gradev, "Workers' representation", 45.

17. Stanojevic and Gradev, "Workers' representation", 45.
18. See discussion paper by A. Bronstein, "Labour Law Reform in EU Candidate Countries: achievements and challenges", available online: http.//www.ilo.org/ public/English/dialogue/ifpdial/download/papers/candidate.pdf.
19. See Ladó and Vaughan-Whitehead, "Social dialogue", 80.
20. Csilla Kollonay-Lehoczky, "European Enlargement – A Comparative View of Hungarian Labour Law", in G.A. Bermann and K. Pistor (eds.), Law and Governance in and Englarged European Union (Hart Publishing, Oxford and Portland, 2004), 209.
21. For a detailed analysis of the impact of the fundamental social rights in the Charter, see M. Weiss, "The politics of the EU Charter of Fundamental Rights", in B. Hepple (ed.), Social and Labour Rights in a Global Context (Cambridge University Press, Cambridge, 2002), 73.
22. See in this context Catherine Barnard, "The EU Agenda for Regulating Labour Markets – Lessons from the UK in the field of Working Time", in Bermann and Pistor (eds.), Law and Governance, 177.
23. For a detailed analysis, see B. Keller, "Social Dialogue at Sectoral Level: The Neglected Ingredient of European Industrial Relations", in B. Keller and H.W. Platzer (eds.), Industrial Relations and European Integration (Ashgate , Aldershot / Burlington, 2003), 30.
24. For the interrelationship of monetary policy and collective bargaining, see F. Traxler, "European Monetary Union and Collective Bargaining", in Keller and Platzer, Industrial Relations, 85.
25. For a comprehensive overview on all these coordination activities see T. Schulten, "Europeanisation of Collective Bargaining: Trade Union Initiatives for the Transnational Coordination of Collective Bargaining", in Keller and Platzer, Industrial Relations, 58.
26. For such a strategy, see M. Weiss, "Social Dialogue and Collective Bargaining in the Framework of Social Europe", in G. Spyropoulos and G. Fragnière (eds.), Work and Social Policies in the New Europe (European Interuniversity Press. Brussels, 1991), 59.
27. For a comprehensive analysis of this strategy, see European Commission, "Report of the High Level Group on Industrial Relations and Change in the European Union" (Office for Official Publications of the European Communities, Luxembourg 2002); see also C. de la Porte and P. Pochet, "Supple Co-ordination at EU Level and the Key Actors' Involvement", in C. de la Porte and P. Pochet (eds.), Building Social Europe through the Open Method of Coordination (Interuniversity Press, Brussels, 2002), 27.
28. For a very reliable assessment of this development, see J. Goetschy, "European Employment Policy since the 1990s", in Keller and Platzer, Industrial Relations, 137.
29. For a description of the debates leading to this development, see M. Weiss, "Workers' Participation in the European Union", in P. Davies et al. (eds.) European Community Labour Law – Principles and Perspectives (Clarendon Press, Oxford, 1996), 213.
30. OJ 1975 No. L48.

31. OJ 1977 No. L61.

32. OJ 1989 No. L183/1.

33. OJ 1994 No. L254/64.

34. For recent assessments of the factual implementation of the directive, see S. Demetriades, "European Works Councils Directive: A Success Story ?", in Biagi, *Quality of Work*, 49, and T. Müller and H.W. Platzer, "European Works Councils: A New Mode of EU Regulation and the Emergence of a European Multi-level Structure of Workplace Industrial Relations", in Keller and Platzer, *Industrial Relations*, 58.

35. For this effect see Sewerynski, "Employee Involvement", 272.

36. OJ 2001 No. L294/22.

37. For a first evaluation of the directive, see M. Weiss, "Workers' Involvement in the European Company", in Biagi, *Quality of Work*, 63.

38. OJ 2002 No. L80/29.

39. See S. Clauwaert and W. Düvel, "The implementation of the social acquis communautaire in Central and Estern Europe", *ETUI Interim Report*, (European Trade Union Institute, Brussels, 2000).

40. Ladó and Vaughan-Whitehead, "Social dialogue", 80.

41. Ladó and Vaughan-Whitehead, "Social dialogue", 80.

42. Ladó and Vaughan-Whitehead, "Social dialogue", 80.

43. This view is shared by Ladó and Vaughan-Whitehead, see "Social dialogue", 83.

7

Trends and challenges of labour law in Central Europe

ARTURO BRONSTEIN

Introduction

This paper considers the evolution of labour laws in ten Central European countries since they abandoned communist rule at the beginning of the last decade. In alphabetical order these countries are Bulgaria, Czech Republic, Estonia, Hungary, Latvia, Lithuania, Poland, Romania, Slovakia, and Slovenia. In the aftermath of the downfall of communism, all ten countries shared common goals of establishing political democracy, developing a market economy and eventually joining the European Union. In the early 1990s, each applied for EU membership. At its meeting in Copenhagen in 1993, the Council of the European Union decided to welcome their candidatures provided that the EU was satisfied that the applicant countries fulfilled the following criteria (commonly referred to as the "Criteria of Copenhagen "):

Political criteria : stability of institutions guaranteeing democracy, the
    rule of law, human rights and respect for and protection of minorities;
Economic criteria: a functioning market economy as well as the capacity
    to cope with competitive pressure and market forces within the Union;
Institutional criteria: the ability to take on the obligations of membership
    including adherence to the aims of political, economic and monetary
    union, and the transposition of the *acquis communautaire* into the
    national law.

Substantial Community assistance was placed at the disposal of the candidate countries to help them build the capacity required to meet the Criteria of Copenhagen, and the European Commission regularly monitored and assessed their progress. In 2002, the European Union took the view that eight of the Central European candidate countries had met the Criteria of Copenhagen. The exceptions were Bulgaria and Romania, whose political, economic and institutional achievements were considered as lagging behind those of the other countries. On 23 April 2003, the Treaty of Accession was signed in Athens between the fifteen European Union member states and the eight Central European candidate countries that met the Criteria of Copenhagen, together with Cyprus and Malta. After ratification of the Treaty all of these countries officially joined the European Union on 1 May 2004. The applications of Bulgaria and Romania are currently being reassessed, with the expectation that they will join in 2007, together with Croatia which has also been invited to submit its candidature. So far the candidature of another prospective member, Turkey, remains on hold. However, Turkey has been encouraged to intensify and accelerate its political and institutional reform process so as to bring the country closer to EU patterns and eventually join the EU.

The first part of this paper will provide an overview of the labour law patterns that prevailed in Central European countries at the time of the demise of communism. The second part will focus on the challenges these countries faced when they abandoned communism, and the steps they undertook with a view to working out a suitable legal framework for labour market reform and for the organization of sound labour relations within a functioning economy and a democratic society. Within this framework I will consider the position of labour law in these countries vis-à-vis European Community Law (EC Law) and ILO Standards. The final part will address outstanding labour law challenges facing these countries.

Legal systems at the end of the old regime

The ten Central European countries discussed in this paper did not form a homogeneous group when the communist regime came to an end. Countries such as Hungary and Poland had already begun to undertake economic reforms before the downfall of communism, decentralizing decision-making processes and allowing room for private business in commerce, the service sector and agriculture. Conversely, in the three Baltic States (Estonia, Latvia and Lithuania), which had been annexed by the Soviet Union in the early 1940s, Soviet rule applied until independence, and the economy was managed under Soviet-style central planning. To a large extent, rigid central planning and very tight political control over the population were also the prevailing patterns in Bulgaria and Romania, while in the Czech Republic some softening of the regime was already underway when communism collapsed in 1991. Slovenia offered yet another picture. Administrative and management decentralization were important features of Titoist Yugoslavia, making Slovenia, and to a lesser extent Croatia, by far the most developed and Western-looking republics. The legal settings of these countries were also quite varied. The Baltic States, Slovenia, the Czech Republic and the Slovak Republic gained their independence only after the end of communism, which meant that legislation and international obligations of the pre-independence era applied and in certain cases still apply in some of these countries. Overall, three distinct situations emerge, as follows:

• the Baltic States, which had internationally recognized legal status until military occupation and annexation by the Soviet Union in the late thirties;
• the countries which formerly belonged to a wider entity: Slovenia, which was part of the Socialist Federal Republic of Yugoslavia[1], the Czech Republic and the Slovak Republic, which together formed Czechoslovakia; and
• the remaining countries, which did not experience territorial changes at the time of the demise of their communist regimes: Bulgaria, Hungary, Poland and Romania.

At the time of independence in the Baltic states, the basis of the legal system was provided by the laws that then applied in the Soviet Union. In the field of labour law, the legal system was the Code of the Soviet Union, promulgated in 1970 (the so-called "Fundamentals"). These laws were progressively repealed as the Baltic States adopted their own legislation. Regarding international obligations vis-à-vis the ILO, the three Baltic states did not consider themselves bound by the conventions that had been ratified by the former Soviet Union and that had applied in their territory prior to independence. Instead, they confirmed their acceptance of the conventions they had ratified as independent ILO Members before occupation by the Soviet Union,[2] examining the remaining conventions on a case-by-case basis.

Slovenia followed a different approach, accepting the international obligations that applied in its territory before it declared independence from Yugoslavia. It also continued to apply former Yugoslav law, which it progressively repealed and replaced by new legislation. Likewise, the Czech Republic and the Republic of Slovakia also confirmed the validity of both international obligations and federal legislation that applied in the territory of the former Czechoslovakia before it split into two countries.

The third sub-group (Bulgaria, Hungary, Poland and Romania) was made up of states that changed only their political regimes. Because they kept their territorial integrity and statehood, they did not need to address any particular legal problem arising out of a change in international legal status, which meant that all existing international obligations were to be honoured and all existing legislation continued to apply until repealed by new laws.

Some shared patterns

Despite these differences, at the downfall of communism labour laws in all of these countries shared a number of patterns that related closely to the nature of the political and economic system. Labour law was premised on the assumption that the overwhelming pattern of employment was based on a subordinated, permanent and full-time employment relationship, and that work was mainly organized within the framework of large production units or large administrations. There were very few distinctions, if any, between private sector employees and state employees, given that workers in both categories had the same employer and the same kind of employment relationship. On issues such as recruitment and termination of employment, heavy bureaucratic rules and procedures applied, affording far-reaching guarantees to the workers while giving great say to the state-party dominated unions. Discipline at work and penalties for infringement of internal rules, favourite fields for Soviet-minded labour law, were addressed by detailed regulation.[3] The law frequently provided for the settlement of industrial disputes primarily at the workplace level by ad hoc commissions made up of representatives of both labour and management, with a further possibility of appeal.

Another feature of communist-minded labour law was its highly centralized pay structure, which did not take into account structural and market factors. At least in theory, centralized pay structures resulted in relatively narrow disparities in remuneration throughout the different economic sectors. This was not so true in practice, however. For example, when the labour market experienced a structural shortage of manpower, the leading state enterprises were obliged to offer various kinds of bonuses and pay premiums to attract or retain workers.

By far the most significant differences between the labour law systems of Central Europe and those of Western Europe existed in the field of collective labour relations. The shared pattern in Central Europe was the single-union structure. Union membership was quasi-compulsory, indeed necessary, for workers, given that unions were entrusted with the administration of a very large share of the welfare system. Moreover, unions were meant to act primarily as a mechanism for transmitting and implementing policies and decisions taken by the state-party structure.[4]

Although collective bargaining existed formally, its major purpose was to allocate respective responsibilities to management and the workforce in order to meet the production targets of the enterprise within the centralized planning system. Not surprisingly, collective bargaining was carried out at the enterprise level, and strikes were considered a form of sabotage against the state.

The evolution after the demise of communism: major trends

Since the downfall of communism in the new Central European EU members and candidate countries, labour law reform has followed three major trends: (1) the personal scope of labour law has narrowed; (2) the content of labour law has been enriched; and (3) the industrial relations system has been liberalized.

Narrowing the personal scope of labour law stems from the emergence of diverse employment relations and patterns of employment. When the economy was essentially in the hands of the state and operated under a central planning system, there was no real need to make any distinction between the status of civil servants in the public administration and private-law workers in the production sector, given that the latter was also run by the state, indeed, in a very bureaucratic manner. However, the introduction of a market economy and the overall reform of the state in Central Europe led to the recognition of diverse kinds of employment. In market economies, employees may work for a private sector employer, or in government administration, or in public agencies or administrations that do not perform government functions. It follows that labour law applies to the first category of workers only, while public law governs the relations between the state and civil servants, or at least certain categories of government employees. Depending upon the legal and administrative systems of each country, a third and distinct regulation may address the employment relations of employees in the so-called *peripheral administrations*. For example, since 1992, the legislative system of Hungary has included three major Acts covering the individual employment relationship and industrial relations in three categories of employee: (1) employees working in private employment, to whom the Labour Code applies; (2) public employees working for publicly financed institutions such as schools, hospitals, libraries, etc.; and (3) civil servants. Similarly, in Estonia, the law respecting contracts of employment, enacted in 1992, does not apply to civil servants under the Public Service Law who work on the basis of a contract of service.[5] It is possible, however, that some private sector employees work in a public administration or a peripheral administration and would thereby fall under the scope of labour law. In such cases, collective bargaining rights would commonly be addressed by ad hoc regulations.

A second reason that the personal scope of labour law has narrowed is the increase in self-employment that has occurred in all former centrally planned economies. Labour law applies only to workers with employment status. In principle, those who have no formally recognized employment relationship are beyond its scope. It follows that there are considerably fewer potential "customers" of labour law in the new Central European EU members and candidate countries compared to the number of employees to whom labour laws applied under the old regimes. Furthermore, as has recently been suggested by some research undertaken by the International Labour Organization, a growing pattern of hidden or disguised employment, as well as the performance of dependent work outside the scope of an employment relationship, have become features of employment in former Central European communist countries.[6] This is not unlike the circumstances that have emerged in both North America and Western Europe.

While the personal scope of labour law in the new Central European EU members and candidate countries has narrowed, by contrast, the content has been enriched considerably with the introduction of concepts, unknown during the communist regime, related to collective labour relations (social dialogue, freedom of association, free collective bargaining, plant level workers' representation, industrial action) and the individual contract of employment. Issues such as different forms of contract of employment, hiring and termination procedures, transfer of enterprises, modifications in the contract of employment, protection of remuneration, and the effects of an employer's insolvency on the contract of employment, normally need to be addressed in a market economy. Such concepts and issues may be unknown or irrelevant in centrally planned and state-run economies. The need to transpose the *acquis communataire* has also played a major role in this process of enrichment, as the candidate countries have been required to adopt legislation to implement EC law. In addition, the process of labour law reform has been very intensive in areas that, although not addressed by EC law, require regulation for the sake of better and fairer governance of the labour market.

The choice of a model

The adoption of neo-liberal thinking in most, if not all, of the former communist countries has led to the introduction of far-reaching deregulation in labour markets, on the ground that so-called *labour flexibility* would be indispensable in order to increase export-oriented competitiveness, attract foreign investment and create employment opportunities in the emerging private sector. Similar pressures have also come from international moneylenders. To be sure, the idea that flexibility-oriented reforms can contribute substantially to improving the competitiveness of these countries, attract foreign investment and create employment is supported by theoretical analysis and econometric models while it is not by empirical evidence. In fact, it is very likely that the greatest competitive edge enjoyed by Central European countries arises from their relatively low minimum and average wage rates, rather than from any hypothetical low level of their labour standards. At the same time, it is undisputed that highly skilled labour is available in these countries.

It is also true that communist-minded legislation overprotected the individual worker and left management with very few rights to run a competitive organization. Such legislation also put rigid constraints on the functioning of labour relations systems based on the principles of freedom of association and of collective bargaining. With the introduction of a freer collective labour relations system, it became necessary for legislators to review individual labour laws and bring them closer to what was considered the accepted *wisdom* in market economies.

The dominant issue, therefore, became how to choose a workable approach for policy-makers and lawmakers to regulate the labour market within the parameters of a market economy. In view of the weakness, if not the lack, of credible social partners, it was unrealistic to entrust labour market regulation to collective bargaining or other forms of joint decision-making (a practice which, incidentally, prevails in some Nordic countries and Belgium although not in other Western European countries, e.g. the United Kingdom). In practice, all of the former communist countries were required to choose between the essentially *market-minded* Anglo-American model and the essentially *institutionally-minded* Western European approach. Although many of the Central European countries felt strong ideological, and sometimes international financial pressure to adopt a market-minded model, each finally chose the Western European institutionally-minded approach. Such a model was not only closer to their own legal and historical traditions, but also permitted these countries to take into consideration the *acquis communautaire* – i.e. EC law and regulations, including decisions by the European Court of Justice (ECJ) – which they were required to transpose into their national law as a precondition to joining the European Union. In practice, most of these countries looked to German legislation as a reference for their own laws. Many benefited from expertise provided by German and sometimes French experts. Many others received technical advice from the International Labour Organization.

The transposition of the acquis communautaire

To date, the greatest challenge faced by any of these countries has arisen from the need to transpose the so-called *acquis communautaire* into their labour law, one of the preconditions for entry into the EU referenced in the Criteria of Copenhagen.

EC Law is made up of primary regulation (the treaties[7] and, very likely, *jus cogens*) and secondary regulation (EC regulations and directives, and, in practice, rulings of the ECJ). Whereas the treaties and their amendments become binding on EU members only upon ratification, EC regulations and directives are supranational law and do not require ratification to enter into force. Regulations are directly applicable in member states and have general effect. Most regulations contain rules that are essentially technical and only one of them, on Free Movement of Workers within the Community,[8] is really relevant in the labour law field. By contrast, under the EC Treaty, the European Community has been endowed with significant law-making powers in many areas and the catalogue of EC directives in the labour law field is now quite extensive.[9] Directives are binding as to the result to be achieved upon each member state to which they are addressed, but they leave to the national authorities the choice of form and methods. This does not mean, however, that directives have no direct binding effect. Under the preliminary ruling procedure (Article 234 of the EC Treaty), the ECJ has repeatedly instructed national courts to set aside national laws or regulations, including collective agreements, and sometimes even certain practices, that contradicted an EC Directive. Moreover, the effects of EC directives are both *vertical* and *horizontal*; even when they have not been transposed, they may be invoked by individuals against the state as well as between individuals. The ECJ has also ruled that a member state is required to compensate individuals for loss and damage caused by the state's failure to transpose a directive.[10]

Additionally, the ECJ has consistently reaffirmed the direct binding effect of the treaties. In this respect, it is important to recall that the EC Treaty contains core rules relating to freedom of movement for workers (Article 39, formerly Article 48), discrimination (Articles 12 and 13, ex Articles 6 and 6 a) and equal pay (Article 141, ex Article 119). The ECJ has developed extensive case law on the basis of the EC Treaty, especially in the field of equal pay for work of equal value.

The influence of ILO standards and principles on freedom of association and collective bargaining

The third trend in the evolution of labour law in Central European countries relates to the liberalization of the industrial relations systems. Chronologically, this trend was the first to emerge, given that each of the former communist countries experienced political changes well before economic reforms. It is not surprising, therefore, that in the period between 1989 and 1993 most of these countries undertook a first wave of labour law reforms which focused on collective labour relations. Such reforms drew inspiration from ILO Conventions Nos. 87 and 98, as well as from the doctrine of the ILO supervisory bodies on freedom of association and collective bargaining.

The general aim of the reforms was to establish collective representation and collective bargaining structures inspired by reflecting the prevailing industry-based patterns in Western Europe. To a large extent, the German model has served as a reference. This model allocates very distinct faculties and prerogatives respectively to industry-based unions and plant-level works councils. It should be observed, however, that such an approach has not yet been confirmed in practice, as in most Central European countries industry-based collective labour relations are insufficiently developed. This has led to the relocation of the core of industrial relations interactions either upwards to the central level or downwards to the enterprise level, in which case there is some room for conflict between trade unions and non-unionized staff representative bodies.[11]

Czechoslovakia adopted a Collective Bargaining Act in 1991 after former communist trade union regulation was repealed so that the right to form workers' and employers' associations became regulated under a law enacted in 1990. Estonia adopted a new law on trade unions in 1989, and a law on collective labour disputes in 1993. In Hungary, the right to strike was already addressed in a law adopted in 1989. Lithuania adopted a law on collective agreements on 4 April 1991 and a law on collective disputes in 1992. In Poland, two Acts of 1991 regulated trade unions and employers' associations respectively, while a third law addressed the settlement of collective labour disputes. In 1994, an amendment to the Labour Code dealt with collective agreements. In Romania, three laws adopted in 1991, 1996 and 1999 addressed trade unions, collective agreements, and the settlement of industrial disputes respectively. In Slovenia, a 1993 law already established criteria to determine trade union representativeness

A never-ending process of labour law reform

The wave of reforms now underway appears aimed at meeting two different challenges. The first and best known is the transposition of the *acquis communautaire* into national labour law systems. All the new EU members claim that they have already enacted the required laws and regulations. The second challenge arises from the need to adjust labour laws to respond to the same changes and challenges which all European societies currently face and which require striking a fair balance between market constraints and social concerns.

Adjusting labour laws to the social and economic environment would seem to be a never-ending task, not only because the environment constantly changes, but also because government strategies and political options also tend to change with each change in government. This often results in wide-ranging government proposals to amend labour laws; so-called *business friendly* reforms in some cases, and so-called *labour friendly* reforms in other cases. Reforms in Hungary in 2001 and 2002 and in Poland in 2002 provide noteworthy examples of these tendencies. Similarly, in Slovakia a new Labour Code, adopted in 2001, was amended even before it entered into force in April 2002. Yet another reform process was carried out and completed in 2003, after the government that won the election the previous year determined that the Code was not flexible enough to encourage private initiative. In Lithuania, despite a new Labour Code adopted in 2003 consolidating a number of reforms undertaken since 1991, a committee is already working out proposals to regulate different types of contracts of employment that deviate from the so-called standard employment relationship. Work on reforms to the law on trade unions and on a new law addressing pay indexation is also underway. In Romania, business circles and international financial institutions are currently challenging the Labour Code adopted in December 2002. Finally, the Czech Republic envisages adopting a new Labour Code by 2005.

Some remnants from the past

Despite the market economy orientation of the reforms, labour legislation still includes a number of remnants from the old regulatory regimes. A tacit assumption that labour law primarily addresses employment relations in large organizations would seem to be a widely shared approach. In fact, apart from some rules on the use and the renewal of fixed-term contracts of employment (for example in Slovakia), it is hard to find special provisions addressing small enterprises. The lack of ad hoc rules for small enterprises is especially noteworthy with respect to termination of employment. Some countries have considered it indispensable to include rules in their labour codes concerning appointment or promotion by competition, or the contract of employment of individuals who have been appointed to a job by popular election.[12] Some include provisions prohibiting the appointment of relatives of employees in state or municipal enterprises, while others still provide for detailed disciplinary procedures.[13] Such rules normally belong to the domain of civil service staff regulations, and would seem misplaced in private labour law. Also noteworthy in Central Europe are the detailed provisions on civil liability of employees that exist in a number of labour laws. Elsewhere this question is generally addressed under civil law.[14] Another remnant of old labour regulation is the employee's record book,[15] although it would seem that it now serves merely an administrative function. This would certainly not raise the same objections now that it raised during the old regime, when it implied a threat to workers whose political opinions deviated from the official wisdom. It is also worth noting that some existing provisions may eventually come under the scrutiny of the European Commission or the ECJ on the ground that they discriminate against women; for example, provisions that prohibit underground work by women, or state that women may not be employed in work *that is harmful to their body*.[16] Finally, several labour codes still provide for the settlement of labour disputes by enterprise-level labour dispute commissions, with a possibility for further appeal before the judiciary, as was the practice during the communist regimes.[17]

The current structure of labour law in Central European countries

Like most of Western Europe, Central European countries share the Roman-Germanic legal tradition. Hence, law-making essentially follows a top-down process. Labour regulation consists of statutory law, and the state is the usual initiator of the labour law reform process.[18] The labour law systems in all Central European countries recognize the distinction between collective and individual labour relations although in several countries they are both integrated in a single legal instrument, typically a labour code.

Unlike in Western Europe, codification is common in Central Europe, although some countries do not have labour codes.[19] However, even where such codes exist, they are not *codes* in the sense of the French codification and it is common for separate laws on a number of issues to exist alongside the Labour Code (especially to address collective labour relations). Many labour codes formally date back to the old regime: 1965 in Czechoslovakia, 1974 in Poland, 1986 in Bulgaria. In the early seventies, the Baltic countries adopted labour codes based on the Fundamentals of Labour Legislation of the former Soviet Union. Slovenian labour law followed a different pattern, as the former Yugoslavia had a peculiar system of self-management and social ownership that had an important legal bearing on labour regulation. All of these codes have been revised extensively since the early nineties. Thus, in practice it would not make much sense to continue to refer to them as the codes adopted in the sixties or seventies, as is still the case in some countries.[20] In any event, whether these are new codes, like those of Lithuania, Slovakia or Romania, consolidated texts of legislation more or less recently adopted, or separate texts of laws, the legislative drafting process has generally been very careful. The existing legal texts are coherent, well-structured, systematic and fairly easy to understand, even in their translated versions.

Individual labour relations are based on the private law concept of the contract of employment or the employment relationship, which presupposes legal subordination of the employee vis-à-vis his or her employer, with reciprocal rights and obligations on each side of the contract. It is legally presumed that a contract of employment is entered into for an unlimited duration, and in a majority of countries the possibility of concluding fixed-term contracts of employment is restricted by law (although recent reforms have eased the use of such contracts). As in Western Europe, termination of employment is extensively regulated; none of the Central European countries has followed the US doctrine of employment at will.

Provisions on collective labour relations address collective bargaining and agreements as well as the settlement of industrial disputes and strikes. By contrast, labour law does not always address trade union regulation. In some countries, trade unions are simply civil associations under the civil law; consequently, there is no need for a specific trade union law. In a few cases, for example in Poland, there is a special law on employers' associations.

Under the legal systems in these countries, collective agreements bind the parties and those whom the parties represent. In all countries, it is legally possible for a collective agreement to be extended so that it becomes binding on third parties as well. However, extension calls for a number of conditions relating to the level of the collective agreement (in principle only sector-level or national-level agreements can be extended) and representativeness of the parties that are seldom met in practice.

Some particular issues

Contract of employment

The contract of employment, or the employment relationship, forms the basis of what are commonly referred to as *individual employment relations.* The law may provide for a legal definition of the contract of employment and such definitions in comparative law are diverse. Neither the ILO nor the EC legal systems undertake to define the contract of employment; instead, they assume that the relevant national law will do so. Some national laws include such definitions, while others do not. However, all national laws must address certain issues relating to the form of the contract of employment, and most if not all of the labour laws in Central European countries demand that a written contract formalize the employment relationship. It is worth noting, however, that under EC law the employer is only required to provide an employee with *written particulars of the essential aspects of the contract of employment.*[21]

The most controversial issues related to the contract of employment concern hiring procedures, probation, fixed-term employment relationships, supply of labour by third parties, so-called *atypical employment relationships,* and termination of employment and protection against unjustified dismissal. Although some of these issues have been addressed by labour law in the new Central European EU members and candidate countries, others have not. Aspects of fixed-term employment and termination of employment (collective dismissals) are addressed by EC Directives and the ILO has adopted international standards on certain forms of supply of labour by third parties (i.e. temporary employment agencies), part-time work, and individual and collective termination of employment.[22]

Hiring procedures

Two issues are relevant to this subject, and relate respectively to the role of public and private employment services in the supply of manpower to enterprises, and the measures that should be taken under national law to guarantee that job applicants do not experience discrimination on grounds that are prohibited under EC law or national law. The first issue will be addressed in this section. The second will be dealt with in a subsequent section on discrimination issues.

Private and public intermediation in recruitment

For decades, and for a number of historical reasons, it was common in many countries for placement to be the exclusive responsibility of the state. Pursuant to the adoption of three ILO conventions in the 1930s and 1940s, many countries established public service employment offices and took steps to prohibit placement by fee-charging private employment agencies.

This tendency was subsequently reversed, however. Since the early 1980s, private intermediation in the labour market has been recognized to have a legitimate role alongside the public sector. While there is no EC law on this subject, the ECJ has taken the view that under certain circumstances state monopoly in placement is incompatible with Articles 82 (formerly Article 86) and 86 (formerly Article 90) of the EC Treaty, concerning competition, taxation and approximation of laws (Title VI, formerly Title V).[23] Moreover, after reviewing its previous position on the restriction or prohibition of private employment agencies, in 1997 the ILO adopted the Private Employment Agencies Convention (No. 181). Together with its accompanying recommendation (No. 188), this offers a suitable framework for member states to organize labour market intermediation activities. Some of the new Central European EU members and candidate countries, however, remain bound by the old ILO conventions that provide for the prohibition of private employment agencies, something which they probably should review in light of both the aforementioned decisions by the ECJ and ILO Convention No. 181.[24]

Fixed-term contracts of employment

As stated above, a common but not universal approach in labour law is for the term of a contract of employment to be of an indefinite duration. However, in many circumstances employers may have temporary manpower needs. Also, in certain sectors, occupations and activities, fixed-term employment contracts may better suit the needs of both employers and workers. In principle, the use of fixed-term contracts in such circumstances should not be controversial. Conversely, the use of fixed-term contracts to hire workers to perform permanent tasks on a permanent basis is particularly controversial, especially where such contracts are used primarily to deny workers rights that would otherwise be granted in a permanent employment relationship.

The use of fixed-term contracts of employment is a new issue in Central European countries. The overwhelming pattern of employment under communist regimes was one in which workers benefited from job secu-rity and permanent employment in state-owned organizations. Moreover, structural shortage of labour was a widespread feature in most centrally planned economies. In practice, this meant that enterprises were much more interested in maintaining their workforces than downsizing them. A dramatic change occurred, however, when these countries adopted a market economy, privatized state enterprises and undertook far-reaching structural changes. Such activities not only had an impact on the employ-ment of workers, but also raised the need to reassess and revise rules and regulations governing the contract of employment. Against this back-drop, fixed-term employment, together with termination of employ-ment, arguably became the most controversial and emotional issue to be addressed within labour law reform.

All Central European countries have introduced significant flexibility into their hiring and termination practices. Such flexibility includes the use of fixed-term employment. Nonetheless, the allegation remains that they have not done enough and pressure has been put on governments to move further to deregulate the contract of employment. It should be recalled, however, that policy-makers and lawmakers in EU candidate countries did not have unlimited capacity to regulate this issue for they were bound by EC law which demands, at a minimum, that national law provide for safeguards to ensure compliance with EC directives on, inter alia, fixed-term employment, transfer of enterprises and collective redundancies.[25] Latvia and Slovenia are further bound by the ILO Ter-mination of Employment Convention, 1982 (No. 158), which both have ratified.

It is beyond the scope of this paper to discuss the ideas forwarded by those favouring and opposing liberalizing the use of fixed-term con-tracts. It is worth noting, however, that this issue is closely connected to protection against unjust dismissal, given that workers hired under fixed-term arrangements do not enjoy such protection. This suggests that an employer's need to use fixed-term arrangements increases proportion-ately with the level of protection against dismissal that the law affords to permanent workers, and decreases when such protection lessens. In fact, all governments that have promoted reforms to expand the use of fixed-term contracts have claimed that the prevailing model of permanent employment, with its far-reaching protection against dismissal, creates rigidities that are not compatible with an economic environment that is highly competitive and also highly unpredictable. A further assumption is that far-reaching employment security acts to deter hiring; employers fear that it would be difficult to dismiss redundant employees in the event of an economic downturn. The fact that no reliable data has been collected in support of these assumptions does not mean that they should be dismissed lightly.[26]

Fixed-term contracts of employment are addressed under EC law by Council Directive 1999/70/EC of 28 June 1999, which has given binding effect pursuant to a framework agreement concluded by both sides of industry at the European level.[27] This agreement acknowledges that "employment contracts of an indefinite duration are the general form of employment relationships and contribute to the quality of life of the workers concerned and improve performance" (general considerations, para 6). The agreement requires EU members to take measures, first to prevent fixed-term workers from being discriminated against solely because they have a fixed-term contract or relation, and second to prevent abuse arising from the use of successive fixed-terms contracts or relationships.[28] Other provisions state that employers should facilitate access to training for fixed-term employees, and should inform these workers about the vacancies that become available in the enterprise. Fixed-term employees must also be taken into consideration for the purposes of calculating the threshold above which workers' representative bodies may be constituted in the enterprise.

Apart from the directive, EU members have wide discretion on the actual regulation of fixed-term contracts of employment. Not surprisingly, approaches under national labour law are diverse. One major difference relates to the grounds for recourse to fixed-term contracts. In some countries, this is left open with the sole proviso that recourse to fixed-term employment shall be justified "on an objective reason". In others (including a majority of Central European countries[29]), the use of such contracts is restricted to a pre-established list. A third option consists in leaving the use of fixed-term contracts to the discretion of the employer, subject to certain restrictions referring to the maximum length and the number of renewals, as required under the EC framework agreement. In any event, it should be kept in mind that the framework agreement recalls that "the use of fixed-term contracts based on objective reasons is a way to prevent abuses" (General considerations, No. 7). While regulating this issue, consideration should also be given to the ILO Termination of Employment Convention, 1982 (No. 158), whereby "adequate safeguards shall be provided against recourse to contracts of employment for a specified period of time, where the aim is to avoid the protection resulting from this Convention" (i.e. protection against unjustified dismissal).[30]

It follows that there is no single European approach to regulating fixed-term contracts of employment. Within the framework that is set up by international and community law, each country remains at liberty to design its own policy addressing this point.

Temporary agency work

The basic feature of temporary work is the "triangular relationship" between a user undertaking, an employee and an intermediary. A temporary agency worker enters into a contract of employment with an agency, which then dispatches the worker to perform work for a third party, the user enterprise. The latter assigns the worker's tasks and supervises the execution of the work. The formal employment relationship remains with the agency, which assumes the responsibilities of the employer vis-à-vis the worker as well as third parties, in particular the social security institutions.

Temporary agency work is an important feature of the labour market in several EU Member states. According to a 1999 study published by the European Foundation for the Improvement of Living and Working Conditions, temporary work had a participation rate of 1.4 per cent of equivalent full-time employment throughout the European Union. The highest rates of participation of temporary work in the labour market were found in the Netherlands (4 per cent), Luxembourg (3.5 per cent), France (2.7 per cent) and the UK (2.1 per cent), while in Germany, Italy and Spain it accounted only for 0.7, 0.2 and 0.8 per cent of equivalent full-time employment, respectively.[31]

Temporary work has frequently been associated with lack of integration in the enterprise, emotional stress due to the volatility of employment, poor working conditions, exposure to occupational hazards and vulnerability to various abuses. Bad practices and trafficking of manpower have further contributed to the negative image of temporary work, especially in the 1960s and 1970s. This in turn provided grounds for several European governments to take measures to prohibit or tightly regulate the practice. Since then, however, many of the problems associated with temporary work have been overcome. To a great extent this has been due to the combined action of state regulation and state labour inspection, social dialogue, collective bargaining and the efforts that the professional associations of temporary work enterprises have made to impose an ethos on their profession. As very few of the new Central European EU members and candidate countries have regulated temporary agency work,[32] it would seem important that they consider the usefulness of establishing a regulatory framework within which such work could evolve.

Regulatory approaches to temporary agency work vary within the European Union. Some countries have very limited specific regulations (e.g. Denmark, Ireland, the UK) while some others have more or less detailed regulation on this question (e.g. Belgium, France, Germany and Spain). Social dialogue, collective bargaining and corporate codes of conduct have also played an important role in regulating temporary work. Where regulations exist, their aims are to establish administrative supervision of the temporary work agency and protecting temporary workers. Administrative authorization or licensing of temporary work agencies is mandatory in Austria, Belgium, France, Germany, Italy, Portugal and Spain, but not in the Netherlands. A number of countries make licensing conditional on the temporary work enterprise providing a financial guarantee to ensure that obligations vis-à-vis the workers and third parties (e.g. social security) will be met. Protection of temporary agency workers can cover a wide variety of issues, including the obligation of a written contract, wage and paid leave entitlements, maternity leave, training, trade union rights, and protection against occupational hazards.

EC regulation of temporary agency work consists of a directive addressing certain aspects of safety and health of fixed-term and temporary workers.[33] The purpose of this is to ensure that fixed-term and temporary agency workers will receive the same level of safety and health protection afforded to regular workers of the user enterprise. This directive authorizes EU members to prohibit assigning fixed-term or temporary agency workers to work that poses a particular danger to their safety or health, and particularly to certain work that requires special medical surveillance, as defined in national legislation. Preparation of a second directive addressing working conditions for temporary workers is now underway and a proposal has already been disclosed by the Commission.

Temporary work is also addressed by the ILO Private Employment Agencies Convention, 1997 (No. 181)[34] and its accompanying Recommendation No. 188, from which member states may draw very useful guidance to regulate this matter. Under Convention No. 181, it is not mandatory for temporary work agencies to be licensed, provided that adequate regulation exists. In addition, a member that ratifies the Convention must take the necessary measures to ensure adequate protection for temporary agency workers in relation to freedom of association, collective bargaining, minimum wage, working time and other working conditions, statutory social security benefits, access to training, occupational safety and health, compensation in case of occupational accidents or diseases, compensation in case of insolvency and protection of workers claims, maternity protection and benefits, and parental protection and benefits. To this end, the ratifying state must determine and allocate the respective responsibilities of the temporary work agency and the user enterprises in relation to most of these issues. The exception is freedom of association, which enjoys an absolute guarantee. The convention also guarantees other rights, as follows: (1) workers shall not be discriminated against on the basis of race, colour, sex, religion, political opinion, national extraction, social origin, or any other form of discrimination covered by national law and practice, such as age or disability; (2) they shall not have to pay fees to temporary work agencies for the placement services that they receive; and (3) measures shall be taken to protect the personal data of workers that may have been gathered by the temporary work agency.[35] Amongst other provisions, the recommendation adds that private employment agencies should not knowingly recruit for, or place workers in jobs involving unacceptable hazards or risks or where they may be subjected to abuse or discriminatory treatment of any kind. The recommendation also foresees that temporary agency workers should, where appropriate, have a written contract of employment specifying their terms and conditions of employment. At a minimum, these workers should be informed of their conditions of employment before beginning their work assignments. Additionally, temporary work enterprises should not make workers available to a user enterprise to replace striking workers of that enterprise.

Dependent work under civil or commercial contracts

The use of civil or commercial contracts in lieu of a contract of employment raises a different kind of problem. At stake is the recognition of labour law protection and, frequently, of social security protection for workers who perform tasks or provide services for a third party under objective conditions of dependency. Misclassification, disguised employment relationships and grey areas between what constitutes dependent and independent work contribute to this phenomenon, which in most countries is very likely on the increase. The existence of this problem is being increasingly acknowledged. A recent study by the European Foundation for the Improvement of Living and Working Conditions on "Economically dependent workers, employment law and industrial relations"[36] has undertaken a comparative overview of this phenomenon in the EU and Norway and on its effects on the protection of workers. Data gathered by the ILO also shows that this problem is widely shared by most of the new Central European EU members and candidate countries.

Several countries have already addressed the issue and worked out rules that establish criteria for distinguishing between dependent and independent employment. Case law has added further criteria for establishing when these workers should be recognized as having employee status. Social dialogue has also put this problem on its agenda, leading to some very encouraging results.[37] The ILO addressed this question at its 91st Session in June 2003, in which an agenda item on the Employment Relationship was included for a General Discussion.[38] This led to the adoption of conclusions that inter alia, proposed that the ILO adopt a recommendation centred on disguised employment.[39] In March 2004 the ILO Governing Body decided to include this point in the Agenda of the 94th Session of the ILO Conference, to be held in June 2006.

Termination of employment

Two conflicting approaches to termination of employment exist in comparative labour law. On the one hand, there is the US doctrine of employment at will which was formulated in 19th Century US case law. According to this doctrine, which despite many exceptions[40] remains the basic rule in the United States, an employer may terminate the employment of an employee without notice at any time, *whether with good reason, with bad reason or with no reason at all.* By contrast, in a majority of countries in the world, the rule is that a worker's employment cannot be terminated unless there is a ground for termination relating to the conduct or the capacity of the worker, or connected to the economic situation of the enterprise.

The Charter of Fundamental Rights of the European Union has endorsed the latter approach. Article 30 states that every worker has the right to protection against unjustified dismissal, in accordance with Community law and national laws and practices. The implementation of this principle is left to the discretion of EU member states and each must adopt rules to address collective terminations on economic grounds in keeping with Council Directive 98/59/EC of 20 July 1998 on the approximation of the laws of the member states relating to collective redundancies.[41] In addition, countries that have ratified the ILO Termination of Employment Convention, 1982 (No. 158)[42] must take measures to protect employees against unjust termination. Unlike EC law, ILO Convention No. 158 addresses both individual and collective termination of employment.

Although most countries have taken measures to protect workers against unjust dismissal, approaches in comparative law are diverse on issues such as procedures for termination, financial consequences of termination, recourses in case a worker challenges his or her termination, and avenues for redress. Arguably, the most controversial issue concerns the remedies that can be ordered by a tribunal or labour court that, on appeal, has determined that the termination was unjustified. In some countries, the tribunal can decide that the termination is void, and order that the worker be reinstated with back pay.[43] In other countries it can decide that the termination is unjustified but not void, in which case only financial compensation will be required. In a third group of countries, the tribunal is given the right to choose between ordering reinstatement or compensation.[44] A further possibility may consist in the tribunal establishing a distinction in the grounds of the termination, declaring the termination void only when it has been made on prohibited grounds (for example discrimination or victimization), and unjustified in other cases. The tribunal will order reinstatement with compensation in the first case and compensation only in the second case.[45] In some countries the employer may refuse to reinstate a worker, in which case the worker will be entitled to compensation only, while in some others the employer must abide by an order of reinstatement. In certain countries a worker has the option of seeking reinstatement or compensation. Approaches also vary with regard to the actual amount of compensation (which is distinct from severance pay[46]) to which a worker would be entitled in the case of unfair dismissal.[47]

The labour laws of the new Central European EU members and candidate countries share a number of features with the German Protection against Dismissal Law. However, while the German law does not cover small enterprises employing less than ten workers,[48] it would seem that dismissal protection regulation in Central European countries applies to all enterprises, regardless of their size. Also, most of these laws impose reinstatement as the normal remedy even when it may not be a workable solution with regard to a number of circumstances that the court may take into account. Unlike Central European laws, the German law allows the labour court to refrain from ordering reinstatement when it considers that such a remedy would be impractical. In such a case, the court will order the employer to pay compensation.

Finally, it should be acknowledged that reinstatement as a remedy does not always work. For example, it might not be a workable remedy in small enterprises or where management positions are concerned. On the other hand, reinstatement might be considered a suitable remedy when a dismissal has been based on a prohibited ground (e.g. discrimination, anti-union or retaliatory dismissals, or dismissals in violation of a public policy). There, in addition to protecting an individual worker, the law protects a fundamental right, which could justify "sending a clear message" to indicate that certain forms of rights abuse will not be tolerated.[49]

Equality issues

Non-discrimination in employment and equal pay for equal work or work of equal value are fundamental rights in the European Union. Indeed, the equal pay principle (formerly Article 119, now Article 141 of the EC Treaty) is the sole social provision that was included in the original Treaty of Rome of 1957. Originally, former Article 119 was largely meant to serve economic purposes, i.e. to avoid social dumping to the detriment of countries, which like France, had adopted equal pay legislation pursuant to the ILO Equal Remuneration Convention, 1951 (No. 100). However, the ECJ has since stated that the economic aim pursued by Article 119 of the Treaty, namely the elimination of distortions of competition between undertakings established in different member states, is secondary to the social aim pursued by the same provision, which constitutes the expression of a fundamental human right. The European Council adopted two directives in 1975 and 1976 dealing respectively with the equal pay and equal treatment principles,[50] thus providing a legal basis for the European Court of Justice to develop far-reaching case law. Subsequently, in June 2000, the Council adopted a directive dealing with the principle of equal treatment of persons irrespective of racial or ethnic origin. Some months later this was followed by a directive establishing a general framework for combating discrimination on the grounds of religion, belief, disability, age or sexual orientation as regards employment and occupation.[51] Finally, in September 2002, the 1976 Equal Treatment Directive was amended by a new directive,[52] which defined terms such as "direct" and "indirect" discrimination, and specified that harassment and sexual harassment are included within the meaning of "discrimination" and, accordingly, are prohibited. Under the new directive, EU members must make the necessary arrangements for a body or bodies for the promotion, analysis, monitoring and support of equal treatment of all persons without discrimination on the grounds of sex. These bodies may form part of agencies charged at national level with the defence of human rights or the safeguard of individuals' rights. EU members are also required to promote social dialogue between the social partners with a view to fostering equal treatment, through the monitoring of workplace practices, collective agreements, codes of conduct, research or exchange of experiences and best practices.

Although these directives have already been transposed into the legal systems of the new EU members, their actual implementation raises challenges. It remains a regrettable fact that in market economies the labour market tends to be "gender biased". Moreover, discrimination on other grounds, such as those addressed in the directives adopted in 2000, reflects some forms of societal behaviour that have not yet been completely eradicated. In the field of equal pay and gender discrimination it is important for all of the new Central European EU members and candidate countries to be fully familiar with the case law developed by the European Court of Justice, which has, for example, extensively developed the concepts of "indirect discrimination", "equal pay for work of equal value", as well as that of the "objective reasons" underlying acceptable exceptions to the equal pay and equal treatment principles.[53]

A substantial element of anti-discrimination policy is the reversal of the burden of the proof. As a result, during litigation the plaintiff bears only the initial burden of establishing the facts from which it may be presumed that there has been direct or indirect discrimination. Once such facts have been established, it is up to the respondent to demonstrate that the reason for apparent unequal treatment is justified on grounds that are compatible with national and EC law.[54] It is important for litigants and the judiciary alike to be fully aware of the legal bearing of such a rule, as there is a tendency to believe that it contradicts general evidentiary principles on the administration of the evidence in civil litigation. However, this rule simply means that mere allegations by plaintiffs will not be deemed sufficient to establish the facts from which it may be presumed that direct or indirect discrimination existed, and mere generalizations by respondents will not be deemed sufficient to establish that the alleged discriminatory treatment is justified on grounds that are compatible with national and EC law.[55] It remains unclear, however, whether the labour law of new Central European EU members and candidate countries has rightly transposed these rules and principles.

Protection of workers' privacy is another important element of anti-discrimination policy. There is a risk that job applicants may be required to provide personal data, or submit to pre-employment tests that could be used to discriminate against them. Genetic tests and HIV tests, as well as questionnaires enquiring into a job applicant's trade union membership, religious beliefs or political opinions may belong in this category.

With regard to pregnancy tests, it is critical to note that under EC law it is mandatory for the employer to assess the risk to pregnant or breastfeeding workers of exposure to hazardous agents, processes or working conditions, and if necessary to make appropriate accommodations, including transferring the woman to another job.[56] However, the ECJ has ruled that it would be illegal for an employer to refuse to employ a pregnant woman on a permanent contract where the job entails exposure to harmful substances as the prohibition to work in a hazardous environment must be limited to the period of time during which a female worker is pregnant or breastfeeding her child.[57]

Under the Data Protection Directive, 1995,[58] member states must prohibit the processing of personal data that reveals racial or ethnic origin, political opinions, religious or philosophical beliefs, trade union membership, and the processing of data that concerns health or sex life. More specific guidance on the protection of personal data for employment purposes may be drawn from the ILO Code of Practice on the Protection of Workers' Personal Data.[59]

Collective bargaining and collective representation

The weakness of the collective bargaining systems in Central European countries stems from a number of factors and, arguably to a large extent, relates to the fact that free collective bargaining, like free unionization and membership in employers' organizations, is a relatively new issue in their industrial relations systems. Decreasing unionization rates, institutional weakness of both employers' and workers' organizations, privatization and dismantling of the big production units that made up the core of the economy during communism, together with the sharp increase of so-called *atypical* forms of employment, are doubtless contributory factors that help explain collective bargaining weaknesses.

Legislation concerning the rights and obligations of social partners, as well as industrial relations structures and general procedures, is already in place in all countries concerned. However, the rules are relatively new and not yet consolidated. In all likelihood, they will be subject to some revision in the years to come. Two areas which deserve special reconsideration and legal clarification are the representativeness of social partner organizations and the relations between trade unions and non-unionized staff representation bodies. In some countries, problems requiring the attention of law-makers could include those related to collective bargaining machinery and procedures, extension of collective agreements to third parties, relations between collective agreements concluded at different levels, duration and renunciation of the agreements, and the legal effects of collective agreements after they have been renounced.

At present, however, the major difficulty stems from the fact that the practice of collective bargaining presupposes the existence of behavioural patterns and a culture of collective action that has not had time to take root in the relatively short period that has elapsed since the downfall of communism. Such difficulties must be weighed against the political will to support collective bargaining not only as a means of promoting and implementing EC social and labour policy, but also as a tool for achieving social stability at national, sectoral and enterprise levels. It is a fact that collective bargaining within the European Union benefits from very strong institutional and political support. In no small part, this explains why, despite a difficult worldwide economic and structural environment, collective bargaining has suffered fewer setbacks in Western Europe than it has suffered elsewhere in world. Such support would seem indispensable if Central European countries consider that, in addition to EC law, transposition of the *acquis communautaire* should also include the endorsement of the industrial relations cultures and values that prevail in Western Europe. Eventually this should strengthen collective bargaining in the countries that joined the EU in 2004.

Conclusion

This paper has highlighted changes in the labour law of ten Central European countries since communist rule came to an end. Five dimensions have been strategically important in facilitating these changes: (1) the political decision to adopt a market economy and democracy and to apply for EU membership; (2) the choice of EU values over ultra-liberal recipes to reshape labour law; (3) the central role of the state in the revision of the labour law with a view to integrating the *acquis communautaire;* (4) the substantial help that these countries have received from the European Community; and (5) the ILO standards and principles on freedom of association and collective bargaining that were taken as common rules for reshaping the institutional framework of the industrial relations systems. In all of the new EU members, each factor has been instrumental in formulating a labour law system which, despite national differences, is generally homogeneous and reflective of the "European Social Model."

Much work still lies ahead. In view of the tight time-frame within which the reforms have been carried out, it is unreasonable to expect that they have had enough time to consolidate. Undoubtedly, further reforms will be forthcoming. Moreover, a great deal of work is now required to strengthen law-implementation and law-enforcement machineries in many of the new Central European EU members and candidate countries. It is also clear that Central European countries will need to pay considerable attention to strengthening their social partners and social dialogue institutions, in particular collective bargaining, given that Central European labour regulation to date remains essentially a state-driven process.

The European Union has just experienced the biggest expansion in its history. The original six founding members of 1957 have become 25 members and very likely they will be 28 in 2007.[60] Together with this unprecedented expansion the EU has also contemplated the adoption a constitution to replace the original treaties. To this end a draft constitution was initially worked out in a convention, after which in October 2003 the EU Intergovernmental Conference initiated discussions in Rome, which led to the text of the constitution being formally signed on 29 October 2004.[61] In addition to giving expanded law-making powers to the Community, the constitution would have integrated the Charter of Fundamental Rights in the European Union, which to date has been unenforceable. No doubt this would have led to embedding the values of the European Social Model in the labour law systems of both current and candidate EU member states.

Notes

1. The Socialist Federal Republic of Yugoslavia disintegrated in 1991. Its successor state was the Federal Republic of Yugoslavia, which is made up only of Serbia and Montenegro while the status of the autonomous region of Kosovo, now under local administration with UN supervision, has not yet been resolved. The Federal Republic of Yugoslavia has now taken the name of *Serbia and Montenegro*, and it is likely that both entities will become full independent states within a timeframe of three years as from the time of writing. Besides, the former Republic of Bosnia-Hercegovina is now made up of two distinct entities, namely the Muslim-Croat Federation of Bosnia-Hercegovina and the Srpska Republic. While both entities formally make up a single state, they enjoy significant autonomy, including extended law-making and law-enforcement competences.
2. Estonia, Latvia and Lithuania had respectively ratified 18, 17 and 7 conventions before they were annexed by the Soviet Union. By November 2004 they had respectively ratified 32, 45 and 39 ILO conventions.

3. Something which would seem to have been necessary, as high absenteeism and low discipline at work were very common features in all communist countries.
4. Yugoslavia departed, however, from this pattern as decision-making at the enterprise level was to a large extent decentralized, having regard to the self-management and social ownership concepts which made up the underlying philosophy of the political regime.
5. It does not apply to family work in family farming enterprises.
6. See the studies on the scope of the employment relationship in Bulgaria, the Czech Republic, Poland, the Russian Federation and Slovenia, available on the ILO's website, online: http://www.ilo.org/public/english/dialogue/ifpdial/ll/wp.htm.
7. Essentially the Treaty of the European Community, or Treaty of Rome (1957) later amended by the Single European Act, 1987, and the treaties of Maastricht (1992), Amsterdam (1996) and Nice (2001), and the Treaty of the European Union or Treaty of Maastricht (1992), also amended by the treaties of Amsterdam and Nice. In October 2004 a Constitutional Treaty was signed in Rome and is now opened for ratification.
8. Council Regulation 162/68, OJ 1968 No. L257.
9. Under Article 137 (ex Article 118) the Community can adopt directives by qualified majority in the following fields:

improvement in particular of the working environment to protect workers' health and safety;
working conditions;
information and consultation of workers;
integration of persons excluded from the labour market, without prejudice to Article 150;
equality between men and women with regard to labour market opportunities and treatment at work.

Unanimity is required for the EC to regulate in the following areas:

social security and social protection of workers;
protection of workers where their employment contract is terminated;
representation and collective defence of the interests of workers and employers, including codetermination;
conditions of employment for third-country nationals legally residing in Community territory;
financial contributions for promotion of employment and job-creation, without prejudice to the provisions relating to the Social Fund.

The following questions are expressly excluded from the scope of Article 137: pay, the right of association, the right to strike and the right to impose lock-outs.
10. Joined cases C-6/90 and C-9/90, *Andrea Francovich, Danila Bonifaci and Others* v. *Italy* [1991] ECR I-5357.

11. See also Giuseppe Casale, "Collective Bargaining and the Law in Central and Eastern Europe: Recent Trends and Issues", Report submitted to the VII. European Regional Congress of the International Society for Labour Law and Social Security, Stockholm, September 2002, available online:http://www.juridicum.su.se/stockholmcongress2002/casale_english.pdf.

12. For example, the Labour Code of Bulgaria, Arts. 83, and 89 to 97. Similar provisions exist in the labour laws of Estonia and Lithuania.

13. For example, the Labour Law of Latvia, Art. 90, and the Labour Code of Lithuania, Art. 97.

14. The sole reason to address employees' liability in a labour law would be to limit the employee's accountability only to claims that have been the result of his/her illegal action, wilful action or gross negligence, thus departing from the general civil law and common law rule whereby any fault or any negligence can be a source of civil liability. Under labour law the approach is that the employee will not be made accountable for damages that are the result of simple carelessness, on the understanding that such damages are a business risk; see, for example, the Labour Code of Slovakia, Art. 179, or that of Lithuania, Art. 246, which however includes a provision (Art. 256) providing that in certain circumstances a "full liability clause" may be included in a contract of employment.

15. Estonia, Law on Contracts of Employment, Art. 20.

16. Labour Code of the Czech Republic, Art. 150. Estonia, Law on Contracts of Employment, s. 25. It is likely that these provisions have been removed in the most recent revisions of these laws. However, a translated text of such laws was not yet available when this paper was written.

17. See, for example, Labour Code of Lithuania, Arts. 285–303.

18. The Nordic countries and Belgium depart, however, from this approach, as central level collective bargaining usually plays a role at least as important as statutory law. In Denmark central level bargaining is indeed the major source of labour regulation, with the state playing a secondary role, normally to extend labour protection so that it covers workers that are not protected by collective agreements.

19. Estonia, Latvia and Slovenia do not have a unified Labour Code. Lithuania has recently adopted a Labour Code, which has merged into a single text various separate bodies of labour legislation which had been adopted since the early 1990s. All the other countries have a Labour Code.

20. See, e.g., Labour Code of the Czech Republic (1965), Labour Code of Poland (1974), and so on.

21. A written contract of employment is not mandatory under EC Law, as the latter only prescribes that the employer shall be obliged to notify in writing an employee "of the essential aspects of the contract or employment relationship". See Article 2 of Council Directive 91/533/EEC of 14 October 1991 on an employer's obligation

to inform employees of the conditions applicable to the contract or employment relationship, OJ 1991.

22. Council Directive 99/70/EEC of 28 June 1999 concerning the framework agreement on fixed-term work concluded by ETUC, UNICE and CEEP, OJ 1999 No. L175. Council Directive 98/59/EEC of 20 July 1998 on the approximation of the laws of the member states relating to collective redundancies, OJ 1998 No. L 225, which has replaced two previous directives on the same subject, adopted in 1975 and 1992 respectively. ILO Termination of Employment Convention, 1982 (No. 158) and Recommendation (No. 166), Part-time Convention, 1994 (No. 175) and Recommendation (No. 182) and Private Employment Agencies Convention, 1997 (No. 181), and Recommendation (No. 188).

23. Cases C-41/90 *Höfner and Elser* v. *Macrotron GmbH.* [1991] ECR I-01979 and C-55/96 *Job Centre Coop. arl* (rendered on 11 December 1997).

24. Already in 1919 the Unemployment Recommendation (No. 1) advocated that each Member of the International Labour Organisation "take measures to prohibit the establishment of employment agencies which charge fees or which carry on their business for profit". In 1933 the ILO adopted the Fee-charging Employment Agencies Convention (No. 34) which provided for the abolition of employment agencies operating for profit. Convention No. 34 was revised by the ILO Fee-charging Employment Agencies (revised) Convention, 1949 (No. 96), which offered a choice to member states between prohibiting or (tightly) regulating fee-charging employment agencies. Though officially "shelved" by the ILO, Convention No. 34 is still binding on countries that have not denounced it, as is the case of Bulgaria and Slovakia. Convention No. 96 has been denounced by a majority of EU members that had previously ratified it. It remains, however, binding on Poland which has decided to apply Part II (prohibition). Within the group of new EU members only Hungary, the Czech Republic and Lithuania have ratified Convention No. 181, which has also been ratified by Finland, Italy, the Netherlands, Portugal and Spain.

25. Council Directive 2001/23/EEC of 12 March 2001 on the approximation of the laws of the member states relating to the safeguarding of employees' rights in the event of transfers of undertakings, businesses or parts of undertakings or businesses, OJ 2001 No. L082; Council Directive 98/59/EEC of 20 July 1998 on the approximation of the laws of the member states relating to collective redundancies, OJ 1998 No. L225; Council Directive 1999/70/EEC of 28 June 1999 concerning the framework agreement on fixed-term work concluded by ETUC, UNICE and CEEP, OJ 1999 No. L175.

26. For example, the use of fixed-term manpower in Germany is three times less than it is in Spain, though it would not seem credible to affirm that employment protection in Germany is weaker than it is in Spain.

27. Council Directive 1999/70/EEC of 28 June 1999 concerning the framework agreement on fixed-term work concluded by ETUC, UNICE and CEEP, OJ 1999 No.L175.

28. Clause 5 of this agreement provides as follows:

> 1. To prevent abuse arising from the use of successive fixed-term employment contracts or relationships, Member States, after consultation with social partners in accordance with national law, collective agreements or practice, and/or the social partners, shall, where there are no equivalent legal measures to prevent abuse, introduce in a manner which takes account of the needs of specific sectors and/or categories of workers, one or more of the following measures:
>
> > (a) objective reasons justifying the renewal of such contracts or relationships;
> > (b) the maximum total duration of successive fixed-term employment contracts or relationships;
> > (c) the number of renewals of such contracts or relationships.
>
> 2. Member States after consultation with the social partners and/or the social partners shall, where appropriate, determine under what conditions fixed-term employment contracts or relationships:
>
> > (a) shall be regarded as "successive"
> > (b) shall be deemed to be contracts or relationships of indefinite duration.

29. For example, in Bulgaria fixed-term contracts of employment may not be concluded for more than three years, and are limited to temporary or seasonal work (Labour Code, Art. 68). In Estonia there is a limitative list under s. 27.2 of the Law on Contracts of Employment. A limitative list also exists in Latvia, and fixed-term contracts of employment may not be entered into for more than two years, including renewals (Labour Law, ss. 44 and 45). In Lithuania the maximum duration of a fixed-term contract can go as far as five years, but "it shall be prohibited to conclude a fixed-term employment contract if work is of a permanent nature, except for the cases when this is provided by laws or collective agreements" (Labour Code, Art. 109.2). By contrast, no limitations would seem to exist in the Czech Republic. In Poland the restrictions on the use of fixed-term contracts of employment that exist under the Labour Code had been suspended in 2002 until the country effectively joined the European Union; the current status of this provision is, however, unclear. In Slovakia under Article 48 of the Labour Code the maximum duration of a fixed term contract of employment is limited to three years, but it can be renewed in enterprises employing less than 20 employees.

30. To this end, under paragraph 3.2 of the ILO Recommendation No. 166, the following policy is recommended :

> (a) limiting recourse to contracts for a specified period of time to cases in which, owing either to the nature of the work to be effected or to the circumstances under which it is to be effected or to the interests of the worker, the employment relationship cannot be of indeterminate duration;

(b) deeming contracts for a specified period of time, other than in the cases referred to in clause (a) of this subparagraph, to be contracts of employment of indeterminate duration;

(c) deeming contracts for a specified period of time, when renewed on one or more occasions, other than in the cases mentioned in clause (a) of this subparagraph, to be contracts of employment of indeterminate duration.

31. Donald Storrie, "Temporary Agency Work in the European Union" (European Foundation for the Improvement of Living and Working Conditions, Dublin, 2002). This study can be consulted online: http://www.fr.eurofound.eu.int/publications/files/EF0202EN.pdf.

32. Poland has recently regulated this issue. A general description of the new law on temporary agency work can be consulted at the website of the European Industrial Relations Observatory, online: http://www.eiro.eurofound.ie/2003/08/InBrief/PL0308103N.html.

33. Council Directive 91/383/EEC of 25 June 1991 supplementing the measures to encourage improvements in the safety and health at work of workers with a fixed-duration employment relationship or a temporary employment relationship, OJ 1991 No.L206 .

34. The Czech Republic, Hungary and Lithuania had already ratified this Convention in November 2004.

35. This presentation on the scope and the gist of Convention No. 181 is done without prejudice to the view on this convention that may be taken by the ILO supervisory bodies.

36. Available online:http://www.eiro.eurofound.ie/2002/05/study/TN0205101S.html.

37. Particularly noteworthy is the approach that has been followed in Ireland, where the social partners have agreed upon a *Code of Practice in determining employee status.* See the Report of the Employment Status Group established under the Programme for Prosperity and Fairness, online: http://www.revenue.ie/pdf/ppfrep.pdf.

38. The ILO Report, on *The Scope of the Employment Relationship,* is available online: http://www.ilo.org/public/english/standards/relm/ilc/ilc91/pdf/rep-v.pdf.

39. Available online: http://www.ilo.org/public/english/standards/relm/ilc/ilc91/pdf/pr-21.pdf.

40. Exceptions to the *at will* doctrine may exist under the common law, as exemplified by the concept of wrongful dismissal. Statutory law, especially but not only on discrimination, has also established exceptions to the *at will* rule. Further sources of protection against dismissal may be the explicit or implied terms of the individual contract of employment, and the collective agreement by which an enterprise may be bound.

41. This directive has revised and repealed a former directive, adopted already in 1975.

42. Convention No. 158 has been ratified by the following countries: Cyprus, Finland, France, Latvia, Luxembourg, Portugal, Slovenia, Spain, Sweden and Turkey.

43. Bulgaria, LC, Arts. 344–15; Czech Republic, LC, ss. 61; Estonia LCE, ss. 117; Latvia, LL, ss. 124 and 126

44. Poland, LC, Art. 45, Slovenia, Employment Act, Art. 118.

45. Hungary, LC, s. 100.

46. Severance pay is the amount of money that the worker would be entitled to receive when his or her employment is terminated for a valid reason, other than summary dismissal on the ground of gross misconduct. Compensation is damages to which the worker would be entitled in the case of unfair dismissal.

47. However, it should be recalled in this connection that under Directive 2002/73/EEC amending the 1976 Directive on Equal Treatment of Men and Women, which on this point has confirmed an early decision of the ECJ, compensation or reparation for the loss and damage sustained by a person injured as a result of gender discrimination shall be "dissuasive and proportionate to the damage suffered"; it cannot "be restricted by the fixing of a prior upper limit, except in cases where the employer can prove that the only damage suffered by an applicant as a result of discrimination within the meaning of this Directive is the refusal to take his/her job application into consideration".

48. Until December 2003 the law applied to enterprises employing five or more workers. The threshold was increased to ten workers as from 1 January 2004. However, employees in companies with more than five but fewer than eleven employees, will keep their statutory protection if employed before 1 January 2004.

49. To a large extent, the Employment and Industrial Relations Act, 2002, of another new EU member, Malta, has followed such reasoning. Under this law (Article 81) reinstatement would be permitted when the Industrial Tribunal "considers that it would be practicable and in accordance with equity, for the complainant to be reinstated or re-engaged by the employer". However, it will not order reinstatement "where the complainant is employed in such managerial or executive post as requires a special trust in the person of the holder of that post or in his ability to perform the duties thereof" (except where the complainant was appointed or selected to such post as aforesaid by his fellow workers). If there is no specific request for reinstatement, or the Tribunal has decided not to make an order for reinstatement, "the Tribunal shall make an award of compensation which shall take into consideration the real damages and losses incurred by the worker who was unjustly dismissed, as well as other circumstances, including the worker's age and skills as may affect the employment potential of the said worker".

50. Council Directive 75/117/EEC of 10 February 1975 on the approximation of the laws of the member states relating to the application of the principle of equal pay for men and women, OJ 1975 No. L045, and Council Directive 76/207/EEC of 9 February 1976 on the implementation of the principle of equal treatment for men and women as regards access to employment, vocational training and promotion, and working conditions, OJ 1976 No. L039.

51. Council Directive 2000/43/EEC of 29 June 2000 on the principle of equal treatment between persons irrespective of racial or ethnic origin, OJ 2000 No. L180, and Council Directive 2000/78/EEC of 27 November 2000 establishing a general framework for equal treatment in employment and occupation, OJ 2000 No. L303.

52. Directive 2002/73/EEC of the European Parliament and of the Council of 23 September 2002 amending Council Directive 76/207/EEC on the implementation of the principle of equal treatment for men and women as regards access to employment, vocational training and promotion, and working conditions, OJ 2002 No. L269.

53. Under EC law indirect discrimination is deemed to exist where an apparently neutral provision, criterion or practice would put persons of one sex at a particular disadvantage compared with persons of the other sex, unless that provision, criterion or practice is objectively justified by a legitimate aim, and the means of achieving that aim are appropriate and necessary.

54. See, for example, Article 4 of Council Directive 97/80/ECC of 15 December 1997 on the burden of proof in cases of discrimination based on sex, whereby "when persons who consider themselves wronged because the principle of equal treatment has not been applied to them establish, before a court or other competent authority, facts from which it may be presumed that there has been direct or indirect discrimination, it shall be for the respondent to prove that there has been no breach of the principle of equal treatment." The same rule exists under Article 10 of Council Directive 2000/78/EEC of 27 November 2000, establishing a general framework for equal treatment in employment and occupation.

55. For example, in *Helga Nimz* v. *Freie und Hansestadt Hamburg* [1991] ECR I-297 (case C-184/89) the ECJ was asked to make a preliminary ruling on a collective agreement which provided for automatic pay increases for full-timers and part-timers after respectively six and twelve years of service, and it was unchallenged that part-timers were mainly female staff. While it was argued that the greater experience of full-time employees justified the indirect sex discrimination, the ECJ considered that it is a mere generalization that full-timers acquire competences and capabilities pertaining to their work faster than part-timers or that greater experience per se justifies greater pay.

56. Council Directive 92/85/EEC of 19 October 1992 on the introduction of measures to encourage improvements in the safety and health at work of pregnant workers and workers who have recently given birth or are breastfeeding, OJ 1992 No. L348.

57. In *Mahlburg* v. *Land Mecklenburg,* Case 207/98 [2000] ECR I-549, the ECJ held that such refusal would be contrary to Article 2 (1) of the Equal Treatment Directive.

58. Directive 95/46/EEC of the European Parliament and of the Council of 24 October 1995 on the protection of individuals with regard to the processing of personal data and on the free movement of such data, OJ 1995 No. L 281.

59. Available online: http://www.ilo.org/public/english/support/publ/pdf/protect.pdf. Catherine Barnard, *Labour Market Integration: Lessons from the European Union,* Chapter 8 in this volume.

60. The European Union started as the European Common Market in 1957. It was then made up of six members: Belgium, France, Germany, Italy, Luxembourg and the Netherlands. In January 1973 it was joined by Denmark, Ireland and the United Kingdom. In 1981 it was further extended to Portugal and Spain. In 1990 the former German Democratic Republic adhered to the Federal Republic of Germany, thus further extending the territorial scope of the EU. In 1995 the EU welcomed Austria, Finland and Sweden. The Czech Republic, Cyprus, Estonia, Hungary, Latvia, Lithuania, Malta, Poland, Slovakia, and Slovenia joined in May 2004; and Bulgaria, Croatia and Romania are currently at the "applicant" stage of the membership process. Three other countries, Iceland, Lichtenstein and Norway, have established special links with the EU through the Agreement on the European Economic Area, EEA 1992. While Switzerland did not ratify the EEA agreement it has signed seven bilateral agreements with the EU, and is negotiating some more agreements.

61. Text available online: http://europa.eu.int/constitution/constitution_en.htm.

8

Labour market integration: lessons from the European Union

CATHERINE BARNARD

Introduction

Labour migration is as old as the hills. Workers move from areas of high unemployment to those regions where jobs are more plentiful. While economists highlight the economic benefits of labour migration, labour lawyers are more concerned with the rights and entitlements of those individuals – and their families – who have moved. Since its inception, the European Union has provided a structured framework in which transnational migration can occur, principally through the provisions of the European Community Treaty establishing the right of free movement of persons. These provisions enshrine so-called "fundamental freedoms" which grant individuals both the right to move and the right to claim certain welfare benefits in the host state on the same terms as nationals. This is a highly sensitive area. The aim of this paper is to question the basis on which mobility rights have been granted before examining whether the situation in the EU is unique and whether it has wider lessons for international migration.

Free movement of workers

Although the original EEC Treaty talked of free movement of persons, reference to the free movement of *persons* was misleading: The original Treaty gave no general right of free movement for all persons. To enjoy such a right, the individual had to hold the nationality of one of the member states (with nationality being a matter for national – not Community – law)[1] and be economically active either as a worker under Article 39(1), or as a self-employed person under Article 43. For our purposes the Article 39 rights are of greatest interest.

Article 39(1) provides that workers should enjoy the right of free movement[2] which, according to Article 39(2), includes freedom from discrimination based on nationality between workers of the member states, respecting employment, remuneration and other conditions of work and employment.[3] Article 39(3) then adds that free movement comprises the right:

- to accept offers of employment actually made;
- to move freely within the territory of the member states for this purpose;
- to stay in the member state for the purpose of the employment; and
- to remain in the member state after having been employed.[4]

Despite the existence of these rights, most workers have not taken advantage of their right to move for a variety of social, cultural and linguistic reasons. In an attempt to encourage workers to move, in the 1960s the European Community adopted a series of measures giving rights to workers and their families in an attempt to encourage workers to exercise their rights of free movement. The most important of these measures was Regulation 1612/68[5] which provided workers with: the right to access a job on non-discriminatory terms; equal treatment while doing that job; and certain rights for their family members. When enacting this Regulation, the Council:

> took into account, first, the importance for the worker, from a human point of view of having his entire family with him and, secondly, the importance, from all points of view, of the integration of the worker and his family into the host Member State without any difference in treatment in relation to nationals of that State.[6]

The need to integrate the migrant worker into the community of the host state is seen most clearly in Article 7(2) of Regulation 1612/68, which requires that social advantages be provided to migrant workers on a non-discriminatory basis. In *Even*[7] the European Court of Justice defined "social advantages" broadly to include all benefits:

> which, whether or not linked to a contract of employment, are generally granted to national workers primarily because of their objective status as workers *or by virtue of the mere fact of their residence on the national territory* and the extension of which to workers who are nationals of other Member States therefore seems suitable to *facilitate their mobility* within the Community.[8]

The concept of social advantage accordingly includes benefits granted as of right,[9] on a discretionary basis,[10] and those granted after employment ends (e.g. a pension).[11] It also covers benefits not directly linked to employment, such as language rights,[12] death benefits,[13] rights for a dependent child to obtain finance for studies,[14] and rights to be accompanied by unmarried companions.[15] These benefits do not necessarily "facilitate mobility", as the *Even* formula requires, but they do facilitate the integration of the migrant worker into the host state.[16]

The striking feature of the decision in *Even* is that it indicated, by its reference to "residence on the national territory", that Article 7(2) applied not just to benefits granted by the host state to its workers,[17] but also to its residents.[18] This meant that both migrant workers *and* their families could enjoy the social advantages offered by the home state.[19] The Court justified this development on the grounds that Article 7(2) was essential to both encourage free movement of workers and their families (without whom the worker would be discouraged from moving),[20] and also to encourage their integration into the working environment of the host state.[21] As the Court said of Regulation 1612/68 on free movement of persons in *Baumbast*:

> for such freedom to be guaranteed in compliance with the principles of liberty and dignity, the best possible conditions for the integration of the Community worker's family in the society of the host Member State.[22]

The importance of extending equal treatment to social advantages for family members can be seen in the *Christini*[23] decision. The French railway (SNCF) had a scheme which offered a fare reduction for people with large families. Christini, an Italian mother residing in France who was the widow of an Italian who had worked in France, was refused the fare reduction on the grounds of her nationality. The SNCF justified this on the grounds that Article 7(2) applied only to advantages connected with a contract of employment. The Court disagreed, arguing that in view of the equal treatment Article 7(2) was designed to achieve, the substantive area of application had to include all social and tax advantages, regardless of any direct connection with an employment contract. This included fare reductions for large families. The Court added that Article 7(2) applied to all persons lawfully entitled to remain in the host state, irrespective of whether the "trigger" for the rights – the worker – was alive. Hence, strong emphasis was placed on the need for integration to encourage workers to take advantage of their rights of free movement and to remain in the host state.

At first sight, this line of case law entitling foreign workers and their families to social advantages on a non-discriminatory basis appears to impose considerable burdens on the exchequers of the host state. In fact, these decisions have not proved to be so controversial because the migrant workers are, or have been, economically active and have therefore contributed to the exchequer of the host state. There is a certain amount of boot-strapping going on. In order to encourage movement of the economically active, migrant workers will receive benefits if they need them; once they have migrated they will contribute to the exchequer and so they should be entitled to benefits.

This explanation is not adequate when dealing with the case of a migrant who is not economically active. Their situation is considered below. These individuals likely have a greater need of social welfare than those who are economically active, yet because they have not contributed to the host state's system, the logic outlined above would suggest that they should not be entitled to benefits. Yet, in certain circumstances, the European Court of Justice has required the host state to pay these individuals welfare benefits in the name of solidarity.

Free movement of citizens

The concept of "Citizenship of the Union", was introduced by the Maastricht Treaty in 1992, and formed a key part of the Union's response to an increasing sense of alienation felt by many nationals towards the EU. Yet, the rights actually conferred on EU citizens by the Treaty appeared rather spartan.[24] The provision offering the greatest potential for citizenship building[25] was Article 18(1) which laid down the right of EU citizens to move and reside freely within the territory of the member states, subject to the limitations and conditions laid down by the Treaty and the measures adopted to give it effect. These conditions include the limits laid down in the Residence Directives of the 1990s[26] which essentially allow for the free movement of students, the retired, and persons of independent means, provided that they have sufficient medical insurance and resources. In the early days it was not clear whether Article 18(1) merely codified the existing case law under Article 39 or whether it went further and gave rights of free movement to those who were not economically active. Three important decisions, *Martínez Sala*,[27] *Grzelczyk*,[28] and *Baumbast*[29] indicate that the Court now supports the broader interpretation of Article 18(1).

Martínez Sala was a Spanish national who had been living in Germany since 1968 the age of twelve. She had various jobs and various residence permits in that time. When she had a baby in 1993, she did not have a residence permit but she did have a certificate confirming that she had applied for an extension of the permit. The German authorities refused to give her a child- raising allowance on the grounds that she was neither a German national nor did she have a residence permit. If she had been a worker she would have been entitled to the benefit as a social advantage under Article 7(2) of Regulation 1612/68. Given her background, this was unlikely.[30] The Court therefore considered her situation under the citizenship provisions.

It held that as a national of a member state lawfully residing in the territory of another member state,[31] Martínez Sala came within the personal scope of the citizenship provisions.[32] She therefore enjoyed the rights laid down by Article 17(2) which included the right not to suffer discrimination on grounds of nationality under Article 12 in respect of all situations falling within the material scope of the EC Treaty.[33] This was held to include the situation where a member state delayed or refused to grant a benefit provided to all persons lawfully resident in the territory of that state on the basis that the claimant did not have a document (a residence permit) that nationals were not obliged to have.[34] On this basis, the Court concluded that Martínez Sala was suffering from direct discrimination on the grounds of nationality contrary to Article 12.[35]

This case suggests that citizens lawfully resident in a host state can rely on the principle of non-discrimination with respect to all benefits falling within the Treaty's material scope, including those benefits covered by Regulation 1612/68, irrespective of whether they are economically active. In this way, the introduction of Union citizenship exploded the "linkages" which EC law previously required for the principle of non-discrimination to apply (i.e. being engaged in an economic activity or having a family relationship with an economic actor).[36] The Court confirmed this in *Baumbast*:[37]

> The Treaty on European Union does not require that citizens of the Union pursue a professional or trade activity, whether as an employed or self-employed person, in order to enjoy the rights provided in Part Two of the EC Treaty, on citizenship of the Union.

Two things remained unclear after the *Martínez Sala* decision. First, whether migrant citizens could benefit from the full range of social advantages enjoyed by nationals from the first day of their arrival in the host states: second, whether the limitations laid down by the Residence Directives[38] continued to have relevance. These issues were explored in the *Grzelczyk* decision.[39]

Grzelczyk, a French national studying at a Belgian university, supported himself financially for the first three years of his studies but then applied for the minimex (the Belgium minimum income guarantee) at the start of his fourth and final year. While Belgian students could receive the benefit, migrant students could not[40] and so Grzelczyk suffered direct discrimination contrary to Article 12.[41] The question was whether Article 12 applied to his case. The Court began by noting that:

> Union citizenship is destined to be the fundamental status of nationals of the Member States, enabling those who find themselves in the same situation to enjoy the same treatment in law irrespective of their nationality, subject to such exceptions as are expressly provided for.[42]

Referring to *Martínez Sala,* the Court said that because Grzelczyk was a citizen of the Union and was lawfully resident in Belgium, he could rely on Article 12 in respect of situations falling within the material scope of the EC Treaty[43] that involved "the exercise of the fundamental freedoms guaranteed by the Treaty and those involving the exercise of the right to move and reside freely in another Member State, as conferred by Article [18(1)] of the Treaty".[44]

The Court then turned to the limits imposed by Article 1 of the Students' Directive 93/96, namely that the migrant student had to have sufficient resources. The Court distinguished between maintenance grants where Article 3 of the Directive expressly permitted discrimination against non-nationals and social assistance (like the minimex) to which Article 3 did not apply. The Court also held that while a member state could decide that a student no longer fulfilled the conditions of his right of residence based on his or her recourse to social assistance and could withdraw his or her residence permit (or decide not to renew it),[45] such actions could not be the *automatic* consequence of a migrant student accessing to the host state's social assistance system.[46] The Court continued that beneficiaries of the right of residence could not become an "unreasonable" burden on the public finances of the host state.[47] It concluded that the Students' Directive:

> thus accepts a certain degree of financial solidarity between nationals of a host Member State and nationals of other Member States, particularly if the difficulties which a beneficiary of the right of residence encounters are temporary.[48]

The implications of this ruling were spelt out in *Baumbast,*[49] this time in respect of Directive 90/364 on persons of independent means.[50]

Baumbast, a German national, had been working in the UK first as an employee and then as a self-employed person. He brought his family with him and they continued to reside there even after his work had ceased, funding themselves out of their own savings. They also had comprehensive medical insurance for treatment in Germany which did not cover them for emergency treatment in the UK. On this basis, the Secretary of State refused to renew Mr Baumbast's residence permit and the residence documents of his wife and children.

The Court insisted on reading the limitations in Directive 90/364 as subject to the principle of proportionality.[51] It noted that, Baumbast satisfied the terms of the directive with the exception of the failure to have adequate medical coverage.[52] However, the Court held that the reference to limitations and conditions in Article 18(1) of the EC Treaty had to be applied "in compliance with the limits imposed by Community law and in accordance with the general principles of that law, in particular the principle of proportionality".[53] The Court concluded that because the Baumbast family had not become a financial burden on the state, it would amount to a disproportionate interference with the exercise of the right of residence conferred on him by Article 18(1) if he were denied residence on the ground that his sickness insurance did not cover emergency treatment given in the host member state.[54]

The careful articulation of the proportionality principle in Baumbast helps to explain *Grzelczyk*. Grzelczyk could not be refused a minimex under Article 1 of Directive 93/96 because he had been lawfully residing in Belgium for three years during which time he had had sufficient resources (and medical insurance). Now that he was suffering "temporary difficulties", it would be disproportionate for Belgium to deny him the minimex.

At first glance, this case law suggests that migrant citizens who are not economically active now have the right to claim all benefits available in a host state on the same terms as nationals unless the benefits are expressly excluded by Community law.[55] If this analysis is correct, then citizenship of the Union leads to what Iliopoulou and Toner describe as the "perfect assimilation" approach, where the treatment of Community migrants is placed on a completely equal footing with nationals of the host Member State unless Community law specifically provides otherwise.[56]

When examined carefully, however, the cases do not support the full assimilationist approach. They actually support an incremental approach to residence and equality – the longer migrants reside in the member state, the greater the number of benefits they receive on equal terms with nationals. Therefore, Grzelcyzk, a relatively short-term resident, received the minimex for a temporary period. By contrast, Martínez Sala, a long-term resident (she had lived in Germany for 25 years) received child benefit on the same terms as nationals. The difficult question that arises here is, on what basis are these non-economically active migrants entitled to benefits to which they have not contributed? The answer may lie at least in part in the principle of solidarity mentioned by the Court of Justice in *Grzelczyk*. Solidarity is one of the defining values of the European Union. The Laeken declaration describes Europe:[57]

> as the continent of humane values, the Magna Carta, the Bill of Rights, the French Revolution and the fall of the Berlin Wall; the continent of liberty, solidarity and above all diversity, meaning respect for others' languages, cultures and traditions. The European Union's one boundary is democracy and human rights.

Solidarity has also made a number of appearances in the Constitutional Treaty; it appears in the Preamble,[58] in the statement of the Union's values,[59] and again in the Union's objectives.[60]

Solidarity as a concept originated in the social welfare systems of the member states. At the national level, it is used to justify government demands that one social group (e.g. those who are employed) make con-tributions (e.g. pay taxes) to help support another (e.g. those who are unemployed) on the grounds that they share a commonality of interests, mutual dependence and unity of purpose.[61] The financial implications of the solidarity principle were noted by Advocate General Fennelly in his opinion in *Sodemare*:[62] "Social solidarity envisages the inherently uncommercial act of involuntary subsidization of one social group by another."[63]

Martínez Sala seems to have benefited from such national solidarity. She was fully integrated into the host state's community, having spent most of her life in Germany.[64] Accordingly the Court required her to be treated as a national.

While national solidarity can be understood as arising from a sense of community denied from a complex mix of nationality, common heritage, social and cultural traditions, a similar sense of obligation cannot neces-sarily be found at the *transnational* level. Yet, as *Grzelczyk* and *Baumbast* show, the Court has used the introduction of Union citizenship to justify ruling that there is sufficient solidarity at the transnational level (nationals taxpayers pay their taxes to help provide benefits for their fellow nationals in need *and* for migrant EU citizens who are in temporary need). Union citizenship is further used to justify requiring the host state to pay benefits to the non-economically active migrant, at least on a limited basis (the minimex to Grzelczyk in respect of temporary difficulties[65] and, by extension, to provide emergency healthcare to Baumbast, should he need it).

The basis for such transnational solidarity lies both in the fundamental human rights to which the Union is committed (nobody should starve or go without basic healthcare), and in the fact that the principle of citizenship of the Union is common to both nationals and migrants alike. When viewed from this perspective, the principle of citizenship provides the means as well as the ends: the means because it justifies using the solidarity principle to give migrants – even temporary migrants – rights; the ends because true Union citizenship will only be realized when there is genuine solidarity between the citizens of all member states of the kind found in the national systems. Again we can see a process of boot-strapping taking place – citizenship (imposed from above) is used to justify taking limited steps in the name of solidarity and solidarity is used to foster a growing sense of citizenship from the bottom up.

How extensive is the obligation to pay benefits? Although it is early days, it could be argued that the case law suggests a spectrum. At the one end is Martínez Sala, who is fully integrated into the host state and so enjoys full equal treatment (the payment of the benefit on exactly the same terms as nationals). At the middle lies Grzelczyk, who is only partially integrated, and so enjoys only limited equal treatment (he receives the benefit on the same terms as nationals but only until he becomes an unreasonable burden on public funds when his right of residence can be terminated). At the other end of the spectrum should be those migrant citizens who have just arrived in the host state. While Article 18(1) gives them the right to move and reside freely in the host state,[66] the logic outlined above suggests that they should not enjoy equal treatment in respect of social welfare benefits (e.g. the minimex) although they might receive some social advantages on a non-discriminatory basis (e.g. emergency medical help, as Baumbast suggests[67]) because they are not yet integrated into the host state's community. This was the view taken by Advocate General Ruiz-Jarabo Colomer in Collins.[68] Collins, who was Irish, arrived in the United Kingdom and promptly applied for a job-seeker's allowance which was refused on the grounds that he was not habitually resident in the UK. The Advocate General distinguished Grzelczyk,[69] and concluded that Community law did not require providing the benefit to a citizen of the Union who had so recently entered the host with the purpose of seeking employment, while lacking any connection to the state or link with the domestic employment market.[70]

The incremental approach to the principle of equal treatment suggested by the case law was recognized by Advocate General La Pergola in *Stöber*. He said that the ultimate purpose of the citizenship provisions was to bring about *increasing* equality between citizens of the Union, irrespective of their nationality.[71] The idea is further fleshed out in the Directive on Citizens' Rights.[72] This Directive is intended to replace the various directives on workers, the self employed and service providers, in addition to the three Residence Directives. It envisages three categories of migrants. The first group are those wishing to enter the host state for up to three months.[73] They are not subject to any conditions (e.g. as to resources, medical insurance) other than holding a valid identity card or passport. They enjoy the right to reside in the host state for themselves and their families and the right to equal treatment but they have no entitlement to social assistance during the first three months of their stay.

The second group are those residing in the host state for more than three months. They have a "right to residence"[74] if, for example, they are engaged in gainful activity in an employed or self-employed capacity, or they have sufficient resources for themselves and their family members not to become a burden on welfare programmes of the host member state during their stay and have comprehensive sickness insurance coverage in the host member state. Those who qualify have the right to engage in gainful activity and the right to equal treatment.

The third group are those residing in the host state for more than five years.[75] These citizens (and their family members who are not nationals but who have resided with the Union citizen for five years) have the right of permanent residence.[76] None of the conditions applicable to the second group apply to those seeking permanent residence. As with the second group, the third group also enjoy the right to work and to equal treatment. In addition, they can enjoy student maintenance in the form of grants or loans.[77]

From solidarity to non-discrimination?

Although there are strong arguments about entitlement to benefits in the host state based on transnational solidarity deriving from EU citizenship, there is considerable hostility to such an approach. This opposition is seen in references to welfare tourists frequently raised in the press, particularly in light of the recent expansion of the EU to the East (embracing eight formerly Communist countries with significantly lower levels of income).[78] It may be for this reason that the Court has recently moved away from the language of solidarity, placing a greater reliance instead on the principle of non-discrimination. This can be seen in *Collins*[79] and also, more recently, in *Trojani*.[80]

It will be recalled that Collins was a newly arrived Irish man seeking work in the UK. The Court made clear that, as a work seeker, the rights he enjoyed under Article 39 and Regulation 1612/68 were limited to equal treatment in respect of access to employment and that he did not enjoy equal treatment in respect of social (financial) advantages under Article 7(2). The Court then considered the effect of its recent case law on citizenship. Referring to its decision in *Grzelczyk*, the Court said that "in view of the establishment of citizenship of the Union", it was no longer possible to exclude from the scope of Article 39 benefits of a "financial nature intended to facilitate access to employment in the labour market of a Member State". On its face, this appears to be a highly significant development because it confirms that orthodox tenets of the Court's earlier case law (in particular on workers) must now be read subject to a "citizenship" interpretation. The Court then subjected the "habitual residence" requirement to a conventional discrimination analysis. It noted that because the rule disadvantaged those who had exercised their rights of free movement (therefore indirectly discriminatory) it would be lawful only if the UK could justify it based on objective considerations unrelated to nationality and proportionate to the aim of the national provisions. Following the earlier case of *D'Hoop*,[81] the Court accepted that it was legitimate for a national legislature to wish to ensure that there was a genuine link between the person applying for the benefit and the employment market of that state and that the link could be determined by establishing that the claimant has "for a reasonable period, in fact genuinely sought work" in the UK. The Court added that while the residence requirement was appropriate to attain the objective, it was only proportionate if it rested on clear criteria known in advance, judicial redress was available, and the required period of residence was not excessive. Thus, in *Collins* the force of the citizenship rhetoric was curtailed by the discrimination analysis which allowed an indirectly discriminatory measure to be objectively justified.

Where the discrimination at issue is direct, no such objective justifications are available. This was the case with *Trojani*. Trojani, a French national was a short-term resident in Belgium. He had been living in a Salvation Army hostel where he did various jobs for about 30 hours a week as part of a "personal socio-occupational reintegration programme" in return for board and lodging and some pocket money.[82] As with Grzelczyk, Trojani was denied the minimex on the grounds that he was neither Belgian, nor a "worker" under Regulation 1612/68. While the Court of

Justice left it up to the national court to decide whether Trojani was in fact a worker, it also considered the rights he might derive from being a citizen. The Court said that he did not derive the right to reside in Belgium from Article 18 due to his lack of resources.[83] However, the Court did say that he could benefit from the fundamental principle of equal treatment laid down in Article 12 since he was lawfully resident in Belgium.

This case law suggests that the Court is now focusing on the question of legal residence: if migrants are legally resident in the host state then they should receive the same benefits as nationals. While unobjectionable as a matter of principle, it still raises the question as to the basis for the entitlement especially if they have not contributed to the exchequer of the host state. One possible answer may lie in some (unarticulated) sense of solidarity (possibly of the national rather than the transnational variety) buttressed by the notion of European citizenship. Some support for this view can be found in Advocate General Geelhoed's opinion in *Ninni-Orasche*.[84] Mrs Ninni-Orasche, an Italian, married an Austrian national in 1993. Under Austrian law she was given leave to enter and reside in Austria.[85] She did various casual jobs until 1996, when she started studying at an Austrian university. The Austrian authorities rejected her request for study financing because she did not satisfy the criteria laid down in *Lair*.[86] The Advocate General said that she could not rely on the Students' Directive 93/96 to obtain the financing because, unlike Grzelczyk, she was just starting her course and Article 3 of the Directive expressly precluded her from obtaining maintenance grants in the host state. The Advocate General also considered her other capacity – that of legal resident living in another member state "in a capacity which is not connected primarily with the exercise of the fundamental economic freedom".[87] When viewed from this perspective, he said that the restrictions contained in Article 18(1) did not apply. The Advocate General continued that Article 17, read in conjunction with Article 12, applied and could, "in specific circumstances, confer a right to equal treatment even where social advantages which are not granted under the directives on residence are concerned".[88] He referred to the need for a minimum degree of financial solidarity towards those residents who are students but hold the nationality of another member state, and concluded that a resident like Mrs Ninni-Orasche with a "demonstrable and structural link to Austrian society" could not be treated in Austria "as any other national of a third country".[89] For this reason, he said that she enjoyed the right to equal treatment unless unequal treatment could be objectively justified.[90]

Conclusions

In this paper I have argued that the concepts of integration and solidarity, which have been justified (particularly in recent years) in the name of Union citizenship, have been central to facilitating the movement and integration of migrants in the EU. However, the sensitivity of such concepts, combined with the expansion of the EU to the East, seems to have made the Court wary of articulating these justifications clearly in the recent case law. This may be due to the fear that notions of transnational solidarity could serve to undermine, rather than reinforce, ideas of Union citizenship.

So what lessons does the EU example provide for labour market integration more generally? It would seem that the more homogenous the group, especially in terms of income levels and an ability to contribute (the workers example in the EU context), the greater the acceptance that migrants should receive benefits. As the degree of homogeneity declines, and no financial contribution is made to the exchequer of the host state, the greater the resistance to benefits. Even in the EU context where some (rather artificial) concept of homogeneity is imposed from above in the form of EU citizenship, ambitious attempts to use notions of transnational solidarity appear to be replaced by more tentative references to non-discrimination for those legally resident. This places the ball firmly back into the host state's court to grant residence or, at least, to remove those who are not legally resident.

Notes

1. See generally Christopher Greenwood, "Nationality and the Limits of Free Movement of Persons in Community Law" (1987) 7 *Yearbook of European Law* 185, at 187–93; Andrew Evans, "Nationality Law and the Free Movement of Persons in the EEC: with Special Reference to the British Nationality Act 1981" (1982) 2 *Yearbook of European Law* 173.
2. Subject to derogations on the grounds of public policy, public security and public health.
3. EEC Treaty, Art. 39(2).
4. EEC Treaty, Art. 39(3).
5. OJ 1968 No. L257/2, amended by Regulation 312/76 (OJ 1976 No. L3/2) and Council Regulation 2434/92 (OJ 1992 No. L25/1). Measures previously existed which protected the national labour market: Regulation 15/1961 allowed a migrant worker to take a job in another member state if, after three weeks, no national was available to take the job. This was changed by Regulation 38/1964 and Directive 64/240.

6. Case C-249/86, *Commission* v. *Germany* [1989] ECR 1263, para. 11.

7. Case 207/78, *Criminal Proceedings against Even* [1979] ECR 2019.

8. Para. 22, emphasis added.

9. See e.g. Case C-111/91, *Commission* v. *Luxembourg*; Case C-85/96, *Martínez Sala* [1998] ECR I-2691, para. 28.

10. Case 65/81, *Reina* v. *Landeskreditbank Baden-Württemberg* [1982] ECR 33, para. 17.

11. See e.g. Case C-57/96, *Meints* v. *Minister van Landbouw, Natuurbeheer en Visserij* [1997] ECR I-6689, para. 36 (payment to agricultural workers whose employment contracts are terminated); Case C-35/97, *Commission* v. *France* [1998] ECR I-5325 (supplementary retirement pension points).

12. Case 137/84, *Criminal proceedings against Mutsch* [1985] ECR 2681, para. 18 (criminal proceedings in the defendant's own language).

13. Case C-237/94, *O'Flynn* v. *Adjudication Officer* [1996] ECR I-2617 (social security payments to help cover the cost of burying a family member).

14. Case C-3/90, *Bernini* v. *Minister van Onderwijs en Wetenschappen* [1992] ECR I-1071; Case C-337/97, *Meeusen* [1999] ECR I-3289, para. 15

15. Case 59/85, *Netherlands* v. *Reed* [1986] ECR 1283, para. 28.

16. Evelyn Ellis, "Social Advantages: A New Lease of Life" (2003) 40 *Common Market Law Review* 639 at 648.

17. This includes those who are not resident in the territory of the providing state: Case C-57, *Meints* [1997] ECR I-6689, para. 50; Case C-337/97, *Meeusen* [1999] ECR I-3289, para. 21.

18. AG Jacobs in Case C-43/99, *Leclerce and Deaconescu* v. *Caisse nationale des prestations familiales* [2001] ECR I-4265, para. 96. Steve Peers, " 'Social Advantages' and Discrimination in Employment: Case Law Confirmed and Clarified" (1997) 22 *European Law Review* 157 at 164.

19. Compare with the early decision in Case 76/72, *Michel S.* v. *Fonds national de reclassement social des handicapés* [1973] ECR 457, para. 9, where the Court limited social advantages to workers.

20. See e.g. Case 94/84, *ONEM* v. *Deak* [1985] ECR 1873.

21. See also Joined Cases 389 & 390/87, *Echternach and Moritz* v. *Minister van Onderwijs en Wetenschappen* [1989] ECR 723; Case C-308/93, *Bestuur van de Sociale Verzekeringsbank* v. *Cabanis-Issarte* [1996] ECR I-2097.

22. Case C-413/99, *Baumbast and R* v. *Secretary of State for the Home Department* [2002] ECR I-7091, para. 50.

23. Case 32/75, *Fiorini (née Christini)* v. *SNCF* [1975] ECR 1085. See also Case C-278/94, *Commission* v. *Belgium* [1996] ECR I-4307 (tideover benefits); Case C-185/96, *Commission* v. *Greece* [1998] ECR I-6601 (attribution of large family status).

24. They included the right to vote in local and European elections in the host State (Article 19); the right to diplomatic and consular protection from the authorities of any member state in third countries (Article 20); the right to petition the European

Parliament and the right to apply to the ombudsman in any one of the official languages of the EU (Article 21).

25. AG La Pergola in Case C-85/96, *Martínez Sala* v. *Freistaat Bayern* [1998] ECR I-2691, para.18.

26. Council Directives 90/364/EEC ([1990] OJ No. L180/26) on the rights of residence for persons of sufficient means (the "playboy directive"), Directive 90/365/EEC on the rights of residence for employees and self-employed who have ceased their occupational activity ([1990] OJ No.L180/28) and Directive 90/366/EEC ([1990] OJ No. L180/30) on the rights of residence for students.

27. Case C-85/96, [1998] ECR I-2691.

28. Case C-184/99, [2001] ECR I-6193, para.31, echoing AG La Pergola in Case C-85/96, *Martínez Sala* [1998] ECR I-2691, para.18.

29. Case C-413/99, *Baumbast and R* v. *Secretary of State for the Home Department* [2002] ECR I-7091.

30. It was for the national court to make the final decision.

31. This was merely probative and not constitutive of the right to residence.

32. Para. 61.

33. Para. 62.

34. Para. 62.

35. Para. 64.

36. Siofra O'Leary, "Putting Flesh on the Bones of European Union Citizenship" (1999) 24 *European Law Review* 68 at 77–8.

37. Case C-413/99, [2002] ECR I-000, para. 83. See also AG Jacobs' views in Case C-148/02, *Garcia Avello* [2003] ECR I-000, para. 61 and AG Cosmas' even grander claims in Case C-378/97, *Wijsenbeek* [1999] ECR I-6207, para. 85: "Article [18] does not simply enshrine in constitutional terms the *acquis communautaire* as it existed when it was inserted into the Treaty and complement it by broadening the category of persons entitled to freedom of movement to include other classes of person not pursuing economic activities. Article [18] also enshrines a right of a different kind, a true right of movement, stemming from the status as a citizen of the Union, which is not subsidiary in relation to European unification, whether economic or not."

38. See residence directives at note 26 above

39. Case C-184/99, [2001] ECR I-6193.

40. Para. 29.

41. Para. 30.

42. Para. 31.

43. Para. 32.

44. Para. 33, citing Case C-274/96, *Bickel and Franz* [1998] ECR I-7637.

45. Para. 42.

46. Para. 43.

47. Para. 44.

48. Para. 44.

49. Case C-413/99, [2002] ECR I-000, para.91.

50. [1990] OJ No. L180/26.

51. Para. 91.

52. Para. 92.

53. Para. 91.

54. Para. 93.

55. An example of an express exclusion is maintenance grants for students in Art.3 of Directive 93/96.

56. Anastasia Iliopoulou and Helen Toner, "Case C-184/99, *Rudy Grzelczyk v. Centre public d'aide sociale d'Ottignies-Louvain-la-Neuve*, Judgment of the Full Court of 20 September 2001, CR I-6193" (2002) 39 *Common Market Law Review* 609 at 616.

57. European Council Meeting in Laeken, Presidency Conclusions, 14/12/01, 00300/1/01, p.21.

58. "Believing that reunited Europe intends to continue along the path of civilisation, progress and prosperity, for the good of all its inhabitants, including the weakest and most deprived; that it wishes to remain a continent open to culture, learning, and social progress; and that it wishes to deepen the democratic nature of its public life, and to strive for peace, justice and solidarity throughout the world."

59. Article I-2: "The Union is founded on the values of respect for human dignity, liberty, democracy, the rule of law and respect for human rights. These values are common to the Member States in a society of pluralism, tolerance, justice, equality, solidarity and non-discrimination." "Solidarity" can also be found in the existing Article 2 EC.

60. Article I-3, para. 3 provides: "It shall combat social exclusion and shall promote social justice and protection, equality between women and men, solidarity between generations and protection of children's rights. It shall promote economic, social and territorial cohesion, and solidarity among Member States." Para. 4 says: "In its relations with the wider world, the Union shall uphold and promote its values and interests. It shall contribute to peace, security, the sustainable development of the earth, solidarity and mutual respect among peoples, free and fair trade, eradication of poverty and protection of human rights and in particular children's rights, as well as to strict observance and development of international law, including respect for the principles of the United Nations Charter."

61. See also Marise Cremona, "EU Enlargement: Solidarity and Conditionality", inaugural lecture, delivered at Queen Mary College, University of London, 12 March 2003.

62. Case C- 70/95, *Sodemare SA, Anni Azzurri Holding SpA and Anni Azzurri Rezzato Srl v. Regione Lombardia* [1997] ECR I-3395.

63. Para. 29.

64. See also the views of AG Ruiz-Jarabo Colomer in Case C-138/02, *Collins* [2003] ECR I-000, para. 65 who disagreed with the assimilationist approach (para. 63).

65. Case C-184/99, *Grzelczyk* [2001] ECR I-6193, para. 44.

66. See also AG Geelhoed in Case C-413/01, *Franca Ninni-Orasche* v. *Bundesminister für Wissenschaft, Verkehr und Kunst* [2003] ECR I-000.

67. Although on the facts of *Baumbast* his length of residence suggested that his case might be closer to the full integration end of the spectrum. See also Case C-274/96, *Bickel and Franz* [1998] ECR I-7637 on access to translation services in court.

68. Case C-138/02, *Brian Francis Collins* v. *Secretary of State for Work and Pensions* [2003] ECR I-000.

69. Para. 66.

70. Para. 76.

71. Joined Cases C-4 and 5/95, *Stöber and Pereira* [1997] ECR I-511, para. 50.

72. Directive 2004/58/EC (OJ 2004 No. L229/35).

73. Article 6.

74. Article 7.

75. There are certain exceptions to the four-year rule, e.g. those reaching pension age or suffer a permanent incapacity or frontier workers.

76. Article 16.

77. Those with the right of residence and who are engaged in gainful activity may also have the right to student maintenance.

78. In the UK attention has been focused in particular on the influx of students from the enlargement countries. For a flavour of the debate see Liz Lightfoot, "Students face EU fight for Places", *Daily Telegraph*, 4 March 2004, p. 1; L. Clark, "Britain faces huge bill for upkeep of students from EU", *Daily Mail*, 22 March 2004, p. 2. T. Miles, "Warnings over Influx of EU college Students", *Evening Standard*, 4 March 2004, p. 24.

79. Case C-138/02, *Collins* v. *Secretary of State for Work and Pensions*, judgment of 23 March 2004

80. Case C-456/02, *Trojani* v. *Centre public d'aide sociale de Bruxelles*, judgment of 7 September 2004.

81. Case C-224/98, [2002] ECR I-6191.

82. Para. 9.

83. Para. 36.

84. Case C-413/01, *Franca Ninni-Orasche* v. *Bundesminister für Wissenschaft, Verkehr und Kunst* [2003] ECR I-000.

85. Para. 81.

86. Case 39/86, [1988] ECR 3161, namely there had to be a link between the previous occupational activity and the studies.

87. Para. 91.

88. Para. 92.

89. Para. 96.

90. Para. 98.

PART IV

The Americas

9

Labour rights in the FTAA

LANCE COMPA

Introduction: rejection or engagement?

Negotiations on the Free Trade Agreement of the Americas (FTAA) bring advocates of a strong social dimension in hemispheric economic integration to a fork in the road: a path of rejection and a path of engagement. On the rejection path, critics point to flaws and failings in existing trade-labour linkages in the Americas. Ten years after the adoption of the North American Free Trade Agreement (NAFTA) and its labour side agreement, the three member countries of the North American Agreement on Labour Cooperation (NAALC), demonstrate job and wage stagnation, growing inequality in labour markets, and continuing violations of workers' rights.[1]

Similarly, more than a decade after the creation of the Common Market of the Southern Cone (Mercosur) and five years after its Social-Labour Declaration, workers in Brazil, Argentina, Paraguay and Uruguay face wrenching problems of job and wage losses and social inequality. So do workers of the Caribbean Community (CARICOM), in spite of the far-reaching Declaration of Labour and Industrial Relations Principles (1993) and the Charter of Civil Society (1994).[2] In sum, the social provisions of trade pacts have failed to protect human rights, workers' rights and labour standards.

The flaws and failings of these labour instruments lead to one conclusion: an effective workers' rights regime in the FTAA is an impossible goal, and seeking one is a lost cause. In addition, promoting a social dimension in the FTAA, like the NAALC and other regional trade-labour instruments, is aiding and abetting abuses by transnational companies and investors. It gives political cover to weak-kneed legislators who can vote in favour of the FTAA claiming that they support workers' rights when in fact the trade-labour link is "toothless" (the favorite epithet of critics).

Instead, advocates must turn all their energies to torpedoing any agreement. For activists who adopt this view, it means convincing their governments to reject a hemispheric trade pact or, where elections are imminent, supporting and electing legislators and presidents who will repudiate FTAA talks.

This paper advocates for the advancement of the engagement path. Not from any rose-coloured view of existing labour rights-trade links whose flaws and failings are manifest. Rather, from a short-term analysis that parliaments and presidents in the Americas are unlikely to renounce a hemispheric trade agreement, and from a longer-term view that workers can benefit from expanding trade and investment linked to human rights and labour rights protection.

NAFTA countries show no inclination to abandon the FTAA. Hopes of anti-FTAA activists that the election of Luis Inacio da Silva as Brazil's president would crash hemispheric trade negotiations have faded. Lula had earlier characterized FTAA proposals as a US plan for economic "annexation" of Latin America, but upon taking office he declared he would bargain hard for an agreement beneficial to Brazil and the other Mercosur countries.[3]

If labour rights advocates refuse to promote a workers' rights chapter in the FTAA, they could end up with an FTAA with no labour provision at all. And, if they succeed in killing the FTAA, they can celebrate for one night and wake up the next morning to find that not much has changed. The United States and Canada, the developed country engines of the hemispheric economy, will continue to seek bilateral trade agreements with countries eager for expanded access to North American markets and more investment in their economies.

Hemispheric trade and investment with insufficient regard for workers' rights will continue with or without an FTAA. Multinational companies and banks might have to account for slightly higher risk premiums in making production and investment decisions without FTAA guarantees, but they will not walk away from profitable deals. Many countries in Latin America and the Caribbean will jump at the chance for a competitive edge vis-à-vis other developing countries through bilateral deals with the United States and Canada. Mexico and Chile have done so, and Costa Rica with Canada. Since access to US and Canadian markets is the main goal of other countries in the hemisphere, the NAALC and its variations will likely be the sole model for a workers' rights clause, as it was in the Canada–Chile, Canada–Costa Rica, and United States – Chile agreements.

Without an overall trade agreement containing stronger labour rights linkage than that of the NAALC model, advocates will have no central forum or mechanism for dealing with workers' rights in the Americas. This paper suggests that labour rights advocates can and should shape a new viable social dimension in hemispheric trade and demand its inclusion in the FTAA.

The emphasis of this paper is on a viable, not a definitive or triumphant, solution. Workers and their advocates do not triumph in the current conjuncture of economic and political forces. They do not will their way to victory with the sharpness of their criticism or the strength of their denunciations; they hold their losses and make small gains where possible. Workers' advocates must coldly calculate what can be done with the reality they are dealt, hoping the outcomes will advance the longer-term struggle for social justice.

Start over or build on what's been done?

Commitment to a workers' rights clause in the FTAA raises another issue. Should labour rights advocates scrap existing rights models in the hemisphere like the NAALC and its progeny (the United States–Chile, Canada–Chile and Canada–Costa Rica labour pacts), the Mercosur's Social-Labour Declaration, or the CARICOM social charter? Jettisoning those models, advocates could demand a totally new worker rights system with international standards to which national laws must conform and an oversight body empowered to levy economic sanctions on violators. This paper argues for an incremental approach integrating positive features of labour rights instruments and mechanisms already in place in the hemisphere.

For some, the European Union (EU) provides an example. Its structure includes a commission, parliament and a council setting Europe-wide labour standards ("directives") by which national laws must abide. It empowers the European Court of Justice to find violations and to order countries to change their laws to come into compliance with EU standards. Indeed, the EU has all the trappings of a "hard law" legal system like that of national systems.[4]

But for all its strengths, the EU is not the best model for the Americas. Countries involved in FTAA talks are not even remotely contemplating EU-style structural integration. Moreover, the EU social dimension is not nearly as strong as its institutional framework suggests. Directives setting European labour standards are few, and they cover less thorny issues such as health and safety, parental leave, and employee "works councils" entitled to information and consultation, but not to collective bargaining. The EU treaty specifically *excludes* collective bargaining, union organizing and the right to strike from Europe-wide standard setting.[5] These issues are so embedded in national institutions, histories, cultures and class struggles that no European country is willing to hand them over to supranational rule.

Various European social charters broadly address labour rights and labour standards. In December of 2000, the Charter of Fundamental Rights of the European Union was adopted at a summit meeting in Nice. The Nice charter replaced the 1989 Community Charter of Basic Social Rights. An EU "convention" crafting a new union treaty had proposed incorporating the charter into the EU's constitutional structure, supposedly making it binding and enforceable, but such a move is still far from complete.[6]

The charter and its forerunners have always been non-binding "side agreements" to the EU treaty. They are important as guiding principles and points of reference for EU institutions, but they do not yield enforceable rights. National authorities and national courts can ignore them. Countries sometimes even ignore orders from the European Court of Justice (ECJ) on cases stemming from violations of Europe-wide directives, which are supposed to be binding and enforceable. For example, for a decade, France ignored an ECJ order to repeal its labour law prohibiting night work by women. The ECJ held that the law discriminated against women, but there is no European police or European marshal to enforce that court order.[7]

Creating a supranational tribunal empowered to overrule national laws and courts risks turning the wrong direction. For example, the ECJ struck down a German state's affirmative action law favouring women's movement into public sector supervisory jobs. The court held that this was "reverse discrimination" forbidden by EU equality directives, and ordered Germany to nullify their law.[8]

Even if the EU's social dimension were a robust one driving labour standards higher and punishing workers' rights violators (granted that it *is* more advanced than Americas' models), importing it into a trade pact is impractical. Both large and small countries in this hemisphere are not going to say, "We're at sea on workers' rights, we don't know how to do this, so we'll borrow the EU model." They are going to negotiate a homegrown social dimension to hemispheric trade.

Binding, enforceable international labour standards remain an overarching goal for worker rights advocates. However, getting from here to there in a single bound in an FTAA is not possible, especially when so much economic disparity marks the negotiating parties. Smaller, weaker countries naturally fear that universal standards will be applied to them, but not to bigger economic powers. Moreover, each country has its own political and jurisdictional barriers to supranational labour authority. For example, Canadian provinces already enjoy and jealously guard provincial sovereignty in most labour affairs. They are not interested in surrendering their power to the federal government, let alone to a new international authority.

On the trade union side, activists in other countries look at the condition of workers' rights in the United States and recoil at the prospect of homogenized labour standards tending toward the US model. US trade unionists ought to be equally sceptical about solving their own problems through some kind of international legal legerdemain. Trade-labour instruments are not going to reverse deficiencies in US law – NLRB election rules, striker replacements, contingent workers' lack of protection and others – without action by Congress.[9] These are problems for US workers to tackle through their own organizing and political action, not by demanding a silver bullet in a trade and labour pact.

The embedded national framework of labour rights and labour standards did not take shape casually. In each country, it resulted from national histories replete with anti-colonial wars, civil wars, constitutional crises, domestic regional conflicts and class struggles. Thirty-four countries sitting down to negotiate a social dimension to a hemispheric trade agreement are not going to undo those histories and defer to an untested supranational authority.

Many governments involved in FTAA talks have already committed themselves to addressing workers' rights in trade arrangements. Their specific labour agreements are still evolving, but they are enough to lay a foundation for new movement in FTAA negotiations. Instead of a harsh demand that governments leap into the unknown with a new supranational system, a softer demand to build upon blocks already in place is one that a strong civil society movement can persuade governments to adopt.

Labour rights in existing regional trade agreements

I am not going to recite all of the institutional structures, procedures, case histories and other aspects of labour rights provisions related to various regional trade agreements. However, a brief description of the main features of the NAALC, the Mercosur Social-Labour Declaration, and the CARICOM Social Charter will set the stage for what follows. This paper aims to explore the prospect of weaving together the "best practices" into a new plan that labour rights advocates can support and that governments can accept.[10]

The NAALC

The NAALC sets forth eleven "Labour Principles" that the three signatory countries have committed themselves to promote:

- freedom of association and protection of the right to organize;
- the right to bargain collectively;
- the right to strike;
- forced labour;
- child labour;
- minimum wage, hours of work and other labour standards;
- non-discrimination;
- equal pay for equal work;
- occupational safety and health;
- workers' compensation; and
- migrant worker protection.

The NAALC signatories have pledged to effectively enforce their national labour laws in these eleven subject areas, and have agreed to be subjected to critical reviews of their performance by the other countries.

With regard to the eleven labour principles, these countries adopted six "obligations" for the effective enforcement of these principles. These obligations include:

- a general duty to provide high labour standards;
- effective enforcement of labour laws;
- access to administrative and judicial fora for workers whose rights are violated;
- due process, transparency, speed, and effective remedies in labour law proceedings;
- public availability of labour laws and regulations, and opportunity for "interested persons" to comment on proposed changes; and
- promoting public awareness of labour law and workers' rights.

Key to understanding the NAALC is to highlight the two things that it does *not* do. Firstly, it does not set new common standards to which countries must adjust their laws and regulations. Instead, the NAALC stresses sovereignty in each country's internal labour affairs, recognizing "the right of each Party to establish its own domestic labour standards".

Secondly, the NAALC does not create a supranational tribunal that hears evidence, decides guilt or innocence in labour disputes or orders remedies against violators. This role is left to national authorities applying national law. Nor does it create a supranational judicial review body to hear appeals from decisions of national tribunals and overrule decisions that arguably fail to "enforce" the NAALC. Decisions by the national courts are left undisturbed by the NAALC.

Instead of an international enforcement system, the NAALC countries have created an oversight, review and dispute resolution system designed to hold each other accountable for performance in the eleven defined areas of labour law. Oversight is conducted by a review body of *another* government. Then, depending on the subject area, an evaluation and arbitration is held by an independent, non-governmental committee or panel.

Under this process, trade unionists and their allies file complaints on one or more of the labour principles in a new institutional structure that provides for investigations, public hearings, written reports, government-to-government consultations, independent evaluations, non-binding recommendations and other "soft law" measures common to most international agreements. At each stage of this process, advocates can intervene to press for favourable outcomes.

A National Administrative Office (NAO) in the labour department of each country receives complaints ("public communications" or "submissions" in NAALC parlance) from the public related to any of the eleven labour principles. There are no restrictions on who may file a complaint. In the interest of having the process as open and accessible as possible, the regulations of each NAO set a fairly low threshold of acceptance for review.[11]

The scope of such reviews is "labour law matters arising in the territory of another Party". This is an unusual but critical feature of the NAALC. Employers, workers, unions and allied NGOs must file their submissions with the NAO in another country, not the country where alleged violations occurred, to commence the review process. The United States and Canada hold public hearings on complaints with transcripts and sworn testimony. The Mexican NAO holds private "informative sessions".

The NAOs issue public reports on the submissions that they have accepted for review. The public report contains a key make-or-break conclusion: whether or not it recommends ministerial consultations. If no recommendations are made, the matter is closed. If recommendations are provided, the matter moves forward. These ministerial consultations are open-ended efforts to resolve a problem before it enlarges. They have generally led to further hearings, special research reports, seminars and conferences, worker education programmes and the like.

A "hard law" edge has been applied to three of the labour principles: those covering minimum wages, child labour, and occupational safety and health. An independent arbitral panel is empowered to fine an offending government for a "persistent pattern of failure to effectively enforce" domestic labour law. If the fine is not paid, the panel can apply trade sanctions on the firm, industry, or sector where the workers' rights violations occurred.[12]

In sum, the NAALC is not a full-fledged international enforcement mechanism. It is not intended to resolve specific complaints and to issue orders to reinstate workers unjustly discharged, orders to recognize and bargain with trade unions, orders to remove children from unlawful labour, orders to adjust pay for women to equal that of men, orders to install air filters to reduce health hazards, orders to provide compensation to injured workers, and other remedies associated with labour law enforcement. These matters are left to national legislation and national enforcement mechanisms.

The NAALC is intended as a review mechanism by which member countries open themselves up to investigation, reports, evaluations, recommendations and other measures so that over time enhanced oversight and scrutiny will generate more effective labour law enforcement. To the extent that legislative responses can be fashioned within national systems, rather than imposed by a supranational power, oversight under the NAALC can change the climate for labour law reform in each country to achieve greater adherence to NAALC principles and obligations.

Mercosur and the Social-Labour Declaration

When the Common Market of the South (Mercosur)[13] took shape in 1991, a reference to "social justice" in the Preamble of the Treaty of Asunción was the only nod to a social dimension in regional trade plans. Mercosur countries quickly realized the need to respond to the demands of workers, trade unions and allied civil society forces for instruments and mechanisms to ensure that expanding regional trade did not create new incentives for social dumping and worker exploitation to obtain a competitive advantage. That same year, labour ministers of the member countries responded to demands from labour and civil society by adopting the Montevideo Declaration insisting that the trade group address labour and social issues.

The 1994 Protocol of Ouro Preto finalized Mercosur's institutional structure and created two new organisms on labour matters: "Working Group 10" (WG10) and a new body called the Economic and Social Consultative Forum. WG10 is composed of labour ministry officials of each Mercosur member government in a tripartite government-labour-business structure, with one representative from each sector in each of the four countries. Labour and business representatives have the right to participate and vote in committees on conclusions and recommendations to send to the full Working Group.

A parallel structure is established within each country. Country committees have often invited non-governmental organizations like consumer groups, international organizations like the ILO, and labour centrals that might not have a seat on the committee to participate in committee meetings. Both national committees and WG10 have contracted with experts for special working groups or technical committees on particular subject matters.

WG10 also created a permanent Labour Market Observatory. The Observatory is a technical organ designed to provide "real-time" comparative information on labour market indicators to Mercosur governments to help them coordinate employment policies. Like other Mercosur social initiatives, the Observatory has a tripartite institutional structure. A 12-member management council named by WG10 oversees a secretariat of experts from each country selected by the country's tripartite national section.

The Economic and Social Consultative Forum (ESCF) is a setting for trade unions, employers and non-governmental organizations to voice their views and concerns about economic integration in the region. Like other Mercosur institutions, the ESCF is tripartite in structure, but with a key distinction: the Forum does not include government representatives. The three sectors of the ESCF are labour, business and NGOs.

Each of the four Mercosur countries have nine seats on the ESCF, creating a plenary body of 36 members. Each country may choose through its internal processes its nine members, with the sole requirement that labour and business seats be equal. Thus, for example, labour and business could have two seats each, opening up five seats to NGOs. In practice, these countries have generally chosen three labour and three business representatives, with three NGO representatives joining them in the national delegation. NGO participants have come from consumer, environmental, educational, legal and other civil society groups.

The ESCF began functioning in 1996 after its four national sections were formed. It is strictly an advisory body, able only to forward non-binding recommendations to governments. The Forum provides space for civil society sectors in each country to learn about each other's concerns, to develop institutional rules, procedures and customs for tripartite work, and to seek common ground on social aspects of regional economic integration. These were important precursors to the new framework created by the Social-Labour Declaration of Mercosur.

Social-Labour Declaration of Mercosur

The Social-Labour Declaration of 10 December 1998 and the move to create a Mercosur Social-Labour Commission are the most significant developments in the region. Emitted not by a working group or even a council of ministers, but by the heads of state of the four Mercosur member countries, the declaration has exceptional solemnity and authoritativeness. The creation of a new, permanent Social-Labour Commission gives added impetus to the social dimension in Mercosur.

In its Preamble, the declaration invokes ILO Conventions such as the 1998 ILO Declaration on Fundamental Principles and Rights at Work, the Universal Declaration of Human Rights, the 1995 Copenhagen summit and other multilateral and regional human rights instruments. The content of the declaration covers the usual core labour standards – freedom of association, child labour, forced labour and non-discrimination. However, it ranges beyond the usual core to address migrant workers' rights, the right to strike, social dialogue, employment and unemployment, training, health and safety, labour inspection and social security.[14]

The declaration does not establish harmonized norms and has no linkage to the Mercosur trade regime imposing economic sanctions for violations of workers' rights – key trade union goals for a social charter. Rather, the member countries "commit themselves to respect the fundamental rights inscribed in this declaration and to promote its application in conformity with national law and practice and with collective contracts and agreements". In its closing article, the declaration states: "The States Party emphasize that their Declaration and its follow-up mechanisms cannot be invoked or used for other ends not contained herein; prohibited, in particular, is its application to trade, economic, and financial matters."

Social-Labour Commission

The declaration's application and follow-up clause creates a tripartite Mercosur Social-Labour Commission that reports to the Common Market Group (CMG). Composed of twelve government, labour and business members (one per sector per country), the Commission is empowered to act by consensus to:

- review annual reports from governments;
- develop recommendations;
- examine "difficulties and mistakes in the application and fulfilment" of the declaration;
- write its own analyses and reports on application and fulfilment; and,
- shape proposals for modifying the text of the declaration.

Each government must submit an annual report to the Commission on changes in national law and practice on matters addressed in the declaration, on progress in promoting the declaration, and on difficulties in applying it. Based on an examination of these reports, the Commission prepares a comprehensive report to the CMG.

As with the NAALC, Mercosur governments are reluctant to cede sovereign power over labour matters to a new, untested supranational authority or to create international norms that trump national law. Employers complain that the Social-Labour Declaration is too favourable to the trade union agenda and fails to promote much needed (from their perspective) flexibilization of labour law and practice in the region. However, they count as a victory the fact that the declaration does not have linkage to trade disciplines with potential for economic sanctions.

Unions see the declaration as lacking "teeth" precisely because it does not establish harmonized standards or trade sanctions against labour rights violators. Furthermore, it fails to halt harmful (from their point of view) trends toward greater flexibility, whether such changes stem from de facto moves by management or from labour law reforms often demanded by the International Monetary Fund or other international financial institutions. In the trade unions' view, such flexibilization undermines workers' rights won through decades of struggle, including the struggle against military dictatorships in all four Mercosur countries.

At the same time, trade unions welcome the significant role afforded to labour in the tripartite structure of the Commission. They have seen a broadening and deepening of social dialogue, which they view as progress in the long march toward an effective social dimension in trade.[15]

The Caribbean Community (CARICOM) and the Charter of Civil Society

CARICOM is an association of Caribbean nations created in 1973 to develop a common market and coordinated policies among its member states.[16] Faced with the rise of regional trade agreements around them, and in particular, the new comparative advantages afforded to Mexico under NAFTA, CARICOM countries accelerated efforts to overcome strong distinctions and rivalries and built an effective trade group.[17]

CARICOM's social dimension is grounded in the Charter of Civil Society of the Caribbean Community, signed in 1994 and adopted by the countries in 1997. The purpose of the Charter is captured in the following statement by the commission:

> CARICOM needs normative moorings; we have found widespread yearning for giving the community a qualitative character – values beyond the routine of integration arrangements to which [economic integration] can be made to conform. The Charter can become the soul of the Community which needs a soul if it is to command the loyalty of the people of CARICOM.[18]

The Charter of Civil Society is a comprehensive human rights instrument composed of 27 articles. Most notably, in comparison with similar international efforts, the CARICOM Charter subjects private actors – "social partners"[19] – as well as states to its oversight mechanism.

The first grouping of articles covers classical civil and political rights – human dignity and the right to life, liberty and security of the person; equality before the law; political freedom; freedom of association, expression and religion. Article X on cultural diversity shifts the instrument's focus to economic and social rights as reflected in its clauses on indigenous peoples, women, children and the disabled; access to education and training; health; participation in the economy; environmental rights; and good governance.

Two articles of the Charter relate to a social dimension. Article XIX on Workers' Rights is the longest article of the Charter. It guarantees to "every worker" the right to form or belong to a trade union, to bargain collectively, to reasonable hours and pay, to withhold his or her labour, to a safe workplace, and not to be subjected to unfair labour practices. An exception is made for public employees which is said to be "reasonably justifiable in a free and democratic society".

Article XIX enumerates the obligations of governments to:

- safeguard workers' right to freely choose occupations;
- recognize the desirability of decent pay;

- provide machinery for recognition and certification of trade unions freely chosen by a majority of workers;
- sensitize workers, unions and employers as to their respective and mutual obligations;
- provide protection against arbitrary dismissal;
- provide machinery for industrial dispute resolution;
- provide maternity leave and return-to-work rights after pregnancy;
- establish standards to ensure a safe and healthy workplace;
- provide adequate social security; and
- ensure social and medical assistance to retired persons.

Article XXII on Social Partners states briefly the undertaking of each government to establish a framework for genuine consultation among its social partners on the objectives, contents and implementation of national economic and social programmes and their respective roles and responsibilities in good governance.

The follow-up mechanism in Article XXV calls for periodic reports to the CARICOM Secretary-General on measures adopted and progress achieved in compliance with the Charter. Reports are to indicate "factors and difficulties, if any" affecting implementation. Governments are advised to consult with social partners in preparing the reports, and establish in each country a National Committee to oversee Charter implementation. The National Committee is to be made up of government representatives, representatives of the social partners, and "other persons of high moral character and recognized competence in their respective fields of endeavor".

The Charter contains a complaint mechanism by which citizens may file with their National Committee "reports of allegations of breaches of, or non-compliance with" the Charter. Significantly, complaints may cite violations "attributed to the state or to one or more social partners".

The National Committee must notify the state or social partner named in the complaint and request comments on the allegation. The complaint, comments and the Committee's "own views" are then reported to the Secretary-General for forwarding to the Conference of Heads of Governments of the Caribbean Community. The deliberations of the Conference and any recommendations are sent back to the government and the National Committee of the country involved.

No further action is contemplated under the CARICOM Charter in situations alleging violations of Charter provisions, including workers' rights. The Charter establishes an oversight system relying on peer pressure and moral force to change behaviour or to correct injustices. There is no linkage to CARICOM trading arrangements and no plan for economic sanctions against human rights and workers' rights violators.

Gleaning positive elements

An institutional role for civil society actors

In FTAA talks to date, governments have declared their intention to engage civil society on a social dimension in trade. Labour rights advocates should demand action through a labour rights chapter promoting a strong institutional role for civil society actors. The NAALC and NAALC-like agreements are weak on civil society involvement. They allow private parties to file complaints under the agreement, but after an initial filing there is no right of appeal or advancement to higher levels of the procedure. Such advancements are entirely controlled by governments.

NAALC-style agreements include trade union and employer representatives on advisory committees, but these committees are largely inactive. Applying the labour agreement is strictly a government-to-government operation with civil society marginalized.

In contrast, Mercosur and CARICOM provide valuable models of openness to civil society and respect for social actors. Mercosur created a civil society Economic and Social Consultative Forum (ESCF) for business, labour and NGOs to develop recommendations on human rights, labour and environmental matters in its member countries. Like other Mercosur institutions, the ESCF is tripartite in structure, but the three parts are non-governmental. Each of the four countries have nine seats on the ESCF, making for a plenary body of thirty-six members. Each country may choose through its internal processes the nine members to be drawn from business, trade union and NGO communities. The sole proviso is that business and labour representatives must be equal in number. In practice, countries have come up with three representatives from each constituency: labour, business and NGOs. NGO participants come from consumer, environmental, educational, legal and other civil society groups.

Mercosur has also created a Social-Labour Commission (SLC) under the declaration with ample space for trade union participation in setting a social agenda for member countries. The twelve-member SLC includes one labour, business and government representative from each of the four parties. This commission reviews annual government reports on labour law and practice, progress in promoting the declaration, and problems in applying it. The SLC examines each country's report and prepares its own comprehensive analysis and recommendations to Mercosur's governing body, including proposals for changes to the declaration.

The Mercosur SLC is complemented by a national labour-business-government commission in each country, as well as sectoral commissions in textile, transportation, agriculture, telecommunications and other industries. Again, results should not be overstated. Recommendations flowing from this tripartite process are non-binding. However, requiring country self-reporting and forging consensus critiques and recommendations with the labour movement's full, equal participation is a valuable model for a hemispheric institutional setting. Moreover, the SLC has fostered innovative regional developments such as cross-border collective bargaining (for example, between Volkswagen and metalworkers unions in Brazil and Argentina)[20] and the unusual step of joint child labour and job safety inspections by multinational teams of enforcement officials from labour departments of member countries.

Borrowing from European discourse, CARICOM's Charter of Civil society sets out obligations not only for member governments, but also for "social partners" including trade unions, corporations and NGOs. In each country, a national committee made up of government officials, representatives of the social partners, and respected independent scholars and experts oversees the implementation of this Charter.

Complaint mechanisms

A strong institutional role guaranteeing a permanent "seat at the table" for trade unions and other civil society actors is an important feature in Mercosur and CARICOM's social dimension. This is lacking in the NAALC and its progeny. However, participatory mechanisms leading to consultations and recommendations are not enough. A robust complaint system is needed to give a voice and recourse to workers victimized by labour rights violations and to advocates who can act on behalf of victims. Mercosur and CARICOM lack such a mechanism, whereas the NAALC has something important to offer.

The NAALC and its offshoots have several positive elements of a complaint mechanism to weave into a new FTAA labour rights system. For one, the NAALC has no "standing" requirement that only victims or only trade unions or only citizens can file complaints about workers' rights violations. "Any person", meaning any individual or any organization, alone or in concert, regardless of citizenship, can file a complaint (called a "public communication" in the soft diplomatic language of the NAALC) about violations of one or more of the eleven labour principles and the failure of a government to effectively enforce related laws.

In practice, most NAALC complaints have been submitted jointly by trade unions, human rights organizations, independent worker support groups and others from two or three countries working from a cross-border alliance. Indeed, the NAALC's unusual requirement for complaints about violations in one country to be filed in another member country (to avoid conflict with national labour law bodies) forces advocates to work collaboratively in international coalitions, a valuable spin-off effect of the NAALC.

A new hemispheric labour rights regime should preserve the ample use of consultation with complainants, public hearings, commissioned research and detailed reports like those by the National Administrative Offices (NAOs) of the NAALC countries. Public hearings, in particular, allow affected workers and their advocates to state their claims through dramatic first-hand testimony. Hearings also create opportunities for protests, press conferences and other elements of strategic media campaigns.

Another favourable element in the NAALC complaint system is the absence of a requirement that complainants "exhaust" national mechanisms before resorting to the NAALC. Exhaustion of national remedies is a requirement of the Inter-American Commission and Court of Human Rights, for example. This severely crimps the timeliness of using it, since in most countries appeal procedures can take years before a case is finally resolved. Under the NAALC, aggrieved workers and their advocates can file unfair labour practice charges with their national authorities on Monday and with another country's NAO on Tuesday.

Targeting corporate abusers

CARICOM countries recognized that in the context of regional economic integration, the power of multinational corporations over workers' rights and labour standards often exceeds the governments' power to regulate them. Thus, CARICOM expressly allows complaints against corporations as well as governments for violations of workers' rights provisions in the Charter of Civil Society.

NAALC complaints technically run against governments' failure to effectively enforce national laws. In practice, targeted governments have been joined in the dock by corporate abusers of workers' rights. Cases are called the *GE case*, the *Sony case*, the *Duro Bag case* (all cases "against" Mexico), the *Sprint case* ("against" the United States), the *McDonald's case* ("against" Canada) and so on. Enforcement is the focus of the NAALC, but the questions "enforcement of what?" and "enforcement against whom?" cannot be delinked from the inquiry. When the US NAO first sought public comment on its proposed regulations, employer groups demanded a prohibition on naming any corporation in a complaint or in an NAO report.[21]

Workers' rights violations do not occur in a vacuum; they occur in a defined place and time, and usually in a place of employment. Fortunately, the US NAO rejected this employer demand so that complaints could weave together allegations about countries' failure to effectively enforce their laws in connection with specific workers' rights abuses by corporations.[22]

In the years since it took effect, NAFTA's labour side agreement has given rise to a varied, rich experience of international labour rights advocacy. Nearly thirty complaints and cases on behalf of workers in all three countries have arisen under the NAALC. They embrace workers' organizing and bargaining efforts, occupational safety and health, migrant worker protection, minimum employment standards, discrimination against women, compensation for workplace injuries, and other issues.

A rapid summary of just a few cases demonstrates how advocates get results. Gains are not made through direct enforcement by an international tribunal, but through indirection, by exploiting the spaces created by this new labour rights instrument to strengthen cross-border ties among labour rights advocates and to generate unexpected pressures on governments and on transnational enterprises. To be effective, labour rights advocates using the agreement must seek help from their counterparts across the border.

- In 1996, the provincial government of Alberta announced plans to privatize workplace health and safety enforcement. Labour inspectors would have become independent contractors. The public employees' union declared it would file a NAALC complaint charging Alberta with not just a failure, but with a complete abdication of its responsibility to effectively enforce health and safety laws. The government dropped its plan.[23]
- In 1996, Mexican labour authorities dissolved a small democratic trade union in the fisheries ministry when that agency merged with a larger

environmental ministry, who held larger pro-government bargaining rights. Together with US human rights groups, the dissident union filed a NAALC complaint in the United States alleging failure to enforce the Mexican constitutional guarantee of freedom of association. At a public hearing in Washington, DC, Mexican government officials and leaders of both Mexican unions, labour law experts from both countries, and US labour and human rights advocates testified, generating wide publicity in both countries and a sharply critical report by the US NAO. As a result, the smaller dissident union regained its registration and has continued its activity in the democratic union movement.[24]

- A 1997 complaint by a coalition of US and Mexican labour, human rights and women's rights groups challenged the widespread practice of pregnancy testing in the maquiladora factories. A public hearing in Texas exposed the involvement of well-known US companies such as General Motors and Zenith which led to a US NAO report confirming the abuses.[25] Several US multinational firms announced that they would halt the practice and advocacy groups in Mexico launched new efforts seeking legislative reform to halt pregnancy testing in employment. In 2003, Mexico adopted a new far-reaching anti-discrimination law prohibiting pregnancy testing and other forms of discrimination against women.[26]

- A 1999 complaint to the US NAO by flight attendants' unions in the United States and Mexico charged Mexico with failing to enforce the right to freedom of association by denying flight attendants represented by a "wall-to-wall" pro-government union at the TAESA airline the right to form an independent union. A March 2000 public hearing in Washington, DC buttressed the workers' claims and demonstrated international support for Mexican flight attendants who undertook protest actions in major airports. Later in 2000, in a parallel situation at another airline, the Mexican government reversed its stance and allowed flight attendants to vote separately on union representation to avoid a new round of international scrutiny.[27]

- Canadian and US unions filed a NAALC complaint with the US NAO in 1998 after McDonald's closed a Montreal restaurant where workers had formed a union. The complaint targeted flaws in Quebec's labour law that allowed companies to close work sites based on anti-union motivation. When the US NAO accepted the complaint and scheduled public hearings, Quebec trade unions, employer federations, and labour department officials agreed to resolve the matter in a labour code reform bill rather than have Quebec's labour policies aired in a US public hearing. The unions withdrew their complaint and the hearing was cancelled.[28]

- Twenty-five unions, health and safety advocacy groups, human rights organizations and an allied community support network filed a major complaint with the US NAO in 2000 for workers suffering egregious health and safety violations at two Auto-Trim manufacturing plants in the *maquiladora* region. The 100-page complaint reflects long and careful collaboration among the filing organizations, a high level of technical competency and legal argument, and a powerful indictment of the government's failure to enforce health and safety laws.[29] These advocates filed a parallel complaint with Canada's NAO, and the two complaints led to a series of public hearings and sharply critical reports. Mexico claimed to strengthen its health and safety enforcement in response to the complaints. The labour-community coalition was not satisfied, but claimed for its part the creation of a permanent new network of health and safety advocates in North America.

- The Washington state apple case is a rich example of strategic use of the NAALC and how it can foster new ties of solidarity. More than 50,000 Mexican workers labour in the orchards and processing plants of the largest apple-growing region in the United States. Employers crushed their efforts throughout the 1990s to form trade unions, to bargain collectively, to have job health and safety protection, to end discrimination, and to attain other workplace gains. In 1997, the Teamsters union and the United Farm Workers agreed to develop a NAALC case on these issues. They reached out for support from Mexican unions, farm worker advocacy groups, and human rights organizations, and filed a NAALC complaint with the NAO of Mexico. In December of 1998, a hearing was held in Mexico City, with widespread media coverage.[30] The Mexico NAO report and follow-up ministerial consultations initiated a campaign involving workers which lasted for over a year and attained a number of gains for workers.[31] For example, international scrutiny under the NAALC helped convince two large apple warehouse companies to agree to a "card-check" certification which led to union recognition.[32]

In each of the aforementioned examples, new alliances were built among groups that had hardly ever communicated until the NAALC complaint gave them a concrete venue for working together. For leaders and activists of independent Mexican trade unions in particular, access to international allies and to a mechanism for scrutiny of repressive tactics long hidden from international public view provided strength and protection to build their movement.[33]

This accounting is not meant to overstate the NAALC's impact. Each of the examples provided are more complicated than these capsule summaries can convey, and the advantages gained are uneven. Asking workers to turn to the NAALC to air their grievances must be joined by honest cautions that it cannot directly result in regained jobs, union recognition, or back pay for violations. Unions and allied groups have to weigh the value of using the NAALC in light of staff time, energy and resources that might be allocated elsewhere when a specific payoff in new members or new collective agreements cannot be promised. Gains come obliquely, over time, by pressing companies and governments to change their behaviour, by sensitizing public opinion, by building ties of solidarity, and by taking other steps to change the climate for the advancement of workers' rights.

The NAALC allows transnational social actors to demand investigations, public hearings and government consultations on workers' rights violations. Advocates now have the opportunity to strategize and plan together in a sustained fashion, gathering evidence for drafting a complaint, crafting its elements, setting priorities, defining demands, launching media campaigns, meeting with government officials to set the agenda for a hearing and to press them for thorough reviews and follow-up, preparing to testify in public hearings, engaging technical experts to buttress a case with scientific elements (a health and safety case, for example), influencing the composition of independent experts' panels and the terms of reference of their investigation among other concrete tasks.

This is not meant to be a wide-eyed endorsement of using the NAALC at every opportunity. Choices about resource allocation and measurement of potential gains have to be made. Actors face unavoidable compromises using instruments and procedures created by governments more attuned to corporate concerns than to workers' interests. But given the structurally defensive position of workers in a corporate-dominated system, sole reliance on denunciation, confrontation and rejection, while scorning involvement in efforts to link workers' rights to trade or to use the inevitably flawed agreements that follow, surrenders the chance for a savvy, strategic exploitation of pressure points found in international human rights and labour rights instruments, however flawed they may be, compared with what labour rights advocates would create on their own without governments or transnational enterprises to contend with.

Research and oversight bodies

The NAALC created a small permanent Secretariat (originally placed in Dallas, Texas, but now in Washington, DC) to serve as the research and administrative arm of the council of labour ministers. A half-dozen economists, lawyers and labour policy experts from the three member countries have produced valuable, book-length comparative labour law and labour market studies, along with shorter guides to workers' rights.[34]

Mercosur has created a social-labour *Observatorio* to monitor developments and produce reports and analyses on labour markets and workers' rights in member countries.[35] The Observatorio has produced valuable comparative studies on child labour, discrimination, social dialogue, migration, job creation, training and other important topics.

The NAALC Secretariat and the Mercosur *Observatorio* provide solid models for a new, hemispheric labour rights research and reporting body. Such new body should have an adequate staff and budget to carry out an expanded programme, and it should have guarantees of greater independence in its work. Its mandate should also include strengthened oversight on the efficacy of labour rights mechanisms in a hemispheric agreement, "blowing the whistle" when governments and companies violate workers' rights and exposing failures to provide effective enforcement and remedies.

Enforcement

The ever-present question of "teeth" in labour rights-trade linkage arises in the FTAA context. Critics have lambasted all the models discussed in this paper for lacking teeth, for not providing specific remedies like reinstatement of workers dismissed for union organizing, recognition of independent unions, enforceable orders to halt pregnancy testing in *maquiladora* factories, and other on-the-ground targets of NAALC or CARICOM complainants.

Such criticism is fair. However, we have to recognize that countries are not going to set up a supranational mechanism that can overturn national labour laws and overrule national supreme courts in labour cases. Instead, international labour rights mechanisms provide new opportunities to foster organizing and solidarity. Advocates make gains indirectly, when using these labour rights mechanisms as part of a broader strategy of workplace organizing and cross-border solidarity campaigns. We can shape even farther-reaching opportunities in a hemispheric setting.

The NAALC and its progeny have some teeth in the form of potential fines or trade sanctions against countries or sectors that violate workers' rights. However, no case has ever reached such a point. Only member governments, not social actors, can invoke the sanctions phase of the NAALC process.

Applying sanctions is unlikely while governments control the process. They too often put superficial cooperation ahead of honest engagement and criticism on workers' rights violations. However, preserving the sanctions option is a critical goal in FTAA negotiations to drive home the truth that labour rights and trade are bound up with each other and that, under certain circumstances, violators will be punished. Realistically, economic sanctions should only be a last, extreme resort when all intermediate opportunities for settling problems have been exhausted. But unless the *possibility* of sanctions exists, stubborn companies and governments can resist change with impunity.

A possible innovation in the FTAA would be to allow complaining parties like workers, unions and NGOs to "appeal" cases to higher levels, forcing the creation of independent evaluation committees and arbitral panels that can make binding recommendations and impose sanctions. This would further engage civil society actors in the process and provide new opportunities for negotiated settlements before any sanctions are applied.

Effective enforcement of national law

The NAALC and agreements modeled on the NAALC (United States – Chile, Canada–Chile, Canada–Costa–Rica) all make "effective enforcement" of national labour laws a central obligation of the parties, distinct from a need to change laws to comply with new supranational standards. This is a reasonable starting point for a new hemispheric agreement, as long as national laws comport with fundamental rights.

The capacity for enforcement is critical to protecting workers' rights. One need only see the re-emergence of apparel sweatshops in many US cities or the well-documented failure of US authorities to protect workers' organizing rights to appreciate that effective enforcement of national law is a general problem, not one limited to poor countries. Fixing it should be a priority in hemispheric trade. This threshold promise to improve performance by enforcing national laws is one that countries can readily accept.

International standards

Commitment to enforcing national laws creates a threshold problem: what about laws that are inadequate or that outright violate workers' rights? This is a central problem in current negotiations between the USA and Central American countries on a Central America Free Trade Agreement (CAFTA). Several of these countries' laws fall short of compliance with international standards on fundamental workers' rights.[36]

Here is where a strong normative statement setting baseline standards comes into play. The NAALC and NAALC-based agreements all contain eleven "labour principles" covering freedom of association, forced labour, child labour, discrimination, safety and health, migrant worker protection and more. CARICOM's Charter of Civil Society and Mercosur's Social-Labour Declaration go further, addressing all the NAALC principles as well as social dialogue, job training and promotions, protection against dismissal, maternity leave, social security and other issues.

It is worth noting at this point that all of these instruments extend beyond the ILO's four-part definition of core labour standards: freedom of association, elimination of forced labour, abolition of child labour and elimination of discrimination at work. Indeed, labour rights advocates in the Americas can make an important stand by not limiting their discourse to ILO core standards. The ILO's core definition is important, but focusing just on them invites the logical conclusion that other labour rights and standards, mostly dealing with economic and social rights, are less worthy of attention because they fall outside the "core". Governments in this hemisphere have already created broader definitions of workers' rights. Labour rights supporters should build upon this "core-plus" approach in the FTAA.

A sustained independent review process

Implicit in the charter-like statements on workers' rights in the Americas is an assumption that countries' laws honour them. In many cases, they do not. Central American countries are not alone in the region in falling short of international norms. Mexico's labour law makes it difficult for workers to dislodge a corrupt, undemocratic union. Chile's labour code bars company-wide and industry-wide bargaining. Ecuador and other countries' labour laws allow employers to string together "temporary" employment contracts to frustrate workers' organizing rights. US labour

law fails to protect the rights of millions of workers to organize by excluding them from coverage under the National Labour Relations Act or other
protections of the right to organize. Furthermore, Canada has come under
consistent criticism from the ILO for denying associational rights to various categories of public employees.[37]

At least some elements of most countries' labour laws violate international standards. It would be unrealistic to expect wholesale, immediate,
pro-worker labour law reforms throughout the hemisphere as part of
a trade deal. However, the implicit commitment to meet basic norms
of decency expressed in existing labour rights clauses in the Americas
can be made explicit. As part of a hemispheric agreement, countries
could agree to thoroughly review their labour laws with help from
a neutral, non-governmental international body such as the International Society for Labour Law and Social Security or the International
Industrial Relations Association, or perhaps in collaboration with ILO
experts, that can shape recommendations and a plan for change where
needed.

The purpose of a sustained review process would not be to hold trade
hostage until every nation's labour code is pristine. Rather, the goal is
to create incentives for positive labour law reforms by accelerating trade
benefits for countries moving swiftly in order to bring their laws into
compliance with international norms. In other words, we should reverse
the race to the bottom dynamic, not only by removing incentives to keep
low labour standards to attract investment, but by adding incentives to
harmonize labour standards upward to gain trade benefits.[38]

Conclusion

A comprehensive overview of helpful and harmful language in existing
labour rights agreements in the Americas is beyond the scope of this paper.
The purpose of this paper has been to provide some examples for the
argument that governments negotiating a hemispheric trade pact should
include a viable workers' rights chapter by building upon models that
have already been freely adopted. For example, the United States, Mexico
and Canada can say to Central American, Mercosur and Caribbean island
countries, "We like the way you developed an institutional role for trade
unions and NGOs; let's weave together the best threads of what we have
each accomplished in a new cloak of protection for workers' rights in
this hemisphere." This way, the larger countries can approach the smaller
countries on the basis of equality, not imposition.

This is not to say that labour rights advocates should be content with patching together current models. We should also demand new provisions that advance workers' interests. For example, an FTAA labour rights chapter should specify that a substantial portion of the budget of a labour rights commission or secretariat created under the labour agreement ought to be devoted to cross-border educational work such as conference support and research grants to trade unions and non-governmental organizations.

Another clause should provide heightened transparency in hemispheric labour affairs, requiring a "labour information audit" of companies involved in FTAA commerce. Audit information should be provided to and posted on the website of an FTAA labour secretariat with information such as corporate ownership structure, the location of facilities and their products or service lines, the number of employees, their salaries, benefits and working hours, the unionization status of any groups of employees, copies of collective bargaining agreements, and other relevant information.

In addition, a clause based on the principle of compliance with national law should be incorporated. This would allow targeted trade sanctions against companies found guilty of repeated violations of national labour laws linked to labour principles or other charter-like statements in an FTAA labour rights chapter.

This is all easy to say in a policy paper. The hard part in months and years ahead will be building a cross-border movement of trade unions and allies to demand an effective labour rights chapter in a hemispheric trade agreement – and a credible threat to defeat an agreement if governments fail to include such a chapter.

The fate of the FTAA does not hinge only on labour rights. Other "killers" stalk an agreement, like NAFTA's "investor-state" chapter letting corporations sue governments for regulatory actions harming profits and corporate pressure to privatize basic social services. Other social demands, if unmet, should also force labour advocates to join a struggle to defeat the FTAA, like the need for environmental protection, debt relief, equitable agricultural trade, guarantees of democracy, and sustainable development policies that include North-South economic aid.

Labour rights advocates are not alone in their struggle to build a strong social dimension into the architecture of hemispheric trade and investment. We should offer to engage governments with realistic proposals for a viable labour rights chapter in an agreement of the Americas building upon what countries have already done and not demand totally new and untested instruments and mechanisms. We should also be ready to join allies in other social movements to kill an FTAA that fails a broad test of social justice.

Notes

1. See, for example, Economic Policy Institute, "NAFTA at Seven: Its impact on workers in all three countries" (2001) online: http://www.epinet.org/content.cfm/ briefingpapers_nafta01_index; Gordon H. Hanson, "What Has Happened to Wages in Mexico Since NAFTA? Implications for Hemispheric Trade", National Bureau of Economic Research, Working Paper 9653 (2003), online: http://papers.nber.org/papers/ w9563. For some recent journalistic treatment in the United States, see Tessie Borden and Sergio Bustos, "Hurt by NAFTA, Mexican Farmers Head North", *Arizona Republic*, 19 June 2003, p.1D and Katherine Yung, "El Paso No Longer Believes in NAFTA after Garment Industry Fades, Jobless Ranks Mount", *Dallas Morning News*, 13 April 2003 p.1D.

2. See, for example, Suzanne Duryea, Olga Jaramillo and Carmen Pagés, "Latin American Labour Markets in the 1990s: Deciphering the Decade" (Inter-American Development Bank, 2003), available online: http://www.iadb.org/sds/doc/ PANlaborEAR4.pdf; see also the country labour market reports produced by the Global Policy Network, available online at http://www.gpn.org.

3. See Raymond Colitt, "Free Trade Area of the Americas: Brazil's government-elect drops hostility to proposal; Lula's party backs free trade area talks" *Financial Times*, 8 November 2002, p. 11. For a comprehensive discussion of FTAA regional politics (written prior to Lula's election), see Christopher M. Bruner, "Hemispheric Integration and the Politics of Regionalism: The Free Trade Area of the Americas (FTAA)" (2002) 33 *University of Miami Inter-Amerian Law Review* 1.

4. For a valuable analysis and comparison, see Edward Mazey, "Grieving Through the NAALC and the Social Charter: A Comparative Analysis of their Procedural Effectiveness" (2001) 10 *Michigan State Universtiy – D.C.L. Journal of International Law* 239.

5. For more on these exclusions from EU competence, see European Industrial Relations Observatory, "Social policy provisions of draft EU constitutional Treaty examined", available online: http://www.eiro.eurofound.ie/2003/08/Feature/ EU0308204F.html.

6. For journalistic analysis of the status and debates on the EU's charter of rights in the new treaty, see Edward Rothstein, "Europe's Constitution: All Hail the Bureaucracy" *New York Times*, 5 July 2003, p. B9; "Your darkest fears addressed, your hardest questions answered – Europe's constitution", *The Economist* (American Edition), 21 June 2003. A recent legal analysis can be found in Manfred Weiss, "The Social Dimension as Part of the Constitutional Framework", in Reiner Hoffmann et al. (eds), *European Integration as a Social Experiment in a Globalized World* (Hans Böckler Stiftung, Düsseldorf, 2003), 31–46.

7. See European Industrial Relations Observatory, "France and EU in legal tussle over women's right work", available online: http://www.eiro.eurofound.eu.int/1999/05/Feature/ FR9905183F.html.

8. See Case 450/93, *Kalanke* v. *Frei Hansestadt Bremen,* [1995] ECR I-3051, [1996] 1 CMLR 175. The *Kalanke* decision was later softened by the ECJ in Case 409/95, *Marschall* v. *Land Nordrhein-Westfalen* [1997] ECR I-6363, [1998] 1 CMLR 547, and by the 1997 Treaty of Amsterdam, which contained a new clause, Article 141(4), which reads:

> With a view to ensuring full equality in practice between men and women in working life, the principle of equal treatment shall not prevent any Member State from maintaining or adopting measures providing for specific advantages in order to make it easier for the under-represented sex to pursue a vocational activity or compensate for disadvantages in professional careers.

For extended discussion, see Christopher D. Totten , "Constitutional Precommitments to Gender Affirmative Action in the European Union, Germany, Canada and the United States: A Comparative Approach" (2003) 21 *Berkeley Journal of International Law* 27; Sean Pager, "Strictness and Subsidiarity: An Institutional Perspective on Affirmative Action at the European Court of Justice" (2003) 26 *Boston College International and Comparative Law Review* 35.

9. See, for example, Human Rights Watch, "Unfair Advantage: Workers' Freedom of Association in the United States under International Human Rights Standards" (2000), available online: http://www.hrw.org/reports/2000/uslabour.

10. For important, creative contributions to this discussion from Canadian perspectives, see Pierre Verge, "La place des droits relatifs au travail dans le projet d'integration des Ameriques" *Les Cahiers de Droit* (Université Laval, 2003); James Mercury and Bryan Schwartz, "Creating the Free Trade Area of the Americas: Linking Labour, the Environment, and Human Rights to the FTAA" (2001) 1 *Asper Review of International Business and Trade Law* 37.

11. See "Revised Notice of Establishment of United States National Administrative Office and Procedural Guidelines", 59 Fed. Reg. 16,660–62 (1994); "Regulation of the National Administrative Office of Mexico", *Diario Oficial de la Federación,* 28 April 1995; "Canadian NAO Guidelines for Public Communications", available at the Canadian NAO website, online: http://labour.hrdc-drhc.gc.ca/doc/ialc-cidt/eng/e/guidlns-e.html.

12. Through a complex legal mechanism, Canada guarantees that it would pay any fines required under the NAALC, and is thus insulated against economic sanctions. See NAALC Annex 41A.

13. The four Mercosur members are Argentina, Brazil, Paraguay and Uruguay. Chile and Bolivia are associate members.

14. For extended description and discussion, see Geraldo von Potobsky, "La Declaración Sociolaboral del Mercosur" in *Revista del Ministerio del Trabajo* (Ministry of Labour of Argentina, 1999).

15. Author interviews with trade union and employer representatives and advisors, São Paulo and Brasilia, Brazil, 19–25 August 1999.

16. CARICOM members are Antigua and Barbuda, Belize, the Bahamas, Barbados, Dominica, Grenada, Guyana, Haiti, Jamaica, Montserrat, Saint Lucia, Saint Vincent and the Grenadines, Saint Kitts and Nevis, Suriname, and Trinidad and Tobago. Associate members are Anguilla, British Virgin Islands, and Turks and Caicos Islands.

17. For a recent discussion, see Peter Richards, "Economy: Caribbean Region Preparing for Globalization" *Inter-Press Service*, 16 October 2002.

18. Cited in CARICOM Secretariat statement on *Declaration of Industrial and Labour Relations Principles*, 6 January 1999.

19. "Social partners" are defined in Article I as "the government of a State, Associations of Employers, Workers' Organizations and such Non-Governmental Organizations as the State may recognize".

20. See "Contrato Coletivo entre a Volkswagen do Brasil Ltda. e Volkswagen de Argentina S.A. e o Sindicato dos Metalurgicos do ABC, Sindicato dos Trabalhadores nas Industrias e Oficinas Metalurgicas, Mecanicas e de Material Eletrico e Eletronico de Taubete, Tremembe e Distritos, a Confederacao Nacional dos Metalurgicos da CUT, e o Sindicato de Macanicos e Afins de Transporte Automotor da Republica da Argentina e as Comissoes Internas de Fabrica", 16 April 1999.

21. See, "Comments on Implementation of US National Administrative Office", Letter of 15 Febuary from US Council for International Business to US NAO, on file with US NAO (1994).

22. For more discussion of the shaping of NAO procedures, see Lance A. Compa, "The First NAFTA Labour Cases: A New International Labour Rights Regime Takes Shape" (1995) 3 *United States – Mexico Law Journal* 159.

23. See Allan Chambers, "Privatization of labour rules raises fears: Law may face NAFTA challenge", *Edmonton Journal*, 6 September 1996, p. 1; "Province's Halt of Privatization Plan Ends Looming NAFTA Complaint", *Inside NAFTA*, 25 December 1996, p. 14.

24. See US NAO, "Public Report of Review", NAALC Submission No. 9601 (1997).

25. See US NAO Case No. 9701, "Submission Concerning Pregnancy-Based Sex Discrimination in Mexico's Maquiladora Sector" (1997) and US NAO, "Public Report of Review", NAALC Submission No. 9701 (1998).

26. See John Nagel, "Mexico's President Fox Signs New Anti-Discrimination Law", *BNA Daily Labour Report*, 11 June 2003, p. A-4.

27. See US NAO, "Public Report of Review", NAALC Submission No. 9901 (2000).

28. See Associated Press "U.S. labour body probes anti-union move in Quebec", *Toronto Star*, 21 December 1998, p. D3; see also letter dated 14 April 1999 from Claude

Melançon, lawyer for Teamsters Canada, to Irasema Garza, US NAO Secretary, on file with US NAO.

29. See US NAO, "Public Report of Review", NAALC Submission No. 2000–01 (2001).

30. See, for example, Molly Moore, "Mexican Farmhands Accuse U.S. Firms: Panel Hears Washington Apple Pickers", *Washington Post*, 3 December 1998, p. A-36; Elizabeth Velasco, "Trabajadores agrícolas denuncian explotación en EU", *La Jornada*, 3 December 1998, at p. 41; Arturo Gomez Salgado, "Denuncian migrantes violaciones labourales", *El Financiero*, 3 December 1998, p. 19.

31. See *Informe de Revisión Comunicación Pública Mex 9802* (Public Report of Review of Mexico NAO Submission No. 9802), August 1999.

32. See Florangela Davila, "Judge Confirms Teamsters' Victory", *Seattle Times*, 20 October 1999. Following a change in national Teamster leadership, the union could not consolidate its victory, and later renounced bargaining rights at one of the plants. See Lynda V. Mapes, "Unionizing of Apple Workers Unravels", *Seattle Times*, 8 December 2001.

33. For more on this point, see Bertha Lujan, "Los sindicatos frente al ACLAN", in Graciela Bensusán (ed.), *Estándares labourales después del TLCAN* (Ebert/FLACSO, 1999).

34. The Secretariat's publications are generally available online: http://www.naalc.org.

35. Online: http://www.observatorio.net.

36. For detailed description of the shortfalls in those countries' laws and how a labour rights clause in the CAFTA should correct them, see Carol Pier, "El Salvador's Failure to Protect Workers' Human Rights: Implications for CAFTA", *Human Rights Watch Briefing* (May 2003); Sandra Polaski, "How to Build a Better Trade Pact with Central America", *Carnegie Endowment for International Peace (CEIP) Issue Brief* (July 2003); "Central America and the U.S. Face Challenge – and Chance for Historic Breakthrough – on Workers' Rights", *CEIP Issue Brief* (February 2003). They are available respectively on the websites of Human Rights Watch and the Carnegie Endowment for International Peace.

37. Information on workers' rights problems in all these countries and others in the hemisphere can be reviewed at the website of the ILO's Committee on Freedom of Association and Committee of Experts on the Application of Ratified Conventions, with cases organized by region and by country, online: http://webfusion.ilo.org/public/db/standards/normes/libsynd/index.cfm?lang = EN.

38. For an elaboration of this strategic approach, see Sandra Polaski, "Trade and Labour Standards: A Strategy for Developing Countries", *Carnegie Endowment of International Peace Briefing Paper* (2003).

10

Globalization and the just society – core labour rights, the FTAA, and development

BRIAN LANGILLE

Introduction – a familiar response to a possible FTAA labour rights agenda

The philosopher Nietzsche observed that "the most common form of stupidity is to forget what it is you are trying to do". There is a lot of truth in that remark. We often confuse our real objectives with mere epiphenomena – most typically we confuse our true goals with our means for achieving them. So, in an effort to take Nietzsche's observation seriously, we should start with some basic questions about our purposes. Why are we here? Why do nation states enter into international treaties regarding trade and other aspects of economic integration? What do labour ministries, labour law, and labour market policy have to do with these agreements? In particular, what should be the attitude of governments in the Americas regarding the "trade and core labour standards" debate?

There is a traditional, or at least familiar, reply to this last question. It goes like this.

Central and South American countries might be deeply distrustful of a labour rights agenda in a possible FTAA for the following reasons. First, and fundamentally, the "trade and labour issue" is a side show made necessary by domestic and political demands within the United States, and by the resulting conditionality of the Trade Promotion Authority granted by the US Congress. Second, these politics are essentially the by-product of several domestic political forces – protectionist interests, on the one hand, and misguided anti-globalization forces on the other. The result is that these forces must be, at least, appeased by appearing to attend to issues such as labour rights and environmental concerns. (Also at hand are other external pressures which must be heeded. In particular, the European Union's General System of Preferences presents a similar political reality, albeit in a slightly different form.) Third, these politics are offensive in part because they attempt to export domestic policy and in part because of the hypocrisy involved in such an exercise. Fourth, the core labour rights agenda represents a cost because it increases labour costs, adds inflexibility, pushes growth in the informal sector, deters investors and hinders trade performance. Fifth, as a result, the object of the exercise is to minimize and marginalize this agenda with a view to containing the costs involved in negotiation and implementation of any such arrangement. In short, the labour rights agenda is an unfortunate cost inflicted upon negotiations for economic integration within the Americas. The overall objective is to minimize this cost.

While some of the claims made in this line of reasoning may, unfortunately, be accurate – I believe the conclusions drawn are very wrong. The purpose of this paper is to explain why. The paper pursues this objective in the following way. The next section starts with some very basic thinking (as Nietzsche recommends) about our true goals (i.e. reminders of what it is we are trying to do) and their relationship to globalization. I suggest that clear thinking is blocked here by a framework of thought regarding the relationship between just societies on the one hand, and globalization on the other, which is shared by pro and anti globalization (and pro and anti labour rights) forces. In fact, by paying attention to observed reality and our best thinking about what it is we are trying to do we can overcome this blockage and articulate a new and positive approach at an abstract level. The third section then addresses specifically the labour rights aspect of this general and positive view of the relationship between globalization and the just society. The final section then briefly addresses the problem of "informality" in Latin American labour markets. The conclusion draws attention to the ways in which thinking about a labour rights dimension of a possible FTAA must change in the South, and in the North.

Globalization and the just society – the basics of a positive approach

We can begin by taking Nietzsche's advice and recalling what our central problems really are, and what it is that we can and really should be trying to do about them. In my view this approach leads to the following line of thinking:

Here are the most significant facts about our world. There are (roughly) 6 billion people living on the planet. Of these, 3 billion live on less than two dollars a day and 1.2 billion live in what the World Bank describes as "absolute poverty" of less than one dollar a day.[1] This is our problem.

Here is the most important and controversial phenomenon of our time – globalization. By globalization we mean not simply trade liberalization but international economic integration in which barriers to the mobility of capital, goods, services, data, ideas (but not, nearly to the same extent, people) are lowered and, in conjunction with revolutions in communications and transportation, technologies, enable the construction of networks of international investment, production, and consumption (I refer to this as the globalization and information revolution (or GIR) following the lead of my fellow Canadian, Tom Courchene.)[2]

Here, then, is our most obvious challenge – how can the globalization and information revolution be channelled, harnessed, mobilized, called in aid of, and be put to work in overcoming our most significant problem? Or, more simply, how can globalization and the information revolution foster the development of a world which is more just?

But there is a barrier to answering this vital question. While clear thinking is required in order to answer our question, our thinking here is, in fact, often muddled and confused. Our thinking frequently falls into an unfortunate but very common pattern or way of understanding our crucial question. This is the broader view of globalization which is referred to above and of which the package of views on the labour agenda is part. This "received wisdom" or conventional way of thinking goes, roughly, as follows. Globalization is an external phenomenon bearing or putting pressure upon our societies – including our labour markets and our labour market policies and institutions. Many people believe that this pressure exerted by globalization is, to say the least, unwholesome. On this view globalization increases inequality (both globally and within states), causes local job losses, imposes a set of Western, or American, or European or "market" values, undermines local cultures and patterns of social behaviour, is unfairly tilted towards the already rich and powerful, exacerbates the existing disadvantages of those already marginalized, erodes domestic sovereignty by subjecting local policies to undesirable competitive pressures which lead to suboptimal policy decisions because of international collective action problems, challenges the ability of individual states to raise the revenue (taxes) to fund social programmes, and so on. In short, globalization means a world run by economists, trade theorists, the chief executive officers of transnational corporations, whose chief goal is to advance market values over social values. The opposing view is equally familiar. Globalization means increased trading opportunities bringing with it the mutual windfalls of the theory of comparative advantage, increased international investment – a most critical requirement in a world in which wealth is so unevenly distributed, a world in which transnational corporations can introduce technology and knowledge which enhance the lives of local citizens, create jobs and the tax base for improved educational, health, and social services, in which states will be subjected to good competitive pressure which will illuminate and help eliminate harmful corruption, inept administration and poor policy choices. In short, globalization means more and better distributed world wealth.

While these scenarios are both familiar and very different, they *share* a picture or vision of the relationship between globalization and societies. On this view, globalization bears upon individual societies and the causal arrow runs in one direction only. This is a view which unites the pro and anti globalization forces. They see globalization bearing upon societies but see different results flowing from the application of this force – one group sees bad results, the other sees good ones. This is a widely shared framework of thought – even among those who have thought long and hard about these issues. It is sort of a glass bottle in which the debate has been placed. Without even seeing it the debate keeps bumping up – like a fly inside a bottle – against the limits imposed by the framework of thought in which the debate has been cast.[3] So, for example, Dani Rodrik writes that the most daunting challenge posed by globalization is "ensuring that international economic integration does not lead to domestic social disintegration",[4] and the United Nations Millennium Declaration articulates its understanding of the problem as follows: "We believe that the central challenge we face today is to ensure that globalization becomes a positive force for all the world's Peoples."[5] So too the recent report of the World Commission on the Social Dimension of Globalization suggests, even in its title, that Globalization is a "thing" (a process) which needs to be made fair, rather than simultaneously a driver of, and deeply dependent upon, "fairness".[6]

While Rodrik articulates the problem in terms of avoiding the "bad", and the Millennium Goals World Commission stake their claim in terms of securing the "good", what unifies is the common framing of the issue – that our problem is that globalization is, to put it simply, the "central challenge" to, or promise for, depending on one's view, the people and societies of the world. Globalization drives human societies – and the potential is seen as both positive and negative, depending on your view.

This brace of familiar views – which still frames and organizes much of current thinking about globalization – has been researched, examined, tested, and argued about in forums ranging from obscure academic journals to the streets of Seattle, Genoa, Quebec City, and beyond. One of the most interesting outcomes of this study and debate has not been the resolution of our controversy. Rather, something more interesting has been going on. What we are witnessing is a gradual recognition that this received way of understanding the globalization debate is stale, unhelpful, inconsistent with our observed reality, and intellectually incoherent.

This is true for two reasons.

First, this received wisdom is locked into a very familiar and inadequate understanding of the central dynamic of globalization. It is based upon an outdated paradigm. But it is a powerful paradigm. Second, the received wisdom has lost touch with Nietzsche's warning – it has lost sight of what our real goals are.

The old paradigm was a paradigm which underwrote much of modern labour law (in Canada, for example), international labour law (the ILO, for example), and development theory (the "Washington consensus", for example), and on this paradigm there was a segregation (professional, conceptual, institutional) of the economic forces of globalization from "the social and political" realm. They were segregated, sequenced, and locked into a zero sum game. This old paradigm leads to a view, for example, of domestic labour law which sees its chief justification as the need to come to the rescue of workers thought of as people "in need of protection". And at the international level, to a view of the ILO as protecting against real prisoners' dilemmas caused by states making rational choices to lower labour standards. On this view the economic (getting prices right) is prior to and separate from the social (including basic issues of democracy, human rights, equality concerns, etc.), the latter being conceived of as a set of luxury goods which might be purchased with the fruits of economic progress generated elsewhere. All of this is reflected in an institutional division of labour, both domestically and internationally, between the financial institutions and ministries on the one hand (the Bretton Woods institutions, ministries of finance), and the social ones (the ILO, ministries of labour) on the other.

The crucial point is that the foundations upon which this simple and shallow view rests are shifting. Recent factual findings and clearer normative thinking (especially that which focuses upon the need to think carefully about our true ends as opposed to our means, or instrumentalities, for achieving them) have led to a wide variety of claims about an emergent "integrated theory" of development, of the Human Development Index, of the Comprehensive Development Framework, among other things. This involves a re-conceptualization of development theory (and of domestic labour law, and the ILO, as well). At its core is the idea that the formulation underlying the shallow view (globalization → society), needs to be supplemented by another formulation (society → globalization), and to see the two as linked in a (potentially, at least) virtuous circle of mutual reinforcement. To return to the words of Rodrik and the Millennium Goals, our real problem is not simply to ensure that "international economic integration does lead to domestic social disintegration" *but also* that domestic social disintegration does not lead to international economic disintegration, and, more positively, that domestic social integration drives international economic integration.

To put this in a very short form, the old paradigm saw the forces of globalization and the information revolution (GIR) bearing upon the construction of just societies (JS) – making it, depending upon one's view, either easier or harder to do so. Thus, GIR → JS. The new comprehensive view sees the causal arrow running in both directions in an at least potentially virtuous circle of reinforcement, i.e. GIR ↔ JS.

Thus our central policy dilemma needs to be reformulated in terms of this central question – *how can globalization foster **and be fostered by** just societies?*

The second reason that our old paradigm and structure of thought was inadequate is that it was not based upon, and is in fact disconnected from, a real normative foundation which would generate not only the political support, but also the intellectual case for globalization. This was because the old debate and old paradigm proceeded without any real clarification or identification of our true ends – what it is all about – as opposed to our mere means, modality, instrumentalities, methods, for achieving those ends. To put it simply, the old paradigm had no account, other than self-serving technical ones, of what it was we were trying to do. As a result, it fell prey to Nietzsche's observation that the most common form of stupidity is forgetting what it is we are trying to do.

In short, we need an account of why we are discouraged and disheartened by the fact that 3 billion live on less than two dollars a day and 1.2 billion live on less than one dollar a day. This will in turn explain to us our own understanding of what constitutes a just society and why we pursue that end. It will let us understand the link between just societies and globalization. This is a tall order. But it is one that has been filled by some much needed modern thinking, especially that of Amartya Sen.[7] Sen's core insights are as follows. First, our concern – our true goal – is not simply to raise GDP per capita. Raising GDP per capita is a means to our true goal which is to improve the real lives of real human beings

– to make those lives longer, healthier, happier, more fulfilling – to let people be subjects of their lives rather than mere objects buffeted by forces over which they have no control. In short, our goal is to give people the "real capability to lead lives we have reason to value". This is what Sen calls human freedom. So, raising GDP per capita, the drafting of an international labour code, or the creation of a Free Trade Agreement of the Americas – all of these are not ends in themselves – but means to the end of real human freedom.

Human freedom can be blocked in a number of ways. As Sen writes:

> Sometimes the lack of substantive freedoms relates directly to economic poverty, which robs people of the freedom to satisfy hunger, or to achieve sufficient nutrition, or to obtain remedies for treatable illnesses, or the opportunity to be adequately clothed or, sheltered, or to enjoy clean water or sanitary facilities. In other cases, the unfreedom links closely to the lack of public facilities of social care, such as the absence of epidemiological programs, or of organized arrangements for health care or educational facilities, or of effective institutions for the maintenance of local peace and order. In still other cases, the violation of freedom results directly from a denial of political and civil liberties by authoritarian regimes and from imposed restrictions on the freedom to participation in the social, political and economic life of the community.[8]

Development is the process of removing these obstacles to human freedom.

Human freedom is not only the goal – the destination – it is also the path. This is because different sorts of human freedoms – economic, political, social – interact in complex ways. For example:

> Political freedoms (in the form of free speech and elections) help to promote economic security. Social opportunities (in the form of education and health facilities) facilitate economic participation. Economic facilities (in the form of opportunities for participation in trade and production) can help to generate personal abundance as well as public resources for social facilities. Freedoms of different kinds can strengthen one another.[9]

This is a view which takes market freedoms seriously – indeed sees them as an important aspect of human freedom in and of themselves and not simply justified on an instrumental basis.

These insights are both profound, yet very obvious. These are the ideas animating the quest for post-Washington consensus – a Comprehensive Development Framework, the Human Development Index, the

Millennium Goals – and explain what our best research shows us. This is that the fundamental failure of the old paradigm was the isolation of economic freedoms from social and political ones. This led to a belief that freedoms could be sequenced and segregated – a view of social and political freedoms as a set of "luxury goods" which could be purchased, after the event, with the fruits of prior economic progress generated by economic freedoms alone. This was the core idea of the Washington consensus. The problem is – the world does not work that way. What we now see is that our empirical reality and best theoretical reasoning, not to mention our most fundamental beliefs, lead to the demonstration of the shallowness of this view. A new view is called for. At the core is the idea that human freedoms, including but not exclusive to economic freedoms, are valuable in themselves but even more critically from a policy perspective, that they interact and are mutually supporting in complex ways. In short, development of just society is a "package deal". Successful globalization is both driven by and driving the creation of successful societies. This is the key insight of our new view. It is within this context that one must turn to the issue of the construction of a possible free trade agreement of the Americas. And it is from this perspective that one must address the specific issue of labour rights within such an undertaking.

While we could refer to other evidence of the increasing salience of this way of thinking, let me refer simply to one contribution. Nicholas Stern, until recently the Chief Economist of the World Bank, has articulated a view deeply congruent with the above thinking. In his way of talking the "old paradigm" – the Washington consensus point of view rested upon "one pillar" – the creation of an appropriate investment climate.[10] What development theory has learned "the hard way"[11] is that this pillar needs to be seen as deeply intertwined with, and in a mutually reinforcing relationship with, a "second pillar" which Stern labels "individual empowerment". The first pillar is really the Washington consensus – fiscal discipline, market-determined exchange and interest rates, protection of property rights, liberalization, privatization, and openness to trade. What that consensus left out was "governance and institutions, the role of empowerment in democratic representation, the importance of country ownership, and the social costs and the pace of transformation".[12] Building on these "two pillars", Stern specifies a number of "key lessons", the foremost of which is that "the state is not a substitute for the market, but a critical complement". Stern elaborates: "we have learned that markets need government and government needs markets; and that government action is crucial to the ability of the people to participate in economic opportunity. These lessons point to an active state which fosters an environment where contracts are enforced and markets can function, basic infrastructure works, there is provision for adequate health, education, and social protection, and people are able to participate in decisions which affect their lives".[13]

And, perhaps most significantly for our purposes Nicholas Stern sums up this new understanding with a reference to Sen, as follows:

> These lessons from development experience point to the strategy proposed here. But before we can define strategy we have to set objectives. Our perspective on the goals of development have changed substantially in the last 20 years. We now look beyond incomes to health and education, or human development. But it is deeper than that. We now see the objectives or ends of development as concerning the ability of people to shape their own lives or "development as freedom" as Amartya Sen has put it. . . . We have learned that the empowerment is both an end and a means of development.[14]

The link to our issue – labour rights and a potential FTAA

Now we must be more specific. This new and purposeful approach to globalization and development requires us to rethink the traditional response to set our course to a possible labour agenda within a FTAA. I would not be surprised to encounter some resistance to our discussion thus far – a discussion of labour rights within a possible FTAA beginning with such general and "philosophical" considerations. Practical people charged with making choices in the real world need concrete policy options – not general considerations for further reflection. But the point of reminding ourselves of our basic values and the fundamental shift in international development theory is *deeply pragmatic*. And there is real risk that this pragmatism will be lost by falling – in the name of tough-mindedness and "realism" – into our familiar way of understanding our issue. That is, there is a tight link between alleged tough-mindedness, and the old paradigm.

The point of our long and general introduction is precisely to give pause to those who might find such a pattern of thought appealing. The questions which Sen and Stern and others pose for such a line of thinking include the following:

- Is there a positive case for core labour standards as part of our new understanding of an adequate strategy for growth and economic development?

- Is a concern with human capital policy at the periphery or at the core of an agenda for growth and economic development – within an FTAA structure or elsewhere?
- Are core labour rights a cost or a benefit to societies?
- What is the link between economic progress and respect for core labour rights?
- Are core labour rights to be solely conceived of as an expensive if legitimate concern with fundamental human freedom, or also as crucially instrumental to economic growth?

These are deeply pragmatic questions of profound consequence to the issue of how we conceive of the project of economic integration in the Americas. Recall, our fundamental question is "what are we trying to do?" The project of economic integration in the Americas is not an *end* in itself (whatever that would mean) – but as with all international arrangements – an important potential *means* of helping all nations construct just societies in which citizens enjoy real human freedom, i.e., longer, fuller, more meaningful lives they have reason to value and over which they have some control. If our new approach to development is an improvement on the old, then the question is whether core labour rights are best conceived of as both an important constitutive element of human freedom (important in and of themselves) *and* an important means to that goal. Rather than a cost, a benefit. Rather than a threat, an opportunity. Rather than marginalized, at the core of an economic agenda. Rather than a brake on successful globalization, one of its drivers.

Key to our new understanding of the ingredients required for the construction of durable, economically flourishing, and just societies is the understanding that economic growth and the institutions of the just society are linked in a mutually supporting relationship. Free markets are, on the one hand, imbedded in, made possible by and dependent upon the just society, and on the other hand, they help sustain and are in themselves an important aspect of that society. Economic freedoms, social opportunities, and political rights and freedoms interact in a mutually reinforcing manner. This is the package deal. The old framework of thought – markets *versus* society – is dead. If the FTAA is to be an important means to our real goals, then it will do so only if it helps individual nations see, commit to, and move along the path to this integrated view. But again, the point of such an exercise is not simply that globalization is inevitable, although it might be. As the president of one developing country recently put it, "Globalization can do without us, but we can't do without it."[15]

Rather, comprehensive regional or global arrangements are important for two reasons. First, they benefit individual states in so far as they are able to commit to a comprehensive project of development. But, second, they are also instrumentally significant for the other signatories to the agreement. There are significant "public goods" aspects, or positive externalities, for all states from a mutual agreement to pursue a rational project of joint development interaction. Expanded markets, social stability, political stability and security, are important not only within states, but across states.

But how, precisely, are we to conceive of the labour rights agenda within this general overview? In my view, labour rights lie at the core of new integrated view, and of Nicholas Stern's "two pillars" which constitute another articulation of the integrated view. Labour rights are central to the creation of a mutually reinforcing interrelationship between the market and the social and political institutions in which it is imbedded – and, as a result, are central to the realization of a positive interrelationship with the dimensions of international economic integration – creating the conditions for growth, investment, employment, public and private infrastructure, which in turn attracts investment, expands markets, and so on.

Let us start with economic growth.

A key concept in any discussion of labour rights and standards is productivity. Higher wages or higher labour costs are never the issue – the issue is never labour costs per se, but rather, net unit labour costs or "the costs of labour for each unit of production after taking productivity into account". Paul Krugman, the American economist and public commentator is famous for observing "productivity isn't everything – but in the long run, it is almost everything".[16] Krugman expands on this point by noting, simply:

> At the most basic level the rate at which an economy's potential grows is the sum of two terms: the rate at which the number of able and willing workers expands, and the rate at which the productivity of the average worker rises.[17]

Or, to make the same point in a slightly different way:

> In the long run, barring some catastrophe, the rate of growth of living standards in a country is almost exactly equal to the annual increase in the amount that an average worker can produce in an hour.[18]

Or, as the ILO succinctly formulated the matter:

GDP growth $=$ employment growth $\times$ labour productivity growth.[19]

There is, as Krugman points out, a natural limit to the number of workers a nation can put to work – full employment, however defined.[20] This means that in the long run, as Krugman puts it, the real and not naturally limited or capped factor in the equation of economic growth is the rate of productivity growth of the average worker.

The obvious policy questions is – "what can a country do to improve the productivity of its workers?" Krugman responds to this obvious question in the following way:

> There are three main things that an economy can do to raise the productivity of its workers. It can raise the quantity and quality of its business capital, it can improve the public capital that supports the private economy; and it can improve the quality of its workforce, what is sometimes called human capital.[21]

Human capital policy is critical in our most fundamental economic equation. At the end of the day, and as Krugman acknowledges, human capital policy involves, most basically, "the education of the nation's children".[22]

Education is undoubtedly a public good of enormous consequence, especially in an integrated world and in light of our new understanding of what makes for durable and successful economies and societies. The role of the state in providing it is critical. It is intimately linked to Stern's approach – the importance of empowerment and ownership, participation, and the construction of the basic institutions of society and the market. But continuous improvement in the education of the nation's children, whether at the primary, secondary or tertiary levels, is not enough. As Carneiro and Heckman put it:

> Human capital accumulation is a dynamic process. The skills acquired in one stage of the life cycle affect both the initial conditions and the technology of learning at the next stage. Human capital is produced over the life cycle by families, schools and firms, although most discussions of skill formation focus on schools as the major producer of skills, despite a substantial body of evidence that families and firms are major producers of abilities and skills. A major determinant of successful schools is successful families. Schools work with what parents bring them. They operate more effectively if parents reinforce them by encouraging and motivating children. Job training programs, whether public or private, work with what families and schools supply them, and cannot remedy 20 years of neglect.[23]

As our theory notes, it is the complimentarity and interactivity of the state and market – of social, political, and economic rights – which is the keystone of an evolving "post-Washington consensus". Obviously, as Krugman points out,[24] it takes time for children to get an education and to enter the workforce. This is a long-term strategy and there must be a workforce to enter, one in which education (i.e. educated workers) can be utilized – "exploited" in the best sense of that word. But as Carneiro and Heckman forcefully point out education, critical as it is, is part of a larger "package deal". The World Bank recently reinforced this point in a report on the importance of tertiary education for development:

> Knowledge by itself does not transform economies, nor is there any guarantee of positive returns to investments in research and development or in other products of tertiary education. Numerous countries, including large ones such as Brazil, India and Russia, have invested heavily in building up capacity in science and technology without reaping significant returns. This is because scientific and technological knowledge yields its greatest benefits when it is used within a complex system of institutions and practices known as a national innovation system (NIS).

> An NIS is a web made up of the following elements: a) knowledge-producing organizations in the education and training systems; b) the appropriate macroeconomic and regulatory framework, including trade policies that affect technology diffusion; c) innovative firms and networks of enterprises; d) adequate communication infrastructures; e) other factors such as access to the global knowledge base and certain market conditions that favour innovation. Tertiary education systems figure predominately in this framework serving not only as the backbone for high-level skills but also as a network base for information sharing.[25]

It is important not to read this passage as an impossible to achieve list of prerequisites available only to the OECD nations – rather, it is critical to read it in light of Sen's and Stern's reminders of the interconnectivity and "package deal" nature of our endeavour. It is precisely an educated population which will make available innovative firms which will drive political processes to sound investment and infrastructure policies, enabling firms to participate successfully in trade, which will in turn fund educational improvements, and so on and so on. One of the most important lessons of this thinking is that the idea sequencing is undesirable. Economic freedoms, social opportunities, and political rights rise, and fall, together. In my country, Canada, these lessons are at the core of our national policy debate. It is true that in Canada we spend a great deal of time discussing our politically funded system of medical care. In Sen's language this is one of the basic guarantees against non-freedom. But Canada is also a country which is deeply dependent on an open and rules-based trading system. It is also a country which takes seriously the idea that knowledge – the ability to produce it and to utilize it – is the key to growth. In fact one of Canada's leading economic policy thinkers, Tom Courchene, has articulated the following "mission statement" for Canada:

> To design a sustainable, socially inclusive and internationally competitive infrastructure that ensures a quality of access for all Canadians, so that they may develop, enhance and employ their skills in human capital in Canada, thereby enabling them to become full citizens in the information-era of Canadian and global societies.[26]

> This mission statement provides not only the social goal towards which any global order governance structure ought to strive, but as well, the emphasis on human capital and citizen information empowerment provides the means of ensuring citizens will maximize their ability to participate in any governance regime.[27]

Careful readers will note the deep complimentarity here between Courchene and Sen. Courchene is advocating a comprehensive policy prescription for Canada – a rich OECD society. Sen is laying bare the basis of development – what it is and how to get it. Yet both focus upon human freedom (and empowerment, participation, opportunity) as a goal, *and* the best means to achieve it.

At one level this is terribly simple – if you want real human freedom, and we do – start with real human freedom. The dificult part is understanding the complex interaction of different sorts of human freedom – economic, social and political.

If human capital is critical to productivity growth, which is the basis of economic growth, and if human capital must be seen as imbedded and part of a "package deal", our next question is "what is the link between core labour standards and a new understanding of the role of education, knowledge and human capital?" If Krugman is right in identifying human capital – along with private capital and public capital (infrastructure) – as one of the three margins upon which policy-makers can engage to improve their societies – what does this mean for labour rights?

First, consider the following basic point. As a general matter human capital policy will, or at least should, always have pride of place in a globalized world. One of the central characteristics of the integrated world is that while goods, parts, data, ideas, and crucially capital, are highly mobile, labour is relatively less so. Without underestimating the potential of "brain drains" (with which we in Canada have much experience) labour will, for both legal, linguistic and deeply human reasons, always remain relatively less mobile than other factors of production.

The key to a new approach to labour law and labour market policy is to set it within a new framework of development that takes into account freedom, economic growth, the role of productivity, and the place of human capital policy therein. If education is the goal at the most basic level, it is the structuring and mobilization of that human capital through the complex workings of the labour market that is also of core concern. It is within this general overall framework of thought that we need to assess the role of labour rights in a possible FTAA.

It is in this light that there is a possibility of seeing positive benefit – rather than mere costs which we would rather, but cannot, avoid.

Our questions thus become, among others:

- What is the positive case for core labour rights?
- How do core rights cohere with the new post-Washington consensus?
- How does respect for core rights foster mobilization and utilization of human capital?
- How does respect for core labour rights lead to productivity growth otherwise foregone?
- Is the story of human capital as the essential element of development and growth peculiar to the OECD nations?
- Is the structure of the Latin American labour markets, particularly "informality", a barrier to the adoption of a human capital policy, including sound institutions and real respect for core labour rights?
- Is collective bargaining part of this story or not? (Will the real World Bank please stand up?)
- Is the story limited to core rights?
- Is the core labour rights agenda a recipe for locking-in unhelpful and unproductive labour law regimes?
- Does respect for core rights, even if theoretically desirable in the abstract, also have a negative affect on attracting FDI and upon trade performance?

In what follows I attempt to address at least some of these vital questions. First, a brief note about core labour rights. There is now a well defined international consensus about the core rights regarding (1) discrimination, (2) child labour, (3) forced labour and (4) freedom of association and free collective bargaining. The rapid agreement on the core during the last decade or so is really quite an accomplishment by international diplomatic and legal standards. From the Copenhagen Summit, to the WTO ministerials in Singapore and Doha, to the ILO declaration of 1998, to the World Bank, the OECD, and beyond there is now no disagreement on the identity of the core rights agenda. Of great importance is the "process" nature of core rights which is critical for their fit with both economic and development theory, as well as fundamental human rights and deep moral commitments.[28]

It will be surprising if these basic freedoms were not part of a "post-Washington consensus/development as freedom" agenda. But it is central to this new way of thinking that these basic ways of thinking be viewed as not only ends in themselves, but as having crucial instrumental value as well. The freedoms from child labour, forced labour, and discrimination in the work place create no controversy about their status as freedoms valuable in and of themselves. Often, however, policy-makers need reminders of the fundamental, and upon reflection, non-controversial point about their additional instrumental significance. Recall our basic equation:

$$\text{GDP growth} = \text{growth in number of workers} \times \text{growth in productivity of each.}$$

Our initial policy question is, therefore, how does respect for the four core labour rights affect both labour market size and productivity – i.e. both variables on the right-hand side of our equation?

Let us start with discrimination. Excluding certain sectors, say women, from the labour market altogether is an obvious problem. It cuts the potential growth of the country's economy in half. Many observers believe that this is a current and core problem in many parts of the world. The problem is obviously damaging when the discrimination takes the form not only of exclusion from the workforce, but exclusion from education and, as a result, certain higher value added (more productive) labour market sectors. Discrimination of this sort is simply economically irrational.

There is also no long-term economic defence of child labour. Education is, at the end of the day, the key to productivity growth (see Krugman, above), and employment of the children of the nation in ways which undermine this educational development is, straightforwardly, economically counterproductive. This is not to say that there are not other economic complications, certainly in the short run. For example, eliminating child labour could be seen in basic economic theory as reducing labour supply.[29] But these concerns go to the modalities of achieving economically rational long-term policies. Galli's recent analysis "The Economic Impact of Child Labor" presents a comprehensive and sympathetic sorting out of the long-term and short-term implications of child labour.[30] She finds that in the long run child labour perpetuates household poverty through lower human capital accumulation, perpetuates poverty through enhanced fertility, can slow down long-run growth and social development through reduced human capital accumulation, might affect girls more than boys thus fuelling gender inequality in education, and does not attract foreign direct investment.

Forced labour is also not only a profound violation of human rights, but in the long run a direct assault on instrumental efficiency as a direct interference with market forces. Again, in the shorter term, it may increase labour supply, but in a manner which is fundamentally inconsistent with market (efficiency) principles. In the long term it is, as with child labour and discrimination, antithetical to a human capital development strategy.

To put it simply, violations of the rights of children, and of adults due to discrimination and forced labour, have not only profound human rights implications but are counterproductive from an instrumental point of view. Discrimination not only excludes eligible members of the workforce, but precludes human capital development. Child labour and forced labour, while perhaps superficially increasing labour market participation, are in the long run fatal to human capital formation which is the real source of productivity growth. What of the final core labour rights, freedom of association and the right to free collective bargaining? One of the most debilitating aspects of the general debate about both domestic and international labour law has been the continued resistance of policymakers to empirical data and continued reliance upon uninformed a priori belief when it comes to the issue of the economic effects of collective bargaining. (This is not to say that there are not defective and dysfunctional collective bargaining regimes – but this is an issue that I return to below when it is argued that international agreements can be a cure rather than a recipe for such systems.)

As always, the issue is not wage costs per se but wage costs taking into account productivity. It is widely known that unions achieve a wage mark

up for their members.[31] But the interesting question is the effect on productivity. What is the *net* cost of unions? The answer to this question turns
out to be complex and involves sound empirical enquiry and weighing
up of the wage costs and efficiency gains. And the answer is that "it all
depends" – i.e. "it is indeterminate",[32] and depends upon the quality of
the relationship between labour and management, among other things.
The key point is that in addition to their "monopoly effects" unions have
productivity enhancing effects – and the interesting question is why some
firms achieve a positive sum in this calculation, while others do not. But
to concentrate upon the microeconomic effects of unions – as revealing as
this is to some – is to miss the main point of what we increasingly appreciate – both as an empirical matter and as a matter of theory as expounded
by those such as Stern and Sen. This is the point that the effects of respect
for the rights of freedom of association and collective bargaining – and
other core rights – do not operate solely at the microeconomic level and
in isolation. Rather they are best understood as part of the more complex
interaction of the economic, the social and the political arenas, which is
the core insight of any post-Washington consensus. Recall that our basic
formula is: growth = > number of workers × > productivity of each. As
Krugman points out, there are three dimensions of productivity policy –
private capital, public capital, human capital. It turns out that, as Sen and
others point out, there is an interactivity between these three dimensions –
critically, for us, between human capital policy and "public infrastructure".
This point is best viewed through the lens of a number of recent studies
which try to explain why societies which invest in respect for core labour
rights are more, not less, successful in attracting FDI and in their trade
performance, i.e. better able to successfully engage globalization as *and
because* they create more just societies.

   One of the most striking developments in the last decade of debate
about labour rights and globalization was the publication in 1996 of the
OECD study *Trade, Employment, and Labour Standards: A Study of Core
Workers' Rights and International Trade*.[33] This study and a follow up one in
2000 (*International Trade and Core Labour Standards*) were critical in the
movement to reassess conventional thinking about international labour
standards. This movement is an important contribution to the development of our post-Washington consensus world. It challenged directly the
view that respect for core rights was "costly" in terms of attracting foreign
direct investment or in terms of trade performance. As such, it caused
developed countries to reassess their worries about a "race to the bottom"
sort of competition resulting from globalization. And it was a wake-up

call to the developing world about the correct policy course regarding core labour rights. That is, it is a direct contradiction of the stock set of views set out at the beginning of this paper.

The 1996 OECD study, while acknowledging the difficulty of carrying out a complete empirical analysis of the links between core standards and trade and investment, did go on to make the following very important observations. First, the OECD found that "the core labour standards do not play a significant role in shaping trade performance".[34]

The OECD went on to observe:

> The view that argues that low-standards countries will enjoy gains in export market share to the detriment of high-standards countries appears to lack solid empirical support. These findings also imply that any fear on the part of developing countries that better core standards would negatively affect either their economic performance or the competitive position in world markets has no economic rationale. On the contrary, it is conceivable that the observance of core standards would strengthen the long-term economic performance of all countries.[35]

On the second crucial question on the relationship between respect for core labour standards and investment, the OECD in 1996, again while acknowledging the difficulty of a final empirical assessment, noted that "core labour standards are not primary factors in the majority of investment decisions of OECD companies".[36]

And with particular reference to freedom of association and its relationship to trade liberalization, the OECD stated:

> The results reveal a relatively clear pattern. The more successful the trade reform in terms of the degree of trade liberalization, the greater is the respect of association rights in the country.
> ... the clearest and most reliable finding is in favour of a mutually supportive relationship between successfully sustained trade reforms and improvements in association and bargaining rights. This positive two-way relationship appears to be strongest after trade reforms have been in place for several years ... Similarly, there was no case where freedom of association and bargaining rights impeded trade liberalization. This means, at least for these countries, that fears that freer trade could lead to an erosion of these standards, or that improved compliance with them could jeopardize trade reforms are unfounded.[37]

A number of studies have addressed the core issues of concern to us as identified by the 1996 and 2000 OECD reports. A very useful recent summary of this other work is found in the much quoted ILO paper by

Kucera: "The Effect of Core Workers' Rights on Labour Costs and Foreign Direct Investment: Evaluating the 'Conventional Wisdom'".[38] This paper, and its key findings, are reflected in the official ILO document "Investment in the Global Economy and Decent Work" (March 2002).[39]

Other studies by Rodrik[40] and Flanagan[41] have and continue to reach similar conclusions. The result is no longer surprising. And more importantly, we see why. Even if respect for core rights was simply a cost, which it is not, the evidence has always been that labour costs are not a dominant factor in investment decisions. A widely cited survey ranked investment location criteria in order of importance and on a scale of 0–5 as follows:

- growth of market (4.2)
- size of market (4.1)
- profit perspectives (4.0)
- political and social stability (3.3)
- quality of labour (3.0)
- legal and regulatory environment (3.0)
- quality of infrastructure (2.9)
- manufacturing and services environment (2.9)
- cost of labour (2.4)
- access to high technologies (2.3)
- fear of protectionism (2.2)
- access to financial resources (2.0)
- access to raw materials (2.0)[42]

Cost of labour ranks very low in this survey – lower than quality of labour, political and social stability, and quality of infrastructure. But the key conclusion to draw from all of this is that the impact of respect for core labour rights cannot be seen in isolation. Rather, respect for core labour rights is part of a productivity strategy which is part of a human capital strategy. This in turn is part of a larger and more complex "package" of interactions between private capital, public capital and human capital – or, in Sen's terms, between political rights, economic freedoms and social opportunities. In one sense this is obvious – all we need do is look at the most successful and competitive societies in the world – take the Scandinavian countries for example. The problem is not "what do we want?" or "is it possible to have it?" – but rather, "how do those who do not have it, get it?" The lesson here is that welcoming a labour rights agenda is part of the answer – not part of the problem. Indeed, resisting the development of a positive human capital policy package is a recipe for problems. It is necessary to approach development comprehensively – i.e.

with respect for Sen's insights about the interconnectivity of economic, social and political freedoms. Labour rights, as all else, need to be seen through this lens. As Kucera puts it:

> In short no solid evidence is found in support of the "conventional wisdom" that foreign investors favour countries with weaker worker rights. These findings are consistent with prior studies, suggesting that the burden of proof ought to shift to those arguing the case in favour of the "conventional wisdom." In addition to empirical evidence are presented theoretical grounds for calling into question the logic of the "conventional wisdom." Along these lines, a broader view of the economics of worker rights is argued for, beyond the labour cost–labour productivity relationship. For while this relationship provides a two-sided, cost-benefit approach, there are more than two sides to the story, at least as regards FDI location and economic growth. That is, the effects of worker rights may be transmitted not only through the labour cost–labour productivity nexus, but also through enhancing political and social stability (particularly regarding rights of freedom of association and collective bargaining) and levels of human capital (particularly regarding child labour and gender inequality).[43]

Or, as Flanagan puts his final conclusion:

> Contrary to the race to the bottom hypothesis, the analysis did not find significant linkages between export performance or FDI inflows and the measures of labour standards. In sum, the paper finds no evidence that countries with global standards gained competitive advantage in international markets. Poor labor conditions often signal low productivity or are one element of a package of nation characteristics that discourage FDI influence or inhibit expert performance.[44]

This is, in fact, the labour law specific version of the more general story told by Sen and Stern. The complex interaction of labour rights, human capital, productivity growth, and political and social stability, is one dimension – a very important dimension – of a new approach to healthy and competitive economies and societies.[45]

Informality

But then it is said that the problem of the informal economy in Latin America alters the normal calculus and makes the emerging consensus more difficult to apply or even believe. Is this true?

At a conceptual level it is hard to see why. After all, the question is one of growth in productivity – not the particular legal questions of whether that productive activity is channelled through the device of an employment contract, conventionally understood. Employment is a legal category but, for example, we should note that the International Labour Organization is called the International *Labour* Organization and not the International *Employment* Organization. And its campaign is for "decent work" not, "decent employment". The fundamental social problems to be solved remain the same regardless of legal category. Core rights should be adaptable to all modes of engaging in productive activity. But the concerns about the informal economy raise other more specific issues. As Galli and Kucera write:

> Latin America has experienced in recent decades a steady and substantial increase in the share of workers characterized by informal employment status. From 1990 to 1997, for instance, the share of informal employment for a group of 14 Latin American countries increased from 51.8 to 57.7%, based on a definition of informal employment used by the International Labour Organization including non-agricultural employment in small firms, self-employment and service. One reason for concern regarding the growing share of informal employment in Latin America is that such employment is often characterized by poor work conditions, including low labor standards.[46]

The link between this reality and the labour standards agenda is the belief that higher labour standards – in particular freedom of association and collective bargaining – reduce employment in the formal sector and contribute to the informalization of the economy. This is a common view. But Kucera and Galli demonstrate that for the civic rights of freedom of association and collective bargaining, this view does not hold. They carefully distinguish these basic rights from other substantive entitlements to employment security through job security regulations. Their findings, and others at the World Bank, are summarized by Sengenberger as follows:

> A recent empirical study based on 14 countries in Latin America in the 1990s found a clear cyclical pattern for the share of informal employment. It acted as a buffer for formal employment in large firms, resulting in robust pro-cyclical employment in the formal private sector and robust counter-cyclical employment in small firms and self-employment. Countries with stronger civic rights, including freedom of association, collective bargaining and civil liberties, and also countries with higher wage shares tended to have higher proportions of formal employment and lower shares of informal employment, even controlling for GDP per capita. This finding is contrary to the proposition that higher labour standards in the formal economy

lead to increased informalization. The authors concluded that increasing
the share of formal employment required both the strengthening of civic
rights and growth-promoting macro-economic policy (Galli and Kucera,
2002). The findings of this study confirm the findings of earlier empirical
analysis that political liberties, which almost always go hand in hand with
the freedom of unions to organize, are associated with less dualism in labour
markets and a larger formal economy (World Bank, 1995).[47]

William Maloney's recent and provocative "Informality Reconsidered" is,
in many ways, consistent with the findings of Galli and Kucera – that
inefficient substantive labour law – not core labour rights in the form
of freedom of association and collective bargaining – is responsible for
the "attractiveness" of the formal sector, for both employers and workers.
Maloney writes:

> More fundamentally, informal employment firms of relatively low technol-
> ogy and capital intensity can only be attractive if the overall level of labor
> productivity in the formal sector is also low. To the degree that current
> legislation impedes investment in physical and human capital, or prevents
> the efficient organization and operation of firms, it perpetuates the low
> levels of productivity throughout the economy.[48]

Conclusion

What is the overall lesson? The overall lesson is that much of what has
passed for conventional and correct thinking for a significant stretch of
time leading up to the relatively recent past, is simply incorrect. What Sen
and Stern have articulated at the level of conceptual overview is more than
substantiated by empirical study at the level of detail and concerning the
specific issue of core labour rights. The lesson is that core labour rights are
part of any successful effort to build a competitive society and economy –
one that is just, *and because so*, competitive in a globalized world, which
in turn helps it build a more just society, *and so on*. There is a "package"
of policies which are necessary ingredients for sustainable societies and
economies which both drive and are driven by globalization. What this
means for our concrete and current purpose – labour rights in the context of a possible Free Trade Agreement of the Americas – is actually quite
straightforward at the level of principle. In short, all countries to all such
potential agreements have to re-evaluate their reasons for engaging the
labour rights agenda. For countries such as Canada the name of the game
is no longer that we ought to pursue the labour rights agenda in order to
avoid a "race to the bottom". For developing countries the name of the
game is that they should no longer contest such an agenda in the name

of avoiding costly and unwanted protectionist-driven political agendas emanating from the North. Leaving aside the motivations of some advocating the labour agenda from the North, successful development requires attention to the labour agenda. And the point of hemispheric economic integration, properly undertaken, is that there are positive externalities (economic, in terms of security, etc.) to all parties from an agreement upon integration based upon increasing levels of development for all. If we take the labour rights/productivity/human capital/ comprehensive development strategy seriously, then because our basic thinking has changed (from a negative/cost view to a positive/benefit view) the basic structure of any such labour component in a possible FTAA must also change. Respect for core labour rights is to be promoted in our *mutual* interests. On this view the point of a labour agenda is part of a positive development agenda. The core modalities in any such agreement must be incentives and capacity building – not sanctions and punishment. The new view empowers countries in Latin America to seek concrete financial and technical aid and assistance in developing a core labour rights infrastructure. Without going into institutional details, the ILO regional offices and multidisciplinary teams could be funded and mobilized to these ends. Shortcomings on core labour rights are occasions for assistance and progress, not sanctions and exclusion.

The impetus for such an agreement should come from the South, but should be welcomed in the North because of its possible contribution to a larger, more successful, more stable set of regional economies with resulting mutual gain for all. In so far as existing labour practices – regarding collective bargaining for example – are considered as inefficient in terms of substantive outcomes, or even in terms of the standards of *real* freedom of association and free collective bargaining, then an FTAA labour agenda is best seen as an opportunity to provide institutional push and resources for positive reform.

Others have made the *strategic* case for a warmer reception in the past of developing countries to the labour rights agenda.[49] This paper makes the *principled* case for such a change in thinking. Our best thinking, our deepest normative views, and our latest empirical research clearly point to the need to break out of the straightjacket of our old ways of thinking about development, globalization and the role of labour policy. The reality is that this act of liberation simply consists in seeing that this particular international emperor has no clothes. The result will be that a positive and new agenda – undertaken with a new motivation - will be made available to us. One further consequence will be the end of marginalization of labour law and labour ministries and their repositioning at the centre of a productivity/human capital/comprehensive development strategy. For these reasons, and in this way, labour rights are a key component of a possible FTAA.

Notes

1. James D. Wolfensohn, "Opening Remarks at the International Conference on Poverty Reduction Strategies" (Paper presented to the IMF/World Bank international conference, January 2002).
2. Thomas J. Courchene, *A State of Minds: Towards a Human Capital Future for Canadians* (Institute for Research on Public Policy, Montreal, 2001).
3. I borrow this idea from Wittgenstein who famously said the aim of philosophy is "to show the fly the way out of the fly-bottle". Ludwig Wittgenstein, *Philosophical Investigations* (Blackwell, Oxford, 1953), at para. 309.
4. Dani Rodrik, *Has Globalization Gone Too Far?* (Institute of International Economics, Washington, DC, 1997), 2.
5. *United Nations Millenium Declaration*, UN MD, 55th Sess., UN Doc. A/RES/55/2 (2000), online: http://www.un.org/millennium/declaration/ares552e.pdf.
6. World Commission on the Social Dimension of Globalization, *A Fair Globalization: Creating Opportunities for All* (Report) (ILO–World Commission on the Social Dimension of Globalization, Geneva, 2004).
7. Amartya Sen, *Development As Freedom* (Oxford University Press, New York and Oxford, 1999).
8. Sen, *Development*, 4.
9. Sen, *Development*, 11.
10. Nicholas Stern, "Dynamic Development: Innovation and Inclusion" (Munich Lectures on Economics, November 2002).
11. Stern, "Dynamic Development", at 9.
12. Stern, "Dynamic Development", at 9.
13. Stern, "Dynamic Development", at 6.
14. Stern, "Dynamic Development", at 7.
15. Statement by President Mkapa of Tanzania, National Dialogue on the Social Dimensions of Globalization (Dar es Salaam, August 2002).
16. Paul Krugman., *The Age of Diminished Expectations*, 4th edition (MIT Press, Cambridge, Mass., 1994), 13.
17. Paul Krugman, *Peddling Prosperity* (W.W. Norton and Co., New York, 1994), 124.
18. Krugman, *Peddling Prosperity*, 56.
19. ILO, *World Employment Report 1995*, 189; Courchene, *A State of Minds*.
20. Many commentators have noted that the fundamental problem with many under-developing states has been the exclusion – particularly along gender lines – of significant numbers from the labour market either altogether or from educational opportunities leading to higher value added jobs.
21. Krugman, *Peddling Prosperity*, 125.

22. Krugman, *Peddling Prosperity*, 127.
23. For an extended and illuminating analysis in the context of the US policies in this regard, see Pedro Carneiro and James Heckman, "Human Capital Policy" (NBER working paper 9495, Feb. 2003).
24. Krugman, *Peddling Prosperity*, 128.
25. Jamil Salmi, *Constructing Knowledge Societies: New Challenges for Tertiary Education* (World Bank, 2002), 21, online: http://www.worldbank.org/education/tertiary
26. Thomas J. Courchene, "A Mission Statement for Canada" (2000) 21 *Policy Options/Options politiques* 6.
27. Thomas J. Courchene, "Imbedding Globalization: A Human Capital Perspective" (Canada House Lecture, 23 October 2001).
28. Attached as Appendix A is a summary of the core ILO conventions relating to the core rights taken from Werner Sengenberger, *Globalization and Social Progress: The Role and Impact of International Labour Standards* (Friedrich-Ebert-Stiftung, Bonn, 2002), 47.
29. Robert J. Flanagan, "Labor Standards and International Competitive Advantage" (Stanford University, 2002), at 6, online: http://www.iza.org/iza/en/papers/ transatlantic/1_flanagan.pdf.
30. Rossana Galli, "The Economic Impact of Child Labour", ILO Discussion Paper DP/128/2001 (International Institute for Labour Studies, Geneva, 2001), at 21.
31. Toke Aidt and Zafiris Tzannatos, *Unions and Collective Bargaining : Economic Effects in a Global Environment.* (World Bank, Washington, DC, 2002).
32. Richard B. Freeman and James L. Medoff, *What Do Unions Do?* (Basic Books, New York, 1985); Morley Gunderson et al., *Union – Management Relations in Canada*, 4th ed. (Addison-Wesley, Don Mills, 1982), 395; Aidt and Tzannotos, *Unions*.
33. Organization for Economic Development, *Trade, Employment, and Labour Standards: A Study of Core Workers' Rights and International Trade* (OECD, Paris, 1996). ("*OECD 1996*").
34. *OECD 1996*, 105.
35. *OECD 1996*, 105.
36. *OECD 1996*, 123.
37. *OECD 1996*, 111–112. In a 2000 follow-up study the OECD reviewed data and analysis made available since 1996 and addressed itself to the same set of questions covered regarding labour standards and trade performance and investment. A principle finding of the OECD 1996 study was that there is no evidence that countries with low core standards enjoy a better global export performance than high standard countries. The OECD 2000 study states that this finding has not been challenged by literature appearing since the 1996 study was completed. Regarding labour standards and foreign direct investment the OECD 2000 study concludes: "In sum, there is no robust evidence that low-standard countries provide a haven for foreign firms."

Other main conclusions of the 2000 Study can be summarized as follows:

- Strengthened core labour standards can increase growth and efficiency by raising skill levels in the work force and encouraging innovation and higher productivity.
- Countries that develop democratic institutions – including core labour rights – will weather the transition to trade liberalization with smaller adverse consequences than countries without such institutions.
- Trade interventions are not an optimal instrument to abolish exploitative child labour and expand human capital formation. In some circumstances a ban on child labour may be effective, but there are limits to such a policy and a ban can actually worsen the conditions of households.

38. David Kucera, 'The effects of core workers rights on labour costs and foreign direct investment: evaluating the "conventional wisdom"', ILO DP/130 (2001).
39. Working Party on the Social Dimension of Globalization, "Investment in the Global Economy and Decent Work", 283rd Session., ILO Doc. GB.283/WP/SDG/2 (2002).
40. Dani Rodrik, "Labor Standards in International Trade: Do They Matter and What Do We Do About Them', in R. Z. Lawrence et al., *Emerging Agenda For Global Trade: High Stakes for Developing Countries*, (Overseas Development council, Washington, DC, 1996)
41. Flanagan, "Labor Standards".
42. Fabrice Hatem, *International Investment*, UN Economic and Social Council, UN Doc. E/1997/67 (1997), cited in Kucera, "The effects", and elsewhere.
43. Kucera, "The effects", at 33.
44. Flanagan, "Labor Standards".
45. Charles P. Oman, *Policy Competition for Foreign Direct Investment* (OECD Development Centre, Paris, 1999). All of these points are very nicely summarized by Oman:

> No discussion of rules-based competition among governments to attract foreign direct investment, especially among governments in developing and emerging economies would be complete without mention of the tremendous importance some investors – especially those seeking sites for long-term investment in major production capabilities to serve regional and global markets, i.e. those which governments are generally most eager to attract – attach to the stability and predictability of the operating environment of their chosen investment sites. This observation brings us back, of course, to the importance of the fundamentals, notably the political and macroeconomic stability, along with market size and growth potential, and the availability of infrastructure and human resources. The point, however, is that countries that do reasonably well on the fundamentals are now finding that strengthening their judiciary system, or having a judiciary system that is seen both at home and abroad as fair and consistent . . . can be a powerful attraction – or its absence a significant deterrent to many investors.

And with specific reference to labour market deregulation Oman puts the point as follows:

> The point to be emphasized for our purposes, however, is that governments in OECD countries – at the subnational or national level – compete for FDI primarily with one another, and do so largely within their own geographical region. The negative effects of that competition include some governments' overblown fear of losing FDI to low-wage countries, or a "race to the bottom" in global labour standards caused by developing countries.
>
> This does not mean, of course, that it would not be preferable for all countries to enforce core labour standards, not does it mean that competition among governments to attract FDI may not act as a deterrent to a socially optimal raising of labour standards . . . What it means is that policymakers and OECD countries must overcome their fear of losing FDI to low-wage countries and must, in any case, use means other than weakening their protection of workers rights and their enforcement of labour standards to attract FDI. Policymakers in developing emerging economies must also use rules-based means to attract FDI other than those that involve any downgrading of local labour standards, and they have no reason not to respect and enforce core labour standards.

Another powerful presentation of a similar set of views is offered in Rodrik, 'Labor Standards':

> Healthy societies have a range of institutions which make . . . colossal coordination failures less likely. The rule of law, the high-quality judiciary, representative political institutions, free elections, independent trade unions, social partnerships, institutionalized representation of minority groups and social insurance are examples of such institutions. What makes these arrangements function in institutions of conflict management is that they entail a double "commitment technology": they warn the potential "winners" of social conflict that their gains will be limited, and they assure the "losers" that they will not be expropriated. They intend to increase the incentives for social groups to cooperate by reducing the payoff to socially uncooperative strategies.

46. Rossana Galli and David Kucera, "Labor Standards and Informal Employment in Latin America" (2004) 32/5 *World Development* 809–28.
47. Sengenberger, *Globalization and Social Progress*.
48. William F. Maloney, "Does Informality Imply Segmentation in Urban Labor Markets? Evidence from Sectoral Transitions in Mexico" (1999) 13/2 *World Bank Economic Review* 275–302.
49. See, for example, Sandra Polaski, "Trade and Labor Standards: A Strategy for Developing Countries (Carnegie Endowment for International Peace, Washington, DC: 2003), 7–16.

Appendix A

Convention No.	Title and Aim of Convention	Ratifications (August 2002)
No. 29	*Forced Labour Convention (1930)* Requires the suppression of forced or compulsory labour in all its forms. Certain exceptions are permitted, such as military service, convict labour properly supervised, emergencies such as wars, fires and earthquakes.	*161*
No. 87	*Freedom of Association and Protection of the Right to Organize Convention (1948)* Establishes the right of all workers and employers to form and join organizations of their own choosing without prior authorization, and lays down a series of guarantees for the free functioning of organizations without interference by public authorities.	*141*
No. 98	*Right to Organize and Collective Bargaining Convention (1949)* Provides for protection against anti-union discrimination, for protection of workers' and employers' organizations against acts of interference by each other, and for measures to promote collective bargaining.	*152*
No. 100	*Equal Remuneration Convention (1951)* Calls for equal pay and benefits for men and women for work of equal value.	*161*
No. 105	*Abolition of Forced Labour Convention (1957)* Prohibits the use of any form of forced or compulsory labour as a means of political coercion or education, punishment for the expression of political or ideological views, workforce mobilization, labour discipline, punishment for participation in strikes, or discrimination.	*157*

Appendix A (cont.)

Convention No.	Title and Aim of Convention	Ratifications (August 2002)
No. 111	*Discrimination (Employment and Occupation) Convention (1958)* Calls for a national policy to eliminate discrimination in access to employment, training and working conditions, on grounds of race, colour, sex, religion, political opinion, national extraction or social origin, and to promote equality of opportunity and treatment.	*156*
No. 138	*Minimum Age Convention (1973)* Aims at the abolition of child labour, stipulating that the minimum age for admission to employment shall not be less than the age of completion of compulsory schooling.	*116*
No. 182	*Worst Forms of Child Labour Convention (1999)* Calls for immediate and effective measures to prohibit and eliminate the worst forms of child labour, including all forms of slavery, the use of child labour for prostitution, pornography, illicit activities, and work harmful to the health, safety and morals of children.	*129*

11

The future of labour integration: the South American perspective

Introduction – the FTAA

In 1994, the leaders of 34 American nations established the Free Trade Area of the Americas (FTAA), an organization that today involves some 800 million people and a combined gross domestic product of more than US$13 billion. Given the historical and cultural differences among its members, especially where industrial relations are concerned, the FTAA's achievements have been monumental. Over the last decade, Latin America has curbed inflation, decreased import tariffs and, as a result, has stimulated its economic growth. Unfortunately, however, the FTAA's economic and social shortcomings are as salient as its accomplishments. With the organization's final phase of negotiations nearing their end, poverty and inequality still remain widespread throughout Latin America. Moreover, despite the FTAA's important objective of ensuring fair international trade, the diversity and, at some points, incompatibility of domestic labour laws and policies have only been marginally addressed during the FTAA negotiations. Consequently, many Latin Americans now question the wisdom of increasing competition with more efficient economies, particularly those of the United States and Canada.

Economic advantages and disadvantages of the FTAA

From an economic perspective, Latin America's continued participation in the FTAA has both benefits and burdens. On the one hand, membership in the FTAA would not only allow Latin American countries to explore current technology and refined business practices, but would also afford them the opportunity to purchase industrial inputs at a lower price. More importantly, the FTAA offers Latin American economies a valuable opportunity to consummate their entrance into the planet's largest and most fluid market, an attractive option given the fact that, since the FTAA's emergence, its members' economic performance has steadily improved. In the 1980s, for instance, economic growth among the FTAA's members reached an annual average of 3.26 per cent. In the subsequent decade, this rose to 3.55 per cent. In Central America, annual growth also jumped from 1.35 per cent during the 1980s to 4.45 per cent in the 1990s. Similarly, the Andean Region's economic growth went from 1.67 to 2.76 per cent a year, Mercosur grew from 1.62 to 3.32 per cent, and NAFTA grew from 3.26 to 3.55 per cent. Although the greatest benefactor of this arrangement in the 1990s was the United States, with an average annual growth rate and an economy that have almost doubled over the last two decades. America's success provides a strong incentive for other nations to maintain their membership in the FTAA.

On the other hand, Latin America's continued membership in the FTAA would allow nations with stronger economies to continue to exploit nations with weaker ones, thereby potentially increasing trade disparities among FTAA states. Further, existing protective practices and economic inequalities threaten established trade restrictions on products of particular interest to poorer countries – most notably, sugar, fish, meat, textiles, clothing, tobacco, orange juice, soybeans and steel. Many barriers already exist in this respect. In 2001, for instance, the American Congress approved the Trade Promotion Authority (the TPA), which deemed most American agriculture products, textiles and clothing to be "sensitive" items not immediately subject to free trade. Subsequently, a quota system and tariff increases made it very difficult to export steel to the United States. In 2003, the United States passed anti-terrorism legislation, which limited migration and labour movement across its borders. Additionally, the United States continues to apply quotas for many products and to impose anti-dumping measures via legislation such as its Trade Act.[1]

While the aggregate GNP of the FTAA's members in 2004 reached US $13 billion, only a handful of countries were responsible for the bulk of this economic output. As one might expect, the United States generated an astounding 80 per cent of this wealth. The nations comprising NAFTA generated 89 per cent. Adding Brazil, this figure increases to 94 per cent. Clearly, most of the FTAA's GNP can be attributed to four countries.[2] This dependence has made Latin Americans suspicious of America's promise that free trade will help "lift nations and workers".[3]

The social debate

The FTAA also presents challenges from a social perspective. While Latin America's continued membership in the FTAA promises to create more jobs, improve labour capabilities, and raise real wages, the road to economic viability seems laden with several formidable pitfalls. To begin with, technological advances may eventually contribute to Latin America's rising unemployment and informal labour. Many people claim that productivity and regulatory disparities will favour more developed nations and further marginalize labourers in poorer nations. The introduction of higher labour and environmental standards is seen by many as having a negative effect on the competitive advantage of less developed nations. In short, the social benefits are under debate.

In fact, after several years of structural adjustment in Latin America during the 1990s, unemployment did not decrease, but increased from 6 to 10 per cent, while informal work rose from about 50 to 57 per cent.[4] Some blame the excessive commercial regulations that in many countries made economic activities unaffordable to small entrepreneurs who were less prepared to cope with technological changes and the effects of globalization, which complicated rising unemployment and informal labour.[5] Others blame a large part of Latin America's unemployment and informality on high payroll taxes and severance payments, as well as rigid labour codes.[6] Regardless of its cause, however, the labour area's disappointing performance has lead to Latin America's widespread scepticism of free market policies. In many countries, anti-neo-liberalism is increasingly finding support and, with it, countries, particularly Argentina, Brazil, Ecuador, Venezuela and Peru, are shifting toward populist and left-wing government. In fact, recent studies sponsored by the United Nations suggest that approximately 55 per cent of Latin Americans are willing to support dictatorships promising to reduce poverty and inequality.[7]

As the 2005 deadline for the FTAA's final negotiations approaches, the debate on the labour question has intensified. In Brazil, for example, the Workers Party has branded the FTAA as a mere ploy to annex Brazilian markets to American ones, and, accordingly, a serious threat to domestic production and national employment. In Argentina, labour unions fear that the FTAA will have the same disastrous effects as the intervention of the IMF, which resulted in the country's default and economic collapse. In Peru, the labour press referred to the FTAA as a weapon of mass destruction in Latin America. Notably, Lula, Brazil's president and

Kirchner, Argentina's president, have invited Peru and Venezuela to join Mercosur and, with this move, it appears that they intend to build a strong alternative trading block in the FTAA's final negotiation phase. Further, sceptical of current protectionism, business is pressuring governments to take retaliatory measures. Similarly, suspecting the further decline of working conditions and a further trade imbalance, labour unions are demanding that governments accept social conditions proposed during the Uruguay Round of GATT.

Labour laws in Mercosur

Several regional economic agreements, which include direct or indirect references to labour relations, have been established in Latin America during the last 25 years.[8] One of these is Mercosur, formed in 1991 by Brazil, Argentina, Paraguay and Uruguay, which, aside from a few products, established a free trade zone with no import tariffs.

The highest institution of Mercosur is the Common Market Council (CMC), comprised of member states' presidents and foreign ministries. Mercosur's executive authority is the Common Market Group (CMG), formed by representatives of its members' foreign ministries, economic ministries and the presidents of central banks.

Mercosur began to address labour issues more explicitly in 1995, when its members' ministries of labour agreed to form a special committee (SGT10) to deal with employment, social security, health and safety, and migrant workers concerns. Representatives from governments, businesses and labour unions are also partners in the Socio-Economic Forum (SEF), and, as such, are invited to make recommendations to the CMG and CMC. Following a recommendation made by those Ministries, Mercosur agreed to create the Consultative SEF under the following terms:

> (a) it is of fundamental importance to eliminate all kinds of non-tariff barriers which may affect trade among the four countries; (b) it is important to harmonize the macroeconomic policies and the national laws; (c) it is urgent to create a committee of social policies to cover labour, education, health and social security; (d) it is indispensable to create a tribunal for conflict resolution.[9]

Mercosur's initial success is demonstrated by the fact that international trade among the four countries increased 200 per cent in the 1990s. After 1999, however, commerce was severely affected mainly due to Brazil's currency devaluation and its consequent financial crises, as well as Argentina's default on its external debt. Between 2000 and 2002, and particularly in 2004, economic trade was affected by severe crisis. Argentina, in particular, has raised several protectionist barriers to free trade. The future of Mercosur is now uncertain.

In the area of labour, one of Mercosur's first efforts to integrate its members' diverse labour laws occurred when the SEF's union representatives proposed an agreement on the eleven ILO Conventions already ratified by its members. The proposal involved Convention No. 11 (the right to association in agriculture), No. 14 (industrial workers' weekend rest), No. 26 (methods to establish minimum wages), No. 29 (forced labour), No. 81 (labour inspection), No. 95 (wage protection), No. 98 (the right to collective bargaining), No. 100 (equal remuneration), No. 105 (the elimination of forced labour), No. 111 (the elimination of discrimination), and No. 159 (job training). Unfortunately, the CMC rejected this proposal, maintaining that Mercosur's members still had conflicting interests that needed to be resolved before a labour pact could be signed. A later attempt was made to move the nations to agree on a Social Charter on Fundamental Labour Rights. This agreement would have included Convention Nos. 29 and 105 (prohibiting forced labour), No. 98 (protecting the freedom of association), Nos. 100 and 111 (preventing discrimination), and No. 138 (preventing child labour). Predictably, the effort to establish a set of international labour standards failed. Argentina vetoed this proposal, arguing that no agreement on labour rights could be reached before Mercosur approved a fiscal monitor. Instead, Argentina proposed the creation of a "Labour Relations System of Mercosur" and a "Labour Relations Board of Mercosur". Mercosur's other members considered these proposals to be unacceptable, however.

Despite Mercosur's failure in 1995 to achieve agreement on the above-mentioned ILO Conventions, the CMC made significant progress when it signed the "Declaración Sociolaboral" in 1998 (Social-Labour Declaration). This recognizes individual rights, collective rights, employment policies, labour inspection, social security, and conflict resolution procedures.[10] Mercosur's members agreed to respect the rights enumerated in this agreement when enforcing their respective labour laws and practices. Mercosur's members also announced their desire to create a "Comissão Sociolaboral Regional" (Regional Labour Commission), which would promote and monitor the protection of the rights addressed in the Social-Labour Declaration. To date, however, this Commission remains merely a proposal. Hence, no concrete regulatory mechanism exists to monitor members' compliance with respective national labour

standards. Moreover, the Socio-Economic Forum has been meeting errat-
ically, and it lacks sufficient power to transform its founders' original
intentions into effective practices. Yet, in 2002 the CMC approved the
creation of a Permanent Tribunal of Appeal (composed of five lawyers
with a mandate of six years) to resolve commercial disputes. Although
labour disputes may be brought before this Tribunal, it has not heard a
single case.[11]

Much law, little compliance

In each of Mercosur's four member nations, legislation respecting individual rights is very detailed. Yet, where collective rights or collective
bargaining is concerned, this legislation is vague. This is a deficiency that
cannot be modified through the collective bargaining process.

Argentina's 1994 Constitution establishes a minimum wage, maximum
working hours (8 hours a day and 48 per week), a paid vacation entitlement, freedom of association, health and safety protection, equal pay
for the same work and the requirements for valid collective agreements.
Ratified ILO conventions also have a constitutional status and, thus,
require constitutional changes to be denounced. The Argentinian labour
courts do not have a "normative power" permitting judges to extend the
results of a judicial decision to many firms and segments of the labour
force, as might be done in Brazil. Unlike in Brazil, however, the Minister
of Labour may exercise this power.

In Brazil, labour protection is outlined in the country's 1988 Constitution, the Brazilian Labour Code (CLT) and other legislation. Brazil's Constitution has about 40 provisions addressing labour concerns, while the
CLT has more than 900 detailed articles respecting individual rights, bargained agreements, labour court procedures, health and safety, and regulations for special occupations. Generally, neither Brazil's Constitution nor
the CLT permits parties to alter the terms of the country's laws through the
use of collective bargaining. There are, though, three exceptions: wages,
working hours, and profit share participation. Although trade unions
may bargain for higher wages, they must agree with any conditions that
management may advance. An increase in an employee's daily work hours
must be offset with a decrease in the amount of hours he or she works in
the same week. Where profit sharing is concerned, unions and enterprises
must establish distribution criteria.

Brazil has a particular problem ratifying ILO Convention 87 (freedom
of association). Brazil's 1988 Constitution provides that only one union

is permitted in a particular sector in a particular territory. It also requires compulsory contributions to be paid to unions, regardless of their membership or affiliation. This restriction, however, is presently under discussion. President Lula, a former union leader, fought for twenty years for the ratification of Convention 87. Once elected president, a national labour forum, the Forum Nacional do Trabalho (FNT) was established to ensure Brazil's adoption of that Convention's principles. The FNT, a large tripartite commission with membership exceeding 300 persons, was scheduled to present its recommendations to President Lula in April 2004. However, the work of the FNT has been too slow. To date, FNT has concluded only one reform respecting union organization.

Paraguay also has very detailed legislation specified by its Constitution and national Labour Code. The rigidity of these laws is very similar to the Brazil situation.

Uruguay has no labour code. Individual relations are regulated by a variety of laws and ILO conventions. It is the only country in Mercosur where collective bargaining has a wider range of application. Even so, many issues are established in a top-down manner. For instance, at the federal level, a tripartite council annually defines the value of wages for several categories for the whole country.

The four countries present variations in the types of contracts into which parties may enter. In Argentina and Uruguay, there is a wide range of labour contracts, with special provisions for small and medium enterprises, young workers, seasonal work, etc. In Brazil and Paraguay, such possibilities are restricted. Attempts to reform this rigidity were halted by trade unions and corporatist groups who lobbied legislators.

Variations also exist on working hours, paid vacation, holidays, and the remuneration of weekend work. In Brazil, employees work 8 hours per day, 44 hours per week. In Mercosur's other nations, employees work 48 hours per week. Brazil has a vacation allowance (one-third of the monthly salary) and a rule that employers must pay the non-working days during weekends for contracts where work is paid by the hour.

However, despite the extensive protections embedded in the legislation, the extended legislation in those countries is seldom fully enforced.

Furthermore, in Latin America, informality is the rule. Informal employees are not unionized and do not bargain with their employers. They do not have social security protection. This means that when they are out of work, they cannot rely on any sort of unemployment insurance. When they fall ill, there is no paid leave. When they become older, they receive no retirement benefits. When they die, they leave nothing to their descendants. Additionally, wage differentials among men and women, as well as between racial groups, are much greater in the informal sector than in the formal one. Child labour is more common. A large number of informal workers are self-employed.

In short, a large segment of the Latin American work force lives in countries with generous laws and poor compliance. Take Brazil. In 2002, there were about 75 million Brazilians at work. Of these, 30 million enjoyed social security, whereas 45 million did not. Of these 45 million, about 19 million were non-registered employees, 15 million were self-employed, 6 million were non-wage workers (usually working for parents and relatives), 4 million were non-registered maids, and 1 million were employers. Informality is a large problem that is unlikely to be solved by auditing and labour courts. The Ministry of Labour has about 7,000 labour auditors and the Department of Justice has about 5,000 judges, an alarmingly small number considering the 45 million informal and 30 million formal workers they are required to assist. There are more than two million legal proceedings in the labour courts currently awaiting decision.

Reforms must be made to Brazil's Labour Code and dispute resolution procedures. As previous attempts have demonstrated, though, such change has been difficult to achieve. In the past, trade unionists blamed greater flexibility for workers' problems, particularly unemployment and informality. At other times, although judges complained about the judicial backlog, they resisted decentralization or instituting voluntary dispute resolution mechanisms such as conciliation, mediation or arbitration. In spite of the efforts of the FNT, it is very likely that Brazil's labour laws and judiciary will remain rigid for a long time. As a result, one can expect Brazil's current problems with informality to worsen.

The cost of law

In times of economic stagnancy, high unemployment and an overabundance of labour, unrealistic legislation generates high social costs that, for the majority of firms and workers, frustrates compliance. In Brazil, for instance, social costs have reached 103.46 per cent of the nominal wage because of such legislation. Consider the figures in Table 11.1 below.

None of the items in this table can be negotiated by labour and management. Given the legislation's rigidity and its resultant social costs, firms and workers find it difficult to comply with the law's prescriptions.

Table 11.1. *The cost of legal contracts in Brazil – hourly workers*

Social Costs	Percentage of wages
Group A – Social Obligations	
Social Security	20.00
Severance Fund	8.50
Educational contribution	2.50
Accident contribution (average)	2.00
Social services (SESI/SESC/SEST)	1.50
Vocational training (SENAI/SENAC/SENAT)	1.00
Entrepreneurial promotion (SEBRAE)	0.60
Agrarian reform (INCRA)	0.20
Subtotal A	36.30
Group B –Non-working time I	
Paid weekend	18.91
Vacation	9.45
Vacation Allowance	3.64
Holidays	4.36
Advance notice	1.32
Sick leave	0.55
Subtotal B	38.23
Group C –Non-working time II	
Christmas salary	10.91
Dismissal Penalty	3.21
Subtotal C	14.12
Group D –Cumulative Incidences	
Group A/Group B	13.88
Severance Payment/Christmas salary	0.93
Subtotal D	14.81
GRAND TOTAL	103.46

Source: IBGE (Brazilian Census Bureau), 2000.

Rigidity and generosity are the hallmarks of Latin American labour laws. However, there are variations within Mercosur, each producing significant differences in terms of final labour costs:

- With the exception of Uruguay, all of Mercosur's members have similarly rigid legislation concerning collective bargaining. However, each members' legislation varies in terms of working hours, paid weekends, dismissal procedures, vacation and paid holidays are concerned.
- Argentina, Paraguay and Uruguay have each legislated a 48-hour work week. In Brazil, the only country that pays non-working weekend days for hourly workers, a working week is 44 hours long.
- In Brazil, annual vacation is fixed at 30 days, plus 10 days (paid in cash) as vacation allowance. In Mercosur's other members, vacation entitlement is progressive. In Argentina, individuals employed for up to 5 years by a firm are entitled to 14 vacation days, for between 5 and 10 years to 21 days, and so on. In Uruguay, individuals employed for up to 5 years by a firm are entitled to 20 vacation days. After that, one day is added for every 4 years of additional time in the firm. In Paraguay, individuals employed by a firm for up to 5 years are entitled to 12 days of vacation, for between 5 and 10 years to 18 days, and so on.
- Brazilian firms pay their employees for 12 vacation days a year. In Argentina, Paraguay and Uruguay, employers pay their employees for more than 12 vacation days, but offset this by reducing the number of paid days (Argentina and Paraguay, 10; Uruguay, 5).
- On the other hand, sick leave is entirely paid by the firm in Argentina (and it is very high) whereas in Brazil the firm is responsible for the first 15 days of illness only. The social security system pays for the rest.

These differences substantially affect the social costs of labour. As shown in Table 11.2, the highest impact is in Brazil (103.46 per cent), while the lowest is in Paraguay (41 per cent).

In Brazil, the total social costs (i.e. 103.46 per cent) are universal and applicable to micro, small, medium, large and multinational enterprises. It has been very difficult for smaller firms to cope with these costs as well as with administrative requirements to collect payments. Yet, as Table 11.3 makes clear, smaller firms are responsible for a large part of existing employment.

The micro, small and medium firms in Brazil represent 53 per cent of Mercosur's total employment. These firms are most affected by the high social costs created by Brazil's labour laws and they employ most of the country's informal labour force. Of 13.6 million workers in micro and

Table 11.2. *The cost of legal contracts in Mercosur – hourly workers*

Social Costs	Argentina	Brazil	Paraguay	Uruguay
Annual working hours	2,264	2,015	2,264	2,264
Group A – Social Obligations	Percentage of wages			
Social Security	33.00	20.00	15.50	19.50
Severance Fund		8.50		
Educational Contribution		2.50		
Accident Contribution (average)		2.00		2.00
Social Services		1.50		
Vocational Training		1.00	1.00	
Entrepreneurial promotion		0.60		
Agrarian Reform		0.20		
Subtotal A	33.00	36.30	16.50	21.50
Group B – Non Working Time – I				
Paid weekend		18.91		
Vacation	4.54	9.45	4.77	8.11
Vacation Allowance		3.64		
Holidays	3.24	4.36	3.18	1.62
Advance notice		1.32		
Sick leave	6.78	0.55		
Subtotal B	14.56	38.23	7.95	9.73
Group C – Non Working Time II				
Christmas salary	9.74	10.91	9.55	9.74
Dismissal Penalty	4.00	3.21	4.00	2.00
Subtotal C	13.74	14.12	13.55	11.74
Group D – Cumulative Incidences				
Group A/Group B	4.80	13.88	1.31	2.09
Severance/Christmas Salary		0.93		
Group A/Christmas Salary	3.21		1.57	2.09
Other Incidences	0.92			
Subtotal D	8.93	14.81	2.88	4.18

Table 11.2. (*cont.*)

Social Costs	Argentina	Brazil	Paraguay	Uruguay
Annual working hours	2,264	2,015	2,264	2,264
Group E – Others				
Life Insurance	0.04		0.12	
Wage Tax				1.00
Subtotal E	0.04		0.12	1.00
			2.88	4.18
GRAND TOTAL	70.27	103.46	41.00	48.06

Source: IBGE (Brazilian Census Bureau), 2000.

Table 11.3. *Formal and informal employees in urban areas in Brazil*

	Size			
Sector	Micro / Small	Medium	Large	Total
Manufacture	3,522,689	1,636,721	2,465,939	7,625,349
Commerce	5,457,983	311,642	1,076,120	6,845,745
Service	4,629,485	715,689	10,641,999	15,987,173
Total	13,610,157	2,664,052	14,184,058	30,458,267

Source: IBGE (Brazilian Census Bureau), 2000.

small enterprises, about 9.2 million or 68 per cent have no social protection. Medium firms, particularly in the non-tradable sectors, endure the same difficulties in coping with the cost and bureaucracy of the present legislation.

Core labour standards in Latin American nations

Presently, Latin American labour legislation outlines a wide range of individual rights, such as working hours, resting periods, vacations, holidays, health and security, unemployment and social security. Most Latin American countries have also ratified the ILO conventions dealing with core labour standards. One might argue that, given these protections, Latin American labour codes and regulations promise much more than the

North American equivalents. Latin American laws guarantee workers the
ability to organize unions without state or employer interference. Unionized workers may bargain once a year or whenever it is necessary to renew
their labour contracts. Laws prohibiting discrimination are also becoming
more detailed. All national laws prohibit forced labour. Labour courts and
ministers of labour are aggressively combating slave and bonded labour.
Child labour is also prohibited. If one takes the core labour standards
as measures of basic protections, Latin American countries have a good
record. As Table 11.4 demonstrates, most countries have ratified the conventions outlining the core labour standards:

Table 11.4.

	Ratified conventions							
	Forced Labour		Freedom of Association		Discrimination		Child Labour	
Convention no.	29	105	87	98	100	111	138	182
Argentina	✓	✓	✓	✓	✓	✓	✓	✓
Brazil	✓	✓	No	✓	✓	✓	✓	✓
Paraguay	✓	✓	✓	✓	✓	✓	No	✓
Uruguay	✓	✓	✓	✓	✓	✓	✓	✓
Chile	✓	✓	✓	✓	✓	✓	✓	✓
Venezuela	✓	✓	✓	✓	No	✓	✓	No
Colombia	✓	✓	✓	✓	No	✓	✓	✓
Ecuador	✓	✓	✓	✓	✓	✓	✓	✓

There is no lack of labour protection in Latin America. The problem,
however, is compliance. Although laws are extensive, they do not cover
the majority of people who work in the informal sector, which exceeds 50
per cent of the total workforce in most countries.[12]

Other countries in Latin America have demonstrated the tendency to
approve detailed laws that, both ironically and tragically, are difficult to
enforce. The very high costs of dismissal demonstrate why compliance can
be so difficult. On average, dismissal costs in Latin America are about 35
per cent of annual wages. In Brazil, in addition to paying 8.5 per cent every
month for a severance fund (Fundo de Garantia por Tempo de Serviço),
firms pay a penalty of 40 per cent of the total amount accumulated by the
worker in that fund in cases of dismissal. In practice, firing costs come
close to 150 per cent of an employee's annual salary.

Hence, dismissal costs are much higher than in most of the OECD countries, where they are less than 15 per cent of the annual wage (with the exception of 26 per cent in Spain and 35 per cent in Portugal).[13] Several studies show that the decline in employment associated with rising dismissal costs is much greater in the formal sector than in the aggregate. Conversely, an increase in firing costs is associated with an increase in informal employment. Complicating this problem is the fact that the formal and the informal sectors interact extensively. It is not uncommon for individuals to work for one or two years in the formal sector, move to the informal sector for a year or two, return to the formal sector for some time, then end up in the informal sector for the remainder of their lives. With every movement toward the informal sector, social protection is lost. The time lost is not recovered upon returning to the formal sector. Legislation is not flexible enough to protect individuals where they work; instead, it merely protects their jobs in the formal sector.

Generous legislation and lack of enforcement are largely responsible in Latin America for unemployment and the growth of the informal sector. Curiously, though, resistance to labour reform has been widespread; most countries have only made timid attempts to modernize their labour laws. Moreover, Latin Americans have not been patient enough to allow reform efforts to mature and to achieve positive results. Persistent macroeconomic problems have prevented employment growth and the creation of quality jobs. Faced with this reality, Latin Americans have quickly blamed the labour reforms instead of the problems. Latin American trade unions, the press, the media and lawmakers tend to be opposed to any kind of reform, and particularly those reforms that may reduce legal labour protection or shift protection from a legal to a contractual basis. The protected group (the "included") speak louder than the unprotected group (the "excluded") and manage to thwart any kind of change that might jeopardize the privileges they enjoy.

Consider Brazil's recent pension reform. In Brazil's private sector, the average retirement allowance was US $100 per month. In the public sector, it was US $1,000. For judges, it was US $4,000. A 2003 reform attempted to narrow this disparity gradually. In response, the country's 24,000 judges threatened to close their courts if legislators did not maintain the status quo. The result was that the private sector's 20 million workers were not only forced to accept their US $100 retirement allowances, but were ultimately subjected to more rigid rules concerning retirement and pension.

Informality and inequality usually go together. An unequal society tends to force a large majority of its people into informality and to protect only the few living in the formal market. In general, people in the informal economy have unstable jobs, low income and poor education. The most vulnerable are the young and women, who have little access to land, urban property and legal facilities. For them, unemployment is a luxury, since most of them never had a formal employment contract guaranteeing unemployment insurance. Recourse to the courts is also rare due to bureaucratic complexity, lengthy dispute resolution and high opportunity costs.[14] In Brazil, legal actions appealed to state and federal courts usually take an average of seven years to be resolved. Yet judicial reform has been difficult to achieve. Although the Brazilian Congress has been discussing reform for the last fifteen years, the measures it is proposing will not meet the country's needs.

Implications for the FTAA

The first challenge in establishing a fair labour market in a regional bloc such as the FTAA is to ensure that existing standards are effectively enforced. This issue must take priority over promulgating an exhaustive set of international labour standards. How might the countries involved in the FTAA ensure that enforcement issues are addressed?

It is unlikely that the internationalization of minimum labour standards will take place through confrontation. Instead, cooperation and continuing dialogue are essential in reaching solutions that fulfil mutual interests. During this process, it will be necessary not only to affirm but also to demonstrate clearly that proposed guidelines are not merely protectionist measures.

Recently, both the International Monetary Fund and the World Bank have rejected the idea of conditioning the approval of loans to poor countries on their compliance with the ILO core labour standards. These two organizations recognize, however, the importance of promoting the core labour standards through persuasion and moral pressure.[15]

A realistic approach to the problem is to consider that effective compliance is more likely to improve as countries increase their exports. The FTAA's potential use of trade sanctions to enforce labour standards could backfire. With respect to the United States and Canada, credible communication will be essential in establishing that their concern for better standards is humanitarian, not protectionist. A credible way to show that one derives satisfaction from improving the conditions of the poor is by helping them, by fostering their mastery of new technologies to improve their productivity. This sort of attitude seems to be more efficient than simply imposing trade sanctions and penalties on those who refuse to adopt existing labour standards. What is needed is a climate of sincere collaboration in which violations cannot be excused.

What form of intervention would best achieve this goal? What kind of changes will be necessary to make compliance more realistic?

To maximize compliance, all of the FTAA's members will need to participate fully in the enforcement procedures, which must be negotiated multilaterally and established through a systematic dialogue that respects cultural and economic differences. Obedience depends on feasibility. For instance, it is easy to prohibit child labour; it is not clear, however, whether this prohibition will keep children in school. Children may be moved from the labour market only to be exploited in other ways, such as through prostitution. The mere removal of a child from labour may be a solution, but a possible shift from work to drugs, crime or prostitution is a much bigger problem. Moreover, there is no consensus in the existing literature on the validity of the assumption that respect for core labour standards will thereby improve the lives of workers. OECD studies, for example, concluded that:

- there is no clear correlation between freedom of association and higher salaries;
- the impact of freedom of association depends on a series of other measures to be approved and implemented by states;
- there is no clear association between weak labour standards and an unusual attraction of direct foreign investments in developing countries; and
- as a rule, labour standards play a minor role in determining export prices.[16]

A recent study examined the idea that low labour costs are one of the most fundamental criteria for determining factory location. Surveying hundreds of multinational corporations, the study concluded that the cost of labour weighs into management's calculations after concerns for market growth, market size, the likelihood of profit, political and social stability, labour quality, regulatory environment, infrastructure, and manufacturing and services environment.[17] Surveying multinational corporations in 40 countries, Dani Rodrik found no relationship between, on the one hand, manufacturing and economic performance and, on the other hand, the number of ILO conventions that a country had ratified.[18] Using a methodology capturing the effective implementation of core labour standards, David Kucera found no conclusive evidence supporting the "conventional wisdom" that foreign investors favour countries that afford their workers fewer rights.[19]

In spite of this evidence, lobby groups continue to press a link between labour standards and trade. The issue is now overtly political. Unions in developed countries have advanced the idea that trading with a country with low labour standards is a bad deal. In this campaign they have sought the support of many unions from developing countries. As Paul Krugman points out, "it is a workers against workers battle".[20]

The need to improve the working conditions of poor people is indisputable. The claim that good standards are able, *per se*, to improve these conditions is simplistic. In fact, the issue is much more complex, and requires that attention be directed at reducing strong barriers against product and market competition.

It is clear that the linking of labour standards to international trade faces an enormous number of practical and theoretical barriers. Overcoming these barriers depends much more on small scale, concrete pilot projects than on massive actions to be undertaken within the context of trade liberalization.

What kind of model will the FTAA adopt?

Since the FTAA negotiations began in 1994, the labour question has only been discussed in vague terms. At the joint declaration of the Summit of the Americas, which took place in Denver, Colorado (30 June 1995), the ministers responsible for trade in the 34 nations declared:

> We are committed to the protection of the environment and further obser-
> vance and promotion of workers rights, through our respective govern-
> ments.

At the joint declaration of the Second Trade Meeting (Cartagena, Colombia, 21 March 1995) the ministers declared:

> We recognize the importance of further observance and promotion of
> workers rights and the need to consider appropriate processes in this area,
> through our respective governments.

In 1996, the WTO addressed this topic again, and issued the following ministerial declaration:

> We renew our commitment to the observance of internationally recognized
> core labour standards. The International Labour Organization (ILO) is the
> competent body to set and deal with these standards, and we affirm our
> support for its work in promoting them.

At the FTAA's Third Meeting (Belo Horizonte, Brazil, 16 May 1997), the ministers approved the WTO's decision that labour standards should be addressed primarily through the ILO. Since then, the group's discussions concerning labour standards have tapered off. For instance, at the Fourth Meeting in San Jose, Costa Rica (19 March 1998) the only reference to labour standards was as follows:

> We, the Ministers responsible for trade in the 34 countries reaffirm our commitment to the Singapore Declaration of the WTO – on the question of core labour standards.

The labour movement became dissatisfied with the minimal attention given to labour standards by the ministers during the FTAA's negotiations. During the meeting at Belo Horizonte (Brazil), Brazilian and other Latin American labour unions pressed the authorities to allow them to participate in at least one session. At the Fourth Meeting in 1998, the ministers responded:

> We, the Trade Ministers recognize and welcome the interests and concerns that different sectors of society have expressed in relation to the FTAA. Business and other sectors of production, labour, environmental and academic groups have been particularly active in this matter. We encourage these and other sectors of civil societies to present their views on trade matters in a constructive manner.

At that meeting, the ministers drafted the Principles and Objectives of the FTAA. On the labour question, the draft has the following wording:

> We the Trade Ministers wish to further secure in accordance with our respective laws and regulations the observance and promotion of workers rights, renewing our commitment to the observance of internationally recognized core labour standards and acknowledging that the ILO is the competent body to set and deal with those core labour standards.

In the Fifth Meeting (Toronto, Canada, 4 November 1999), the Ministers simply endorsed the previous commitments.

In the Sixth Meeting of the FTAA (Buenos Aires, Argentina, 7 April 2001), the ministers declared:

> We are grateful for the contributions made by Civil Society and urge to continue to make these contributions in a constructive manner on trade-related issues of relevance to the FTAA. We reaffirm our commitment to raising living standards, improving the working conditions of all people in the Americas and better protecting the environment.

At the XIIth Inter-American Conference of Ministers of Labour in Ottawa (October 2001), the labour ministers and the representatives of workers and employers emphasized the need to respect the ILO's Declaration on Fundamental Principles and Rights at Work (1998) and to include a mechanism for social consultation in the FTAA:

> We declare to have established a working group to deal with labour questions attached to the Summit of Americas to discuss the relationship among globalization, work and employment.

In the Quito declaration (Quito, Ecuador, 1 November 2002), the trade ministries presented the following statement:

> We reiterate that the FTAA negotiations will take into account the wide social agenda . . . but we reject the use of labour or environmental standards for protectionist purposes.

In July 2003, the United States presented a proposal to deal with labour norms in the FTAA. The key points of this proposal are:

- As members of the ILO, the FTAA's members will recognize their individual obligations to comply with the ILO's Fundamentals Declaration. They also guarantee their compliance with their respective national labour laws.
- No member will use the violation of national labour laws as a strategy to affect trade.
- Members will not promote trade or attract investments by diluting the protection offered by their respective labour laws. Where this provision is violated, Chapter XX (Dispute Settlement Procedures) will be applicable.
- Any member is entitled to enquire about any other member's compliance with its national labour laws.
- A cooperative mechanism will be established to promote enforcement of, and compliance with national labour laws, including the following areas: fundamental rights; worst forms of child labour; labour administration; labour inspection; labour courts; capital labour relations; and hours of work, minimum wage, health and safety.
- Members can require arbitration in respect of any alleged non-compliance. The arbitrator may impose fines on the violators. The value of the fines will be calculated taking into account: (a) the impact of the violation on trade; (b) the persistence and duration of the violation; (c) the reasons for non-compliance; (d) the degree of non-compliance;

(e) the efforts made by the nation to comply; and (f) other factors. The maximum fine will be US$15 million per case and per country involved in a bilateral dispute. If the fine is not paid, tariff measures will be applied.

This initial proposal went much further than the "soft" cooperative terms of the North American Agreement on Labour Cooperation (NAALC). In addition to including an array of trade sanctions for violators, the proposal addressed many issues that had not been previously considered, such as working hours and minimum wage. However, it is very unlikely that Latin American nations will accept the terms of this proposal as they are.

Practical choices

Given the present state of the FTAA's final phase of negotiations, what practical choices should be made in the labour area?

The FTAA members have three basic models from which to choose. At one extreme, negotiators might adopt a model that "can bite", such as the proposed social clause to the WTO. Most managers and union leaders of developed countries believe that such a system will ensure compliance. At the other end of the spectrum, negotiators might opt for a model based on moral pressure like the ILO, which embarrasses violators into compliance. Between the two extremes lies a cooperative model, such as the NAALC, which induces compliance by helping violators remedy the causes of their violations.[21]

It seems unlikely that the FTAA will adopt a model with more teeth, given that the WTO has passed the labour question to the ILO. It also seems unlikely that the FTAA will adopt a model based on moral platitude, as American and Canadian union leaders have expressed their frustration with the ILO's system. Thus, it seems as though the NAFTA model has a good chance of being adopted. Under the NAALC system, labour standards are not to be defined by, or imposed from, outside. Instead, nations are required to implement their own labour laws and to respect the ILO's core labour standards. This control mechanism is based on cooperation among the organization's members rather than economic sanctions or moral embarrassment.

The NAALC is the first multilateral agreement linking a regional free trade regime to a government commitment to implement and improve labour principles.[22] In many circles, the NAALC has been criticized for not having enough teeth.[23] In fact, sanctions receive little emphasis in the agreement, since the regime emphasizes cooperation. The NAALC respects its nations' sovereignty. Rather than trying to impose a supranational labour law, it recognizes that labour laws should be legislated by each country.

The NAALC contains several provisions relating to violations, all of them based on a philosophy of cooperation. Pursuant to the agreement, each country created a National Administrative Office to follow and supervise its legal obligations. Unresolved issues are submitted to an Evaluation Committee of Experts, who are responsible for investigating each case and trying a negotiate a solution to effect compliance. If this route fails, the case is presented to a trilateral ministerial council, which will use the same negotiation method or can resort to arbitration.

Many have complained that the NAALC's procedures are too slow, and that sanctions have thus far not been applied. While true to some extent, this is typical of an institution that attempts to achieve solutions through consensus. But the NAALC's effectiveness must be examined on a different footing, namely whether it has established new lines of communication among its members, whether it has prevented recurring violations, and whether its members are more sensitive to the agreement's terms. The answers to all of these questions is yes. The NAALC has implemented gradual solutions that improve labour standards without either eroding its members' sovereignty or applying trade sanctions.

The adoption of a sort of NAALC for the Americas is not a simple matter. Many Latin American nations have legal standards that are too high for realistic compliance under present economic conditions. For example, take the case of child labour in Brazil. Under the Constitution, children under 16 years of age are prohibited to work – with no exception. This is much more stringent than US laws which prohibit certain types of jobs for certain ages. Under the US Fair Labour Standards certain activities are permitted for people under the age of 14. These include working for one's parents in occupations other than manufacturing, mining, or hazardous activities. Also included are those employed as domestic labourers in and around their employers' homes, as well as actors or performers in movies, theatres, radio or television productions.[24]

Most of the activities that are permitted in the United States are prohibited in Brazil. Nevertheless, out of a total Brazilian labour force of about 80 million people, about 4.5 million children under 16 (5.5 per cent) work. Out of these, about 2.1 million are teenagers between 14 and 15 years of age; 1.9 million are in the 10 to 13 age-group; and 400,000 are between 5 and 9 years old.[25] Moreover, among working children between 10 and 13 years of age, 90.5 per cent go to school; among the 14 to 15 year olds, 76.1 per cent attend school. Therefore, working is not necessarily an obstacle to attending school. Only 5 per cent of children work and are not in school.

Brazil is implementing several programmes linking income aid for families to better schools for children ("bolsa-escola") – all with positive results.[26] The goal for 2004 is to enrol 7 million families and 12 million students. The objective is to avoid child labour by attacking its real causes. In the case of Brazil, the causes seem to be related to the poverty of families and inadequate schools.

This means that the enforcement of national regulations regarding child labour is feasible through time even with the constitutional minimum age of 16 in Brazil. If combating child labour is to be a priority within the FTAA, the implementation mechanism has to be based on a gradual, nuanced approach.

Conclusion

With the FTAA negotiations scheduled to conclude in 2005, its members need to begin seriously discussing labour standards in order to resolve diverging interests and legislative regimes.

In Latin America, the basic problem is compliance rather than a lack of laws to protect workers. While the continent has a wealth of labour laws and labour courts, 60 per cent of the labour force is in the informal market, where no such protection exists.

So far, the world has three basic models for incorporating labour standards into international trade. At one extreme, there is the WTO model, which relies on the use of trade sanctions. At the other extreme, there is the ILO model, which applies moral pressure to induce compliance with ratified conventions. Between these extremes lies the NAFTA model, which is based on cooperative mechanisms to elevate labour standards while respecting national laws.

More recently, however, a "procedural system" has emerged. This system proposes that countries focus on procedural standards as opposed to substantive ones. The idea is to agree on a process through which different economic sectors will agree to adopt increasingly high standards on a realistic basis. Based on the assumption that it is fruitless to try to impose substantive standards from above, this model is based on agreement, not punishment. It proposes a gradual move towards negotiated standards among sectors and, later, in the economy as a whole, the provision of the necessary flexibility that developing nations require.[27] Although this model will probably be well-received by most of the FTAA's members, Canada and the United States would probably prefer a system similar to the NAALC.

It is likely that the FTAA's members will end up discussing some variation of the NAALC. Even so, this will be problematic. The NAALC model will demand adjustments. As mentioned, Latin American nations have extensive laws that fully respect core labour standards but have poor compliance mechanisms. The question, however, is not one of improving these mechanisms but rather improving the concrete economic and social conditions of the labour market, thereby facilitating enforcement.

In this sense, a combination of the NAALC model with the "procedural model" may be a way to move toward an agreement on the labour question. Of course, substantive change will require time. The FTAA's members would also benefit from less protectionist behaviour by rich nations in several areas, particularly in agriculture, environment and labour. The 34 nations comprising the FTAA must work for the benefit of all, and not simply take advantage of a regional agreement to meet their respective interests.

Notes

1. Sandra Polonia Rios and Soraya Saavedra Rosar, "As Negociações de Acesso a Mercados na ALCA e a Agenda Brasileira", in Alberto do Amaral Junior and Michelle Raton Sanchez (eds.), *O Brazil e a ALCA*, (Editora Aduaneiras, São Paulo, 2003), 259–88.

2. Simão Davi Silber, "Aspectos Econômicos da Formação da Área de Livre Comércio das Américas", in Alberto do Amaral Junior e Michelle Raton Sanchez (eds.), *O Brazil e a ALCA*, (Editora Aduaneiras, São Paulo, 2003)

3. Robert B. Zoellick, "Trading in Freedom: The New Endeavor of the Americas" (2002) 7/3 *Electronic Journal of the U.S. Department of State*; on line: http://usinfo.state.gov/journals/ites/1002/ijee/toc.htm. Agência Estado, 'Ajudando os Trabalhadores por Meio do Comércio' in *O Estado de S. Paulo*, 21 April 2004; Grant D. Aldonas, "The FTAA: Mapping the Road to Economic Growth and Development" (2002) 7/3 *Electronic Journal of the U.S. Department of State*.

4. Eduardo Lora and Mauricio Oliveira, "Macro Policies and Employment Problems in Latin America" (1998), Washington DC, Inter-American Development Bank, Working Paper no. 372; Samuel Freije, "Informal Employment in Latin America and the Caribbean: Causes, Consequences and Policy recommendations", Primer Seminario Técnico de Consulta Regional sobre Temas Labourales (mimeo) (Panama, 2002).

5. Hernando De Soto, *The Mystery of Capital: Why Capitalism Triumphs in the West and Fails Everywhere Else* (New York, Basic Books, 2000).

6. James Heckman and Carmem Pagés-Serra, "The Cost of Security Regulation: Evidence from Latin American Labour Markets" (2000) 1 *Economia* 109-54.

7. Josias de Souza, "Maioria na América Latina Apoiaria Ditadura Eficiente", in *Folha de S. Paulo*, 21 April 2004.

8. Central American Integration System (1991), Andean Community (1996), Caribbean Common Market (1973), North American Free Trade Agreement (1992) and Free Trade Area of Americas (1994) (OIT, 1999).

9. Oscar Ermida Uriarte, 'Instituciones y Relaciones Laborales del Mercosur', in *El Mercado Comun del Sur: Mercosur: Estudio de Caso sobre una Experiencia de Integración Economica* (Officina Internacional del Trabajo, Lima, 1997).

10. Claudia Ferreira Cruz, "A Declaração Sociolaboural do Mercosul e os Direitos Fundamentais dos Trabalhadores", Dissertação de mestrado, Faculdade de Direito da Universidade de São Paulo (2001).

11. This is very common in Latin American cultures – dispute resolution procedures come before compliance mechanisms. See Wolney de Macedo Cordeiro, *A Regulamentação das Relações de Trabalho Individuais e Coletivas no mbito do Mercosul*, (Editora LTR, São Paulo, 2000).

12. Victor Tokman and Daniel Martinez Fernández, "Los Temas Labourales em el Mercorur", in *El Mercado Comun del Sur: Mercosur: Estudio de Caso sobre una Experiencia de Integración Economica*, (Officina Internacional del Trabajo, Lima, 1997).

13. See Freije, "Informal Employment".

14. Armando Castelar Pinheiro, "Judicial System Performance and Economic Development", Ensaios BNDES, no. 2 (Rio de Janicro, 1997); Álvaro Herrero, and Keith Henderson, *El Costo dse la Resolución de Conflictos en la Pequeña Empresa* (Washington, Banco Interamericano de Desarrollo (mimeo), 2003).

15. Stanley Fischer, "*A Role for Labor Standards in the New International Economy*", Seminar and Panel Discussion (International Monetary Fund, Washington DC, 1999); Robert Holzmann, "A Role for Labor Standards in the New International Economy", Seminar and Panel Discussion, (International Monetary Fund, Washington DC, 1999).

16. OECD, *Trade, Employment and Labour Standards* (OECD, Paris, 1996). Notably, the OECD repeated this research in 2000 with practically the same results, see OECD, *International Trade and Core Labour Standards* (OECD, Paris, 2000).

17. Fabrice Hatem, *International Investment: Toward the Year 2001* (United Nations, New York, 1997).

18. Dani Rodrik, "Democracies Pay Higher Wages" (1999) 114(3) *Quarterly Journal of Economics* 707.

19. David Kucera, "The Effects of Core Workers' Rights on Labour Costs and Foreign Direct Investment: Evaluating the Conventional Wisdom", *Decent Work Research Programme*, Discussion Paper DP/130/2001 (International Institute for

Labour Studies, Geneva, 2001) online: http://www.ilo.org/public/english/bureau/inst/download/dp13001.pdf.

20. Paul Krugman, "Trabalhadores vs. Trabalhadores", *O Estado de S. Paulo*, 22 May 2000, B2.

21. Ericson Crivelli, "Os Trabalhadores e a ALCA: A Construção de um Direito Internacional do Trabaklho Americano", in Alberto Amaral Junior e Michelle Raton Sanchez (org.), *O Brazil e a ALCA* (Editora Aduaneiras, São Paulo, 2003).

22. In 2000 the United States signed a trade agreement with Jordan. This was the first trade document which included workers' rights in the body of the agreement. In the same year the US-Caribbean Basin Trade Partnership Act extended workers' rights to the apparel sector and the US-Cambodia's trade pact did the same for the apparel and textile sectors. Lance Compa, "Workers' Rights in the Global Economy" (2001) 5/1 *Perspectives on Work* 10–12.

23. Rainer Dombois, Erhard Hornberger and Jens Winter, "Transnational Labour Regulations in the NAFTA", Paper presented at the 13th World Congress of the International Industrial Relations Association, Berlin, 2–8 September 2003.

24. Dorianne Beyer, "Understanding and Applying Child Labour Laws to Today's School-to-Work Transition Programs", in *Center Focus* (National Center for Research and Vocational Education, Berkeley, 1995).

25. Simon Schwartzman, *Trabalho Infantil no Brazil*, (OIT, Brasília, 2001)

26. Secretaria da Educação, *Bolsa-Escola, Um Programa de Educação Máxima* (Governo do Distrito Federal, Brasília, 1998); Previdência Social, *Dados da Secretaria de Assistência Social* (Ministério da Assistência e Previdência Social, Brasília, 1999).

27. Anil Verma, "Global Labour Standards: Can we get from here to there?", Paper presented at the 13th World Congress of the International Industrial Relations Association, Berlin, September 8–12 2003.

PART V

The ILO

12

International labour standards in the globalized economy: obstacles and opportunities for achieving progress

WERNER SENGENBERGER

Introduction

Various arguments have been advanced over the years in support of international labour standards (ILS). They include: the contribution that ILS would make to social justice and social peace; the nature of labour standards as part and parcel of basic human rights; the consolidation of national labour legislation; their potential as a basis for national action; and their equally important potential for regulating international competition.[1]

The call for international labour law to regulate international competition arose prior to World War I during the first major wave of international economic integration. At that time, each country could easily trade with any other country. Tariffs were low, and the gold standard facilitated the financing of trade and investment. From its inception in 1919, the International Labour Organization (ILO) claimed that unregulated cross-border trade and investment flows would depress labour conditions and create hardships for workers. The remedy to "social dumping" (as it was called initially) or the "race to the bottom" (as it was later termed in trade union circles) would be international action for the achievement of universal minimum labour standards. To be effective, all potential market players would have to obey the same norms. Actual compliance with the law should keep defectors from gaining an unfair competitive advantage. The application of ILS would have to be coextensive with the size of the labour, commodity and capital markets. The ILO is certainly aware of these functional requirements. Its constitution states explicitly that "fair and humane conditions of labour should be applied, both at home and in individual countries to which their commercial and industrial relations extend" and "the failure of any nation to adopt humane conditions of labour is an obstacle in the way of other nations which desire to improve the conditions in their own countries".

In a way, the ILO's track record of setting and supervising universal labour standards and related jurisprudence looks impressive. To date, 185 legally binding conventions and an even greater number of recommendations have been adopted by the International Labour Conference (ILC). They comprise what has become known as the International Labour Code. In 1998, in its Declaration of Fundamental Principles and Rights at Work, the ILO enunciated "core labour standards", or "workers' fundamental rights". These rights are defined as: the freedom of association and the effective recognition of the right to organize and to collective bargaining; the elimination of all forms of forced and compulsory labour; the effective abolition of child labour; and the elimination of discrimination in respect of employment and occupation. Moreover, the ILO conventions cover substantive standards (economic and social rights) regarding: minimum wages and wage payment; hours of work; holidays and periods of rest; the protection of workers with special needs (such as women prior to and after child birth); migrant workers; home workers; indigenous and tribal populations; occupational safety and health; labour inspection; employment security; social security and social services; the settlement of disputes; full, freely chosen and productive employment; and employment services and human resource development. As of October 2003, the total number of ratifications of ILO conventions by the 174 member states amounted to 7164 and the number of ratifications of fundamental conventions stood at 1214.

Ratification alone does not necessarily mean that a convention is actually respected or implemented. In fact, a recent study found little evidence of a statistical link between ratification of ILO conventions and actual working conditions.[2] Massive violations of ILO norms are observed, even regarding the eight core conventions. All ILO members, by virtue of their acceptance of the ILO constitution, agreed to respect these conventions, and to promote and to realize them in good faith independently from their ratification. Among the worst violations of basic worker rights is the flouting of trade union rights, including the discrimination, intimidation, political persecution and assassination of trade unionists; widespread discrimination against women and minorities; the persistence of forced, compulsory and bonded labour; and extensive use of child labour. Social standards are frequently not met, as is indicated by the vast number of unemployed and underemployed workers, low pay, the non-payment of wages, minimal social protection of the global population, high rates of occupational accidents and occupational diseases, and other deficits in what the ILO nowadays calls "decent work".[3]

Being a voluntary organization, the ILO has limited power to enforce its normative instruments in member countries. Its major means are moral suasion and technical assistance to foster the adoption and implementation of ILS. Attempts have failed to introduce social clauses into the GATT and WTO that would reward compliance with a favourable trade status and sanction non-compliance by excluding countries from trade.

In view of the discrepancy between international labour law and the norms and the realities of prevailing working conditions, this paper aims to address major obstacles that hinder the adherence to, or implementation of, ILS in large parts of the world. In particular, four issues will be raised:

- Are ILS economically beneficial, or do they produce economically adverse effects?
- Are ILS universal as is claimed by the ILO?
- How should we address the diversification of actors that set and enforce ILS?
- How favourable is the global political and economic context for ILS?

It appears that obstacles to full compliance with ILO standards are either associated with, or are reinforced by, the process of economic globalization. This begs the question of whether the present architecture of globalization (which the ILO wishes to direct towards more socially acceptable outcomes) is itself undermining the means and efforts to attain the objectives of the organization.

The economic case made for and against ILS

"Labour law" versus "economic law"

Setting and applying ILS involves direct interference in labour markets and indirect intervention in product markets, with the objective of intercepting destructive, downward directed competition, reducing vulnerability, and allowing workers to exercise countervailing power to upgrade labour conditions and share in the fruits of higher productivity. From its early years, the ILO has always insisted that economic growth alone does not suffice to ensure the improvement of working and living conditions, or to alleviate the vulnerability of certain individuals and groups in the labour market.

This view has been contested by mainstream economics theory, the classic doctrine of which held that employment and working conditions are determined by endogenous economic forces, and that they would depend primarily on the real income of each country. Even after making allowance for variations in the sharing of the national product, hours of work will inexorably be long, wages low, and the conditions of work burdensome if the total real per capita income of the country is low. Labour conditions could not be "artificially" raised beyond that permitted by the pace of economic growth. International action to improve conditions would be futile, and even damaging. It would strike against the "law of economics". The lever for raising each country to the highest level of prosperity is unconditional and unrestricted economic competition, both within and between countries.[4] Therefore the economic policy prescription was exactly the opposite to the ILO's position, which argued that labour should be taken out of competition.

The credo of neo-classical economic theory is also that unfettered market forces and a purely market-determined income distribution create not only the best, but also the fairest economic results, and are therefore in the best interest of workers. For Alfred Marshall, the free market establishes the "true standardization" of work and wages. Competition forces firms to be good employers that pay full attention to efficiency in the workplace. In contrast, imposing ILS on countries would produce "false" standardization of work and wages. Trade unions, collective agreements, minimum wages, the welfare state, etc. are seen to represent monopolies, cartels and other restrictions on competition that create distortions in the labour market and institutional sclerosis in the economy as a whole. They increase production costs by raising the level of wages above the market clearing equilibrium wage, impede efficiency and restrict flexibility, seek rent for advantaged insiders (thereby increasing inequality), deter investments (thereby constraining economic growth), and reduce the overall level of employment. In the final analysis, they are a hindrance to social progress. To quote Jeffrey Sachs (an influential advisor of many governments) in a lecture given at the ILO:

> The greatest damage to growth is in across-the-board labour standards, that dictate either minimum standards or minimum conditions for higher and fairer wages, or worse still, provide for the extension of wages across the economy; in short, the German system applied to South Africa or some

other developing country; . . . the cost of such conditions and strategies could be quite substantial for developing countries, and bring modest, if any, gains to the advanced countries.[5]

This view is echoed by modern international trade economists for whom economic development and the welfare of workers are best served by a liberal trade regime.[6] Constraining trade and cross-border investment would make it more difficult for poverty-stricken developing countries to catch up with economically advanced nations.

In theory and practice, the view that ILS are economically harmful because they raise the cost of production and squeeze firms out of the market has proved to be one of the greatest obstacles to advancing labour standards. Neo-classical economic theory has dominated thinking since the 1970s. Through its influence in standard economics textbooks, it has educated generations of students in large parts of the globe, some of whom have and will become top-level politicians and decision-makers. Neo-liberal policies of the "Washington consensus" have guided the action of the international financial institutions and the World Trade Organization. The World Bank officially endorsed the core ILS only two years ago, but declined to support them by means of its lending and procurement policies. Further, it has remained critical of many substantive ILS. During the last few decades, the economic arguments against ILS have also gained currency among politicians in the Third World. The natural competitive advantage of developing countries is their supply of abundant, low cost, unprotected labour and this should not be taken away by imposing the labour standards of developed countries. Until they reach a higher level of economic development, it is premature for them to adhere to ILS. Mass unemployment, underemployment and poverty create policy priorities other than quality jobs and good working conditions.

Curiously enough, the argument of ILS' excessive cost has also been used in the rich, developed countries to warn against further improvements in labour standards, or even to call for derogation from existing standards, i.e. in view of fierce international competition, social expenses related to standards are not affordable, or would inevitably lead to lower growth and job loss. Krugman (1995) made an additional point. As countries open to the international economy, adherence to ILS raises production costs because, in a free trade regime in which prices are set by international markets, the whole cost of meeting ILS must be absorbed by the firm or the workers. Producers can no longer (as is the case in a closed economy) pass on the cost of standards to the consumers through higher prices. Accordingly, there will be downward pressure on domestic standards unless there is a common international standard for all competitors in a given market.

How sound is the economic case against ILS?

The stated economic arguments against ILS fail on several counts. To some extent they are based on a misunderstanding of ILO norms and ILO policies. The ILO proclaims universality, but not uniformity in the application of its normative instruments. While it indeed insists that core ILS are independent from a country's stage of development, it emphasized early on that substantive standards must respect the special economic, climatic and other circumstances of the member country (Article 19 of the ILO constitution), and flexibility must be practised in its policies of applying ILS. For instance, the ILO does not call (as is often alleged) for the same minimum wage across all countries. Rather, it proposes that each country engages in minimum wage fixing, be it by statute, decree or collective agreement. Thereby, the ILO fully acknowledges that the minimum wage level must respond to a country's degree of development and other economic conditions. It cannot be the same in India and in Canada.

Economic orthodoxy has to be challenged on its assumption that ILS inevitably engender higher labour costs, thereby squeezing firms out of the market and dislocating jobs. The argument is partly wrong and partly exaggerated. Improved labour standards very often lead to higher productivity, which means that unit labour costs (the decisive parameter for international competitiveness) need not rise, and may even decline. Employers that abide by an eight-hour day, a minimum weekly rest period, or an occupational health and safety work standard have frequently found that they are not disadvantaged in relation to competitors who do not observe such rules, because attaining the standards entails higher worker motivation, less fatigue, fewer mistakes and accidents, etc. Furthermore, it should not be assumed that the costs of applying labour standards are inevitably borne by the employer; the costs of many mandated benefits are shifted to workers in the form of lower wages. Moreover, the ILO has shown that, contrary to popular views, the cost of observing ILO conventions (e.g. those on social security or occupational health and safety in developing countries) is not prohibitively high. Finally, failure to observe ILS may turn out to be more costly than compliance with them. For example, in the absence of employment protection, employers may face excessive litigation costs arising from worker dismissals. A study by the World Bank concluded that equal education and vocational training for women and men and the absence of discrimination in the labour market would have yielded a 50 per cent higher rate of economic growth in South Asia since the 1960s, and a 100 per cent higher rate in Sub-Saharan Africa.[7]

While the costs of applying standards are mostly direct, ascertainable, immediate and localized, the benefits tend to be indirect, intangible, and resist easy metrics. It is only when the negative effects of lower standards accumulate (e.g. in the form of poverty, crime and social disintegration) that people become fully aware of the economic and social utility of standards.

Unfortunately, the economics commonly applied to ILS are rather poor. They tend to be limited to micro-economic aspects, ignoring macro-economic implications. Equity and distributional issues are neglected, and it is beset with simplifications and very crude unrealistic assumptions. This has recently been vocally and relentlessly demonstrated by Joe Stiglitz, winner of the 2001 Nobel Prize in Economics.[8] To pass sound judgement on ILS, they must be looked at in a wider economic, social and political perspective. They are enacted when a significant number of ILO member countries are confronted with the same labour issue or problem, and other countries have already carved out policies and measures that can resolve the problem. ILO instruments embody the collective wisdom of member states from all over the world, and the accumulated experience of more than 80 years of history. Their adoption requires approval from a majority of delegates from governments, employers and workers in the International Labour Conference.

Economic, social and political dividends of applying ILS

Efforts must be made to enhance the economic logic applied to ILS to demonstrate their economic, social and political dividends.[9] Examples of the benefits of ILS include:

• Minimum standards give rise to dynamic efficiency, and minimum wage fixing and other minimum terms of employment alter the competitive regime of business. If the option to compete through sub-standard wages and poor working conditions is closed, efforts must be made to compete in other, more constructive ways. Firms have to attain a minimal level of productivity to meet the prescribed floor so that they can afford to pay the cost of usages and other conditions of work. Minimum terms of employment spur employers to improve management, technology, products, processes, work organization and worker competence. Firms unable to reach the standard will be squeezed out of the market by more efficient firms.

- Worker participation based on freedom of association, collective bargaining and social dialogue are ways of fostering cooperation and mutual trust, which enhance both micro- and macro-economic performance. This effect is brought about in various ways: workers contribute knowledge and experience to improve managerial decision-making; conflicting interests can be accommodated peacefully through consultation and negotiation; collective agreements make business conditions predictable and accountable, providing increased certainty in investment decisions; collective bargaining makes wage-setting more transparent, thereby avoiding discontent. Strong collective organization in the labour market and coordinated collective bargaining tend to contain, rather than cause, inflationary pressures (or at least accomplish this better than decentralized patterns of bargaining). Tripartite social dialogue at the national level facilitates the stabilization of macro-economic conditions, which is an essential prerequisite for high levels of employment. Such conditions have also facilitated the transition from centrally planned to market economies.
- Employment and income security can have various positive impacts. Secure workers are more willing to take risks and to pass on their expertise to other workers and management and they are better prepared to cooperate in technological and organizational change. Worker security and labour market flexibility are not conflicting, but rather are mutually compatible objectives. Protecting workers from job and income loss assumes even greater importance in open economies, which are more susceptible to external crises, greater competitive pressure, and see faster and more volatile structural change. In this situation, protecting workers from social risks is the positive alternative to protectionism imposed by import restrictions and subsidies. This is one reason why developing countries that seek to improve access to Northern markets should be just as interested in this standard as developed countries.
- The elimination of forced labour and child labour is not exclusively a moral imperative; it provides a net economic advantage. Forced labour retards development because it keeps capital and labour in a pre-modern state that depends on such labour for its continued existence. Child

labour may secure the survival of families, but it does so at the very high price of reducing life expectancy and years of working life. It prevents education and skills-development, thus lowering labour productivity and hampering development in the long run. In addition, child labour increases labour supply and drives wage levels down.

- Equal opportunities and equal treatment in employment avoids social conflict and favours higher economic growth. Discrimination amounts to the exclusion of workers from employment either generally or from particular activities, thereby reducing human resource capacity. It results in the waste or under-utilization of talent and labour market skills. Discrimination and the failure to provide equal pay for work of equal value are both demoralizing and demotivating, and may cause serious conflict at the workplace.

- ILS can be instrumental in attaining a degree of wage and income equality, which is conducive to development, social cohesion and democracy. Wage differentials are smaller where trade unions influence wage structures and wage payment systems. Social transfer systems, social safety nets and social services tend to diminish income disparities, strengthen aggregate demand, avoid or reduce poverty, and prevent political upheaval.

- Policies to promote full, productive and freely chosen employment are central to any development effort. The quantity of employment need not be pitted against the quality of employment. To quote Amartya Sen, a leading development economist: "Fighting unemployment should not be used as an excuse for doing away with reasonable conditions of work for those already employed."[10] Large-scale labour surplus is a major impediment to implementing ILS. It tilts the power equation in the labour market drastically in favour of employers. It makes it difficult, if not impossible, to raise wage levels, and there is little or no incentive to invest in labour to make it more productive. There is a vicious cycle of low wages, poverty and high population growth. Child labour, prison labour, low real wages and insufficient levels or coverage of social security tend to increase the supply of labour. This causes real wages to decline further, in turn, raising poverty and child labour, and culminating in a self-perpetuating trap of surplus labour and low or absent labour standards. What is required is a package of expansionary macroeconomic policies and active labour market policies to help match supply and demand, as well as social security measures and minimum wages to intercept and cushion the depressive forces, and ultimately to turn these vicious spirals into virtuous spirals of development.

Evidence of the dividends of ILS

Recent findings from empirical research on the impact of ILS are largely consistent with the positive effects noted above. Recent econometric studies by the OECD, ILO and academics investigated the links between the application of core labour standards and economic performance in a fairly large number of countries, including many developing countries.[11] It was found that standards are apt to enhance productivity, GDP growth, trade, foreign direct investment, and employment. They reduce the adverse effects of opening national economies and ease the adjustment to market liberalization. Trade union strength poses no obstacle to successful international economic integration.

Countries that do not respect core labour standards receive a proportionally small share of global investment. In fact, the bulk of the worldwide volume of trade and of foreign direct investment (FDI) is located in the most developed countries that, on average, command high labour standards. However, there are exceptions to these general findings. Some emerging economies in South-East Asia, where violations of trade union rights have been observed, have received important shares of FDI flows. It can be concluded that while in the aggregate there is no evidence of a "race to the bottom", there are indications that this does occur in some regions and sectors, especially in labour-intensive manufacturing industries. Further evidence for this interpretation comes from research into the criteria used for locating FDI. The majority of investors rated the size and the growth of markets very highly, and they also viewed the political and social stability of the host countries and the quality of the labour force to be important. However the cost of labour was not among the high-ranking factors.[12] A recent study by the World Bank on East Asia revealed that labour rights were conducive to export performance in that region. This finding dispels the common assumption that the region's weak standards have played a role in its export competitiveness and ability to attract foreign investment.[13]

Among the most compelling evidence of economic advantages of ILS is a study of the countries of Northern Europe. By virtually any statistical indicator used, they rank at the top or near the top in respect of the implementation of ILS and economic achievement. These are characterized by high rates of worker and employer organization and collective bargaining coverage, highly developed welfare states, high real wages and gender equality coexisting with high average economic growth, high rates of employment, advanced technologies, world class competitiveness, low inflation, positive trade, fiscal and current account balances, and high levels of social and political stability. Yet, they are among the least protectionist countries worldwide.[14]

The issue of universality

The ILO considers its normative instruments to be universally valid and applicable. At various points in its history, the ILO was confronted with the issue of whether, in a world of great development diversity, it would not be preferable to adopt regional standards instead of global ones. The ILO has always resisted such a move. Recently, when the ILO adopted "decent work" as its overarching promotional objective under Director-General Juan Somavia, it reasserted its claim that ILO goals, principles and standards apply everywhere, and that they apply not only to wage workers, or sections of wage workers, but also to the self-employed, home workers, and those who work on their own account.

At present, the debate on the principle of universality centres on the related issues of the informal economy and cultural diversity.

Applicability of ILS to the informal economy?

It has been argued that the ILO approach to ILS focuses on organized sectors and the formal economy, and that ILS are not relevant or suited to the informal economy, the economic activities of which are not recognized, recorded, protected or regulated by public authorities. Ardent critics go further. They charge that ILS (especially substantive standards such as employment and income protection, minimum wages, safety at work and maternity protection) are a major cause for the emergence and growth of the informal economy.

The charges levelled against ILS are serious, mainly because the informal economy has not proved to be a transient or residual phenomenon as the ILO and many development theorists had assumed. In fact, in recent decades the informal economy in many developing countries has increased rather than declined. The share of informal employment in Africa and Latin America has been estimated to about 60 per cent. In Africa, 93 percent of the newly created jobs in the 1990s were informal. In Latin America and Asia, the shares were 60 and 40 per cent respectively. Between 60 per cent and 80 per cent of the informal economy labour force in these regions are women.[15] Informal activities have also expanded in

developed countries and countries undergoing transition, although from
a much lower level.

In part, the expansion of informal employment is linked to international trade and investment. The traditional informal sector consisted of
survival activities like shoe shining, street vending, garbage collecting and
other small-scale self-employment at the margins of the urban economy.
With economic globalization, however, a new type of informal enterprise
has emerged through various types of sub-contracting. Such informal
enterprise is subordinate to formal firms, and helps to supply the high-
income market. Informal production is not only for the domestic market,
but also increasingly for export. The drive towards increasing exports has
led state enforcement agencies to turn a blind eye to systematic violations
of existing labour codes by export firms. Often, there is no formal removal
of existing worker protection, but a pattern of selective omission, causing a
proliferation of informal enterprises. Employers no longer give workers a
formal contract but rather contract with them informally as independent
contractors.[16] In addition, special export processing zones (EPZs) have
been created which are off limits for many ILS and in which taxation and
labour controls are relaxed in order to attract foreign capital. The suppression of ILS in EPZs includes fundamental worker rights, such as freedom
of association and collective bargaining. While both domestic and foreign
investors may want to take economic advantage of relaxed labour regulation, it is often local authorities that drive the relaxation process in the
belief that this will attract business, while the investor may well be ready
to accept higher costs if there is political stability, infrastructure, domestic demand for the produced goods and services, and well-functioning
industrial relations.[17]

The ILO attempted to respond to the provocative expansion of informal
employment in a debate of the issue in 1991. The International Labour
Conference saw itself caught in a "dilemma". Should the ILO and its constituents promote the informal economy as a provider of employment and
income or seek to extend regulation and social protection to it and thereby
possibly reduce its capacity to provide jobs and incomes to an expanding
labour force? In 2002, the ILC dealt again with the informal economy
and many delegates recognized that the ILO had moved closer to a broad
and in-depth understanding of its nature. The Conference concluded that
there are a variety of reasons for informal work and that the barriers to
entry into the economic mainstream constrain employment creation in
the formal economy. The barriers include inadequate governance, unemployment in the formal economy, under-employment and poverty, higher

wages in the formal economy (acting as incentive for sub-contracting and outsourcing to low wage countries) and the absence, or ineffective implementation, of appropriate legislation and social protection. The situation is exacerbated by inadequate government policies such as restrictive registration laws and high taxes. The structural adjustment programmes advocated by international financial institutions (especially overshooting macro-economic stabilization) has contributed to the growth of informal activities. The Conference made it clear that informalization has resulted not from the application of ILS, but rather from the failure to enact and apply them. It urged ILO constituents to develop laws, policies and institutions that would implement ILS.[18]

ILS cannot be the root of expanding informal employment because informalization has also occurred and spread (and is actually most pervasive) where employment protection legislation is limited or non-existent. In the meantime, ILO research based on 14 countries in Latin America in the 1990s found that countries with stronger civic rights, including freedom of association and collective bargaining, and also countries with higher wage shares, tended to have higher proportions of formal employment and lower shares of informal employment, even controlling for relative GDP per capita.[19]

Objections to ILS on cultural grounds

The universalism of ILS has also been challenged on cultural grounds. It has been argued that ILS are the product of Western materialist culture, the offspring of the Judaeo-Christian system of beliefs, or an expression of the Protestant ethic. As such, they would be incompatible or alien to other cultures, traditions and religions and therefore should not be imposed on them. Some critics have gone as far as to call ILS a form of cultural imperialism. Whilst hostility to ILS based on the claim of cultural imperialism is prevalent in several regions, it exists mainly in Asia[20] and it shows up very strongly in relation to ILO norms that prescribe freedom of association and freedom from discrimination. For example, in a hearing concerning ILO Convention no. 111 on equality of treatment in the 1980s, a representative of the Islamic Republic of Iran stated before the ILO Committee of Experts that all normative instruments of the ILO and other international organizations that are not in conformity with the principles of Islam are null and void in the Republic.

Are the aims of ILS culturally specific, and do they correspond to a particular political system? As Francis Maupin reminds us, ILS are not value neutral in the sense that they imply a pluralist concept of society, and a reformist and voluntarist approach to social justice and social progress. The content of ILS is not predefined or decreed but it is contingent on the reconciliation of conflicting, or even antagonistic, interests of the parties to the employment relationship.[21] This vision is clearly manifested in the Preamble of the ILO's Constitution. The pluralist social model contrasts with the centralist, or monolithic, model of communism. This was reflected in the purely formal acceptance of the rights of freedom of association and collective bargaining in the former communist countries, in spite of their ratification of the relevant ILO conventions.

While it is true that cultures differ widely, and that these differences must be respected, cultural relativism with regard to ILS becomes highly questionable and in fact unacceptable where it restricts basic liberties, or creates destitution, inequitable income distribution and risk of personal injury at work. It is implausible that a worker in Ghana, Bangladesh or El Salvador is less keen than a Swiss or Canadian worker to avoid the loss of limb and life in a work accident. Should technical knowledge and experience embodied in relevant ILO conventions and technical cooperation programmes not be brought to bear due to differing cultures, customs, religion and income levels of a country? How can it be justified that workers in certain countries should not be supported by a trade union when it comes to settling labour disputes? To take another illustration, child labour has been justified with reference to local culture, tradition, and pressing poverty in family households, which makes the work of children an economic necessity. While it is undeniable that child labour may add to family income, it also tends to perpetuate poverty by destroying the productive capacity of children and by preventing schooling or vocational education that could make them more productive as adults. According to ILO research, child labour often merely replaces adult labour. The latter is given preference because children are more pliable and docile and make fewer demands than adults. For the same reason, ever more children are used as soldiers. Large labour oversupply in developing countries makes it easy to play one worker or group of workers against another. The issue of poverty is not merely a concern about living standards in an absolute sense; at stake is the fair sharing of a firm's product, and also the sharing of the national product.

Universal respect for rights at work does not conflict with the principles of Islam, as is often asserted. There are analogies between Islamic precepts and ILO standards. On this point, extensive reference can be made to the Declaration of Human Rights in Islam, adopted by all member states of the Organization of the Islamic Conference on 5 August 1990 in Cairo (hence known as the Cairo Declaration).

ILO standards should also not be confused with particular lifestyles or materialist values. Such charges are rarely credible. In Asian countries where governments have rejected certain worker rights on grounds of "separate Asian values" and on their opposition to materialist values, leaders have no qualms about embracing capitalist markets and consumerist culture.[22] The motives for evoking relativism of universal worker rights, and the resulting resistance to standards, can frequently be traced to national politics. For example, freedom of association is denied by authoritarian regimes because they view trade unions as a type of political opposition, or they charge that trade unions would raise wages excessively, thereby threatening national cost competitiveness.

The rationale for ILS to regulate competition should not be seen exclusively in terms of a North-South conflict. Economic competition today is as harsh, and even more intense, between Southern countries, as it is between North and South. With regard to ILS, the clash today is not so much between civilizations, but primarily between cultural and free market fundamentalists on the one hand, and those who claim universal principles and human rights on the other.

Diversification of actors for setting and enforcing ILS

In the section above, we described the tensions created by universal ILS in a world with a great variety of forms of employment, culture and civilization. These tensions have proliferated with the growth of ILO membership, and the related disparities of economic, social, political and cultural conditions within and between member countries.

Leaving aside the diversification of the ILO's membership, the organization is now being challenged by the diversification of the agents engaging in establishing and controlling the application of labour standards. Conventionally, it has been the ILO, together with national governments, that were exclusively charged with defining and enforcing ILS. Meanwhile, a host of other actors, including multinational companies, trade and industry groups, labour unions, and a diverse group of non-union NGOs have entered the arena. We are witnessing a twin process of "privatization" of action in the promotion of labour standards, and the "politicization" of this private action.

There is a great variety of private international action in this field. NGOs and consumer groups observe and pressure transnational companies to accept more responsibility for employment and working conditions, particularly among their foreign suppliers and subcontractors. Labelling practices for export products have been proliferating. Prominent examples include "Rugmark", a foundation concentrating on child labour in the carpet industry, and the "Clean Clothes Campaign", an international NGO network focusing on the working conditions in the global garment industry. In the flower industry, labels are designed to advertise acceptable working conditions, including protection against toxic pesticides. Multinational enterprises have established corporate codes of conduct and auditing protocols that determine whether firms in their supply chains actually comply with these codes. More recently, we have seen investors adopt ethical codes that include ILS. Pertinent clauses in pension funds are an example of this attitude. Companies (often for the benefit of their investors) have set up the codes to deflect criticism about their perceived anti-social conduct. Optimistic observers believe that the codes could lead to a "race to the top" by generating inter-firm competition to improve local standards and avoid social dumping.[23] In its fullest version, every firm in the supply chain would report wages, hours of work and other working conditions, features of industrial and labour relations, workforce profiles, and other elements of social performance under its purview. Monitors would then provide rankings of firms that would be made publicly available. The "Global Compact", set up between the UN, global employers and global trade unions in 1999, places demands on companies for transparency of corporate social responsibility in general, and for respecting ILS in particular.

The diversification of agents dealing with ILS has been harshly criticized by labour lawyers and others on the basis that such activities will result in a loss of coherence in standard setting, monitoring and control. If a variety of new actors establish their own labour standard regimes, they would restrict their concern selectively to some ILS and neglect others. Supervision and enforcement would remain outside of public control. This would result in the loss of a unified approach to the breadth and depth of standards, would erode the erstwhile universality of standards, and would allow protection of worker rights to be set according to the interests of the most powerful actors. "If a multinational enterprise or a government can satisfy its (international) obligations by abiding by a fuzzy set of core standards promoting civil rights, what incentive does it have to accept (or in the case of a government to ratify) any existing non-core ILO standards relating to economic and social rights. Can a system that does not address economic and social rights be rightly termed an international labour standards system?"[24]

While it would indeed be problematic if a hierarchy of ILS emerged, and the new actors could "pick and choose" their standards ad libitum from the international labour code, one should not deny the potential benefits of monitoring and enforcing private ILS in principle. A broadening of forces taking interest and responsibility should be welcomed. This includes the growing number of activists in NGOs, among them many young people, who do not accept the violation of worker rights anywhere in the world. In fact, one of the effects of globalization and the advancement of modern communication technology is that we are better and faster informed about labour conditions around the globe.

New actors have also arrived on the scene because the conventional supervisors lack capacity. This phenomenon is particularly evident in the case of national governments of developing and transitional countries, which have retrenched their budgets and public services. This has diminished the resources available for monitoring ILS and inspecting labour conditions. Further, technical competence for supervision of standards has declined due to uncompetitive salary levels in the public administration.

In view of the shortcomings of governance in the conventional ILO approach, the advent and multiplication of new actors in relation to ILS is an opportunity. Transnational business activity has seen a phenomenal rise in the last quarter of the last century. UNCTAD estimates the present number of transnational corporations (TNCs) at 63,000, and their foreign affiliates at 690,000. It is hard to imagine that without their cooperation ILS can be imposed on the world economy. The diversification of stakeholders becomes a problem, however, where it leads to a dilution of ILS, or where private codes of conduct and labelling devices are used to supplant public regulation. Appropriate independent monitoring and transparent verification (auditing, inspection, etc.) of private action can go some way to prevent degradation of ILS. Also, guidelines based on international agreements, including the ILO's Tripartite Declaration of Principles Concerning Multinational Enterprises, and the OECD Guidelines for Multinational Enterprises can support and enhance the social conduct of TNCs. The international trade union movement has also developed guidelines for union involvement in private sector codes of conduct.[25]

The ILO itself has still to come to grips with the new "realities" that confront the classic system of ILS, and in particular the new mosaic of actors and means of action. After the failure of another attempt to include a social clause within the global trading regime in 1994, the ILO's Governing Body decided to examine alternative ways and means of enforcing and promoting ILS. In 1996, when the ministers of trade stipulated in their WTO

Ministerial Singapore Declaration at the First Ministerial Conference that the ILO is the relevant and legitimate organization in the multilateral system in charge of ILS, the ILO set up a working party on the Liberalization of Trade. This was followed by the establishment in 2000 of an independent World Commission on the Social Dimension of Globalization, consisting of 21 eminent personalities from diverse national backgrounds and expertise, and six ex-officio members of the ILO's Governing Body. Since then the Commission has published a report entitled "A Fair Globalization: Creating Opportunities for All". It calls for a greater voice for non-state actors. "The contributions of business, organized labour, civil society organizations (CSOs), and of knowledge and advocacy networks to the social dimensions of globalization should be strengthened."[26]

The global political and economic context of ILS

ILS can only be successful if they receive political backing from sufficiently powerful forces, both national and international. The immediate and most important stakeholder for ILS is the international labour movement, but it alone will not be strong enough to ensure the enactment and enforcement of standards. Support from other stakeholders is required. Whether and to what extent other constituents – employers and governments – favour cooperation and progress on ILS remain unclear. It depends on the world view, interests, relative market power, and strategy of each party. At almost any point in labour history there have been farsighted employers who understood that regulating competition through standards would be in their interest, and would further rather than impair profitability. At the same time there have been those who prefer to win competitive advantages in individual, opportunistic ways, thus rejecting a common standard. Likewise, trade unions have opted variably for the "wide front" or the "strong point" to further their interests, and governments have been schizophrenic in their commitment to cooperate across national borders.

The evolution of ILS has not proceeded in a continuous, linear fashion, but has been subject to political and economic cycles. Strikingly, great progress was achieved in the years following the two World Wars. From the experience of World War I, it was concluded that there could be no international peace without social peace. This led to that "great moment of daring and adventure" (famously stated by Albert Thomas) of establishing the ILO in 1919. Observers have pointed to another motive behind that event, namely the Bolshevik revolution in 1917, which gave rise to concerted tripartite effort in the capitalist world to contain the spread of communism by advancing a reformist approach to social progress. In fact, the rivalry between political systems that lasted until 1990 acted as a spur for social policy because it was felt necessary for each camp to ensure the loyalty of its satellite nations and garner support from the many third world countries. The end of East-West confrontation terminated the systems contest and reduced efforts to court the developing world, as was reflected in the strong decline of development aid in the 1990s. Furthermore, the end of the cold war has relaxed joint international efforts. It led workers, employers and governments in the capitalist countries to revert from a period of converging interests in response to a common external threat, to a more "natural" state of diverging interests and roles.[27] This, in turn, weakened the will for cooperation among the groups in general, and also in the ILO. At the same time, it resulted in more natural interest configurations in the former communist countries, including more genuine freedom of association, collective bargaining, and the right to strike.

An alternative hypothesis would suggest that the fortunes of the ILO, and ILS in particular, vary with the economic cycle. Under this theory, one may explain the most prolific period of standard setting in the ILO after World War II as a sort of international "New Deal" in response to the experience of the great depression in the late 1920s and 1930s. Thus, many of the most important ILO instruments were enacted between 1948 and 1964. They include the conventions on freedom of association (No. 87) in 1948, the right to organization and collective bargaining (No. 98) in 1949, equal pay for men and women (No. 100) in 1951, social security (No. 102) in 1952, the abolition of forced labour (No. 105) in 1957, freedom from discrimination (No. 111) in 1958, and full, productive and freely chosen employment (No. 122) in 1964. The experience of economic depression alone, however, would not have been sufficient to produce the concerted action for standard setting in that period. The other necessary ingredient was a power shift in the labour market, caused by exceptionally high rates of economic growth and almost full employment in the industrialized countries and beyond. The 1950s and 1960s were the "golden age of capitalism", as some economists called it, and the heyday of "social corporatism", during which trade unionism reached its highest density rates, and employers were most willing to cooperate in view of the ubiquitous shortage of labour. Public revenues were plentiful, which allowed the expansion of social spending and the welfare state.

Since the 1970s, global economic conditions have deteriorated. GDP growth slowed from an average 5.3 per cent in the 1960s to 3.5 per cent in the 1970s, 3.1 per cent in the 1980s, and 2.3 per cent in the 1990s. In the 1980s and 1990s, world per capita output increased by merely 33 per cent, compared to an 83 per cent increase in the previous two decades. Long-term economic growth declined everywhere except in some parts of Asia. Unemployment in the OECD countries rose from an average 3 per cent in the 1960s to 7.4 per cent in the 1990s, with the rise being even faster in the EU countries. Global unemployment has reached record levels of 180 million. Including underemployed workers, one third of the world's labour force either has no job or is underemployed. Except in the high growth countries of Asia, real wages have either stagnated or declined, and the share of total income that goes to labour has shrunk virtually everywhere. Tax revenues have also declined, thereby diminishing the financial scope for the welfare state.

It is controversial to what extent the adverse economic trends are due to economic globalization or neo-liberal policies, or both. It appears that such policies created an unfavourable economic environment for ILS. Trade unions have fallen on hard times, and in the large majority of countries their membership rates have been declining.[28] The fast expansion of the informal economy in much of the developing world has exacerbated the trend. Unions have hardly set foot there, and in some countries, such as Pakistan, they are legally prevented from organizing this sector. Many EPZs have been kept "trade union free". The liberalization of trade and capital markets has opened up new and better options for capital investment, such as the exit-option of relocating production and services across national borders. The mere threat of shifting plants is frequently enough to diminish the bargaining power of worker organizations, which in turn makes union organization more difficult.[29]

As a result of international economic integration, governments are in the grip of global forces as well, such as TNCs that are able to "punish" countries for what they view as "unfavourable" national conditions (the income of the world's six largest multinationals exceeds that of 64 nation states with 58 per cent of the global population). Hence, governments have seen their sphere of autonomy in the social policy field diminish. Many believe that high social spending, and the taxes and contributions required to finance such policies, will hurt the competitive position of their economy. More than 100 countries now offer tax holidays to foreign investors, expecting to attract more foreign capital and stimulate exports. Fearing capital flight, many communities make concessions on wages, taxes and regulations to retain corporate investment. The drawback for economic development is obvious – it reduces the fiscal revenues required for investment in social infrastructure and for strengthening social institutions. All this has left its mark in the international political arena by discouraging policy-makers from advancing ILS vigorously; it may even entice them to scale down ILS.

To escape this vicious cycle, a concerted policy shift at the international level is needed. Globalization as such is not to blame for negative economic outcomes; the policies in practice are. More expansionary macro-economic policies, a stronger commitment to labour standards, and a new emphasis on multilateralism are essential components needed to make the outcome of economic integration beneficial for workers and their families.

Summary and conclusions

At the dawn of the ILO's 85th year, its normative framework remains controversial. In the midst of the second big wave of economic globalization, and in particular the surge of cross-border investment flow, the need for a solid social dimension in the process of economic integration is as acute as ever. To set an effective social floor in the global economy, and to promote constructive instead of destructive competition, ILS must be forcefully applied everywhere.

This view, however, is contested by various opponents on varying grounds. The dogmatism of neo-liberal economics and the neo-liberal political agenda still makes for a very uneasy relationship with ILS. This economic orthodoxy insists that labour conditions are the product of economic development, and that unfettered free market forces produce optimal outcomes for growth and hence for employment and working conditions anywhere. This deterministic posture, and its insensitivity to history and institutions, is at odds with the philosophy behind ILS, which holds that while growth is conducive to the improvement of labour conditions it alone will not improve them. ILS are both an output *and* an essential input to social progress, or in other words, both ends *and* means of economic development. Emanating from its pluralist vision of the economy and society, the ILO envisages social progress resulting from an open-ended process of reconciliation of conflicting interests through association, consultation, negotiation and other forms of social dialogue. Nevertheless, freedom of association and collective bargaining are still frequently disputed as antithetical to markets. On the whole, economic orthodoxy has been a major obstacle to the advancement of ILS. Yet, it may be seen as a sign of hope that two Nobel prize winners in economics, Amartya Sen and Joseph Stiglitz, have challenged this orthodoxy, and have strongly endorsed ILS. There is no inconsistency in principle between ILS and good economic performance. Rather, the two are mutually supportive. Understanding this would lead nations to ratify and implement ILS for economic, and not purely for moral, reasons. Applying ILS makes the economy more productive, offsetting any cost of standards. To be effective and sustainable, markets need the underpinning of social institutions. The protectionism that let the multilateral system of trade collapse and provoked the great economic depression in the 1920s was also a result of similar insufficient social provision.

Next to free market fundamentalism, it has been political and cultural fundamentalism that opposes the system of values and norms of the ILO. Looking behind the rhetoric, however, it turns out that often it is not really the universalism of ILS, but rather national politics that blocks the observance of standards. Cultural tradition, local values, and religious dogmas serve as a pretext, or an effective ideology, for defending the power positions of particular individuals or groups, and denying internationally-agreed rights to women, children, ethnic minorities, trade unionists and others.

The largest barrier to the advancement of ILS has been the global economic and political environment. The end of the cold war has opened up new opportunities for the pursuit of ILS in the former communist countries. At the same time, it has ended the contest between the communist and the capitalist worlds that had driven each camp to solicit adherence from smaller countries by offering social support. Curiously enough, the end of the cold war has diminished the incentives for cooperation between government, employers and workers in the social policy field. An even greater impediment to ILS is the shift of power in the labour market in recent decades, resulting from low growth, high unemployment and underemployment, and reduced public budgets in most corners of the world. A large surplus of labour acts as a strong disincentive to improve labour conditions at a time when it is most needed. The ability of capital, both financial and real, to be moved freely beyond national borders has exacerbated the power imbalance. International cooperation, including the commitment to implement standards, would be the effective remedy in this situation, but the necessary political will appears lacking. Paradoxically, as globalization advances and the need for concerted international action grows, parochial attitudes and opportunistic local behaviour predominate.

Rights are essential to, but not sufficient for, economic and social development. Respect for and the enforcement of rights are subject to economic and political cycles. A protective norm tends to be worth less when there is no trade union to demand compliance. Public inspection of safety standards at work tends to be relaxed when jobs are at stake, and safety and other standards have little chance of being implemented in a country that suffers from a lack of capacity or technical competence in the public administration. An enabling framework of institutions and administrative resources is imperative to translate rights into reality.

To overcome the barriers, it may help if a wide spectrum of civil society actors assumes responsibility to monitor, supervise and enforce ILS. This has increasingly occurred recently, leading to new means of action and control, such as product labels, codes of conduct and ethical investment schemes. At the same time, there are risks in going beyond the classic ILO approach to ILS through non-governmental action, such as substituting hard law with soft law, and fragmented or selective implementation of labour standards. Transparency and independent control procedures might diminish the risks. It should also be pointed out that, to the extent that the new means of action are limited to products designed for the export market, this approach does not help to ensure ILS for workers – often the majority – who produce or work exclusively for the domestic market.

Finally, the proliferation of actors also provides new opportunities for ILS. There is an urgent need to take the case for standards beyond the realm of diplomats, experts, and the tripartite constituency of the ILO to the national and international levels. Nothing could be more encouraging for the future of ILS than a growing number of young people caring about and advocating good labour conditions at home and abroad in the ILO's tradition of peaceful and considered action.

Notes

1. Nicolas Valticos, "Fifty years of standard-setting activities by the International Labour Organization" (1969) 100(3) *International Labour Review* 201–8.
2. Robert J. Flanagan, "Labour standards and international economic advantage", in Robert J. Flanagan and William B. Gould (eds.), *International Labour Standards: Globalization, Trade and Public Policy* (Stanford University Press, Palo Alto, 2002).

3. ILO, "Reducing the decent work deficit: A global challenge", Report of the Director General, International Labour Conference, 89th Session (Geneva, 2001).
4. Herbert Feis, "International labour legislation in the light of economic theory" (1927) 4 *International Labour Review* 492.
5. Jeffery Sachs, "Globalization and employment", Public Lectures, International Institute for Labour Studies (Geneva, 18 March 1996).
6. Jagdish Bhagwati, "A view from the academia", in US Department of Labour, Bureau of International Labour Affairs, *International Labour Standards and Global Economic Integrations,* Proceedings of a Symposium (Washington DC, 1994).
7. Elizabeth King and Andrew Mason, *Equality and Development* (The World Bank, Washington DC, 2000).
8. Joseph E. Stiglitz, "Employment, social justice and societal well-being" (2002) 141(1-2) *International Labour Review* 9–15.
9. For a synthesis of the available research on the beneficial effects of ILS, see Werner Sengenberger, *Globalization and Social Progress: The Role and Impact of International Labour Standards* (Report prepared for Friedrich-Ebert Foundation, Bonn, 2002).
10. Amartya Sen, "Work and rights" (2000) 193(2) *International Labour Review* 114.
11. *International Trade and Core Labour Standards,* (OECD, Paris, 2000) 39-42; David Kucera, "Core labour standards and foreign direct investment" (2002) 141 *International Labour Review* 31–69.
12. Fabrice Hatem, *International Investment: Towards the Year 2001* (United Nations, New York, 1997), 14, 47, 55–6.
13. *East Asia Integrates: A Trade Policy for Shared Growth* (World Bank, Washington DC, 2003), 26–7.
14. Phillipe Egger and Werner Sengenberger (eds.), *Decent Work in Denmark: Employment, Social Efficiency and Economic Security* (ILO, Geneva, 2003), 38–42.
15. ILO, "Decent Work and the Informal Economy", Report VI, International Labour Conference, 90th Session (Geneva).
16. Alejandro Portes, "By-passing the rules: the dialectics of labour standards and informalization in less developed countries", in Werner Sengenberger and Duncan Campbell (eds.), *International Labour Standards and Economic Interdependence* (International Institute for Labour Studies, Geneva, 1994).
17. "Your voice at work", Global Report under the Follow-up to the ILO Declaration on Fundamental Principles and Rights at Work (ILO, Geneva, 2000).
18. ILO, "Decent Work"; Amartya Sen, "Our culture, their culture", in *New Republic,* 1 April 1996, 4; Xiaorong Li, "Asian Values and the universality of human rights" (1996) Vol. 16, no. 2, *Report from the Institute for Philosophy and Public Policy,* Maryland, 1.
19. Rossana Galli and David Kucera, "Labour standards and informal employment in Latin America", Discussion Paper (International Institute of Labour Studies, Geneva, 2002).
20. See Amartya Sen, "Our culture, their culture". Xiaorong Li, "Asian Values".

21. Francis Maupin, "Le renouveau de débat normatif à l'OIT de la fin de la guerre froide à la mondialisation", in *International Labour Standards Department Discussion Paper* unpublished (ILO, Geneva, 2002), 6.

22. Li, 'Asian Values', 2.

23. Charles F. Sabel, Dara O'Rourke and Archon Fung, *Ratcheting Labour Standards: Regulation for Continuous Improvement in the Global Workplace* (World Bank, Washington DC, 2000), 31.

24. Philip Alston and James Heenan, "The role of international labour standards within the trade debate: the need to return to fundamentals" Discussion Paper, International Labour Standards Department, (ILO, Geneva, 2002), 15.

25. International Conference of Free Trade Unions, "The international trade union movement and the new codes of conduct", online: http://www.icftu.org/.

26. ILO's World Commission on the Social Dimension of Globalization, "A Fair Globalization: Creating Opportunities for All" (2004), xiv.

27. Maupin, "Le renouveau de débat", 4.

28. ILO, "Organizing for social justice", 49–56.

29. See, for example, Kate Bronfenbrenner, "Uneasy terrain: the impact of capital mobility on workers, wages and union organizing", Report Submitted to the US Trade Deficit Review Commission, New York State School of Industrial and Labour Relations, (Cornell Universiy, Ithaca NY, 2000), 8.

13

The growing importance of the International Labour Organization: the view from the United States

EDWARD POTTER

Introduction

For most people in the United States, the International Labour Organization (ILO) is virtually an unknown multilateral organization. However, in our globalized world, it is becoming increasingly important. Much of this increased importance is being driven by US trade and investment policies whose seeds go back to the 1950s. This itself is ironic. Although American policy since the failed Bricker Amendment in the 1950s has been that domestic laws should not be made by the consequences of ratified treaties, the United States is nevertheless using the ILO and its conventions as a tool to raise basic worker rights in other countries. At the same time, a law that was passed in 1789 to address the consequences of the acts of pirates could possibly result in ILO standards de facto amending domestic labour and employment law in the United States.

Although joining the ILO in 1934, the United States did not seriously adhere to the ILO constitutional obligation to ratify ILO conventions until 1980. As a consequence, the United States had ratified just seven conventions prior to 1980, the last in 1953. Six were maritime conventions, and the seventh endorsed the transfer of the ILO from the League of Nations to the United Nations. Since 1980, the United States has ratified another seven conventions, two of which are fundamental ILO conventions concerning forced labour and the worst forms of child labour. Another fundamental convention concerning equal treatment has been before the Senate Foreign Relations Committee since 1998.

From the point of view of US business, until the fall of the Berlin Wall in 1989, the primary justification for participating in the ILO was to fight communism and to limit the scope of new international labour standards being negotiated at the annual June ILO Conference. Ratification of ILO conventions by the United States was something to be opposed unless there were no legal differences between the requirements of the conventions and existing US law and practice. Since 1990, however, US business has viewed the ILO as a vital tool to address worker rights in a global economy.

Taking labour standards out of competition

At the end of the twentieth century, globalization and increased international competition have led to calls to link labour standards and international trade. However, the idea of removing labour conditions as a factor in international competition is not a new idea. In the early 1800s, it was advocated by two industrialists, Robert Owens of Wales and Daniel Legrand of France. The first proposal for an international treaty on labour legislation was made in 1833 by Charles Hindley, a member of the British Parliament. In 1890, Otto von Bismarck convened a congress in Berlin for the purpose of establishing an international labour parliament to legislate multilateral labour conventions. The effort failed. Nevertheless, the concern that differing labour conditions could create a competitive advantage for one country's goods and services over those of another was one of the principal reasons for the formation of the ILO.

As the last remaining vestige of the League of Nations that was established in the Treaty of Versailles as part of the peace process following World War I, the Geneva-based ILO is the third largest of the 23 specialized United Nations agencies today.[1] Its principal purpose in 1919 and now is to establish minimum labour standards through conventions and recommendations, so that the terms and conditions of employment can be taken out of global competition. A convention is a multilateral treaty that creates an international obligation on the part of a ratifying state to meet the convention's requirements. A recommendation provides international guidance but has no binding effect. Since 1919, the ILO has adopted 185 conventions and 193 recommendations.

The adoption of international labour standards

The philosophy and purpose of the ILO when it was formed was to promulgate minimum labour standards, i.e. basic labour standards below which no nation should fall. When the first ILO Conference met in Washington DC in October 1919, it adopted six international labour standards concerning hours of work in industry, unemployment, maternity protection, night work for women, minimum age, and night work for young persons in industry. Presumably these were the most important labour standards issues of the day. In its first decade, the ILO Conference adopted 26 conventions and 30 recommendations. In its second decade in the 1930s during the Great Depression, the ILO had its most prolific era, adopting 37 conventions and 26 recommendations.

Beginning in the 1950s, the pace of adoption of international labour standards began to slow. In the 1980s, 16 conventions and one protocol were adopted; in the 1990s, 13 conventions and 3 protocols were adopted. It is particularly notable that the great majority of conventions in the last two decades were adopted by close voting margins. This suggests the absence of a strong international consensus. Currently, over half of these conventions (18) had 9 or less ratifications, while 8 others had 19 or fewer ratifications. That is, nearly 80 per cent of the international labour standards adopted by the ILO Conference in the last two decades have been ratified by 10 percent or less of the member states. The three conventions that were adopted by wide voting margins, and that addressed general principles — labour statistics, the worst forms of child labour and vocational rehabilitation — have had much higher levels of ratification ranging from 42 to over 130 ratifications.

In 1930, the ILO adopted its first human rights treaty concerning the abolition of forced labour (Convention No. 29). In the late 1940s and in the 1950s, the ILO adopted five other human rights treaties concerning freedom of association (Convention No. 87), the right to organize and collective bargaining (Convention No. 98), equal remuneration (Convention No. 100), forced labour (Convention No. 105) and equal treatment (Convention No. 111). These conventions, along with the 1930 forced labour convention, are the most heavily ratified conventions having been ratified by 120 to 150 nations. In June 1999, the ILO Conference unanimously adopted a convention prohibiting the worst forms of child labour (Convention No. 182). It has become the fastest ratified convention in ILO history with over 130 ratifications.

The levelling effect of ILO standards is incomplete

As multilateral treaties, ILO conventions have no levelling effect on labour standards unless all nations ratify them. Today, these conventions cover virtually every aspect of conditions of employment. ILO standards range from basic matters such as freedom of association and the worst forms of child labour to more technical issues such as wage setting, social security and chemical safety.

The ILO's goal of removing labour standards from competition, however, is far from being achieved. Even for the most ratified conventions, primarily concerning fundamental worker rights — freedom of association, right to organize, collective bargaining, forced and child labour, and equal opportunity — it remains the case that over half of the world's workers do not work in countries that have ratified these conventions. This is because three large countries – China, India and the United States – have ratified few of the fundamental labour standards. At the same time, 54 per cent of the ILO membership have ratified all eight fundamental ILO standards.[2]

The ratification rate and coverage for the more technical conventions, particularly those negotiated in the last 20 years, is substantially lower. More significantly, nearly 70 per cent of the 175 ILO member nations have ratified 25 percent or less (45 or fewer) of all adopted ILO conventions. In sum, the strategy of taking labour standards out of international competition through ratified conventions has not succeeded.

The changing global context for labour standards

The economic realities of the world today are vastly different than they were during the nineteenth century and most of the last century. Until the mid-1900s, a nation's economic standing and the standard of living of its people depended largely on the abundance of natural resources, the availability of adequate capital and labour within its borders, and certain cultural factors. The location of production was tied to these factors. At their birth, many countries had the good fortune to be well-endowed with natural resources, which increased the opportunity of their people to become relatively rich. Being well-off during the nineteenth and twentieth centuries allowed those countries to save more, invest in more plant and equipment, educate their labour forces and have higher productivity and incomes.

The importance of these factors as a comparative advantage for developed countries and their people began to dissipate in the 1960s with the diffusion of technology, instantaneous telecommunications, rapid and relatively inexpensive intercontinental transportation, and educational advances by developing countries. Today, natural resources endowments matter less overall in terms of comparative advantage. Technology, capital and trained workers are more readily available in many countries, rather than just a few. No longer do developed countries and their citizens necessarily have a comparative advantage in both domestic and international markets.

Unlike when the ILO was formed and dominated by a relatively few industrialized countries, the ILO today is dominated by over 130 developing countries. In the twenty-first century, the frame of reference for international labour standards is different than for most of the history of the ILO. First, the economic realities of the global economy are fundamentally different from the world economy that preceded it. Second, the economic interests of the citizens of developed and developing countries frequently conflict over issues of comparative advantage and perceptions of protectionism. The global economy has resulted in substantial, and in some cases dramatic, economic growth in some developing countries. At the same time, structural adjustment is occurring in many developed nations that previously dominated their own domestic markets as well as other markets in the world economy.

The global economy has meant that developing and developed countries (i.e., their companies and employees) compete head-to-head in the world market-place as never before. The global economy is viewed as a zero sum game of economic losers and winners, and job losers and gainers. To be sure, industrialized countries can ease (but not eliminate) the pain by being at the cutting edge of technology, by pursuing new and growing market niches, and by retraining their citizens. On the other hand, developing countries without infrastructure and markets are particularly concerned about high and sometimes expensive labour standards that developed countries did not have to meet during their economic development. The basis for such concern is primarily that these standards will compromise their primary comparative advantage — lower production costs.

Nonetheless, since the end of World War II, one of the key issues has been whether to establish a linkage of trade and labour standards as a means of preventing a "race to the bottom," assuring "fair trade", at least in theory, through the use of trade sanctions and economic penalties. A key aspect of the issue has been whether such sanctions, if established, should be administered through the ILO or through a trade organization such as the World Trade Organization (WTO).

ILO Declaration on Fundamental Principles and Rights at Work

In every trade round since the 1950s under the General Agreement on Tariffs and Trade (GATT) – the predecessor multilateral trade organization to the WTO – the US negotiating objective has been to link worker rights and trade. Near the conclusion of the Uruguay Round, then Vice

President Al Gore went to Marrakesh to seek a working party within the new WTO to study the relationship of "internationally recognized labour standards" and trade. That effort failed.

Within the ILO, the US attempt to establish a working party on worker rights in the WTO resulted in the ILO Governing Body (the ILO's board of directors) forming the Working Party on the Social Dimensions of the Liberalization of International Trade in June 1994 to address the linkage question. Two years of discussion in the Working Party enabled the ILO to be in a strategic position to take action when the WTO trade ministers reached the following agreement at the conclusion of their inaugural December 1996 ministerial conference:

> We renew our commitment to the observance of international recognized core labour standards. The International Labour Organization (ILO) is the competent body to set and deal with these standards, and we reaffirm our support for its work in promoting them. We believe that economic growth and development fostered by increased trade and further trade liberaliza- tion contribute to the promotion of these standards. We reject the use of labour standards for protectionist purposes, and agree that the comparative advantage of countries, particularly low-wage, developing countries, must in no way be put into question.[3]

As a result of the pressure to link worker rights and trade in the WTO, and in recognition of the ILO's primary responsibility with respect to work- ers, the ILO Conference adopted on 18 June 1998, without dissenting vote, a Declaration on Fundamental Principles and Rights at Work (the "Fundamental Declaration"), which is applicable to all ILO member nations. Adoption of the Fundamental Declaration was a top priority for the US Government and US business.

The Fundamental Declaration commits all ILO members to "respect, to promote and to realize . . . the principles concerning fundamental rights" that are the subject of eight ILO human rights conventions.[4] Because the legal basis for the substance of the Fundamental Declaration is drawn from the ILO Constitution, the Fundamental Declaration represents a solemn commitment by virtue of ILO membership and requires no additional action by member nations. The Fundamental Declaration has follow-up procedures to hold ILO members accountable for their commitment to seek to achieve the goals and objectives of the fundamental ILO conven- tions. Under annual review and global reporting procedures, the follow- up constitutes a political track in the ILO to address egregious or "worst case" violations of fundamental worker rights.

Under the Fundamental Declaration, the 175 ILO member nations promise to seek to achieve the goals and objectives, but not the legal requirements, of the fundamental ILO conventions. As such, the Fundamental Declaration is not a new international labour standard but rather an embodiment of the fundamental principles of ILO membership. The principles are:

- freedom of association and the effective recognition of the right of collective bargaining;
- the elimination of all forms of forced or compulsory labour;
- the effective abolition of child labour; and
- the elimination of discrimination in respect to employment and occupation.

Although the Fundamental Declaration is not a new labour standard per se, it represents the ILO at its very best in the global economy. Besides addressing fundamental workplace human rights issues, the Fundamental Declaration is also significant in that protectionism and comparative advantage were the dominant issues of concern for developing countries in the four years of discussions leading to adoption of the Fundamental Declaration. One consequence of the adoption of the Fundamental Declaration has been the substantially increased number of ratifications of the fundamental conventions.

The Fundamental Declaration and its follow-up are based on the view that "sunshine", in the form of peer review, publicity, and targeted technical assistance, will do much more − and more quickly − to promote fundamental worker rights than the sledgehammer approach of trade sanctions that will be strongly resisted by developing countries.

The impact of US trade policy

In addition to US efforts to establish a working party to study the effect of labour standards on trade and the importance the United States placed on adoption of the Fundamental Declaration, US trade and investment policy has had other consequences that have increased the importance of the ILO.

Beginning in the 1980s, the US Congress began to link trade preferences, political risk insurance and other benefits in trade legislation with "internationally recognized worker rights" that are based on ILO standards. As defined in numerous US trade laws,[5] "internationally recognized worker rights" include:

- the right of association;
- the right to organize and bargain collectively;
- a prohibition on the use of any form of forced or compulsory labour;
- a minimum age for the employment of children; and
- acceptable conditions of work with respect to minimum wages, hours of work, and occupational safety and health.

Under these trade statutes, complaints may be brought alleging that the country concerned is not "taking steps" to achieve the enumerated worker rights.

In August 2002, as a condition of giving the President of the United States trade promotion authority (formerly known as "fast track" authority), Congress established trade negotiating objectives that require incorporation of the Fundamental Declaration and "core labour standards/internationally recognized worker rights" within any bilateral or regional trade agreement with the possibility of economic trade penalties. As specified in the Trade Act of 2002,[6] the overall US trade negotiating objectives include:

- "To promote respect for worker rights and the rights of children consistent with the core labour standards of the ILO."
- "To seek provisions in trade agreements [that] do not weaken or reduce the protections afforded in domestic . . . labour laws as an encouragement of trade."
- "To promote universal ratification and full compliance with ILO Convention No. 182 [concerning the worst forms of child labour]."

More particularly, the labour negotiating objectives include "strengthen[ing] the capacity of . . . trading partners to promote respect for core labour standards".

In a lack of precision in legislative drafting by the US Congress, "core labour standards" were given the same definition as the trade law concept of "internationally recognized worker rights", as opposed to the ILO definition. Unlike the North American Agreement on Labour Cooperation (NAALC), which is a side agreement to the North American Free Trade Agreement (NAFTA), workers' rights must be included in the trade agreement. Moreover, with respect to dispute settlement and enforcement, the United States' principal negotiating objectives must be treated "equally with respect to: resort to dispute settlement; availability of equivalent dispute settlement procedures; and availability of equivalent remedies".

As the largest economy in the world with one-third of all gross domestic product, these US trade requirements ratchet up considerably the importance of the ILO and its fundamental labour standards at the beginning of the twenty-first century.

The increasing ILO role in the context of US trade agreements

On 20 January 1999, Cambodia and the United States entered into a three-year Trade Agreement on Textile and Apparel. The agreement was amended and extended for another three-year period at the end of 2001. The agreement sets an export quota for garments from Cambodia to the United States, while seeking to improve working conditions and respect for basic workers' rights in Cambodia's garment sector by promoting compliance with – and effective enforcement of – Cambodia's Labour Code as well as internationally recognized core labour standards. The amended agreement offers a possible 18 per cent annual increase in Cambodia's export entitlements to the United States, provided Cambodia supports: "The implementation of a program to improve working conditions in the textile and apparel sector, including internationally recognized core labor standards, through the application of Cambodian labor law." Under the agreement, the US Government must make a determination by 1 December of each year as to whether working conditions in the Cambodian textile and apparel sector substantially comply with Cambodia's labour laws and standards.

Following the signing of the agreement, Cambodia and the United States requested ILO technical assistance to prepare a project proposal to support the implementation of the article of the trade agreement concerned with the improvement of working conditions. Following this request, the ILO consulted extensively with the Cambodian Ministry of Social Affairs, Labour, Vocational Training and Youth Rehabilitation, the Garment Manufacturers Association in Cambodia, the Cambodian trade union movement and representatives of the United States Government. As a result, a technical cooperation project with a budget of $1.4 million over a three-year period was agreed upon in May 2000. The project commenced in January 2001 under the direction of a Chief Technical Advisor appointed by the ILO to manage the project in accordance with the agreed project document. The US mission has participated closely with the ILO to ensure that core labour standards are met under the US trade agreement with Cambodia.

The basic objective of the project is to improve working conditions in Cambodia's textile and apparel sector through:

- establishing and operating an independent system to monitor working conditions in garment factories;
- providing assistance in drafting new laws and regulations where necessary as a basis for improving working conditions and giving effect to the labour law;
- increasing the awareness of employers and workers of core international labour standards and workers' and employers' rights under Cambodian labour law;
- increasing the capacity of employers and workers and their respective organizations to improve working conditions in the garment sector through their own efforts; and
- building the capacity of government officials to ensure greater compliance with core labour standards and Cambodian labour laws.

Presently, under its Trade Promotion Authority (TPA), the United States is negotiating a Central American Free Trade Agreement (CAFTA) involving five countries: Costa Rica, Guatemala, El Salvador, Honduras and Nicaragua. Unlike the other TPA negotiations that have occurred so far, there is a legitimate question of whether these countries laws in substance contain requirements that are equivalent to the ILO's eight fundamental conventions. Consequently, on a low profile basis, the ILO is conducting an audit of the law and practice of the five countries as a result of an agreement between the United States and the CAFTA countries. In addition, an ILO monitoring agreement similar to that conducted in Cambodia is being considered.

Moreover, for the past four years, the ILO has received up to $75 million annually from the United States – more than the annual US dues subscription to the ILO – in support of ILO technical assistance programmes under the Fundamental Declaration technical assistance programme and under the ILO's child labour technical assistance programme. In addition, and again with US financial support, the ILO is performing technical cooperation programmes funded by the Department of Labour in Morocco and Southern Africa. These projects involve strengthening labour systems and capacity and relate directly to TPA agreements being negotiated.

Corporate social responsibility

In the face of the excesses of Enron and WorldCom, among others, and with revenues exceeding $7 trillion and foreign direct investment more than double any other country, it is not surprising that US companies have come under increasing pressure to adopt codes of conduct respecting corporate social responsibility, and are subject to a variety of corporate campaigns. For the most part, these codes – Global Compact, Ethical Trading Initiative, SA 8000, and the Fair Labour Association, for example – are based on ILO standards, in particular the eight fundamental conventions. Thus, ILO standards are increasingly the basis for how many US multinationals assess both their domestic and overseas operations, and supply chains. At the same time, third party monitoring by organizations such as Verité, Social Accountability International and the Fair Labour Association apply ILO standards in whole or in part.

One very interesting development is the use of ILO procedural mechanisms and standards as part of union-initiated corporate campaigns against companies.

Committee on Freedom of Association

By virtue of reference in the ILO Constitution to freedom of association, the ILO Governing Body established a Committee on Freedom of Association (CFA) in 1950 to address complaints concerning trade union rights. Over 3000 such complaints have been filed. The procedure is applicable to all governments, including those like the United States that have not ratified ILO Conventions Nos. 87 and 98 concerning freedom of association, the right to organize and collective bargaining. Although the procedures concern governmental denial of, or failure to protect, trade union rights, there have been three instances where the CFA procedure has been utilized to challenge the actions of foreign-owned companies in high profile organizing campaigns in the United States.[7]

Tripartite Declaration of Principles concerning Multinational Enterprises and Social Policy

In 1977, the Governing Body adopted the Tripartite Declaration of Principles concerning Multinational Enterprises and Social Policy (the "Tripartite Declaration"). The most detailed of the existing multilateral guidelines that address workplace practices of multinational companies, the Tripartite Declaration is composed of 58 paragraphs that encompass the full breadth of workplace issues from freedom of association to training and education, to occupational safety and health, to child labour. Each paragraph is footnoted in an addendum with relevant ILO conventions that address company policies in the area. The guidelines have been periodically updated by footnoting newly adopted ILO conventions that are relevant to the content of the Tripartite Declaration.

Most recently, in November 2000, the Governing Body considered and adopted amendments to the text of the Tripartite Declaration. Although the addendum to the Tripartite Declaration, which references relevant ILO conventions and recommendations, has been updated on numerous occasions, the Governing Body's 2000 amendments were the first changes to the Tripartite Declaration's text. The first amendment to the Tripartite Declaration called on all concerned parties (i.e., multinational enterprises, governments, employers and workers) to "contribute to the realization of the ILO Declaration on Fundamental Principles and Rights at Work and Its Follow-up, adopted in 1998". The second amendment added Convention No. 138 (minimum age for admission to employment) and No. 182 (prohibition and immediate action for the elimination of the worst forms of child labour) to the list of core conventions that governments are urged to ratify if they have not yet done so. The third amendment called on multinational companies, as well as national enterprises, to "respect the minimum age for admission to employment or work in order to secure the effective abolition of child labour", with a footnote referencing Convention Nos. 138 and 182.

As a result of a complaint concerning a US multinational's planned lay-offs in the United Kingdom and elsewhere in Europe in 1984, the ILO Governing Body established a detailed procedure and jurisdictional criteria for considering requests for interpretation of proper multinational company behaviour under the Tripartite Declaration.[8] The totality of the corporate campaign, including the results of the Tripartite Declaration case, resulted in the US multinational abandoning its lay-off plans across Europe. Thus, the prospect of being held accountable for ILO standards or the Fundamental Declaration is increasingly important to US multinational companies.

Secondary boycotts and ILO conventions

In 2000, the Offshore Mariners United Union (OMU) began an organizing campaign directed at the some 70 boat companies that operate in the offshore oil and gas industry in the Gulf of Mexico. Some of these companies have more ships than the US Navy. The OMU targeted a mid-size US company, Trico Marine Services, Inc. ("Trico"), headquartered in New Orleans, Louisiana. Trico's principle business is servicing and supplying oil rigs. However, after almost 19 months, the OMU had been unable to gain recognition of the employees working at Trico. The National Labour Relations Board concluded, moreover, that Trico had not engaged in any unfair labour practices during the organizing campaign. With its failure to enlist employee support at Trico, the OMU decided to redirect its efforts overseas.

Subsequently, after Trico successfully enjoined a world-wide boycott by the International Seafarers Federation in the British courts,[9] the OMU initiated a secondary boycott in Norway through a Norwegian affiliate against the Trico subsidiary, Trico Supply ASA. The boycott was based on the alleged denial of US workers' right to freedom of association. Nearly 20 countries have statutes that permit secondary boycotts based on human rights and economic harm in other countries. Although Trico Supply ASA had three collective bargaining agreements and good relations with the Norwegian maritime unions, Norwegian unions planned to refuse service of Trico Supply ASA's boats in the North Sea.

On 18 October 2001, in the face of Trico's threat of a legal injunction and damages, the Norwegian Oil and Petrochemical Union filed a lawsuit against Trico Supply ASA seeking court approval for the boycott by its oil rig and dock members who worked with Trico Supply vessels or handled equipment and material transported by the vessels. The entire case turned on whether US labour law failed to protect workers' rights at a level commensurate with ILO Conventions Nos. 87 and 98, which conventions have not been ratified by the United States. Notably, however, the United States had ratified Convention No. 147 concerning minimum maritime standards in 1988. Each nation ratifying Convention No. 147 commits, inter alia, to implement the general goals of Convention No. 87, which was incorporated in the appendix of Convention No. 147.

Following opening arguments, the case was settled in November 2002. With the prospect of future secondary boycott cases of this kind and the large overseas foreign direct investment of US multinationals, the case highlights the potential importance of ILO standards on both domestic and foreign operations even when the United States itself has not ratified those standards.

Alien Tort Claims Act

Soon after ratification of the US Constitution by the 13 states, the new Congress enacted the Alien Tort Claims Act (ATCA), which was part of the Judiciary Act of 1789. This one-sentence statute states:

> The district courts shall have original jurisdiction of any civil action by an
> alien for a tort only, committed in violation of the law of nations or a treaty
> of the United States.

The ATCA was intended to show the European powers that the fledgling United States would not tolerate the acts of pirates attacking merchant ships in the Caribbean.

The ATCA remained dormant for nearly two centuries until 1980 when the Second Circuit Court of Appeals decided *Filartiga* v. *Pena-Irala*.[10] *Filartiga* dealt with the 1976 torture and murder of Joel Filartiga by a Paraguayan police official. The official fled to the United States where the family of the victim was able to track him down. The suit was by an alien plaintiff against an alien in the United States for torture that had taken place in Paraguay. Significantly, the Second Circuit held that the ATCA allowed foreigners to sue in US courts for all torts committed in violation of the law of nations, not as the term was understood in 1789, but as international law is contemporaneously interpreted.[11]

It was not until the late 1990s and in the twenty-first century that the full impact of the *Filartiga* decision could be seen. US courts have subsequently held that:[12]

- the ATCA confers tort jurisdiction over all violations of international law as contemporaneously interpreted;
- foreign plaintiffs are not compelled to bring cases in their national courts wherever possible before US jurisdiction is granted; and
- multinational companies may be targeted as defendants, not only when they act in concert with a foreign state, but also if their actions can be construed as knowingly aiding and abetting the acts of the foreign state in violation of the law of nations.

Presently, there are over 50 ATCA lawsuits in the United States involving over 200 US multinational companies. Several of these cases are connected with ILO conventions, and two are particularly notable. First, on 18 September 2002, in a landmark decision, the Ninth Circuit Court of Appeals ruled in *Doe I* v. *Unocal Corporation*.[13] that companies can be held liable in US courts for "aiding and abetting" human-rights violations committed abroad.

In *Unocal*, Burmese villagers sued under ATCA, claiming that government soldiers forced them to help build a large natural gas pipeline in Myanmar (formerly Burma). They alleged that Unocal, a partner in the construction project, knew of human rights abuses, including murder, rape, and forced labour, yet provided financial, logistical and moral support to the Myanmar military despite this knowledge. The international law element of proof was established by virtue of the US ratification of ILO Convention No. 105 concerning forced labour as well as the "law of nations" concerning murder and rape.

The Ninth Circuit panel reversed the trial court's grant of summary judgment in favor of Unocal and remanded the case for trial. Using standards developed by international criminal tribunals such as the Nuremberg Military Tribunals, the International Criminal Tribunal in Rwanda and the International Tribunal for the former Yugoslavia, the majority opinion held that individuals and companies can be liable for "aiding and abetting" human rights violations through "knowing practical assistance, encouragement, or moral support which has a substantial effect on the perpetuation of the crime". The concurring opinion found potential ATCA liability against Unocal under more familiar standards of US federal law used for imposing joint venture and agency liability.

Similarly, in *Estate of Rodriguez* v. *Drummond Co., Inc.*,[14] decided by the District Court of Alabama on 23 April 2003, the plaintiffs alleged that trade union leaders in Columbia were killed by agents or employees of Drummond Company, who operated a coal mine and a supporting rail line and port in Columbia. The plaintiffs specifically alleged that the defendant hired paramilitary security forces to silence the leaders of the union by means of violence, murder, torture and unlawful detention. Although the district court dismissed the ATCA claim, it concluded that, although ILO Convention No. 87 has not been ratified by the United States, freedom of association and Convention 87 are "generally recognized principles of international law."

This finding by a conservative judicial jurisdiction in the United States is significant for two reasons. First, until this decision, freedom of association had not been seen as a generally recognized principle of US law,[15] nor has it been viewed as a preemptory norm of international law.[16] Although one would expect most ATCA complaints to involve torture, murder and other widely accepted and acknowledged norms of the "law of nations", the Alabama district court decision raises the prospect that US courts will find the eight fundamental ILO conventions to constitute the "law of nations." This is reinforced by the fact that 54 per cent of the entire ILO membership has ratified all eight fundamental conventions.

Second, and perhaps more importantly for purposes of domestic US labour and employment law, it raises the real possibility over time that US courts could apply ILO standards in domestic law cases even though

the United States has not ratified the relevant ILO Conventions. Traditionally, US courts have been quite reluctant to incorporate customary
international law into US law. As established by the Supreme Court in
its 1900 decision in *The Paquete Habana*,[17] US courts will treat rules of
customary international law as part of "the law of the land" and will apply
these rules as appropriate in cases coming before them, at least in the
absence of contrary legislation or executive policy. Experience has been
sparse regarding direct incorporation of customary human rights policy
into US domestic law. While rare, such decisions appear to be based on
the ground that domestic law required such a result, rather than on an
invocation and incorporation of international human rights standards.[18]
Such cases have not involved, to date, domestic workplace issues, but the
Drummond decision could presage the growing importance of ILO standards in the US workplace even when the United States has not ratified
the standard.

Implications of ILO standards on US domestic workplace law

In 1984, I wrote a short booklet on what ratification of ILO Conventions Nos. 87 and 98 would mean for US law and practice, assuming they
were ratified on an unqualified basis.[19] Nearly 20 years later, except for
the flipping and flopping of the Supreme Court on federal-state jurisdiction with respect to public sector workers, the implications identified in
that book remain valid. Unqualified ratification of one or both of those
conventions would redirect US labour policy significantly. To mention
just two: the conventions would broaden the right to strike but give representation rights to minority unions; and they would revoke or modify
substantial portions of the Landrum-Griffin Act, but would remove limits
on disaffiliations of local unions from international unions.

Similarly, as presently applied, unqualified ratification of the ILO's 1930
forced labour treaty (Convention No. 29) would prohibit states and the
federal government from privatizing the operation of prisons, something
now occurring in a dozen states and proposed in the first budget of the
Clinton Administration. Moreover, ratification of the ILO's treaty on equal
pay for work of equal value (Convention No. 100) would redirect equal
pay for equal work to equal pay for comparable work in the United States.

Because all of these questions are complicated issues, it is unlikely
that the relevant conventions could be ratified until the legal differences
are resolved legislatively and politically. To the extent that they are ratified (in terms of enactment of relevant legislation by both the House of

Representatives and the Senate and, where necessary, at the state level), they would have significant implications for US labour and employment policy.

Conclusions

As a result of the numerous charters and covenants that emerged after the formation of the United Nations, a broad coalition of isolationist and conservative Americans began to fear for US sovereignty. In particular, they saw treaties such as the UN Declaration on Human Rights as seeking to regulate domestic economic and social behaviour to a degree never achieved by the Brain Trusters in the Franklin Roosevelt presidency. If the New Deal had failed to completely socialize America, it appeared to conservatives that the United Nations was determined to finish the job. When three Supreme Court justices, including the Chief Justice, cited the UN Charter and the NATO treaty in support of their argument that Truman had the right to seize the steel mills in *Youngstown Sheet & Tube Co.* v. *Sawyer*,[20] Senator John Bricker from Ohio introduced into the Senate in February 1952, as Senate Joint Resolution 130, the "Bricker Amendment" to the Constitution. It read:

- Section 1. A provision of a treaty which conflicts with this Constitution shall not be of any force or effect.
- Section 2. A treaty shall become effective as internal law in the United States only through legislation which would be valid in the absence of treaty.
- Section 3. Congress shall have power to regulate all executive and other agreements with any foreign power or international organization. All such agreements shall be subject to the limitations imposed on treaties by this article.
- Section 4. The congress shall have power to enforce this article by appropriate legislation.

Although the Bricker Amendment started out with 56 co-sponsors, as is well-documented in Robert Caro's biography of President Lyndon Johnson,[21] it eventually went down to defeat in the US Senate, 42–50, with 4 not voting (a watered-down version, the "George proposal", lost by a single vote).

Although the Bricker Amendment effort failed, the operative foreign policy of the United States since the Eisenhower Administration has been that US domestic law will not be made by the treaty route. With the growing importance of the ILO, as reflected especially in US trade policy, increasing focus on the actions of multinational companies, and Alien Tort Claims Act litigation, US law and practice might in the future be changed through judicial application of treaties that the United States has not ratified.

Notes

1. The New York-based United Nations and Geneva-based World Health Organization are first and second, respectively.
2. The eight fundamental conventions are:
   Convention No. 87 concerning freedom of association and the right to organize;
   Convention No. 98 concerning the right to organize and collective bargaining;
   Convention No. 29 concerning the abolition of forced labour;
   Convention No. 105 concerning the abolition of forced labour;
   Convention No. 100 concerning equal remuneration;
   Convention No. 111 concerning equal treatment;
   Convention No. 138 concerning minimum age;
   Convention No. 182 concerning the worst forms of child labour.
3. World Trade Organization, Singapore Ministerial Declaration (Doc. WT/MIN(96)/DEC, 18 Dec. 1996), para. 4.
4. Convention Nos. 87, 98, 29, 105, 100, 111, 138 and 182. Although adopted after completion of the Fundamental Declaration, Convention No. 182 was immediately added to the conventions encompassed by the Fundamental Declaration by the ILO Governing Body.
5. This includes the Generalized System of Preferences, which grants trade preferences to over 140 developing nations, 19 U.S.C § 2462 and the Trade Act of 1988, 19 U.S.C § 2411.
6. Pub. L. No. 107–210, 19 U.S.C. § 3101 et seq.
7. See *Complaint Against the Government of the United States Presented by the International Association of Machinists and Aerospace Workers and the American Federation of Labor and Congress of Industrial Organizations,* Report No. 253 Case No. 1401; *Complaint Against the Government of the United States Presented by the United Mine Workers of America (UMWA), the American Federation of Labor and Congress of Industrial Organizations (AFL-CIO) and the Miners' International Federation (MIF),* Report No. 262 Case No. 1467; and *Complaint against the Government of the United States presented by the United Food and Commercial Workers International Union (UFCW), the American Federation of Labor and Congress of Industrial Organizations (AFL-CIO) and the International Federation of Commercial, Clerical, Professional and Technical Employees (FIET),* Report No. 284, Case No. 1523.

8. See ILO, Tripartite Declaration of Principles Cconcerning Multinational Enterprises and Social Policy (3rd ed.) online: http://www.ilo.org/public/english/employment/multi/download/english.pdf, 25–6.

9. Unpublished bench ruling.

10. 630 F.2d 876, 879 (2d Cir. 1980).

11. But see *Tel-Oren* v. *Libyan Arab Republic*, 726 F.2d 774 (D.C. Cir. 1984).

12. See Gary C. Hufbauer and Nicholas K. Nitrokostas, *Awakening the Monster: The Alien Tort Statute of 1789* (Institute for International Economics, Washington DC, 2003) and the cases cited therein.

13. 2003 U.S. App. LEXIS 2716 (9th Cir. 2003)[*Unocal*].

14. 256 F. Supp.2d 1250 (N.D. Alabama, 14 April 2003).

15. See American Law Institute, *Restatement of the law, the foreign relations law of the United States / as adopted and promulgated by The American Law Institute at Washington, D.C., May 14, 1986* (American Law Institute Publishers, St Paul, 1987) § 701; Comment, Vol. 2, 152.

16. American Law Institute, *Restatement of the law* at § 702.

17. 175 U.S. 677 (1900).

18. See *Rodriguez-Fernandez* v. *Wilkenson*, 654F.2d 1382 (10th Cir. 1981) affirming 505 F. Supp. 787 (D. Kan. 1980).

19. Edward E. Potter, *Freedom of Association, the Right to Organize and Collective Bargaining: The Impact of U.S. Law and Practice of Ratification of ILO Conventions No. 87 and No. 98* (Labor Policy Association, Washington DC, 1984).

20. 343 U.S. 579 (1952).

21. Robert Caro, *The Years of Lyndon Johnson: Master of the Senate* (Alfred A. Knopf, New York, 2002), at 528–41.

PART VI

Labour rights

14

Securing gender justice: the challenges facing international labour law

MARY CORNISH, FAY FARADAY AND VEENA VERMA

Introduction

Widespread gender inequality continues to be entrenched in global labour markets notwithstanding the positive gains women have made and the existence of international norms and legal obligations which prohibit such discrimination. The international labour law system, originally developed on the basis of the male model of "standard" employment", is now evolving to address the protection of women's work. This includes addressing the shift to the new "feminized" global economy where women's jobs are often precarious, substandard and low wage, where many women have no formal job at all, and where women continue to bear the many burdens of family and community responsibilities.[1]

The international labour law system has been fundamentally challenged by the forces of globalization which seek to move large volumes of goods, services, information and capital across international borders with low friction and high velocity.[2] Workers', and particularly women workers', rights stand in the way of this global whirlwind as labour lacks capital's mobility advantage and is subject to the threat of global capital moving to regions with lower standards. The international business community has had significant success in requiring nation states to ease, not legislate or not enforce labour and equality protections so as to attract and retain transnational companies and permit local businesses to compete in the global production system. The result has been structural adjustment programmes, privatization of state services, anti-collective bargaining laws and business-friendly export processing zones. As stated in a UN report, "economic systems which value profits, often do so at the expense of female labour."[3] Yet for poor women, their greatest asset is their labour. The international equality seeking community, including the UN, ILO, trade unions and NGOs have spent many years working to develop effective instruments and measures to meet this global equality crisis. While developing and obtaining signatories to international equality instruments is an important part of building an engendered labour law system, the challenge is to implement those instruments so that they offer real protection to women in this globalized context.

The first section of this chapter summarizes the current worldwide gendered patterns of inequality and female poverty which must be addressed by an engendered labour law framework. The second section reviews the current formal international labour law framework in the area of gender discrimination including key ILO, UN and regional instruments. The third section distils from these instruments the key gender equality standards and principles which represent the international consensus on the obligations of state actors and social partners. The final section identifies the key issues which must be addressed by policy-makers, legislators and civil society in order to transform labour markets. It also reviews some of the lessons learned in this process and some examples of good practices which are starting to deliver on the gender justice promised by these international standards.

Women's labour – the context of global inequality

The global labour market for women has been marked by five significant trends that, while displaying some progress in women's share of both jobs and wages, demonstrate the persistent systemic gaps that exist between men and women across the spectrum of employment rights and benefits. These five trends are:

- women's increased participation in the labour force;
- women's modest gains in remuneration;
- the continuing occupational segregation and income gaps between male and female workers;
- women's continuing struggle to reconcile employment and family responsibilities; and
- women's concentration in the informal economy.

Industrialized and developing countries alike share these trends, although the burden of inequality falls greatest on women workers where poverty, the informal economy, weak employment regulation, racial and ethnic discrimination and violence are most pronounced.[4] So, while there has been improved equality, quantitatively, in women's global labour market participation, this has yet to yield true socio-economic equality and empowerment for women.[5]

Women's increased participation in the labour force

Over the last twenty years, women worldwide have increased their share of non-agricultural labour market employment, a shift which has been linked to an expansion in export-led industrial development associated with globalization.[6]

While the female share of wage employment continues to grow gradually in most economically healthy countries,[7] employment levels approach parity with that of men in less than half the countries for which data is available.[8] While in the transition economies 91 women are economically active for every 100 men, and in East Asia the ratio is 83:100, in the Middle East, North Africa and South Asia, for every 100 men employed, only about 40 women are economically active.[9]

Women's wages improving gradually

The past twenty years have also seen an improvement in women's average monthly wage in the vast majority of 63 countries with available figures, although by 1998–9 none of these countries had yet achieved equal average wages.[10] While progress to equality in wages has been very uneven, it has extended beyond OECD countries and into the developing world: selected Latin American states, for example, have shown anywhere from 1 per cent (Ecuador) to 19 per cent (Paraguay) gains in women's average income in non-agricultural sectors relative to men's between the early and late 1990s.[11]

Continuing occupational segregation of women and men

While these first two trends reveal some progress, they also obscure the pervasive, worldwide trends concerning the nature and quality of women's labour force participation and the extent and persistence of prevailing wage gaps in the wake of market integration and globalization.[12] The inequality facing the world's women is still staggeringly widespread and systemic. Women represent 60 per cent of the world's 550 million working poor.[13]

Within both the formal and informal economy, the occupational segregation of men and women by gender continues worldwide with men dominating higher-paying "production" jobs and women dominating lower-paying "care giving" or "home-based" jobs. Studies show that low pay and flexibility are associated with typically "female" occupations primarily because they are "female".[14] At the same time, women are also excluded from "male" occupations because of the human capital discrimination they face given their unequal access to education.[15] This gendered job segregation, stereotyping and undervaluation of women's work underpins the worldwide gender order with men's work considered superior economically, socially and legally.[16]

Women's full integration into the labour market continues to be resisted and surrounded by patriarchichal stereotypes, prejudices, misconceptions and culturally based expectations about gender roles and what constitutes "valuable work".[17] The rising importance of religious fundamentalism has also contributed to reassertion of traditional women's roles.[18] These powerful gendered perceptions of women's inferior status persist even though the international community recognizes formally that gender inequality tends to lower labour productivity, intensify the unequal distribution of resources and contribute to the non-monetary aspects of poverty – lack of security, opportunity and empowerment.[19] Women and girls still bear the largest and most direct costs of these inequalities which inhibit sustainable development and global poverty reduction.[20]

The challenge of reconciling employment and family responsibilities

Further compounding these disadvantages are the challenges women face in continuing to bear the double burden of balancing the demands of paid work and those of "unpaid care work" in sustaining families and communities. Domestic and child care responsibilities involved in social reproduction continue to be borne overwhelmingly by women and this impacts on the economic choices that are available to women and the choices women make which lead to "contingent" work.[21] The extent to which women suffer from a "time poverty"[22] caused by their many responsibilities is greatly exacerbated as women are forced to take on added domestic obligations as states roll back, privatize and eliminate public services, as the population ages, as global poverty increases, and as HIV/AIDS rises internationally.[23]

Women's concentration in the informal economy

Although women's labour force participation has increased, this growth has come largely in the informal economy through self-employment, part-time employment, casual and temporary employment and home-based low income work.[24] Relative to work in the standard economy, work in the informal economy is highly vulnerable, with very low pay and irregular income, is excluded from legal and regulatory frameworks and therefore lacks access to employee and social security benefits.[25] Women in the informal sector have less property and fewer assets; are largely under-compensated; are prevented from obtaining the necessary credit to sustain themselves and their families; and are less able to access and enforce their rights, than their male counterparts.[26]

While both men and women are moving to the informal economy, women and other disadvantaged workers, such as racial and ethnic minorities and the disabled, usually predominate in that sector.[27] In 2003, about two-thirds of the female work force participating in the developing world (outside of agriculture) was through the informal economy.[28] Many women engaged in this sector work in home-based work, street vending, and in the worst cases are trafficked as sex workers across national borders.

The predominance of women in the informal economy reflects the disadvantages women face in the labour market and the economic restructuring of the new economy. Non-standard work is becoming the new standard model of production. With the increasing shift to performance-based pay, "home-based" work, export processing zones and use of migrant workers, there is an increasing specific demand for cheap female labour.[29] This type of employment is generally not unionized and operates without the protections offered by the ILO core labour standards.[30] Contractualization or flexibilization of labour means that many regular jobs are being replaced by "temporary" workers with no benefits, many of whom are women.[31] In India, home-based bidi making is the largest non-agricultural occupation for women and home-based work is the lowest paying work sector for women. With trade liberalization, many women have lost their livelihoods in the agricultural sector and face discrimination as producers in gaining access to the new economy activities.[32]

The global push to force large numbers of female labourers, migrants and other minority work groups outside of the formal labour market is not a discrete phenomenon of the developing world. In more industrialized countries, the informal and non-standard sector is also expanding to include new workers into the labour force and to absorb workers from the formal sphere who have been rendered redundant by economic crisis, downsizing or structural adjustment.[33] In the United States and Japan, for example, women's share of part-time employment has risen throughout the 1990s to just under 70 per cent.[34]

Globalization has undoubtedly opened some opportunities for women in more industrialized and developing countries to improve their position and enter "new economy" sectors of the global labour force. Yet, even women who are able to obtain "standard" employment face discrimination in terms of the type of standard employment to which they have access and the terms and conditions of that employment. At the same time, the gaps in terms of wages and the treatment of those women who do make it into better paying administrative or managerial positions and the balance of female earners, who remain in more marginal, underpaid and "feminized" sectors of the global economy continue to widen.[35]

Women also continue to be disproportionately affected by the lack of employment in the private sector and the reduction of jobs in the public sector, which drive them into informal and non-standard work and perpetuate cycles of "permanent temporary employment or no employment at all".[36] At the same time, public sector funding crises, privatization and social sector restructuring have reduced women's access to day care, basic education and retraining, and other employment-enhancing strategies.[37]

It is clear then that the number of women internationally who are engaged in "decent work" – measured by the ILO as available, freely chosen, productive, sustainable, equitable, secure and dignified – still lags far behind that of the world's men.[38] Globally, women continue to work in environments characterized by unfair labour practices and work conditions: they face discrimination, unequal and low wages, and few opportunities for participation in decision making, career advancement and long-term employment stability.[39] At the same time that women continue to experience such widespread and continued exploitation and the need for increased labour market equality protections, globalization forces have moved to limit such regulatory protections. While even the regulation of "standard" work has suffered in this context, as women are pushed further outside of the formal networks and deeper into the informal non-standard sphere, their quest for labour market justice becomes even more remote.

The next section reviews the formal international and regional labour law mechanisms which are currently in place to protect the rights of women workers to equality in employment.

International labour law gender equality system

The international labour law system is made up of many intersecting and overlapping instruments including treaties, conventions, declarations, resolutions, decisions and recommendations. Together these instruments form the world's legal framework within which women's specific rights can be strengthened, states' positive obligations can be clarified, and effective mechanisms can be established and improved to monitor compliance with international obligations. Since the adoption of the ILO's Equal Remuneration Convention in 1951, and continuing to the present with the UN Commission on Human Right's 2003 adoption of the Resolution Integrating the Human Rights of Women throughout the United Nations System, world governments have highlighted the importance of establishing global rules to recognize women's rights as human rights and to redress all forms of gender discrimination. As this review discloses, there has been an increasing recognition of the systemic and multi-layered nature of women's labour market discrimination.

Treaties and conventions

Treaties and conventions are the most important mechanisms within the labour law system because once they are negotiated, signed and ratified, they become legally binding and enforceable against the laws and actions of each signatory state. This section focuses specifically on those treaties and conventions which set out the international principles, norms, and standards that are critical to the realization of women's labour market equality.

Key ILO instruments and mechanisms

The ILO's first major gender equality instrument was the 1951 Convention Concerning Equal Remuneration for Men and Women for Work of Equal Value.[40] This convention signalled the ILO's commitment to equality of economic rights and was the first instrument to address the differences between formal equality ("equal pay for equal work") and a more substantive and systemic notion of equality ("equal pay for work of equal value"). The new standard recognized the systemic differences between men's and women's work and required national governments and workplace parties to carry out an objective appraisal and evaluation of this work, and implement comparable pay schemes for different work of comparable value. The convention departed from earlier commitments to gender equality by obliging member states to take positive "action" to achieve pay equity and by following up on the effectiveness of these actions through reporting mechanisms, a complaints procedure and external monitoring.[41]

In 1958, the ILO took another step towards labour market gender equality by adopting the Convention Concerning Discrimination In Respect of Employment and Occupation.[42] This convention defined the parameters of discrimination in employment broadly as encompassing any distinction, exclusion or preference which has the effect of nullifying or impairing equality of opportunity or treatment in employment or occupation. It requires that signatory states declare and pursue a national policy aimed at eliminating all discrimination including sex-based discrimination.[43]

Since the early 1980s, recognizing the multiple layers of women's disadvantage, the ILO has built on these core conventions to address women's specialized needs as workers by adopting the Maternity Protection Convention.[44] This convention protects women from termination in relation to pregnancy/maternity, guarantees women the right to return to the same or equivalent position at the same pay rate following maternity leave, and requires member states to take appropriate measures to ensure that maternity does not constitute a source of discrimination.[45] The Workers with Family Responsibilities Convention[46] further requires signatory states to implement national policies which enable persons with family responsibilities to engage in employment without discrimination.

The Termination of Employment Convention[47] provides that sex does not constitute a valid ground for termination. The Part-time Work Convention[48] – particularly significant for the predominant number of women who split their days between family care and part-time work – aims to ensure equality in protection between part-time workers and full-time workers, particularly with respect to the right to bargain collectively; access to occupational health and safety; and the right to work free from discrimination. The Home Work Convention[49] requires signatory states to adopt and regularly review a national policy on home work aimed at promoting equality with other wage earners.

Supporting these specialized conventions[50] are those ILO Conventions protecting the principles of the right to equal treatment, full participation and non-discrimination in the work place which were elevated in status in the 1998 Declaration of Fundamental Principles and Rights at Work and its Follow-up.[51] Of the eight conventions encompassed by the Declaration, the following are most relevant to securing women's economic rights: Convention No. 87 on freedom of association and protection of the right to organize 1948; Convention No. 98 on the right to organize and collective bargaining 1949; Convention No. 100 on equal remuneration for men and women for work of equal value, 1951; and Convention No. 111 on discrimination in respect of employment and occupation 1958. The 1998 Declaration requires compliance with the eight "fundamental conventions" whether or not a member state has ratified them because these principles are fundamental to ILO membership. The ILO requires member states to submit annual reports on implementation and compliance with the Declaration.[52]

Key UN instruments and mechanisms

Other UN bodies are increasingly taking an important role in enforcing gender labour market equality.[53] Numerous UN instruments complement the ILO conventions set out above, and more importantly demonstrate the fundamental intersection between promoting labour market gender equality and promoting basic human rights.

Women's rights are protected in the International Bill of Human Rights which consists of three cornerstone documents – the Universal Declaration of Human Rights (UDHR),[54] the International Covenant on Civil and Political Rights (ICCPR)[55] and the International Covenant on Economic Social and Cultural Rights (ICESCR).[56]

The UDHR affirms women's right to: equal pay without discrimination; a standard of living adequate for the health and well-being of the individual and her family; and the right of all mothers and children to receive special care and assistance and the same social protection as all other individuals.[57] The ICCPR ensures that men and women have the ability to fully enjoy their civil and political rights and that all persons are equal before the law and entitled to equal protection under the law, free from discrimination.[58] The ICESCR enhances the protection of women's economic rights by giving more definition to work rights and requiring that member states create just and favourable working conditions including fair wages and equal remuneration without distinction based on gender.[59]

The 1981 Convention on the Elimination of all Forms of Discrimination Against Women (CEDAW)[60] is the most comprehensive UN Convention dealing with gender equality. It addresses the multi-faceted nature of women's discrimination and the need for comprehensive social, political and economic remedies, sets up an agenda for national action towards the complete legal protection of women's rights[61] and monitors enforcement by requiring member states to report every four years on compliance.[62] CEDAW also sets out a number of specific and important employment protections such as women's right to: the same employment opportunities as men; application of the same criteria for selection in matters of employment; free choice of profession and employment; promotion, job security and all benefits and conditions of service that are granted to men; vocational training and retraining; equal remuneration, benefits, and equal treatment in respect of work of equal value; equality of treatment in evaluation of the quality of work; protection of health and safety in working conditions; and the right not to be discriminated against due to pregnancy or family responsibilities.[63]

Following CEDAW, a number of UN Declarations were issued to strengthen gender equality internationally and to mobilize member states into taking concrete action to realize this objective. In 1986, the UN Declaration on the Right to Development[64] emphasized non-discrimination, security, empowerment, and development rights as human rights. The Vienna Declaration and Programme of Action[65] adopted following the 1993 World Conference on Human Rights, affirmed the human rights of women as an inalienable, integral and indivisible part of human rights and demanded gender mainstreaming across all UN institutions and activities. The 1995 UN Copenhagen Declaration on Social Development[66] reinforced these principles by calling for greater transparency and equality in governance and administration institutions in order to create sustainable foundations for social and economic development.

In that same year, following the UN Fourth World Conference on Women, member states adopted the Beijing Declaration and Platform for Action.[67] The Beijing Declaration renewed the world's commitments to eliminating all forms of discrimination against women and girl children, and the Platform for Action committed signatories for the first time to a detailed agenda for achieving this objective over a five-year period.[68] The strategic objectives set out in the Platform for Action call on member states, employers, employees, trade unions and women's organizations to promote women's economic rights and independence in order to: secure access to employment, appropriate working conditions and control over economic resources; facilitate women's access to resources employment, markets and trade; strengthen women's economic capacity and commercial networks; and eliminate occupational segregation and all forms of employment discrimination.[69]

As a follow up in June 2000, the UN General Assembly after reviewing country status reports, issued a resolution on Further Actions and Initiatives to Implementing the Beijing Declarations and Platform for Action which signalled the need to accelerate implementation of the Platform for

Action and the need for more sustainable signs of an increase in women's equality internationally.[70]

Regional mechanisms

With the world divided into many economic regions, regional mechanisms are increasingly an important means for addressing women's labour market equality. This section provides a brief snapshot of some of the more prominent regional instruments that have been developed.

The European Economic Community recognized equality between men and women as a fundamental principle and gender mainstreaming as a priority objective in all of its activities. This was reinforced in the Treaty of Amsterdam, the Charter of Fundamental Rights of the European Union, and by numerous binding EC regulations, and directives.[71] The many directives adopted by member states to harmonize standards across borders focus on the following areas to promote equality between women and men:

- establishing a general framework for equal treatment in employment and occupation;[72]
- equal pay for work of equal value[73];
- equal treatment in access to employment, vocational training, promotion, and working conditions;[74]
- the burden of proof in cases of discrimination based on sex;[75]
- equal treatment in social security[76] and occupational security schemes[77];
- equal treatment for those engaged in self-employment and protection for self-employed women during pregnancy and motherhood;[78]
- measures to improve safety and heath of pregnant workers, and workers who have recently given birth and who are breast-feeding;[79]
- parental leave.[80]

Within the Inter-American human rights system, the Inter-American Commission on Human Rights, the Inter-American Court of Human Rights, the Inter-American Commission on Women, and the Special Rapporteurship on the Rights of Women collectively work to enforce equality and non-discrimination. The American Declaration on the Rights and Duties of Man recognizes the right to equality before the law; the right to protection for mothers and children; the right to work and fair remuneration; and the right to social security. The 1969 American Convention on Human Rights confirms that all individuals have a right to equal protection before and under the law, and the right to progressive development. Further conventions to protect civil, political and economic, social and cultural rights have expanded on these equality rights for women.[81]

Further regional mechanisms in North America[82] and in the Caribbean Community[83] (CARICOM) provide additional means for addressing women's equality in the labour market. In the North American Agreement on Labour Cooperation, a side agreement to the North American Free Trade Agreement, the United States, Mexico and Canada have committed themselves to promoting 11 specific Labour Principles which are annexed to the Agreement. Of particular relevance to the economic rights of women are the principles of: prohibition on forced labour; minimum employment standards; elimination of employment discrimination; equal pay for women and men; and protection of migrant workers.

In the Asia Pacific Region, the Association of Southeast Asian Nations (ASEAN) adopted the Declaration of the Advancement of Women in the ASEAN Region in 1988 to reinforce the Bangkok Declaration of 1967, the Declaration of ASEAN Concord of 1976, and the Manila Declaration of 1987 and to strengthen regional cooperation, collaboration and coordination for the purpose of advancing the role and contribution of women in the region's progress. In 1998 the Asia Pacific Economic Conference (APEC) Ministerial Meeting on Women recommended developing a Framework for the Integration of Women in APEC. The ASEAN Sub-Committee on Women (ASW) is also working towards implementing a plan of action to address regional priorities of: trafficking and violence against women; implementation of CEDAW and other international instruments related to women; intensifying the efforts of the ASEAN Network for Women in Skills Training; and gender mainstreaming in the development programmes of ASEAN member countries.[84]

In June 2002, the New Economic Partnership for African Development in Durban enacted resolutions that affirm a commitment to gender equality in the labour market. For example, the Durban Declaration on Mainstreaming Gender and Women's Effective Participation in the African Union confirms member states' commitments to women's empowerment as enshrined in the Constitutive Act of the African Union.[85] The Protocol to the African Charter on Human and Peoples' Rights on The Rights of Women in Africa, adopted in July 2003, affirms the principles of non-discrimination under the African Charter on Human and Peoples' Rights. It also reinforces the African Platform for Action and the Dakar Declaration of 1974, and gives the African Commission on Human and People's Rights increased jurisdiction to deal with issues of gender inequality.[86]

International gender equality principles and standards

As the previous section demonstrates, international labour law has begun the process of transforming itself from its traditional focus on the regulation of male-dominated "standard" workplaces, to taking a more systemic, inter-disciplinary and inter-institutional approach. This approach recognizes that securing gender justice for women in labour markets requires much more than enacting new labour laws. Equality measures must be taken to address the social, political and economic factors at the root of women's labour market discrimination as identified in the first section of this chapter: women's increasing labour force participation; persistent income discrimination; the continuing ghettoization of women's work particularly in the increasing informal economy, and the many burdens of reconciling work and family life.[87]

The international gender equality mechanisms reviewed in the previous section have established a new set of universal gender equality standards to govern the actions of signatory state actors and where appropriate other social partners. The following standards, distilled from these mechanisms, while far from being implemented now reflect a worldwide consensus on the nature of labour market inequalities facing women and the steps which need to be implemented to redress those inequalities:

- Labour market equality for women and securing economic rights are priorities which warrant immediate attention and demand concerted action from all governments. Every available measure must be explored and the maximum available resources must be allocated towards securing these objectives. The achievement of equality for women in all aspects of life is a fundamental precondition for achieving a sustainable, just and developed society.[88]
- Gender-based employment discrimination is systemic in nature. Traditional patterns of conduct and conceptions of what constitutes "valuable work" must be transformed in order to achieve greater workplace equality, including equal access to all benefits enjoyed by workers in the formal sector, and recognizing also that women's full participation in all aspects of the labour market is imperative.[89]
- Securing gender justice requires a multi-faceted approach with measures requiring governments and now civil society including employers and trade unions to take proactive steps coordinated through national action plans to address gender equality on a systematic basis.[90] A comprehensive national strategy must be developed which recognizes and addresses the specific features of inequality which are facing women in the many different communities within a country.

- Women's right to equal pay for work of equal value is a fundamental labour standard and human right of the highest priority. Government has a pressing legal obligation to take positive steps to eradicate gender-based wage discrimination and to enact, modify and strengthen legislation in order to prevent all discrimination in employment practices including discrimination based on family status, non-standard work, and during periods of pregnancy or parental leave.[91]
- Governments have an obligation to recognize the precarious position of female migrant workers and must implement measures to protect this group against involuntary confinement, forced labour, trafficking, and all other forms of labour and human rights abuse.[92]
- Governments have a legal obligation to apply a gender perspective in the creation and implementation of labour laws ensuring also that women play an active role in this process, recognizing that the right to work and define work conditions is fundamental to the right to development; recognizing also that women experience work differently than men and their rights to development may be obstructed by violence, time poverty and unequal access to education; and recognizing that the empowerment of women and full participation on the basis of equality are pressing international objectives.[93]
- Governments have a legal obligation to ensure and guarantee equality outcomes.[94] Government must enforce adherence to workplace equality laws by public authorities and institutions.[95] It has an added obligation to take all appropriate measures to eliminate discrimination against women by any person, organization or enterprise and must ensure that labour equality standards are achieved in both the public and private sector.[96]
- As a follow up to the Beijing Platform for Action and Beijing+5, employers (including private sector employers) have an obligation to take proactive steps to implement equal pay for work of equal value, to eliminate gender segregation in the labour force, and to review, analyse and reformulate wage structures for female-dominated jobs with a view to raising their status and earnings.[97]
- The achievement of equality is interconnected with the achievement and operation of other fundamental labour rights, including freedom of association and the right to collective bargaining. The methods devised to achieve labour market gender equality must recognize that collective bargaining is an important mechanism for eliminating wage discrimination and for securing adequate work conditions.[98] In the process of formulating legislation and taking steps to eradicate

discrimination, and protect fundamental human rights, Governments have a legal obligation to consult employers, trade unions, and civil society.[99]

- Governments have a legal obligation to create effective enforcement mechanisms for ensuring compliance with international and national labour law standards. All labour complainants must have direct access to a competent tribunal that can: adjudicate their rights; issue and enforce an effective remedy; and impose sanctions for non-compliance. Effective enforcement also requires access to legal aid for vulnerable persons seeking to enforce their rights.[100]
- Ongoing monitoring, reporting and follow up within a defined time-frame are necessary in order to ensure the practical implementation and realization of gender equality and full labour participation.[101]

Some issues to consider, lessons learned and good practices

While establishing these international gender equality standards reflects considerable progress, efforts to secure gender justice are systematically undermined by the refusal, inability or lack of capacity of governments and institutions to implement these standards and the widespread inability of women to exercise these rights in their day to day lives. There are many diverse issues which need to be addressed by policy-makers, legislators and social partners in order to implement the promise of these standards. This section addresses some of these key issues, reviews various lessons learned and identifies examples of good practices.

Structural inequalities

The structural and persistent inequalities outlined in the first section of this chapter and which permeate the economic, social, and political lives of men and women constitute a powerful barrier to the implementation of these gender equality standards. Gender inequality is so entrenched in the world's labour markets that progress must be made on many fronts in order for women to be able to break out from the web of inequalities they face in education and health and by reason of violence. Engendering the labour law system requires more than just enacting better workplace labour laws and enforcement measures, although these are an essential step. For women, securing gender justice in the world's labour markets requires a combination of transformative measures which are aimed at every aspect of women's inequality. The lack of resources and capacity in many countries to undertake such systemic measures is problematic and necessitates a careful approach by state actors and social partners with international assistance in order to plan measures which are realistically implementable.

Understanding gender differences

Women's experiences at work and in society vary dramatically from men's and these differences vary by country and region and within countries. While the lack of decent work is a worldwide issue, the particulars of the gender discrimination are dependent on the country and on women's age, location, education level, class and ethnicity.[102] Securing gender justice requires at its most fundamental level that equality measures are based on a specific and clear understanding of the social, economic and political labour market barriers facing women in a particular country, region and local area.

While it may seem obvious that policies and laws should be based on accurate information, the international labour law system historically ignored the circumstances and needs of women's work by focusing on men's "standard" work and even on women holding "standard" work while ignoring the needs of those women for protections such as pregnancy leave and equal pay. Protecting the rights of women workers in the new economy requires that the many diverse employment and unemployment circumstances facing women are addressed. As men also increasingly find themselves in this new "feminized" economy, they will also benefit from the labour law system addressing women's economic issues.[103]

Gender mainstreaming, planning and pro-active intervention

The collection and analysis of gender information noted above is essential to the development of the National Plans for implementing gender equality called for by the Beijing Platform of Action. Engendering labour market policies and law means making visible and then addressing women's concerns, needs and aspirations. Policy and law-making must be gender aware and responsive, not gender blind. This approach, known as "gender mainstreaming", is the cornerstone of the Beijing Platform and CEDAW. This requires not just making programmes or policies more accessible to women but the simultaneous mobilization of legal instruments, financial resources and a country's analytical and organizational capabilities to develop balanced relationships between men and women. State actors and social partners must therefore redefine their mandates to proactively intervene and address the measures needed to improve women's equality and establish goals and timetables for those measures.[104]

A recent important initiative which draws effectively on the lessons learned from years of struggling to redress gender discrimination is the European Union's Community Framework Strategy on Gender Equality (2001–2005). The Community Framework Strategy is comprehensive, embracing all Community policies in an effort to promote gender equality either by adjusting general policies and/or by implementing concrete actions specifically targeted in a proactive way at a particular situation facing European women. The Strategy addresses five interrelated fields and then develops specific operational objectives within those areas: promoting gender equality in economic life; equal participation and representation; equal access and full enjoyment of social rights for men and women; gender equality in civil life; and change in gender roles and stereotyping.[105]

The dual focus of the Community's strategy is a marked departure from previous Community initiatives which, despite the CEDAW and Beijing requirements had focused on specific compartmentalized programmes. The new Strategy brings together under one umbrella all the different initiatives in order to facilitate clear assessment criteria, monitoring tools, setting of benchmarks, gender proofing and evaluation.[106] While recognizing that gender mainstreaming is necessary to include and address women's issues in general policy and legal planning, the Strategy also recognizes that such mainstreaming will only be effective if it is buttressed by specific initiatives which target women's unique needs.[107] Gender mainstreaming, without a simultaneous political and resource commitment has sometimes been used as a way of eliminating funded gender specific policies and departments. The Community Framework Strategy recognizes this problem by adopting a dual track strategy.

Taking on patriarchichal values and constraints

A recent important ILO study, "Quality of Women's Employment: A Focus on the South", by Kanchana N. Ruwanpura reflects on the considerations and measures which must be taken to implement labour market gender protections. This study underscores the need to specifically acknowledge and address the dynamics of the social, cultural and patriarchichal values and institutions which affect the perceptions of women and their work. Effective measures to provide more and better jobs for women require state actors and social partners to develop mechanisms which address these social and institutional labour market constraints. Otherwise, women's attempts to secure a better position in the labour market will continue to be frustrated by social and cultural norms which label women as secondary or marginal.[108] Promoting equality requires promoting long-lasting changes in parental roles, family structures, institutional practices, the organization of work and time, personal development and independence, and the involvement of men.

Targeting the occupational segregation of women

The worldwide occupational segregation of women has become the central mechanism for perpetuating women's secondary status and the patriarchy system. Such segregation reinforces the gender division of labour, pays low wages, and maintains women's economic dependence and weakened power in the labour market.[109] The use of cheap female labour by capital in the new economy as highlighted in the second section of this chapter has reinforced women's employment ghettos. With the benefit of data showing the gender-based structure of labour market occupations, measures can be taken to improve the conditions of current women's employment as well as to allow women to gain access to "male-dominated" work with social protections.[110]

Affirmative action or employment equity measures and laws are necessary to attack the occupational segregation of women both horizontally and vertically.[111] An example of the type of specific initiatives which are required is the ILO's International Programme on More and Better Jobs for Women. This programme provides assistance to countries to meet ILO equality standards and the requirements of the Beijing Platform for Action and Copenhagen Declaration on Social Development.[112] As many countries lack the institutional capacity to engender their labour law framework, this ILO programme steps in to provide needed support.

Pay equity measures

Measures to address gender-based pay inequalities require a multi-faceted approach tailored to a country's needs and can include: laws establishing minimum wages; promoting collective bargaining in the areas where women work; establishing pay equity laws to require women's jobs to be paid on a comparable basis to men's jobs; and, finally, special measures for improving the income received by women from the informal economy including sectoral wages and other income-enhancing measures. International human rights instruments combined with the experience implementing ILO Convention No. 100 lead to the following guiding principles for pay equity laws: wage discrimination is systemic in nature; traditional patterns of conduct must be transformed in order to achieve equality; and discrimination-free wages must be identified by reviewing, analysing and reformulating wage structures for female-dominated jobs with a view to raising their status and earnings.

Accommodating women's domestic and child care responsibilities

A critical feature of the disadvantage women experience in the labour market flows from their domestic and child care responsibilities which often lead to their taking low or non-paying "flexible" jobs with little or no protection. Labour market laws and policies must adapt to recognize the links between family and work, to fairly distribute the costs and responsibilities of social reproduction among women, men and society and to adopt measures which accommodate for these social reproduction responsibilities.[113] Parental leave policies are a way to acknowledge and cross-subsidize the economic costs of parenting which have historically fallen on women's shoulders.[114] Supportive measures such as child care are needed to level the playing field for women. Otherwise, the new globalized employers looking for cheap and flexible labour will continue to take advantage of the vulnerable situation of female parents and capital will continue to exploit women by taking advantage of their need for flexible work.[115]

Addressing the needs of women in the informal economy

Given women's predominance in the informal sector, the first step is to use gender data to understand country and region specific information about where women are found within the informal sector. The next step is to develop labour protections which will address the needs of these particular workers. This means rethinking labour law protections to adapt to the needs of this very diverse sector. For many women in the informal economy, their status is most likely to be that of own account, self-employed or home-based workers. Many home-based workers who previously produced crafts are now being drawn into industrial production and experiencing further exploitation. Labour protections in this context may mean measures to provide equitable access to micro-credit, marketing information and other entrepreneurial supports. Successful strategies in this area focus on providing such workers with networking and educational opportunities which build towards self-reliance, independence and improved productivity. As example is the successful SEWA programme in India which has these objectives.[116] Other important initiatives have been taken to improve the income and conditions of street vendors, an occupation which is one of the few readily accessible avenues of employment to women. The 1995 Bellagio International Declaration of Street Vendors calls on governments to develop national policies to improve vendors' conditions, including improving licensing, involving vendors in urban development plans and providing access to child care.[117] As women occupy the lowest paid, lowest skilled jobs in the informal sector, other measures include providing training for women to undertake the specialized higher status and paying "male" jobs in the informal sector which are often held by men.[118]

Organizing women workers and promoting core labour standards

The informalization of the economy has weakened the power of trade unions and collective voice representation. Workers are often no longer in a traditional one-site workplace which historically facilitated union organizing. Home workers and small workshops are often "invisible" and difficult to organize.[119] Where organizing has been successful, such as the unionization of certain domestic workers in Namibia or the organizing of market traders in Côte D'Ivoire and Burkina Faso, this has often been attributed to such efforts being supported by ILO projects which provide the women with access to funds, marketing and training initiatives. This highlights the critical importance of institutional support and capacity building in facilitating the collective voice representation of women workers.[120] It also points to the need to promote compliance with the ILO's core labour standards which include freedom of association and the right to be free from discrimination in employment.[121]

Empowering the voices of women and their representatives

Transformative labour market reforms are those which empower women as partners and active agents in the reform process. While trade unions provide an important collective voice for women to promote equality measures, most women worldwide either have no access to a union or have not joined unions because they have been undemocratic or male-dominated. Women NGOs both at the local and national level have played and continue to play an indispensable role in advocating for reforms with local and national businesses and governments. This role must be supported by state and international actors and institutions.

Consumer campaigns

An emerging new protection for women workers worldwide has been the waging of consumer campaigns to improve the conditions of workers from the developed world who are employed by supply chain contractors to apparel or manufacturing companies. Women in these transnational industries, frequently in export processing zones, often remain disproportionately vulnerable to abusive labour conditions because of their limited employment opportunities. Businesses maximize profits by establishing operations where commercial imperatives are unrestricted by effective labour legislation.[122]

As a response to globalization's persistent erosion of world labour standards, consumer campaigns have led to auditing to establish fair workplace practices by organizations such as Verité on behalf of buyers such as Gap, Liz Claiborne and Tommy Hilfiger.[123] While these campaigns have raised a number of issues and concerns, overall they have achieved a remarkable degree of success as a potential further source of international employment governance.[124] Campaigns by NGOs and trade unions highlight the social consequences of manufacturing as commercial considerations alongside quality and price.[125] This is done through publicizing global labour abuses and then working to establish more socially viable options through corporate codes of conduct and auditing mechanisms.[126] While such campaigns rely on individual consumers, NGO's are ultimately critical to catalysing and channelling consumer purchasing power's influence into concrete change.[127] Starbucks' April 2000 adoption of fair trade coffee following anti-sweatshop activist successes, for example, illustrates exactly this effect.[128]

Unfortunately, the importance of image to transnationals often leaves them struggling to improve public relations instead of employment policy, with many either slipping away from inconvenient rights commitments or simply weathering the publicity storm. Effectively monitoring suppliers for labour-standard adherence is difficult and expensive for corporations[129] in an environment where shoppers react far more strongly to negative than positive human rights records.[130] There is also concern that such campaigns should not take the place of governmental measures to enforce core labour standards. As well, such campaigns often undergo significant resistance to including measures facilitating union organization, particularly where consumer support for union rights is weak.[131]

Yet, this often high-profile consumer advocacy has helped to give more prominence to labour rights on the public agenda. Resulting attention from policy-makers has had both bi- and multilateral impacts, ranging from the inclusion of incentives for industrial unionization in the 1999 Cambodian-US trade negotiations to Kofi Annan's "Global Compact" appeal in the same year for transnational business to respect nine core principles, including human and labour rights.[132]

Trade agreements and transnational corporations

National markets are significantly affected by forces and laws outside the country, including international or regional trade arrangements, the requirements of international financial institutions and transnational corporate business practices. Trade liberalization policies often tend to define social and economic regulation as "trade barriers". These forces are limiting the ability of individual states to exercise control over their labour market policies. Trade agreements negotiated at the transnational level have a profound impact on public policy, making it more difficult for governments to control their labour markets. The negotiation of trade agreements has been widely criticized for the lack of substantive labour and social protections including the protection of core labour standards as well as the lack of transparency.[133] Women's NGOs and unions are lobbying organizations such as the World Bank and the World Trade Organization to take steps to ensure that financing, development and trade practices promote gender equality rather than inequality. The current move to include "services" in trade agreements, a sector where women are clustered, will also have equality implications. The World Bank has enacted policies to integrate gender into its work and has taken significant steps but the progress is slow given the required time, resources and commitment needed from client countries.[134] Progress is even slower on the trade front.[135] There is considerable debate and research on how labour and human rights protections can be best addressed in a trade context, including whether core labour standards should be negotiated into trade agreements or left to the enforcement procedures of the ILO.[136]

Conclusion

As the preceding review illustrates, engendering the international labour law system is a complex multi-faceted process. Harnessing the full potential of a country to compete in a globalized world requires unleashing the full productive potential of its labour force. Nation states will not develop or prosper without ensuring the full participation of women and men in all aspects of social, political and economic life. Results-based, outcome-directed steps must be taken by international bodies, states, employers and unions to ensure that the international labour equality standards transcend to the national and local level in order that gender equality can become the reality for the world's women in their daily lives.

As women are empowered and work with advocacy, trade union and other civil society organizations, the process of "globalization from below" works towards the recognition and enforcement of women's employment rights. Such movements working with state and international actors and institutions seek to regulate and control the inequitable practices of the "globalization from above" forces – the movement of corporate enter-prises, markets and capital.[137] An engendered international labour law system will play a key role in bringing a measure of balance and equality to this struggle.

Notes

1. M. Cornish, "Engendering Citizenship and Labor Market Regulation – Interna-tional and Canadian Perspectives", presented at 5th Annual World Bank Gender and Law Conference, World Bank, Washington DC, 18–19 March 2003.

2. H. Arthurs, "Reinventing Labor Law for the Global Economy: The Benjamin Aron Lecture" (2001) 22(2) *Berkeley Journal of Employment and Labour Law* at 273.

3. See "Preliminary Report of the Special Rapporteur on Violence Against Women, its Causes and Consequences", cited in C. Chinkin, "Canada Women's Continued Economic Inequality" (2001) Gender and Globalization, UN Chronicle, online: http://www.globalpolicy.org/socecon/inequal/0221.htm; "A Fair Globalization: Creating Opportunities for All", Report of the World Commission on the Social Dimension of Globalization (ILO, Geneva, 2004), at 46–7 (World Commission, "Fair Globalization").

4. Cornish, "Engendering Citizenship", at 47.

5. ILO, *Global Employment Trends for Women 2004* (ILO, Geneva, 2004), at 1. See also, Diane Elson, "Progress of the World's Women", UNIFEM Biennial Report (UN Development Fund for Women, New York, 2000); *Time for Equality at Work: Report of the ILO Director General*, UN ILOOR, 2003, Report 1B, 92-2-112871-7 (ILO "Time for Equality"); World Commission "Fair Globalization", at 48.

6. Elson, "Progress of the World's Women", at 30.

7. The female employment share is rising throughout the developed world, the Caribbean, and Latin America. Asian countries have experienced only

moderate increases as women were most affected by the late 1990s financial crisis. Both women and men show losses in transition economies and Sub-Saharan Africa. See ILO "Time for Equality", at 41

8. Elson, "Progress of the World's Women", at 30. See also Cornish, "Engendering Citizenship", at 3–5.

9. ILO, "Global Employment Trends for Women", at Table 2.1

10. See *Progress of the World's Women: UNIFEM Biennial Report,* UN IFEMOR, 2000 at 92 [UNIFEM, 'Progress of Women 2000'].

11. ILO, "Time for Equality", at 54.

12. Note that in some countries indicators which point to a reduction in the gender wage gap are the result of the depression of men's wages rather than an increase in women's wages. See UNIFEM, 'Progress of Women 2002', at 37. See generally Cornish, "Engendering Citizenship", at 3.

13. ILO, "Global Employment Trends for Women", at 15.

14. K. Ruwanpura, "Quality of Women's Employment: A Focus on the South" (2004), Decent Work Research Programme, International Institute for Labour Studies, at 10–12, online: International Institute for Labour Studies, http://www.ilo. org/public/english/bureau/inst/research/crbien.htm; and R. Anker, "Theories of Occupational Segregation by Sex: An Overview" (1997), online: International Labour Review, http://www.ilo.org/public/english/support/publ/revue/ articles/ank97–3.htm.

15. Ruwanpura, "Quality of Women's Employment", at 10.

16. Ruwanpura, "Quality of Women's Employment", at 5–6.

17. See generally Cornish, "Engendering Citizenship", at 3–4. See generally, ILO, "Time for Equality", at 47–54. Women are also denied access to men's work because of the different "human capital" they bring to the labour market. For example, women outnumber men 2-to-1 among the world's 900 million illiterates. See Elson, "Progress of the World's Women", at 21.

18. See A. Obando, "Women Facing Globalization: The Impact of Neo-Liberal Globalization on the Economic, Social and Cultural Rights of Women", Women's Human Rights Net (2003), online: http://www.whrnet.org/docs/issue-globalisation.html.

19. See World Bank Gender and Development Group, *Gender Equality and the Millennium Development Goals* (World Bank, Washington DC, 2002), at 1.

20. Elson, "Progress of the World's Women", at 21. See generally, Cornish, "Engendering Citizenship", at 4.

21. Ruwanpura, "Quality of Women's Employment", at 5 and 22. See Cornish, "Engendering Citizenship", at 4; J. Fudge and L. Vosko, "Gender Paradoxes and the Rise of Contingent Work: Towards a Transformative Political Economy of the Labour Market", in Wallace Clement and Leah Vosko (eds.), *Changing Canada: Political Economy as Transformation* (University Press, Montreal and Kingston, 2003), 183–209.

22. See Elson, "Progress of the World's Women", at 60. See also United Nations, *The World's Women 2000: Trends and Statistics* (New York: UN, 2000).

23. See Elson, "Progress of the World's Women 2002", at 58–9. For example, Women in Eastern Europe and Central Asia work an average of 70 hours a week. Cornish, "Engendering Citizenship", at 4.

24. Cornish, "Engendering Citizenship", at 3–4.

25. ILO, "Global Employment Trends for Women" (2004), at 3–4, 10–12. See also International Labour Conference, *Women and Men in the Informal Economy: A Statistical Picture*, (Geneva: ILO, 2002) at 26 (ILC, "Informal Economy").

26. See *Working out of poverty: Report of the ILO Director General*, UN ILOOR, 2003, 92-2-112870-9 at 26–9. (ILO, "Poverty") See also Cornish, "Engendering Citizenship", at 3–5.

27. Cornish, "Engendering Citizenship", at 3–5.

28. See ILO, "Poverty", at 26.

29. K. Rittich, "Feminization and Contingency: Regulating the Stakes of Work for Women", in J. Conaghan, R. L. Fischl and K. Klare (eds.), *Labour Law in an Era of Globalization, Transformative Practices and Possibilities* (Oxford University Press, Oxford, 2002), at 117–36.

30. S. Russell-Brown, "Labor Rights as Human Rights: The Situation of Women Workers in Jamaica's Export Free Zones" (2003) 24 *Berkeley Journal of Employment and Labor Law* at 179–201.

31. Centre for Women's Resources, "The Life and Struggle of Women Workers under Contractualization", Asia Pacific Research Network (2003), online: http:www.aprnet.org.

32. Ruwanpura, "Quality of Women's Employment", at 9 and 25; World Commission, "Fair Globalization", at 47–8.

33. Fudge and Vosko, "Gender Paradoxes", at 197–9.

34. See International Labour Conference, *Decent Work and the Informal Sector*, UN ILOOR, 2002, Agenda Item Six, 92-2-112429-0, at 36–7. See also ILC, 'Informal Economy' at 28.

35. For example, although women made substantial advances in securing administrative and managerial positions through the mid-80s to mid-90s, their share of these types of jobs ultimately remained below 30 per cent in 43 of the 50 countries surveyed in UNIFEM'S biennial report. Elson, "Progress of the World's Women", at 91–5. Wage differentials are significant in those developing countries engaged in export-led industrialization or those that have export processing zones: ILO Director, "Time for Equality", at 45 and 52.

36. See generally Cornish, "Engendering Citizenship", at 4.

37. See M. Cornish, "Employment and Pay Equity in Canada – Success Brings Both Attacks and New Initiatives" (1996) 22 *Canada-United States Law Journal* 265–83; see also Cornish, "Engendering Citizenship", at 3–5.

38. See R. Anker et al., *Measuring decent work with statistical indicators,* Working Paper No. 2 (ILO Policy Integration Department, Geneva, 2002) on the concept of decent work indicators. See also Elson, "Progress of the World's Women 2002", at 30–7 regarding inequalities between working men and women.

39. K. Rittich, "Feminization and Contingency", at 122–5; and Ruwanpura, "Quality of Women's Employment", at 6–12.

40. Convention Concerning Equal Remuneration for Men and Women for Work of Equal Value, (ILO Convention No. 100), 29 June 1951, 165 U.N.T.S. 303 (entered into force 23 May 1953).

41. See M. Cornish, E. Shilton and F. Faraday, "Canada's International and Domestic Human Rights Obligations to Ensure Pay Equity: Obligations to Design an Effective Enforceable and Proactive Pay Equity Law", Research paper prepared for the Federal Pay Equity Review Task Force, Justice Canada, Ottawa (October 2002), online: http://canada.justice.gc.ca/en/payeqsal/2307.html (Cornish et al., "Pay Equity").

42. Convention Concerning Discrimination in Respect of Employment and Occupation, (ILO Convention No. 111), 25 June 1958, 362 U.N.T.S. 31 (entered into force 15 June 1960).

43. ILO Convention No. 111, at Arts. 1(b), 2.

44. Maternity Protection Convention, (Revised) (ILO Convention No. 183), International Labour Conference, Provisional Record, 88th Session Geneva, 15 June 2000, (entered into force 07 July 2002).

45. ILO Maternity Protection Convention, at Arts. 6, 8, 9 and 10.

46. Convention on Workers with Family Responsibilities, (ILO Convention No. 156), International Labour Conference, 67th Session Geneva, 23 June 1981 (entered into force 11 August 1983).

47. Termination of Employment Convention, (ILO Convention No. 158), International Labour Conference, 67th Session Geneva, 22 June 1982 (entered into force 23 November 1985).

48. Part Time Work Convention, (ILO Convention No. 175), International Labour Conference, 81st Session Geneva, 24 June 1994. (entered into force 28 February 1998).

49. Home Work Convention, (ILO Convention No. 177), International Labour Conference, 83rd Session Geneva, 20 June 1996 (entered into force 22 April 2000).

50. For other ILO Conventions which can be used to protect the rights of women workers, see generally: Underground Work (Women) Convention, 1935 (No. 45); Protection of Wages Convention, 1949 (No. 95); Social Policy (Basic Aims and Standards) Convention, 1963 (No. 117); Employment Policy Convention, 1964 (No. 122); Maximum Weight Convention, 1967 (No. 127); Minimum Wage Fixing Convention, 1970 (No. 131); Paid Educational Leave Convention, 1974 (No. 140); Rural Workers' Organizations Convention, 1975 (No. 141); Human Resources Development Convention, 1975 (No. 142); Employment Promotion and

Protection against Unemployment Convention, 1988 (No. 168); Night Work Convention, 1990 (No. 171).

51. *Declaration on Fundamental Principles and Rights at Work,* Geneva Conference, International Labour Conference, 86th Session, Geneva, June 1998 ("ILO 1998 Declaration").

52. Cornish et al., "Pay Equity".

53. In addition to the instruments and enforcement mechanisms set out below, there are also UN representatives and working groups that are critical in promoting and enforcing women's economic rights. Some of these include the UN Commission on the Status of Women, UN Special Rapporteurs, the Commission and Sub-Commission on Human Rights.

54. Universal Declaration of Human Rights, G.A. Res. 217 (III), UN GAIE, 3d Session, Supp. No. 13, UN Doc. A/810 at 71 (1948).

55. International Covenant on Civil and Political Rights, 16 December 1966, 999 UNTS 171.

56. International Covenant on Economic, Social and Cultural Rights, 16 December 1966, 993 UNTS.

57. General Assembly, UDHR at Arts. 16, 23 and 25.

58. International Covenant on Civil and Political Rights, at Arts. 7, 22 and 23.

59. International Covenant on Economic, Social and Cultural Rights, at Arts 6, 7, 8 and 10

60. Convention on the Elimination of All Forms of Discrimination Against Women, G.A. Res. 34/180, GAOR, 34th Session, Supp. No. 46 at 193 (1979).

61. By ratifying the convention, states are committed to: incorporating the principle of equality of men and women in their legal system; abolishing all discriminatory laws and adopting appropriate ones prohibiting discrimination against women; establishing tribunals and other public institutions to ensure the effective protection of women against discrimination; and ensuring elimination of all acts of discrimination of women by persons, organizations or enterprises.

62. See Convention on the Elimination of All Forms of Discrimination Against Women, at Part V; see also Cornish et al. "Pay Equity". See generally, UN "Division for the Advancement of Women", online: http://www.un.org/womenwatch/daw/cedaw.

63. Convention on the Elimination of All Forms of Discrimination Against Women, at art.11.

64. Declaration on the Right to Development, G.A. Res. 128, annex, U.N. GAOR, 41st Session, 97th plen. mtg., Supp. No. 53, at 186, U.N. Doc.A/41/53 (1986) ("Right to Development").

65. Vienna Declaration and Programme of Action, 12 July 1993, U.N. Doc A/CONF 157/23.

66. Report of the World Summit on Social Development, Copenhagen, 6–12 March 1995, UN Doc. A/CONF/166/9 (19 April 1995), Chap. 1, Annex 1.

67. United Nations, *Report of the Fourth World Conference on Women*, Beijing, China, 4–15 September 1995, A/CONF.177/20, 17 October 1995, Beijing, chap. 1, Resolution 1, Annex 1 ("Beijing Declaration") and Annex II ("Beijing Platform for Action").

68. See Cornish et al., "Pay Equity".

69. Beijing Platform for Action, at Strategic Objectives F.1, F.2, F.5.

70. Further Actions and Initiatives to Implement the Beijing Declaration and Platform for Action, GA Res. S-23/3, UN GAOR, 23rd Spec. Session, UN Doc. A/RES/S-23/3 (2000) ("Beijing + 5 Resolution").

71. EU Citizens can use the Charter of Fundamental Rights of the European Union to contest any decision which has been taken by any Community institution or member state who is implementing EU law, where a particular decision discriminates on the basis of sex. In addition, the European Social Charter requires member states to report to a Committee of Experts every two years on: the implementation of social rights related to work conditions; the right to protection of health and social security; and the rights of employed women. For more on this subject see: Employment and Social Affairs, "Simplification and improvement of legislation in the area of equal treatment of men and women" (2003), online: http://europa.eu.int/comm/employment_social/news/2003/jul/consultation_ en.html; and ILO, "Equal Opportunities in the European Union", online: http://www.ilo.org/public/english/ employment/gems/eeo/eu/eu_ main.htm

72. EC Council Directive O.J.L. 2000 303/16 on establishing a general framework for equal treatment in employment and occupation.

73. EC Council Directive 75/117 on the approximation of the laws of the members states relating to the application of the principle of equal pay for men and women, O.J.L. 1975 045/19.

74. EC Council Directive 2002/73, [2002] O.J.L. 269/15, on the implementation of the principle of equal treatment for men and women as regards to access to employment, vocational training and promotion, and working conditions.

75. EC Council Directive 97/80, [1998] O.J.L. 014/6, on the burden of proof in cases of discrimination based on sex.

76. EC Council Directive 79/7, [1998] O.J.L. 014/6, on the implementation of the principle of equal treatment for men and women in occupational social security schemes.

77. EC Council Directive 96/97, [1997] O.J.L. 046/11, on the implementation of the principle of equal treatment for men and women in occupational social security schemes.

78. EC Council Directive 86/613, [1986] O.J.L. 359/56, of 11 December 1986 on the application of the Principle of Equal Treatment between men and women engaged in an activity, including agriculture, in a self-employed capacity, and on the protection of self-employed women during pregnancy and motherhood.

79. EC Council Directive 92/85, [1992] O.J.L. 348/1, of 19 October 1992 on the introduction of measures to encourage improvements in the safety and health at work of pregnant workers who have recently given birth and are breast-feeding.

80. EC Council Directive 96/34, [1996] O.J.L. 145/4, of 3 June 1996 on the Framework agreement on parental leave.

81. See: Inter-American Convention on the Granting of Civil Rights to Women; the Inter-American Convention on the Granting of Political Rights to Women; American Convention on Human Rights; and the American Protocol to the American Convention on Human Rights in the Area of Economic, Social and Cultural Rights. For a more complete listing of resolutions in this area, see online: Inter-American Commission on Human Rights, http://www.cidh.oas.org/basic.eng.htm; see also "Regional Mechanisms", online: http://www.ilo.org/http://www.ilo.org/public/english/ employment/gems/eeo/inter/toc_main.htmpublic/english/employment/ gems/eeo.

82. See M. Cornish and V. Verma, *Enforcing International Standards in the Americas in an Era of Free Trade* (Canadian Bar Association, Ottawa, 30–31 May 2002). See generally online: North American Agreement on Labour Cooperation, http:// www.naalc.org/english/infocentre/whatisclc.htm.

83. The Carribean Community (CARICOM) mechanisms which address equal employment opportunities of women are: the Charter of Civil Society for the Caribbean Community; the Model Harmonization Act Regarding Equal-ity of Opportunity and Treatment in Employment and Occupation; The Employment (Equal Opportunity and Treatment) Act; the Model Legislation on Equal Pay; and the Model Legislation on Sexual Harassment. For more on this issue see: CARICOM online, ILO website, http://www.ilo.org/public/ english/employment/gems/eeo/cover/caricom_ main.htm

84. The Asia Pacific Gender Equality Network supports these mechanisms by address-ing regional issues of feminization of poverty and gender inequality in decision-making. For more on this issue, see Asia Pacific Economic Cooperation, ILO, online: http://www.ilo.org/public/english/employment/gems/eeo/inter/apec.htm. See also Asia Pacific Gender Network, UNDP, online: http://www.undp.org. ph/apgen/home1.htm; and Association of Southeast Asian Nations, ASEAN, online: http://www.aseansec.org/8685.htm.

85. In this declaration, member states called for: the appointment of a Commis-sioner with an exclusive mandate on gender issues; the establishment of a special-ized Technical Committee on Gender; operationalization of the African Women's Committee on Peace and Development, and the African women's network in the Working Group for the elaboration of the ECOSOCC Protocol; and guarantees of gender balance in all the organs of the African Union within a reasonable timeframe.

86. For more on this issue see "African Decade of Education", African Union, online: http://www.achpr.org; and "Basic Documents", African Commission on Human and People's Rights, online: http://www.achpr.org/html/basicinstruments.html.

87. Cornish, "Engendering Citizenship", at 7–16; and Chinkin, "Canada Women's Inequality".

88. United Nations, Beijing Declaration, at para. 7; United Nations, Beijing Platform for Action, at para. 4–5; Convention on the Elimination of All Forms of Discrimination Against Women, at Arts. 2 and 24; International Covenant on Economic, Social and Cultural Rights, at Art. 2.; Right to Development, at Preamble, Art.2(d).

89. Convention on the Elimination of All Forms of Discrimination Against Women at Preamble, Art.11(1); International Covenant on Economic, Social and Cultural Rights at Arts. 7(a) and 11.1; ILO, Convention No. 111, at Art.2(b)(vi).

90. Convention on the Elimination of All Forms of Discrimination Against Women; Beijing Declaration; and the Resolution Integrating the Human Rights of Women throughout the United Nations System.

91. ILO Convention No. 100 at Arts. 2.1 and 3.3; ILO Constitution, at Preamble; ILO 1998 Declaration; ILO Convention No. 111, at Art. 2(b)(v); General Assembly, UDHR at Art. 23.2; International Covenant on Economic, Social and Cultural Rights, at Art. 7(a)(i); Convention on the Elimination of All Forms of Discrimination Against Women, at Arts. 11.1 and 12.

92. See UN International Convention on the Protection of the Rights of Migrant Workers and Their Families, G.A. res. 45/158, annex, 45 U.N. GAOR Supp. (No. 49A), at 262, U.N. Doc. A/45/49 (1990), (entered into force 1 July 2003); UN Convention on the Suppression of Traffic in Persons and of the Exploitation and Prostitution of Others, 96 U.N.T.S. 271, entered into force July 25, 1951; UN Declaration of Elimination of Violence Against Women, G.A. res. 48/104, 48 U.N. GAOR Supp. (No. 49) at 217, U.N. Doc. A/48/49 (1993) (DEVAW).

93. ILO Workers With Family Responsibilities Convention, at Art. 7; ILO, Convention No. 111, at Art. 2(b)(iii); Right to Development, at Art.8; International Covenant on Economic, Social and Cultural Rights, at Art. 6(10) & 10.1; Convention on the Elimination of All Forms of Discrimination Against Women, at Art. 10(h), Art. 11.2(c); DEVAW at Art.2, Art.4; Beijing Declaration, at para. 82, 179(c), 180 (a), 190.

94. ILO Convention No. 100, at Art. 2; International Covenant on Economic, Social and Cultural Rights, at Art. 3; Convention on the Elimination of All Forms of Discrimination Against Women, at Arts. 2, 11 and 24; General Assembly, UDHR; Beijing Platform for Action, at para.165(a).

95. Convention on the Elimination of All Forms of Discrimination Against Women, at Art. 2(d).

96. Convention on the Elimination of All Forms of Discrimination Against Women at Art. 2(e); Convention No. 111, at Arts. 2 and 3.

97. Beijing Platform for Action, at para. 178(a), (h), (l) and (o).
98. ILO 1998 Declaration, at para. 178(h); General Assembly, UDHR at Art. 20.1 and 23.4; International Covenant on Economic, Social and Cultural Rights, at art. 8.1(a); International Covenant on Civil and Political Rights, at Art. 22.1.
99. Beijing Declaration, at para. 20.
100. International Covenant on Civil and Political Rights, at art. 3; Convention on the Elimination of All Forms of Discrimination Against Women, at art. 2(b)(d); Beijing Platform for Action, at para. 178(l).
101. See regarding reporting, monitoring and follow up: ILO Convention No. 100; International Covenant on Economic, Social and Cultural Rights; International Covenant on Civil and Political Rights; Convention on the Elimination of All Forms of Discrimination Against Women; Beijing Declaration; Beijing Platform for Action; and Beijing + 5 Resolution.
102. Ruwanpura, "Quality of Women's Employment", at 22.
103. Cornish, "Engendering Citizenship".
104. Cornish, "Engendering Citizenship".
105. The European Commission, "Community Framework Strategy on Gender Equality", European Commission (2001–2005), online: http://www.europa.eu. int/comm/employment_social/equ_pp/strategy/ 22_en.html (EC, "Community Framework")
106. EC, "Community Framework".
107. EC, "Community Framework", at 3
108. Ruwanpura, "Quality of Women's Employment", at 6.
109. Ruwanpura, "Quality of Women's Employment", at 6.
110. Ruwanpura, "Quality of Women's Employment", at 16.
111. Ruwanpura, "Quality of Women's Employment", at 11.
112. See L. Lim, "More and Better Jobs for Women: An Action Guide – An ILO Follow up to the Fourth World Conference on Women and the World Summit for Social Development" (International Labour Office, Geneva, 1996).
113. Fudge and Vosko, "Gender Paradoxes", at 202–4.
114. K. Rittich, "Feminization and Contingency", at 132.
115. Ruwanpura, "Quality of Women's Employment" at 6–8; and see Obando, "Women Facing", at 1–2.
116. Ruwanpura, "Quality of Women's Employment", at 17; and Cornish, "Engendering Citizenship", at 8.
117. M. Cohen, "Women Street Vendors: The Road to Recognition", 20 *SEEDS* (Population Council, New York, 2000).
118. Ruwanpura, "Quality of Women's Employment", at 19.
119. Ruwanpura, "Quality of Women's Employment", at 20–1; Decent Work and the Informal Economy Report VI, Geneva, ILO, 2002.
120. Ruwanpura, "Quality of Women's Employment", at 21.

121. Cornish and Verma, "Enforcing International Standards"; Cornish, "Engendering Citizenship", at 14.

122. K. Elliott and R. Freeman, "White Hats or Don Quixotes? Human Rights Vigilantes in the Global Economy", Working Paper 8102 (Massachusetts, National Bureau of Economic Research; A. Blackett, "Global Governance, Legal Pluralism and the Decentred State: A Labor Law Critique of Codes of Corporate Conduct" (2001) 8 (2) *Indiana Journal of Global Legal Studies* 401–47.

123. Ruwanpura, "Quality of Women's Employment", at 21.

124. Blackett, "Global Governance", at 401.

125. Blackett, "Global Governance", at 401, Elliot and Freeman, "White Hats", at 16.

126. Elliott and Freeman, "White Hats".

127. Blackett, "Global Governance", at 28.

128. Blackett, "Global Governance", at 29.

129. Blackett, "Global Governance", at 22.

130. Elliott and Freeman, "White Hats", at 9.

131. Blackett, "Global Governance", at 430–1, 436–40.

132. Elliott and Freeman, "White Hats", at 29–31.

133. Cornish and Verma, "Enforcing International Standards".

134. World Bank, *Workers in an Integrating World* (Oxford University, Washington DC, 2002).

135. S. Polaski, "Trade and Labour Standards: A Strategy for Developing Countries", Carnegie Endowment for International Peace, Issue Brief (2003).

136. Polaski, "Trade and Labour"; Cornish and Verma, "Enforcing International Standards".

137. Chinkin, "Canada Women's Inequality".

15

International labour law and the protection of migrant workers: revitalizing the agenda in the era of globalization

RYSZARD CHOLEWINSKI

" . . . Labour is not a commodity"
"All human beings, irrespective of race, creed or sex, have the right to pursue both their material well-being and their spiritual development in conditions of freedom and dignity, of economic security and equal opportunity"

Declaration of Philadelphia 1944.[1]

Introduction

The protection of migrant workers raises profound challenges for the role and efficacy of international labour law in the era of globalization. It is easy to be sceptical about future developments. The process of globalization has arguably widened the income gap between the traditional migrant receiving and sending countries, and the demand for cheap labour in the context of increasing and intense pressures to reduce labour costs threatens the continuation of an established international regime protecting the employment and human rights of migrant workers. The richer countries appear to hold all the cards in this process with the result that poorer countries have nominal bargaining power regarding the treatment of their workers abroad. Moreover, the standards adopted by the ILO and the UN to provide for migrant workers remain poorly ratified and inadequately implemented and the prospects for numerous further ratifications appear rather slim despite the considerable efforts undertaken to promote these standards, especially by civil society. Official resources for the promotion of the ratification of these instruments have also been lacking, a position often attributable to a perceived collusion among major receiving countries as well as between competent authorities in sending countries and private recruitment agencies not to further the issue of the protection of migrant workers.

This bleak picture depicting inaction and a chronic lack of political will on behalf of states at the international level, however, should be contrasted with the dynamism that labour migration generates in both sending and receiving countries. A number of sending countries view labour migration as an indispensable cog in the wheel of their economic development. With the remittances generated by the labour of their workers abroad often exceeding the income from development assistance, a number of sending countries have developed elaborate domestic policies that seek to promote the employment of their nationals overseas. Similarly, receiving countries experiencing structural labour shortages in both skilled and low-skilled sectors caused by demographic developments, which are characterized by ageing populations, and changes to employment practices, in themselves stimulated largely by globalizing trends, are competing for the readily available labour supply located in poorer sending countries. Consequently, receiving countries are also sometimes making complex amendments to their national immigration legal systems in order to accommodate and manage the entry and residence of diverse categories of migrant workers. Against the background of these dynamic developments in both sending and receiving countries, irregular movements take place,[2] facilitated by unscrupulous labour intermediaries and agents, and often fuelled by overly restrictive measures established by individual receiving countries and regional integration blocs, such as the European Union.

This dynamic response to labour migration at the national law and policy levels in the era of globalization contrasts starkly therefore with the inertia evident in the international community of states with regard to the acceptance of international labour and human rights standards protecting migrant workers and members of their families. Moreover, these standards are seen as dated and inflexible in the context of new economic and social realities and in the light of contemporary international labour migration trends.

This chapter begins with an overview of international labour law and its application to migrant workers and traces the specific protections that have been developed first by the ILO and then under the auspices of the UN. The focus is on universal rather than regional or bilateral standards, although it should be underlined that regional initiatives in particular are playing an important role in protecting migrant workers.[3] The chapter then considers the challenges facing international labour law for protecting migrant workers in the era of globalization. It examines the approaches and initiatives that are being developed to supplement and complement the international labour standards applicable to migrant workers. It concludes that these standards continue to be relevant and important and that their erosion cannot be squared with an agenda to protect migrant workers as human beings and with efforts to promote the orderly transnational movements of persons for the purpose of employment.

International Labour Organization and migrant workers

For a long time, the ILO was considered the principal organization concerned with the welfare of migrant workers. Indeed, it is constitutionally mandated to concern itself with this group.[4] In addition to the ethical rationale of protecting human beings in their working environment, the need for international regulation in this area was premised essentially on a utilitarian objective, namely to offset any economic and competitive disadvantages that might apply if governments were left to tackle these problems alone.[5] Such reasoning therefore has resonance for the ILO's continued relevance in the light of the economic challenges raised by globalization.

While the ILO has adopted specific instruments concerning migrant workers, all ILO standards, with very few exceptions,[6] apply to all workers regardless of nationality. Moreover, the eight fundamental conventions of the ILO[7] have special importance, as recognized by the ILO Declaration on Fundamental Principles and Rights at Work adopted by the International Labour Conference in June 1998.[8] The Declaration imposes obligations on all member states, including those that have not ratified the instruments in question, by virtue of their membership in the Organization to respect, promote and realize in good faith the principles concerning the fundamental rights which are the subject of those conventions.[9] The instruments discussed below relating to migrant workers are not considered as core ILO conventions, although the Declaration underscores the need to devote "special attention to the problems of persons with special needs, particularly the unemployed and migrant workers".[10]

The two legally binding instruments relating to migrant workers are Convention No. 97 of 1949 (C97) and Convention No. 143 of 1975 (C143), which are both buttressed by non-binding recommendations.[11] These conventions are concerned not only with the protection of migrant workers while in the country of employment but also apply to the whole labour migration continuum from entry to return. C97 covers the conditions governing the orderly recruitment of migrant workers and also enunciates the principle of their equal treatment with national workers in respect of working conditions, trade union membership and enjoyment of the benefits of collective bargaining, accommodation, social security, employment taxes and legal proceedings relating to matters outlined in the convention.[12] Its other objective is to ensure the orderly flow of migrants from countries with labour surpluses to countries with labour shortages, which is reflected in a number of its provisions as well as the annexes.[13]

While the state-organized context of fulfilling this objective is no longer applicable to many cases of labour migration, which is frequently organized by private intermediaries and increasingly spontaneous,[14] a number of states nonetheless seek to retain an element of control by actively managing the flow of migrant workers between them. This is evident in the recent proliferation of bilateral labour agreements between receiving and sending countries,[15] a development which ensures the continued relevance of the standards set out in C97 and the accompanying recommendation. The scope of C143 is broader. Adopted at a time when particular migration abuses, such as the smuggling and trafficking of migrant workers, were attracting the attention of the international community,[16] which is also the case today,[17] this instrument devotes a whole part to the phenomenon of irregular migration and to inter-state collaborative measures considered necessary to prevent it.[18] In keeping with the ILO's ethical prerogative of social justice and protecting all workers in their working environment, Article 1 of C143 imposes an obligation on states parties "to respect the basic human rights of *all* migrant workers",[19] which also confirms the applicability of this instrument to irregular migrant workers. While the ILO Committee of Experts on the Application of Conventions and Recommendations initially viewed this provision as applying essentially to traditional civil and political rights,[20] such a restrictive position is not reiterated in the Committee's more recent assessment of the migrant worker instruments.[21] This wider interpretation is particularly important given that most of ILO standard-setting can be reduced effectively to the right of everyone to just and favourable conditions of work recognized in Article 23 of the Universal Declaration of Human Rights (UDHR)[22] and Article 7 of the International Covenant on Economic, Social and Cultural Rights (ICESCR).[23] Moreover, Article 9(1) of Part I of C143 emphasizes explicitly that irregular migrant workers should be entitled to equal treatment in respect of "rights arising out of past employment as regards remuneration, social security and other benefits". Part II of C143, however, is limited to the integration of lawfully resident migrants with a view to promoting their equality of opportunity and treatment. Particularly enlightening provisions in this Part are contained in Article 10, which obliges states parties to declare and pursue a national policy designed to guarantee and promote equality of opportunity and treatment of migrant workers in a number of fields, including those that arguably go beyond the confines of their immediate working environment, such as cultural rights. One should similarly consider Article 14(a), by virtue of which states parties are only permitted to restrict free choice of employment for lawfully resident migrant workers to a maximum of two years. The liberal nature of some articles in C143, in contrast to more restrictive provisions in the complementary UN Convention on the Protection of the Rights of All Migrant Workers and Members of Their Families (MWC)[24] considered in Section 3 below, are partly explicable by the unique tripartite structure of the ILO where trade union and employer representatives participate actively in the adoption of international labour standards at the annual International Labour Conference and in the interim decision-making of the Governing Body. As noted by Virginia Leary, however, the advantages of tripartism have not been exploited fully in practice by workers' organizations by actively promoting measures concerning migrant labour in the same way as they have done in relation to other more "conventional" areas, such as freedom of association.[25] More generally, she concludes that "the lack of interest of ILO constituents – governments, labour, and employer organizations – inhibited ILO work on migrant labour despite formal commitments to regulating such labour since its founding".[26]

This last point is reinforced when the status of ratification of these ILO instruments is considered. In contrast to the fundamental "core" conventions of the ILO, the attempts at identifying legally binding international principles for the protection of migrant workers have not been generally well received by member states. While 42 states have ratified C97,[27] the broader C143 has received just 18 ratifications, with only four countries, all constituting the former Yugoslavia, having ratified the instrument since 1985.[28] Clearly, some of the liberal provisions identified above, which contrast starkly with national law and practice, constitute considerable legal impediments to the acceptance of these conventions.[29] This overall low rate of ratifications is exacerbated by the impossibility of states parties making reservations to particular labour standards, even though it is possible to selectively ratify parts of ILO instruments, such as the two parts of C143.[30]

The ILO has embarked recently on a new "integrated approach" to migrant workers, the principal objective of which is to "mainstream" the protection of this group in all its other activities (see the section "ILO and an 'Integrated Approach'" below). Nonetheless, it would be incorrect to conclude that the adoption of specific labour standards relating to migrant workers has had little or no impact in practice. First, while relatively few states have ratified the applicable instruments; those states that have accepted them encompass a diverse range of countries in all parts of the globe and, most importantly, include both sending and receiving countries, which is presently not the case with the ratification status of the UN's MWC discussed below. Second, ILO standards constituted the catalyst and model for the adoption of the MWC and many of these standards are reiterated in that instrument. But a number of the ILO standards represent also the highest level of protection afforded migrant workers at the international level given the deficiencies of the MWC in certain key areas such as trade union rights and access to employment. Third, ILO standards have made an impact in broad terms on domestic law in ILO member states and not merely in those countries that have formally accepted them as is underscored by the Committee of Experts in its 1999 General Survey.[31] With regard to ratifying states, the Committee has requested states parties on several occasions to re-examine their national law and practice in the light of the principles in these instruments.[32]

United Nations Convention on Migrant Workers

Given the ILO's constitutional concern for migrant workers, the need for the UN to intervene in this area was somewhat contentious. The reasons vary, ranging from the broader human rights mandate of the UN to the largely self-centred wishes of states to regulate the content of the final text without the formal intervention of other non-state parties, such as the social partners and civil society.[33] Given this latter justification, however, it is somewhat ironic that so few states (and no receiving countries) seem prepared to ratify the MWC and that the considerable efforts of civil society have been largely instrumental for its entry into force on 1 July 2003.[34]

The broader human rights mandate of the UN means that the MWC is in theory able to meet most of the concerns and interests of migrant workers and members of their families. As with the ILO standards, the MWC goes beyond the treatment of migrant workers in the country of employment and covers the entirety of the migration process, particularly with a view to the prevention of abuses. Part VI is devoted to this question and calls upon states parties to cooperate to prevent irregular migration and the exploitation of migrant workers, and to impose sanctions on smugglers, traffickers and employers of irregular migrant workers.[35] Moreover, because migrant worker remittances are a crucial economic benefit to sending countries in the developing world, the MWC also recognizes the right of migrant workers to transfer their earnings and savings and requires states parties to take appropriate measures to facilitate such transfers.[36] Given its broader scope, the MWC clearly protects irregular migrants as well as regular migrants and in Part III lists the fundamental rights to which all migrant workers should be entitled. Fernand de Varennes, however, argues that Part III "is much more than a reiteration of relevant international human rights provisions" because it emphasizes:

- that migrants – not just citizens – are entitled to the full protection of most international human rights standards [and]
- the necessity of clarifying the legal consequences of the proper application of general human rights standards to the particular situation of migrants.[37]

In addition to underlining the application of many of the traditional civil and political rights found in other more general human rights instruments to all migrant workers and their families, the MWC clarifies that basic economic, social and cultural rights apply to both regular and irregular migrant workers. It also contains some particularly positive provisions, such as the comprehensive procedural and substantive safeguards against expulsion found in Article 22. Despite these liberal provisions, however, some of the standards agreed to in the MWC clearly reflect its more state-centred ethos in contrast to the tripartite "tone" of ILO instruments. A significant provision in this respect is the so-called "sovereignty clause" in Article 79, which underlines that migrant worker admission policies remain within the jurisdiction of states parties:

> Nothing in the present Convention shall affect the right of each State Party to establish the criteria governing admission of migrant workers and members of their families. Concerning other matters related to their legal situation and treatment as migrant workers and members of their families, States Parties shall be subject to the limitations set forth in the present Convention.[38]

Further, as noted above, some of the more enlightened concepts in C143 have been watered down considerably in the MWC, such as access to employment where states parties are permitted to retain far more discretion. Moreover, while the MWC contains a more detailed definition of migrant worker than that found in ILO instruments, the rights of certain specific categories of temporary migrants, such as seasonal workers, project-tied workers or specified-employment workers, are curtailed explicitly in Part V of the MWC or remain entirely unprotected, such as in the case of students and trainees who are excluded from its scope (see also the section "Temporary migrant worker programmes" below).[39] The attempt in Part III of the MWC to list most of the basic human rights applicable to all migrant workers has also led to some rather odd results. In particular, a cursory reading of the convention's text would suggest that irregular migrant workers have no right to *form* their own trade unions. While such a reading might conform to the position adopted in certain individual state laws and would arguably, in certain limited circumstances, be in line with the rather controversial exception in Article 16 of the European Convention on Human Rights (ECHR),[40] which permits restrictions on the political activities of non-nationals in the context of the rights to freedom of expression, peaceful assembly and association,[41] it is nonetheless clearly contrary to the more general protections afforded by the UDHR and the ICESCR as well as Article 2 of the ILO Convention No. 87 of 1948 on Freedom of Association and Collective Bargaining.[42] Indeed, the ILO supervisory Committee on Freedom of Association, which draws its mandate from the ILO Constitution, concluded in March 2001 that the Spanish Foreigners' Law restricting migrants' trade union rights by making their exercise dependent on authorization of their presence or status in Spain was not in conformity with the broad scope of Article 2.[43] The Committee stated that Article 2 of Convention No. 87 covers all workers with the only permissible exceptions relating to the army and the police as provided for in Article 9.[44]

Shortcomings and gaps in the international labour migration and human rights standards concerning migrant workers

Despite the comprehensive nature of ILO labour standards pertaining to migrant workers and the vast coverage of the MWC, shortcomings and omissions have been identified. In its General Survey on C97 and C143 in 1999, the ILO Committee of Experts pointed to a number of developments, which are not fully addressed in these instruments and which are largely attributable to the way the migration landscape has changed since they were first adopted:

- the decreasing significance of the role of the state in the recruitment of migrant labour and the increasing importance of private agents and intermediaries (as discussed in the previous section above);
- the feminization of migrant labour with the overrepresentation of women migrant workers in "extremely vulnerable positions", particularly in the sex sector, characterized by a strong bond of subordination between the employer and employee and the exclusion of the sectors concerned from the protection of labour law;
- the increasing short-term nature or temporariness of labour migration;
- the considerable growth in irregular migration and the need to balance control measures in countries of employment with measures to facilitate labour migration and to protect migrant workers; and
- the growth of certain means of transport, such as air travel, which renders some of the provisions out of date.[45]

In particular, the protection challenges posed by the feminization of the migrant labour force and the increasing resort to temporary work are not adequately reflected in these instruments or in the MWC.

Feminization of the migrant labour force

Women migrant workers find themselves frequently in unregulated low-skilled employment in destination countries, such as domestic work, as carers for children and the elderly, or in so-called sex work.[46] Furthermore, this employment tends to be irregular, unprotected by labour legislation and, often in the case of sex work, facilitated by criminal trafficking networks. Indeed, the economic pressures of globalization, discussed in Section 6 below, have arguably exacerbated the exploitation of migrant women.[47] While the ILO and UN conventions contain specific provisions combating trafficking,[48] they do not instruct party-states to devote particular attention to the types of employment in which women predominate. Certain categories of workers, such as seasonal workers in the MWC, in which male migrants predominate, are identified separately,[49] but there is no specific reference to domestic work. However, a note of caution should be advanced against the identification of separate categories of migrant workers in these instruments as this does not necessarily advance their protection. Indeed, the specific categories, including seasonal workers, listed in the MWC, are accompanied by somewhat lesser safeguards (see the following section). In this regard, the ILO Committee of Experts contends also that a revision of the categories of "artistes" and "members of the liberal profession" in the ILO instruments may well be necessary, "particularly in light of the extent of the phenomenon of women migrant workers being recruited for such employment only to find themselves working in the sex sector".[50]

Temporary migrant worker programmes

The growth in temporary work opportunities for migrants has resulted in a number of difficulties in ensuring their protection. In a comparative study of six temporary migrant worker programmes in five countries (Germany, Kuwait, Singapore, Switzerland and the United States), the following protection problems were identified in some of these schemes: their time-limited duration; the lack of possibilities to switch to a more secure residence status and for family reunion; restrictions on employment (to a specific employer and employment sector), wages and savings; the absence of social protection; and other restrictions unrelated to employment, such as a prohibition on marrying citizens and becoming pregnant (in the case of temporary migrant workers and female domestic workers in Singapore).[51] A study focusing on the legal status of migrants admitted for employment in selected European countries drew similar conclusions. As a general rule, migrant workers admitted on a short-term basis encountered obstacles, in particular to liberalize their employment opportunities and to access a secure residence status and the full range of social security in the country of employment.[52] Therefore, it would seem that the increase in temporary migrant labour is often accompanied by the proliferation of a confusing array of different legal statuses, which tend on the whole to dilute further the protections afforded such migrant workers in the country of employment.[53] Moreover, temporary migrant workers are vulnerable to certain abuses in the recruitment process, which is a particular problem faced by unskilled workers using the services of private recruitment agents who compete intensely for the sale of their labour to employers in the destination country. Such abuses include deliberate misinformation about the working and living conditions in the country of employment and the charging of excessive fees. The requirement that employers sponsor migrant workers also results in abuses such as late payment of wages, contract substitution, restrictions on freedom of movement, and, in some cases, physical or sexual intimidation.[54]

Importantly, C97, C143 and the MWC do not generally distinguish between migrant workers admitted for settlement and those admitted for short-term employment in terms of their protection, although some adjustments are made to cater for particular categories of temporary work. C143 excludes specific categories of temporary migrant workers from Part II, including artists and members of the liberal professions who have entered the country on a short-term basis, students and trainees, and certain types of protect-tied migrants.[55] On the other hand, the MWC provides that all workers, except students and trainees who are excluded entirely,[56] can benefit from the rights in Parts III and IV, although, in Part V, states parties may limit some of the rights in Part IV in respect of certain categories of temporary migrant workers, such as seasonal workers, project-tied workers, and specified-employment workers. This limitation is set in general terms in Article 59(1) in respect of seasonal workers, who are entitled to those rights in Part IV "that can be applied to them by reason of their presence and work in the territory of the State of employment and that are compatible with their status in that State as seasonal workers, taking into account the fact that they are present in that state for only part of the year". While this provision would appear to enable states parties to exclude seasonal workers from such rights as vocational training and family reunion, it has been argued that it is a flexible clause which does not *require* states parties to exclude seasonal migrants from these rights and thus reflects the drafters' intention "to secure the widest possible rights for this category of temporary migrant workers".[57]

As far as project-tied and specified-employment migrant workers are concerned, both are excluded from the following rights in Part IV: access to vocational guidance and placement services and vocational training, social housing, and free choice of employment.[58] In addition, project-tied migrant workers are excluded from further rights in Articles 53 to 55 concerning equal treatment with national workers in respect of protection against dismissal, unemployment benefits, access to public work schemes intended to combat unemployment, access to alternative employment in the event of loss or termination of work, and equal treatment in respect of the exercise of a remunerated activity, while their family members are excluded from any right to free choice of employment.[59] Some of the other rights provided for in Part IV are also modified in Part V in respect of project-tied migrants, namely social security protection, which is to be provided, subject to any bilateral or multilateral agreements in force for the states concerned, by the social security system of the country of origin or habitual residence.[60] While the provisions concerning this particular category of migrant workers appear to have been adopted as a compromise position to take account of the fact that most such workers at the time of drafting were found in the Gulf States and in recognition that certain rights such as free access to employment and social housing were largely meaningless for this group,[61] it is arguable nonetheless that the restrictions in terms of their employment conditions are not compatible entirely with the general standards existing elsewhere in both UN human rights and ILO instruments.

The growth in temporary migrant worker programmes in a number of receiving countries is one of the features of the "flexibilization of labour", which has been caused by globalization further discussed below ("Protecting migrant workers in the era of globalization"). The comparative study of these programmes concludes that, though different in design, they have generated similar adverse consequences supporting the negative argument that they do not work.[62] In addition to the particular vulnerabilities suffered by temporary migrant workers and noted above, these consequences include: the emergence of "immigrant sectors" in the host economy that employ, primarily or exclusively, foreign workers; the tendency of programmes to become longer in duration and larger in size than originally envisaged; the opposition of local workers to the introduction and expansion of programmes; and the emergence of irregular migrant workers, who together with local employers, circumvent these programmes.[63] However, rather than recommend that such programmes be dispensed with, the study proposes several policy principles for making them work, and thus benefiting receiving countries' economies by meeting their structural demand for labour, on the basis that most countries simply do not possess viable alternatives to temporary migrant worker programmes.[64] Interestingly, four of the policy principles proposed would, if implemented, augment migrant workers' rights: (i) an element of free movement within the receiving country's labour market, which would reduce the worker's dependence and thus vulnerability on his or her sponsor, i.e. the employer, and also increase the efficiency of the host country's labour market by enabling migrant workers to respond to wage differentials; (ii) the establishment of clear rules and procedures for the transfer of migrant workers into programmes that grant them permanent residence (and for their return home if permanent residence is not granted), in recognition of the fact that in practice a proportion of temporary migrant workers are permitted in any event to stay indefinitely in the host country and to bring their families; (iii) legalization of the status of all migrant workers who have been illegally employed in the host country for a certain amount of years without having been apprehended and deported by existing law enforcement measures, which is in the interest of all regular workers (both national and foreign) because of the existence of labour market competition from irregular workers, who are in the position to undermine the wages and working conditions of the former; and (iv) the implementation of a unified temporary worker programme to accommodate all skill levels (which is not the position presently because most countries operate more liberal programmes for skilled migrant workers), on the basis that the decisive factor in the employment of a migrant worker is whether his or her skill level is in demand in the host economy.[65] These proposals indicate vividly that affording protection to migrant workers is associated closely with the efficiency and success of such programmes.

Obstacles to ratification

In addition to the "protection gaps" identified above, the reluctance of states to agree to legally binding multilateral instruments regulating international labour migration and protecting the rights of migrant workers remains a chronic problem. In conducting its General Survey in 1999 on the principal ILO instruments on migrant workers, the Committee of Experts, in addition to the legal difficulties that a number of liberal provisions give rise to as noted in Section 2 above, identified the following principal obstacles to their ratification:

- the incompatibility of national legislation with the instruments' provisions in many sending and receiving countries;
- the lack of financial resources to implement the instruments in the context of the additional workload for national labour administrations that implementation would entail;
- the existence of a difficult economic situation and high unemployment rates in some countries with the result that preference is given to national over foreign labour;
- the relative novelty of international labour migration for a number of countries (e.g. Azerbaijan, China, Romania and Tajikistan) and the need to develop appropriate national measures;
- the specificity of the labour market in certain countries (for example, the high proportion of foreigners in the labour force in countries such as Bahrain and Luxembourg);
- the view of some major sending countries (e.g. Mexico and Pakistan) that the instruments are primarily concerned with addressing labour shortages in countries of employment rather than the needs of sending countries.[66]

Some of these obstacles also apply to the non-ratification of the MWC, such as its incompatibility with national legislation in many countries and the technical implementation challenges it poses for domestic administrations given the size of the text and its complexity. Other obstacles relate to the general lack of awareness and knowledge of the MWC, the absence of adequate promotional activity, and, most importantly, lack of political will.[67] In an interesting empirical study undertaken for UNESCO on obstacles to the ratification of the MWC in seven countries in the Asia-Pacific region, Nicola Piper and Robyn Iredale identify two major hurdles applicable to sending and receiving countries respectively. First, sending countries fear that ratification will result in a loss of labour markets in destination countries to their non-ratifying competitors. The authors argue that this hurdle can be offset by collaboration among sending countries in the region and the encouragement of regional leadership by a country such as the Philippines, which is widely regarded to be the model sending country in the Asia-Pacific and which has undertaken innovative steps to protect its workers abroad as discussed in the section "Innovative national approaches" below. Second, receiving countries face sensitive political obstacles connected with the protections afforded by the MWC to irregular migrants as well as the perception that it requires the admission of family members of migrant workers. The study concludes that before ratification of the MWC can be contemplated in receiving countries, efforts should focus on changing domestic laws and policies, which can then be complemented by the drafting of a non-binding recommendation or declaration.[68]

Protecting migrant workers in the era of globalization

The era of globalization sets forth a number of challenges for the protection of migrant workers and indeed all persons in their working environment. Growing economic interdependence among states is a well-recognized feature of globalization,[69] as is the freer flow of information, ideas and human values.[70] In the economic sphere, globalization is not only characterized by liberalization of trade, services, investment and capital but also by transnational movements of persons to better their lives and in response to employment opportunities elsewhere. The dynamics of these processes and their impact on both sending and receiving countries have resulted in an increase in international labour migration. In most sending countries, globalization is seen as "contributing to migration pressures, since only a few developing countries have succeeded in exporting manufactures and as a consequence income and wage differentials between the developed and the less developed regions have further widened".[71] Consequently, sending countries have experienced a "serious social and economic dislocation associated with persistent poverty, growing unemployment, loss of traditional trading patterns and . . . a 'growing crisis of economic security'".[72] It is hardly surprising therefore that this insecurity, with little prospect for improvement in the short to medium term, motivates citizens in those countries to improve the economic conditions for themselves and their families by seeking employment abroad. The more intense competition generated by globalization has also resulted in a profound restructuring of employment in developed and industrialized countries as well as in a number of developing countries, particularly in lower skilled sectors, such as agriculture, food-processing, construction, and manufacturing, and low-wage services such as domestic work, home health care and the sex sector. Because companies and employers operating in these labour-intensive sectors cannot relocate abroad, they have introduced other measures to remain competitive, including downgrading manufacturing processes, deregulation, and the introduction of flexibility into their labour force, with a greater emphasis on cost-cutting and sub-contracting. Given that available or unemployed national workers are unwilling to fill these jobs for a variety of reasons, namely poor pay, dangerous conditions, the low status of these jobs and the existence of alternative welfare provision, migrant workers and increasingly irregular migrants have stepped in to fill the demand.[73]

Although the processes of globalization have contributed to the growing labour migration pressures in sending countries and the demand for such labour in receiving countries, the movement of workers (the most abundant factor of production in labour-sending countries) has not been facilitated in the same way as the flow of capital, goods and services. Indeed, the result has actually been the restriction of such movements.[74]

While these developments, particularly those in receiving countries concerned with deregulation and flexibilization of employment practices, undermine the traditional protections afforded to all workers, they are especially damaging to migrant workers because their exploitation is often seen as a tool in maintaining competitiveness at the expense of formal employment and human rights protections.[75] In this economic climate, therefore, the need to protect all workers and particularly migrant workers, both those lawfully resident and those in an irregular situation, is becoming paramount. Indeed, this was one of the reasons for the adoption of the ILO Declaration on Fundamental Principles and Rights at Work as recognized in its final recital: "Whereas it is urgent, in a situation of growing economic interdependence, to reaffirm the immutable nature of the fundamental principles and rights embodied in the Constitution of the [ILO] and to promote their universal application."[76]

Supplementary and complementary approaches to standard-setting

The relatively low rate of ratification of international labour instruments together with their poor implementation has resulted in the development of alternative significant approaches to the protection of migrant workers, some of which are connected with the promotion of the acceptance of the above standards while others exist independently of this objective. Such approaches can be seen in recent arguments propounded by the ILO; activities in the UN and particularly the reports and activities of the Special Rapporteur on the human rights of migrants; the work and programmes of intergovernmental organizations, such as the International Organization for Migration (IOM) and UNESCO; the growing mobilization of civil society; and innovative national approaches by sending countries to protect their workers in light of the inertia existing at the international level. While not an exhaustive overview,[77] this part of the chapter illustrates the growing solidarity of certain actors in the international community with labour migrants and their plight, which has revitalized the agenda regarding the protection of this particularly vulnerable group of workers.

ILO and an "integrated approach"

The ILO Committee of Experts recommended two options to the Governing Body for addressing the difficulties posed by the relatively low rate of ratification of C97 and C143: (i) to maintain the status quo by recognizing the problems member states experience in accepting any legally binding international standards on labour migration accompanied by a vigorous promotion of the existing standards, with the possible elaboration of supplementary protocols to address the gaps and shortcomings in these instruments; or (ii) the complete revision of the two instruments, preferably into one single detailed or framework convention.[78] In response, the Governing Body earmarked a general discussion on migrant workers based on an "integrated approach" at the June 2004 International Labour Conference. Such an approach would recognize that:

> ... the issues raised by migrant workers for economic and social policy on the one hand, and the protection of human rights on the other, cut across practically all spheres of the normative and technical activities of the ILO ... An integrated approach would thus comprise a programmatic response to the issues of migrant workers in a cooperative and comprehensive process among the various concerned ILO sectors and units. It would also allow for a more comprehensive review of the question of whether and how the instruments need to be revised.[79]

The integrated approach would "offer an opportunity to examine in greater depth the need for social dialogue in fostering consensus on migration policy at national and international levels" given that "tripartism is not yet accepted as an operative principle in structuring decision-making in this important area of public policy", and would also enable the ILO to consider how to "further elaborate and strengthen its role beyond standard-setting in promoting more orderly forms of labour migration".[80] The Governing Body suggested that issues for discussion might include: international labour migration in the era of globalization, with a focus on the formulation of policy responses to ensure that the rights of migrant workers are safeguarded while at the same time enabling them to contribute to the growth and development of countries of employment and countries of origin; policies and structures for more orderly labour migration; and the improvement of the protection of migrant workers through standard-setting, which would consider whether existing ILO standards should be promoted or revised, as well as their complementarity with the MWC.[81] In preparation for the conference discussion on migrant workers, the ILO's International Migration Programme sent to all its member state governments a comprehensive survey on international labour migration, which was to be completed by the beginning of September 2003.[82] The aims of the survey were to obtain the latest information on: the ways in which labour migration and the treatment of migrant workers are being regulated or managed through laws, policies and administrative action; the role played by bilateral and multilateral treaties (with a focus on ILO instruments); and how the social partners participate in the process.[83]

UN activities: Special Rapporteur on the human rights of migrants and the World Conference against Racism

The Special Rapporteur on the human rights of migrants was appointed by the UN Commission on Human Rights at its 55th Session in 1999 for an initial three-year period with a view to examining "ways and means to overcome the obstacles existing to the full and effective protection of the human rights of this vulnerable group, including obstacles and difficulties for the return of migrants who are non-documented or in an irregular situation",[84] and with the following functions:

- to request and receive information from all relevant sources, including migrants themselves, on violations of the human rights of migrants and their families;
- to formulate appropriate recommendations to prevent and remedy violations of the human rights of migrants, wherever they may occur;
- to promote the effective application of relevant international norms and standards on the issue;
- to recommend actions and measures applicable at the national, regional and international levels to eliminate violations of the human rights of migrants;
- to take into account a gender perspective when requesting and analyzing information, as well as to give special attention to the occurrence of multiple discrimination and violence against migrant women.[85]

Ms Gabriela Rodríguez Pizarro from Costa Rica was appointed as the Special Rapporteur and her mandate was extended for a further three years by the Commission on Human Rights at its 58th Session in 2002.[86] As noted by Patrick Taran, the appointment of a Special Rapporteur in this field indicates that the human rights abuses suffered by migrants warrant the same attention of the international community as torture and violence against women.[87] While her mandate is broad and covers the human rights of all migrants, the Special Rapporteur's work and activities hold special resonance for the situation of migrant workers. Indeed, she has issued three general reports, which include an examination of the situation of migrant workers.[88] In her general report, submitted to the 59th Session of the Commission on Human Rights in 2003, the Special Rapporteur describes the urgent appeals she sent to, and normal communications with, governments concerning the treatment of migrant workers in a diverse range of countries of employment, for example: physical abuses suffered by Bolivian migrant workers and their families in Argentina;

the plight of a pregnant Indonesian domestic worker accused of adultery in the United Arab Emirates; the living, work and health conditions of (mostly) irregular migrant workers in the Spanish region of Andalusia; and the situation of Haitian labour migrants working in the sugar cane fields of the Dominican Republic.[89]

Moreover, the Special Rapporteur has played an important role in promoting the MWC. Rather curiously, however, while the two Commission on Human Rights resolutions concerned with her mandate and its renewal request states to effectively protect and promote migrant rights with explicit reference to the core human rights treaties and also urge states to ratify the Convention against Transnational Crime and its Anti-Trafficking and Smuggling Protocols,[90] there is no explicit mention of the MWC. This again probably reflects the sensitivities of many countries to the mere existence of this instrument.

The Special Rapporteur's mandate to consider the particular position of migrant women is especially relevant to highlighting the human rights abuses suffered by women migrant workers. In her first country visit to Canada, the Special Rapporteur's report contains a separate section on the situation of live-in caregivers, which underlines the generally positive features of this programme, but also highlights some of the problems faced by this group of migrants, such as difficulties in reporting mistreatment in their employment because of the need for a positive reference from the former employer in order to obtain work elsewhere.[91] The report draws attention also to the problems of temporary workers and specifically agricultural workers employed under agreements with Mexico and the Caribbean countries,[92] such as the long hours some are required to work and pressures exerted on them by their employers not to complain in the event of abuse.[93] The Special Rapporteur encourages the Canadian Government to ratify the MWC.[94] Since her visit to Canada, the Special Rapporteur has also visited and reported on Mexico,[95] the Mexican-US border,[96] and the Philippines.[97] The MWC figures prominently in two reports. In the report focusing on the Mexican-US border, the Special Rapporteur also encourages the United States to consider ratifying the MWC.[98] With regard to Mexico, which has ratified the instrument, the Special Rapporteur's comments focus on harmonizing domestic legislation and policy with the MWC and implementation of its provisions.[99]

The entry into force of the MWC will not diminish the importance of the work of the Special Rapporteur, particularly given the current low rate of ratifications of this instrument and the persistent reluctance of receiving countries to commit themselves to its provisions.[100] A notable example of the Special Rapporteur's broader role in raising the profile of the human rights of migrants was her participation in the preparatory meetings for the 2001 World Conference against Racism, Racial Discrimination, Xenophobia and Related Tolerance in Durban, as well as the conference itself, which contributed to the inclusion of 45 paragraphs on migrants in the conference's Declaration and Programme of Action.[101] These "soft law" instruments contain a number of specific references to migrant workers, particularly the Declaration's reaffirmation of the necessity of eliminating racial discrimination against migrant workers in respect of employment, social services, including education and health, as well as access to justice,[102] and the Programme of Action's call to states:

> . . . to design or reinforce, promote and implement effective legislative and administrative policies, as well as other preventive measures, against the serious situation experienced by certain groups of workers, *including migrant workers*, who are victims of racism, racial discrimination, xenophobia and related intolerance.[103]

The Programme of Action underlines further that "special attention should be given to protecting people engaged in domestic work and trafficked persons",[104] and states are urged to consider signing and ratifying C97 and C143 and the MWC.[105]

International Organization for Migration

While not a standard-setting organization like the ILO, the IOM is committed to the principle that "humane and orderly migration benefits migrants and society"[106] and seeks to implement this principle in all its programmes, projects and activities. Increasingly, the IOM has highlighted the protection of the human rights of migrants as an integral aspect of its operations.[107] The IOM Constitution mandates activities in the labour migration field in the context of the provision of migration services.[108]

In May 2002, the IOM launched a new Labour Migration Service Area, which acts as the focal and coordinating point for the development of IOM projects and technical support in, inter alia, the following thematic areas:

• government capacity building in labour migration management by training officials and policy advice with a view to assisting developing countries and countries in transition, particularly in Africa and Asia, to promote foreign employment of part of their labour force;

- pre-departure training and orientation of labour migrants;
- administration of selective bilateral labour migration programmes, particularly the pre-selection and transportation of migrants;
- reception and better integration of migrant workers in host countries by reinforcing the capacity of civil society;
- enhancement of the development impact of remittances by facilitating transfers as well as the exchange of migrant ideas, knowledge and experience.[109]

While these activities span the whole migration spectrum from departure to return, they contribute to the protection of migrant workers by focusing in particular on the lawfulness of the movements. Moreover, they provide assistance to both sending and receiving countries for strengthening their institutional capacities concerning the travel, reception and treatment of migrant workers. The IOM has also played a coordinating role in promoting regional dialogue by bringing together government officials from countries involved in international labour migration. One recent meeting was the ministerial-level consultations of Asian labour-sending countries, convened in Colombo, Sri Lanka, in April 2003, which included among its recommendations the need to protect migrant workers from exploitative practices in recruitment and employment and provide them with appropriate services, such as pre-departure information and assistance, welfare assistance during their stay abroad and reintegration assistance on their return home.[110]

United Nations Educational, Scientific and Cultural Organization

Through its International Migration and Multicultural Policies Section, UNESCO disseminates information about the MWC and promotes its signature and ratification. Greater protection for the human rights of migrant workers and their families is seen as an integral element in UNESCO's work on promoting social cohesion and integration of migrants in culturally diverse societies, thus combating their marginalization and exclusion.[111] The International Migration Section has produced a useful information kit on the MWC,[112] which contains an overview of its principal provisions, the background to its adoption and entry into force, some basic facts about international migration, and also attempts to dispel a number of the myths about obstacles to its ratification. Most pertinently, the information kit underscores that the MWC "is not an instrument for more liberal immigration policies":

It does not propose any new set of rights that would be specific to migrants. It only ensures that human rights are properly applied to migrant workers. States that already respect human rights and that have ratified other human rights instruments therefore have no reason to resist ratifying the Convention.[113]

The role of civil society

The increasing attention devoted to the rights and conditions of migrant workers by the international community is attributable in large part to the role of civil society and particularly NGOs. The work of NGOs can be divided broadly into three fields of activity, which overlap and complement one another. The first is concerned with intense lobbying on the promotion of the ratification of the MWC. In March 1998, NGOs, together with a number of international and intergovernmental organizations, such as the Office of the UN High Commissioner of Human Rights, UNESCO, ILO, IOM, and the International Confederation of Free Trade Unions, set up the International Steering Committee for the Campaign for the Ratification of the Migrants Rights Convention.[114] Whereas only eight countries had ratified the instrument at that time, the success of this venture is reflected in the fact that the MWC received the necessary 20 ratifications to enter into force in July 2003 and has now been ratified by 25 states.[115] Other pertinent accomplishments include the proclamation by the UN General Assembly of 18 December (the date of the adoption of the MWC in 1990) as International Migrants' Day,[116] and the appointment of the Special Rapporteur on the human rights of migrants. Migrant NGOs, such as December 18, Migrant Rights International, the International Catholic Migration Commission, and the Migrant Forum in Asia, have led the activities centring on the ratification of the MWC.[117] The second field of activity concerns long-established NGOs, such as Amnesty International, Human Rights Watch and the World Council of Churches, which have also begun to voice their concerns about the treatment of migrant workers. For example, Human Rights Watch, which is a member of the International Steering Committee, runs a project on migrants' rights drawing particular attention to abuses suffered by irregular migrants, including undocumented workers.[118] Furthermore, the plight of irregular migrant workers in Europe has been given further prominence by the establishment of an NGO coalition, the Platform for International Cooperation on Undocumented Migrants (PICUM), to identify their concerns and to promote respect for their human rights.[119] Thirdly, NGOs often fill the "protection gap" by providing migrant workers with services, which are the subject of state obligations identified in the legal instruments on migrant workers, such as the provision of information and orientation services to migrants in countries of origin as well as return and reintegration assistance, and housing, education, health care, social welfare and legal services in countries of employment.[120]

Innovative national approaches

In the absence of the acceptance by receiving and sending countries of a robust international regime protecting the rights of migrant workers and with a pragmatic acknowledgment that the international labour migration system is heavily weighted in favour of receiving countries, sending countries have sought to develop innovative national "self-help" approaches. The Philippines, a model sending country in this respect, has rooted its migrants' protection policy in a form of Institutional Capacity Building (ICB).[121] In the view of the former Administrator of the Philippine Overseas Employment Administration (POEA), Tomas Achacoso, ICB should rank alongside other mechanisms protecting and promoting the welfare of migrant workers, such as standard-setting and enforcement, supervision of private recruitment and welfare services.[122] The "self-help" orientation of this approach is apparent:

> Much lip service has been given to the goal of promoting and protecting the rights and welfare of [overseas contract workers] but few are willing to attempt to build it. We must stop hoping for some *deus ex machina* to show the way – we only have ourselves. We should never forget that structures condition people but people create and transform structures.[123]

The Philippines is a sending country, which, like Pakistan and Sri Lanka, operate a "state-managed" policy actively promoting the employment of their nationals overseas.[124] The advantages of such a system over private recruitment, however, can only be realized if an adequate public infrastructure organizing and promoting foreign employment is put into place.[125]

The focus of the Philippines' government's policy is concerned with enforcing combatting contractual obligations between migrant workers and employers and the practice of "contract-substitution" whereby contracts signed by workers in the country of origin and approved by the national authorities are substituted by less protective contracts before departure or on arrival in the country of employment.[126] The Philippines has adopted three devices (both legal and non-legal) to counter the difficulties existing in this area. First, employers cannot recruit workers directly in the Philippines and must undertake recruitment through agencies registered and licensed by the POEA. Employers then have to agree to be jointly responsible with the agency in the Philippines under its law for any claims and liabilities arising in connection with the implementation of the employment contract. This legal device favours migrant workers by recognizing the practical obstacles faced in seeking a remedy in the country of employment, although foreign employers retain control over the selection of workers in sending countries and can also impose a "performance bond" not exceeding the cost of a one-way airfare to ensure repatriation to the country of origin in the event of non-performance of the worker's contractual obligations.[127] A second non-legal device involves the conclusion of informal understandings with embassies and consular officials in receiving countries to issue visas only to Filipino workers approved by the POEA or on the employment conditions under which such workers migrate to those countries.[128] A third device is the compulsory Pre-Departure Orientation Seminar designed to assist and provide information to workers who have succeeded in obtaining employment to prepare for work and life abroad.[129]

Conclusion: the continuing need for international labour and human rights standards

While the processes of globalization threaten to undermine further the fragile international regime in place for the protection of migrant workers, the employment and human rights standards discussed in this chapter remain of fundamental importance to the realization of a dignified and orderly system of international labour migration. In a recent work entitled *Elusive Protection, Uncertain Lands: Migrants' Access to Human Rights*, Bimal Ghosh advances what he terms as three "powerful" arguments why it is in the interests of nation-states to protect all migrants (and not only migrant workers).[130] Ghosh depicts the tension states experience between their concern for human rights and fulfilment of their political, strategic and commercial interests, giving rise to "the cleavage between the declarations of principles or even formal commitments by governments at the international level, and their actual performance at home, especially in relation to non-nationals".[131] His first argument is rooted in ethics and law and accords with the general consensus and recognition that human rights apply to all without any distinctions, including distinctions based on citizenship status.[132] The remaining arguments, while not undermining the rationale for a universal set of human rights

standards, are pragmatic and utilitarian and based on the individual interests of states in protecting their citizens abroad. This is a goal best achieved
through international cooperation and agreement on reciprocal obligations towards non-nationals resident and working in their territories, and
through "the collective interest of nation states in maintaining orderliness
in the movement of people across countries as an important element in
global peace and security".[133] While these arguments are not necessarily new, they attempt to rationalize persuasively the apparent "unholy"
alliance between ethical principles and state interests, which echoes some
of the justifications advanced for the development of international labour
standards at the dawn of the ILO's creation when it was implicitly accepted
that the advancement of the principle of social justice, enshrined in the
ILO Constitution and cited in the prelude to this chapter, was also very
much in the economic interests of states.

Migrant workers, and in particular certain vulnerable categories,
such as women domestic workers, and temporary and irregular labour
migrants, continue to suffer abuses and malpractices at the hands of
employers, government officials and the general population in receiving countries, while the standards that have been painstakingly devised
to enable them to lead a dignified existence when resident and employed
abroad have lain largely dormant. As described in the second part of this
chapter dealing with the ILO and migrant workers, however, a particularly welcome feature of the last decade has been a palpable mobilization
by international organizations, NGOs and civil society in response to the
continuing ill treatment and injustices experienced by migrant workers
and in support of the ratification of the MWC. Somewhat paradoxically
therefore, while globalization is perceived generally as a threat to the
application of existing labour and human rights standards, by bringing
together the diverse and geographically distant voices in support of labour
migrants, it has also enabled this movement to gain momentum and play
an increasingly important role in the struggle to achieve a just and fair
deal for migrant workers in terms of their employment and general life
conditions.

Notes

1. Declaration of Philadelphia concerning the Aims and Purposes of the International Labour Organization (ILO), Sections I(a) and II(a) respectively. The
   Declaration was adopted by the International Labour Conference in 1944 and
   incorporated as an annex into the revised ILO Constitution of 1946 (when the

ILO also became the first specialized agency of the UN). For the Constitution and Declaration, see ILO Constitution and Declaration of Philadelphia, online: http://www.ilo.org/public/english/about/.

2. The ILO International Labour Migration website states that of the 80 to 97 million migrant workers and their dependants in the world today, about 15 per cent are estimated to be in an irregular situation. See "Current dynamics of international labour migration: Globalisation and regional integration" (ILO 2002), online: http://www.ilo.org/public/english/protection/migrant/about/index.htm.

3. The quintessential system of international labour protection for migrant workers is found in the European Union where equal treatment between workers who are nationals of member states and who exercise their free movement rights flows from the Treaty Establishing the European Communities, OJ 2002 C 325/33, (EC Treaty), in particular Article 12 EC (non-discrimination on the grounds of nationality) and Article 39 EC (free movement of workers), which have been implemented by detailed secondary legislation. Equivalent rights are also afforded to nationals of Iceland, Liechtenstein and Norway under the European Economic Area Agreement (EEA), OJ 1994 L 1/1. Although non-EU nationals working in EU Member States are not covered by the free movement regime, certain groups of third-country nationals are privileged by virtue of Association Agreements that their country has entered into with the EU (see e.g. the Association Agreement with Turkey, OJ 1973 C 113/1, and implementing measures). Moreover, under the terms of Title IV of Part Three of the EC Treaty, which grants the EU competences regarding asylum and immigration, the European Commission has proposed a Council directive on the conditions of entry and residence of third-country nationals for the purpose of paid employment and self-employed economic activities (COM (2001) 386 final of 11 July 2001), which would establish a uniform system for the entry of third-country nationals into EU Member States to fill labour market shortages and guarantee them equal treatment with EU citizens in respect of, inter alia, working conditions, access to vocational training, health care and housing. In contrast, general free movement of labour is not a feature of the North American Free Trade Agreement (NAFTA) between Canada, Mexico and the United States. This agreement only facilitates the entry of specified skilled professionals and business persons into these countries. See NAFTA, Chapter 16 (http://www.nafta-sec-alena.org/english/index.htm). The Council of Europe has also adopted multilateral instruments of relevance to the protection of migrant workers, including the European Convention on the Legal Status of Migrant Workers, Strasbourg, 24 November 1977; ETS No. 93. A major limitation of this and other treaties, however, is their limited personal scope given that they only apply on the basis of reciprocity to nationals of other contracting parties. For a detailed overview of the convention, see E. Guild, "The European Convention on the Legal Status of Migrant Workers (1977): An Analysis of its Scope and Benefits" (1999) Doc.

CDMG (99) 11. While there are no human rights standards pertaining specifically to migrant workers in Latin America, the Inter-American Commission on Human Rights recently established the Special Rapporteurship on Migrant Workers and Members of Their Families. See J. Fitzpatrick, "The Human Rights of Migrants", in T. A. Aleinikoff and V. Chetail, (eds.), *Migration and International Legal Norms* (T.M.C. Asser Press, The Hague, 2003), 169 at 170. Furthermore, in September 2003, the Inter-American Court of Human Rights issued a landmark Advisory Opinion on the legal status and rights of undocumented migrants in response to a request by Mexico. The Court ruled, inter alia, that the migratory status of persons cannot constitute a justification for depriving them of the enjoyment and exercise of their human rights, including those related to work and that migrants, upon taking up a work-related role, acquire rights by virtue of being workers that should be recognized and guaranteed independently of their regular or irregular situation in the state of employment. Advisory Opinion OC-18/03 of 17 September 2003, Series A No.18 (available only in Spanish), para. 8, online: Inter-American Court of Human Rights, http://www.corteidh.or.cr/index-ingles.html.

4. Second recital of the Preamble to the revised ILO Constitution: "Whereas conditions of labour exist involving such injustice, hardship and privation to large numbers of persons as to produce unrest so great that the peace and harmony of the world are imperilled; and an improvement in these conditions is urgently required; as, for example . . . [*inter alia*] *protection of the interests of workers when employed in countries other than their own*". Emphasis added.

5. V. A. Leary, *International Labour Conventions and National Law: The Effectiveness of the Automatic Incorporation of Treaties in National Legal Systems* (Martinus Nijhoff, Dordrecht, 1982), at 6.

6. A significant exception is Convention No. 111 of 1958 concerning Discrimination in respect of Employment and Occupation, which does not delineate nationality as a prohibited ground of discrimination (Article 1(1)(a)). Indeed, Article 1(1)(b) provides expressly that additional grounds of discrimination may be determined by the member state concerned in consultation with the social partners and other appropriate bodies. See also H. K. Nielsen, "The Concept of Discrimination in ILO Convention No. 111" (1994) 43 *International and Comparative Law Quarterly* 827 at 840. However, discrimination between nationals and migrant workers on the basis of other listed grounds, such as race, sex or religion, would not be permissible without an objective justification.

7. Conventions No. 29 of 1930 concerning Forced or Compulsory Labour and No. 105 of 1957 concerning the Abolition of Forced Labour; No. 138 of 1973 concerning Minimum Age for Admission to Employment and No. 182 of 1999 concerning the Prohibition and Immediate Action for the Elimination of the Worst Forms of Child Labour; No. 87 of 1948 concerning Freedom of Association and Protection of the Right to Organize; No. 98 of 1949 concerning the Application of the Principles of the Right to Organize and Bargain Collectively; No. 100 of 1951 concerning Equal

Remuneration for Men and Women Workers for Work of Equal Value; and No. 111 of 1958 concerning Discrimination in respect of Employment and Occupation.

8. International Labour Conference, 86th Session, Geneva, June 1998, ILO Declaration on Fundamental Principles and Rights at Work (ILO, "Declaration on Fundamental Principles"), online: http://www.ilo.org/dyn/declaris/ DECLARATIONWEB.INDEXPAGE.

9. ILO, Declaration on Fundamental Principles, at para. 2. The Declaration contains a "promotional follow-up" enabling the ILO Governing Body to request, on an annual basis, reports from those ILO Member States which have not ratified these conventions to supply information on the efforts undertaken to give effect to the fundamental rights and freedoms (Annex, Part I).

10. ILO, Declaration on Fundamental Principles, at Recital 4.

11. See respectively Conventions No. 97 of 1949 concerning Migration for Employment (Revised) and No. 143 of 1975 concerning Migrations in Abusive Conditions and the Promotion of Equality of Opportunity and Treatment of Migrant Workers, referred to simply as the Migrant Workers (Supplementary Provisions) Convention. Recommendations No. 86 of 1949 concerning Migration for Employment (Revised), which includes an Annex containing a model bilateral labour migration agreement, and No. 151 of 1975 concerning Migrant Workers accompany the conventions.

12. The equal treatment provision is Article 6 of C97.

13. See in particular the informational provisions in Articles 2 and 3 and the state obligation in Article 4 to take measures "to facilitate the departure, journey and reception of migrants for employment".

14. International Labour Conference, 87th Session, Geneva, June 1999, Report III (1B), *Migrant Workers: General Survey on the Reports of the Migration for Employment Convention (Revised) (No. 97), and Recommendation (Revised) (No. 86), 1949, and the Migrant Workers (Supplementary Provisions) Convention (No. 143), and Recommendation (No. 151), 1975* (Geneva: International Labour Office, 1999) ("General Survey 1999"), para. 657; E. Guild and H. Staples, "Labour Migration in the European Union", in P. De Bruycker, (ed.), *The Emergence of a European Immigration Policy* (Bruylant, Brussels, 2003), 171 at 177–82.

15. OECD, Note by the Secretariat, *Bilateral Labour Agreements: Evaluation and Prospects,* OECD and the Swiss Federal Office of Immigration, Integration and Emigration (IMES) Seminar on Bilateral Labour Agreements and Other Forms of Recruitment of Foreign Workers, Montreux, 19–20 June 2003 (on file with the author), para. 11.

16. R. Böhning, former Director, ILO Multidisciplinary Advisory Team Southeast Asia and the Pacific (SEAPAT), speaking at the Regional Workshop on the ILO in Manila, 11–12 January 1999, organized by the Canadian Human Rights Foundation, the Ateneo Human Rights Center and the Asia Foundation.

17. For example, in June 2000, immigration officials in the English port of Dover discovered 58 deceased Chinese nationals in the container of a lorry. They had died of asphyxiation while attempting to enter the United Kingdom unlawfully. See T. Reid et al., "58 Die in Lorry Ride to Hope", *The Times*, 20 June 2000.

18. See Part I of C143 on Migrations in Abusive Conditions.

19. Emphasis added.

20. International Labour Conference, 66th Session, Geneva, 1980, Report of the Committee of Experts on the Application of Conventions and Recommendations, *General Survey of the Reports relating to Conventions Nos. 97 and 143 and Recommendations Nos. 86 and 151 concerning Migrant Workers* (ILO, Geneva, 1980), paras. 256–7.

21. General Survey 1999, at 96.

22. GA Res. 217 A (III) of 10 December 1948.

23. 16 December 1966; 993 UNTS 3.

24. GA Res. 48/158 of 18 December 1990. However, not all the provisions in C143 can be considered liberal. For example, in keeping with other international human rights instruments, no explicit right to family reunification for migrant workers is recognized. An obligation is merely imposed on states parties "to facilitate" family reunification (Article 13(1)).

25. V. Leary, "Labour Migration", in *Migration and International Legal Norms*, 231–2.

26. V. Leary, "Labour Migration", at 232.

27. Algeria, Bahamas, Barbados, Belgium, Belize, Bosnia and Herzegovina, Brazil, Burkina Faso, Cameroon, Cuba, Cyprus, Dominica, Ecuador, France, Germany, Grenada, Guatemala, Guyana, Israel, Italy, Jamaica, Kenya, Madagascar, Malawi, Malaysia (Sabah), Mauritius, Netherlands, New Zealand, Nigeria, Norway, Portugal, Saint Lucia, Serbia and Montenegro, Slovenia, Spain, Tanzania (Zanzibar), The former Yugoslav Republic of Macedonia, Trinidad and Tobago, United Kingdom, Uruguay, Venezuela, Zambia.

28. Benin, Bosnia and Herzegovina, Burkina Faso, Cameroon, Cyprus, Guinea, Italy, Kenya, Norway, Portugal, San Marino, Serbia and Montenegro, Slovenia, Sweden, The Former Yugoslav Republic of Macedonia, Togo, Uganda, and Venezuela.

29. General Survey 1999, at 643.

30. C143, Article 16(1). In General Survey 1999, at 106, the Committee of Experts notes that only one state party, Norway, has made a declaration under this provision excluding Part I of C143.

31. See General Survey 1999, at 646 and 647.

32. For example, see the Committee's individual Observations to the Spanish Government regarding its obligations under C97 in respect of the violent attacks perpetrated against Moroccan agricultural workers and their families in the region of Andalusia in February 2000. International Labour Conference, 89th Session, Geneva, June 2001, Report III (1A), *Report of the Committee of Experts on the*

Application of Conventions and Recommendations (Geneva, International Labour Office, 2001), see online: ILOLEX database, http://www.ilo.org/ilolex/english/index.htm.

33. See R. Cholewinski, *Migrant Workers in International Human Rights Law: Their Protection in Countries of Employment* (Clarendon Press, Oxford, 1997), 141–2; P. Taran, Statement by the ILO to the Expert Meeting on Clarifying and Expanding the Rights of Non-Nationals, organized by the Open Justice Initiative, New York, 9–10 November 2003, online: http://www.ilo.org/public/english/bureau/exrel/events/statements/2003/migrants-osj.htm.

34. As of 30 January 2004, the MWC has been ratified by the following 25 States: Azerbaijan, Belize, Bolivia, Bosnia and Herzegovina, Burkina Faso, Cape Verde, Colombia, Ecuador, Egypt, El Salvador, Ghana, Guatemala, Guinea, Kyrgyzstan, Mali, Mexico, Morocco, Philippines, Senegal, Seychelles, Sri Lanka, Tajikistan, Timor Leste, Uganda and Uruguay. For the efforts of civil society and particularly NGOs, see the section "Supplementary and complementary approaches to standard-setting" in this chapter.

35. Part VI of the MWC is entitled "Promotion of Sound, Equitable, Humane and Lawful Conditions connected with International Migration of Workers and Members of their Families." The first provision in this Part, Article 64(1), requires states parties to consult and cooperate with one another in this respect.

36. See respectively MWC, Articles 32 and 47.

37. F. de Varennes, "Strangers in Foreign Lands: Diversity, Vulnerability and the Rights of Migrants", Discussion Paper (UNESCO, 2003), online: http://www.unesco.org/most/paper_devarennes.pdf.

38. See the discussion in L. Bosniak, "Human Rights, State Sovereignty and the Protection of Undocumented Migrants under the International Migrant Workers' Convention", in B. Bogusz, A. Cygan, R. Cholewinski and E. Szyszczak (eds.), *Irregular Migration and Human Rights: Theoretical, European and International Perspectives* (Brill Academic Publishers, forthcoming).

39. MWC, Article 3(e). See also W. R. Böhning, "The Protection of Temporary Migrants by Conventions of the ILO and the UN", paper presented to the International Institute for Labour Studies Workshop on Temporary Migration, September 2003, at 6.

40. 20 March 1952; ETS No. 9.

41. Indeed, Article 16 ECHR has been interpreted restrictively by the European Court of Human Rights. See *Piermont v. France* (1995) 20 EHRR 301.

42. Article 2 of Convention No. 87 is unequivocal: "Workers and employers, *without distinction whatsoever*, shall have the right to establish and, subject only to the rules of the organization concerned, to join organizations of their own choosing without previous authorization". Emphasis added. For an analysis of this provision, see J. Hodges-Aeberhard, "The Right to Organize in Article 2 of Convention

No. 87 – What is meant by Workers 'Without Distinction Whatsoever'?" (1989) 128 *International Labour Review* 177.

43. See Case No. 2121 (23 March 2001); ILO, Committee on Freedom of Association, *Report No. 327*, Vol. LXXXV, 2002, Series B, No. 1, at 561

44. The Committee, at 562, invited the ILO Governing Body to recommend the Spanish Government "as concerns the legislation in cause, to take into account the terms of Article 2 of Convention No. 87 according to which workers, without distinction whatsoever, have the right to join organizations of their own choosing".

45. General Survey 1999 at 657–62. The latter point is made specifically with reference to Article 5 of C97 requiring member states to ascertain that migrant workers and members of their families are in reasonable health, both at the time of departure and on arrival.

46. See also P. Taran and E. Geronimi, *Globalization, Labour and Migration: Protection is Paramount, Perspectives on Labour Migration 3E* (ILO, Geneva, 2003), at 10.

47. See H.S. Mattila, "Protection of Migrants' Human Rights: Principles and Practice" (2000) 38 *International Migration* No. 6, 53 at 62–3, citing L. L. Lim, *The Analysis of Factors Generating International Migration*, UN ACC Task Force on Basic Social Services for All Working Group on International Migration, Paper No. IV/3 (ILO, Geneva, 1998).

48. In particular, see Article 6(1) of C143 and generally Part VI and, more specifically, Article 68(1)(c) of the MWC. The international legally binding measures against trafficking and human smuggling are now found, in a criminal law context, in the Protocols to the UN Convention against Transnational Crime (GA Res. 55/25 of 15 November 2000) on combating trafficking in persons, especially women and children, and on smuggling of migrants by land, air and sea.

49. See MWC, Articles 2(2)(b) and Article 59.

50. General Survey 1999, at 658.

51. M. Ruhs, *Temporary Foreign Worker Programmes: Policies, Adverse Consequences, and the Need to Make them Work*, Perspectives on Labour Migration 6 (ILO, Geneva, 2003), at 8–9.

52. R. Cholewinski, *The Legal Status of Migrants Admitted for Employment: A Comparative Study of Law and Practice in Selected European States*, Doc. MG-ST (2002) 2 (Council of Europe, Strasbourg, 17 October 2002), at 106–8, 109.

53. To a degree, such a finding supports theoretical arguments that migrants' enjoyment of rights is connected integrally with the existence of complex systems of differentiation at the national level. See L. Morris, *Managing Migration: Civil Stratification and Migrants' Rights* (Routledge, London, 2002).

54. Ruhs, *Temporary Foreign Worker Programmes*, 13–15.

55. C143, Articles 11(2)(b), (d) and (e). The latter are defined as "employees of organisations or undertakings operating within the territory of a country who have been admitted temporarily to that country at the request of their employer to

undertake specific duties or assignments, for a limited and defined period of time, and who are required to leave that country on the completion of their duties or assignments" and "essentially concerns persons with special qualifications who go to a country to carry out specific short-term technical assignments". See Böhning, "The Protection of Temporary Migrants", at 3.

56. MWC, Article 3(e).

57. Böhning, "The Protection of Temporary Migrants", at 4.

58. MWC, Articles 61 and 62.

59. Specified-employment workers, on the other hand, are only excluded further from the right to equal treatment with national workers in respect of access to alternative unemployment in the event of loss or termination of work, and their family members cannot benefit from free access to employment. MWC, Articles 62(1) and (2).

60. MWC, Article 61(3).

61. Böhning, 'The Protection of Temporary Migrants", at 4–5.

62. Ruhs, *Temporary Foreign Worker Programmes*, 23.

63. Ruhs, *Temporary Foreign Worker Programmes*, 10–23.

64. Ruhs, *Temporary Foreign Worker Programmes*, 24–5.

65. Ruhs, *Temporary Foreign Worker Programmes*, 26–31.

66. General Survey 1999, at 629–35.

67. Cholewinski, *Migrant Workers in International Human Rights Law*, 202; P. Taran, "Human Rights of Migrants: Challenges of the New Decade" (2000) 38 *International Migration* 7–51, at 22.

68. N. Piper and R. Iredale, "Identification of the Obstacles to the Signing and Ratification of the UN Convention on the Protection of the Rights of all Migrant Workers 1990: The Asia Pacific Perspective", UNESCO (2003), online: http://portal. unesco.org/shs/en/ev.php@URL_ID = 3170&URL_DO = DO_TOPIC&URL_ SECTION = −465.html. As regards the concerns of receiving countries about family reunion, Article 44(2) of the MWC only requires states parties to "facilitate" the reunification of certain close family members. While this is not a strict obligation, clearly any laws and policies prohibiting the reunification of families outright or deliberately impeding such reunification would violate this provision. It is also arguable that the adoption of a non-binding recommendation or declaration would be a step backwards given that such an instrument usually precedes the adoption of a legally binding instrument (or, as is the case with an ILO convention, accompanies it and also augments rights; thus Recommendations No. 86 of 1949 concerning Migration for Employment (Revised), which includes an annex containing a model bilateral labour migration agreement, and No. 151 of 1975 concerning Migrant Workers accompany the conventions).

69. Taran and Geronimi, *Globalization, Labour and Migration*, 2.

70. B. Ghosh, *Elusive Protection, Uncertain Lands: Migrants' Access to Human Rights* (IOM, Geneva, 2003), at 12.

71. International Labour Office, Governing Body, 283rd Session, Geneva, March 2002, Second Item on the Agenda, *Date, place and agenda of the 92nd Session (2004) of the International Labour Conference* [Agenda, Point 4: Migrant workers (general discussion based on an integrated approach)], Doc. GB.283/2/1 at 110.

72. Taran and Geronimi, *Globalization, Labour and Migration*, 2. See also P. Stalker, *Workers Without Frontiers: The Impact of Globalization on International Migration* (ILO, Geneva, 2000).

73. Taran and Geronimi, *Globalization, Labour and Migration*, 3–4. Intrinsic to these developments is the unprecedented expansion in these countries of the informal sector or the "underground economy", which is reliant on "cheap, docile, and often irregular, immigrant workers, while avoiding taxes". See Ghosh, *Elusive Protection*, 13–14.

74. T.D. Achacoso, "The Role of the State in Managing an Overseas Employment Programme", unpublished paper (October 2003) [on file with the author].

75. Taran and Geronimi, *Globalization, Labour and Migration*, 6.

76. ILO Declaration on Fundamental Principles, at Recital 7.

77. This section focuses on approaches specifically concerning migrant workers. With regard to migration generally, there have recently been a number of global and regional intergovernmental initiatives, which clearly will also impact on international labour migration. Of particular interest is the establishment in December 2003 of the independent Global Commission on International Migration (GCIM), a state-led initiative in response to the UN Secretary-General's call for a more comprehensive examination of "the various dimensions of the migration issue": see UN, General Assembly, 57th Session, *Strengthening of the United Nations: an agenda for further change*, Doc. A/57/387 (9 September 2002), at 10, para. 39, online: UN http://www.un.org/reform/pdfs/sgreport.pdf. The Commission has a three-fold mandate: to place international migration on the global agenda; to analyse gaps in current approaches to migration and examine its relationship with other areas, such as, economic development, labour supply and demand, remittances and trade; and to make recommendations to the Secretary General and other stakeholders on how to strengthen national, regional and global governance on international migration, which will also include proposals on ways to improve the conditions of the individual migrant. See online: Global Commission on International Immigration, http://www.gcim.org/.

78. General Survey 1999, at 666–7.

79. Migrant Workers (general discussion based on an integrated approach), at 108.

80. Migrant Workers (general discussion based on an integrated approach), at 109–10 respectively.

81. Migrant Workers (general discussion based on an integrated approach), at 111.

82. "International Labour Migration Survey" (ILO Office, Geneva 2003), online: http://www.ilo.org/public/english/protection/migrant/projects/survey/index.htm.

83. "International Labour Migration Survey", at iii.

84. CHR Res. 1999/44, of 27 April 1999 (adopted without a vote), para. 3. This was also one of the principal recommendations of the report of the Working Group of intergovernmental experts on the human rights of migrants (E/CN.4/1999/80), convened by the Commission on Human Rights in 1997.

85. CHR Res. 1999/44, at 3.

86. CHR Res. 2002/62 of 25 April 2002 adopted without a vote and endorsed by UN Economic and Social Council (ECOSOC) Decision 2002/266 of 25 July 2002 (E/2002/INF/2/Add.2).

87. Taran, "Human Rights of Migrants", at 36–7.

88. See E/CN.4/2001/83 (9 January 2001), E/CN.4/2002/94 (15 February 2002), and E/CN.4/2003/85 (30 December 2002).

89. E/CN.4/2003/85 at paras. 75–6, 79–80, 83–4 and 85–7 respectively.

90. See CHR Res. 1999/44 at 2 and CHR Res. 2002/62 at 3 and 24.

91. E/CN.4/2001/83/Add.1 (21 December 2000), at 65–8.

92. Copies of these agreements are available online: Human Resources Development Canada, http://www.on.hrdc-drhc.gc.ca/english/ps/agri/welcome.shtml.

93. E/CN.4/2001/83/Add.1 at 69–70.

94. E/CN.4/2001/83/Add.1 at 88.

95. E/CN.4/2003/85/Add.2 (30 October 2002). Online: http://www.unhchr.ch/ Huridocda/Huridoca.nsf/0/02ba799ae4d4e896c1256c800050885e/$FILE/ G0215406.pdf.

96. E/CN.4/2003/85/Add.3 and Corr.1 (30 October 2002). Online: http://www. unhchr.ch/ Huridocda/ Huridoca.nsf/ 0/ 5b6e3e148f22c3fbc1256c8e00335f80? Opendocument.

97. E/CN.4/2003/85/Add.4 (1 November 2002). An important conclusion of the Special Rapporteur in the report on the Philippines, at 2 (Executive Summary), concerns the inadequacy of domestic legislation in protecting women migrants, particularly against abuses relating to sex work.

98. E/CN.4/2003/85/Add.3 and Corr.1 at 67.

99. E/CN.4/2003/85/Add.2 at 52.

100. V. Leary, "Labour Migration", 237–8.

101. E/CN.4/2002/94 at para. 82. For the Declaration and Programme of Action, see A/CONF.189/12 (25 January 2002).

102. E/CN.4/2002/94 at para. 82. For the Declaration and Programme of Action, see A/CONF.189/12 (25 January 2002), at 17, para. 51.

103. E/CN.4/2002/94 at para. 82. For the Declaration and Programme of Action, see A/CONF.189/12 (25 January 2002), at 40, para. 67. Emphasis added.

104. E/CN.4/2002/94 at para. 82. For the Declaration and Programme of Action, see A/CONF.189/12 (25 January 2002), at 40, para. 67.

105. E/CN.4/2002/94 at para. 82. For the Declaration and Programme of Action, see A/CONF.189/12 (25 January 2002), at 42, paras. 78(b), (i) and (k).

106. See IOM Mission Statement (http://www.iom.int/en/who/main_mission.shtml).

107. In this regard, see the IOM policy paper on "Effective Respect for Migrants' Rights" (http://www.iom.int/en/who/main_policies_effrespect.shtml).
108. Preamble, Recital 2 and Article 1(c) of the Constitution; IOM Council, 86th Session, 2003, *International Labour Migration Trends and IOM Policy and Programmes*, Doc. MC/INF/264 (6 November 2003) at 5, para. 21.
109. Preamble, Recital 2 and Article 1(c) of the Constitution; IOM Council, 86th Session, 2003, *International Labour Migration Trends and IOM Policy and Programmes*, Doc. MC/INF/264 (6 November 2003) at 5, para. 23; IOM, *Labour Migration Activities in 2002* (IOM, Geneva, March 2003).
110. IOM Press Briefing Note: Asian Labour Migration Ministerial Consultation Ends (4 April 2003), online: http://www.iom.int/en/archive/pbn040403.shtml#item3).
111. Compare de Varennes, "Strangers in Foreign Lands", at 34.
112. United Nations Convention on Migrants' Rights (UNESCO, Paris, 2003).
113. United Nations Convention on Migrants' Rights (UNESCO, Paris, 2003), at 4.
114. For the Campaign's website, see online: http://www.migrantsrights.org/.
115. Taran, "Human Rights of Migrants", at 36 elaborates on the origins and activities of the International Steering Committee.
116. GA Res. 55/93 (4 December 2000).
117. See respectively, http://www.december18.net/web/general/start.php (December 18); http://www.migrantwatch.org/ (Migrants Rights International); http://www.icmc.net/docs/en (International Catholic Migration Commission); and http://www.asian-migrants.org/ (Asian Migrant Centre/Migrant Forum in Asia).
118. See Human Rights Watch web site pages on "Defending the Rights of Migrants and Asylum Seekers in Western Europe", online: http://www.hrw.org/campaigns/migrants/.
119. See the PICUM online: http://www.picum.org/.
120. Taran, "Human Rights of Migrants", at 39.
121. Defined by the ILO as "the process through which individuals and organizations in any country strengthen their abilities to mobilize the resources needed to overcome economic and social problems and to pursue economic opportunities in order to achieve a better standard of living as generally defined in that society". D. Rondinelli, "Institutions and Market Development: Capacity Building for Economic and Social Transition" (Enterprise and Cooperative Department, ILO, Geneva, 1998), cited by Achascoso, "The Role of the State", at 16, who contends however that this definition does not focus sufficiently on the social and administrative aspects of the process.
122. Achacoso, "The Role of the State", at 17.
123. Achacoso, "The Role of the State", at 29.
124. V. Leary, "Labour Migration", at 229.
125. See M. I. Abella, *Sending Workers Abroad* (ILO, Geneva, 1997), at 57.
126. Other recruitment malpractices listed in the ILO's *International Labour Migration Survey*, at 8, include: offers of non-existing jobs; charging recruitment fees *supra* the legal limits; misleading information about jobs, remuneration and benefits;

withholding a worker's travel and/or identification documents; and smuggling or trafficking.

127. Achacoso, "The Role of the State", 19–21.

128. Achacoso, "The Role of the State", 21–2.

129. Achacoso, "The Role of the State", 22–3. A mandatory Pre-Employment Orientation Seminar for prospective applicants for overseas employment precedes this Seminar. Achacoso, "The Role of the State", at 23.

130. B. Ghosh, *Elusive Protection, Uncertain Lands: Migrants' Access to Human Rights* (IOM, Geneva, 2003), at 43–6.

131. Ghosh, *Elusive Protection*, 43. In this regard, Mr David Weissbrodt, the Special Rapporteur on the rights of non-citizens of the UN Sub-Commission on the Promotion and Protection of Human Rights, writes in his final report: "In general, international human rights law requires the equal treatment of citizens and non-citizens . . . There is, however, a disjuncture between the rights that international human rights law guarantees to non-citizens and the realities that non-citizens must face." E/CN.4/Sub.2/2003/23 (26 May 2003), paras. 1 and 2.

132. E/CN.4/Sub.2/2003/23 (26 May 2003), at 6; Cholewinski, *Migrant Workers*, 47 et seq.

133. Ghosh, *Elusive Protection*, 45.

BIBLIOGRAPHY

Achacoso, T. D., *The Role of the State in Managing an Overseas Employment Programme* (October 2003) [unpublished]

Adams, George, *Canadian Labour Law* (2nd edn, Canada Law Book, Aurora, revised 2004)

Adams, Roy J., *Assessing the Extent of Freedom of Association and the Effective Right to Bargain Collectively in Light of Global Developments* (ILO, Research & Publications, Geneva), online: http://www.ilo.org

Adams, Roy, "On the Convergence of Labour Rights and Human Rights" (2001) 56 *Relations Industrielles/Industrial Relations* 199

Adams, Roy, "Implications of the International Human Rights Consensus for Canadian Labour and Management" (2002) 9 *Canadian Labour and Employment Law Journal* 125

African Commission on Human and People's Rights, *Basic Documents*, online: http://www.achpr.org/html/basicinstruments.html

Agência Estado, "Ajudando os Trabalhadores por Meio do Comércio", *O Estado de S. Paulo*, 21 April 2004

Aggarwal, Mita, "International Trade, Labour Standards, and Labour Market Conditions: An Evaluation of the Linkages", Working Paper No. 95-06-C U.S. (Office of Economics, International Trade Commission, 1995)

Aidt, Toke and Zafiris Tzannatos, *Unions and Collective Bargaining: Economic Effects in a Global Environment* (World Bank, Washington DC, 2002)

Alcock, Anthony, *History of the International Labor Organization* (Octagon Books, New York, 1971)

Aldonas, Grant D., "The FTAA: Mapping the Road to Economic Growth and Development" (2002) 7(3) *Electronic Journal of the U.S. Department of State*, online: http://usinfo.state.gov/journals/ites/1002/ijee/ftaa-aldonas.htm

Alesina, Alberto and Roberto Perotti, "The Welfare State and Competitiveness" [unpublished], cited in Dani Rodrik (ed.), *Has Globalization Gone too Far?* (Institute for International Economics, Washington DC, 1997), 45

Alexander, Jason McKenzie and Brian Skyrms, "Bargaining With Neighbors: Is Justice Contagious?" (1999) 96 *Journal of Philosophy* 588–98

Alston, Philip and James Heenan, "The role of international labour standards within the trade debate: The need to return to fundamentals", Discussion Paper, International Labour Standards Department (ILO, Geneva, 2002)

American Law Institute, *Restatement of the law, The foreign relations law of the United States / as adopted and promulgated by The American Law Institute at Washington, D.C., May 14, 1986* (American Law Institute Publishers, St Paul, Minnesota, 1987)

Anker, R., "Theories of Occupational Segregation by Sex: An Overview" (1997), online: International Labour Review, http://www.ilo.org/public/english/support/publ/revue/articles/ank97–3.htm

Anker, R. et al., *Measuring Decent Work with Statistical Indicators*, Working Paper No. 2 (ILO Policy Integration Department, Geneva, 2002)

Ankerl, Geza, "Towards a Social Contract on a World-wide Scale: solidarity contracts", Research Series, no. 47 (International Institute for Labour Studies, International Labour Office, Geneva, 1980)

Appelbaum, Richard, William L. F. Felstiner and Volkmar Gessner (eds.), *Riles and Networks: The Legal Culture of Global Business Transactions* (Hart Publishing, Oxford, 2001)

Armstrong, Tim, "Labour Issues in International Trade Agreements: Two Solitudes? Where Does Canada Stand vis-à-vis the Integration of Labour Standards and International Trade Agreements? Are We Making Progress?" (2000) 4 *Behind the Headlines* 57

Arthurs, Harry W., "Protection against Judicial Review" (1983) 43 *Revue du Barreau* 277–90, reprinted in Canadian Institute of Administrative Justice, *Judicial Review of Administrative Rulings* (Editions Yvon Blais, Montreal, 1983)

Arthurs, Harry W., "Understanding: Industrial Relations Research and Policy in Canada from 1969 to 1984 . . . and Beyond" (1984) 39 *Relations Industrielles* 753

Arthurs, Harry W., "Labour Law in the New Economy", Remarks to the Conference of Labour Board Chairs of Canada (9 August 1995) [unpublished]

Arthurs, Harry W., "Labour Law without the State" (1996) 46 *University of Toronto Law Journal* 1

Arthurs, Harry W., "Globalization of the Mind: Canadian Elites and the Restructuring of Legal Fields" (1998) 12:2 *Canadian Journal of Law and Society* 219

Arthurs, Harry W., "The New Economy and the New Legality: Industrial Citizenship and the Future of Labour Arbitration" (1999) 7 *Canadian Labour and Employment Law Journal* 45

Arthurs, Harry W., "The Hollowing out of Corporate Canada?", in Jane Jenson and Boaventura de Sousa Santos (eds.), *Globalizing Institutions: Case Studies in Social Regulation and Innovation* (Ashgate Press, London, 2000), 29

Arthurs, Harry W., "The Role of Global Law Firms in Constructing or Obstructing a Transitional Regime of Labour Law", in Richard Applebaum, *Rules and*

Networks: the legal Culture of Global Business Transactions (Hart, Portland, Oregon, 2001), 273–300

Arthurs, Harry W., "Reinventing Labor Law for the Global Economy" (2001) 22(2) *Berkeley Journal of Employment and Labor Law* 271–92

Arthurs, Harry W., "Private Ordering and Workers' Rights in the Global Economy: Corporate Codes of Conduct as a Regime of Labour Market Regulation", in Joanne Conaghan, Richard Michael Fischl and Karl Klare (eds)., *Labour Law in an Era of Globalization: Transformative Practices and Possibilities* (Oxford University Press, 2002), 471–88

Arthurs, Harry W., "Corporate Codes of Conduct: Profit, Power and Law in the Global Economy", in Wesley Cragg (ed.), *Ethics Codes, Corporations and the Challenge of Globalization* (Edward Elgar Press, Northampton, 2005), 51–71

Arthurs, Harry W., "Corporate Self-regulation: Political Economy, State Regulation and Reflexive Labour Law", in Ton Wilthagen and Rolf Rogowski (eds.), *Reflexive Labour Law: Studies in International and European Employment Law and Labour Market Policy* (Kluwer Law International) [forthcoming]

Arthurs, Harry W. and Brent Arnold, *Does the Charter Matter?* [forthcoming]

ASEAN, Association of Southeast Asian Nations, online: http://www.aseansec.org/8685.htm.

Asian Migrant Centre/Migrant Forum in Asia, online: http://www.asian-migrants.org

Aspinwall, Mark, "Globalization, Exit and Free Social Riders: A Dysfunctional Integration Theory" (1998) 33 *European Journal of Political Research* 323

Associated Press, "U.S. labour body probes anti-union move in Quebec", *Toronto Star*, 21 December 1998, D3

Avi-Yonah, Reuven S., "Globalization, Tax Competition and the Fiscal Crisis of the Welfare State" (2000) 113 *Harvard Law Review* 1573

Axelrod, Robert, *The Evolution of Cooperation* (Basic, New York, 1985)

Bagwell, Kyle and Robert W. Staiger, "The Simple Economics of Labor Standards and the GATT", in Alan V. Deardorff and Robert M. Stern (eds.), *Social Dimensions of U.S. Trade Policies* (University of Michigan Press, Ann Arbor, 2000), 195–231

Bagwell, Kyle and Robert W. Staiger, *The Economics of the World Trading System* (MIT Press, Cambridge, Massachusetts, 2002)

Baird, Douglas G., Robert H. Gertner and Randal C. Picker, *Game Theory and the Law* (Harvard University Press, Cambridge, Massachusetts, 1994)

Banks, Kevin, "Trade, Labor, and International Governance", Doctoral Dissertation, Harvard Law School (2003)

Banks, Kevin and Tequila Brooks, *Legal Rights of Migrant Agricultural Workers in North America* (Commission for Labor Cooperation, Dallas, Texas, 2000)

Banks, Kevin, Lance Compa, Leonico Lara and Sandra Polaski, *North American Labor Relations Law – A Comparative Guide to the Labor Relations Law of*

Canada, Mexico and the United States (Commission for Labor Cooperation, Washington DC, 2000)

Barnard, Catherine, "The EU Agenda for Regulating Labour Markets: Lessons from the UK in the Field of Working Time", in G.A. Bermann and K. Pistor (eds.), *Law and Governance in the Enlarged European Union* (Hart Publishing, Oxford and Portland, 2004), 177–208

Barré, Philippe, "Production des normes de temps de travail et décentralisation organisée de la négociation collective en Europe", in Claude Durand and Alain Pichon (eds.), *La puissance des normes* (L'Harmattan, "Logiques sociales", Paris, 2003), 237–54

Basu, Kaushik, "Child Labour: Cause, Consequence, and Cure, with Remarks on International Labour Standards" (1999) 37 *Journal of Economic Literature* 1083–119

Basu, Kaushik, "Globalization and Marginalization: A Re-examination of Development Policy", Working Paper no. 026 (Bureau for Research in Economic Analysis of Development (BREAD), 2003)

Bausili, Anna V., "Rethinking the Methods of Dividing and Exercising Powers in the EU: Reforming Subsidiarity and National Parliaments", Jean Monnet Working Paper 9/02 (NYU School of Law), online: http://www.jeanmonnetprogram.org/

BBC, "Blair confirms EU constitution poll", *BBC News – World Edition,* 20 April 2004, online: http://news.bbc.co.uk/2/hi/uk_news/politics/3640949.stm

Baylis, John and Steven Smith (eds.), *The Globalization of World Politics: An Introduction to International Relations* (Oxford University Press, 1997)

Beatty, David, *Putting the Charter to Work: Designing a Constitutional Labour Code* (McGill-Queens University Press, Kingston and Montreal, 1987)

Beatty, David, *The Ultimate Rule of Law* (Oxford University Press, 2004)

Beatty, David and Steven Kennett, "Striking Back: Fighting Words, Social Protest and Political Participation in Free and Democratic Societies" (1988) 67 *Canadian Bar Review* 573

Belanger, Jacques, A. Giles and J. Grenier, "Patterns of Influence in the Host Country: A Study of ABB in Canada" (2003) 14 *International Journal of Human Resource Management* 469

Belser, Patrick, "Does Latin American & Caribbean Unemployment Depend on Asian Labor Standards?", Working Paper No.380 (Inter-American Development Bank, 1998)

Berik, Günseli, "What Happened after Pakistan's Soccer Ball Industry Went Child Free", Paper presented to the Conference on Child Labor, Graduate School of Social Work, University of Utah (7–8 May 2001)

Betten, Lammy, *International Labour Law: Selected Issues* (Kluwer, Deventer, 1993)

Bewley, Truman F., *Why Wages Don't Fall During a Recession* (Harvard University Press, Cambridge, Massachusetts, 1999)

Beyer, Dorianne, "Understanding and Applying Child Labor Laws to Today's School-to-Work Transition Programs", *Center Focus* (National Center for Research and Vocational Education, Berkeley, California, 1995)

Bhagwati, Jagdish, "A view from the academia", *International Labor Standards and Global Economic Integrations,* Proceedings of a Symposium (US Department of Labor, Bureau of International Labour Affairs, Washington DC, 1994)

Bhagwati, Jagdish, "The Demands to Reduce Domestic Diversity among Trading Nations", in Jagdish Bhagwati and Robert Hudec (eds.), *Fair Trade and Harmonization: Prerequisites to Free Trade?* (MIT Press Cambridge, Massachusetts, 1996), 9–40

Bhagwati, Jagdish, "Free Trade and Labour", *Financial Times,* 29 August 2001

Bhagwati, Jagdish, "NAFTA 'a pox on the world trading system'" in *Free Trade Today* (Princeton University Press, New Jersey, 2002), 95

Biagi, Marco, "Changing Industrial Relations – A Few Comments on the Report of the High-Level Group on Industrial Relations and Managing Change in the European Union", in Michele Tiraboschi (ed.), *Marco Biagi, Selected Writings* (Kluwer Law International, The Hague/London/New York, 2003), 29–44

Binmore, Ken, Alan Kirman and Piero Tani, *Introduction, Frontiers of Game Theory* (MIT Press, Cambridge, Massachusetts, 1993)

Bisson-Rapp, S., "Exceeding our Boundaries: Transactional Employment Law Practice and the Export of American Lawyering Styles to the Global Market" [forthcoming]

Blackett, Adelle, "Whither Social Clause? Human Rights, Trade Theory and Treaty Interpretation" (1999) 3 *Columbia Human Rights Law Review* 1

Blackett, Adelle, "Global Governance, Legal Pluralism and the Decentred State: A Labor Law Critique of Codes of Corporate Conduct" (2001) 8(2) *Indiana Journal of Global Legal Studies* 401–47

Blackett, Adelle, "Mapping the Equilibrium Line: Fundamental Principles and Rights at Work and the Interpretative Universe of the World Trade Organization" (2002) 65 *Saskatchewan Law Review* 369

Blackett, Adelle and Colleen Sheppard, "Collective Bargaining and Equality: Making Connections" (2003) 4 *International Labour Review* 419–57

Blanpain, Roger, *European Labour Law* (8th rev. edn, Kluwer Law International, The Hague, 2002)

Böhning, W. R., *The Protection of Temporary Migrants by Conventions of the ILO and UN,* Paper presented to the International Institute for Labour Studies Workshop on Temporary Migration, Geneva (September 2003)

Borden, Tessie and Sergio Bustos, "Hurt by NAFTA, Mexican Farmers Head North", *Arizona Republic,* 19 June 2003, 1D

Bosch, J., "MERCOSUR: Recent Experience and Future Prospects for Social and Labour Institutions", Panel No.2 of the XIIth Inter-American Conference of Ministers of Labour, First Meeting of Working Group 1 (9–11 April 2002), transcript online: http://www.xii.iacml.org

Bosniak, L., "Human Rights, State Sovereignty and the Protection of Undocumented Migrants under the International Migrant Workers' Convention", in B. Bogusz, A. Cygan, R. Cholewinski and E. Szyszczak (eds.), *Irregular Migration and Human Rights: Theoretical, European and International Perspectives* (Brill Academic Publishers forthcoming)

Bronfenbrenner, Kate, "Uneasy Terrain: The impact of capital mobility on workers, wages and union organizing", Report Submitted to the US Trade Deficit Review Commission, New York State School of Industrial and Labor Relations (Cornell University, Ithaca, New York, 2000)

Bronstein, A., "Labour Law Reform in EU Candidate Countries: Achievements and Challenges", online: http://www.ilo.org/public/English/dialogue/ifpdial/download/papers/candidate.pdf

Brosnan, Sarah F. and Frans B. M. De Waal, "Monkeys Reject Unequal Pay" (2003) 435 *Nature* 297–9

Brown, Drusilla K., "A Transaction Cost Politics Analysis of International Child Labor Standards", in Alan V. Deardorff and Robert M. Stern (eds.), *Social Dimensions of U.S. Trade Policies* (University of Michigan Press, Ann Arbor, 2000), 246–64

Brown, Drusilla F., Alan V. Deardorff and Robert M. Stern, "Child Labor: Theory, Evidence, and Policy", in Kaushik Basu, Henrik Horn, Lisa Román and Judith Shapiro (eds.), *International Labor Standards: History, Theory, and Policy Options* (Blackwell, Malden, Massachusetts, 2003)

Brown, Drusilla K., Alan V. Deardorff and Robert M. Stern, "The Effects of Multinational Production on Wages and Working Conditions in Developing Countries", Working Paper 9669 (National Bureau of Economic Research, 2003)

Browne, Harry and Beth Sims, *Runaway America: U.S. Jobs and Factories on the Move* (Interhemispheric, London, 1993)

Bruner, Christopher M., "Hemispheric Integration and the Politics of Regionalism: The Free Trade Area of the Americas (FTAA)" (2002) 33 *University of Miami Inter-American Law Review* 1

Busse, Matthias and Sebastian Braun, "Export Structure, FDI and Child Labour", Discussion Paper 216 (Hamburgisches Welt-Wirtschafts-Archiv (HWWA), 2003)

Cairns, Walter, *Introduction to European Union Law* (2nd edn, Cavendish Publishing Ltd, London, 2002)

Camerer, Colin F., *Behavioral Game Theory: Experiments in Strategic Interaction* (Russell Sage Foundation, New York and Princeton University Press, New Jersey, 2003)

Cameron, Jamie, "The Second Labour Trilogy: a comment on *R. v. Advance Cutting, Dunmore v. Ontario*, and *R.W.D.S.U. v. Pepsi-Cola*" (2002) 16 *Supreme Court Law Review* 66

Campbell, Duncan, *Globalisation and strategic choices in tripartite perspective: An agenda for research and policy issues*, DP/46/1991 (New Industrial Organisation Programme, International Institute for Labour Studies, International Labour Office, Geneva, 1991)

Canada, Privy Council Office, *Canadian Industrial Relations: The Report of the Task Force of Labour Relations* (December 1968) (Chair: H.D. Woods)

Canadian Auto Workers Newsletter, *Line in the Sand,* online: http://www.caw.ca/news/allCAWnewsletters/lineinthesand/

Capra, Fritjof, *The Tao of Physics* (3rd edn, Shambhala Publications, Boston, 1991)

Card, David and Alan B. Krueger, *Myth and Measurement: The New Economics of the Minimum Wage* (Princeton University Press, New Jersey, 1995)

CARICOM Secretariat, *Statement on Declaration of Industrial and Labour Relations Principles* (6 January 1999)

Carlsson, Hans and Eric van Damme, "Equilibrium Selection in Stag Hunt Games", in Ken Binmore, Alan Kirman and Piero Tani (eds.), *Frontiers of Game Theory* (MIT Press, Cambridge, Massachusetts, 1993), 237–53

Carnegie Endowment for International Peace, "Central America and the U.S. Face Challenge – and Chance for Historic Breakthrough–on Workers' Rights", *CEIP Issue Brief* (February, 2003)

Carraro, Carlo, "Modelling International Policy Games: Lessons from European Monetary Coordination" (1997) 24 *Empirica* 163–77

Casale, Giuseppe, "Collective Bargaining and the Law in Central and Eastern Europe: Recent Trends and Issues", Report submitted to the VII European Regional Congress of the International Society for Labour Law and Social Security, Stockholm (September 2002), online: http://www.juridicum.su.se/stockholmcongress2002/casale_english.pdf

Caro, Robert, *The Years of Lyndon Johnson: Master of the Senate* (Alfred A.Knopf, New York, 2002)

Castel, Jean Gabriel and Janet Walker, *Canadian Conflicts of Laws* (Butterworths, Markham, Ontario, 2002)

Cavalluzzo, Paul, "The Rise and Fall of Judicial Deference", in Neil Finkelstein and Brian Rogers (eds.), *Recent Developments in Administrative Law* (Carswell, Toronto, 1987) 213–42

CBC News Poll, CBC News (2001), online: http://cbc.ca/news/indepth/summit_poll.html

Centre for Women's Resources, "The Life and Struggle of Women Workers under Contractualization" (Asia Pacific Research Network, 2003), online: http:www.aprnet.org

Chambers, Allan, "Privatization of labour rules raises fears: Law may face NAFTA challenge", *Edmonton Journal*, 6 September 1996, 1

Charnowitz, Steve, "The Influence of International Labor Standards on the World Trading Regime: A Historical Overview" (1987) 126 *International Labour Review* 565

Chau, Nancy H. and Ravi Kanbur, "The Adoption of Labour Standards Conventions: Who, When, and Why?", Discussion Paper 2904 (Centre for Economic Policy Research, 2001), online: http://www.cepr.org/pubs/dps/DP2904.asp

Chinkin, C., "Canada Women's Continued Economic Inequality", Gender and Globalization, UN Chronicle (2001), online: http://www.globalpolicy.org/socecon/inequal/0221.htm

Cholewinski, R., *Migrant Workers in International Human Rights Law: Their Protection in Countries of Employment* (Oxford: Clarendon Press, 1997)

Cholewinski, R., *The Legal Status of Migrants Admitted for Employment: A Comparative Study of Law and Practice in Selected European States*, Doc. MG-ST (2002) 2 (Council of Europe, Strasbourg, 17 October 2002)

Chwe, Michael Suk-Young, *Rational Ritual: Culture, Coordination, and Common Knowledge* (Princeton University Press, New Jersey, 2001)

Clark, L., "Britain faces huge bill for upkeep of students from EU", *Daily Mail*, 22 March 2004, 2

Clarkson, Stephen, *Uncle Sam and US: Globalization, Neoconservatism and the Canadian State* (University of Toronto Press, Ontario, 2002)

Clauwaert, S. and W. Düvel, "The Implementation of the Social Acquis Communautaire in Central and Eastern Europe", *ETUI Interim Report* (European Trade Union Institute, Brussels, 2000)

Cohen, Monique, "Women Street Vendors: The Road to Recognition", 20 *SEEDS* (Population Council, New York, 2000)

Colitt, Raymond, "Free Trade Area of the Americas: Brazil's government-elect drops hostility to proposal; Lula's party backs free trade area talks", *Financial Times*, 8 November 2002, 11

Columbia Encyclopedia, s.v. "European Union" (6th edn, Columbia University Press, New York, 2003), online: www.bartleby.com/65/

Compa, Lance A., "The First NAFTA Labor Cases: A New International Labor Rights Regime Takes Shape" (1995) 3 *United States – Mexico Law Journal* 159

Compa, Lance, "Workers' Rights in the Global Economy" (2001) 5(1) *Perspectives on Work* 10–12

Compa, Lance and Jeffrey S. Vogt, "Labor Rights in the Generalized System of Preferences: A 20-Year Review" (2003) 22(2/3) *Comparative Labor Law & Policy Journal* 199–238

Constitutional Law Group (The), *Canadian Constitutional Law* (Emond Montgomery Publications, Toronto, 2003)

Copleston, Frederick, "Book One", *A History of Philosophy* (Doubleday, New York, 1985) 38–46

Cordeiro, Wolney de Macedo, *A Regulamentação das Relações de Trabalho Individuais e Coletivas no mbito do Mercosul* (Editora LTR, São Paulo, 2000)

Coriat, B., "Penser à l'envers: Travail et organisation dans l'entreprise japonaise" (Bourgeois, "Choix-essais", Paris, 1991)

Cornish, M., "Employment and Pay Equity in Canada – Success Brings Both Attacks and New Initiatives" (1996) 22 *Canada–United States Law Journal* 265–83

Cornish, M., "Engendering Citizenship and Labor Market Regulation – International and Canadian Perspectives", Paper presented at 5th Annual World Bank Gender and Law Conference, World Bank, Washington DC (18–19 March 2003)

Cornish, M. and V. Verma, *Enforcing International Standards in the Americas in an Era of Free Trade* (Canadian Bar Association, Ottawa, 30–31 May 2002)

Cornish, M., E. Shilton and F. Faraday, "Canada's International and Domestic Human Rights Obligations to Ensure Pay Equity: Obligations to Design an Effective Enforceable and Proactive Pay Equity Law", Research paper prepared for the Federal Pay Equity Review Task Force, Justice Canada, Ottawa (October, 2002), online: http://canada.justice.gc.ca/en/payeqsal/2307.html

Courchene, Thomas J., "A Mission Statement for Canada" (2000) 21 *Policy Options/Options politiques* 6

Courchene, Thomas J., "Imbedding Globalization: A Human Capital Perspective" (Canada House Lecture, 23 October 2001)

Courchene, Thomas J., *A State of Minds: Towards a Human Capital Future for Canadians* (Institute for Research on Public Policy, Montreal, Quebec, 2001)

Cox, Archibald, Derek C. Bok, Robert A. Gorman and Matthew W. Finkin, *Labor Law, Cases and Materials* (12th edn, Foundation Press, University Casebook Series, Westbury, 1996)

Crandall, Robert W., *Manufacturing on the Move* (Brookings Institution, Washington DC, 1993)

Cremona, Marise, "EU Enlargement: Solidarity and Conditionality", Inaugural lecture delivered at Queen Mary College, University of London (12 March 2003)

Crivelli, Ericson, "Os Trabalhadores e a ALCA: A Construção de um Direito Internacional do Trabaklho Americano", in Alberto Amaral Junior and Michelle Raton Sanchez (eds.), *O Brazil e a ALCA* (São Paulo, Editora Aduaneiras, 2003)

Cruz, Claudia Ferreira, "A Declaração Sociolaboural do Mercosul e os Direitos Fundamentais dos Trabalhadores", Dissertação de mestrado, Faculdade de Direito da Universidade de São Paulo (2001)

d'Espagnat, Bernard, *Physical Review Letters* 49 (1981): 1804.

Dahlby, Bev, "Payroll Taxes", in Allan Maslove (ed.), *Business Taxation in Ontario* (University of Toronto Press, Ontario, 1993)

Danielsen, Dan and Karl Klare, "Trade, Labour & Catfish: A Case Study", Paper
    presented at INTELL 7, Kyoto, Japan (26–29 March, 2004)
Davidov, Guy, "The Three Axes of Employment Relationships: A Characterization
    of Workers in Need of Protection" (2002) 52 *University of Toronto Faculty of
    Law Review* 357
Davies, Paul, Silvana Sciarra, Antoine Lyon-Caen and Spiros Simitis, *European Com-
    munity Labour Law : Principles and Perspectives* (Clarendon Press, Oxford,
    1996)
Davis, Dennis, Patrick Macklem and Guy Mundlak, "Social Rights, Social Citizen-
    ship and Transformative Constitutionalism: A Comparative Assessment", in
    Joanne Conaghan, Richard Fischl and Karl Klare *Labour Law in an Era of
    Globalization: Transformative Practices and Possibilities* (Oxford University
    Press, 2002), 511–34
Davis, Mike, *Prisoners of the American Dream: Politics and Economy in the History
    of the U.S. Working Class* (Verso Press, London, 1986)
Deacon, Bob, "The Prospects for Equitable Access to Social Provision in a Global-
    izing World", in Andrea Krizsan and Violetta Zentai (eds.), *Reshaping Glob-
    alization* (Central European University Press, Hungary, 2002), 109
December 18, Migrant Rights International, online: http://www.december18.net/
    web/general/start.php
Dehejia, Vivek H. and Yiagadeesen Samy, "Trade and Labour Standards – Theory,
    New Empirical Evidence, and Policy Implications", Working Paper No. 830
    (CESifo, 2002)
Demetriades, S., "European Works Councils Directive: A Success Story ?", in M.
    Biagi (ed.), *Quality of Work and Employee Involvement in Europe* (Kluwer Law
    International, The Hague, 2002), 49
Department of Foreign Affairs and International Trade, "Trade and Investment
    Report – Mercosur", online: http://dfait-maeci.gc.ca/latinamerica/ merco-
    suren.asp
DeVault, James M., "Political Pressure and the U.S. Generalized System of Prefer-
    ences" (1996) 22 *Eastern Economic Journal* 35–46
Dezalay, Yves and Bryant Garth, *Dealing in Virtue: International Commercial Arbi-
    tration and the Construction of a Transnational Legal Order* (University of
    Chicago Press, Illinois, 1996)
Dezalay, Yves and David Sugarman (eds.), *Professional Competition and Profes-
    sional Power: Lawyers, Accountants and the Social Construction of Markets*
    (Routledge, London/New York, 1995)
Dicey, Albert V., *The Law of the Constitution* (10th edn, ed. E. C. S. Wade, Macmillan
    & Co. Ltd, London, 1960)
Dixit, Avinash, "Strategic Aspects of Trade Policy", in Truman F. Bewley (ed.),
    Advances in Economic Theory Fifth World Congress (Cambridge University
    Press, Massachusetts, 1987), 329–62

Dombois, Rainer, Erhard Hornberger and Jens Winter, "Transnational Labour Regulations in the NAFTA", Paper presented at the 13th World Congress of the International Industrial Relations Association, Berlin (2–8 September 2003)

Drache, Daniel, "Lean Production in Japanese Auto Plants in Canada" (1994) 2(3) *Canadian Business Economics* 45

Drezner, Daniel, "Who Rules? State Power and the Structure of Global Regulation", Paper presented at the 97th annual meeting of the American Political Science Association, San Francisco, California (September, 2001)

Duryea, Suzanne, Olga Jaramillo and Carmen Pagés, "Latin American Labour Markets in the 1990s: Deciphering the Decade" (Inter-American Development Bank, 2003), online: http://www.iadb.org/sds/doc/PANlaborEAR4.pdf

Economic and Social Commission for Asia and the Pacific, *Sexually Abused and Sexually Exploited Children and Youth in Pakistan: A qualitative account of their health needs and available services in selected provinces*, UN ESCAP, 2001, ST/ESCAP/2123, online: http://www.unescap.org/esid/hds/sexual/pakistan. pdf

Economic Policy Institute, "NAFTA at Seven: Its Impact on Workers in all Three Countries" (2001), online: http://www.epinet.org/content.cfm/ briefingpapers_nafta01_index

Economist, The (American Edition), "Your darkest fears addressed, your hardest questions answered – Europe's constitution", 21 June 2003

Edmonds, Eric and Nina Pavcnik, "Does Globalization Increase Child Labour? Evidence From Vietnam", Working Paper 8760 (National Bureau of Economic Research, 2002)

Egger, Phillipe and Werner Sengenberger (eds.), *Decent Work in Denmark: Employment, Social Efficiency and Economic Security* (ILO, Geneva, 2003)

Elliott, K. and R. Freeman, "White Hats or Don Quixotes? Human Rights Vigilantes in the Global Economy", Working Paper 8102 (National Bureau of Economic Research, Massachusetts, 2001)

Elliott, Kimberly Ann and Richard B. Freeman, *Can Labor Standards Improve Under Globalization?* (Institute for International Economics, Washington DC, 2003)

Ellis, Evelyn, "Social Advantages: A New Lease of Life" (2003) 40 *Common Market Law Review* 639

Ellis, Ron, "An Administrative System in Jeopardy: Ontario's Appointments Process" (1998) 6 *Canadian Labour & Employment Law Journal* 53

Elmslie, Bruce and William Milberg, *Free Trade and Social Dumping: Lessons From the Regulation of US Interstate Commerce* (May/June 1996) 39 *CHALLENGE* 46–52

Elson, Diane, *Progress of the World's Women: UNIFEM Biennial Report* (United Nations Development Fund for Women, New York, 2000)

Employment and Social Affairs, "Simplification and improvement of legislation in the area of equal treatment of men and women" (2003), online: http://europa.eu. int/comm/employment_social/news/2003/jul/ consultation_en.html

Employment Status Group, *A Code of Practice in Determining Employee Status*, Programme for Prosperity and Fairness, online: http://www.revenue.ie.pdf/ ppfrep.pdf

Etherington, Brian, "Arbitration, Labour Boards and the Courts in the 1980s: Romance Meets Realism" (1989) 68 *Canadian Bar Review* 405

Etherington, Brian, "An Assessment of Judicial Review of Labour Laws under the *Charter*: Of Realists, Romantics, and Pragmatists" (1992) 24 *Ottawa Law Review* 685

European Commission, *Community Framework Strategy on Gender Equality* (2001– 2005), online: http://www.europa.eu.int/comm/employment_social/equ_pp/ strategy/ 22_en.html

European Commission, "Report of the high level group on industrial relations and change in the European Union" (Office for Official Publications of the European Communities, Luxembourg 2002)

European Foundation for the Improvement of Living and Working Conditions, *Economically Dependant Workers, Employment Law and Industrial Relations*, online: http://www.eiro.eurofound.ie/2002/05/study/TN0205101S. html

European Industrial Relations Observatory Online (EIROnline), *Industrial relations in the EU, Japan and USA, 2001* (2002), online: http://www.eiro.eurofound.ie/

European Industrial Relations Observatory Online (EIROnline), *Industrial relations in the EU Member States and candidate countries* (2002), online: http://www.eiro.eurofound.ie/

European Industrial Relations Observatory, "France and EU in Legal Tussle Over Women's Right Work", online: http://www.eiro.eurofound.eu.int/1999/05/ Feature/FR9905183F.html

European Industrial Relations Observatory, "Industrial Relations in the Candidate Countries" (2002), online: http://www.eiro.eurofound.eu.int/2002/07/ feature/TN0208102F.htm

European Industrial Relations Observatory, "Social Policy Provisions of Draft EU Constitutional Treaty Examined", online: http://www.eiro.eurofound.ie/ 2003/08/Feature/EU0308204F.html

European Union, *2003 Adopted Employment Guidelines*, online: http://europa.eu. int/comm/employment_social/employment_strategy/guidelines_en.ht

European Union, *2004 Proposal for Employment Guidelines*, online: http://europa.eu.int/>comm/employment_social/employment_strategy/guidelines_en. ht

Evans, Andrew, "Nationality Law and the Free Movement of Persons in the EEC: with Special Reference to the British Nationality Act 1981" (1982) 2 *Yearbook of European Law* 173

Feenstra, Robert, "Integration of Trade and Disintegration of Production in the Global Economy" (1998) 12:4 *Journal of Economics Perspectives* 31–50

Feis, Herbert, "International labour legislation in the light of economic theory" (1927) 4 *International Labour Review* 492

Ferner, Anthony, "Country of Origin Effects and HRM in Multinational Companies" (1997) 7 *Human Resource Management Journal* 19

Fischer, Stanley, "A Role for Labor Standards in the New International Economy", Seminar and Panel Discussion, International Monetary Fund, Washington DC (1999)

Fitzpatrick, J., "The Human Rights of Migrants", in T.A. Aleinikoff and V. Chetail (eds.), *Migration and International Legal Norms* (T.M.C. Asser Press, The Hague, 2003) 169

Flanagan, Robert J., "Labor Standards and International Competitive Advantage", in Robert J. Flanagan and William B. Gould (eds.), *International Labor Standards: Globalization, Trade and Public Policy* (Stanford University Press, Palo Alto, California, 2002)

Flood, J., "Mega-lawyering in the Global Order – The Cultural, Social and Economic Transformation of Global Legal Practice" (1996) 3 *International Journal of the Legal Profession* 169

Follows, John W., *Antecedents of the International Labour Organization* (Clarendon Press, Oxford, 1951)

Free Trade Area of the Americas, *Miami Ministerial Declaration*, Eighth Ministerial Meeting, Miami, Florida (20 November 2003), online: http://www.ftaa-alca.org/ministerials/Miami/Miami_e.asp

Free Trade Area of the Americas, *Ministerial Declaration of Quito*, Seventh Ministerial Meeting, Quito, Equador (1 November 2002), online: http://www.ftaa-alca.org/ministerials/quito/Quito_e.asp

Freeman, Richard B. and James L. Medoff, *What Do Unions Do?* (Basic Books, New York, 1985)

Freije, Samuel, "Informal Employment in Latin America and the Caribbean: Causes, Consequences and Policy Recommendations", Primer Seminario Técnico de Consulta Regional sobre Temas Labourales (mimeo) (Panamá, 2002)

Frenkel, Stephen, "Patterns of Workplace Relations in the Global Corporation: Toward Convergence?", in Jacques Belanger et al. (eds.), *Workplace Industrial Relations and the Global Challenge* (ILR Press, Ithaca, New York, 1994), 247

Frundt, Henry J., *Trade Conditions and Labor Rights: U.S. Initiatives, Dominican and Central American Responses* (University Press of Florida, Gainesville, 1998)

Fudenberg, Drew and Eric Maskin, "The Folk Theorem in Repeated Games with Discounting or with Incomplete Information" (1986) 54(3) *Econometrica* 533–54

Fudenberg, Drew and Jean Tirole, *Game Theory* (MIT Press, Cambridge, Massachusetts, 1991)

Fudge, J. and L. Vosko, "Gender Paradoxes and the Rise of Contingent Work: Towards a Transformative Political Economy of the Labour Market", in Wallace Clement and Leah Vosko (eds.), *Changing Canada: Political Economy as Transformation* (University Press, Montreal and Kingston, 2003), 183–209

Fudge, Judy, Eric Tucker and Leah Vosko, "Employee or Independent Contractor? Charting the Legal Significance of the Distinction in Canada" (2003) 10 *Canadian Labour and Employment Law Journal* 193

Galli, Rossana and David Kucera, "Labor Standards and Informal Employment in Latin America" (2004) 32(5) *World Development* 809–28

Galli, Rossana, "The Economic Impact of Child Labour", ILO Discussion Paper DP/128/2001 (International Institute for Labour Studies, Geneva, 2001)

Garrett, Geoffrey, "Global Markets and National Politics: Collision Course of Virtuous Circle?" (1998) 52(4) *International Organization* 787–824

Garrett, Geoffrey, *Partisan Politics in the Global Economy* (Cambridge University Press, Cambridge, 1998)

Garth, Bryant, "Transnational Legal Practice and Professional Ideology" (1985) 7 *Michigan Year Book of International Legal Studies* 3

Gauvin, Michel and Charles-Philippe Rochon, *Labour Legislation in Canada: Major Developments and Trends 1989–2003* (HRSDC, 2003)

Gereffi, Gary, "The Organization of Buyer Driven Global Commodity Chains: How US Retailers Shape Overseas Production Networks", in Gary Gereffi et al. (eds.), *Commodity Chains and Global Capitalism* (Praeger, Westport, Connecticut, 1994), 95–122

Ghosh, B., *Elusive Protection, Uncertain Lands: Migrants Access to Human Rights* (IOM, Geneva, 2003)

Giddens, *The Consequences of Modernity* (Stanford University Press, California, 1990)

Gillingham, John, *Coal, Steel, and the Rebirth of Europe, 1945–1955* (Cambridge University Press, Cambridge, 1991)

Glenn, H. Patrick, *Legal Traditions of the World* (Oxford University Press, 2000)

Global Policy Network, *Country Labour Market Reports*, online: http://www.gpn.org

Godard, John, "Labour Unions, Workplace Rights and Canadian Public Policy" (2003) 4 *Canadian Public Policy* 29

Goetschy, J., "European Employment Policy since the 1990s", in B. Keller and H.W. Platzer (eds.), *Industrial Relations and European Integration* (Ashgate, Aldershot / Burlington, Ontario, 2003), 137–60

Goodhart, David, "Social Dumping within the EU", in David Hine and Hussein Kassim (eds.), *Beyond The Market: The EU and National Social Policy* (Routledge, London, 1998), 70–90

Granut, C. de, "La mondialisation de l'économie: Éléments de synthèse", Forecasting and Assessment in Science and Technology, Working Paper (Commission of the European Communities, Brussels, 1990)

Green, Robert A., "Antilegalistic Approaches to Resolving Disputes Between Governments: A Comparison of the International Tax and Trade Regimes" (1998) 23 *Yale Journal of International Law* 79–139

Greenwood, Christopher, "Nationality and the Limits of Free Movement of Persons in Community Law" (1987) 7 *Yearbook of European Law* 185

Guild, E. and H. Staples, "Labour Migration in the European Union", in P. de Bruycker (ed.), *The Emergence of a European Immigration Policy* (Bruylant, Brussels, 2003), 171

Guild, E., "The European Convention on the Legal Status of Migrant Workers (1977): An Analysis of its Scope and Benefits", Doc. CDMG (99) 11 (1999)

Guillen, Ana M. and Manos Matsaganis, "Testing the 'Social Dumping' Hypothesis in Southern Europe: Welfare Policies in Greece and Spain During the Last 20 Years" (2000) 10 *Journal of European Social Policy* 2

Gunderson, Morley et al., *Union – Management Relations in Canada* (4th edn, Addison-Wesley, Don Mills, 1982)

Gunderson, Morley, "Harmonization of Labour Policies Under Trade Liberalization" (1998) 53 *Relations Industrielles* 1

Haile, Daniel, Abdolkarim Sadrieh and Harrie A.A. Verbon, "Self-Serving Dictators and Economic Growth", Working Paper 1105 (Center for Economic Studies and IFO Institute of Economic Research, 2003) online: http://www.CESifo.de

Hanson, Gordon H., "What Has Happened to Wages in Mexico Since NAFTA? Implications for Hemispheric Trade", Working Paper 9653 (National Bureau of Economic Research, 2003), online: http://papers.nber.org/papers/w9563

Hanusch, Horst and Marcus Balzat, "A New Era in the Dynamics of European Integration?", online: IDEAS at University of Connecticut Department of Economics using RePEc data, http://www.wiwi.uni-augsburg.de/vwl/institut/paper/261.pdf

Harrison, Bennett, *Lean and Mean: The Changing Landscape of Corporate Power in the Age of Flexibility* (Basic Books, New York, 1994)

Harrod, Jeffrey, "Social Relations of Production, Systems of Labour Control and Third World Trade Unions", in Roger Southall (ed.), *Trade Unions and The New Industrialization of the Third World* (Zed Books Ltd, London, 1988), 41–58

Harvey, Pharis, J., "The North American Agreement on Labour Cooperation: A Non-Governmental View", paper presented to a conference on Social Clauses and Environmental Standards in International Trade Agreements: Links,

Implementation and Prospects, Brussels (31 May 1996), online: http://www.laborrights.org/publication/naalc.html

Hatem, Fabrice, *International Investment*, UN Doc. E/1997/67 (UN Economic and Social Council, 1997)

Hatem, Fabrice, *International Investment: Toward the Year 2001* (United Nations, New York, 1997)

Hatem, Fabrice, *International Investment: Towards the Year 2002* (Renouf Pub. Co. Ltd, Paris, 1998)

Hayter, William, "Bill 7: Advance or Retreat?" (1996) 4 *Canadian Labour & Employment Law Journal* 331

Heckman, James and Carmem Pagés-Serra, "The Cost of Security Regulation: Evidence from Latin American Labour Markets" (2000) 1 *Economia* 109–54

Heidegger, Martin, *The Thing* in *Poetry, Language, Thought*, trans. by Albert Hofstadter (Harper & Row, New York, 1971)

Held, David, Anthony McGrew, David Goldblatt and Jonathan Perraton, *Global Transformations: Politics, Economics and Culture* (Stanford University Press, California, 1999)

Hepple, Bob, "The Future of Labour Law" (1995) 24 *Industrial Law Journal* 303

Hepple, Bob, "New Approaches to International Labour Regulation" (1997) 26 *Industrial Law Journal* 353

Herbert, Nick, *Quantum Reality: Beyond the New Physics* (Doubleday, New York, 1985)

Herrero, Álvaro and Keith Henderson, *El Costo de la Resolucion de Conflictos en la Pequeña Empresa* (Banco Interamericano de Desarrollo (mimeo), Washington DC, 2003)

Hodges-Aeberhard, J., "The Right to Organize in Article 2 of Convention No. 87 – What is Meant by Workers 'Without Distinction Whatsoever'?" (1989) 128 *International Labour Review* 177

Hogg, Peter, *Constitutional Law of Canada, Student Edition* (Carswell, Scarborough, Ontario, 2003)

Holzmann, Robert, "A Role for Labor Standards in the New International Economy", Seminar and Panel Discussion (International Monetary Fund, Washington DC, 1999)

Howse, Robert, "The Labour Conventions Doctrine in an Era of Global Interdependence: Rethinking the Constitutional Dimension of Canada's External Economic Relations" (1990) 16 *Canadian Business Law Journal* 160

Howse, Robert, "The World Trade Organization and the Protection of Workers" Rights" (1999) 3 J*ournal of Small and Emerging Business Law* 131

Howse, Robert and Makua Mutua, *Protecting Human Rights in the Global Economy: Challenges for the World Trade Organizaztion* (Rights and Democracy, Montreal, 1999), online: International Centre for Human Rights and

Democratic Development, http://www.ichrdd.ca/111/english/commdoc/publications/globalization/wtoRightsGlob.html

Hufbauer, Gary C. and Nicholas K. Nitrokostas, *Awakening the Monster: The Alien Tort Statute of 1789* (Institute for International Economics, Washington DC, 2003)

Human Resources and Skills Development Canada, News Release, "Labour Ministers from Canada, Brazil and Mexico present IACML report to the Trade Ministers of the Americas" (20 November 2003), online: www.hrsdc.gc.ca/en/cs/comm/news/2003/021120b/shtml

Human Rights Watch, "Defending the Rights of Migrants and Asylum Seekers in Western Europe" , online: http://www.hrw.org/campaigns/migrants/

Human Rights Watch, "Unfair Advantage: Workers' Freedom of Association in the United States Under International Human Rights Standards" (2000), online: http://www.hrw.org/reports/2000/uslabour

Hussain, Mahmood and Keith E. Maskus, "Child Labour Use and Economic Growth: An Econometric Analysis" (July 2003) 26 *World Economy* 993–1017

Iliopoulou, Anastasia and Helen Toner, "Case C-184/99, Rudy Grzelczyk v. Centre public d'aide sociale d'Ottignies-Louvain-la-Neuve, Judgment of the Full Court of 20 September 2001, CR I-6193" (2002) 39 *Common Market Law Review* 609

Inter-American Conference of Ministers of Labour, Ottawa *Declaration* and *Plan of Action*, XIIth IACML (19 October 2001)

Inter-American Conference of Ministers of Labour, "Feasibility Study for an Inter-American Co-operation Mechanism for Professional Labour Administration", XIIIth IACML (26 September 2003)

Inter-American Conference of Ministers of Labour, Salvador *Declaration* and *Plan of Action*, XIIIth IACML (26 September 2003)

Inter-American Conference of Ministers of Labor Working Group 1, *Labor Dimensions of the Summit of the Americas Process: Globalization, Employment and Labor*, Report presented at the 8th FTAA Ministerial meeting, Miami, Florida (November 2003), online: http://www.oas.org/documents/ ConferenciaTrabajoBrazil/ReportetrabajoGrupo1_eng.pdf

International Catholic Migration Commission, online: http://www/icmc.net/docs/en

International Confederation of Free Trade Unions, *Annual Survey of Violations of Trade Union Rights, 1999* (Brussels, 1999)

International Confederation of Free Trade Unions, *A Trade Union Guide to Globalisation* (Brussels, December 2001)

International Confederation of Free Trade Unions, *Report for the WTO General Council Review of the Trade Policies of Canada* (Geneva, 12 and 14 March 2003), online: http://www.icftu.org, under Trade & Labour Standards: Country Reports: WTO & Labour Standards on Trade & Labour Standards

International Conference of Free Trade Unions, "The International Trade Union Movement and the New Codes of Conduct", online:http://www.icftu.org/

International Labour Conference, *ILO Declaration on Fundamental Principles and Rights at Work* (Geneva, 18 June 1998), online: http://www.ilo.org/dyn/declaris/declarationweb.index

International Labour Organization, "Asia Pacific Economic Cooperation", online: http://www.ilo.org/public/english/employment/gems/eeo/inter/ apec.htm

International Labour Organization, "Current dynamics of international labour migration: Globalisation and regional integration" (Geneva, 2002), online: http://www.ilo.org/public/english/protection/migrant/about/index.htm

International Labour Organization, "Equal Opportunities in The European Union", online: http://www.ilo.org/public/english/employment/gems/eeo/eu/eu_main.htm

International Labour Organization, "International Labour Migration Survey" (International Labour Office, Geneva, 2003), online: http://www.ilo.org/public/english/protection/migrant/projects/survey/ index.htm

International Labour Organization, "Regional Mechanisms", online: http://www.ilo.org/public/english/employment/gems/eeo/inter/toc_main.htmpublic/english/employment/gems/eeo

International Labour Organization, "Your Voice at Work", Global Report under the Follow-Up to the ILO Declaration on Fundamental Principles and Rights at Work (Geneva, 2000)

International Labour Organization, *About the ILO,* online: http://www.ilo.org/public/english/about/history.htm

International Labour Organization, *Code of Practice on the Protection of Workers' Personal Data,* online: http://www.ilo.org/public/english/support/publ/pdf/protect.pdf

International Labour Organization, *Conventions and Recommendations,* online: ILOLEX database, http://www.ilo.org/ilolex/english/index.htm

International Labour Organization, *Decent Work and the Informal Economy*, Report VI, International Labour Conference, 90th Session (International Labour Office, Geneva, 2002)

International Labour Organization, *Employment Statistics in the Informal Sector*, Report III, 15th International Conference of Labour Statisticians (Geneva, 19–28 January 1993)

International Labour Organization, *Freedom of Association and Collective Bargaining*, Report III (Part 4B): General Survey of the Committee of Experts on the Application of Conventions and Recommendations on the Freedom of Association and the Right to Organize Convention (No. 87), 1948, and the Right to Organize and Collective Bargaining Convention (No. 98), 1949, International Labour Conference 81st Session (International Labour Office, Geneva, 1994)

International Labour Organization, *Freedom of Association, Digest of Decisions and Principles of the Freedom of Association Committee of the Governing Body of the ILO* (4th rev. edn, International Labour Office, Geneva, 1996)

International Labour Organization, *Global Employment Trends for Women 2004* (Geneva, 2004)

International Labour Organization, *ILO Declarations, International Labor Conventions and Recommendations,* online: http://www.ilo.org/public/english/comp/civil/standards/iloder.htm

International Labour Organization, *R163 Collective Bargaining Recommendation, 1981,* online: ILOLEX database, http://www.ilo.org/ilolex/english/index.htm

International Labour Organization, *Recommendation on Disguised Employment,* online: http://www.ilo.org/public/english/standards/relm/ilc/ilc91/pdf/pr-21.pdf

International Labour Organization, *Reducing the Decent Work Deficit: A Global Challenge,* Report of the Director General, International Labour Conference, 89th Session (Geneva, 2001)

International Labour Organization, *Report of the Committee of Experts on the Application of Conventions and Recommendations,* International Labour Conference, 89th Session, Report III (1A) (International Labour Office, Geneva, 2001), online: ILOLEX database, http://www.ilo.org/ilolex/english/index.htm

International Labour Organization, *Report of the Director-General: Organizing for Social Justice,* Report I (B), Global Report under the Follow-up to the ILO Declaration on Fundamental Principles and Rights at Work, International Labour Conference 92nd Session (International Labour Office, Geneva, 2004)

International Labour Organization, *The Scope of the Employment Relationship,* online: http://www.ilo.org/public/english/standards/ relm/ilc/ilc91/pdf/rep-v.pdf

International Labour Organization, *Tripartite Declaration of Principles Concerning Multinational Enterprises and Social Policy* (3rd edn), online: http://www.ilo.org/public/english/employment/multi/download/english.pdf

International Labour Organization, *Women and Men in the Informal Economy: A Statistical Picture,* International Labour Conference (International Labour Office, Geneva, 2002)

International Labour Organization, *World Employment Report 1995* (International Labour Office, Geneva, 1995)

International Labour Organization, *World Labour Report 1997–98: Industrial Relations, Democracy and Social Stability* (International Labour Office, Geneva, 1997)

International Labour Organization's Committee on Freedom of Association and Committee of Experts on the Application of Ratified Conventions, online:

http://webfusion.ilo.org/public/db/standards/normes/libsynd/index.cfm?
lang = EN

International Labour Organization's International Programme on the Elimination of Child Labour and National Commission for Child Welfare and Development (Pakistan), *Combating Child Trafficking, Sexual Exploitation and Involvement of Children in Intolerable Forms of Child Labour: Pakistan country report* (1998).

International Labour Organization's World Commission on the Social Dimension of Globalization, *A Fair Globalization: Creating Opportunities for All* (February 2004) online: ILO Homepage, http://www.ilo.org/public/english/ wcsdg/docs/report.pdf

International Labour Organization's World Commission on the Social Dimension of Globalization, *The Social Dimension of Globalization* (March 2003) online: ILO Homepage, http://www.ilo.org/public/english/wcsdg/ globali/globali.htm

International Organization for Migration, "Asian Labour Migration Ministerial Consultation Ends", Press Briefing Note (4 April 2003), online: http://www.iom.int/en/archive/pbn040403.shtml#item3

International Organization for Migration, "Effective Respect for Migrants Rights", online: http://www.iom.int/en/who/main_policies_effrespect.shtml

International Organization for Migration, "Mission Statement", online: http://www.iom.int/en/who/main_mission.shtml

International Program on the Elimination of Child Labor, *Child Labor in the Soccer Ball Industry: A Report on the Continued Use of Child Labor in the Soccer Ball Industry in Pakistan* (International Labor Rights Fund, 1999), online: http://www.laborrights.org/projects/ foulball/index.html

Jacoby, Sanford, "The Duration of Indefinite Employment Contracts in the United States and England: An Historical Analysis" (1982) 5 *Comparative Labor Law Journal* 84

Jain, H. C. and Subba Muthuchidambam, "Ontario Labour Law Reforms: A Comparative Study of Bill 40 and Bill 7" (1996) 4 *Canadian Labour & Employment Law Journal* 311

Jain, H. C. and Subba Muthuchidambam, *Ontario Labour Law Reforms: A History and Evaluation of Bill 40* (IRC Press, Kingston, Ontario, 1995)

Javillier, Jean-Claude, *Droit du travail*, No. 94–95 (7th edn, Paris, LGDJ, 1999)

Jenkins, Rhys, "Corporate Codes of Conduct, Self Regulation in a Global Economy", Technology, Business and Society Programme Paper Number 2 (April 2001), online: United Nations Research Institute for Social Development, http://www.unrisd.org

Johnston, George A., *The International Labour Organization: Its Work for Social and Economic Progress* (Europa Publications Limited, London, 1970)

Kapleau, Philip, *Three Pillars of Zen* (Beacon Press, Boston, Massachusetts, 1967)

Katz, Harry C., "The Decentralization of Collective Bargaining: A Literature Review and Comparative Analysis" (1993) 47(1) *Industrial and Labor Relations Review* 3–22

Kay, Stephen J., "Recent Changes in Latin American Welfare States: Is There Social Dumping?" (2000) 10 *Journal of European Social Policy* 2

Keller, B., "Social Dialogue at Sectoral Level: The Neglected Ingredient of European Industrial Relations", in B. Keller and H. W. Platzer (eds.), *Industrial Relations and European Integration* (Ashgate, Aldershot / Burlington, Ontario, 2003), 30–57

Kenworthy, Lane, "Economic Integration and Convergence: A Look at the US States" (1999) 80 *Social Science Quarterly* 4

Kilcoyne, John, "Developments in Employment Law: The 1986–87 Term" (1988) 10 *Supreme Court Law Review* 183

King, Elizabeth and Andrew Mason, *Equality and Development* (The World Bank, Washington DC, 2000)

Knez, Marc J. and Colin F. Camerer, "Creating Expectational Assets in the Laboratory: Coordination in Weakest-Link Games" (1994) 15 *Strategic Management Journal* 101–19

Knez, Marc J. and Colin F. Camerer, "Increasing Cooperation in Prisoner's Dilemmas by Establishing a Precedent of Efficiency in Coordination Games" (2000) 82(2) *Organizational Behavior & Human Decision Processes* 194–216

Kohl, H. and H.W. Platzer, "Labour Relations in Central and Eastern Europe and the European Social Model" (2003) 9 *Transfer* 11

Kollonay-Lehoczky, Csilla, "European Enlargement – A Comparative View of Hungarian Labour Law", in G.A. Bermann and K. Pistor (eds.), *Law and Governance in an Enlarged European Union* (Hart Publishing, Oxford and Portland, 2004) 209–38

Krueger, Alan B., "The Political Economy of Child Labour", in K. Basu, H. Horn, L. Román and J. Shapiro, *International Labour Standards* (Blackwell, Oxford, 2003) 248–55

Krugman, Paul, "Trabalhadores vs. Trabalhadores", *O Estado de S. Paulo*, 22 May, 2000, B2

Krugman, Paul, *Peddling Prosperity* (W.W. Norton and Co., New York, 1994)

Krugman, Paul, *The Age of Diminished Expectations* (4th edn, MIT Press, Cambridge, Massachusetts, 1994)

Kucera, David, "Core Labour Standards and Foreign Direct Investment" (2002) 141(1–2) *International Labour Review* 31–69

Kucera, David, "The Effects of Core Workers Rights on Labour Costs and Foreign Direct Investment: Evaluating the 'Conventional Wisdom'", *Decent Work Research Programme*, Discussion Paper No. 130/2001 (International Institute for Labour Studies, Geneva, 2001), online: http://www.ilo.org/public/english/bureau/inst/download/dp13001.pdf

Kumar, Vidya S. A., "A Critical Methodology of Globalization: Politics of the 21st Century?" (2003) 10 *Indiana Journal of Global Legal Studies* 87

Kuttner, Thomas, "Constitution as Covenant: Labour Law, Labour Boards and the Courts from the Old to the New Dispensation" (1988) 13 *Queens Law Journal* 32

Kuttner, Thomas, "Federalism and Labour Relations in Canada" (1997) 5 *Canadian Labour and Employment Law Journal* 195

Ladó, M., "EU Enlargement: Reshaping European and National Industrial Relations" (2002) 18 *The International Journal of Comparative Labour Law and Industrial Relations* 101

Ladó, M. and D. Vaughan-Whitehead, "Social dialogue in candidate countries: what for?" (2003) 9 *Transfer* 64

Langille, Brian, "Canadian Labour Law Reform and Free Trade" (1991) 23 *Ottawa Law Review* 3

Langille, Brian, "Competing Conceptions of Regulatory Competition in Debates on Trade Liberalization and Labour Standards", in William Bratton et al. (eds.), *International Regulatory Competition and Coordination: Perspectives on Economic Regulation in Europe and the United States* (Clarendon Press, Oxford, 1996), 479–90

Langille, Brian, "Judicial Review, Judicial Revisionism and Judicial Responsibility" (1986) 17 *Revue Générale de Droit* 169

Langille, Brian, "The Coherence Agenda – A New Approach to International Labour Obligation", Department of Foreign Affairs and International Trade (2002) [unpublished]

Leary, V. A., *International Labour Conventions and National Law: The Effectiveness of the Automatic Incorporation of Treaties in National Legal Systems* (Martinus Nijhoff, Dordrecht, 1982)

Leary, Virginia, "The Paradox of Workers' Rights as Human Rights", in Lance Compa and Stephen Diamond (eds.), *Human Rights, Labor Rights and International Trade* (University of Pennsylvania Press, 1996), 22–47

Leeb, Gavin, "A Global Experience Up Close and Personal: Ontario Government Workers Resist Privatization" (2002) 9 *Canadian Labour & Employment Law Journal* 7

Lewis, David K., *Convention: A Philosophical Study* (Harvard University Press, Cambridge, Massachusetts, 1969)

Li, Xiaorong, "Asian Values and the universality of human rights" (1996) 16(2) *Report from the Institute for Philosophy and Public Policy, Maryland* 1

Lightfoot, Liz, "Students face EU fight for Places", *Daily Telegraph*, 4 March 2004, 1

Lim, L. L., "More and Better Jobs for Women: An Action Guide – An ILO Follow up to the Fourth World Conference on Women and the World Summit for Social Development" (International Labour Office, Geneva, 1996)

Lim, L. L., *The Analysis of Factors Generating International Migration*, UN ACC Task Force on Basic Social Services for All Working Group on International Migration, Paper No. IV/3 (ILO, Geneva, 1998)

Locke, Richard and Kathleen Thelen, "Apples and Oranges Revisited: Contextualized Comparative Labour Politics" (1995) 23 *Politics & Society* 3

Lora, Eduardo and Mauricio Oliveira, "Macro Policies and Employment Problems in Latin America", Working Paper No. 372 (Inter-American Development Bank, Washington DC, 1998)

Lujan, Bertha, "Los sindicatos frente al ACLAN", in Graciela Bensusán (ed.), *Estándares labourales después del TLCAN* (Ebert/FLACSO, 1999), 165–76

Macmillan, Margaret, *Paris 1919: Six Months that Changed the World* (Random House Publishing, New York, 2002)

Maloney, William F., "Does Informality Imply Segmentation in Urban Labor Markets? Evidence from Sectoral Transitions in Mexico" (1999) 13(2) *World Bank Economic Review* 275–302

Maskus, Keith, "Should Core Labour Standards be Imposed through International Trade Policy", World Bank Policy Research Working Paper No. 1817 (The World Bank Group, 1997)

Mattila, H. S., "Protection of Migrants' Human Rights: Principles and Practice" (2000) 38(6) *International Migration* 53

Maupin, Francis, "Le renouveau de débat normatif à l'OIT de la fin de la guerre froide à la mondialisation' [unpublished], cited in *International Labour Standards Department Discussion Paper* (ILO, Geneva, 2002)

Mazey, Edward, "Grieving Through the NAALC and the Social Charter: A Comparative Analysis of their Procedural Effectiveness" (2001) 10 *Michigan State University – D.C.L. Journal of International Law* 239

McCormack, Judith, "Comment on 'The Politicization of the Ontario Labour Relations Framework in the 1990s'" (1999) 7 *Canadian Labour & Employment Law Journal* 325

McCormick, John, *The European Union: Politics and Policies* (2nd edn, Westview Press, Boulder, Colorado, 1999)

McKennirey, John, "Labor in the International Economy" (1996) 22 *Canada-U.S. Law Journal* 183

McMillan, John, *Game Theory in International Economics* (Harwood, Chur, Switzerland, 1986)

McNeil, Michael, "Unions and the *Charter*: The Supreme Court of Canada and Democratic Values" (2003) 10 *Canadian Labour and Employment Law Journal* 3

Meier, Gerald, *Leading Issues in Economic Development* (Oxford University Press, 1964)

Mendoza, Enrique, Assaf Razin and Linda Tesar, "Effective Tax Rates in Macroeconomics: Cross-Country Estimates of Tax Rates on Factor Incomes and Consumption" (1994) 34 *Journal of Monetary Economy* 297

Mendoza, Enrique, Gian Maria Milesi-Ferreti and Patrick Asea, "On the Ineffectiveness of Tax Policy in Altering Long-run Growth: Harberger's Superneutrality Conjecture", Center for Economic Policy Research Discussion Paper No. 1378 (CEPR, 1996)

Mercosur, *Observatorio*, online: http://www.observatorio.net

Mercury, James and Bryan Schwartz, "Creating the Free Trade Area of the Americas: Linking Labour, the Environment, and Human Rights to the FTAA" (2001) 1 *Asper Review of International Business and Trade Law* 37

Migrants Rights International, online: http://www.migrantwatch.org/

Miles, T., "Warnings over Influx of EU College Students", *Evening Standard*, 4 March 2004, 24

Milkman, Ruth, *Japan's California Factories: Labor Relations and Economics Globalization* (Institute of Industrial Relations, Los Angeles, California, 1991)

Mill, John Stuart, "Employment of Children in Manufactories", in Ann P. Robson and John M. Robson (eds.), *Newspaper Writings August 1831–October 1834*, vol. 23 *Collected Works of John Stuart Mill* (University of Toronto Press, 1986), 398–401

Mitchell, Daniel J.B. and Katherine G. Abraham, "Shifting Norms in Wage Determination" [1985(2)] *Brookings Papers on Economic Activity* 575–608

Mittelman, James H., "How Does Globalization Really Work?" in James H. Mittelman (ed.), *Globalization: Critical Reflections* (Lynne Rienner Publishers Inc., Colorado, 1996) 229–42

Mkapa, President of Tanzania, "National Dialogue on the Social Dimensions of Globalization" (Dar es Salaam, August 2002)

Monahan, Patrick, *Storming the Pink Palace: The NDP in Power: A Cautionary Tale* (Lester Publishing, Toronto, Ontario, 1995)

Monterrey, *Declaration of Nuevo Léon* (13 January 2004), online: http://www.ftaa-alca.org/Summits/Monterrey/NLeon_e.asp

Moore, Molly, "Mexican Farmhands Accuse U.S. Firms: Panel Hears Washington Apple Pickers", *Washington Post*, 3 December 1998, A-36

Moran, Theodore H., *Beyond Sweatshops: Foreign Direct Investment and Globalization in Developing Countries* (Brookings Institute, Washington DC, 2002)

Morici, Peter and Evan Schulz, *Labour Standards in the Global Trading System* (Economic Strategy Institute, Washington DC, 2001)

Morris, L., *Managing Migration: Civil Stratification and Migrants' Rights* (Routledge, London, 2002)

Mosley, Hugh, "The 'Social Dumping' Threat of European Integration: A Critique", in Brigitte Unger and Frans van Warden (eds.), *Convergence or Diversity?*

Internationalization and Economic Policy Response (Ashgate Publishing Ltd, Aldershot, 1995) 182–99

Mulcahy, R. E., *Subsidiarity, New Catholic Encyclopedia* (McGraw Hill, New York, 1967), vol. 13

Mullan, David, "Judging the Judgment of Judges: *CUPE v Ontario (Minister of Labour)*" (2003) 10 *Canadian Labour & Employment Law Journal* 431

Murry, Jill, *Corporate Codes of Conduct and Labour Standards,* International Labour Organization Bureau for Workers' Activities, online: http://www.itcilo. it/english/actrav/telearn/global/ilo/GUIDE/JILL.HTM.

Nadeau, Robert and Menas Kafatos, *The Non-Local Universe: The New Physics and Matters of the Mind* (Oxford University Press, 2001)

Nagel, John, "Mexico's President Fox Signs New Anti-Discrimination Law", *BNA Daily Labour Report,* 11 June 2003, A-4

Nielsen, H. K., "The Concept of Discrimination in ILO Convention No. 111" (1994) 43 *International and Comparative Law Quarterly* 827

Nielsen, R., *European Labour Law* (DJOF Publishing, Copenhagen, 2000)

Nielson, Laura, "Paying Workers or Paying Lawyers: Employee Termination Practices in the United States and Canada" (1999) 21 *Law and Social Policy* 247

O'Leary, Siofra, "Putting Flesh on the Bones of European Union Citizenship" (1999) 24 *European Law Review* 68

O'Rourke, Dara, *Outsourcing Regulation: Analyzing Non-Governmental Systems of Labour Standards and Monitoring,* online: http://web.mit.edu/dorourke/ www/PDF/OutsourcingReg.pdf

Obando, A., "Women Facing Globalization: The Impact of Neo-Liberal Globalization on the Economic, Social and Cultural Rights of Women" (Women's Human Rights Net, 2003), online: http://www.whrnet.org/docs/issue-globalisation.html

Ohno, Kenichi, "The Case for a New System", in *Bretton Woods: Looking to the Future,* Commission Report Staff Review Background Papers (Bretton Woods Commission, Washington, 1994) C-5 - C-12

Oman, Charles P., *Policy Competition for Foreign Direct Investment* (OECD Development Centre, Paris, 1999)

Organization for Economic Co-operation and Development, "International Trade and Core Labour Standards", Policy Brief (Paris, 2000), online: http://www.oecd.org/dataoecd/2/36/1917944.pdf

Organization for Economic Co-operation and Development, *Bilateral Labour Agreements: Evaluated and Prospectus,* Note by the Secretariat, OECD and the Swiss Federal Office of Immigration, Integration and Emigration (IMES) Seminar on Bilateral Labour Agreements and Other Forms of Recruitment of Foreign Workers, Montreux (19–20 June 2003)

Organization for Economic Co-operation and Development, *Trade, Employment and Labour Standards: A Study of Core Workers' Rights in International Trade* (Paris, 1996)

Organization for Economic Co-operation and Development, *Harmful Tax Competition: An Emerging Global Issue* (1998)

Ostrom, Elinor, "Toward a Behavioral Theory Linking Trust, Reciprocity, and Reputation", in Elinor Ostrom and James Walker (eds.), *Trust and Reciprocity: Interdisciplinary Lessons from Experimental Research* (Russell Sage, New York, 2003)

Pager, Sean, "Strictness and Subsidiarity: An Institutional Perspective on Affirmative Action at the European Court of Justice" (2003) 26 *Boston College International and Comparative Law Review* 35

Paterson, Robert et al., *International Trade and Investment Law in Canada* (2nd edn, Carswell, Toronto, 2003)

Peers, Steve, "'Social Advantages' and Discrimination in Employment: Case Law Confirmed and Clarified" (1997) 22 *European Law Review* 157

Petrella, Riccardo, "Une même logique inégalitaire sur toute la planète", *Le Monde Diplomatique*, January 1991, 6

Picciotto, Sol, "The Regulatory Criss-Cross: Interaction between Jurisdiction and the Construction of Global Regulatory Networks", in William Bratton et al. (eds.), *International Regulatory Competition and Coordination: Perspectives on Economic Regulation in Europe and the United States* (Clarendon Press, Oxford, 1996), 89–123

Pier, Carol, "El Salvador's Failure to Protect Workers' Human Rights: Implications for CAFTA", Human Rights Watch Briefing (May 2003)

Pinheiro, Armando Castelar, "Judicial System Performance and Economic Development", Ensaios BNDES, No. 2 (Rio de Janeiro, 1997)

Piore, Michael, "Trade and the Social Structure of Economic Activity", in Susan Collins (ed.), *Imports, Exports and the Aerocan Worker* (Brookings Institutions Press, Washington DC, 1998) 257–86

Piper, N. and R. Iredale, "Identification of the Obstacles to the Signing and Ratification of the UN Convention on the Protection of the Rights of all Migrant Workers 1990: The Asia Pacific Perspective" (UNESCO, 2003), online: http://portal.unesco.org/shs/en/ev.php@ULR_ID = 3170&ULR_DO = DO_TOPIC&URL_SECTION = -465.html

Pitkin, Hannah F., *The Concept of Representation* (University of California Press, Berkeley/Los Angeles/London, 1972)

Platform for International Cooperation on Undocumented Migrants, online: http://www.picum.org/

Polaski, Sandra, "How to Build a Better Trade Pact with Central America", Carnegie Endowment for International Peace (CEIP) Issue Brief (July, 2003)

Polaski, Sandra, "Trade and Labour Standards: A Strategy for Developing Countries", Carnegie Endowment for International Peace (CEIP) Issue Brief (2003)

Poppi, C., "Wider Horizons with Larger Details: Subjectivity, Ethnicity and Globalization", in Alan Scott (ed.), *The Limits of Globalization: Cases and Arguments* (Routledge, London, 1997), 284–305

Porte, C. de la and P. Pochet, "Supple Coordination at EU Level and the Key Actors' Involvement", in C. de la Porte and P. Pochet (eds.), *Building Social Europe through the Open Method of Coordination* (Interuniversity Press, Brussels, 2002), 27

Portes, Alejandro and John Walton, *Labor, Class and the International System* (Academic Press, New York/London, 1981)

Portes, Alejandro, "By-passing the Rules: The Dialectics of Labour Standards and Informalization in Less Developed Countries", in Werner Sengenberger and Duncan Campbell (eds.), *International Labour Standards and Economic Interdependence* (International Institute for Labour Studies, Geneva, 1994)

Pothier, Dianne, "Twenty Years of Labour Law and the Charter" (2002) 40 *Osgoode Hall Law Journal* 369

Potobsky, Geraldo von, "La Declaración Sociolaboural del Mercosur", *Revista del Ministerio del Trabajo* (Ministry of Labour of Argentina, 1999)

Potter, Edward E., *Freedom of Association, the Right to Organize and Collective Bargaining: The Impact of U.S. Law and Practice of Ratification of ILO Conventions No. 87 and No. 98* (Labor Policy Association, Washington DC, 1984)

Previdência Social, *Dados da Secretaria de Assistência Social* (Brasília, Ministério da Assistência e Previdência Social, 1999)

Rae, Bob, *From Protest to Power: Personal Reflections on a Life in Politics* (Viking, Toronto, Ontario, 1996)

Reid, Michael, *Mercosur: A Critical Overview* (Mercosur Study Group, Chatham House, London, 2002)

Reid, T. et al., "58 Die in Lorry Ride to Hope", *The Times*, 20 June 2000

Reshef, Yonatan and Sandra Rastin, *Unions in the Time of Revolution: Government Restructuring in Alberta and Ontario* (University of Toronto Press, Ontario, 2003)

Richards, Peter, "Economy: Caribbean Region Preparing for Globalization", *Inter-Press Service*, 16 October 2002

Rios, Sandra Polônia and Soraya Saavedra Rosar, "As Negociações de Acesso a Mercados na ALCA e a Agenda Brasileira", in Alberto do Amaral Junior and Michelle Raton Sanchez (eds.), *O Brasil e a ALCA* (Editora Aduaneiras, São Paulo, 2003) 259–88

Rittich, K., "Feminization and Contingency: Regulating the Stakes of Work for Women", in J. Conaghan, R. L. Fischl and K. Klare (eds.), *Labour Law in an Era of Globalization, Transformative Practices and Possibilities* (Oxford University Press, 2002) 117–36

Robertson, Roland, "Mapping the Global Condition: Globalization as the Central Concept", in Mike Featherstone (ed.), *Global Culture: Nationalism, Globalization and Modernity: Theory Culture and Society, Special Issue* (Sage Publications, London, 1990), vol. 7(2–3), 15–30

Rodrik, Dani , "Labor Standards in International Trade: Do They Matter and What Do We Do about Them?", in Robert Z. Lawrence, Dani Rodrik and John Whalley (eds.), *Emerging Agenda for Global Trade: High Stakes for Developing Countries* (Overseas Development Council, Washington DC, 1996), 35–79

Rodrik, Dani, *Has Globalization Gone Too Far?* (Institute for International Economics, Washington DC, 1997)

Rodrik, Dani, "Democracies Pay Higher Wages" (1999) 114(3) *The Quarterly Journal of Economics* 707

Rondinelli, D., "Institutions and Market Development: Capacity Building for Economic and Social Transition" (Enterprise and Cooperative Department, ILO, Geneva, 1998)

Rose, Joseph B., "The Assault on School Teacher Bargaining in Ontario" (2002) 57: 1 *Relations Industrielles* 100

Rothstein, Edward, "Europe's Constitution: All Hail the Bureaucracy", *New York Times*, 5 July 5 2003, B9

Rousseau, Jean-Jacques, *Discours sur l'Origine et les Fondements de l'Inégalité*, Seconde Partie, 3 Oeuvres Complètes (1755) (Jean Starobinski edition, Pléiade edition, 1964)

Rubery, Jill and Damian Grimshaw, *The Organization of Employment: International Perspectives* (Palgrave, Basingstoke, 2003)

Rugman, Alan, *The End of Globalization* (Random House, London, 2001)

Ruhs, M., "Temporary Foreign Worker Programmes: Policies, Adverse Consequences, and the Need to Make them Work" 6 *Perspectives on Labour Migration* (International Labour Office, Geneva, 2003)

Russell-Brown, Sherrie L., "Labor Rights as Human Rights: The Situation of Women Workers in Jamaica's Export Free Zones" (2003) 24 *Berkeley Journal of Employment and Labor Law* 179–201

Ruwanpura, K., "Quality of Women's Employment: A Focus on the South" (2004), Decent Work Research Programme, International Institute for Labour Studies, online: http://www.ilo.org/public/english/bureau/inst/research/crbien.htm

Sabel, Charles F., Dara O'Rourke and Archon Fung, *Ratcheting Labour Standards: Regulation for Continuous Improvement in the Global Workplace* (World Bank, Washington DC, 2000)

Sachs, Jeffery, "Globalization and Employment", Public Lectures, International Institute for Labour Studies (Geneva, 18 March 1996)

Salazar-Xirinachs, José M., "The Summit Process and Plan of Action: Goals and Strategies for Hemispheric Integration", in Willi Momm (ed.), *Labour Issues in the Context of Economic Integration and Free Trade: A Caribbean Perspective* (ILO Subregional Office for the Caribbean, 1999), 147–58

Salgado, Arturo Gomez, "Denuncian migrantes violaciones labourales", *El Financiero*, 3 December 1998, 19

Salmi, Jamil, *Constructing Knowledge Societies: New Challenges for Tertiary Education* (World Bank, 2002), online: http://www.worldbank.org/education/tertiary

Samuelson, Paul, "International Trade and Equalization of Factor Process" (1948) 7 *Economic Journal* 163

Santos, Boaventura De Sousa, *Toward a New Common Sense: Law, Science and Politics in Paradigmatic Transition* (Routledge, New York, 1995)

Scheuerman, William E., "Globalization and the Fate of Law", in David Dyzenhaus (ed.), *Recrafting the Rule of Law* (Hart Publishing, Oxford, 1999), 243–66

Scheuerman, William, "Globalization", in Edward N. Zalta (ed.), *The Stanford Encyclopedia of Philosophy, Fall 2002 Edition* (Stanford Metaphysics Research Lab, Center for the Study of Language and Information, 2002), online: http://plato.stanford.edu/archives/fall2002/entries/globalization

Schor, Juliet B., *The Overworked American: The Unexpected Decline of Leisure* (Basic Books, New York, 1991)

Schulten, T., "Europeanisation of Collective Bargaining: Trade Union Initiatives for the Transnational Coordination of Collective Bargaining Relations", in B. Keller and H.W. Platzer (eds.), *Industrial Relations and European Integration* (Ashgate, Aldershot / Burlington, Ontario, 2003), 112–36

Schwartzman, Simon, *Trabalho Infantil no Brasil* (OIT, Brasília, 2001)

Sciabarra, Chris M., *Marx, Hayek, and Utopia* (State University of New York Press, Albany, 1995)

Secretaria da Educação, *Bolsa-Escola, Um Programa de Educação Máxima* (Governo do Distrito Federal, Brasília, 1998)

Sen, Amartya, "Isolation, Assurance, and the Social Rate of Discount" (1967) 81(1) *Quarterly Journal of Economics* 112–24

Sen, Amartya, "Our Culture, their Culture", *New Republic*, 1 April 1996, 4

Sen, Amartya, *Development As Freedom* (Oxford University Press, New York and Oxford, 1999)

Sen, Amartya, "Work and Rights" (2000) 193(2) *International Labour Review* 114

Sengenberger, Werner, *Globalization and Social Progress: The Role and Impact of International Labour Standards* (Friedrich-Ebert-Stiftung, Bonn, 2002)

Sewerynski, M., "Employee Involvement and EU Enlargement – Polish Perspective, in M. Biagi (ed.), *Quality of Work and Employee Involvement in Europe* (Kluwer Law International, The Hague / London / New York, 2002), 270

Sharpe, Calvin, "Integrity Review of Statutory Arbitration Awards" (2003) 54 *Hastings Law Journal* 311

Shotwell, James T. (ed.), *The Origins of the International Labor Organization* (Columbia University Press, New York, 1934), vol. 1

Silber, Simão Davi, "Aspectos Econômicos da Formação da Área de Livre Comércio das Américas", in Alberto do Amaral Junior e Michelle Raton Sanchez (eds.), *O Brazil e a ALCA* (Editora Aduaneiras, São Paulo, 2003)

Sklair, Leslie, *Globalization: Capitalism and its Alternatives* (Oxford, New York, 2002)

Skyrms, Brian, *The Stag Hunt and the Evolution of Social Structure* (Cambridge University Press, 2004)

Slinn, Sara, "The Effect of Compulsory Certification Votes on Certification Applications in Ontario: An Empirical Analysis" (2003) 10 *Canadian Labour & Employment Law Journal* 367

Smiley, Donald V., *The Federal Condition in Canada* (McGraw-Hill Ryerson, Toronto, Ontario, 1987)

Soto, Hernando de, *The Mystery of Capital: Why Capitalism Triumphs in the West and Fails Everywhere Else* (Basic Books, New York, 2000)

Souza, Josias de, "Maioria na América Latina Apoiaria Ditadura Eficiente", *Folha de S. Paulo*, 21 April 2004

Spar, Debora, "Foreign Investment and Human Rights: International Lessons" (1999) 42(1) *CHALLENGE* 55–80

Stalker, P., *Workers Without Frontiers: The Impact of Globalization on International Migration*, (ILO, Geneva, 2000)

Stanford, Jim, Christine Elwell and Scott Sinclair, *Social Dumping under North American Free Trade* (Canadian Centre for Policy Alternatives, Ottawa, 1993)

Stanojevic, M. and G. Gradev, "Workers' Representation at Company Level in CEE countries" (2003) 9 *Transfer* 31

Stern, Nicholas, "Dynamic Development: Innovation and Inclusion", Munich Lectures on Economics (November 2002)

Stiglitz, Joseph E., "Employment, Social Justice and Societal Well-being" (2002) 141(1–2) *International Labour Review* 9–29

Stone, Katherine, "Mandatory Arbitration of Individual Employment Rights: The Yellow Dog Contract of the 1990s" (1996) 73 *Denver University Law Review* 1017

Stone, Katherine, *From Widgets to Digits: Employment Regulation for the Changing Workplace* (Cambridge University Press, Cambridge, 2004)

Storrie, Donald, "Temporary Agency Work in the European Union" (European Foundation for the Improvement of Living and Working Conditions, Dublin, 2002), online: http://www.fr.eurofound.eu.int/publications/files/EF0202EN.pdf

Summers, Clyde, "Employment at Will in the United States: The Divine Right of Employers" (2000) 3 *University of Pennsylvania, Journal of Labor and Employment Law* 65

Sunstein, Cass R., "On the Expressive Function of Law" (1996) 144 *University of Pennsylvania Law Review* 2021

Taran, P. and E. Geronimi, *Globalization, Labour and Migration: Protection is Paramount, Perspectives on Labour Migration 3E* (International Labour Office, Geneva, 2003)

Taran, P., "Human Rights of Migrants: Challenges of the New Decade" (2000) 38 *International Migration* 7–51

Taran, P., "Statement by the ILO to the Expert Meeting on Clarifying and Expanding the Rights of Non-Nationals", Organized by the Open Justice Initiative, New York (9–10 November 2003), online: http://www.ilo.org/public/english/bureau/exrel/events/statements/2003/migrants-osj.htm

Teubner, Gunther (ed.), *Global Law Without a State* (Tyne & Wear, Gateshead, 1997)

Tokman, Victor and Daniel Martinez Fernándes, "Los Temas Labourales em el Mercorur", *El Mercado Comun del Sur: Mercosur: Estudio de Caso sobre una Experiencia de Integración Economica* (Officina Internacional del Trabajo, Lima, 1997)

Traxler, F., "Farewell to Labour Market Associations? Organized versus Disorganized Decentralization as a Map for Industrial Relations", in F. Traxler (ed.), *Organized Industrial Relations in Europe: What Future?* (Aldershot, Ashgate, 1995), 3–20

Trubek, David et al., "Global Restructuring and the Law: Studies of the Internationalization of Legal Fields and the Creation of Transnational Arenas" (1994) 44:2 *Case Western Reserve Journal of International Law* 407

Twining, William, *Globalization and Legal Theory* (Butterworths, London, 2000)

UNICEF, ILO, Declare Soccer Ball Industry Child Labour Free, *Pakistani Newswire*, 27 April 2002

United Nations, *Report of the Fourth World Conference on Women*, Chapter 1, resolution 1, annex 1 and 2, A/CONF.177/20 (Beijing, 1995)

United Nations, *Report of the World Summit on Social Development*, Chapter 1, annex 1, Doc. A/CONF/166/9 (Copenhagen, 1995)

United Nations, *Millenium Declaration*, UN MD, 55th Session, UN Doc. A/RES/55/2 (2000), online: http://www.un.org/millennium/declaration/ares552e.pdf

United Nations, *The World's Women 2000: Trends and Statistics* (New York, 2000)

United Nations, *Decent Work and the Informal Sector*, ILOOR, International Labour Conference, Agenda Item Six, 92-2-112429-0 (2002)

United Nations, *Strengthening of the United Nations: an agenda for further change*, General Assembly, 57th Session, Doc. A/57/387 (9 September 2002), online: http://www.un.org/reform/pdfs/sgreport.pdf

United Nations, *Time for Equality at Work: Report of the ILO Director General*, ILOOR, Report 1B, 92-2-112871-7 (2003)

United Nations, *Working out of poverty: Report of the ILO Director General*, ILOOR, 92-2-112870-9 (2003)

United Nations, "Division for the Advancement of Women", online: http://www.un.org/womenwatch/daw/cedaw

United Nations Conference on Trade and Development, *World Investment Report* (1994)

United Nations Conference on Trade and Development, *Trade and Development Report 1997* (1997)

United Nations Commission on Trade and Development, *World Investment Report 2003: Overview*, online: www.unctad.org/en/docs//wir2003overview_en.pdf

United Nations Development Programme, *Asia Pacific Gender Network*, online: http://www.undp.org.ph/apgen/home1.htm

Uriarte, Oscar Ermida, "Instituciones y Relaciones Labourales del Mercosur", in *El Mercado Comun del Sur: Mercosur: Estudio de Caso sobre una Experiencia de Integración Economica* (Officina Internacional del Trabajo, Lima 1997)

Urwin, Derek, *The Community of Europe* (2nd edn, Longman, Essex, 1994)

US Bureau of Democracy, Human Rights and Labor, *Country Reports on Human Rights Practices, Pakistan-2001* (US Department of State, 2002), online: http://www.state.gov/g/drl/rls/hrrpt/2001/sa/8237.htm

US Council for International Business, "Comments on Implementation of US National Administrative Office", Letter to US NAO (15 Febuary 1994)

Valticos, Nicolas, "Fifty Years of Standard-setting Activities by the International Labour Organization" (1969) 100(3) *International Labour Review* 201

Van Horn, Carl E. and K. A. Dixon, "The Disposable Worker: Living in a Job-Loss Economy", 6:2 Work Trends, John J. Heldrich Center for Workforce Development, Rutgers University and Center for Survey Research and Analysis, University of Connecticut, Rutgers University (2003), online: http://www.heidrich.rutgers.edu

Van Huyck, John B., Raymond C. Battalio and Richard O. Beil, "Tacit Coordination Games, Strategic Uncertainty, and Coordination Failure" (1990) 80(1) *American Economic Review* 234–48

Varennes, F. de, "Strangers in Foreign Lands: Diversity, Vulnerability and the Rights of Migrants", Discussion Paper (UNESCO, 2003), online: http://www.unesco.org/most/paper_devarennes.pdf

Velasco, Elizabeth, "Trabajadores agrícolas denuncian explotación en EU", *La Jornada*, 3 December 1998

Verge, Pierre, "La place des droits relatifs au travail dans le projet d'integration des Amériques" *Les Cahiers de Droit* (Université Laval, Quebec, 2003)

Verma, Anil, "Global Labour Standards: Can we get from here to there?", paper presented at the 13th World Congress of the International Industrial Relations Association, Berlin (8–12 September 2003)

Voegelin, Eric, *The New Science of Politics* (University of Chicago Press, Illinois, 1952)

Wai, Robert, "Countering, Branding, Dealing: Using Economic and Social Rights in and around the International Trade Regime" (2003) 14 *European Journal of International Law* 35

Webb, Sidney and Beatrice, *Industrial Democracy* (Longmans Green, London, 1897)

Weber, Roberto, Colin Camerer, Yuval Rottenstreich and Marc Knez, "The Illusion of Leadership: Misattribution of Cause in Coordination Games" (2001) 12(5) *Organizational Science* 582–98

Weigall, David, *The Origins and Development of the European Community* (Leicester University Press, 1992)

Weiler, Paul, "The *Charter* at Work: Reflections on the Constitutionalizing of Labour and Employment Law" (1990) 40 *University of Toronto Law Journal* 117

Weiss, Linda, *The Myth of the Powerless State* (Cornell University Press, Ithaca, New York, 1998)

Weiss, M., "Social Dialogue and Collective Bargaining in the Framework of Social Europe", in G. Spyropoulos and G. Fragnière (eds.), *Work and Social Policies in the New Europe* (European Interuniversity Press, Brussels, 1991), 59–74

Weiss, M., "'Workers' Participation in the European Union", in P. Davies et al. (eds.), *European Community Labour Law – Principles and Perspectives* (Clarendon Press, Oxford, 1996) 213–36

Weiss, M., "The Politics of the EU Charter of Fundamental Rights", in B. Hepple (ed.), *Social and Labour Rights in a Global Context* (Cambridge University Press, 2002), 73–94

Weiss, M., "Workers' Involvement in the European Company", in M. Biagi (ed.), *Quality of Work and Employee Involvement in Europe* (Kluwer Law International, The Hague / London / New York, 2002), 63–82

Weiss, M., "Industrial Relations and EU-Enlargement", in R. Blanpain and M. Weiss (eds.), *Changing Industrial Relations and Modernisation of Labour Law* (Kluwer Law International, The Hague, 2003), 439–48

Weiss, M., "The Social Dimension as Part of the Constitutional Framework", in Reiner Hoffmann et al. (eds.), *European Integration as a Social Experiment in a Globalized World* (Dusseldorf, Hans Böckler Stiftung, 2003), 31–46

Weiss, M. and K. Petkov, "The Social Dimension", in R. Langewiesche and A. Toth (eds.), *The Unity of Europe: Political, Economic and Social Dimensions of*

EU Enlargement (European Trade Union Institute, Brussels, Belgium, 2001), 123–40

Wick, Ingeborg, "Workers' Tool or PR Ploy?: A Guide to Codes of International Labour Practice" (3rd rev. edn, Friedrich-Ebert-Stiftung, Bonn and SÜDWIND Institut für Ökonomie und Ökumene, Siegburg, 2003), online: http://www.suedwind-institut.de/Workers-tool-2003.pdf

Wilken, David, "Manufacturing Crisis in Workers' Compensation" (1998) 13 *Journal of Law and Social Policy* 124

Wittgenstein, Ludwig, *Philosophical Investigations* (Blackwell, Oxford, 1953)

Wolfensohn, James D., "Opening Remarks at the International Conference on Poverty Reduction Strategies", Paper presented to the IMF/World Bank international conference (January 2002)

Wood, Adrian, *North-South Trade, Employment and Inequality: Changing Fortunes in a Skill-Driven World* (Clarendon Press, London, 1995)

Working Party on the Social Dimension of Globalization, "Investment in the Global Economy and Decent Work", 283rd Session, ILO Doc. GB.283/WP/SDG/2 (2002)

World Bank, *Collective Bargaining and Country Economic Performance: A Review of the Empirical Literature* (2000) [unpublished]

World Bank, "Workers in an Integrating World, 2002" (Oxford University, Washington, DC, 2002)

World Bank, *East Asia Integrates: A Trade Policy for Shared Growth* (Washington DC, 2003)

World Bank Gender and Development Group, *Gender Equality and the Millennium Development Goals* (World Bank, Washington, 2002)

World Trade Organization, *Singapore Ministerial Declaration*, Doc. WT/MIN(96)/DEC (18 December 1996)

WTO Panel Rules in India's Favour (World Trade Organisation Panel Dismisses EU's GSP Scheme), *India Business Insight*, 7 September 2003

Yates, C., "The ILO Declaration on Fundamental Principles and Rights at Work: The Limitations to Global Labour Standards", in Maureen Irish (ed.), *The Auto Pact and Beyond* (London: Kluwer Law International, 2004), 243–56

Yung, Katherine, "El Paso No Longer Believes in NAFTA after Garment Industry Fades, Jobless Ranks Mount", *Dallas Morning News*, 13 April 2003, 1D

Zoellick, Robert B., "Trading in Freedom: The New Endeavor of the Americas" (2002), 7(3) *Electronic Journal of the U.S. Department of State*, online: http://usinfo.state.gov/journals/ites/1002/ijee/ftaa-aldonas.htm

Working in other industries: Violation of Labour Rules in Sialkot District, *Pakistani Newswire*, 3 March 2002

INDEX

Aachen, Congress of (1818), 16
Achacoso, Tomas, 431
Adams, Roy, 118
Africa
  gender equality, 388
  informal economies, 341
agency workers
  CEE countries, 204, 207–9
  European Union, 208
  ILO Convention, 204, 208–9
  licensing agencies, 208
Aix-la-Chapelle, Congress of. See
    Aachen
Algeria, 437
Americas
  CARICOM. See CARICOM
  FTAA. See FTAA; Summit of the
    Americas
  gender equality instruments, 387–8
  labour standards, 8–10, 39
  Mercosur. See Mercosur
Amsterdam Treaty, 23–4, 180, 387–8
Anguilla, 272
anti-dumping tariffs, 156–7, 305
anti-globalization protests, 34, 39
Antigua and Barbuda, 272
arbitration, 59
Argentina
  anti-neoliberalism, 306
  Bolivian migrants, 426
  cross-border collective bargaining,
    258, 259
  debt default, 307–8
  and FTAA, 306
  labour contracts, 310
  labour laws, 309
  and Mercosur, 30, 245, 308

  protectionism, 307–8
  social costs, 313
Arthurs, Harry, 129, 131
ASEAN, 388
Asia
  gender equality, 388
  migrant workers, 422
  values, 343, 345
Australia, Generalized System of
    Preferences, 166
Austria, 17, 208
Auto-Trim, 263
Avi-Yonah, Reuven, 106
Azerbaijan, 421, 438

Bahamas, 272, 437
Bahrain, 421
Baltic states
  labour codes, 202
  post-communist legal position,
    192–3
Bangladesh, 149–50
Barbados, 272, 437
Barré, Philippe, 118
Beijing Declaration, 386–7, 390, 392,
    394
Belgium, 21, 107, 169, 177, 197, 208,
    218, 437
Belize, 272, 437, 438
Benin, 437
Berlin Congress 1890, 357–8
Bern Conference 1890, 17
Bern Conference 1906, 17
Biagi, Marco, 108, 109, 112, 118, 132
Bible, Exodus, 116–18
Bismarck, Otto von, 357–8
Bohr, Niels, 115

Bolivia, 438
Bosnia-Herzegovina, 216, 437, 438
boycotts, 367–8
Brazil
    anti-neo-liberalism, 306
    child labour, 324–5
    cross-border collective bargaining,
        258, 259
    currency devaluation, 307
    freedom of association, 309–10
    and FTAA, 32, 246, 306
    labour conditions, 310, 311
    labour contracts, 310
    labour laws, 309–10
    legal procedures, 318
    and Mercosur, 30, 245
    pension reform, 317
    ratification of ILO conventions, 437
    science and technology investment,
        286
    social costs, 311, 313–15
    termination of employment, 316
Bricker, John, 356, 372–3
British Virgin Islands, 272
Brussels Conference 1856, 16
Bulgaria
    communist regime, 192
    and EU membership, 191–2
    labour code, 202, 218
    post-communism, 191, 193–4
    temporary workers, 220
    termination of employment, 221
Burkina Faso, 396, 437, 438
Bush, George H. W., 27
business, right to conduct a business,
        25

CAFTA, 267, 365
Cairo Declaration, 344
Cambodia, 364–5
Cameroon, 437
Campbell, Duncan, 112–13
Canada
    Alberta labour inspectors, 261
    bilateral treaties, 246, 247
    collective bargaining, 119–20, 124
    constitutional rights, 63–4
    flexible employment, 59–60

freedom of association, 262–3
    and FTA, 26, 77
    future labour law, 56–65
    Generalized System of Preferences,
        166
    and globalization, 52–3, 54, 56–7
    and ILO conventions, 61
    labour case law, 52–3, 63–4
    labour standards, 63–4, 77, 278
    labour tribunals, 64
    migrant workers, 427
    mission statement, 286–8
    and NAALC, 251, 263
    and NAFTA, 26
    and neo-liberalism, 57
    Ontario labour law, 58
    privatization of labour law, 58–9
    provincial jurisdictions, 61, 249
    public employees' rights, 268
    recent labour history, 77–8
    transnational firms, 53–4
    US influence, 53, 56–7
Cape Verde, 438
CARICOM
    Charter of Civil Society, 245, 247,
        256–8, 267
    and corporate abuse, 260
    creation, 256
    economic effect, 245
    enforcement of rights, 257–8
    gender equality, 387, 388
    members, 272
    social partners, 256, 258–9
Carneiro, Pedor, 285, 286
catfish, 156–7
Catholic Church, 129
CEDAW, 385–6, 392
CEE countries
    agency workers, 207–9
    collective bargaining, 172, 185–6,
        195, 196, 199–200, 202–3,
        214–15
    communist regime
        collective bargaining, 195
        labour laws, 194–5
        legacy, 200–1
        trade unions, 194–5
    contracts of employment, 202, 203

Copenhagen criteria, 191–2, 198
employee participation, 172, 186
employee status, 209–10
employers' associations, 171, 186, 202
employment agencies, 204
equality issues, 213
EU membership, 7–8, 25–6, 169, 192, 234
freedom of association, 199–200
historical legacy, 7–8, 200–1
industrial relations, 170–3
  EU impact, 41, 185–7
  ILO impact, 199–200
labour laws
  codification, 201–2
  communist regime, 194–5
  continuous process, 200
  current structures, 201–3
  discriminatory laws, 201
  German model, 198, 199, 211
  ILO influence, 199–200
  model, 196–8
  post-communism, 8, 191–2, 195–8
legal system at end of communism, 192–5
legal theory v. practice, 172–3, 185
legalistic approach, 172
neo-liberalism, 7, 8, 196–8
public and private law, 195–6
recruitment procedures, 203–4
self-employment, 196
and small enterprises, 201
social dialogue, 185–6
temporary workers, 204–7
termination of employment, 210–12
trade unions, 170–1, 186, 194–5, 202
transposition of acquis communautaire, 185–7, 191, 196, 197, 198–203, 215
tripartite arrangements, 171
wage rates, 197
Central America Free Trade Agreement (CAFTA), 267, 365
Central and Eastern Europe. See CEE countries
Chau, Nancy, 151

child labour
  benefits of abolition, 338–9
  Brazil, 324–5
  and core ILO principles, 20
  EU Charter of Fundamental Rights, 25
  FTAA, 38
  ILO Conventions, 303
  Mercosur, 254
  NAALC, 28, 250, 252
  soccer balls, 144
  stag hunt model, 149–50
  United States, 324
  unjustifiability, 289–90
Chile, 97, 246, 247, 267
China, 359, 421
Churchill, Winston, 46
citizenship
  equal treatment of EU citizens, 228–36
  EU citizenship, 228
  EU directive, 234
civil society
  See also NGOs
  and CARICOM, 256, 258–9
  and FTAA, 258–9
  and Mercosur, 253–4, 259
  and migrant workers, 430–1
Clean Clothes Campaign, 346
Clinton, Bill, 27, 371
Coca-Cola, 113
collective bargaining
  CEE countries, 172, 185–6, 195, 196, 199–200, 202–3, 214–15
  and decentralization, 118–20
  and democracy, 123
  Doorn Declaration, 177
  EU Charter of Fundamental Rights, 25, 174
  EU countries, 25, 176–80, 215, 248
  European metalworkers, 177–8
  ILO Convention, 126, 132, 302, 349, 384, 416
  and international competition, 89
  Mercosur, 259
  NAALC, 250

collective bargaining (*cont.*)
  state intervention, 128–9
  and subsidiarity, 108, 118–20, 123–7,
    129, 132
Colombia, 370, 438
competition
  comparative advantage, 82, 92
  economic integration, 80–1
  EU regulatory competition, 83
  high labour standards, 86
  horizontal pressures, 88
  and labour costs, 81–2, 88–94, 334
  regulatory competition, 83–4, 120,
    350–1
  and social spending, 84
  specialization, 80
  taxation levels, 84, 93
  US regulatory competition, 84
  vertical pressures, 88
conflict of laws, 60–1
constitutional rights, 63–5
consumer campaigns, 397–8
contracting out, US labour rights, 59
contracts of employment
  CEE countries, 202, 203
  employee status, 209–10
  European Union, 203
cooperation
  international labour processes,
    43
  NAALC, 29
  stag hunt model, 146–52
  Summit of the Americas, 37–8
core labour standards
  benefits, 337–41
  effects, 341
  and export processing zones, 342
  and FDI, 86
  ILO Declaration, 10, 19–20, 360–2,
    384–5
  and IMF, 318
  international consensus, 288–94
  Latin America, 315–18
  meaning, 254, 332, 362
  soft law, 62
  and women, 396
  and World Bank, 289, 318, 335, 337
  and WTO, 289, 320, 323, 333, 361

corporate social responsibility
  Canadian promotion, 59
  Committee on Freedom of
    Association, 366
  international dimension, 41–2
  proliferation of codes of conduct, 59
  Tripartite Declaration, 366–7
  and United States, 365
Costa Rica, 246, 247, 365
Côte d'Ivoire, 396
Council of Europe, 434
Courchene, Tom, 276, 287
crimes, international crimes, 370
Croatia, 192, 193
Cuba, 437
culture, and gender equality, 343,
    393–4
Cyprus, 7–8, 169, 170, 221, 437
Czech Republic
  communist regime, 192
  EU membership, 7–8, 169
  and ILO conventions, 219, 221
  labour code, 218
  post-communism, 191, 193, 200,
    218
  temporary workers, 220
  termination of employment, 222
Czechoslovakia, 193, 199, 202

Danielsen, Dan, 156–7
Dante Alighieri, 108
data protection, 214
decentralization. *See* subsidiarity
Delors, Jacques, 22
democracy, 123, 128, 131–2
Denmark, 17, 208, 218
deregulation, 8, 22
developing countries
  foreign direct investment, 90
  and ILO standards, 41, 92
  infrastructures, 88
  labour cost competition, 88,
    89–91
  labour standards, 95
  Latin America, 246
  mobile industries, 89–90
  negotiations over labour standards,
    155

and race to the bottom theories,
  87–8, 92
segmentation of international
  economy, 91
trade unions, 90
development
  basis, 287
  and international labour standards,
    339
  post-Washington Consensus, 280–2,
    289, 291
  theories, 278–9, 280
  UN conventions, 386
  Washington Consensus, 278, 281–2
discrimination. *See* equal treatment
domestic labour laws
  basis, 278
  bottom-up process, 65
  CEE countries, 172–3
    communist regime, 194–5
    post-communism, 8, 191–2,
      195–8
  codification, 201–2
  declining role of governments, 2
  enforcement, 94, 96, 266, 269
  exhaustion of ideas, 2
  and flexible employment, 59–60
  future in a global world, 56–65
  and GATS, 59
  and globalization, 1–5, 6, 51–4
  human rights discourse, 61–3
  Latin America, 315–18
  Mercosur countries, 315
  non-compliance, Latin America,
    309–11, 316–18
  politicization, 58
  privatization, 58–9
  reflexive labour law, 59
  regulatory competition, 83–4, 120,
    350–1
  regulatory motivations, 87
  role of corporations, 54–6
  state motivations, 87
  and transnationalization of
    employment, 60–1
  without states, 131
  v. workplace reality, 2
Dominica, 272, 437

Drezner, Daniel, 103
Drummond Company, 370
Ducpetiaux, Edouard, 16

economic integration
  effect of labour standards, 94–6
    emerging consensus, 83–94,
      162–3, 291
    received wisdom, 77
    theories, 79–83
  factors, 79
  and fragmentation, 91, 109
  and globalization, 110
  international competition, 80–1
  leverage of mobility, 80
  and race to the bottom, 77–8
Ecuador, 267, 306, 437, 438
education, 285–7, 289
Egypt, 438
Einaudi, Luigi, 45
El Salvador, 365, 438
Elmslie, Bruce, 93
employee participation. *See* worker
    participation
employee status, 209–10
employers' associations
  CEE countries, 171, 186, 202
  European Union, 175
employment agencies. *See* agency
    workers
English language, and globalization,
    113
Enron, 365
equal pay
  European Union, 22, 212
  ILO Convention, 302, 349, 383, 384
  international law, 339, 390
  measures, 394–5
  United States, 371
equal treatment
  benefits, 339
  and burden of proof, 213
  Canada, 58, 64
  CEE countries, 213
  core ILO principle, 20
  cultural objections, 343, 393–4
  EU Charter of Fundamental Rights,
    25

equal treatment (*cont.*)
   EU citizens, 228–34
   EU law, 212–14
   EU solidarity, 232–3
   EU solidarity or non-discrimination,
      234–6
   EU workers, 226–8, 229
   and genetic/HIV tests, 213
   ILO Convention, 303, 343, 349, 384,
      385
   justification, 289
   Mercosur, 254
   NAALC, 28, 250
   pregnancy, 214
   social advantages, 226–8
   unilateral US laws, 156
Estonia
   communist regime, 192–3
   contracts of employment, 218
   EU membership, 7–8, 169
   labour code, 218
   post-communism, 191, 195
   temporary workers, 220
   termination of employment,
      222
   trade unions, 199
ethical investment, 346
Ethical Trading Initiative, 366
Euclid, 4
European Companies, 183
European Convention on Human
   Rights, 416
European Court of Justice
   compliance record, 248
   jurisprudence, 198–9
   model for FTAA, 248
European Metalworkers Federation,
   178
European Trade Union Institute
   (ETUI), 179
European Union
   agency workers, 208
   Amsterdam Treaty, 23–4, 180,
      387–8
   balance of powers, 26
   CEE enlargement, 7–8, 25–6, 169,
      192
      impact, 41, 185–7

Charter of Fundamental Rights,
   24–5, 173–4, 184, 210, 216, 248,
   387, 388
citizenship, 228, 234
collective bargaining, 119, 176–80,
   215, 248
competitiveness factors, 92
Constitution, 25, 173, 175, 216
contracts of employment, 203
Copenhagen criteria, 191–2, 198
direct effect of legislation, 198–9
Doorn Declaration, 177
emergence of social dimension, 21–2
employee information rights, 183–4
employee participation, 174, 181–5
employment policy, 180–1
employment status, 209
enforcement of labour laws, 62
enlargement, 169, 216
equal pay, 22, 212
equal treatment. *See* equal treatment
European Companies, 183
European monetary union, 177
European Works Councils, 181–2
free movement of citizens, 228–34
free movement of workers, 225–8
freedom of association, 173
freedom of movement, 8, 225–36
GDP, 169
gender equality, 213, 387, 393
Generalized System of Preferences,
   166
health and safety, 181, 185
industrial relations framework,
   173–85
information rights, 25, 183–4
institutions, 44
labour dimension, 20–6, 39, 40
labour standards, 20, 174–5
Laeken Declaration, 232
languages, 169
legal residence, 236
life-long learning, 177
Maastricht Treaty, 23, 228
migrant workers, 434
and nationalisms, 112
nationality discrimination and
   workers, 226–8

nature, 20, 174
non-binding declarations, 24
origins, 20–1, 169
pregnant workers, 214
proportionality, 231
redundancies, 181
regulatory competition, 83
Single European Act, 22, 175
Social Action Programme, 21–2
social and labour jurisdiction, 24
Social Charter, 22–3, 248
social dialogue, 175–6
Social Fund, 21, 24
social model, 215, 247
solidarity, 173–4, 230, 232–3, 234–6
sources of law, 198–9
students, 230, 236
subsidiarity, 122–3
temporary workers, 206–7
termination of employment, 210
trade unions, 173
transfers of undertakings, 181
working time, 174, 185
European Works Councils, 181–2
exhaustion of local remedies, 260
export processing zones, 342, 350

Fair Labour Association, 366
family responsibilities, 384, 395
Filartiga, Joel, 369
Finland, 219, 221
fixed-term contracts. See temporary
workers
Flanagan, Robert, 293, 294
flexible employment, 59–60, 205–6,
420, 423
Folk Theorem, 151
forced labour
benefits of abolition, 338–9
and core ILO principles, 20
ILO Conventions, 302, 349
Mercosur, 254
NAALC, 28, 250
unjustifiability, 290
foreign direct investment
developing countries, 90
effect of labour standards on, 84–5,
86, 301, 319, 340

factors, 85
OECD countries, 85
United States, 92
France, 17, 21, 169, 207, 208, 221, 248,
437
Frankfurt Conference 1857, 16
free market
See also neo-liberalism
invisible hand theory, 129–30
and just society, 283–4
and labour law, 334
and real economy, 130–1
and US unilateral labour standards,
156
free movement of citizens, 228–34
free movement of workers
See also migrant workers
EC Treaty, 198, 225
European Union, 225–8
social advantages, 226–8
free riders, 149
free trade. See free market; trade
freedom of association
benefits, 338
Brazil, 309–10
CEE countries, 199–200
core ILO right, 20, 128, 132
EU Charter of Fundamental Rights,
25
EU countries, 25
European Union, 173
ILO Committee on Freedom of
Association, 366
ILO Convention, 302, 349, 384,
416
and McDonald's, 262–3
Mercosur, 254
Mexico, 262
NAALC, 250, 262–3
and subsidiarity, 128
US law, 370
FTA, 26, 77
FTAA
See also Summit of the Americas
creation, 304
horizontal cooperation, 37–8
human rights, 34
ILO principles, 38

FTAA (*cont.*)
  Inter-American Conference of
    Ministers of Labour, 35–9, 41,
    42
  investment chapter, 269
  labour dimension, 20, 33–9, 40, 41,
    43
  labour rights. *See* FTAA labour rights
  and Latin America, 304
  and NAFTA, 246
  opponents, 246
  social dimension, 245
FTAA labour rights
  approaches, 245–9, 320–3
  building on existing models, 268–9
  choice of model, 325
  civil society actors, 258–9
  complaint mechanisms, 259–60
  and education, 285–7
  effective enforcement of domestic
    laws, 266, 269
  enforcement, 265–6
  EU model, 247
  exhaustion of local remedies, 260
  existing regional agreements, 249–58
  familiar responses, 274–5
  and human capital policy, 285–8
  ILO model, 322, 323
  impact on labour issues, 9–10
  incremental approach, 247
  independent review, 267–8
  and international standards, 267
  and just society, 275–94
  and Latin American practices,
    318–20
  and Mercosur, 32–3
  NAALC model, 323–4, 326
  oversight bodies, 265
  positive approach, 275–82
  procedural system, 325–6
  race to the bottom, 296–7
  targeting corporate abusers, 260–4
  transparency, 269
  treaty options, 247–9
  viability of norms, 247

Galli, Rossana, 295–6
game theory
  experimental stag hunt games, 151–2
  and international labour law, 149–51
  Prisoner's Dilemma, 148–9, 153,
    157
  repeated games, 151
  and sanctions, 157–8
  stag hunt, 7–8, 146–9, 157
  and trade agreements, 150, 153
  and unilateralism, 156
Gap, 397
Garrett, Geoffrey, 86
GATT. *See* WTO
gender equality
  affirmative action, 248, 394
  Canadian institutions, 58
  CEE countries, 201
  consumer campaigns, 397–8
  Copenhagen Declaration, 394
  core labour standards, 396
  cultural values, 343, 393–4
  empowerment of women, 396–7
  equal pay. *See* equal pay
  EU Charter of Fundamental Rights,
    25
  European Union, 213, 387, 393
  family responsibilities, 384, 395
  gender differences, 392
  gender mainstreaming, 392–3
  global patterns of inequality, 11,
    378–82
  ILO instruments, 383–5
  and informal economies, 380–2,
    395–6
  and international financial
    institutions, 398
  international labour instruments,
    382–8
  international standards, 389–91
  key issues, 391–8
  occupational segregation, 379–80,
    394
  pervasive global inequality, 377
  regional mechanisms, 387–8
  and religious fundamentalism,
    380
  structural inequalities, 391–2
  and trade agreements, 398
  UN instruments and mechanisms

Beijing Declaration, 386–7, 390, 392, 394
CEDAW, 385–6, 392
development instruments, 386
generally, 385–7
General Motors, 262
Generalized System of Preferences, 144, 154, 156, 166
genetic tests, 213
Germany
affirmative action, 248
and Bern Conference 1890, 17
Doorn Declaration, 177
founding EC member, 21, 169
labour model, 198, 199, 211, 334
licensing of employment agencies, 208
metalworkers' trade union, 177–8
migrant workers, 418
nineteenth century labour laws, 17
ratification of ILO conventions, 437
temporary workers, 207, 219
Ghana, 438
Ghosh, Bimal, 432–3
Gifford, Kathie Lee, 143
Global Compact, 59, 346, 366
globalization
and Canada
future of labour law, 56–65
labour case law, 52–3
characteristics, 1–2
common sense assumptions, 51–4
concept, 109–16, 276
compound interdependence, 111–16
deterritorialization, 110
diversity of views, 276–8
economic integration, 110
globalized localism, 113–14
glocalization, 113
long-term process, 111
narrow and broad views, 110–11
social interconnectedness, 110
speed of change, 111
conflict of laws, 60–1
and domestic labour laws, 6, 51–4
economically driven, 3
fear of, 51, 65–6

flexible employment, 59–60, 205–6, 420, 423
fragmentation, 91, 109
and gender inequality, 378–82
labour law without states, 131
and labour standards, 1–5, 77–8, 94–6, 359–60
emerging consensus, 83–94, 162–3, 291
theories, 79–83
lex laboris, 52, 53, 54
lex mercatoria, 52
and migrant workers, 11, 409–10, 422–4
and neo-liberalism
politicization of labour law, 58
privatization of labour law, 58–9
research projects, 51–4
transnationalization of employment, 60–1
glocalization, 113
Gore, Al, 361
Greece, social expenditure, 101
Grenada, 272, 437
Grenadines, 272
Guatemala, 365, 437, 438
Guehenno, Jean-Marie, 1
Guillen, Ana, 101
Guinea, 437, 438
Gunderson, Morley, 93
Guyana, 272, 437

Haiti, 272
Harrison, Bennett, 105
health and safety at work
EU employee participation, 181, 185
and ILO, 154–5
Mercosur, 254
NAALC, 28, 250, 252, 263
Heckman, James, 285, 286
Hepple, Bob, 113
Heraclitus, 116
Hindley, Charles, 357
HIV tests, 213
home work, 384, 395–6
Honduras, 144, 365
Hugo, Victor, 46
human capital policy, 285–8, 291

human rights
  CARICOM, 256
  international crimes, 370
  labour law discourse, 61–3
  Summit of the Americas, 34
  women. *See* gender equality
Human Rights Watch, 430
Hungary
  communist economic reforms, 192
  communist regime, 193
  EU membership, 7–8, 169
  and ILO conventions, 219, 221
  post-communism, 191, 193–4, 195,
      199, 200
  termination of employment, 222

Iliopoulou, Anastasia, 231
ILO
  and Canada, 61
  centrality, 10–11, 40, 43, 44
  and child labour, 144
  Committee on Freedom of
      Association, 366
  Constitution, 331, 336, 344
  contemporary position, 19–20
  conventions. *See* ILO conventions
  data protection, 214
  decentralization, 118, 125–6
  Declaration of Fundamental
      Principles 1998, 10, 19–20,
      40, 332, 360–2, 384–5, 409,
      424
  on effects of core standards, 340
  and employment status, 210
  freedom of association, 128,
      132
  on gender equality, 393
  gender equality programmes, 394
  global context, 348–51
  history, 17–19, 357–8
    economic origins, 19
    origins, 16, 17, 331–2
    political origins, 18
    social origins, 18, 333
    Washington Conference 1919, 357
  influence, 44
  on labour costs, 336
  membership, 19

and Mercosur, 31, 254
and migrant workers, 416–17
  integrated approach, 424–5
and minimum wage, 336
and non-state actors, 345–8
pluralist approach, 10, 344, 351
priorities, 154–5
prospects, 351–3
purpose, 295
recommendations, 19
and regional systems, 20
soft law, 4
standards. *See* ILO standards
structural change and unions, 126
subsidiarity approach, 128, 132
technical assistance
  to Cambodia, 364–5
  to CEE countries, 198
  US funding, 365
track record, 331, 332–3
and transnational companies, 366–7
Tripartite Declaration, 366–7
and United States, 10–11, 356–7, 373
  rights/trade linking, 360–1, 362–5
universality, 341–5
World Commission on Social
    Dimensions of Globalization, 4,
    83, 348
ILO conventions
  agency work, 204, 208–9
  basis, 278–9
  child labour, 303
  collective bargaining, 126, 132, 302,
      349, 384, 416
  equal pay, 302, 349, 383, 384
  equal treatment, 343, 349, 384, 385
  family responsibilities, 384
  forced labour, 302, 349
  freedom of association, 302, 349,
      384, 416
  gender equality, 383–5
  home work, 384
  ineffectiveness, 332–3
  main conventions, 349
  maternity protection, 384
  migrant workers, 409, 411–14
    obstacles to ratification, 421
  part-time work, 384

ratification, 151, 332–3, 358, 421
right to employment, 349
scope, 19
social security, 349
termination of employment, 205,
    206, 210, 384
US ratifications, 356, 371–2
ILO standards
See also international labour law
adoption by CEE countries, 8
and CEE post-communist laws,
    199–200
constitutional templates, 63–5
core standards. *See* core labour
    standards
economic effects, 86
and FTAA, 38, 322, 323
health and safety, 154–5
ineffectiveness, 40–1, 153
influence on US, 366, 371–2
lack of enforcement mechanisms,
    145
Latin America, 315
levelling effect, 359
and Mercosur, 254
migrant workers, 11, 411
proliferation, 143
subsidiarity approach, 132
substantive standards, 332
and US law, 145, 370
IMF, 84, 255, 306, 307, 318
India, 107, 144, 149–50, 166, 286, 359,
    396
Industrial Revolution, 16–17
informal economies
    Africa, 341
    Asia, 341
    growth, 114
    home work, 395–6
    and international labour law, 340–3
    Latin America, 9, 288, 294–6, 310,
        317–18, 341, 343
    street vendors, 396
    women, 380–2, 395–6
information rights, EU, 25, 183–4
Inter-American Conference of
    Ministers of Labour, 35–9, 41,
    42

International Association for the Legal
    Protection of Workers, 17
International Covenant on Civil and
    Political Rights, 385
International Covenant on Economic,
    Social and Cultural Rights, 144,
    385, 412, 416
international crimes, 370
international financial institutions,
    278, 398
international labour law
    and anti-globalization protests, 39
    concept, 5, 15, 39–44
    constitutionality, 63–5
    cooperation, 29, 43, 146–52
    corporate social responsibility, 41–2
    diversification of actors, 345–8
    diversity of sources, 144–5
    economic case
        counter-neoliberal case, 336–7
        economic, social and political
            dividends, 331, 337–41
        empirical evidence of benefits, 341
        generally, 333–41
        neo-liberal theory, 333–6
    and FTAA rights, 267
    and game theory, 7–8
    gender equality, 382–8, 389–91
    global context, 348–51
    history, 16–39, 348–50, 357
        early bilateral treaties, 17
        ILO history, 17–19, 357–8
        origins, 16, 331–2
    ILO. *See* ILO; ILO conventions; ILO
        standards
    ineffective enforcement, 62, 143,
        144, 145–6
    institutions, 43–4
    internationalizing process, 63
    law v. practice, 333
    legal issues, 154–7
    literature gap, 143–4
    nature, 3–4
    norms and standards, 40–2
    processes, 42–3
    prospects, 351–3
    regional systems. *See* regional
        systems

international labour law (*cont.*)
  regulatory redundancy, 154–5
  sanction requirement, 153–4, 157–8
  stag hunt model, 149–51
  suitability, 6–7
  and unilateralism, 155–7
  universality, 341–5
    Asian values, 343, 345
    cultural objections, 343–5, 393–4
    informal sector, 340–3
    Islamic values, 343, 344
  working hypotheses, 153–4
International Labour Organization. *See*
    ILO; ILO conventions; ILO
    standards
international law
  crimes, 370
  customary law, 371
  labour. *See* international labour law
  principles, 370–1
  and United States, 370–1
International Organization for
    Migration, 424, 428–9
International Seafarers Federation, 368
International Trade Organization, 95
International Workers' Association, 16
invisible hand theory, 129–30
Iran, 343
Iredale, Robyn, 422
Ireland, 107, 208, 221
Islamic Conference, 345
Islamic values, 343, 344
Israel, 107, 437
Italy, 17, 21, 129, 169, 207, 208, 219,
    437

Jamaica, 272, 437
Japan, 114, 381
Jethro, 116–18
Johnson, Lyndon, 372
just society, 275–82

Kanbur, Ravi, 151
Kay, Stephen, 101, 102
Kenya, 437
Keynes, John Maynard, 1
Klare, Karl, 156–7
Kirchner, President, 307

Krugman, Paul, 284–5, 286, 287, 289,
    291, 320, 335
Kucera, David, 86, 293, 294, 295–6, 319
Kumar, Vidya, 109
Kuwait, 418
Kyrgyzstan, 438

labour costs
  anti-liberalist case, 336–7
  CEE countries, 197
  developing countries, 89–91
  and economic integration, 81–2
  empirical studies, 82
  Mercosur countries, 311–15
  neo-liberalist theory, 334–6
  OECD countries, 85, 86
  and productivity, 284–5, 289–94
  significance, 87, 88–94
  and unions, 291
  variables, 82
labour law. *See* domestic labour laws;
    international labour law; labour
    standards
labour standards
  See also ILO standards
  Americas, 8–10, 39
  CARICOM, 256–8, 267
  constitutional status, 3
  developing countries, 95, 155
  effects
    competitiveness, 86
    emerging consensus, 83–94,
      162–3, 291
    global context, 359–60
    race to the bottom, 77–8, 94–6,
      162–3
    received wisdom, 77
    studies, 319
    theories, 79–83, 333–41
  enforcement regimes, 94, 96, 143
  European Union, 174–5
  and foreign direct investment, 84–5,
    86, 301, 319, 340
  FTAA. *See* FTAA labour rights
  ILO. *See* ILO standards
  increased scrutiny, 143
  international norms, 40–2
  and international trade, 85–7

internationalizing process, 63
and just society, 275–82
literature gap, 143–4
Mercosur, 31–2, 247, 254, 267, 315
NAALC, 40, 250, 252, 267
regulatory competition, 83–4
segmentation of international
    economy, 91
skilled and unskilled workers, 80
state intervention, 128–9
trade linking by US, 360–1,
    362–5
and unit labour costs, 81–2
US seafarers, 367–8
vulnerable workers, 11
Laeken Declaration, 232
Langille, Brian, 103
Latin America
  anti-neo-liberalism, 306
  competition between developing
      countries, 246
  core labour standards, 315–18
    non-compliance, 309–11,
        316–18
  dictatorships, 306
  and FTAA
    economic pros and cons, 304
    prospects, 318–20
    social debate, 306–7
    unemployment, 306
  industrial relations, 9–10
  informal sector, 9, 288, 294–6, 310,
      317–18, 341, 343
  unequal society, 317–18
  vulnerable groups, 318
Latvia
  communist regime, 192–3
  EU membership, 7–8, 169
  and ILO conventions, 221
  labour code, 218
  post-communism, 191
  termination of employment, 205,
      222
League of Nations, 357
Leary, Virginia, 413
Legrand, Daniel, 357
lex laboris, 52, 53, 54
lex mercatoria, 52

Lithuania
  collective bargaining, 199
  communist regime, 192–3
  contracts of employment, 218
  EU membership, 7–8, 169
  and ILO conventions, 219, 221
  labour code, 202, 218
  post-communism, 191, 200
  temporary workers, 220
Liz Claborne, 397
local remedies doctrine, 260
Luxembourg, 21, 169, 177, 207, 221,
    421

Maastricht Treaty, 23, 228
Macedonia, 437
Madagascar, 437
Malawi, 437
Malaysia, 107, 437
Mali, 438
Maloney, William, 296
Malta, 7–8, 169, 170, 222
Marshall, Alfred, 334
Marx, Karl, 44
Marxism, 121
Matsaganis, Manos, 101
Maupin, Francis, 343
Mauritius, 437
McDonald's, 262–3
Mercosur
  achievements, 30–2
  and civil society, 253–4, 259
  domestic labour laws, 315
  Economic and Social Advisory
      Forum, 31–2, 253–4, 258
  economic effect, 245
  foundation, 307
  and FTAA, 32–3
  Fundamental Declaration, 31
  growth, 305
  and ILO conventions, 31, 254
  informal economies, 310
  institutions, 307
  labour dimension, 20, 29–33, 40
  labour inspections, 254
  Labour Market Observatory, 31, 253,
      265
  mandate, 30

Mercosur (*cont.*)
  membership, 30, 307
  Montevideo Declaration, 253
  Multilateral Treaty on Social
      Security, 31
  non-compliance with labour laws, 9,
      309–11
  Ouro Preto Protocol, 31, 253
  Social and Labour Commission, 32,
      255, 258–9
  Social and Labour Declaration,
      31–2, 247, 254, 267, 308–9
  social costs, 311–15
  Socio-Economic Forum, 307, 309
  and sovereignty, 255
  trade and labour standards, 39,
      252–5
  Treaty of Asunción, 30, 252
  Working Group 10, 31–2, 253
Mexico
  bilateral treaties with US and
      Canada, 246
  freedom of association, 262
  health and safety at work, 263
  labour laws, 267
  migrant workers, 421, 427
  MWC ratification, 438
  and NAALC, 27, 251, 261–2
  and NAFTA, 26
  pregnancy testing, 262, 265
migrant workers
  civil society, role, 430–1
  European Convention on Human
      Rights, 416
  flexibilization of labour, 420, 423
  free movement of EU workers, 198,
      225–8
  and globalization, 11, 409–10, 422–4
  homogeneity, 237
  innovative national approaches,
      432
  integrated approach by ILO, 424–5
  international law
      complementary approaches,
          424–32
      continuing need, 432–3
      Council of Europe, 434
      European Convention on Human
          Rights, 416

  European Union, 225–8, 434
  ILO conventions, 11, 409, 411–14,
      421
  Mercosur, 254
  NAALC, 28, 250, 263
  NAFTA, 62, 434
  shortcomings, 416–21
  UN Migrant Workers Convention,
      414–16, 418–19, 422
  International Organization for
      Migration, 424, 428–9
  mainstreaming, 414
  PICUM, 430
  temporary work, 418–21
  UN activities, 426–8
  UNESCO work, 424, 429–30
  United States, 263, 427
  women, 390, 417–18
Milberg, William, 93
Mill, John Stuart, 150
minimum wages, 28, 250, 252, 336
Mitchell, Daniel, 104
Montenegro, 216, 437
Montserrat, 272
Morici, Peter, 99
Morocco, 365–7, 438
Moses, 116–18
multinationals. *See* transnational
      companies

NAALC
  and American developing countries,
      246
  and Canadian jurisdictions, 61
  cases, 260–4
  civil society actors
  cooperation, 29
  economic effect, 245
  effectiveness, 29, 264, 324
  enforcement mechanisms, 28–9,
      251–2, 259–60, 266
  freedom of association, 250, 262–3
  gender equality, 388
  generally, 27–9, 250
  health and safety at work, 28, 250,
      252, 263
  impetus, 27
  labour principles, 40, 250, 252, 267
  model for FTAA, 323–4, 326

negotiations, 27–8
obligations of members, 250
scope, 39, 62–3, 252
Secretariat, 29, 44, 265
source of international labour law,
144, 145
and sovereignty, 251, 324
transnational corporate abuse, 260–4
NAFTA
and FTAA, 246
growth, 305
labour dimension, 20, 29, 39–40
migrant workers, 62, 434
NAALC. *See* NAALC
and sovereignty, 26–7
trade and labour standards, 39
Namibia, 396
national laws. *See* domestic labour laws
nationalism, and EU, 112
nationality discrimination
EU citizens, 228–34
EU meaning, 225
EU workers, 226–8
neo-liberalism
and Canada, 57
case against international standards,
333–6
CEE countries, 7, 8, 196–8
counter-case on international
standards, 336–7
and human rights, 61
and labour law, 334–6
post-Washington Consensus, 280–2,
289, 291
and subsidiarity, 128–31
Washington Consensus, 278, 281–2,
335
NEPAD, 388
Netherlands, 21, 169, 177, 207, 208,
219, 437
New Zealand, 95, 119, 437
Newton, Isaac, 130
NGOs, 345, 347, 397, 430–1
See also civil society
Nicaragua, 365
Nietzsche, Friedrich, 274, 275, 278, 279
Nigeria, 437
non-discrimination. *See* equal
treatment

non-state actors. *See* civil society
Norway, 209, 368, 437

OECD
effect of labour standards, 86, 87, 91,
92, 289, 291–2, 319, 340
globalization effects, 83
TNC guidelines, 347
OECD countries
foreign direct investment, 85
labour intensive industries, 91
nature of competition, 89
trade, 85–7
unemployment, 350
unit labour costs, 85, 86
Oman, Charles, 300–1
Organization of American States,
Inter-American Conference of
Ministers of Labour, 35–9, 41,
42
outsourcing, 145–6
Owen, Robert, 16, 17, 357

Pakistan, 144, 149–50, 350, 421, 431
Paraguay, 30, 245, 310, 313
part-time work, 384
Peru, 306, 307
pesticides, 145
Philippines, 422, 427, 431–2, 438
PICUM, 430
Piper, Nicola, 422
piracy, 369
Pius XI, Pope, 120–1
Poland
See also CEE countries
agency workers, 221
communist regime, 192, 193
employers' associations, 202
EU membership, 7–8, 169
and ILO conventions, 219
labour code, 202, 218
post-communism, 191, 193–4, 199,
200
Solidarnosz, 170
termination of employment, 222
Portugal, 17, 208, 219, 221, 437
pregnancy testing, 262, 265
pregnant workers, 214, 384
Prisoner's Dilemma, 148–9, 153, 157

privatization of labour law, 58–9
processes, international labour
    dimension, 42–3
productivity, and labour costs, 284–5,
    289–94
proportionality, 121, 127, 231
Ptolemy, 4

Quadragesimo Anno, 120–1
quantum reality, 115

race to the bottom
    and economic integration, 77–8
    emerging consensus, 83–94, 162–3,
      291
    empirical studies, 83–94
    European Union, 22
    foreign direct investment, 84–5
    and FTAA labour rights, 296–7
    and ILO origins, 19, 331, 332–3
    and international trade, 85–7
    and Mercosur, 30
    and NAALC, 27
    regulatory competition, 83–4, 120,
      350–1
    and subsidiarity, 120, 121–3
    theories, 6, 79–83, 87
redundancy, EU employee
    participation, 181
regional systems
    CARICOM. See CARICOM
    EU. See European Union
    FTAA. See FTAA; Summit of the
      Americas
    and gender equality, 387–8
    and ILO, 20
    international labour dimension,
      20–39
    Mercosur. See Mercosur
    NAFTA. See NAFTA
religious fundamentalism, 380
residence, EU legal residence, 236
right to work
    EU Charter of Fundamental Rights,
      25
    ILO Convention, 349
    US 'right to work' legislation, 84
Rodriguez Pizarro, Gabriela, 426

Rodrik, Dani, 92, 99, 104, 106, 277,
    279, 293, 301, 319–20
Romania
    communist regime, 192, 193
    and EU membership, 191–2
    labour code, 202
    migrant workers, 421
    post-communism, 191, 193–4, 199,
      200
Roosevelt, Franklin, 372
Rousseau, Jean-Jacques, 147, 151
Rugmark, 346
Russia, 18, 286, 348
Ruwanpura, Kanchana, 393

SA 8000, 366
Sachs, Jeffrey, 334
Saint Kitts and Nevis, 272
Saint Lucia, 272, 437
Saint Vincent, 272
San Marino, 437
Santos, Boaventura de Souza, 113–14
Scheuermann, W. E., 110
Schultz, Evan, 99
seafarers
    boycotts, 367–8
    piracy, 369
Sen, Amartya, 153, 279–80, 282, 286,
    287, 291, 294, 296, 339, 352
Senegal, 438
Sengenberger, Werner, 295–6
Serbia, 216, 437
Seychelles, 438
Silva, Luis Inacio da, 246, 306, 310
Singapore, 97, 418
Skyrms, Brian, 152
Slovakia
    EU membership, 7–8, 169
    and ILO conventions, 219
    labour code, 202
    post-communism, 191, 193,
      200
    temporary workers, 201, 220
Slovenia, 188
    EU membership, 7–8, 169
    historical legacy, 202
    and ILO conventions, 221
    labour code, 218

post-communism, 191, 192–3, 200
ratification of ILO conventions, 437
termination of employment, 205,
222
small enterprises, CEE countries, 201
Social Accountability International,
366
social dialogue
European Union, 175–6
Mercosur, 254
new EU members, 185–6
social dumping. *See* race to the bottom
social welfare
and economic integration, 84
EU citizens, 228–34
EU solidarity, 232–3
EU solidarity or non-discrimination,
234–6
EU students, 230
ILO Convention, 349
Mercosur, 31, 254
solidarity
Christian doctrine, 121
EU citizens, 8, 173–4, 230, 232–3
EU solidarity v. non-discrimination,
234–6
strategies, 264
sovereignty
and Mercosur, 255
and NAALC, 251, 324
and NAFTA, 26–7
Spain
and ILO conventions, 219, 221
licensing of employment agencies,
208
migrant workers, 416, 427, 437
ratification of ILO conventions, 437
social expenditure, 101
temporary workers, 207, 219
specialized markets, 80
Sri Lanka, 431, 438
stag hunt
experimental games, 151–2
game theory, 7–8, 146–9
international labour law as, 149–51
and sanctions, 157
value of cooperation, 146–52
Starbucks, 397

state intervention
See also domestic labour laws
human capital policies, 285–7
labour law without states, 131
national innovation systems, 286
and workers' rights, 128–9
Stern, Nicholas, 281–2, 286, 291, 294,
296
Stiglitz, Joseph, 337, 352
street vendors, 396
strike, right to, 25, 199, 250, 254
students, EU, 230, 236
subsidiarity
collective bargaining, 108, 118–20,
123–7, 129, 132
concept, 6–7, 108
and democracy, 128, 131–2
equality of social and economic
interests, 128–31
European Union, 122–3
and freedom of association,
128
functional dimension, 127–31
implications of decentralization,
116–20
and power, 116–18
and proportionality, 121, 127
and race to the bottom, 120,
121–3
social relations, 120–1
state intervention, 128–31
structural dimension, 121–7
and worker participation, 127–8
Summit of the Americas
See also FTAA
Belo Horizonte 1997, 321
Buenos Aires 2001, 321–3
Cartagena 1995, 320
Declaration of Nuevo Léon, 38
Denver 1995, 320
Miami 1994, 33
Monterrey 2004, 38
Ottawa 2001, 322
Quebec City 2001, 34–5
Quito 2002, 322
San Jose 1998, 321
Santiago 1998, 34
Toronto 1999, 321

Suriname, 272
Sweden, 221, 437
Switzerland, 418

Tajikistan, 421, 438
Tanzania, 437
Taran, Patrick, 426
taxation, 84, 93, 350
technical assistance, 8, 198, 364–5
temporary workers
    CEE countries, 204–7
    European Union, 206–7
    flexibility, 205–6
    migrants, 418–21
    unfair dismissal, 205
termination of employment
    CEE countries, 210–12
    European Union, 210
    German model, 211
    ILO Convention, 205, 206, 210, 384
    Latin America, 316–17
    unfair dismissal, 205, 211
textiles, 92, 346
Thatcher, Margaret, 22
Thomas, Albert, 348
Timor Leste, 438
Togo, 437
Tommy Hilfiger, 397
Toner, Helen, 231
trade
    See also free market; WTO
    free trade and real economy, 130–1
    OECD countries, 85–7
    and race to the bottom theory, 85–7
    social dimension, 9
    US rights/trade linking, 360–1,
        362–5
trade agreements
    cooperation model, 150, 153
    enforcement mechanisms, 62
    and gender equality, 398
trade unions
    CEE countries, 170–1, 186, 194–5,
        202
    costs, 291
    decline, 2, 350
    developing countries, 90
    Doorn Declaration, 177

Estonia, 199
ETUC, 175, 178–9
European metalworkers, 177–8
European Metalworkers Federation,
    178
European Trade Union Institute
    (ETUI), 179
European Union, 173, 175
    and international competition, 89
    and structural changes, 126
    United States, 84, 249
training, 254
transfers of undertakings, EU, 181
transnational companies
    Canada, 53–4, 61
    centralization, 55–6
    conflict of laws, 60–1
    and consumer campaigns, 397–8
    European Companies, 183
    FTAA and corporate abuse, 260–4
    growth and influence, 54–6, 347
    management lawyers, 53
    national character, 55
    OECD guidelines, 347
    outsourcing, 90
    punitive behaviour, 350
    size, 55
    social responsibility. See corporate
        social responsibility
    subsidiaries, 112–13
    taxation policies, 350
    Tripartite Declaration, 366–7
    and US Alien Tort Claims Act,
        369–71
    vulnerability, 56
Trico, 367–8
Trinidad and Tobago, 272, 437
Truman, Harry, 372
Turkey, 192, 221
Turks and Caicos Islands, 272
Twinning, William, 112

Uganda, 437, 438
unemployment
    and dismissal costs, 317
    global unemployment, 350
    and international labour standards,
        339

Latin America, 306
and Mercosur, 254
OECD countries, 350
UNESCO, 422, 424, 429–30
unfair dismissal, 205, 211
UNICE, 175
UNICEF, 144
United Arab Emirates, 427
United Kingdom, 95, 119, 122, 207,
208, 437
United Nations
gender equality instruments, 385–7
Beijing Declaration, 386–7, 390,
392, 394
CEDAW, 385–6, 392
on gender inequality, 377
Global Compact, 59, 346, 366
lack of enforcement mechanisms,
145
and migrant workers
activities, 426–8
Migrant Workers Convention,
414–16, 418–19, 422
Millennium Declaration, 277, 279,
281
women's human rights, 383
World Conference against Racism,
428
United States
African Growth and Opportunity
Act, 156
Alien Torts Claims Act, 145, 154,
368–71
anti-discrimination laws, 156, 371
anti-dumping practices, 156–7, 305
anti-terrorism legislation, 305
banana workers cases, 145, 154, 156
bilateral treaties, 97, 246, 247
Bricker Amendment, 356, 372–3
and CAFTA, 365
and Canadian labour cases, 53
Caribbean Basin Economic Recovery
Act, 156
catfish industry, 156–7
child labour, 324
Civil Rights Act, 145
collective bargaining, 119, 124
contracting out of labour rights, 59

corporate social responsibility, 365
foreign direct investments, 92
freedom of association, 370
FTA, 26
and FTAA labour standards, 322–3
Generalized System of Preferences,
144, 154, 156
and ILO, 10–11, 356–7, 373
anti-communism tool, 356–7
application of ILO standards, 370
domestic labour law, 371–2
ratification of conventions, 356,
359, 371–2
technical assistance, 365
integration of Canadian economy,
56–7
International Labour Rights Fund,
145
international law, application, 370–1
intra-state competition, 88, 93
labour laws, 266, 267
migrant workers, 263, 427
and NAALC, 27, 251
and NAFTA, 26, 305
Offshore Mariners United union,
367–8
part-time female employment,
381
prisons, 371
regulatory competition, 84
'right to work' legislation, 84
secondary boycotts, 367–8
sources of international labour law,
144, 145
sweatshops, 266
termination of employment, 210
textile agreement with Cambodia,
364–5
Trade Act 2002, 156
trade/rights linking, 360–1, 362–5
trade union laws, 84, 249
unilateralism, 145, 155–7
Universal Declaration of Human
Rights, 144, 254, 385, 412, 416
Unocal, 369
Uruguay
labour contracts, 310
labour laws, 310

Uruguay (*cont.*)
  and Mercosur, 30, 245
  ratification of conventions, 437, 438
  social costs, 313

Venezuela, 306, 307, 437
Verité, 366
Vietnam, 156–7

wages
  abundance of labour, 81
  CEE countries, 197
  minimum wages, 28, 250, 252,
    336
  women, 379
Washington Consensus, 278, 281–2,
  335
Weiss, M, 102
women
  affirmative action, 248, 394
  empowerment, 396–7
  EU night work, 248
  family responsibilities, 380, 395
  home work, 395–6
  increased participation in labour
    force, 379
  informal economy, 380–2, 395–6
  and international law, 382–8, 389–91
  migrant workers, 390, 417–18
  occupational segregation, 379–80,
    394
  organizing, 396
  pregnancy, 214, 262, 265, 385–7
  wage improvement, 379
worker participation
  CEE countries, 172, 186

European Companies, 183
European information rights, 183–4
European Union, 174, 181–5
European Works Councils, 181–2
  and subsidiarity, 127–8
workers compensation, NAALC, 250
working time, EU, 174, 185
World Bank
  on absolute poverty, 275
  and core labour rights, 289, 318, 335,
    337
  on education, 286, 337
  and gender equality, 398
  and informal Latin American
    employment, 295–6
  labour rights in East Asia, 340
  and regulatory competition, 84
World Commission on Social
    Dimensions of Globalization,
    83, 277
World Conference against Racism, 428
Worldcom, 365
WTO
  and core labour rights, 289, 320, 323,
    333, 361
  GATS, 59
  Generalized System of Preferences,
    144, 154, 156, 166
  and human rights, 62
  social clause debate, 20

Yugoslavia, 193, 202

Zambia, 437
Zen, 129
Zenith, 262